Aberdeenshire Library and Information Service
www.aberdeenshire.gov.uk/libraries
Renewals Hotline 01224 661511

HENN, Francis

A business of some
heat

A BUSINESS
OF
SOME HEAT

Othello: What is the matter, think you?

Cassio: Something from Cyprus, as I may divine:
It is a business of some heat . . .

William Shakespeare: Othello,
The Moor of Venice *i.ii.38.*

A BUSINESS OF SOME HEAT

The United Nations Force in Cyprus Before and During the 1974 Turkish Invasion

by

BRIGADIER FRANCIS HENN

with a foreword by

SIR BRIAN URQUHART
KCMG MBE

Pen & Sword
MILITARY

First published in Great Britain in 2004 by
Pen & Sword Military
an imprint of
Pen & Sword Books Ltd
47 Church Street
Barnsley
South Yorkshire
S70 2AS

ISBN 1 84415 081 X

Typeset in Bulmer by
Phoenix Typesetting, Auldgirth, Dumfriesshire

Pen & Sword Books Ltd incorporates the imprints of Pen & Sword Aviation, Pen & Sword
Maritime, Pen & Sword Military, Wharncliffe Local History, Pen & Sword Select, Pen & Sword
Military Classics and Leo Cooper.

For a complete list of Pen & Sword titles please contact
PEN & SWORD BOOKS LIMITED
47 Church Street, Barnsley, South Yorkshire, S70 2AS, England
E-mail: enquiries@pen-and-sword.co.uk
Website: www.pen-and-sword.co.uk

For Monica

Her love has sustained me for more than forty-five years, and never more so than during some anxious days described in this book, which we experienced together.

Peacekeeping operations have generally been considered to be one of the most successful innovations of the United Nations, and certainly their record over the years is one of which to be proud. They have proved to be a most useful instrument of de-escalation and conflict control and have extended the influence of the Security Council into the field in a unique way. I may add that United Nations peacekeeping operations have traditionally shown an admirable degree of courage, objectivity and impartiality. This record, which is a great credit to the Organization, is sometimes overlooked in the heat of partisanship.

Javier Perez de Cuellar:
'Report of the Secretary General
on the Work of the Organization, 1982'.

CONTENTS

Annexes

ACKNOWLEDGEMENTS

When I embarked on this work numerous individuals of different nationalities (some of whom had been members of the United Nations Force in Cyprus but others who had not) responded with enthusiasm to my appeal for information, in particular accounts of their personal experiences during the crisis of the summer of 1974. The outcome was an extensive and unique archive of relevant information that cannot be found elsewhere, and the preservation of which I intend to ensure. These contributions have been invaluable, but such is the volume of the information they contain that limitations of space have allowed only relatively few direct quotations here. For the same reason it is impossible to acknowledge all these contributors individually by name, but on reading my work I hope that most will recognize how their contribution has been reflected in my account of events. I ask them all to accept my profound gratitude for the trouble to which they went in replying to my initial appeal and subsequent questions.

I must express my appreciation, too, to the Librarians of the Old War Office, the Royal United Services Institute for Defence Studies, and especially the United Nations Information Centre in London for their assistance in my research. Others who responded helpfully to my enquiries include the Army and Air Historical Branches of the Ministry of Defence, London, and the Director History and Heritage, National Defence Headquarters, Ottawa, Canada.

In 1974 UNFICYP's Finnish Contingent experienced closer contact than any other Contingent with the intervening mainland Turkish forces. I am accordingly especially grateful to Lieutenant Colonel Pertti Nykänan, who, while Finland's Military Attaché in London, spent much time and trouble in translating for me lengthy extracts from *Kyproksen Kriisi, 1974*, Captain M. Jokihaara's work in Finnish describing with professional perception the operations of the Turkish forces.

I acknowledge with thanks permission by the following to quote from published works as attributed in the text: Lord Callaghan of Cardiff; *Foreign Policy*, 1779 Massachusetts Avenue, Washington DC, USA; Faber and Faber Ltd, 3 Queen Square, London; The Mershon Center, Ohio State University, Columbus, Ohio, USA; I.B. Tauris, Publishers, 6 Salem Road, London; The Penguin Group, 80 Strand, London; Yale University Press, 47 Bedford Square, London; David Higham Associates Ltd, 5–8 Lower John Street, Golden Square, London; Minority Rights Group International, 379 Brixton Road, London; Trigraph Ltd, West Africa House, Hanger Lane, London; The Royal Institute of International Affairs, Chatham House, 10 St James's Square, London; Alithia Publishing,

Nicosia, Cyprus; Polyvios G. Polyviou, Nicosia, Cyprus; Rustem & Brother, Nicosia, Cyprus.

Particular thanks are due to Ken Howard for generously allowing some of his excellent sketches of UNFICYP scenes to be used for the book's jacket, and to the Editor of *The Sun*, London, for permission to reproduce the cartoon by Rigby (p. 444) published in that newspaper on 16 August 1974.

Publication of this book is due in no small measure to the encouragement of Soteris Georgallis, long-serving Press Counsellor at the Cyprus High Commission, London, to whom I am particularly indebted. His enthusiastic support, demonstrated in numerous ways, has been instrumental in securing financial assistance for publication from the Cyprus Government and from the A. G. Leventis Foundation, to both of whom I express my deep appreciation, not least because neither has sought to influence the contents of the book in any way.

I was encouraged at the outset to undertake this work by General Prem Chand, the outstanding Commander of the United Nations Force in Cyprus throughout the period described. We discussed many aspects, he saw and approved of early drafts, and continued to give the undertaking his enthusiastic support right up until his death in November 2003. It is a deep sadness that he was never to see the finished work, but I hope that it will stand as a fitting tribute to him and to all those under his command, who in the service of the United Nations did their utmost to assist the people of Cyprus in their hour of severe tribulation.

A final word of thanks must go to Tom Hartman, who has edited the work with patience, good humour and meticulous attention to detail.

F.R.H.

LIST OF MAPS

GLOSSARY

AA	Anti-Aircraft
ABLAUT	British Forces contingency plan for operational reinforcements
AFH	Austrian Field Hospital
AKEL	Communist Party of Cyprus
ALO	Air Liaison Officer
APC(s)	Armoured Personnel Carrier(s)
APHRODITE	Greek Cypriot Counter-Attack plan
ATL(O)	Air Transport Liaison Officer
ATOC	Air Transport Operations Centre
AUSCON	Austrian Contingent
AUSTCIVPOL	Austrian Civilian Police
BBC	British Broadcasting Corporation
BFBS	British Forces Broadcasting Service
BFNE	British Forces Near East
Bn	Battalion
Bozkurt	Grey Wolf (Senior Turkish Army Officer in Nicosia)
BRITCON	British Contingent
CANCON	Canadian Contingent
CAO	Chief Administrative Officer
CBC	Cyprus Broadcasting Corporation
CBFNE	Commander British Forces Near East
CIA	Central Intelligence Agency (United States)
CIVPOL	(UN) Civilian Police
CMC	Cyprus Mines Corporation
CMO	Chief Medical Officer
COMCEN	Communications Centre
COO	Chief Operations Officer
Coy	Company
CP	Command Post
CPLO	Chief Personnel and Logistics Officer
CTF	Commander Task Force

CTG	Commander Task Group
CYPOL	Greek Cypriot Police
CYTA	Cyprus Telecommunications Authority
DANCON	Danish Contingent
DCOS	Deputy Chief of Staff
DZ	Dropping Zone
EAC	Electricity Authority of Cyprus
ELDYK	Contingent of Greek army stationed in Cyprus
Enosis	Union with Greece
EOKA	Greek Cypriot armed anti-Colonial Government group (1955–59)
EOKA-B	Greek Cypriot armed anti-Cyprus Government group (1971–74)
EVKAF	Religious Foundation of Greek Cypriot Orthodox Church
FAC	Forward Air Controller
FALLACY	British plan for evacuation of families from Cyprus to UK
FAO	UN Food and Agriculture Organisation
FINCON	Finnish Contingent
FPM	Force Provost Marshal
FOCAS	Flag Officer Carriers and Amphibious Ships (Royal Navy)
FSO	Force Signals Officer
GILLFORCE	Nickname for UNFICYP group commanded by Major P. Gill, RA
HE	High Explosive (also His Excellency)
HMC(s)	Higher Military Command(s)
HMS	Her Majesty's Ship
HQ	Headquarters
ICRC	International Committee of the Red Cross
IRCON	Irish Contingent
JATC	Joint Air Traffic Control
JOC	Joint Operations Centre
Junta	Military Regime in Athens
KYP	Greek Intelligence Agency
LO	Liaison Officer
Lynx	Tracked Armoured Reconnaissance Vehicle
LZ	Landing Zone
MA(s)	Military Attaché(s)
MAMS	Mobile Air Movement Section
Metohi	Annex to Monastery
MG	Machine-Gun
MP	Military Police

MPIO	Military Public Information Officer
MTB	Motor Torpedo Boat
Mukhtar	Turkish Cypriot Village Chief
NATO	North Atlantic Treaty Organisation
NEAF	Near East Air Force
NEOC	Near East Operations Centre
NEARELF	Near East Land Forces
O Group	Orders Group
OP(s)	Observation Post(s)
Para	Parachute
Pigs	Nickname for wheeled armoured trucks
PIO	Public Information Officer
PLATYPUS	British Forces contingency plan for logistic reinforcements
PLC	Political Liaison Committee
PLO	Palestine Liberation Organization
RAC	Royal Armoured Corps
RAF	Royal Air Force
RAOC	Royal Army Ordnance Corps
RCT	Royal Corps of Transport
RCLs	106mm Recoilless Rifles
RE	Royal Engineers
Regt	Regiment
REME	Royal Electrical and Mechanical Engineers
RFA	Royal Fleet Auxiliary
RFU	Raiding Force Unit
RM	Royal Marines
RN	Royal Navy
RSM	Regimental Sergeant Major
SASO	Senior Air Staff Officer
SBA(s)	Sovereign Base Area(s)
SCACYP	Scandinavia-Cyprus Air Service
SDS	Signals Despatch Service
SITREP	Situation Report
SPA	Senior Political Adviser
Snapper	Nickname for Soviet wire-guided anti-tank weapon
Sqn	Squadron
SRSG	Special Representative of the UN Secretary General
SWEDCIVPOL	Swedish Civilian Police
SWEDCON	Swedish Contingent
Swingfire	Nickname for British wire-guided anti-tank weapon

Taksim	Union of part of Cyprus with Turkey
TCF	Turkish Cypriot Fighter(s)
TCPE	Turkish Cypriot Police Element
Tekke	Mosque
TG(s)	Task Group(s) (naval), Tactical Group(s) (military)
Tp	Troop
TRU	(Police) Tactical Reserve Unit
UN	United Nations
UNCIVPOL	United Nations Civilian Police
UNDP	United Nations Development Programme
UNEF	United Nations Emergency Force (Middle East, 1956–67)
UNEF 2	United Nations Emergency Force (Middle East, 1973–79)
UNFICYP	United Nations Force In Cyprus
UNHCR	United Nations High Commission(er) for Refugees
UNIFIL	United Nations Interim Force In Lebanon
UNTAG	United Nations Transition Assistance Group (Namibia, 1989–90)
UNTSO	United Nations Truce Supervision Organisation (Middle East)
US	United States of America
USS	United States Ship
USSR	Union of Soviet Socialist Republics
VPO	Vice President's Office
VHF	Very High Frequency
WO	Warrant Officer

FOREWORD

BY
SIR BRIAN URQUHART KCMG MBE
United Nations Under-Secretary General For Special Political Affairs
1974 – 1986

In the summer of 1974, after the Greek colonels had overthrown but failed to kill President Makarios of Cyprus, Turkey invaded the island with full force. A small United Nations peacekeeping Force (UNFICYP) had, since 1964, been maintaining by non-forceful means the delicate equilibrium between Greek and Turkish Cypriots in the island. The brutal Turkish invasion confronted UNFICYP with a uniquely difficult dilemma. The outside world, sympathizing with the underdog, expected UNFICYP to confront the invaders; UNFICYP had neither the mandate nor the military strength to do anything of the kind.

Fortunately the UN Force was commanded by an unusually strong and ingenious team. General Dewan Prem Chand of India was a quiet but determined soldier who had already demonstrated his peacekeeping skills in the UN operation in the Congo; his Chief of Staff was Brigadier Francis Henn. At UN Headquarters in New York I was responsible for preparing the Secretary General's instructions to peacekeeping operations in the field. The Turkish invasion of Cyprus was a constantly changing situation in which detailed instructions from New York would have been irrelevant, not to say irritating for their recipients. Knowing Prem Chand well, we simply asked him to 'play it by ear', one of his favourite phrases, and to let us know how we could back him up in political or other ways.

As we expected, Prem played it by ear magnificently. He and his team used their very small resources and authority to limit the suffering of civilians and refugees, to curb the worst excesses of the invading forces and to work for the earliest reconciliation of the Greek and Turkish Cypriot leaders. When, in violation of an agreement with the UN, the Turkish commander announced that he would take over Nicosia airport, Prem improvised a sufficiently impressive defence to gain time for us in New York to mobilise the Security Council and Henry Kissinger to dissuade the Turks from taking the airport.

As one who was involved with UN peacekeeping from its inception, I have always felt the performance of Prem Chand and his team in Cyprus in the summer of 1974 was a highlight of the UN's peacekeeping history and a remarkable example of what dedicated, resourceful and courageous people with minimal resources can do in a violent crisis. Brigadier Henn's book both tells this fascinating but little-known story and fills an important gap in the history of peacekeeping.

Brian Urquhart

PREFACE

The purpose of this book is to place on record the circumstances and manner in which during 1972–1974 the United Nations Force in Cyprus, commonly known by its acronym UNFICYP, discharged the responsibilities placed upon it by the Security Council. This was a critical period that brought a watershed in the island's long and turbulent history. Members of the Force, both military and civilian, served the United Nations and Cypriots of all communities with selfless courage and devotion, sometimes at grave personal risk. The quarrel was not theirs, but many were wounded and some gave their lives in the effort to end it.

UNFICYP was established by the UN Security Council in March 1964 in consequence of fighting that had erupted the previous December between Greek Cypriots and Turkish Cypriots, thereby posing a threat to international peace and security in the region. The Force's mission was to prevent a recurrence of this intercommunal violence and to assist in the maintenance of conditions conducive to the search for a settlement of the complex underlying constitutional and other problems. During the ensuing decade that search came within reach of success on more than one occasion, but each time the opportunity melted away. The reasons were various. Sometimes it was the influence of external events such as a *coup d'état* in Athens or political stalemate in Ankara; sometimes it was intransigence on the part of one side or the other intent on gaining further advantage; sometimes it seemed little more than lack of political will to make the compromises that a settlement demanded.

Some believe that the very presence of the UN Force and its success in containing intercommunal tensions at a tolerable level contributed, at least in the later years, to a lack of urgency in the search for a settlement. Be that as it may, there can be no doubt that, had greater vision and generosity been displayed during those ten years by both those in Cyprus and those in the two mother-countries of Greece and Turkey, Cypriots of all communities might today be living together in communal harmony, peaceful security and economic prosperity within a united island state. But time was on the side of none – the opportunities were let slip, perhaps for ever, in what proved to be tragedy of epic proportions for the island's peoples.

On 20 July 1974, five days after a *coup d'état* had unseated Archbishop Makarios as President of the Republic of Cyprus, we at UNFICYP's Headquarters, situated on the edge of Nicosia's international airport, watched in dismay as Turkish aircraft struck at targets that often were uncomfortably close and Turkish airborne troops landed in the main Turkish enclave between the capital and the north coast, while a stream of reports flowed in of bombardments by Turkish warships, of troops and tanks coming ashore near Kyrenia, of fighting between them and the Greek Cypriot National Guard, and of angry reprisals by Greek Cypriots against isolated and vulnerable Turkish Cypriot communities elsewhere on the island.

The calamity which for a decade many had feared, but which few believed would ever be allowed to happen, had become a dreadful reality. It seemed that UNFICYP's diligent peacekeeping efforts of the past ten years were, quite literally, going up in smoke. But it was no time for thoughts such as these – the UN Force was on the spot, a disciplined and impartial international military body, present on the island as an instrument of the Security Council, and we were determined to do our utmost to minimize the extent of the human tragedy which with our own eyes we could see was befalling stunned Cypriots of all communities.

The Cyprus problem was described by President Lyndon Johnson as 'one of the most complex on earth'. Scores of works have been devoted to its exhaustive analysis and this book does not aspire to add to these, but, since the role of UNFICYP cannot be seen in proper perspective without an understanding of the historical origins of the problem, the factors that lie at its heart and the sequence of events that led to deployment of the UN Force are summarized in Part 1. Nor is this book the place for a detailed account of the prolonged and ultimately sterile intercommunal negotiations conducted with patient UN support during 1972-74; these too have been well chronicled by others. Nonetheless, it must be appreciated that the UN's task in Cyprus was two-fold: first, peacekeeping – the responsibility of the Force Commander and the troops and civilian policemen under his command; second, peacemaking – the concern of the Mediator (later the Secretary General's Special Representative) and his civilian officials. If, over the years, the former was more successful than the latter, this must not obscure the reality that, while the two are complementary, it is the peacemaking that ultimately is what matters. Peacekeeping can never be an end in itself – it can only create and maintain conditions conducive to the fundamental task, that of the peacemakers searching for a permanent settlement of underlying problems.

The factors that combined to cause the crisis of the summer of 1974 formed an intricate web, the strands of which extended far beyond the confines of the island, and the story cannot be told without some reference to these. But generally this account records the course of events in Cyprus itself and the part played by UNFICYP during that crisis and in the period leading up to it as seen from the viewpoint of one who was himself present throughout at the UN Force's Headquarters. However, during July and August 1974 so much activity was compressed into a few hectic weeks that this account would be very incomplete without the contributions of many others, some of whom themselves played a part in the events described and whose own words sometimes are quoted. Their help, acknowledged elsewhere, has made it possible to piece together a more comprehensive account of UNFICYP's operations at this time than has hitherto been attempted.

No account can omit mention of the actions of the Royal Navy, British Army and Royal Air Force stationed in the British Sovereign Bases in the south of the island or outside it and operating under British, not UN, command. It would be especially inappropriate to do so here since throughout its long service UNFICYP has depended on these British Forces for many aspects of its day-to-day logistic needs. Always, not least in times of special stress, that support has been given unstintingly. Indeed, it has been the quality of this British support which in large measure has contributed to the high reputation enjoyed from the outset by UNFICYP in the annals of UN peacekeeping.

British support was crucial in the difficult weeks of July and August 1974 when it never faltered, even though British Forces themselves were at full stretch rescuing and caring for thousands of people of scores of nationalities caught up in the conflict. Subsequently there was some criticism of the British Labour Government's policy during this crisis, but nothing but praise for Britain's Armed Forces, which demonstrated with high professional competence (as so often before and since) their ever-present need for flexibility, mobility and a capacity to meet the unforeseen.

In October 1973 international peace and security were threatened by a flare-up in the Middle East which became known as the Yom Kippur War. Without warning or prior contingency planning, UNFICYP was called upon to despatch the bulk of three of its military contingents to Cairo to establish as rapidly as possible a new UN Emergency Force (known as UNEF 2) along the Suez Canal; this was accomplished within 48 hours of the Security Council's call. The operation, nicknamed Operation DOVE, in which British Forces too played a key part, was a remarkable exercise in multi-national military cooperation and demonstrated a hitherto unappreciated flexibility in the use of UN Forces. For this reason, but also in view of the consequential reorganization required in Cyprus, this story is told in Part 3 of this book.

Extensive reference to sources has been avoided, although quotations are given appropriate attribution; for those seeking to delve further a bibliography is appended listing relevant published works. In addition numerous unpublished records and documents, including Operations Logs, Situation Reports and Operational Instructions, together with contemporary personal notes, letters and diaries from various sources, have been drawn upon. However, this is not an Official History and, unless otherwise indicated, any views expressed are the author's own and do not necessarily reflect those of the United Nations or anyone else.

Named individuals are referred to generally by the rank, title or appointment held at the time of the events in question. Personal names of Greeks, Turks and Cypriots are liable to have more than one anglicized spelling; that commonly used in UNFICYP has been adopted. The spelling of Cypriot place names also varies, and confusion is compounded where there are different Greek and Turkish names for the same locality; here the practice of the UK Ministry of Defence 1:50,000 scale Map Series K717 (Edition 1-GSGS) published in 1973 has been followed. All times, unless otherwise indicated, are expressed in local Cyprus time, which in summer is six hours in advance of New York time.

Since it is not a purpose of this book to pass judgement on the dispute between Greek and Turkish Cypriots, but rather to record the course of events as seen from the impartial viewpoint of the UN Force, explanation is necessary of the terms used in referring to the two parties. The administration of President Makarios, which after December 1963 was composed exclusively of Greek Cypriots, was recognized by the United Nations as the Government of the Republic of Cyprus. The Turkish Cypriots refused to acknowledge it as such on the grounds that, in breach of the Constitution, they were excluded from it. As a matter of convenience and without prejudice to this argument, UN practice is followed in referring to the Makarios administration as 'the Government' and to the Turkish Cypriot administration, led initially by Dr Fazil Kuchuk and later by Mr Rauf Denktash, as 'the Leadership'.

To avoid monotonous repetition, Greek Cypriots and Turkish Cypriots are referred to in places as, respectively, Greeks or Turks (notwithstanding that members of the two island communities are not to be confused with nationals of the two mainland mother-countries), but only where the context makes plain that the allusion is to Cypriots.

Inaugurating a debate in the House of Lords in 1985 to mark the 40th Anniversary of the founding of the United Nations, Dr Robert Runcie, the then Archbishop of Canterbury, said of its peacekeepers:

> It is seldom realised that the lives of countless men, women and children have been saved by these unsung Peace Forces. They win no battle laurels but they have made a substantive contribution to world peace and stability. These United Nations soldiers have served us splendidly.

It was fitting that in 1988 the Nobel Peace Prize was awarded to the Peacekeeping Forces of the United Nations. Their value and need continues to be demonstrated ever more vividly in the many trouble spots around the world.

F.R.H.

PART ONE

THE ROSY REALM OF VENUS

Fairest isle, all isles excelling,
Seat of pleasures, and of loves;
Venus here will find her dwelling,
And forsake her Cyprian groves.

John Dryden: *Song of Venus.*

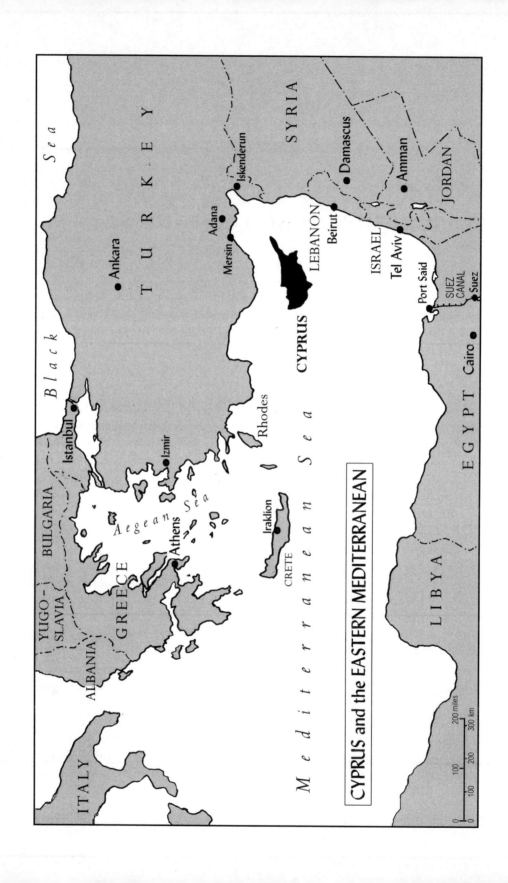

CYPRUS and the EASTERN MEDITERRANEAN

CHAPTER ONE

SEEDS OF CONFLICT

> Different invasions weathered and eroded it, piling monument on monument. The contentions of monarchs and empires have stained it with blood, have wearied and refreshed its landscape repeatedly with mosques and cathedrals and fortresses. In the ebb and flow of histories and cultures it has time and again been a flashpoint where Aryan and Semite, Christian and Moslem, met in death embrace.
>
> Lawrence Durrell: *Bitter Lemons.*

The hot summer of 1974 brought a watershed in the long and often unhappy history of the island of Cyprus. Invasion and bloody conflict were no new experiences for its peoples, who down the ages have suffered more than their fair share of these. But never before had a *de facto* partition been imposed upon the island, with tens of thousands ruthlessly uprooted from homes, property and livelihoods in the heartless process that later became known as 'ethnic cleansing'. It was the consequence of actions by the armed forces of foreign powers acting sometimes with a ferocity that echoed the inhumanity of earlier centuries and with scant regard for the internationally recognized status of the Republic of Cyprus as an independent sovereign state and member of the United Nations.

The seeds of the Cyprus problem were sown deep in time; its history is complex and its ramifications wide. If the part played by the UN Force in the years leading up to that fateful summer is to be seen in clear perspective, an understanding is necessary of the main factors that lie at the heart of the problem, the circumstances in which the Republic was given birth in 1960, the events that led to the deployment of UNFICYP four years later, and the influences exerted by external interests and pressures.

A wry story circulating in Nicosia told of the United States government's misplaced gesture of goodwill in donating a map of the world so projected as to place Cyprus at its centre, thus serving to confirm Cypriots in their self-centred delusion that it was, indeed, their small island around which the remainder of mankind revolved. Cyprus certainly has been the focus for inordinate international attention in recent decades. Why does this small island, tucked away in the north-east corner of the Mediterranean and with a population of a mere 632,000 people, generate such concern? As a Canadian journalist once remarked:

> It's ridiculous that so few people should take themselves so seriously. Even worse is that so many others also take them seriously. When President Makarios turns up at the Commonwealth

Heads of Government Conference in Ottawa next month, "Your Beatitude" will be heard on every side from people who wouldn't turn their heads to greet the Mayor of Vancouver who, if not a Beatitude, at least represents a million people.[1]

Sadly the troubles of the island's long-suffering peoples are not to be dismissed as easily as such light-hearted words suggest.

The heart of the problem of Cyprus, renowned as the birth-place of Aphrodite, Goddess of Love and Beauty, and for long fondly portrayed by romantics as an Arcadian land peopled by friendly folk who pass their days in watching their flocks, tending their vines or gossiping in the shade of village coffee-shops, lies in its geographic situation in the Levant, for it has been this that throughout recorded history has conferred strategic importance on the island. Powers seeking to dominate the region found it necessary to occupy Cyprus for military reasons (and sometimes also for the commercial advantages afforded by its situation and mineral resources). Never strong enough to defend itself, the island was fought over and colonized by a succession of foreign powers from the Mycenaeans, who crossed from the Greek Peloponnese in the 14th Century BC, to the Turks, who in 1571 AD savagely ejected the Venetians and ruled for the next three hundred years. In 1878, in consequence of Disraeli's secret diplomacy, the administration of Cyprus – his 'Rosy Realm of Venus' – passed to Britain, although nominal sovereignty remained with Turkey.[2]

The island's importance has always been a reflection of contemporary interests. For the Venetians Cyprus was an outpost affording protection for their lucrative commerce with the Levant and support for the Crusades. The Turks saw Venetian domination as an intolerable threat to the interests of the Ottoman Empire and to Muslims making the pilgrimage by sea to the holy city of Mecca. As Ottoman power declined, so British concern grew to curb Russian expansion and its threat not only to Asia Minor and the Dardanelles but also to British imperial interests in India and the *Pax Brittanica* of the 19th Century. After eight decades of rule by Britain the emphasis changed yet again with British loss of Empire, the growth of Soviet power and the clash of East-West interests as reflected in the Cold War. The ending of the latter has changed yet again but has not lessened the strategic significance of Cyprus, especially for Turkey, in the troubled world of today.

A glance at the map serves to confirm how the island lies close under the coast of Anatolia, thus commanding the approaches to Turkey's southern ports and airfields.[3] Small wonder if Turkish strategists see Cyprus in terms of their country's defence. While three centuries of rule over the island and the well-being of Turkish Cypriots may be potent factors in Turkish minds, they take second place in the Turks' cold calculations of their national strategic interest.

Their view has long been sharpened by concern (which common membership of NATO has never allayed) of a Cyprus dominated by or, worse, united with the traditional enemy, Greece – a concern voiced by Mr Zorlu, Turkey's Foreign Minister, when speaking in London as long ago as 1955:

> All these south-western ports are under the cover of Cyprus. Whoever controls this island is in the position to control these Turkish ports. If the Power that controls this island is also in control of the western *[Aegean]* islands, it will effectively have surrounded Turkey.[4]

His words were echoed by Foreign Minister Erkin speaking at Lancaster House, London, in 1964. Stressing the strategic importance to Turkey of Cyprus, which he asserted had to be seen geographically as a continuation of the Anatolian peninsula, he concluded:

> All these considerations clearly demonstrate that Cyprus has vital importance to Turkey, not merely because of the existence of the Turkish community in Cyprus, but also on account of its geo-strategic bearing.[5]

A Turkish academic has expounded an even broader view:

> The geo-political situation of Turkey and the outlook of the countries encircling her in the north are such as to force Turkey to keep secure her southern defences. Consequently Cyprus maintains its vital importance . . . as far as Turkey is concerned.[6]

Statements such as these (and many others in the same vein made since) leave no room for doubt that for Turkey the overriding importance of Cyprus is strategic, and that protection of the rights of the Turkish Cypriot minority has been a secondary, though important, consideration.

Asked in 1974 how Britain viewed Turkish interest in Cyprus, Field Marshal Lord Harding of Petherton, who had been Governor of Cyprus from 1955 to 1958, replied:

> The geographical distance between Cyprus and Turkey determines the extent of Turkish interest in Cyprus. Beyond the proportion of the population of Cyprus that is Turkish and in whose future Turkey is definitely interested, the country could not remain indifferent to the future of an island so close to its shores. . . . We did not create Turkish interest in Cyprus. It was always there. And it was quite right and just and legitimate for Turkey to show such interest in Cyprus.[7]

The Cyprus problem cannot be understood without recognition of these fundamental realities.

During the eight decades of British rule there was growing Greek Cypriot agitation for *enosis* (union of the island with Greece) and consequential mounting Turkish concern. The more Greek Cypriots clamoured for this, the louder Turkey warned that this would be met by *taksim* (partition of the island, with a Turkish area annexed to Turkey), a development sometimes referred to as 'double *enosis*'. The proximity of Turkey and its military power lent credibility to this warning, although many on the Greek side failed to recognize this until it was too late. The granting of independence to Cyprus in 1960 under a Constitution which expressly forbade for all time the island's partition or its union with another state brought temporary respite, but, when three years later that Constitution broke down before its ink was properly dry, Turkish fears that the Greek majority was bent on *enosis* were revived. Turkey was determined to forestall any such development and when, ten years later, the ideal opportunity to do so presented itself, it acted swiftly to secure physical control of all northern Cyprus.

The chequered past of Cyprus has given rise to the second main ingredient of the problem – ethnic differences in the population. Until the arrival of the Turks in the late 17th Century the legacy of history had been a population in which Greek influences pre-dominated. The Greek language, together with a Greek cultural tradition, to which Christianity in the Orthodox form was added in early days, combined to create an in-digenous people that felt itself to be Greek in character. These, the Greek Cypriots, saw Greece as the mother-country, for which by the late 19th Century a strong emotional attach-ment had developed and with which political union became a growing aspiration. Following the grant of independence in 1960 such emotions were tempered by realization of what such union might entail; for many the prospect of subjection to the repressive military dictator-ship which seized power in Athens in 1967 was especially unappealing. Nonetheless, the dream of *enosis* remained an ideal embedded in Greek Cypriot emotions, with few daring not to pay at least lip service to it. Makarios himself epitomized this attitude, although latterly sufficiently a realist to warn his community that, so long as Turkey was opposed, *enosis* was unattainable without risk of simultaneous *taksim*.

Greek influences had taken root too deeply to be changed by the arrival in 1571 of the conquering Turks, but that historic event injected a critical new element into the ethnic mix of the population. More than 30,000 soldiers of Lala Mustafa's victorious army were given land and encouraged to settle in Cyprus, and were augmented during the subsequent 300 years by immigrants from Asia Minor. Thus was the Turkish Cypriot community created, and thus were sown the seeds of the island's 20th Century intercommunal problems. Although Turkish Cypriots always constituted a relatively small minority (in 1974 they formed only 18% of the population as compared with the 78% Greek Cypriot majority[8]), differences of language, religion and culture were insuperable obstacles to full integration of the two communities. Turks continued to speak Turkish, to adhere to Islam, to maintain Turkish customs, to educate their children in the Turkish cultural tradition and to refrain from intermarriage with other ethnic groups. For them Turkey was the mother-land to which they looked for political support, economic help and, ultimately, military salvation.

Settled over all the island without discernible pattern, the Turks clung together in the all-Turkish quarters of towns and mixed villages or in exclusively Turkish villages. With the passage of time political, economic and social factors tended to accentuate rather than diminish divisions between the Greek and Turkish communities. These reached their deepest immediately before and after the grant of independence, when Turkish fears of *enosis* and submersion of the minority in the vaunted concept of a 'Greater Greece' were at their most acute. Experiences at the hands of their Greek Cypriot fellow citizens when intercom-munal violence flared left them in no doubt that their fears were well founded. Small wonder if some preferred to describe themselves as 'Cypriot Turks'.

The secular power of the Cypriot Orthodox Church constitutes a secondary, but influen-tial, thread running through the fabric of the island's more recent history. The Church achieved autocephalous (self-regulating) status as a member of the Eastern Orthodox Church as early as the 5th Century, when the Ethnarch of Cyprus was accorded the rights, exercised to this day, to carry a sceptre, wear ceremonial purple and sign his name in red ink. Although the Church's power declined during the four centuries of Lusignan and Venetian rule, during which the Ethnarch was removed and the authority of Rome imposed, paradoxically the advent of the Muslim Turks saw it restored and enhanced. This was because the Turks, whose arrival was greeted by the Cypriots as a welcome release from grinding Venetian oppression, at once set about rooting out all vestiges of the Roman Church, identified in Ottoman minds with Venice. Roman clerics were expelled, cathedrals were converted into mosques and the Cyprus Ethnarch was restored and recognized by the Turks as both the spiritual and the temporal leader of Eastern Orthodox Greeks on the island, this being in conformity with administrative practice in the Ottoman Empire, by which its Christian subjects were ruled by their own prelates. The Archbishop and his subordinate bishops thus became established as the recognized civil administrators and spokesmen for the Greek community. A consequence, however, was to perpetuate the divisions between Greeks and Turks on the island, with the latter looking across the water to Turkey for the conduct of their community's affairs.

British rule, while generally refraining from interference in ecclesiastical matters, achieved some progress in lowering the intercommunal barriers, but did little to promote a common Cypriot identity. A set-back came in 1931, when growing Greek agitation for *enosis* led to riots in which Government House was burnt down.[9] British reaction was firm – repressive measures included deportation of two bishops and others seen as ring-leaders. Although these measures were relaxed progressively before and during the 1939–45 War when Cypriots of both communities rallied to the British cause, in the immediate post-war years *enosis* remained as distant a prospect as ever, in spite of much Greek political manoeuvering.

It was the rise in 1950 of a new, young and forceful Ethnarch, Archbishop Makarios III[10], that gave fresh impetus to the cause. A passionate advocate of *enosis*, he sought to achieve this by securing, as a first step, the right of self-determination for the peoples of the island (in practice the Greek majority) in confident anticipation that at the Church's bidding they would then opt for *enosis*. His activities quickly established him both as ecclesiastical and political leader of the Greek community to a degree reminiscent of the centuries of Ottoman rule, but simultaneously served to sharpen once more the divisions between Greek and Turk on the island, with the latter increasingly looking to mother-land Turkey for support and protection.

The power of the Cyprus Orthodox Church reached its zenith in 1960 with the election of Archbishop Makarios as the new Republic's first President, an office he held in parallel with that of Ethnarch until his death in 1977.[11] Since, uniquely in the Christian world, the laity in Cyprus take part in the election of their Archbishop, his position was doubly strong. Although the religious divide between the island's communities has not in itself been a prime cause for discord,[12] it has tended to exacerbate other differences, rendering it all the more difficult for the Greek Christian majority and the Turkish Muslim minority to reconcile divergent attitudes to the constitutional and other problems that in recent years have bedevilled their contentious island.

CHAPTER TWO

INDEPENDENCE –THE FALSE DAWN

The achievement of independence, and with it the lifting of the controlling and restraining influence of the colonial power, had the effect of intensifying the mutual distrust and fear ingrained in the two communities and of aggravating their intransigence to each other.

Sir Lawrence McIntyre: 'Cyprus as a United Nations Problem',
Australian Outlook, April 1976.

The struggle which failed to win *enosis* but led instead to independence has been well chronicled by others[1]. It was waged on two fronts: externally by pressures exerted at international level in the course of which, in the face of British insistence that Cyprus was the exclusive responsibility of the United Kingdom, both Makarios and the Greek Government sought to involve the United Nations, not least because they saw this as affording a safeguard against military intervention by Turkey; and internally by armed insurrection, a bitter and ruthless business in which wounds were inflicted that endure to this day.

The campaign of violence, launched on 31 March 1955, followed the UN General Assembly's rejection the previous December of Greece's request[2] for a motion concerning the right of self-determination for Cypriots to be inscribed on its Agenda. The campaign was conducted by an initially inept guerrilla group, which gained notoriety as EOKA (*Ethniki Organosis Kyprion Agoniston* – National Organization of Cypriot Fighters), led by a 57-year-old austere former officer of the Greek army of Cypriot birth, Colonel Georgios Grivas, who adopted as cover for his clandestine activities the *nom de guerre* 'Dighenis'.[3] Although sometimes at odds over tactics and timing, the headstrong and unsophisticated Grivas and the astute and subtle Makarios worked hand-in-glove to further the armed struggle. The latter's clear complicity led in March 1956 to his deportation by the British government to the Seychelles, from which a year later he was released to go to Greece (but not back to Cyprus), it having become clear by then that a solution to the island's problems was unlikely without his cooperation.

Initially EOKA's campaign was directed against the British Administration, but it soon took an intercommunal turn. Turkish Cypriots, perceiving that their interest lay in supporting the colonial power, readily cooperated with the British, and violent incidents between Greeks and Turks multiplied as the former realized the extent to which the latter were an obstacle to *enosis*.[4] As intercommunal relations deteriorated, so did tension between the two mother-countries rise. The British Government, by now heavily committed in anti-

EOKA military operations (a State of Emergency had been declared in November 1955), became increasingly anxious to cure the running sore that Cyprus had become, prejudicing not only Britain's international reputation but also the cohesion of NATO's southern flank. Various proposals for a settlement, including those made in 1956 by Lord Radcliffe (the officially appointed Constitutional Adviser), proved fruitless. In 1958 the British Prime Minister, Harold Macmillan, advanced a plan that conceded the right of self-determination, although this was to be exercised only after a seven-year period during which separate communal legislative bodies and municipalities would be permitted and intercommunal passions allowed to cool. Turkey accepted this plan, but Greece and Makarios rejected it on the grounds that it was tantamount to partition.

As violence continued and international anxiety grew as to where this was leading, Paul-Henri Spaak, NATO's Secretary General, convened talks in Paris in December1958 between Britain, Greece and Turkey, at which the concept was addressed of an independent Cyprus neither united with Greece nor partitioned. This concept was known to be acceptable to Makarios, perhaps because of his perception that, since *enosis* was unattainable without the risk of *taksim*, independence might permit progress towards union with Greece at some future date when that risk had been nullified. The Paris talks, conducted in the shadow of the Cold War (which may have concentrated Greek and Turkish minds[5]), augured well, and were followed by a meeting in Zurich in February 1959 between Greek and Turkish ministers (as in Paris, no Cypriots took part), at which agreement was reached on the concept discussed in Paris. This, the Zurich Agreement, set out the basic provisions upon which a Republic of Cyprus was to be established as an independent sovereign State. A week later a settlement incorporating the Zurich Agreement was formalized at a meeting at Lancaster House, London, attended by not only British, Greek and Turkish ministers but also the leaders of the two Cypriot communities.

In a last-minute bid to keep open the door to *enosis* Makarios objected to several aspects of what had been agreed in Zurich, protesting in particular that the Turkish minority was to be given entrenched rights that were excessive. Further, he objected strongly to the proposal that Greece and Turkey should be permitted to station military contingents on the territory of the Republic – a measure which, he argued, was inconsistent with the sovereignty of the new State and without parallel elsewhere. He complained above all that the stipulation that the provisions of the Zurich Agreement were to be regarded as immutable and never open to modification or revision was altogether unrealistic. He looked in vain for support from the Greek Government, which declined to renege on what it had agreed at Zurich. Isolated and under concerted pressure from the remainder, Makarios was obliged to fall into line, asserting subsequently that he had done so only because he had been convinced that partition would otherwise have been imposed on Cyprus, thus allowing the Turks a permanent foothold on the island.

The Zurich and London Agreements were signed at Lancaster House on 19 February 1959 by all participants, including Archbishop Makarios for the Greek and Dr Kuchuk for the Turkish Cypriots, and were accepted on all sides as constituting the foundation for final settlement of the Cyprus problem[6]; as such they were welcomed, not only in Greece and Turkey, but also by the world at large. Makarios returned to Nicosia the following month and action followed to draft the Constitution and give effect to the other requirements of the Agreements. Details were settled only after prolonged negotiation, so that it was not until 16 August 1960 that the Republic of Cyprus came into formal being, with Makarios as President and Kuchuk as Vice President, each having been so elected by the votes of his own community. In September the young Republic was admitted to membership of the United Nations and in 1961 of the British Commonwealth. That same year it joined the Council of Europe and became a founder member of the Non-Aligned Movement. To outward appearances the island had achieved full independent status, but given the nature of what had been agreed at Zurich and in London this was a deceptive veneer.

By a Treaty of Guarantee, to which Britain, Greece, Turkey and Cyprus were parties, each undertook to recognize and to maintain the independence, territorial integrity and security of the Republic as stipulated by the Basic Articles of the Constitution. In view of subsequent events the wording of Article IV of this Treaty is significant:

> In the event of a breach of the provisions of the present Treaty, Greece, Turkey and the United Kingdom undertake to consult together with respect to the representations or measures necessary to ensure the observance of these provisions. In so far as common or concerted action may not prove possible, each of the three guaranteeing powers reserves the right to take action *with the sole aim of re-establishing the state of affairs created by the present Treaty.'* [author's emphasis]

Thus, although there was an obligation to consult, there was no obligation to take any other action. Interpretation of this Article has since given rise to much dispute, in particular whether or not it permitted unilateral military intervention, which (it is argued) is in breach of the UN Charter's stipulation that:

> All Members shall refrain in their international relations from the threat or use of force against the territorial integrity or political independence of any state, or in any other manner inconsistent with the Purposes of the United Nations. *[Article 2, 4]*

What was indisputable is the clearly stated sole aim of any action taken.

Related to that Treaty was a second, a Treaty of Alliance between Greece, Turkey and Cyprus (Britain was not a party), whereby Greece and Turkey was each authorized to station permanently on the island a battalion of its own army. These were to provide training for a Cyprus army, and all three were to participate in a Tripartite Headquarters, the express purpose being to provide for defence against any threat to the independence or territorial integrity of the new Republic.

In order to satisfy its own defence obligations in the region Britain insisted on retaining under British sovereignty two areas on the island's southern coast where, following withdrawal from the Suez Canal Zone in 1954, major military installations had been established. Totalling 255 sq km in extent, these two Sovereign Base Areas (SBAs) were excluded from forming part of the territory of the Republic[7], and the arrangements governing them were incorporated in a third treaty, the Treaty of Establishment, to which all four governments subscribed. In addition to military establishments situated within the two SBAs (which included the strategically important RAF airfield at Akrotiri), there were other facilities elsewhere which Britain wished to continue to use, such as the RAF base at Nicosia airport, port facilities at Famagusta and Limassol, radio and radar sites on Mount Olympus and several training areas and weapon firing ranges located elsewhere around the island. Under the treaty these were designated 'Retained Sites' of various categories, at which Britain would continue to enjoy special rights, even though the sites themselves were republican territory. The British Government undertook on its part to make a grant of £12 million to the Cyprus Government to be spread over a period of five years.[8] Although not mentioned in any of the treaties, there was a tacit assumption that, in addition to satisfying Britain's wider defence obligations, a purpose of retaining the SBAs was also to afford Britain a capability to fulfil its responsibilities under the Treaty of Guarantee comparable to that allowed to Greece and Turkey by the terms of the Treaty of Alliance.

The Constitution for the new Republic provided for the President and Vice President to be respectively Greek and Turkish Cypriots, each having power of veto over decisions of both legislature and executive. They were supported by a Council of Ministers and a House of Representatives, each in the ratio of seven Greeks to three Turks and both elected on separate communal rolls. The integrity of the Constitution was to be safeguarded by a Supreme Constitutional Court of three members – a Greek and a Turkish Cypriot with a neutral President.[9] Other provisions included the establishment of Communal Chambers for each community to deal with matters such as education, religion and culture. Indeed, bi-communal provisions ran right through every facet of the Constitution and became a cause for perpetuating rather than eliminating ethnic divisions. They also resulted in a written Constitution of inordinate length and complexity, including the stipulation that the 48 Basic Articles agreed at Zurich were to be regarded as immutable in perpetuity. That stipulation has been defended on the grounds that agreement would otherwise never have been reached, but it was an unrealistic requirement that was soon to prove a recipe for disaster, illustrating the truth of Edmund Burke's dictum that 'a State without the means of some change is without the means of its conservation'. Nevertheless, at first sight the constitutional problems appeared to have been settled to the reasonable satisfaction of all parties. The Turks believed that the Republic had been founded on the basis of equal partnership between the communities and that the door to *enosis* had been firmly closed, while the Greeks were able to claim achievement of independence, albeit under arrangements that denied them the right of self-determination and which conceded to the minority entrenched rights that they deemed to be excessive in relation to the latter's numbers, abilities and share of the island's economy. In practice what had emerged was an inflexible compromise.

Makarios made no secret that he had accepted the settlement under duress, but Grivas went further, making plain that he saw it as a betrayal of what EOKA had been fighting for and that he acquiesced only in deference to the Greek mother-land. There was also a personal note to Grivas's anger – he had not been consulted by Makarios during the London negotiations and was resentful that as leader of the armed struggle he had been allowed no say in the outcome; to add to his discomfort, it had been agreed in London that he must quit Cyprus. He did so in March 1959 after securing an amnesty for members of EOKA and was flown to Athens, where he was accorded a rapturous reception and the honorary rank of Lieut. General in the Greek army.

Among Greeks 'Dighenis' became the subject of romantic legend, with much being made of his supposed skill in evading capture by the British. Since Grivas is destined to appear prominently twice more on the Cyprus stage, it is pertinent to tell the story of how he survived to do so. The words are those of General Sir Kenneth Darling, then Director of Operations in Cyprus:

> Shortly before the start of the London Conference to which Hugh Foot [*Governor of Cyprus*] had gone, John Prendergast [*Chief of Intelligence*] came to my house and told me that we had run Grivas and some of his closest associates to ground in a house in Nicosia, which was under tight surveillance. He asked for instructions as to what action should be taken. I was thrilled at this news which did not surprise me. It meant that we had George Grivas at our mercy. . . .
>
> At a meeting held by Mr George Sinclair, the Deputy Governor, it was agreed that the only practical course was to instruct John Prendergast to fly to London that night, to give the information to Hugh Foot and to seek instructions as to whether Grivas's head was required on a charger, or whether he should be allowed to stew in his own juice. John Prendergast returned after a short absence to say that we were to adopt the latter course. While this decision was something of a disappointment to those concerned in the hunt for Grivas, they appreciated the long-term hopes on which it was based. For all practical purposes the Emergency was over. It ended on a very satisfactory note; we held the military initiative, we had run EOKA into the ground and we had its legendary leader in our grasp.[10]

General Darling has added a postscript describing the British Army's farewell to Grivas (a diminutive figure, habitually dressed in baggy uniform blouse and breeches) as he left Nicosia for Athens:

> It was thought necessary that Grivas should be seen off by some military officer of not too high a rank. . . . Paul Gleadell [*Darling's Chief of Staff*] made a brilliant choice. He selected Lieut. Colonel Bill Gore-Langton of the Coldstream Guards. He stood all of six feet four inches and, immaculately turned out and unarmed, he would be able to gaze down, maybe with disdain, from a considerable height. But the strongest point in his favour was that he had no right arm, having lost it in the war, and no offence could be interpreted if he did not salute.[11]

It was not long before euphoria at the outcome of Zurich and London gave way to a feeling in both Cypriot communities that matters had been decided over their heads with their voices accorded inadequate hearing, and the belief grew that the solutions adopted were little more than short-term expedients. The Greek Cypriots nursed a deep-felt grievance that the democratic right of the majority to determine its future had been subordinated to the interests of the relatively small minority. For their part the Turkish Cypriots, whose fear of *enosis* and Greek domination were not entirely allayed, became all the more determined not to permit any erosion of their rights as entrenched in the Constitution.

The mainland Turks, who backed their compatriots in this stand, re-affirmed their claim that Cyprus, which had never belonged to Greece, had to be seen geographically as forming part of Turkey. Three centuries of Turkish rule, they asserted, had been interrupted only temporarily by the eighty years of British administration; if Cyprus was not to remain independent, then it must revert to Turkey.[12] For good measure they argued that the democratic concept of majorities and minorities was irrelevant – there were two distinct ethnic communities on the island, who had come together as equal partners in a spirit of compromise. But, pointedly, they added that, if the democratic argument was to be pursued, then the Greeks in Cyprus were no more than a small minority among an overwhelming majority of Turks inhabiting the wider region of Anatolia, of which Cyprus was merely an extension. For Cypriots of both communities the achievement of independence was thus a false dawn. For others it was a paradox such as only Cyprus supplies. Whereas colonial peoples elsewhere struggled for full independence, the Cypriots had gained it without seeming to want it, aspiring rather to exchange their colonial masters for the rule of Athens or Ankara.

Within three years of the Republic's birth disagreements had surfaced and intercommunal antagonisms were revived. Ostensibly the causes lay in disputes concerning matters such as the ratio of Turks to Greeks in government services, the establishment of separate Turkish municipalities in the main towns, taxation and budgetary measures, and the manner in which Greeks and Turks were to be integrated in the army. But the root causes were to be found in the extreme bi-communal character of the Constitution[13] and in the ingrained mutual distrust that had been exacerbated by the intercommunal violence of the EOKA years. It was commonly remarked that Zurich and London had created a Cypriot state but not a Cypriot nation, for, as Sir Arthur Bryant once observed, 'without unity no people can become or remain a nation'. In November 1963, with the Greeks ever more exasperated by what they saw as Turkish intransigence and obstruction of government, President Makarios decided to bring matters to a head. Convinced that the Constitution had been shown to be unworkable, he proposed thirteen amendments, designed (he claimed) to facilitate government and remove some of the causes of intercommunal friction.[14] He presented these as a genuine attempt both to overcome difficulties that were paralysing government and to create a unified Cypriot nation but could not conceal that the proposed amendments all worked to the advantage of the Greek side.[15]

Turkish Cypriots were deeply suspicious of Makarios's motives, for from the outset he had shown no disposition to use his position as President to promote true understanding and reconciliation between the two communities; this may be history's strongest criticism of him. But even had he tried to do so, the duality of temporal and spiritual office combined in his person was not readily acceptable to the Muslim Turks, who saw in this an inherent conflict between his ecclesiastical obligations to his Greek Orthodox flock and his civil responsibilities to the Cypriot people as a whole. Turkish disquiet was well founded, for in his many public utterances Makarios had continued to make no secret of his antipathy to the Turks and his adherence to the dream of *enosis*. Further, the thirteen amendments struck at the heart of the Basic Articles and thus were of direct concern to other signatories of the Treaties. On 16 December 1963 the Turkish Government declared outright rejection, and a sharp increase in intercommunal tensions followed.

Within both communities there were groups which had never given up their arms after the EOKA struggle and secretly remained ready against the day when these might once more be needed. The call came on 21 December 1963 when a spark (the origin of which is disputed) set light to the tense situation in Nicosia and intercommunal violence of singular ferocity flared and spread.[16] Appeals by Makarios and Kuchuk for a ceasefire went unheeded and the Turkish community withdrew behind barricades thrown up around the Turkish quarter. Cooperation between the two communities ceased and Turkish ministers, members of the Legislature, civil servants and policemen withdrew from the government and administration, never to return – the Greeks held that they had resigned, while the Turks protested that they had been prevented by force from exercising their constitutional rights and responsibilities. Henceforward government and administration were in the exclusive hands of the Greek Cypriots, but were seen by the Turkish Cypriots as illegal since neither complied with the provisions of the Constitution.

As fighting intensified troops of the mainland Greek national contingent (ELDYK) left their camp on the outskirts of Nicosia to reinforce the attacks of Greek Cypriot irregulars on the minority community. Complementary action was taken by men of Turkey's national contingent, who went to the aid of their hard-pressed Cypriot brothers, seized St Hilarion Castle, which dominates the northern port of Kyrenia, and took up positions astride the road linking that port with the Turkish quarter of Nicosia. Meanwhile the Turkish fleet put to sea and on Christmas Day Turkish military aircraft flew low over Nicosia – ominous indications of possible military intervention by Turkey. Makarios's protests to the Security Council had little effect and, when it became clear that the situation was beyond containment by the leaders of the island's two communities, recourse was had to the Treaty of Guarantee. With the agreement of Greece and Turkey Britain proposed that troops of the three powers stationed on the island should be formed into a tri-partite force under British command and deployed to assist the government to restore law and order. Fearful of Turkish intervention, Makarios reluctantly agreed, but stipulated that the force be confined to the area of Nicosia. The General commanding British troops in Cyprus, Major General P.G.F. Young, was appointed overall commander, and the British component was deployed from the SBAs to Nicosia on 26 December. It immediately set about halting the fighting, but the tri-partite force, known as the Joint Truce Force, never came into effective being, the Greek and Turkish components having disqualified themselves by their partisan actions.

The gravity of the situation prompted the British Secretary for Commonwealth Relations, Duncan Sandys, to fly to Nicosia on 28 December. He at once established a Political Liaison Committee, of which the Cypriot members were, for the Greeks Clerides (President of the House of Representatives) and Georghadjis (Minister of the Interior), and for the Turks Denktash (President of the Turkish Communal Chamber) and Orek (Minister of Defence); other members were the British High Commissioner, the Ambassadors of Greece and Turkey and the Commanders of the British, Greek and Turkish contingents. Sandys lost no time in setting it to work:

> At the committee's first meeting on Dec. 29 Mr Sandys, who took the chair, asked the Greek and Turkish Cypriot representatives to consider the following matters:
> (1) Arrangements to ensure the complete freedom of movement of British patrols in both sectors of Nicosia.

(2) The withdrawal of Greek and Turkish Cypriot fighters from strongpoints on either side
of the ceasefire line and their replacement by British troops, thereby creating a neutral
zone.

After a 12-hour meeting, the committee agreed on Dec. 30 to the formation of a neutral zone,
and on Dec. 31 to an exchange of hostages.[17]

The agreed neutral zone was delineated on a map by General Young using a green pencil;
ever since this has been known as 'the Green Line', a term that has passed into international
usage to denote comparable territorial divides elsewhere. The three guarantor powers, with
the concurrence of Makarios, also proposed that a UN representative be sent to Cyprus to
observe their operations for the maintenance of intercommunal order, and on 16 January the
Secretary General, U Thant, appointed Lieut. General Gyani of India, previously
Commander of the UN Force in Yemen, as his Special Representative on the island.

Apart from some isolated incidents the first two weeks of 1964 were relatively quiet,
but the British were less than content to find themselves carrying the main burden of maintaining the volatile state of affairs. With memories of the bitter EOKA years still fresh, distaste
for the task was strong and was not lessened by anti-British feelings heaped on the patient
British troops by elements in both communities, ever ready to blame others for their self-
inflicted misfortunes. Some Greek Cypriots, blind to the danger that Turkish military
intervention and even war between Greece and Turkey lurked in the offing, went so far as to
accuse the British soldiers of protecting the Turk 'rebels'. Unwilling to act indefinitely as
policeman, Britain convened a conference in London on 15 January with a view to resolving
the constitutional problems that had precipitated the crisis. It was attended by the Foreign
Ministers of Greece and Turkey and by Clerides and Denktash for the two Cypriot communities. At the opening session, Sandys, once more in the chair, said that British action had
given Cyprus a breathing space and stressed the need now for urgency in using this to find
an honourable and workable solution. He warned that:

> If fighting were to break out a second time, it would be much more difficult to stop it than on
> the last occasion, and Cyprus would once again be faced with all the dangers, internal and
> external, which were so narrowly averted a few weeks ago. The prospect of failure is too grim
> to contemplate. Somehow or other we have got to find a solution.[18]

But this was not to be; positions had hardened to the point of being irreconcilable. While the
Greek Cypriots offered limited safeguards for the Turkish minority, they remained insistent
on changes to the Constitution, which (they argued) had been shown to be unworkable.
More significantly, they demanded revocation of the Treaties of Alliance and Guarantee on
the grounds that these had been imposed on the Republic, infringed its sovereignty and ran
counter to the UN Charter;[19] all these demands were rejected by Turkish Cypriots and Turks
alike. Asserting that it was now patent that the two communities could not subsist together
in harmony under the 1960 arrangements, the Turks made counter-demands for the physical separation of the two under a federal arrangement or else by 'double *enosis*'. These were

rejected in turn by the Greek side, and the conference broke up in mutual recrimination and increased hostility.

In spite of the exertions of the British peacekeepers (now reinforced by a Divisional HQ and additional units under Major General R.M.P. Carver, who took over from Young to allow the latter to resume his responsibilities in the SBAs) the security situation deteriorated with fighting spreading to Limassol, Paphos and other areas. As calls for *enosis* or *taksim* became more vociferous, relations between Greece and Turkey neared breaking point. The clear threat to international peace and security, of which further low-level sorties over Nicosia by the Turkish airforce were evidence, gave rise to mounting concern within both the UN and NATO.

On 24 January 1964, following failure of the London conference and with its forces already stretched by emergencies in Aden and East Africa, Britain proposed with US support that an international peacekeeping force drawn from members of NATO be sent to the island. NATO governments, including those of Greece and Turkey, agreed, albeit with little enthu-siasm on the part of some, but Makarios refused to accept a force that was not subject to UN control.[20] Being convinced that only in this way could the risk of Turkish military inter-vention be obviated, he informed U Thant that Cyprus was ready to accept a UN Force. The Security Council met at Britain's request on 18 February but it took two weeks of debate and behind-the-scenes negotiation before a Resolution was adopted which, *inter alia*, author-ized the establishment of a UN Peacekeeping Force in Cyprus (UNFICYP) for a period of three months. This Resolution – No. 186 of 4 March 1964[21] – recommended that:

> the function of the Force should be, in the interests of preserving international peace and secu-rity, to use its best efforts to prevent a recurrence of fighting and, as necessary, to contribute to the maintenance and restoration of law and order and a return to normal conditions.

Since it was essential for the Force's mission to be complemented by action to settle the underlying problems, the Resolution also authorized the Secretary General to appoint a Mediator, whose task was:

> to use his best endeavours with the representatives of the [*Cypriot*] communities and also with the aforesaid four Governments [*of Cyprus, Greece, Turkey and the United Kingdom*] for the purpose of promoting a peaceful solution and an agreed settlement of the problems confronting Cyprus, in accordance with the Charter of the United Nations, having in mind the well-being of the people of Cyprus as a whole and the preservation of international peace and security.

Paradoxically, the Resolution gave another twist to the differences between Greeks and Turks as each placed its own interpretation on its intent, the former holding that it required the UN Force to act in their support to suppress the Turkish 'rebels', while the latter claimed that it required the Force to side with them to remove the 'illegal' Makarios administration and restore constitutional government.

UNFICYP came into formal being on 27 March 1964 with the arrival of the first UN troops from outside the island, but did not become operational for a further month.[22] In the meantime British troops, who until then had held the ring alone, donned the UN's blue beret and bore the brunt of the increasingly onerous peacekeeping task. The build-up of UN troops was slow, but was completed by the end of May, when the Force totalled 6,400 men drawn from nine countries. Military contingents came from Austria (in the form of a Field Hospital), Canada, Denmark, Finland, Ireland, and Sweden, as well as from the United Kingdom, and were supplemented by civilian police contingents from Australia, Austria, Denmark, New Zealand and Sweden.[23] Reporting on the Force's experiences during its first month of duty, the Secretary General wrote:

> Suspicion and a lack of mutual confidence dominate the relations of the two main communities and preserve the tension, which on occasion increases because of acts of violence and harassment. In this situation the role of UNFICYP is an exceedingly difficult one, in which both constructive initiative and non-interference are inevitably and invariably misinterpreted by one side or the other.[24]

These comments could well have been made at any time during UNFICYP's subsequent long duty on the island.

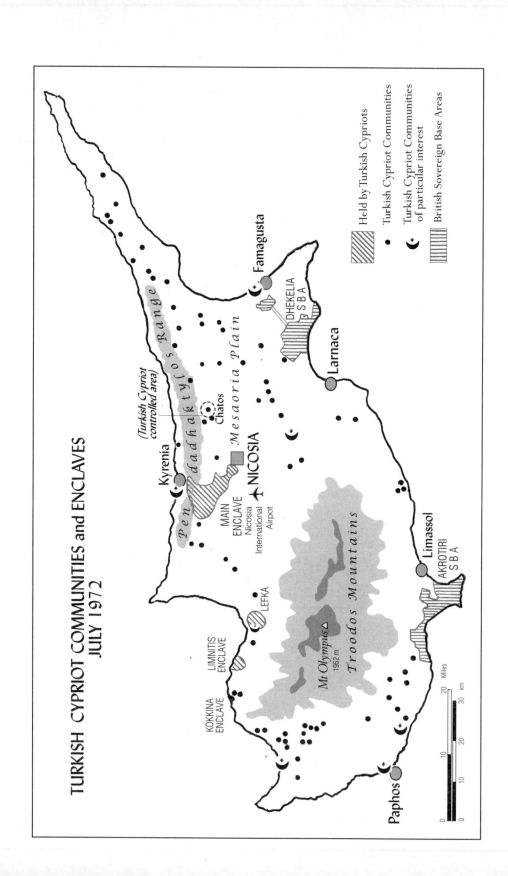

TURKISH CYPRIOT COMMUNITIES and ENCLAVES
JULY 1972

Held by Turkish Cypriots

Turkish Cypriot Communities

Turkish Cypriot Communities of particular interest

British Sovereign Base Areas

Famagusta

DHEKELIA S B A

Larnaca

(Turkish Cypriot controlled area)

Chatos

Mesaoria Plain

Kyrenia

Pen dadhaktylos Range

NICOSIA

MAIN ENCLAVE

Nicosia International Airpot

LEFKA

LIMNITIS ENCLAVE

KOKKINA ENCLAVE

Mt Olympus △
1952 m

Troodos Mountains

Limassol

AKROTIRI S B A

Paphos

Miles

km

0   10   20

0   10   20   30

CHAPTER THREE

FESTERING WOUND

The problem of Cyprus may appear very complicated, but in fact it is very simple. It is the relentless struggle of the Greek Cypriots and their mainland, Greece, to achieve *enosis*, and the efforts and sacrifices of the Turkish Cypriot community and their mother-land, Turkey, to prevent it.

Vedat Celik, speaking to the UN Special Political Committee,
29 October 1974.

The violence of Christmas 1963 marked the beginning of a period of severe tribulation for the Turkish community, which resisted stubbornly all attempts by the Greek majority to bring it to its knees. The blackest years were from 1964 to 1968, when the community at times was reduced to living under virtual siege conditions. That it survived was due in no small measure to the presence of the UN peacekeepers, who exercised a moderating influence, stabilized the security situation (although not always able to prevent some serious incidents), mitigated the harsh conditions under which many Turks existed, and – by no means least – kept the world at large impartially informed of what was happening.

But the threat of Turkey's military power poised a mere 70km away constituted the ultimate sanction that preserved the Turkish Cypriots from expulsion or worse. Their Leadership, resentful of a fancied anti-Turkish bias in UN attitudes and actions, was in no doubt on this score, as Dr Kucuk made plain in early and bitter criticism of UNFICYP:

The fact is that, despite the existence of the United Nations Force in Cyprus, Turkey's determination to protect the Turkish community and the presence of the Turkish army contingent in Cyprus is the only guarantee for the physical existence of Cypriot Turks [*sic*] individually and collectively.[1]

(Turkish criticism of UNFICYP diminished during succeeding years, but the feeling persisted that neither those in New York nor those serving on the island were sufficiently understanding of the predicament of the minority community.)

When in December 1964 intercommunal fighting flared, Turkish Cypriots in the smaller and more isolated communities fled to the security offered by the hastily organized defences of larger communities in towns or Turkish-dominated areas; some Turkish villages were abandoned altogether, as were some mixed villages. Often the vacated properties were destroyed by the Greeks and in many cases the rightful owners were never to return to them.[2] Atrocities and excesses were committed by both sides, but inevitably it was the Turkish minority that suffered the more. With scant regard for age or sex, some were murdered and others were taken hostage or abducted, never to be seen again.

Many refugees, estimated to total some 25,000, congregated in one of three Turkish Cypriot 'enclaves'. The largest was the Nicosia enclave, which stretched from the Turkish quarter of the capital northwards astride the Kyrenia Road to the summit of the Kyrenia Pass; the other two, both far smaller, were situated on the north-west coast at the villages of Limnitis and Kokkina-Mansoura. Others fled to the the Turkish quarters of larger mixed villages, such as Polis in the north-west, or to other areas that were under Turkish control, such as that centred on Chatos (on the Mesaorian Plain 25km north-east of Nicosia) or Lefka (in the mining area 45km west of the capital). Protection of the Nicosia enclave was ensured by troops of the Turkish National Contingent, which remained deployed astride the Kyrenia Road in the key Geunyeli – Orta Keuy sector. Elsewhere the Turks existed as best they could, defended by their own inadequately armed irregulars, the TMT (*Turk Mudufaa Teskilati*), later known as the TCF (Turkish Cypriot Fighters), while hemmed in by armed Greeks.

The latter consisted of irregulars drawn from several disparate factions, of which the old EOKA was the most prominent, but the need to bring these groups under control was clear and Makarios decided to create a Greek Cypriot National Guard into which they could be absorbed. A Bill establishing this force made it illegal for arms to be carried by any Cypriots, Greek or Turk, who were not members of the force or the civilian police.[3] He intended the National Guard (not to be confused with the still-born Cyprus Army) to be the primary armed service of the State, and this it became until differences between him and Athens led to its subversion by its mainland Greek officers.

During a visit to Athens in April 1964 the Archbishop had been assured by the Greek Prime Minister, George Papandreou, of the mother-land's support against Turkey if required, including provision of trained men and military supplies; in return Makarios was required to recognize Athens as the 'National Centre' and authority for determining policy. A Greek army officer, General Karayiannis, was appointed to command the National Guard (a move welcomed by the UN Secretary General on the grounds that this would bring Greek Cypriot extremists under control) but, when Karayiannis proved less successful in this respect than had been hoped, eyes turned to Grivas, still languishing in Greece. The latter's prestige and popularity, coupled with his acquaintance with leaders of the various armed factions, made him an obvious choice for the task of welding them together under the aegis of the National Guard. Summoned from banishment to assume overall command, he landed back on the island in June 1964 and set about this task with the help of the Greek army, which covertly infiltrated a large number of its men in the guise of 'volunteers', together with weapons and equipment including armoured vehicles and artillery. Within a year the National Guard had achieved a strength of 20,000 men, of whom a high proportion were mainland Greeks.

The stubborn resistance of the Turkish Cypriots, bolstered by the Turkish national contingent and sustained by confidence in Turkey's will and ability to preserve them from annihilation, ensured their survival but did not save them from severe privations caused by economic sanctions imposed by the Greek Cypriots. Turkish areas were subject at times to total blockade, while at others foodstuffs and relief supplies imported under international auspices were denied to them by the imposition of duties or other administrative devices.[4] And not only foodstuffs – the Greeks proscribed a wide range of other goods as 'strategic materials', to be denied to the Turks in order to bring an end to their 'rebellion'; items in every day civil use, such as building materials and automobile spares, were included, but, whether proscribed or not, all goods were liable to arbitrary confiscation at check points. Turkish Cypriots were harassed in other ways too. Freedom of movement was often denied and they left their sanctuaries at their peril, for murders and abductions continued. Further, postal and telephone services, payment of pensions and other benefits, registration of births and deaths, issue of passports, supply of water and electricity, distribution of agricultural and educational subsidies and even the very conduct of the judiciary were at times obstructed, suspended or altogether withheld. These actions bore heavily on the Turkish community as a whole, but their impact on the refugees, who had lost home and livelihood, was especially severe.

During the summer of 1964 camps were established on the outskirts of Nicosia, where some 1,500 refugees (over half of them children) lived in tents in the searing heat; another 600 took refuge in the small Kokkina enclave where many lived primitively in caves. The community's hardships were compounded by its losses in agriculture, industry and trade, by cessation of annual government grants hitherto paid for communal purposes, by the loss of schools, mosques and other buildings, and by the ending of employment of over 4,000 who had been in government or private service in Greek areas. In consequence some 56,000 members of the community (25,000 refugees, 23,500 unemployed, and 7,500 disabled), who had been deprived of their normal means of subsistence, had to be sustained. The privations and insecurity experienced during 1964–68 left indelible marks which inevitably influenced future Turkish-Cypriot attitudes.[5]

The concentration of the community within besieged areas was to prove of fundamental importance. The Leadership was obliged to establish its own administration in these areas and soon saw the advantage of keeping them intact and under its control, not only as a bargaining counter but also as a stepping-stone to eventual partition (a policy facilitated by economic support from Turkey). The Leadership ruled the community with an iron hand, allowing its members few contacts with the Greek side and often refusing them permission to return to their own homes in the few cases where the Greeks were willing to allow it; even the sale to Greeks of Turkish-owned real estate was prohibited (albeit not always success-fully). The Greeks failed to grasp the significance of this Turkish policy, mistakenly interpreting reliance on economic support from Turkey as a sign of weakness that would work to Greek advantage the longer matters remained unresolved. As a Greek Cypriot was later to lament:

> Throughout the 1963–74 period there seemed to have been a feeling on the Greek Cypriot side that it was for the Greek side to dictate terms and that eventually the Turkish Cypriot com-munity would be forced by its own self-segregation and economic deprivation that entailed to come to the negotiating table. This was a monumental mistake of basic policy.[6]

The problems confronting UNFICYP on its arrival in mid-1964 were thus formidable, ranging from measures to halt the violence to ways and means of settling economic and other disputes that were potential causes for a resumption of fighting. The Force set about its mission in a variety of ways. Men in blue berets were interposed in areas of close military confrontation, Observation Posts (OPs) or mobile patrols were deployed in areas of special intercommunal sensitivity, and close liaison was maintained with each side at every level – all with the purpose of resolving (or, where possible pre-empting) problems and serving as a channel of communication and mediation; where appropriate, the Force sought to estab-lish a peaceful *modus vivendi* pending settlement of the island's basic difficulties. As year followed year and its mandate was regularly renewed in identical terms[7], UNFICYP succeeded in reducing intercommunal violence to a minimum.

But during the first four years there were numerous local incidents in which exchanges of fire were common; rarely needing to open fire themselves[8], UN soldiers managed to contain most, preventing escalation. However, where either side chose not to cooperate with UNFICYP and was intent on action that went beyond solution at local level, the Force's ability to contain the situation was limited. In the period up to 1968 there were three such occasions; all were potentially disastrous and were resolved primarily as a result of external international pressures. The first occurred in June 1964, when continuing violence in Cyprus caused mounting concern in Turkey to the point that its government decided on military inter-vention. When told of this decision in confidence by Ankara, Washington's reaction was sharp. In a personal letter couched in unequivocal terms, President Lyndon Johnson warned Prime Minister Ismet Inonu of likely grave consequences for Turkey of any such action. On Inonu's own admission this warning was decisive in averting the intended action.[9]

A second crisis developed two months later. Its seeds lay in well-founded allegations that the Turks were smuggling arms through the enclave around Kokkina-Mansoura, in Greek Cypriot anger at the Turkish national contingent's continuing control of the Kyrenia road, and in related problems connected with that contingent's troop rotations; rejection by Makarios of a plan put forward by the American Dean Acheson for an overall settlement of the Cyprus problem was a contributory factor.[10] Matters were brought to a head by National Guard attacks on the two small Turkish enclaves on the north-west coast. Pressures exerted by the UN Secretary General and others proved fruitless and UNFICYP, unable to prevent the attacks, withdrew its troops positioned between the combatants, which did little to enhance the force's credibility or the Turkish community's confidence in it. The fighting lasted for several days, during which the Turks came close to being driven into the sea. That they did not suffer this fate was due to intervention by the Turkish air force, which mounted strikes against National Guard positions and Greek villages in the Tyllyria area, set fire to a Greek Cypriot patrol boat, and threatened retaliation elsewhere across the island. Trusting in earlier assurances of support from both Greece and the Soviet Union, a frightened Makarios declared that, unless the air strikes were called off within two hours, he would order immediate retaliation against Turkish Cypriots throughout the island. It was an empty threat, for Greece was powerless to help, the island being beyond the range of its fighter aircraft, while Moscow cautioned the Archbishop to go no further. Once again the Americans exerted restraint on Turkey, but the latters' intervention had been decisive. The Turkish Cypriots survived bloody but unbowed, while the Greeks had been taught a lesson in the realities of military power that all too soon was forgotten.

The UN's search for a settlement of the Cyprus problem was launched against this background. It was initiated by Sakari Tuomioja of Finland, the Mediator appointed in March 1964, but when, six months later he died, the task was taken over by Dr Galo Plaza of Ecuador, who until then had been the Secretary General's Special Representative (SRSG). In March 1965 Galo Plaza produced a Report containing a penetrating analysis of the Cyprus problem.[11] Although he concluded that the Lancaster House settlement had been shown to be unrealistic, his proposals adhered to the concept of the Republic as an independent unitary state. Both the Greek government and Makarios accepted the Report as a basis for further discussion, but it was rejected out of hand by Turkey, ostensibly on the grounds that, in making proposals to which it had not given its agreement, Galo Plaza had exceeded his remit as Mediator. However, real Turkish objections ran deeper – they centred on Galo Plaza's view that any form of partition or federal government should be excluded, his opinion that the Turkish community had received over-generous treatment under the 1960 Constitution and, above all, his proposal that the Treaties of Alliance and Guarantee should be repealed and replaced by a United Nations guarantee.

The Secretary General, U Thant, declined to accept that Galo Plaza had exceeded his terms of reference, but the Turks insisted that with publication of his Report his role as Mediator was ended; in December 1965 Galo Plaza resigned. No further Mediators were appointed, the responsibilities of the SRSG (at that time Carlos Bernardes of Brazil) being widened to include the mediation function. Bernardes resigned in January 1967 and was succeeded by Dr Bibiano Osorio-Tafall of Mexico, who held the post with distinction for the ensuing seven years.

In the aftermath of Galo Plaza's failed mediation, the Greek and Turkish governments engaged in direct dialogue during 1966 with a view to ending the tensions that were souring relations between them, exacerbating animosities in Cyprus and keeping the Turkish community in conditions of acute hardship. The dialogue dragged on inconclusively into 1967 as fresh developments brought new complications, including a determined attempt by Makarios to gain effective control over the National Guard, which under its mainland Greek officers was seen increasingly to be under the thumb of Athens. Tension between the Archbishop and 'the National Centre' increased during the winter of 1966–67, when Makarios imported a large quantity of weapons from Czechoslovakia; these, he asserted, were needed to re-equip the police, but this placed them beyond the control of Grivas and Athens. Such developments were viewed with apprehension by the Turkish community which feared that without the restraining hand of Athens Makarios might be tempted into some new venture against it. A serious intercommunal incident in April 1967 at the village of Mari, which from its cliff-top position 22km east of Limassol dominates the main road to Nicosia, justified such fears.

However, it was an event outside the island that was to have the most serious consequences for Cyprus. A *coup d'état* in Athens on 21 April 1967 brought to power a military junta led by Colonel George Papadopoulos. Despite the junta's declaration that there would be no change in Greece's Cyprus policy and that the dialogue with Ankara would continue, new uncertainties had been created. The Greek Colonels were narrow in outlook, politically naive, intensely nationalistic and imbued with strong anti-communist emotions; the cohesion of NATO in the prevailing cold war climate was for them the overriding consideration. Thus Turkey, the traditional enemy, was seen as a lesser evil than the Soviet Union and the communist régimes on Greece's northern frontiers. Although committed to *enosis*, the Colonels believed that this could be achieved in such a way, not excluding partition, as to satisfy Turkish aspirations and preserve the cohesion of NATO's southern flank, but when, in September 1967, the Prime Ministers of Greece and Turkey met in Thrace to renew the dialogue, the junta's proposals were rejected. The Turks were adamant that the 1960 arrangements must be maintained and refused to contemplate any settlement that would give any part of Cyprus to Greece.

The collapse of this dialogue was followed in November 1967 by the third major crisis, which in its gravity eclipsed those of 1964 and brought Greece and Turkey to the brink of war. Its seeds were several, but the ostensible cause was an incident deliberately provoked by Grivas, which led to an attack by the National Guard on Turkish Cypriots in and around the villages of Ayios Theodorous and Kophinou (located at the junction of the main roads from Nicosia and Larnaca to Limassol). Inadequate surveillance by UNFICYP of National Guard troop movements resulted in failure to appreciate Grivas's real intentions and UN troops were caught unawares by the scale of the attack, in which artillery, mortars and armoured vehicles were used. Overwhelmed by this weight of arms, the Turks of these villages were obliged to capitulate with the loss of 27 dead and many wounded.[12]

Turkey's reaction was forthright. Threatening military intervention, to which a demonstration over Nicosia by its air force lent credibility, it demanded the immediate withdrawal of the National Guard from the two villages. Makarios and an alarmed Athens compelled Grivas to comply, but Turkish demands went much further: Grivas was to be dismissed and expelled for a second time; all Greek army personnel infiltrated into Cyprus were to be withdrawn; the National Guard itself and all Greek Cypriot para-military bodies were to be disbanded; the weapons imported from Czechoslovakia were to be placed in secure custody; compensation was to be paid for the Turkish Cypriot dead and all harassment of the community was to cease. These demands were backed by the movement of Turkish troops to Greece's Thracian frontier and by the readying of an amphibious force at the southern ports of Iskenderun and Mersin. Alarmed by these developments, the Secretaries General of both the UN and NATO urged restraint, but, as before, it was the Americans who exerted the strongest pressure. Cyrus Vance, despatched to Athens and Ankara to dampen down the crisis, succeeded in averting Turkish military action on terms that marked a turning point in the Cyprus saga.

The price paid by the Greeks for Grivas's rashness was heavy. Grivas himself had already been recalled to Athens where he was placed under house arrest, and the junta undertook to withdraw those military personnel, variously estimated to number between 10,000 and 15,000, in excess of the 950-man-strong battalion allowed by treaty. Makarios agreed to lift the economic sanctions imposed on the Turkish community, but managed to prevaricate over the demand for the disbandment of the National Guard to the point that this was never effected – an irony of history that he must later have sorely regretted. He also successfully resisted UN proposals for extending the powers of UNFICYP with a view to enhancing the Force's peacekeeping role. For its part Turkey agreed to stand down its forces on the Thracian frontier and those threatening Cyprus, and to withdraw from the island its own military personnel in excess of the 650 men permitted by treaty.[13] Meanwhile the Turkish Cypriots exploited Greek discomfort by declaring the establishment of a 'Turkish Cypriot Provisional Administration' to govern the affairs of their community until such time as the 1960 Constitution was restored; this was accorded no international recognition (except by Turkey), but both the UN and foreign governments pragmatically treated with it as necessary. The Kophinou crisis (as it became known) provided stark proof to the Greek Cypriots that in the face of Turkey's military power their ends could not be achieved by force, especially since Greece, even under a military régime, had been shown to be a broken reed. Consequently, after four turbulent years that had deepened intercommunal mistrust, the Cyprus story took a fresh direction. For the next six years – until 1974 – the intercommunal situation outwardly was one of relative calm; violence gave way to negotiation as the means for settling disputes.

It was necessary for the UN peacekeepers to monitor events within the Greek Cypriot community to ensure that incidents did not take an intercommunal turn, but during these six years their primary role consisted in snuffing out minor intercommunal disputes before they could escalate, in overcoming (or at least mitigating) causes of friction in economic and social matters, and more generally in maintaining a climate of calm conducive to the search for a settlement of the underlying problem. In this more stable situation it was possible progressively to reduced the size of UNFICYP, so that from a peak of 6,400 men in 1964 it had contracted to little over 3,000 by the middle of 1972 .

Makarios, who did not disguise his distaste for the military régime in Athens, was quick to recognize the new situation created by the collapse of the Athens-Ankara dialogue and by the Kophinou débâcle. Seeking to strengthen his position, he called a fresh Presidential election and in an electioneering speech in January 1968 advocated preservation of the Republic as an indivisible unitary state. Solutions to constitutional problems should be sought, he declared, by peaceful measures that would afford safeguards to the Turkish minority while ensuring effective government in accordance with democratic principles – in other words, by the Greek majority. His emphasis on retention of an undivided Cyprus stemmed from his perception that the Athens junta was ready to sacrifice part of the island to Turkey in exchange for union of the remainder with Greece – a price for *enosis* he was not willing to pay. Solutions must be sought, he declared, within the limits of what was feasible and not necessarily of what was desirable. The message was clear: since *enosis* was unattainable without risk of partition, it must be put aside, at least for the time being. Some concluded that Makarios had abandoned his commitment to *enosis* and was bent, rather, on retention of an independent Cyprus with him as its President. The Athens junta was now in no doubt that the Archbishop was an obstacle not only to an accommodation with Turkey but also to the dream of incorporating Cyprus in a 'greater Greece', but Makarios received the support of most Greek Cypriots, who in February 1968 re-elected him as President with a resounding majority of 96% over his one opponent.[14] His position thus secured, Makarios was ready to face any challenge from either of the junta or the Turks.

With need for a fresh peacemaking initiative clear, the Security Council in December 1967 authorized the Secretary General to exercise his 'good offices' to assist the parties in reaching a settlement. To this end U Thant proposed direct talks between representatives of the two communities with his Special Representative, Osorio-Tafall, exercising these good offices on his behalf. After delays occasioned by the Presidential election and resolution of procedural matters, the first session took place in Nicosia on 24 June 1968 between Glafkos Clerides and Rauf Denktash, representing respectively the Greek and Turkish communities, and with Osorio-Tafall present. Goodwill was evident on both sides (Clerides and Denktash personally were on good terms) and it seemed that the problems were to be tackled in a constructive and civilized manner; this early promise soon faded. Both sides conceded that there were defects in the 1960 arrangements but views as to how these should be remedied differed profoundly. Prolonged argument, exchanges of detailed written proposals, consultations with Ankara and Athens, and Osorio-Tafall's patient exercise of the UN's good offices failed to bridge fundamental differences on matters such as the degree of local autonomy to be allowed to Turks, renouncement of *enosis* and insistence on retention of a unitary state. After three years of frustrating and sterile talking, the momentum was lost and in September 1971 the negotiations foundered.

Recognizing the risk posed to international peace and security by leaving the Cyprus problem unresolved, U Thant proposed reactivation of the talks on a broader basis – Osorio-Tafall as his representative should now be a party to the talks and Greece and Turkey should each appoint a constitutional expert to be in attendance. This, he expected, would induce greater flexibility on the part of the two negotiators. By January 1972, when Dr Kurt Waldheim succeeded U Thant as Secretary General, all concerned had agreed a formula for the reactivation of the talks on this basis. A fresh complication then intervened.

Early in February it came to light that Makarios had clandestinely imported a further large consignment of Czech arms for the use of para-military forces under his direct control. The disclosure caused an immediate crisis, the Athens junta demanding that the arms be handed over to the National Guard under its Greek commanders and Ankara insisting that they be placed in UN custody. The argument was not resolved until late April, when by common consent they were placed under UNFICYP's control. Although the episode hardened Turkish attitudes, the talks were reactivated in Nicosia in June 1972, when Waldheim himself attended the opening session. It was to prove the last opportunity to settle matters peacefully. Both sides let it slip.

The apparent stability and calm of the post-Kophinou years were accompanied by economic boom on the island, generating a euphoria that blinded many Cypriots, Greeks in particular, to the realities of their inherently volatile situation. The resumption of intercommunal negotiations gave a ray of hope, but no sense of urgency was apparent. Few, even if they discerned it, grasped the significance of an ominous cloud building up from a new direction to darken the sky over Cyprus. Within two years it brought catastrophe on a scale not experienced by Cypriots since the advent of Lala Mustapha's conquering Turks four centuries earlier.

This shadow was cast by an ever-deepening rift between Makarios and the Greek junta. The Archbishop made clear his attitude in explicit terms:

I have always adhered to the principle, and I have on many occasions stated, that my co-operation with the Greek Government for the time being is for me a national duty. The national interest dictates harmonious and close cooperation between Athens and Nicosia. No matter which government of Greece was in power, it was for me the government of the mother-country and I had to cooperate with it. I cannot say that I have a special liking for military régimes, particularly in Greece, the birthplace and cradle of democracy.[15]

The sting was in the tail, but the feeling was mutual.

The Athens Colonels remained convinced that the need to maintain the strength of NATO warranted concessions to the Turks, even if this entailed a measure of 'double *enosis*'. In their eyes the obstacle was Makarios and his insistence on the preservation of the island's unity. To them his affirmations of unswerving allegiance to *enosis* rang hollow, qualified as they were by his reservations on the need to seek solutions within the limits of what was feasible. They concluded that he was no longer a true supporter of Hellenism, committed to union with Greece, and that he preferred retention of his office as President of an independent state rather than subordination to the 'National Centre'. But this was not all. The Archbishop's non-aligned policies gave the fervently anti-communist junta added cause for mistrust, for these were bringing him into close contact with what the Colonels saw as Third-World crypto-communists and leading to a flirtation with Marshal Tito of Yugoslavia, then a potent communist power on Greece's very doorstep. The fact that the Cypriot Communist Party, AKEL (*Anorthotikon Komma Ergazomenon Laon*), which was composed almost exclusively of Greeks, gave Makarios its support added to their anxieties, for AKEL followed the Soviet line in advocating preservation of Cyprus as an unaligned independent state and in opposing *enosis*, which would have allowed the island's absorption into the western alliance.[16]

Makarios's relations with the communist world misled some to speak extravagantly of him as 'the Red Archbishop' and to warn that Cyprus was in danger of becoming 'the Cuba of the Mediterranean' with him as its 'cassocked Castro'. Those who raised this spectre failed to perceive that Makarios was engaged in a Byzantine exercise in expediency, for there is little doubt of his devotion to his Church or his attachment to a democratic Greece – both inconsistent with genuine sympathy for communism. Indeed, Makarios was under no illusion that AKEL needed him more than he needed it – and he did not hesitate to say so. It was, rather, his realization that the policies of the Athens Colonels were serving to undermine the ability of Cyprus to withstand Turkish pressures that caused him to redress the balance by enlisting support elsewhere including Moscow, which to the junta's alarm he visited in July 1971. Paradoxically his adherence to a democratic Greece added to the Colonels' antipathy, for they feared that the Archbishop might become a rallying point for those in the mother-land who sought their downfall and the restoration of democracy. Persuaded for all these reasons that Makarios must go, the Colonels embarked on action to this end and did not shrink from violence.

The first attempt on his life, like those that followed, was a spectacular failure. On 8 March 1970 a helicopter carrying the Archbishop was shot down over the Archbishopric in Nicosia. Although the pilot was severely wounded, he brought the aircraft safely down and Makarios stepped out unharmed. Suspicion at once fell on one of Grivas's old EOKA henchmen,

Polycarpos Georghadjis, who until dismissed a short time earlier had been Minister of the Interior. Before his complicity could be established, Georghadjis was found murdered; investigations were not pursued, but many were convinced that he was the real culprit and had been silenced by Greek officers in the National Guard, who at Athens's bidding had been the true instigators. The attempt was a clear signal that the junta would stop at nothing to oust Makarios, but it rallied popular support behind him and obliged the Colonels to look to other means. Action followed to build up a covert subversive organization on the island and Greek army officers, selected for loyalty to the Athens régime, were posted to key appointments in the National Guard. These officers set out in increasingly blatant fashion to subvert the allegiance of young Greek Cypriots conscripted into the force, instilling in its place loyalty to Athens as the true champion of Hellenism. Their activities assumed increasingly sinister proportions and gave Makarios cause for deep concern and frequent complaint to the junta.

The Colonels' next venture was as inept as it was unsuccessful and can have caused Makarios no more than irritation, except in so far as it demonstrated their implacable opposition to him. Their agents were three bishops of the Cyprus Church, who during 1971 were prevailed upon to campaign for his resignation as President on the grounds that this temporal office conflicted with his responsibilities as Ethnarch. The resulting schism was not serious, for most thought the bishops' case was weak, not least because it had not been advanced until Makarios had already held Presidential office for three years. Desultory argument dragged on until March 1973, when the three bishops declared Makarios unfrocked as Archbishop on the grounds that he had failed to comply with their demand. Their action ended in ignominious failure. Makarios had been quietly mobilizing the support of the Eastern Orthodox Church, which met in July in Major Ecclesiastical Synod; the consequence was the unfrocking and dethronement of the three bishops themselves. Their futile action had done nothing to dent Makarios's political and ecclesiastical popularity, which was reflected in public demonstrations in Cyprus against 'the Judas bishops'.

In September 1971, in angry reaction to Makarios's July visit to Moscow, the junta sent Grivas back from Athens to make his third and final appearance on the Cyprus stage. His mission was to revive EOKA with a view to securing the downfall of Makarios as President on the ground that events had proved him an enemy of *enosis*. Grivas went about his task with the barely concealed support of the National Guard's pro-junta Greek officers. Violence within the Greek Cypriot community, watched by the Turkish community with both satisfaction and anxiety, reached a climax in 1973 with attacks on police stations, government agencies and Makarios supporters. Ironically, it was this internecine Greek quarrel, rather than that between Greeks and Turks, which in July 1974 was to bring Nemesis to the island. As the Soviet President, Leonid Brezhnev, later observed:

> The problems of Cyprus are an open wound which is continuously poisoning the life of the people.

CHAPTER FOUR

INTERNATIONAL DIMENSIONS

Cyprus has been the victim of geography for 3,000 years. . . . It may look only a speck on the map, but contemporary geo-political factors give it a strategic significance out of all proportion to its size.

The Economist, London, 26 July 1974.

If down the ages the fortunes of Cyprus and its peoples have been determined by geo-strategic factors, never was this more evident than in the decades of the Cold War that preceded the collapse of the Soviet Union in 1991. During that period Cypriots and their bitter animosities served as little more than pawns on the board of international power rivalries. Regardless of how some self-centred Cypriots might see it, the fundamental significance of their island and their internal quarrels has lain in the degree to which these exacerbate relations between Greece and Turkey to the prejudice of peace and the balance of power in the Eastern Mediterranean. Conflict between these two uneasy NATO partners would have serious implications for the cohesion of the Alliance's southern flank and consequently its prevention has been a long-standing Western concern. Small wonder that, when weighed in this balance, the national interests of diminutive Cyprus and its divided communities has usually been seen as of secondary importance.

As the dominant partner of the Western Alliance, the United States' attitude has been crucial. At the heart of US policy, so long as the Cold War persisted, lay concern that the Russians would exploit any Graeco-Turkish armed conflict, perhaps by expansion into the Middle East with consequent threat to the West's oil sources and a further spread of communism. Maintenance of the integrity of the Republic of Cyprus was thus seen by the Americans as of lesser importance than preservation of NATO's unity, leading them in turn to advocate settlements of the Cyprus problem, such as the Acheson Plan, that were calculated less to satisfy Cypriot interests than to avert war between Greece and Turkey. Between 1964 and 1974 Washington was at one with Athens in viewing Makarios as an obstacle to a settlement that might remove the principal cause[1] for potential conflict on NATO's southern flank, and US impatience increased as the intercommunal talks in Cyprus dragged on inconclusively. Makarios's contacts with Moscow and other communist régimes added to American disenchantment, and no tears were expected to be shed in Washington in the event of his premature departure from his seat of power in Nicosia. Indeed, there were suggestions that it would be in the US and Western interest to hasten this, a view that was not unwelcome to the Athens junta.[2]

While Greece and Turkey each occupied a key place in NATO strategy, their values were not commensurate. Not only are Turkish military forces far stronger than those of Greece (Turkey's population of more than 35 million outnumbers that of Greece by four to one), but also Turkey has been vital to NATO on account of its common frontier with the erstwhile Soviet Union, its control of the Black Sea exit and the barrier it presented to Soviet expansion into the Mediterranean, Levant and beyond. Some NATO military installations were located on Turkish soil, on which the US also established its own electronic surveillance posts. For all these reasons the Americans inclined towards Turkey, notwithstanding naval and air facilities allowed them in Greece. The significance of this reality was lost on neither Turks nor Greeks. The former, confident of their value in US and NATO calculations, felt free to follow policies more independent than might otherwise have been feasible. For their part the Greeks were obliged ruefully to face the fact that, in spite of their situation as a bulwark for NATO against the communist States on their northern borders, they took second place to Turkey in the West's strategic assessments.[3]

The reverse of this coin was the Soviet Union's interest in the island, of which its large Embassy in Nicosia was clear evidence.[4] Any weakening of the West's position in the Eastern Mediterranean was to Russian advantage, and to this extent friction between Greece and Turkey was not unwelcome. With the twin aims of exploiting differences between NATO allies and preventing Cyprus from being absorbed into the NATO camp Soviet policy was opportunistic. The Russians persistently demanded the withdrawal of all foreign forces from the island and closure of the British bases with the ultimate purpose of establishing a régime sympathetic to the Eastern bloc; it was their aim meanwhile to preserve the neutral and non-aligned status of the Republic and oppose any action that might prejudice this. The Soviet attitude to Graeco-Turkish differences was marked by oscillation, demonstrated at times by Soviet support for the Turks and at others by Soviet warnings to Ankara against action prejudicial to the neutrality or non-alignment of Cyprus. A complication for Moscow was the need to retain the confidence of AKEL, the membership of which was predominantly Greek Cypriot; any too overt support for the Turkish cause would alienate AKEL, whose proclaimed policies served not only to counter agitation for *enosis* but also to exert pressure for closure of the British bases. Cyprus confronted the Russians with a fine balancing act.

Eighty years of British administration left imprints on Cyprus deeper than is sometimes acknowledged today. It also created ties with Britain in economic, social and cultural fields that are closer than might have been expected, given the differences that separate Britons from the two Cypriot ethnic communities. Those imprints were not eradicated, nor were those ties much loosened by the grant of independence – indeed, in some respects they were strengthened, not least by Cyprus's membership of the Commonwealth. Nonetheless, there has been a disposition on the part of some Cypriots to denigrate the achievements of British colonial rule and to blame it for many of their later self-inflicted troubles. The reality is that Britain's legacy was one of which any colonial power could be proud. In 1980 a former senior British colonial official wrote:

It is perfectly true that, since independence, the island has achieved a material prosperity far exceeding that which Britain bequeathed to it at the time of independence. . . . But it is nevertheless true that virtually all the foundations of this remarkable economic and social development were laid during the period of British rule.[5]

Listing the many achievements of the colonial administration under a mere handful of Britons, he also acknowledged the part played by its Cypriot members:

They were the backbone of the Civil Service, and to them belongs most of the credit for establishing such foundations for the progress and prosperity of the island after it became independent. Our finest legacy to Cyprus was the excellence of the locally recruited Civil Service. Many Cypriots today look back nostalgically to the peace and security which they enjoyed under British rule . . . .[6]

The colonial years created close, though sometimes ambivalent, relations between the Cypriots and Britain, but the latter's policy in the post-independence years continued to be governed by considerations similar to those which had induced Britain to acquire the island in 1878. The military commitments which had prompted the move from the Suez Canal Zone to Cyprus in 1954 had mostly disappeared twenty years later, but the importance of the SBAs in the context of Western strategic interests had not diminished:

Cyprus has for the Atlantic Alliance the same importance and significance as it had when Disraeli agreed with the Sultan that we should occupy and administer it as a *place d'armes* to enable us to fulfil our obligations to support the Turks against any further aggression by the Russians against her eastern provinces.[7]

Since the economy of the SBAs is closely linked to that of the Republic, Britain has needed to maintain good relations with Nicosia. Cypriot sensibilities have obliged the British authorities to tread a delicate path, taking care not to antagonize Greek Cypriots by any seeming pro-Turkish bias, while avoiding actions that might give rise to Turkish complaint or cause friction between the Cypriot communities or the mother-countries.

To these ends Britain has generally adopted a low profile in the Cyprus dispute, preserving amicable relations with all sides, encouraging the communities to settle differences by negotiation, refraining from action likely to exacerbate relations between Greece and Turkey, and taking care to avoid giving grounds for criticism of its administration of the SBAs or the use to which they are put.[8] Nevertheless, with memories scarred by the bitter EOKA years there was aversion in many quarters to any renewal of British military involvement in the Cypriots' internal quarrels. This permeated to the highest level of government, if an account of a ministerial meeting of the then Labour government is to be believed:

Friday July 28, 1967. This morning at OPD [*Oversea and Defence Policy Committee*] we turned to an astonishing paper on Cyprus. . . . This paper advised that if the Greek army in Cyprus staged a *coup* against Makarios in order to achieve *enosis*, we should dissent from it but prevent our troops getting engaged in any hostilities. Denis Healey [Defence Minister] and I were the only two people there who had noticed this extraordinary proposal. A Commonwealth country is attacked by a fascist dictatorship and although we have 15,000 armed men there we stand idle. We both thought this totally intolerable and the passage was deleted. . . . When I saw Burke [Sir Burke Trend, Cabinet Secretary] and Harold [Prime Minister Harold Wilson] afterwards, they said: "That's what comes of one member of the Committee reading the papers".[9]

Since Cyprus was now an independent state and member of the United Nations, British obligations (it was argued) could be discharged adequately by participation in UNFICYP. In this way responsibility for keeping the peace between the two communities and preventing their quarrels from spreading wider could properly be laid in the lap of the UN Secretary General rather than on Britain as a guarantor power. So long as some semblance of the 1960 constitutional arrangements was preserved, this was a tenable position. But when in the summer of 1974 those arrangements were utterly shattered, it was not sufficient, at least in Greek Cypriot eyes, to excuse Britain's failure to react more positively in the spirit, if not the letter, of the Treaty of Guarantee.

Such were the geo-strategic realities that circumscribed the foreign policies of the Makarios government. The 1960 treaties had limited the sovereignty of the Republic and imposed special obligations on its part towards the three guarantor powers. Further, the close affinities of the two communities with their respective mother-countries generated pressures that brought the Republic's relations with Greece and Turkey into the realm of the latters' domestic, rather than foreign, affairs. These considerations apart, the Cyprus government was formally non-aligned, as Makarios explained in 1973:

> Since its independence Cyprus has followed a non-alignment policy for reasons of principle and for reasons of substance. We believe that Cyprus's national interests are better served through a non-aligned policy, and our non-participation in political or military blocs makes it easier for us to contribute to the cause of peace.[10]

The corner-stone of his foreign policy lay in support for the UN and its Charter, both because he believed that this was the surest guarantee against Turkish military intervention and because it offered opportunities for economic advancement through UN agencies, such as the UN Development Programme.

The frequent and well-publicized appearances of the Archbishop on the world stage gave him a standing and influence out of all proportion to those of the small island he represented. He was thus able to keep its troubled affairs, especially the Greek-Cypriot case, in the forefront of international attention. Since the non-aligned movement included states which had themselves only recently shed a colonial yoke, his pleas for preservation of Cyprus's integrity fell on sympathetic ears, as did his complaints that the 1960 treaties had been imposed on unwilling Cypriots and constituted unwarranted limitations on his Republic's sovereignty and independence. The advent in 1967 of an undemocratic military régime in Greece lent added weight to his arguments, which the existence of no less undemocratic régimes in some other non-aligned states did not diminish.

The Turkish Cypriots followed Ankara's lead in opposing non-alignment and in advocating adoption of a clear anti-communist stand. They were suspicious of Makarios's contacts with Moscow and other communist régimes and critical of the links afforded by membership of the non-aligned movement. They resented, too, the skill with which the Archbishop exploited membership of this movement in order to present the Greek case. However, since after December 1963 the recognized government of Cyprus lay solely in Greek Cypriot hands, there was little they could do to counter this situation other than, with Turkey's support, to enlist the sympathy of Arab states and the Muslim world. Thus foreign policy was yet another bone of contention between the two Cypriot communities, to be added to the constitutional differences and historical, ethnic, cultural and religious divisions that had already polarized the peoples of this 'rosy realm of Venus' and prevented the realization of a truly Cypriot nation.

Neither the UN peacekeepers on the island nor their masters in New York could ignore the international dimensions of the Cyprus problem, for, apart from responsibilities to the two Cypriot communities, there was an overriding United Nations consideration – the preservation of *international* peace and security, in the interests of which UNFICYP had been established in the first place. As one commentator observed:

When Cyprus catches cold, the rest of the region shows a distinct tendency to sneeze.[11]

PART TWO

THE CYPRUS PEACEKEEPING GAME, 1972-1974

A peacekeeping operation, no matter how successful and efficient, cannot provide the solution of a political problem. It is only a means of keeping that problem under control, maintaining reasonably normal conditions of life for the people of the area, and creating a situation in which a lasting settlement can more fruitfully be sought.

UN Secretary General: *Report on the Work of the Organization*, 1974, p.10.

CHAPTER FIVE

PEACEKEEPING – THE UN CONCEPT

The soldiers seem to have got the hang of it more successfully than most of the civilian public has. Every UN operation has suffered from some degree of misunderstanding of its scope and purpose. . . . There might be less misunderstanding if the United Nations could expound the policy behind its peacekeeping more fully.

The Economist, London, 25 March 1978.

Peacekeeping is not a word that features in the UN Charter but is not a new one in the soldier's vocabulary, for history abounds with military operations conducted in its name. It is a term that has been (and continues to be) applied loosely, and sometimes euphemistically, to a wide spectrum of actions, ranging from the national in support of the civil power, such as practised by the British Army in the heyday of its imperial past or more recently in Ulster, to third-party multi- or unilateral interventions in international or national disputes, such as those of the Anglo-French forces at Suez in 1956, the Turks in Cyprus in 1974, or the Soviets in Afghanistan in 1979. Whatever their point in that spectrum, all such operations are by definition enforcement actions, since the ultimate sanction upon which their credibility depends is readiness to resort to the use of force. Whether governed by the doctrine of minimum force so thoroughly inculcated in the British Army, or whether given the free rein that has characterized the less fastidious methods of some others, the degree of force used is in this context immaterial.

For many years peacekeeping as practised by UN forces embodied a fundamentally different concept, as a former UN Secretary General explained:

The technique of peacekeeping is one of the real innovations of the United Nations. It is a complex and unconventional procedure in which military personnel are used for purposes to which they are not normally accustomed. *It is essentially an enterprise based on voluntary co-operation, restraint and mutual interest in restoring peace and normality.* [author's emphasis] [1]

This concept derives from two principles enshrined in Articles 1 and 2 of the UN Charter, namely that settlements of disputes that threaten international peace and security shall be brought about by peaceful means and that the Organization is founded on the sovereign equality of all its members.

Although provision was made in Chapter VII of the Charter ('Action with Respect to

Threats to Peace, Breaches of the Peace and Acts of Aggression') for enforcement action where other measures have been, or are likely to be, inadequate, the Security Council has been reluctant to invoke this power, preferring instead that UN peacekeeping operations be mounted in accordance with Chapter VI, which provides for the pacific settlement of disputes. Such operations are thus established only with the consent of the state or states concerned, and the UN troops involved may not initiate the use of force either to bring an end to conflict or to maintain peace. It is this that gives to UN peacekeeping its unique character. Failure to understand this lies at the heart of much of the misplaced criticism of UN peacekeeping operations.

Although the UN's founding fathers envisaged in Chapter VII a possible need for a stronger action by military forces acting in the UN name, during the Organization's first four decades its peacekeeping (except in the special circumstances of the Korean War and briefly in Katanga) took only the more pacific Chapter VI path, not least because some member states, in particular the Soviet Union, had reservations as to the propriety of the UN engaging in this activity at all. In 1982 a frustrated UN Secretary General complained:

> Sterner measures for world peace were envisaged in Chapter VII of the Charter, which was conceived as a key element of the United Nations system of collective security, but the prospect of realizing such measures is now deemed almost impossible in our divided international community.[2]

But the collapse of the Soviet Union, the end of the Cold War and more recent outbreaks of conflict in various parts of the world have brought greater readiness on the part of UN members to authorize the sterner measures that earlier were usually denied.

The terms of reference for UN forces, known as 'the Mandate', are embodied in the relevant Security Council resolution establishing the operation. Some UN peacekeepers complain that mandates are insufficiently precise for their purposes and open to differing interpretations by the parties. Such complaints take inadequate account of the political realities, for Security Council resolutions are necessarily framed in the broad terms required to secure adoption by a Council composed of members of often widely differing attitudes and interests. In practice the flexibility inherent in a broadly framed mandate is not without advantage, for subject to the overall direction of the Secretary General it allows a UN Commander in the field to conduct operations with the discretion and flexibility that changing circumstances sometimes require.

This is an important consideration because Security Council mandates are usually framed in the heat of a crisis and are only modified later with difficulty. Successive Secretaries General have displayed skill in the day-to-day direction of UN forces within the framework of such mandates and the confidence that this has generated is reflected in the degree to which it has become accepted Security Council practice to vest this direction in them. More explicit mandates, even if there was realistic prospect of achieving these, might restrict sensible initiative on the part of both Secretary General and Force Commander, and in some circumstances might even prejudice the effective and timely conduct of operations.

Restriction on the use of force by UN troops is a corollary of the requirement to secure the consent of the parties in dispute, for the latter cannot be expected to acquiesce in the deployment of a UN force that might impose its will on them by military means. However, this restriction does not debar the use of force in self-defence, a circumstance which the Security Council holds to include situations where forceful means are used to prevent UN troops from discharging duties stipulated in the mandate. Even so, UN Commanders are reluctant to resort to force, except as a last resort, because an inevitable consequence is forfeiture, if only temporarily, of the confidence and with it the cooperation of the party concerned.

Much hinges on the will and judgement of UN Commanders, who must assess carefully the implications of resorting to force in given situations. In some cases, such as a direct attack on a UN post, the decision may be relatively straightforward; in others, where, for example, UN troops are being prevented by forceful means from carrying out tasks which the Commander judges to lie within the mandate, the decision may be more difficult. In such circumstances Force Commanders need to weigh not only the extent of the support to be expected from the Secretary General (who in turn must take account of likely attitudes both inside and outside the Security Council – in other words, the strength of international will), but also the obvious factor of relative military strengths and capabilities. For UN forces, comparatively weak in terms of numbers and weapons and deployed over wide areas in small vulnerable posts, more often than not find themselves interposed between far stronger forces armed with heavy weapons including tanks and artillery and close air support.

In some situations the use of force will not be a realistic option; indeed, a prudent UN Commander must take care not to permit his troops to create a situation where in this respect their bluff may be called. This is not as disadvantageous as it may seem, for peacekeeping as practised by UN forces under Chapter VI is primarily a political exercise in which their real strength lies less in their military capability (important though this is for their credibility) than in their political muscle exerted through the Security Council and individual member states, especially those troop-contributor governments whose men are immediately involved. If that muscle is strong and the troops on the ground are resolute, relative military strengths are of secondary importance and the need for recourse to the use of force will be rare. Should that muscle be weak, UN forces can find themselves in deep difficulty from which a stronger military capability or increased readiness to resort to force will not easily extricate them. As a former UN Secretary General has explained:

> It is not always realized that peacekeeping operations are the visible part of a complex framework of political and diplomatic efforts and of countervailing pressures designed to keep the peacekeeping efforts and related peacemaking efforts effective. . . . If this framework breaks down . . . there is little that a United Nations peacekeeping force can by itself do to rectify the situation. Indeed in such circumstances it tends to become the scapegoat for the developments that follow.[3]

The validity of those remarks was demonstrated in October 1973, when following the outbreak of the Yom Kippur War it was decided under pressure from the two super-powers to interpose a UN Force (UNEF 2) between the Egyptian and Israeli armies locked in battle

along the Suez Canal. The first UN troops to arrive consisted of a handful of Finns hastily
sent from Cyprus and armed with little more than UN flags. A ceasefire called for by the
Security Council was nominally in force but was being widely ignored, and the Finns,
experienced UN peacekeepers, were immediately ordered to interpose themselves between
the two armies, halt the fighting and establish an effective ceasefire. They did so with
outstanding courage and success. Had they been prevented by force from carrying out this
dangerous mission, they would have been entitled to resort to the use of force, but in the
circumstances it would have been ludicrous even to have contemplated doing so. Their
success in the face of the overwhelming strength of the opposing armies was due to their
resolution and the backing of the powerful international authority with which their daunting
mission was endowed. The experience of the UN Interim Force in Lebanon (UNIFIL),
which was brushed contemptuously aside by the Israeli army's incursion into South
Lebanon in June 1982, provided stark contrast. From the outset UNIFIL had lacked the
degree of international support necessary to ensure that it could properly accomplish its
mandate.

In according consent for the mounting of a UN peacekeeping operation, it is understood
that the state or states concerned commit themselves to cooperating with the UN force,
whose task in a non-enforcement situation would otherwise be impossible. But unless these
governments are able to exercise effective authority, consent and assurances of cooperation
are all but meaningless. The contrast between the experiences of UNEF 2 in Sinai, where
the Governments of Egypt and Israel were in effective control of their forces, and the difficulties encountered by UNIFIL in Lebanon illustrates the point. The Lebanese Government
was weak and ineffective, and elements such as the PLO, Major Haddad's militia and sundry
other diverse armed factions had scant regard for it or for the UN. The uncontrolled activities of these elements caused the Israelis to lose confidence in UNIFIL, which made matters
worse. It is rare, nonetheless, for UN forces to be accorded in full the degree of cooperation
to which they believe themselves entitled, but this does not lessen the need for them to do
their utmost to retain the confidence of all sides in a dispute. Nor does it mean that UN
Commanders should shrink from action which they judge to be impartial and necessary for
the prevention of conflict just because one side disagrees (most UN forces have found themselves temporarily in such a predicament), but it does oblige them to weigh such situations
with care and to assess the extent to which use of force may exacerbate relations with that
party.

The credibility of a UN force in the eyes of the parties is a critical factor in such calculations, for it will certainly suffer unless there is a clear perception that the UN force is not to
be intimidated. Even where the use of force in self-defence is not at issue, the success of any
UN force is related directly to the firmness of purpose it displays and the extent to which it
earns the respect of the parties. An experienced senior UN Commander has gone so far as
to declare: 'My experience in the Sinai is that there is no confidence in a UN force if it never
strikes back.'[4] Such situations may be rare, but, when they do occur, they call for cool heads
on the part of UN Commanders, whose dilemma will seldom be as simple as it may appear
to others. UN forces seek to avoid difficulties of this nature by fostering good relations with
the parties at all levels in order that problems may be anticipated and pre-empted, or, where

this has not been possible, for them to be resolved peacefully. As a third party a UN Force fulfils an important role in this respect, providing a discreet and reliable channel of communication between the disputing parties, who otherwise may have difficulty in speaking to each other, especially in the heat of an acute situation.

Negotiation and mediation are the UN peacekeepers' prime tools, demanding on their part qualities of quiet diplomacy, courtesy, patience and good humour. They may advise, suggest and persuade, but it is not for them to tell the parties what they may or may not do, except where the latter are in clear breach of an agreement to which they have put their name. UN soldiers need to appreciate that in some situations loss of face may be involved, making it difficult if not impossible for the offending party to comply with the peacekeepers' proposed solution – as in all negotiations, the parties should not be driven into a corner but, rather, afforded a line of retreat that can honourably be taken. All this requires of a UN Commander a sound appreciation of the parties' anxieties and difficulties in order accurately to judge how far the latter may be expected to go and the point beyond which they believe their vital interests are threatened.

Sir Brian Urquhart, when UN Under Secretary General responsible for the Organization's peacekeeping operations, was quoted as saying:

> One of the great attributes of peacekeeping is being there. The point is for them [*the UN peacekeepers*] to be there so the people have an excuse to stop fighting.[5]

This over-simplification highlights the third-party nature of UN forces. It is no part of their mission to act in support of one side or the other, but to create the conditions which will encourage both to put aside their weapons and pursue a settlement of their differences in a non-violent way. UN forces need to tread a delicate path in this respect, taking care to avoid any action likely to prejudice or pre-judge the interests of either party. The need for impartiality is self-evident, and the task has been likened by some to that of referee or linesmen in a game of football.[6] The analogy is superficial, not least in its inference that the game is governed by a set of rules which it is the peacekeepers' task to enforce – such rules as may exist govern only their own conduct and not that of the other parties.

The true position is that a UN force, although a third party, is an active player. Its role and purpose are different from those of the others (whose aim is to win on their own terms), but it has a positive part to play in helping matters forward to a satisfactory conclusion – that is, a peaceful settlement acceptable to all sides. Never partisan, but being seen always to be acting with scrupulous disinterest, a UN force has to use its best endeavours to guide the parties to that end. However, impartiality is a matter of subjective judgement and from time to time one or other is sure to accuse, possibly in insulting terms, the peacekeepers of bias. In such circumstances the latter can but maintain a cool mien and meet complaints with courtesy and good humour.

The principle of consent imposes a major constraint upon the manner in which UN peacekeeping operations are mounted and conducted. The agreement of the governments concerned, especially that of the host country whose sovereignty would otherwise be infringed, is a pre-requisite. The principle also usually extends to matters such as the composition of the UN force, including the nationality of its constituent contingents[7], the choice of Force Commander and even the appointment of some of his senior officers, but does not extend to the point that host or other governments may dictate how a UN force goes about its task. However, the principle imposes constraints on the UN force's operations, requiring in particular that members of the force respect the sovereignty of the host government and be punctilious in not usurping functions properly the latter's responsibility. Governments are sensitive on this score and quick to protest where they consider a UN force to have over-stepped the mark. UNFICYP was not blameless in this respect and, even if its transgressions usually were trivial, could always expect to be reminded sharply of the limits of its authority.

The strengths and limitations of the UN's unique concept of international peacekeeping have been summed up succinctly as follows:

> Peacekeeping operations can function properly only with the cooperation of the parties and on a clearly defined mandate from the Security Council. They are based on the assumption that the parties, in accepting a United Nations peacekeeping operation, commit themselves to co-operating with it. . . . Their main strength is the will of the international community which they symbolise. Their weakness comes to light when the political assumptions on which they are based are ignored or overridden.[8]

CHAPTER SIX

UNFICYP'S MANDATE AND DIRECTION

UNFICYP . . . cannot act as an instrument of the Government in helping it extend its authority by force over the Turkish Cypriot community . . . . On the other hand, it cannot assume responsibility for restoring the constitutional position which existed prior to the outbreak of hostilities in 1963 and early 1964, nor to contribute to the consolidation of the present stalemate in the island. Both these courses would basically affect the final settlement of the country's problems, a matter which is in the province of the Mediator and not UNFICYP.

Report by the UN Secretary General
(S/6228, 11 March 1965, para. 274).

The responsibilities of the Mediator on the one hand and UNFICYP on the other were stipulated by the Security Council in Resolution 186(1964) (Annex 1). The Resolution also reminded member states of the UN Charter requirement that they refrain from the threat or use of force against the territorial integrity or political independence of any other state, and called on them to refrain from any action likely to worsen the situation in Cyprus and on the island's two communities to act with utmost restraint. It also recommended that the costs of UNFICYP[1] should be met both by those governments providing contingents and by the Cyprus Government, with the Secretary General empowered to receive voluntary contributions from others.[2] Of particular significance was the Security Council's request for:

the Government of Cyprus, *which has the responsibility for the maintenance and restoration of law and order*, to take all additional measures necessary to stop violence and bloodshed in Cyprus. [author's emphasis]

These words, which were clear recognition of the host government's sovereign authority, were subject to differing interpretations, and on occasions gave rise to dispute between UNFICYP and the two parties, but the UN was consistent in its recognition of the Makarios Administration as the Government of Cyprus, notwithstanding no less consistent Turkish objection that the latter did not conform to the 1960 Constitution and therefore was illegal.

The Security Council vested the overall direction of UNFICYP in the Secretary General.

Command in the field was to be exercised by a Force Commander appointed by the Secretary General with the Council's approval and this officer was to be responsible direct to him. The Secretary General had at the outset issued instructions to the Force Commander stressing that UNFICYP's activities were at all times to be kept within the terms of Resolution 186(1964). These instructions had been contained in confidential communications, but, to allay uncertainties as to how the Force would go about its tasks, the Secretary General then published an *aide-memoire* for general information. An understanding of its salient points is necessary for proper appreciation of UNFICYP's role and actions during the period up to 1974.

First was the stipulation that the Force was to avoid any action designed to influence the political situation otherwise than by contributing to a restoration of quiet [*sic*] and creating a climate in which political solutions could be sought. Second were guiding principles which *inter alia* made clear that, while its composition and size were matters for consultation with governments concerned, the Force was under exclusive UN command with operational control of its units resting at all times with the Force Commander. Third was guidance governing the use of force in self-defence, which required UN troops to refrain from taking the initiative in its use and stressed adherence to the principle of minimum force; this guidance specifically prohibited any action by UNFICYP that was likely to bring it into conflict with either community. Exceptions were where the Force was compelled to act in self-defence or the safety of its members was in jeopardy, or where arrangements accepted by both communities had been, or were likely to be, violated, thus risking a recurrence of conflict. UN troops were required wherever possible to give advance warning of the use of force and not to resort to automatic weapons except in extreme urgency. Any decision to use force was to rest with the UN commander on the spot, who was required to distinguish between those situations where there was no real need to open fire and those in which there was no credible alternative.

Further, the *aide-memoire* indicated how UNFICYP was to deal with threats of attack by armed elements of one community against the other, clarified arrangements concerning ceasefire agreements (UNFICYP was not to interpose its men to enforce a ceasefire where this was not acceptable to the parties, since to do so might lead to direct clashes with them), and stressed the need for UNFICYP to maintain close contact with appropriate officials of the Cyprus Government. Last but by no means least, it made clear that the UN Force must respect the principles and spirit of international conventions governing the conduct of military personnel.

Two further documents regulated UNFICYP's activities. A Status of Forces Agreement[3] set out the relationship of the Force and its members to the Cyprus government, the obligation of the former to respect the laws and regulations of the latter, and the undertaking of the latter to respect UNFICYP's international character and function. It also contained provisions relating to entry to and exit from the Republic; the operation of vehicles and aircraft; the wearing of uniform and carriage of arms; freedom of movement; the provision of premises, communications, public utilities and other facilities; the privileges and immunities of members of the Force; criminal and civil jurisdiction in cases involving UN troops; arrest, transfer of custody and mutual assistance in the investigation of offences; the hiring of local labour and liaison arrangements between UNFICYP and the Government. This Agreement, while bestowing important privileges on UNFICYP, also imposed on it no less important obligations.

The second document was *UNFICYP Force Regulations*, two provisions of which were of fundamental importance. The first related to the international character of the Force:

> The members of the Force, although remaining in their national service, are, during the period of their assignment to the Force, international personnel under the authority of the United Nations and subject to the instructions of the Commander, through the chain of command. *The functions of the Force are exclusively international, and members of the Force shall discharge these functions and regulate their conduct with the interests of the United Nations only in view.* [author's emphasis]

The second was the explicit statement that '*in the field the Force Commander has full command of the Force, including responsibility for deciding the deployment and assignment of tasks to troops placed at his disposal*' [author's emphasis]. There were occasions when these two stipulations were accorded insufficient recognition by some contingents or their parent government.[4] *Force Regulations* also stipulated that, while the Force Commander had general responsibility for good order and military discipline within UNFICYP, each Contingent Commander was responsible for exercising discipline within his own unit in accordance with his own national military code and procedures.

It was a quirk of Resolution 186(1964) that, while it referred to the Government of Cyprus, there was no mention of the two ethnic communities or the reality that it was conflict between these that it was a purpose of UNFICYP to prevent. It was accepted, nonetheless, that the Force's mission was limited to the intercommunal quarrel and did not permit intervention in the internal affairs of either community, even where these were giving rise to violence within that community. In the early days UN recognition of the Makarios administration as the Government, coupled with the acknowledgement in Resolution 186(1964) that responsibility for law and order rested with it, led some Greek Cypriots to brand the Turkish Cypriots as 'rebels' and to expect UNFICYP to act virtually as an arm of the Government in acting to suppress them. Such expectations were quickly dismissed by UNFICYP, which took the pragmatic view that, since there was a dispute to which the Turkish Cypriots were a party, it must deal with the Leadership. The device adopted was to treat with the Leader of the Turkish community (Dr Kuchuk and, later, Rauf Denktash) in his constitutional capacity as Vice President of the Republic, and UNFICYP's contacts with the community were thus through him in that capacity and with his staff as members of the Vice President's Office (VPO).[5] Although demurring, the Greek side accepted the practical necessity for this. For its part the Turkish side did not waver in its view that UNFICYP should have been acting on its behalf to remove what it held to be an unconstitutional régime. Protestations of this nature by each side became less vociferous over the years and more of a formality to be used, it sometimes seemed, when more substantive grounds for twisting the UN tail were lacking. The Secretary General illustrated the dilemma in an early Report:

In cases where disputed military situations arose, UNFICYP . . . of necessity negotiated with both, since the consent of both was in fact required if peaceful solutions were to be found and violence averted. This gave rise, quite unjustifiably, to allegations from some quarters that UNFICYP treated the Turkish Cypriot community as a separate state.[6]

It was a measure of the skill of the UN peacekeepers that, despite occasional sharp disagreements, UNFICYP generally maintained amicable relations with the civil and military authorities of both communities.

Resolution 186(1964) had drawn a clear distinction between the mediation and peacekeeping functions by requiring the Secretary General to appoint both a Mediator and a Force Commander, each being responsible direct to him. In Cyprus the Special Representative of the Secretary General (SRSG) (the Mediator's successor) worked hand-in-hand with the Force Commander and, together with their senior aides (the Senior Political Adviser (SPA) and the Force Chief of Staff), were located in adjacent offices in the 'top corridor' of the Force HQ main building. Consultations between all four were necessarily close and frequent since military activities had political implications impinging on the mediation process, while developments (or more often lack of these) in that process could influence the Force's military operations.

So close was this collaboration that it was the practice for the Secretary General to address most of his communications to the SRSG and Force Commander jointly and for communications from them similarly to be sent in the name of them both.[7] These consisted of memoranda despatched through the routine UN diplomatic pouch service or code-cables transmitted through the UN Radio service.[8] At HQ UNFICYP incoming code-cables were passed initially direct to the SRSG and Force Commander before being seen by the SPA and Chief of Staff, but were not normally accorded wider distribution. Outgoing code-cables were drafted by the Force Commander (or his Chief of Staff) and the SRSG (or his SPA), frequently jointly, and were despatched over the signatures of both. In New York distribution was limited generally to those on the 38th floor of the UN Headquarters building but the very nature of that large multi-national organization rendered preservation of confidentiality difficult. For this reason a special category of cables was used where particularly sensitive matters were involved; these were seen only by the Secretary General and his most senior advisers. Their use in the case of Cyprus was infrequent, but an arrangement of this kind is essential for the effective control of UN Forces, especially in times of crisis, since otherwise the risk of 'leaks' might inhibit frank exchanges between the Secretary General and his commanders and representatives in the field.

This excellent coordination of the UN's peacemaking and peacekeeping activities in Cyprus set an admirable precedent. The SRSG and the Force Commander, neither being subordinate to the other, were enabled to go about their complementary tasks taking due account of each other's interests and responsibilities; important decisions were reached together and agreed advice was tendered jointly. This was an important element in the effective conduct of the UN's operation in Cyprus. In New York the Security Council was content to leave day-to-day direction of UNFICYP to the Secretary General, who maintained routine liaison with governments concerned through their ambassadors to the UN. Except in times of special crisis the Council itself normally met only twice a year (in June and December) to review the situation and renew UNFICYP's mandate. The Secretary General published a Report in advance of these meetings, at which it was usual for the SRSG (and sometimes the Force Commander) to be present.   In the face of Turkey's opposition 'The Question of Cyprus' was regularly inscribed on the agenda of the UN General Assembly, when old sterile arguments were customarily rehearsed at length. Periodic visits by the Secretary General or his senior officials to Nicosia, Ankara and Athens ensured that he was well informed of views and developments surrounding the Cyprus problem generally and the operations of the UN force in particular.

CHAPTER SEVEN

UNFICYP'S COMPOSITION, ORGANISATION AND DEPLOYMENT –JUNE 1972

To me the marvel of all UN forces has been the extraordinary ability of soldiers of utterly different backgrounds, training and language to work together as effectively and courageously as they have, often under conditions that would try the endurance of the most professional armies.

Robert Rhodes James, *The Daily Telegraph*,
London, 29 September 1978.

By the summer of 1972 UNFICYP, now in its ninth year of duty on the island, had settled into a comfortable routine, maintaining a low profile consistent with the climate of intercommunal calm that had prevailed since the Kophinou crisis of 1967. In part this calm was a consequence of the Force's success in preventing escalation of minor incidents, but more particularly it was due to Greek Cypriot realization of the risks, demonstrated at Kophinou, inherent in any attempt to settle matters by force. The need in these circumstances for a peacekeeping Force was questioned by some, who advocated its replacement by a small and less costly UN observer-type mission. Although this concept gained little support (not least because it required revision of Resolution 186(1964) and risked opening up more contentious issues), it had been possible progressively to reduce UNFICYP's strength from 6,400 men in June 1964 to just over 3,000 men in June 1972. The organization of the Force and its chain of command in June 1972 are shown in outline at Annex 2.

The Force Commander was an Indian infantry officer, Major General D. Prem Chand, who had served in a variety of senior posts in the Indian army; aged 53, he had succeeded the 73-year-old Lieut. General Martola of Finland in December 1969. He had gained earlier UN peacekeeping experience during the UN's Congo operation when he served as General Officer Commanding Katanga Area in 1962–63, for which he was awarded the Indian government's Medal for Most Distinguished Service (PVSM). He had retired from the Indian Army in 1967, but had been called upon by the UN Secretary General two years later to take command of UNFICYP.[1] Prem Chand was a soldierly figure whose command of English and inborn qualities of integrity, courtesy and tact, enlivened by a nice sense of humour, enabled him to establish an easy rapport with all with whom he dealt; he was a well known figure throughout the island and a respected and popular visitor to all UNFICYP's contingents.[2] Beneath this easy manner lay common sense, shrewdness and firm resolve, as

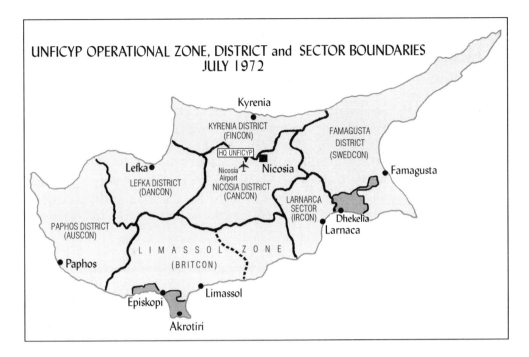

was evident both in his dealings with leaders of both Cypriot communities and in his handling of internal UNFICYP affairs.[3]

His civilian counterpart, the Secretary General's Special Representative (SRSG) who ranked as an ambassador, was Dr Bibiano Osorio-Tafall – known to all as 'Bibi'. He had been appointed to the post in February 1967, when he assumed most of the functions of the Mediator which had fallen to the SRSG's lot on the resignation of Dr Galo Plaza. Then aged 64, he already had wide experience in the service of the UN and quickly acquired a deep and invaluable understanding of the complexities of the Cyprus problem. He enjoyed good personal relations with the leading protagonists in each community and his acute perception of the devious processes of Eastern Mediterranean minds enabled him to give advice that was practical, abounding in common sense and free of unrealistic optimism. Bibi was a short dapper figure with a physical zest and energy that belied both his years and his rotundity. Possessed of a sparkling sense of humour and a fund of good, if sometimes earthy, stories, he was convivial company and an excellent host. He travelled widely throughout the island, which he came to know better than many Cypriots themselves, and was a familiar and welcome visitor to its peoples of all ranks from abbots of monasteries to ordinary village folk of both communities.[4]

Some in Nicosia's diplomatic circle saw Bibi as a 'UN time-server' who displayed little urgency in pursuit of a settlement of the island's problems. The truth is that the UN and Cypriots generally were fortunate to be served at this period by two men as able, dedicated and selfless as Osorio-Tafall and Prem Chand. There was mutual confidence and close personal friendship between them, and the former's departure in June 1974, at the very moment when his talents and experience were most needed, was a severe blow to UNFICYP.

UNFICYP Headquarters

The Force HQ, located in Blue Beret Camp on the eastern perimeter of Nicosia airport and about 10 minutes by car from the centre of the city, was organized broadly on British Army lines, this being a legacy of April 1964, when it had been established with as its nucleus, the British divisional HQ controlling operations until then. It was multi-national in composition, personnel being drawn from troop-contributor countries in approximate proportion to the size of each's contingent. In principle all posts were open to all nationalities but practical considerations led to certain posts being tied to particular countries. At senior level the Chief of Staff initially was a British Brigadier and his Deputy, a Canadian Colonel – a pragmatic arrangement given Britain's preponderance in the Force and the degree of dependence on British logistic support, but in 1968 it became the practice for Britain and Canada alternately to fill these two posts.[5]

The Force's nerve centre was the Joint Operations Centre (JOC), manned on a 24-hour basis by military and civilian police officers and working direct to similarly manned JOCs at subordinate District HQs. The JOC was the responsibility of the Chief Operations Officer of Lieut. Colonel rank, whose Operations Branch included an Air Liaison Officer (ALO) to manage the Force's helicopter support, an Operations Information Section (dealing with the military intelligence function – the latter not being a term used in UN forces on account of connotations thought to be incompatible with their neutral role), and an Operations Economics Section concerned with intercommunal disputes of an economic or social, rather than military, nature. A Military Public Information Officer (MPIO) was also a member of the Branch, his task being to handle the Force's external military public relations and internal matters, including the publication of UNFICYP's weekly journal, *The Blue Beret*, and production of a weekly radio programme for members of the Force.

The Personnel and Logistics Branch, staffed by officers drawn from all contingents, was headed by the Chief Personnel and Logistics Officer (CPLO), also of Lieut. Colonel rank. Since the Force was dependent for most of its needs on British sources in the SBAs, this post was filled by a British officer. Similarly, logistic staff advisers (Transport, Ordnance and Electrical and Mechanical Engineering) were also British, since their advisory function was combined with command of the related British Contingent logistic unit; an exception was the Force Engineer, who in the period 1972–74 was provided by either Canada or Ireland. The Branch's tasks were complicated by differing needs and administrative practices within each contingent, frequent changes in personnel due to six-monthly rotations and the fact that financial control rested, not with the Force Commander and through him with the CPLO, but with the Field Service Branch in New York acting through its representative in Cyprus, the civilian Chief Administrative Officer (CAO). Dependence on logistic backing from British units in the SBAs, which were subject to neither the Force Commander nor any other UN authority, was an added complication.

Force Communications

Fast and reliable communications are vital in peacekeeping Forces because Commanders need to know immediately of incidents, however trivial, which might escalate into something more serious. Within the Force contingents were responsible for their internal communications, using their own national procedures, language and equipment (or in some cases radios hired from British stocks). Above the contingent level procedures were British and the language English. The means of communication throughout the Force were threefold: radio, telephone (and teleprinter) and Signals Despatch Service (SDS), of which radio was the primary. Two radio systems were available at Force HQ – District HQ level. First was a voice net of over 200 Motorola sets, some of which were static base stations with others fitted in the vehicles of key personnel; a few hand-portable sets were also available. The sets afforded two channels, one of which was reserved for operational traffic in English and the other for UN Civilian Police and administrative traffic using whatever tongue was convenient. The large number of users with access to these two channels demanded a high standard of radio discipline. This net was efficient and much used, island-wide coverage being assured by a relay station at Troodos, near the summit of Mt Olympus.[6]

The second radio system, the Force VHF Command Net, was an exclusively military one linking Force HQ with Zone, District and Sector HQs, the Force Reserve, helicopters and the Field Hospital; an automatic rebroadcast facility at Troodos also ensured island-wide coverage. There was little security inherent in either radio nets but two codes were available, one low grade for general use and one higher grade operated by trained signals personnel.

For its external communications UNFICYP relied on a variety of systems. Traffic with New York was transmitted through the UN Radio (which had its own ciphers) or by routine diplomatic pouch service; in cases of urgency consultations were possible using the international civil telephone system. The Nicosia terminal of the UN Radio, situated in Blue Beret Camp, was part of a radio network first established some 30 years earlier to meet the UN's worldwide needs (in the early 1970s technical problems, such as adverse atmospheric conditions, sometimes necessitated traffic from Nicosia being re-routed through the UN Radio at Jerusalem with consequent delays). UNFICYP HQ also had access to British world-wide military communications through the Communications Centre (COMCEN) at RAF Nicosia. This facility was used mainly for British and Canadian Contingent national traffic, but during the 1974 crisis it proved a valuable back-up for the hard-pressed UN Radio. With the exception of the Irish (who relied on the UN Radio for communication with Dublin) other contingents operated their own radio link to their capital.[7]

The Military Contingents

Although now in its ninth year, UNFICYP in 1972 remained a temporary emergency Force subject to six-monthly renewals of its mandate. It was composed of lightly armed infantry[8] with no artillery or tanks, no fixed-wing air support and no naval element. Military contingents were the same in number and nationality as at the outset – a total of seven provided by Austria, Canada, Denmark, Finland, Ireland, Sweden and the United Kingdom. The British and Canadian Contingents, the two largest, consisted of professional soldiers organized in regular units sent to Cyprus for six months at a time as part of their normal military duty. In contrast those of Denmark, Finland and Sweden consisted of battalions formed specially for a six-month tour of duty in Cyprus and comprised a small regular army nucleus together with conscripts, reservists and volunteers recruited for this specific duty; this did not detract from their effectiveness as peacekeepers, not only because these contingents included a proportion of men with previous UN experience but also because individuals were to be found in them possessing useful civilian expertise, notably in the field of economic affairs. Austria's Contingent was organized on similar lines, while Ireland's was composed of regular soldiers drawn from all parts of its army and organized into a single temporary unit for the UNFICYP task (UN service was popular with Irish soldiers, some of whom had several tours of duty in Cyprus or elsewhere to their credit).

Deployment Pattern

In 1972 UNFICYP was deployed throughout the island, with static Observation Posts (OPs) supplemented by mobile patrols established at points of military confrontation or some other special intercommunal sensitivity. Each contingent was allotted its own area of responsibility, designated a District (or in some cases a Zone or Sector). To facilitate liaison with the civil authorities the boundaries of contingents' operational areas were drawn where possible to coincide with those of civil administrative districts, and the Contingent Commander concerned was appointed District Commander[9]. Variations in the island's topography, which ranged from mountains and forests to citrus groves, vineyards and agricultural plains[10], and different ethnic and population patterns confronted each contingent with its own particular problems.

Austrian Contingent (AUSCON)

Until January 1972, when its 1st UN Battalion (strength 275 men) joined UNFICYP to compensate for a reduction in the Irish strength, AUSCON had consisted only of a Field Hospital. On arrival the 1st Battalion had taken over Paphos District with its HQ and administrative base in Duke Leopold V Camp at Ktima-Paphos itself.[11] One company policed the interface between the Greek and Turkish quarters of the town and manned OPs at three Turkish villages further east – Mandria, Anadhiou and Stavrokono. A second company was based at Polis, a mixed village and potential flash-point near the north coast.

Danish Contingent (DANCON)

This Contingent, represented by its 17th Battalion (strength 215 men), was deployed in the UN-designated 'Lefka District' on the southern side of the Bay of Morphou. In this case there was no complementary civil District, the UN's District forming part of the large civil Nicosia District, which covered the whole of central Cyprus. The Danes' HQ and base was in Viking Camp at Xeros, adjacent to the ore milling plant and marine terminal of the Cyprus Mines Corporation. One company was based at Limnitis with one platoon in Kokkina, their tasks being to man a series of OPs on the mountains surrounding these small Turkish coastal enclaves that had been sealed off since the Tillyria fighting of 1964. Three concentric rings of posts were to be seen, identified by the red crescent flags of the Turks on the inside, the blue and white stripes of the Greeks on the outside and the pale blue of the UN between them. Other DANCON posts were maintained at Selemani, Ambelikou and Ghaziveran, all points of earlier and potential intercommunal friction.

Finnish Contingent (FINCON)

The Finnish Contingent's 17th Battalion (strength 270 men) was responsible for Kyrenia District, stretching along the north coast from Stazousa Point in the east to Cape Kormakiti in the west. The UN operational boundary diverged from that of the civil Kyrenia District by extension south to include the main Turkish enclave astride the Kyrenia Road, the northern Nicosia suburbs of Neapolis, Omorphita and Trakhonas, and the villages of Skylloura and Kalokhorio, all of which were part of the civil Nicosia District. FINCON's HQ was located in Kykko Camp, 1km east of UNFICYP HQ. One company was based in the Nicosia suburb of Omorphita and provided OPs along the southern boundaries of the Turkish enclave and the outer extremities of the Nicosia Green Line. A second company, based in Tjiklos Camp near the head of the Kyrenia Pass, manned four OPs established on the peaks of the Pendhadaktylos range, which rise to heights of 900m. These OPs monitored the activities of adjacent Greek and Turkish posts and afforded spectacular views and observation north and south. This company also provided a detachment for the security of workers at an isolated but economically important lime plant at Oneisha.

Canadian Contingent (CANCON)

Except for those parts allotted to the Danes or Finns, the large civil Nicosia District, including the city itself, was the responsibility of the Canadians, whose Contingent HQ and supporting logistic elements were co-located with Force HQ in Blue Beret Camp under the command of the Deputy Chief of Staff, who in his national capacity was also CANCON's Contingent Commander. The operational element consisted of a 540-man-strong battalion-size unit, Lord Strathcona's Horse (Royal Canadians), an armoured unit deployed to Cyprus in the infantry role. Its HQ in Wolseley Barracks, situated just outside the walls of the Old City of Nicosia and close to the Paphos Gate, was also the HQ of UNFICYP's Nicosia District, and its Commanding Officer was the District Commander. The main task of the Canadians was to police the Green Line running across the centre of Nicosia; to this end company bases were established from which a network of OPs was manned and patrols were carried out on foot, in vehicles and even on bicycles.[12]

Swedish Contingent (SWEDCON)

The whole of the east of the island comprised Famagusta District and was the responsibility of the Swedes' 48th UN Battalion (strength 275 men).[13] It covered most of the fertile central plain (the Mesaoria), extensive citrus groves south of Famagusta, the eastern end of the

Pendhadaktylos range, the forest of Kantara and the Karpasia (the island's remote and little developed 'Panhandle' extending out to to Cape Andreas). SWEDCON's HQ was in Carl Gustav Camp, 3km north of the old walled city of Famagusta. Its men manned OPs close to the Old City, which was populated exclusively by Turks, and maintained posts at several outlying points in the widely spread District, including a detachment near Chatos to preempt incipient problems in that Turkish controlled area.

Irish Contingent (IRECON)

Following a reduction of 250 men in January 1972, Ireland's Contingent comprised its 22nd Infantry Group, which at a strength of 130 men represented no more than one company. Since this was insufficient to allow responsibility for a full District, the Irish were allotted the eastern part of Larnaca District on the island's south coast; this was designated UNFICYP's Larnaca Sector. It comprised Larnaca town and its sizeable Turkish quarter and also covered an area of coastal plain, the eastern foothills of the Troodos range and villages on the southern edge of the Mesaoria. Contingent/Sector HQ was in Wolfe Tone Camp[14] on the outskirts of Larnaca, and OPs were maintained in and around the town with a detachment further north at the Turkish village of Louroujina to prevent a recurrence of earlier fighting between it and the neighbouring Greek village of Lymbia.[15]

United Kingdom (or British) Contingent (BRITCON)

The British Contingent, at a strength of 1,030 men, provided over one third of UNFICYP's total. It was composed of two elements: first, an infantry battalion (3rd Bn, The Parachute Regt) of 565 men with its own operational area, and, second, small operational and logistic units supporting the Force as a whole (*see below*). Administrative command was exercised through a small Contingent HQ located in Blue Beret Camp, the Contingent Commander being concurrently the Force Chief of Staff. BRITCON's operational responsibility was for Limassol District and the Kophinou (or western) Sector of Larnaca District, the two together being designated Limassol Zone. It extended along the island's south coast from Cape Kiti in the east to beyond Pissouri village in the west (excluding the British western SBA), and reached up through the slopes of the Troodos to include Mt Olympus, at 1952m the highest point on the island. The battalion's Commanding Officer was Zone Commander, with HQ and base in Polemhidia Camp, high on a hillside 4km north of Limassol. One company, based at Kophinou, was responsible for that sector and manned OPs in its vicinity. A second company was based in Zyyi Camp on the coast 25km east of Limassol; its role was to watch over that mixed village and nearby communications installations and to man an OP near Mari, scene of a serious incident in April 1967. The third company, based in Polemhidia Camp, maintained a patrol base, known as Town OP, in Limassol itself, its task being to monitor relations between Greeks and Turks in the town. The remainder of the Zone was covered by battalion patrols, supplemented by a reconnaissance troop of the Force Reserve (*see below*), which was stationed at Polemhidia under operational command of the Zone Commander.

Force Supporting Operational Units

A British armoured reconnaissance squadron, D Sqn, Royal Scots Dragoon Guards (105 men), constituted (and was known as) The Force Reserve. Equipped with Ferret armoured scout cars, its troops patrolled extensively throughout the island, working in close co-operation with contingents concerned. It was based in Gleneagles Camp, adjacent to HQ UNFICYP at Nicosia airport, with one troop detached under command of Limassol Zone.

Helicopter support for the Force was also provided by the British. It consisted of an Army Aviation Corps Flight (30 men), equipped with four 2/3 man Sioux helicopters, used for reconnaissance and communication purposes, but also capable of casualty evacuation and other light tasks. Heavier needs were met by a detachment of No. 84 Squadron RAF, equipped with four Westland Whirlwind aircraft. The parent squadron, which was responsible for the detachment's technical backing, was not part of UNFICYP but of the UK's Near East Air Force (NEAF) based at Akrotiri, and the detachment itself was not formally under UN command.[16] Responsibility for its day-to-day tasking was delegated to UNFICYP and for all practical purposes it was an integral part of the Force, but was not based in a UN camp but within the confines of the British Retained Site at RAF Nicosia, and for disciplinary purposes its personnel were subject to the jurisdiction of the RAF Station Commander (although UNFICYP required them to observe UN disciplinary orders when on duty outside the SBAs).[17]

The Force signals unit, 644 Signals Troop, was a mixed British/Canadian unit some 80 men strong, of whom two-thirds were British. It operated the Force COMCEN, radio links forward to subordinate HQs, and Blue Beret Camp's telephone exchange; additionally it provided men to operate rear link radios for the Swedes and the Danes, the detachment manning the Troodos relay station and technicians to maintain radio masts at all locations. It was also responsible for line construction and maintenance and for operation of the SDS.

Force Personnel and Logistic Supporting Units

Each Contingent had its own Medical Officer, with medical backing for the Force as a whole provided by a 50-man strong Austrian Field Hospital located at Kokkini Trimithia (6km west of Nicosia airport). As a field unit the latter's resources were limited, but more extensive facilities were available at two British Services hospitals (one Army and one RAF) in the SBAs. Liaison to facilitate this was a responsibility of the Force's Chief Medical Officer (CMO), a British Colonel, who also monitored medical and hygiene standards within the Force and advised HQ staff and contingents on these matters.

The only fully integrated multi-national unit in UNFICYP (apart from Force HQ itself), in which men from every contingent served and lived together, was the Military Police (MP) Company of 50 men based in Blue Beret Camp. It was commanded by a Canadian officer, designated the Force Provost Marshal (FPM) with a Danish officer as his assistant; small detachments were stationed in the main towns. Responsibilities of the Company included watching over the discipline of UN soldiers both on and off duty and ensuring compliance with UNFICYP orders in such matters as traffic discipline, curfews, 'off-limit' premises, wearing of uniform, carriage of weapons and good order generally. It liaised with the civilian police of both communities in cases involving Cypriots and members of UNFICYP, and had a small Special Investigation Section to deal with more serious matters. Offences noted by the Company were reported to the Contingent Commander concerned (to whom any UN soldier taken into custody was handed over at the first opportunity) for action by him in accordance with the national disciplinary code.

All other Force logistic support units were provided by Britain. They consisted of a transport squadron of the Royal Corps of Transport (RCT), an Ordnance Depot of the Royal Army Ordnance Corps (RAOC), a Workshop of the Royal Electrical and Mechanical Engineers (REME) and a small detachment of the Royal Engineers (RE); the total strength of these was some 170 men.[18] UNFICYP's logistic base was located in Camp UNFICYP adjoining the perimeter of the airport and only 1.5km from Blue Beret Camp. It was administered by a small British staff under the Camp Commandant (a major), his Adjutant and the Camp Regimental Sergeant Major (RSM). Also located in the camp was the 'Morphou Gate Guard' responsible for the security of a store of Czech weapons placed in UN custody early in 1972 (*see Chapter 16*).

UN Civilian Police (UNCIVPOL)

Civilian police contingents provided by Australia, Austria, Denmark and Sweden and totalling 170 men also formed part of UNFICYP. Their operational activities were the responsibility of the Force's Police Adviser, Dr Hans Wagner, an Austrian civil servant who was answerable to the Force Commander direct. He was assisted at HQ UNFICYP by a small staff of professional police officers, who also helped to man the HQ's JOC. The Australian policemen provided support for AUSCON and BRITCON, the Austrians for FINCON and CANCON, the Danes for DANCON and also BRITCON, and the Swedes for SWEDCON and IRECON. These UNCIVPOL detachments were not formally subject to the military chain of command, but they provided police representation in JOCs at District level and their activities were coordinated by military commanders where appropriate.

UN Civilian Staff Members

Some 40 male and female civilian UN staff members (as distinct from locally hired civilian employees) worked at UNFICYP HQ but were not formally part of UNFICYP and were responsible to their masters in New York rather than to the Force Commander; they included personal secretaries, clerks and UN Radio technicians and at their head was the Chief Administrative Officer (CAO). Other senior civilian posts were that of the Senior Political Adviser (SPA) (John Miles, an Australian of wide UN experience), a Legal Adviser (Ramon Prieto of Spain) and a Public Information Officer (PIO) (Jean Back of France).[19]

The anomalous position of UN civilian officials serving with UN forces while owing allegiance is to their own masters in New York rather than to the Force Commander has been a feature of most UN operations. In UNFICYP the position of the CAO was the most obvious example of the problem. His financial responsibilities sometimes faced him with difficult choices between obeying the dictate of New York and meeting the wishes of the Force Commander. It was not satisfactory that, while the Force's military Chief Personnel and Logistics Officer was responsible to the Force Commander for efficient logistic support, the purse-strings were held by another individual answerable only to a superior in New York, since this created an inherent risk of friction. UNFICYP was fortunate to be served during the period 1972–74 by two CAOs, Victor Mills and George Ryder, both Americans, whose long experience with UN forces in the field had given each a sympathetic understanding of the needs and problems of their military colleagues. Both established harmonious relations with Lieut. Colonel Mark Pennell, the British officer who throughout this period was the Force's able CPLO, and did their utmost to represent the needs of UNFICYP to superiors in New York. Nonetheless on occasions they felt obliged to exert pressure by bypassing the Force Commander and using their own link with New York.

Comparable difficulties were to be found in the field of radio communications, where there was a split in responsibility as between the civilian Head of the UN Radio and the military Force Signals Officer (FSO); although their tasks were closely related, neither was subordinate to the other. Difficulties arose because, while the latter was responsible for the organization of tactical and other communications within UNFICYP, the former had responsibility for the UN-owned Motorola radio sets so widely used within the Force. Moreover, in times of crisis when pressure on radio communications with New York was intense, imposition of signals traffic priorities was essential. This clearly is a matter for operational staffs but, since the UN Radio was not under the latter's control, decisions were made by the CAO or the UN Radio Head, neither of whom was well placed to make the necessary operational judgements. This split in responsibility for UNFICYP's signals communications was not satisfactory and was an arrangement that would not have been tolerated in military forces other than those of the UN.

CHAPTER EIGHT

LOGISTICS AND FINANCE

The existence of the facilities of the UK Sovereign Base Areas has been of the greatest help to the United Nations. Throughout the life of the Force the United Kingdom has provided the most men and the greatest logistic support. Its financial contributions have been second only to those of the United States. . . . But the burden of the UN operation has been very unevenly shared and UNFICYP has presented the Secretary General with massive financial problems to which there is no ready solution.

> Rosalyn Higgins: *United Nations Peacekeeping –*
> *Documents and Commentary*, Vol. 4, Europe 1946–79.

Failure to ensure adequate logistic backing at the outset has handicapped the early operations of most UN peacekeeping Forces and has imposed hardship on the troops concerned. The urgency with which these operations have usually had to be mounted has been advanced as an excuse, but few military officers would absolve the UN Secretariat in New York of all blame. Its civilian officials have displayed skill in handling the political complexities, but, lacking military expertise, have failed to appreciate fully the importance of planning for and providing from the outset a standard of logistic support that would be accepted as even a minimum in most western armies.[1]

From the start UNFICYP was an exception, the high quality of its logistic backing being the fortuitous consequence of the circumstances in which the Force came into being in 1964, when it took over from and absorbed elements of a British army formation already in place and operating with logistic support provided by military establishments in the SBAs. This support was readily extended to all UN contingents as they arrived in Cyprus and has remained in place ever since. The benefits have been clearly stated:

> A third valuable experience to be gained from UNFICYP is the advantage of having the logistic system the responsibility of one country. . . . The advantages are obvious – a single organization is more economic, more efficient and smooth-running, and so long as there can be a standardisation of the major items of equipment problems of provisioning can be considerably reduced.[2]

Nonetheless, the multi-national composition of the Force inevitably required somewhat complicated arrangements to provide for differing national needs.

Each contingent provided its own basic equipment such as weapons and ammunition, in some cases vehicles, in most cases radios and other items for internal communication, some tentage, national military uniform (the UN supplied items such as blue berets and badges) and items needed for welfare purposes; all other equipment was supplied mostly from British stocks in the SBAs. UNFICYP hired some 400 vehicles from these stocks and, because standardization made for economy, it became UN policy to do this rather than that contingents should provide their own. Some radios and various other items, notably tentage, were also hired from British stocks. Items that contingents were unable to supply themselves and that were not available from this source were purchased or hired by the UN on the open market or else issued from meagre stocks held in the UN Depot at Pisa, Italy, run by the UN Field Service Branch.[3] Apart from a few national specialities, the Force's food was procured by the British army and issued to contingents in accordance with separate ration scales that took account of differing national dietary tastes.[4] Petroleum fuels were obtained from the Shell oil refinery near Dhekelia under contracts negotiated by the British army, and British assistance extended to a variety of other UNFICYP domestic needs, including engagement of local civilian labour[5], provision of base hospital services, and storage for heavier natures of ammunition.

The continuing existence of UNFICYP was dependent on renewal of its mandate at six- (and on occasions three-) month intervals, which did not allow it to incur long-term expenditure. For this reason in 1972, in spite of a sojourn of eight years on the island, standards of accommodation, ranging from tented camps and OPs to old hutted buildings[6], fell well short of what was desirable in the extremes of the Cyprus climate. Although the Status of Forces Agreement stipulated that

> The Government of Cyprus shall provide without cost to the Force and in agreement with the Commander such areas for headquarters, camps and other premises as may be necessary for the accommodation and the fulfilment of the functions of the Force. Without prejudice to the fact that all such premises remain the territory of Cyprus, they shall be inviolable and subject to the exclusive control and authority of the Commander.[7]

responsibility for the provision and maintenance of any new buildings was a bone of contention, the Government arguing that, while ready to maintain existing buildings, it was under no obligation to provide new ones or to carry out other works.[8] This obliged UNFICYP to do what it could within its own resources – old Nissen-type (corrugated iron) huts, long abandoned by the British, were recovered from around the island and refurbished, and contingents displayed energy and initiative in improving camps and OPs by self-help and at their own expense.

Personnel and logistic matters at UNFICYP HQ were the responsibility of the Personnel and Logistic Branch. Because the administration of discipline remained a national responsibility, the load on the Personnel Section of this Branch was lighter than would otherwise have been necessary; much of its work was concerned with the six-monthly personnel rotations and dealing with inquiries into road accidents, which averaged about one a day for the Force as a whole – a statistic that reflected less on UN drivers than on Cypriots notorious for their disregard of traffic discipline. It was the Logistics Section that carried the main load. Under its control rations and general stores were collected daily from British depots in the Eastern SBA and issued to contingents, where these were then broken down for further distribution – in some cases to posts of only 3–4 men who did their own cooking. Some OPs were inaccessible by road, and their needs including kerosine, radio batteries and drinking water, were supplied by helicopter, on foot or even by donkey.[9]

It was the Canadian Government's policy that its contingent should as far as possible be self-supporting. Although dependent on UNFICYP sources for rations and petroleum products, CANCON maintained its own logistic base in Blue Beret Camp, including medical, dental and workshop facilities. From a Force point of view this was not an economical arrangement, and the proportion of the contingent engaged in its own internal logistic and administrative tasks was far higher than that of other contingents. Since these resources were provided at Canadian expense, there could be little complaint, but one consequence was that the Canadians were less well integrated into UNFICYP than members of other contingents.

UNFICYP was an exception in respect not only of the high quality of its logistic support but also in the weakness of its financial situation. Unlike other UN peacekeeping operations (whose costs are borne by the Organization as a whole as provided for in Article 17 of the Charter) the Cyprus operation was funded under the provisions of Resolution 186(1964), which laid the burden on troop-contributor countries and the Cyprus Government alone, with the Secretary General authorized to accept voluntary contributions from others. This arrangement was conceived in the context of a three-month mandate, but as that initial period was further extended year after year it proved wholly inadequate. Repeated appeals by successive Secretaries General to all member states for voluntary contributions generally fell on deaf ears, so that by December 1972 the deficit in the UNFICYP Special Account was US $13.6 million and by 1990 had grown to US $174.5 million; a report by the UN Secretariat that year did not mince its words:

> This arrangement for financing peacekeeping has proven most unsatisfactory and particularly unfair to troop-contributing countries, which have had to shoulder a disproportionate share of the cost. Not only do they absorb their share as envisaged in Resolution 186(1964), which represents about 70 per cent of the total cost of UNFICYP, but the continuous shortfall in voluntary contributions has caused the United Nations to be 10 years in arrears in paying them the sums due for reimbursement of their extra and extraordinary expenses. This unsatisfactory situation has plagued UNFICYP throughout its existence and has persistently grown worse, resulting in an ever larger deficit.[10]

Since each troop-contributor government had negotiated its own financial agreement with the Secretary General, there were variations as between governments. Generally each met certain of its own contingent's costs and reclaimed the remainder from the UN, these (hopefully) being reimbursed from the Special Account. The British, alone of all the governments, met all the costs of its own contingent as well as 70% of the costs of the Force HQ, and charged the UN only for the equipment and services it provided to other contingents. The

Canadians met all the costs of CANCON except for those of men serving in Force HQ, but did a deal with the UN Secretariat under which they waived claims for the latter in exchange for the UN refunding the cost of a weekly military air service between Canada and Nicosia.[11]

Because its men were regular soldiers, whose basic costs remained the same wherever stationed, the Irish Government claimed back only those additional costs entailed by keeping them in Cyprus. But the Austrian, Danish, Finnish and Swedish Contingents all included a high proportion of men who were not regular soldiers but enlisted specifically for service for a limited period in UNFICYP, and for whom there was otherwise no national need; the full costs of their pay, allowances and personal equipment were chargeable to UN funds. Differing national arrangements led to variations between contingents in the special allowances paid for service in Cyprus, and all these factors made it possible to classify contingents as being, in UN terms, either 'high cost' (Austrian, Danish, Finnish and Swedish) or 'low cost' (British, Canadian and Irish). The significance of this became evident when reductions in the size of UNFICYP were under consideration in late 1973.

Voluntary contributions to the UNFICYP Special Account came from many but by no means all UN member states; although not a troop-contributor, the United States was by far the largest financial contributor, which placed the US in a strong position to exert pressure not only on the management of UNFICYP but also on occasions on the conduct of its operations. Generous support also came from the Federal Republic of Germany and Switzerland, neither of which at the time was a member of the UN[12], in marked contrast to the absence of financial support on the part of China, France and the USSR – all permanent members of the Security Council.[13]

Financial control within UNFICYP was exercised by the CAO, who negotiated local contracts and maintained close liaison with the Command Secretary in Episkopi (the British army's financial controller at HQ BFNE). He was answerable direct to the UN Secretariat in New York, and the anomalous position in which he was thus placed has been mentioned already.

Neither CAO nor CPLO, his military colleague, could surmount a fundamental difficulty that bedevils logistic planning in UN Forces. It is a consequence of the Security Council's practice of placing a time limit, usually six months but sometimes less, on a Force's mandate, for there is then no authority for incurring expenditure beyond that date. This inevitably imposes constraints on logistic planning and usually entails uneconomic expenditure, such as the hire of vehicles and equipment when outright initial purchase would have proved less expensive. Difficulties are compounded by the requirement that a UN Force's logistic needs must usually be put out to competitive international tender, a procedure that does not lend itself to speedy results. Notwithstanding the excellent logistic support received from the British SBAs, UNFICYP suffered in some degree on both these counts.

CHAPTER NINE

NATIONAL TIES
AND THE BRITISH CONNECTION

The functions of the Force are exclusively international and members of the Force shall discharge these functions and regulate their conduct with the interests of the United Nations only in view.

UNFICYP Force Regulations

An exchanges of letters between each troop-contributor government and the UN Secretary General confirmed that its contingent was accepted for service in UNFICYP on the explicit understanding that Force Regulations, of which the above was a fundamental provision, would be binding on its members. This did not obviate the need for a government to issue a confidential national directive to its own contingent's Commander setting out his responsibilities to the Force Commander on the one hand and to it on the other. So long as these directives did not conflict with Force Regulations or instructions properly issued by the Force Commander there could be no UN objection. But since no government can be expected to delegate all control of its contingent to the point that blind obedience is required to all orders emanating from a Force Commander, it is inevitable that national directives allow Contingent Commanders some discretion in respect of any instructions they believe to be contrary to their own national policy or practice. Such situations are likely to be rare and, so long as Contingent Commanders inform him of their intention to exercise that discretion, no UN Force Commander can have cause for complaint.

Although the contents of national directives were confidential as between governments and Contingent Commanders concerned, it was evident within UNFICYP that some contained instructions that came close in some respects to infringing the spirit, if not the letter, of Force Regulations. For example, some Contingent Commanders were required to report regularly to home governments not only on their Contingent's activities (a legitimate national concern) but also on the UN mediation effort and political developments more generally – matters that lay well outside the province of these Commanders. In some cases restrictions, not communicated to the Force Commander, were imposed governing the employment of a contingent, as in the case of the Canadians, whose Commander was enjoined not to permit men of his contingent to be placed under the operational command of any other. Since it was accepted operational practice within UNFICYP to form small multi-national groups to deal with particularly acute situations, giving political strength to the Force's action, such a national instruction was a potential obstacle to effective exercise of the Force Commander's authority.

In UNFICYP the British Contingent was under no such constraints. National instructions to its Commander were brief and to the point, reflecting Force Regulations in both letter and spirit while delegating to him discretion in referring to London any orders he considered to be inconsistent with national policy, provided always that he first informed the Force Commander of his intention to do so (during this author's tenure of this command he never had cause to consider doing so). Nonetheless, there were other concerns of a more subtle nature that were peculiar to the British Contingent. Its presence in UNFICYP had set a precedent, for hitherto it had been the practice to exclude permanent members of the Security Council from participation in UN peacekeeping operations. Three experienced international soldiers have pointed out the benefit of Britain's participation:

> Though the United Kingdom's units had not previously been part of a UN Force . . . they did bring to UNFICYP an unparalleled expertise in operational organization and management.[1]

This participation, however, brought some attendant problems, notably in the sensitivities it created. Some Greek Cypriots harboured bitter memories of the colonial era and the EOKA campaign before independence; others were critical of British actions when, after independence, British forces alone held the ring until the arrival of UNFICYP. For their part Turkish Cypriots were resentful of what they saw as the failure of these forces to protect them against Greek terrorism during the early part of 1964. The predicament of the British troops on joining UNFICYP has been summed up thus:

> They had been serving for three months with an admirable record of impartiality, which meant, of course, that they had managed to please neither side. The Greek Cypriots assailed the British for their failure to make the desired distinction between the legal government and the Turkish Cypriot 'rebels'. The Turkish Cypriots expressed their unhappiness over the British inability to stop Makarios's plans of 'genocide'. Increasingly vilified and abused by each side, the British troops, having lost both Greek Cypriot and Turkish Cypriot confidence, were no longer able to make much of a contribution. Indeed, although United Nations officials were reportedly impressed with how quickly and well the British troops became 'Onusians' *(from the French abbreviation ONU for the United Nations Organization)*, the Greek Cypriots refused to accept the British Contingent as part of the Force, preferring to treat the British part of UNFICYP as British rather than as an integral contingent of UNFICYP. The rest of UNFICYP's troops were hailed, trusted and granted respect; the British were an unwanted and ineffective leftover.[2]

These words were written of the situation in 1964, when anti-British sentiment prompted the Greek Cypriot House of Representatives to go so far as to vote unanimously for termination of British participation in the UN Force. While it would be fair to say that during the ensuing ten years the conduct of the British Contingent won increasing respect and silenced all but a few die-hard Cypriot critics, its successive Commanders had to tread warily in the knowledge that in some quarters anti-British feelings remained latent.

There were sensitivities, too, within UNFICYP. Some in other contingents were reluctant to be identified too closely with a contingent that still had about it what was perceived as an aura of colonialism, while others were critical of the British Army's role in Ulster:

> "The Irish arrived" wrote a *Times* correspondent "greatly troubled at the thought of supporting the British in some sinister plot to impose partition on yet another newly independent island." The Canadians, not wanting to be taken as "Brits", repainted all their vehicles and prominently "displayed hundreds of maple-leaf emblems". And the disembarking Finns "brought out their own bicycles and cycled 50 miles to Nicosia rather than use the British lorries waiting for them".[3]

As with Cypriots, feelings of this kind had all but vanished by 1972, thanks to the sensible way in which members of the British and other Contingents had worked (and played) together during the intervening years, but some vestiges remained and could all too easily be re-awakened by insensitive conduct or action.

The position was rendered no easier by the fact that the British Contingent, always the largest numerically, played a dominant part, as evidenced by its tenure of key appointments at Force HQ, its provision of virtually all the Force supporting and logistic units, the adoption of British military practice for many operational and administrative procedures and, not least, the use of English as the primary language. If some nurtured an uncomfortable feeling that beneath it all they were being used in some subtle way to further British interests, this could be no surprise.[4] It was symptomatic of relations between the British and other contingents even as late as 1972 that, whereas all the latter were at pains to parade national emblems on vehicles and uniform, the former displayed only the UN emblem.

The Secretary General had clarified at the outset the position of BRITCON vis-à-vis British forces in the SBAs:

> There is a clear distinction between the troops of the British contingent in the United Nations Force and the British military personnel in Cyprus, such as those manning the British bases not included in the United Nations Force.[5]

Nonetheless, the presence of the Commander British Forces Near East (CBFNE) and his large Headquarters at Episkopi led some to suspect that he exercised some hidden influence over UNFICYP in general and BRITCON in particular. Detecting suspicions of this nature on arrival in mid-1972 to take over as UNFICYP's Chief of Staff from Brig. General E.M.D. Leslie of Canada, I saw it as important to gain the confidence of those with whom I would be working by demonstrating that I was the servant of the UN Force and in no sense Episkopi's creature. To this end I limited personal contacts with British Commanders in the SBAs to the minimum necessary to maintain proper liaison and ensure that UNFICYP received efficient logistic support.

All UNFICYP Contingents received official visitors from their home countries and the two largest, those of Britain and Canada, were liable to receive a constant stream. In the case of the British their number tended not only to impose a considerable load on those who had to look after them but also heightened the impression of excessive British influence in the

Force. For this reason, and because the British army in the SBAs also suffered from a glut of visitors, I agreed with Major General Butler, the Army Commander at Episkopi, some common ground rules by which we should judge whether or not an intending visitor could demonstrate valid official reasons for visiting, thus enabling us to curb casual so-called 'swanners'.[6] Visitors were not confined to those from contingents' homelands – many others, including diplomats from UN member states, had a legitimate interest in the activities of the UN Force and wished to see at first hand how it was going about its task; military attachés of missions in Nicosia featured amongst these. As a UN Force we were glad to welcome all such visitors, to brief them on our activities and to conduct them round contingents, although at a period when the Cold War was still being waged there were sensitivities in some contingents on this account. The Irish, perhaps, were less concerned than most, and one Irish officer found himself the focus of attention of a Soviet military attaché, who invited him to dine from time to time; these occasions were not without their lighter moments, as when the Russian remarked, 'You seem to be having a lot of trouble with the British in Northern Ireland?' – to be met with the reply, 'You don't understand. It's not the British who are the trouble, it's the Irish.'

Although the Ulster situation rendered relations between the Irish and British Contingents a matter of particular delicacy, experience has shown that when men of diverse nationalities and backgrounds come together under the UN's blue beret they readily put aside national interests and prejudices to a degree that is unique. The fact that UN forces are successful in welding together disparate national contingents into an effective whole is due primarily to the fact that all are motivated by common aims and ideals and are imbued with the determination to make the arrangement, whatever the difficulties, a demonstrable working success. The remarkable spirit that permeates and motivates UN peacekeeping forces was demonstrated in UNFICYP in 1973, when 1st Bn, The Parachute Regt joined BRITCON and was deployed in Limassol District, alongside the Irish in Larnaca Sector. The British battalion had recently been involved in the events of 'Bloody Sunday'[7] and there was potential for friction on this account between men of the two contingents. Much to the credit of both there was none, any national feelings being subordinated to the international character of their common task.

CHAPTER TEN

MILITARY AND POLICE FORCES
OF THE TWO COMMUNITIES

The increasing combat efficiency of the military forces on both sides, resulting from the acquisition of better equipment and continuing high training activity, is a matter of serious concern. Far from acting as a deterrent, as is often contended, the increase of military capability augments the danger of escalation.

Report of the UN Secretary General (S/10842),
1 December 1972, para. 75.

By 1972 the military forces of each community were well established with adequate levels of organization, equipment, training and discipline, although quality varied. On the Greek Cypriot side was the National Guard created by Makarios in 1964 and organized in its early years by Grivas. Composed of conscripts, it was commanded and trained by officers and NCOs of the regular Greek army, the numbers of whom had had to be reduced following the 1967 débâcle at Kophinou to a total of about 700 in 1972. During the two years 1972–74 its total strength was 40,000 men, of whom some 12,000 were immediately available with the remaining 28,000 being reservists at short notice for recall. The force was commanded by a mainland Greek Lieut. General, whose HQ was located at Athalassa on the southern outskirts of Nicosia.[1]

The National Guard's roles were to maintain a balanced force of all arms to contain Turkish Cypriot communities and their armed elements in all parts of the island, and to be ready to counter any intervention from Turkey. Primarily an infantry force, it also contained supporting tank, armoured reconnaissance, armoured infantry and artillery units, which afforded an offensive capability; three Raiding Force Units (RFUs), each of 150–200 men sporting green berets, were its elite. Apart from the latter and certain infantry battalions, most units were normally appreciably below operational strength and in some cases were little more than cadres, but full scales of weapons and equipment were held and arrangements for the mobilization of the large number of reservists – not a difficult problem on a small island – ensured that all units could be placed quickly on an operational footing.

Subordinate to National Guard HQ at Athalassa were five Higher Military Commands (HMCs) located in the island's main towns (*Outline Organization at Annex 3*). Within these were one or more Tactical Groups (TGs), which (as the name implies) were tactical formations usually comprising elements of all arms, although it was the National Guard

Commander's policy to retain central control over armoured units and RFUs. Mainland Greek officers wielded complete authority with all posts down to the level of seconds-in-command of companies filled by them. Greek Cypriot officers were few in number, occupied only very junior posts and were excluded from service at National Guard HQ. Potential Greek Cypriot officers were selected from the conscripts by the mainland officers (a prime cause for complaint by Makarios) and then sent to Greece for training. Thus the control and influence of Athens over the National Guard was complete at all levels to the extent that the force's allegiance to the Makarios régime became uncertain.[2]

The mandatory period of conscription for all Greek Cypriots on reaching the age of 18 was two years, and exemption or deferment was not easily obtained. This compulsory service was popular neither with the conscripts nor their parents, which did not make for high morale in most units (the elite RFUs were exceptions). The situation was exacerbated during the period 1973–74 by reports of harsh treatment (alleged in some cases to have resulted in death) meted out by Greek army personnel to recalcitrant recruits and those not amenable to indoctrination against Makarios and his government.

The National Guard's weaponry was a hotch-potch mixture of modern NATO-pattern small arms and old heavier armaments procured from a variety of sources. Of particular importance (since the Turkish Cypriots possessed no armour) were 32 obsolescent Soviet-built T34/85 tanks which formed 23rd Medium Tank Battalion. Maintenance and spare parts for these posed problems; although some had recently been re-engined, in 1974 UNFICYP estimated that not more than half were serviceable at any one time. The remainder of the force's armour consisted of one armoured reconnaissance battalion equipped with 26 Marmon Harrington armoured cars of South African Second World War vintage and one armoured infantry battalion equipped with 32 Soviet-built BTR-152 armoured personnel carriers (APCs). Artillery support was provided by 11 artillery battalions, of which six were field, two were anti-tank and three were anti-aircraft units. All were equipped with a variety of obsolescent pieces, such as Soviet 100mm guns, British 25-pounders, US 75mm howitzers and anti-tank and anti-aircraft weapons of light nature.[3]

The core of the National Guard was its 15 active infantry battalions (at a normal strength of 150–250 men, increased to 550 on mobilization) and its nine militia battalions. All were equipped with mortars, light anti-tank weapons and a variety of small arms. Motor transport in battalions was limited, but a pool of vehicles was held centrally to provide a degree of mobility. The force as a whole was supported by a service battalion consisting of signals, medical, engineer and stores companies.

The Turkish Cypriot Fighters (TCF) were organized and deployed differently, for their role was defensive with little room for manoeuvre. Their task was two-fold: first, to provide protection for Turkish enclaves and local communities, and, second, to afford a secure base in the Nicosia enclave in the event of military intervention by Turkey; in such a contingency TCF elsewhere on the island had to be prepared to hold out until such time as mainland Turkish troops could reach them or a ceasefire was declared. TCF planning took account of the presence in southern Turkey of the Turkish 39th Division, the formation trained and held ready to intervene, and of the Turkish national contingent stationed on the island which in such a contingency also had a key role to play. There was clear military justification for their existence, but the TCF were also of economic importance to the community, for they were sustained almost entirely by Turkey's subvention, which constituted an important source of income for the beleaguered Turkish Cypriots.[4]

The TCF, too, was a conscript force in which all youths on reaching the age of 16 were compelled to serve for two years; coupled with periodic refresher training for older ex-fighters, this ensured that all Turkish Cypriot males capable of bearing arms were ready to do so. Command and training were in the hands of mainland Turks, estimated to number about 150 at any one time. Unlike mainland Greeks in the National Guard, these Turks remained under cover – their presence common knowledge but not admitted by the Leadership. They avoided contact with UNFICYP officers, whose dealings with the TCF had therefore to be conducted through Turkish Cypriot 'front men'. Since the latter could not take decisions without reference to their Turkish masters, delay was neither unusual nor misunderstanding uncommon; further, attitudes sometimes were hardened because Turkish officers could not be seen in Turkish Cypriot eyes to be deferring to UNFICYP pressures. Although formally responsible to the Vice President's Office (VPO)[5], the TCF in reality was under the thumb of the shadowy figure of the *Bozkurt* (Grey Wolf), a senior Turkish army officer who exercised wide power. He not only controlled the TCF and the Turkish national contingent but was believed also to dominate other spheres of the Turkish Cypriot community, acting as something of a Supremo, answerable only to Ankara. His presence on the island and identity were never acknowledged and access to him was denied. Nonetheless, his identity was known to some, as was his office within the premises of the Turkish embassy, whose staff clearly went in some awe of him.

The TCF had an active strength of 4,500 men (including a permanent cadre of 2,300 and the 150 mainland Turks), with an immediately available first-line reserve of 3,200 men and a second line of about 12,300; since all the latter underwent refresher training and kept arms and uniforms at hand in homes or village armouries, the TCF was able quickly to mobilize its full potential of about 20,000 men, who were augmented by a substantial number of Turkish Cypriot girls, trained in the use of small arms and wearing grey uniform with black berets. The TCF were organized (Annex 4) into regiments, battalions and companies, but none were of the strength usually found in such units and sub-units; in keeping with its primary role the most common element was the village detachment, varying in size from 100 to only 10 men. Standards of training and discipline were high, reflecting the martial qualities of Turks and their sometimes harsh methods. The provision of arms, equipment, ammunition and uniforms posed constant problems due to the Greek Cypriots' stranglehold on imports. The TCF had no tanks, armoured cars or APCs (apart from one primitive home-made vehicle trundled out on occasional parades to tease the Greeks) and no artillery.[6] Their armoury was limited to mortars, heavy machine guns, a few light anti-aircraft weapons and a miscellany of small arms and grenades. They had little motor transport to afford mobility, but this was not a serious handicap given their mainly static defensive role. Communications depended primarily on the existing civil telephone system, supplemented by a rudimentary and not always reliable radio network linking outlying villages and communities with the VPO in Nicosia.

Apart from some elderly reservists, who sometimes took over static duties to allow the more active to take leave or participate in exercises and parades (of which the Turks were fond, not least because they boosted the community's morale), the Fighters were smart, fit and determined. Some 500 were specially selected for training in commando-type skills and provided a more mobile guerrilla potential, but flexibility and initiative were otherwise lacking at lower levels. Although morale generally was higher than in the National Guard, there was a decline in the early 1970s (when some desertions were reported), possibly reflecting the Turkish community's growing disillusion and economic depression as compared with Greek Cypriot prosperity. To counter this decline a number of TCF were sent to Turkey for training as officers and in 1974 a re-equipment programme was in train and new accommodation for Fighters was being built in some villages.

In June 1974 the TCF's main strength was concentrated for the defence of the key enclaves in the island's north, with the remainder responsible for local defence of isolated village communities and Turkish quarters of towns. This deployment was mirrored by that of the National Guard, which retained relatively small numbers to contain the Turks in the isolated areas, the bulk of its strength being concentrated in the Nicosia-Kyrenia and the Famagusta-Chatos areas in order to contain the Turkish enclaves and controlled areas, counter any landings by sea or air from Turkey and provide a mobile armoured force able to react in any direction required.

The concentration of National Guard units in Famagusta District appeared at first sight to indicate an appreciation that any Turkish intervention was likely to include a seaborne landing on beaches north of Famagusta with a view to the early capture of that port (then the island's best) and a rapid armoured/infantry thrust across the good going of the Mesaoria to link up with Turkish Cypriots in the Chatos area and the Nicosia enclave. This may have been an element in National Guard thinking, but the true reason for this deployment was more prosaic; like armies elsewhere the force's peacetime locations were dictated less by tactical considerations than by the availability of camps; a legacy of the British colonial era was a surfeit of these in Famagusta District.

The main enclave lying between Nicosia and the Kyrenia Pass was an area vital to the Turks. It contained the camps of the Turkish national contingent and the Turkish quarter of the capital, covered most of the length of the Kyrenia Road and included the ancient Castle of St Hilarion, which dominated the port of Kyrenia and contained an important radio communication link with Turkey. Also situated within this enclave was an airstrip near the village of Aghirda, which in spite of a difficult approach due to the proximity of the mountains was usable by aircraft of the C130 type. Defence of the northern part of the enclave was the responsibility of the TCF's Boghaz Regiment, with the southern part that of the Nicosia Regiment; the centre sector and its highly vulnerable narrow neck was guarded by the Turkish national contingent. The enclave's perimeter was secured by rudimentary but well constructed posts sited to afford mutual support but with little depth. Since the terrain afforded reasonable going with few natural obstacles the enclave was vulnerable to any armoured thrust aimed at slicing it in half and isolating the Turks in Nicosia from succour from the north.

On the Greek Cypriot side responsibility for containing the enclave rested with the National Guard's 3rd HMC, whose 9th and 11th TG guarded respectively its southern and western flanks and whose 3rd and 12th TG secured the northern and eastern flanks. These formations could readily be supported by the bulk of the National Guard's tank, armoured reconnaissance, APC, artillery and RFU resources, all of which could be rapidly brought to bear. Manning the Green Line in Nicosia, which marked the southern limit of the enclave, was the task of 211th Infantry Battalion, one of only four that were maintained at full strength.

The Chatos area was of particular importance – to the Turks because it embraced a clutch of Turkish villages and fertile land on the Mesaoria and to the Greeks because it was close to one of the island's most important water sources, the perennial spring at Kythrea.[7] The area presented a difficult problem for the Turks since there were no natural obstacles on which to base its defence, and because it was dominated in the north by the Pendhadaktylos mountains and bounded on the south by the Nicosia – Famagusta road, both of which were under Greek control. A further concern of both sides was the disused airstrip at Tymbou; this was an all-weather strip built by the British, which was capable of being brought quickly back into use.[8] The island's Panhandle, although a remote and little developed area, was another area of significance, partly on account of its proximity to Turkey and partly on account of its sizable Turkish Cypriot population. A TCF battalion was centred on the village of Galatia at the Panhandle's base, its tasks in the event of Turkish military intervention being to seal off the peninsula pending the arrival of the mainland forces and to assist in a link-up with Turks in the Chatos and Famagusta areas. The TCF possessed neither air nor naval elements but since Turkey lay close this was of little moment – air and naval support was readily available from mainland bases should this be required. (Several military Forward Air Controllers (FACs) were stationed within the enclave for the purpose of directing Turkish air strikes in the event of a Turkish intervention, and the conical tops of the minarets of mosques all around the island were coated in gleaming aluminium paint, a purpose, it was believed, being to provide ready recognition of Turkish villages and localities by Turkish pilots.)

The air and naval elements on the Greek side were small and no match for those of Turkey. The National Guard's air wing belied its name, since it consisted of only one light aircraft, a Piper Colt used primarily for reconnaissance, and about 300 men, the majority of whom were engaged in operating a chain of six radar stations sited to cover the northern, eastern and southern approaches to the island, but with a reliability that was uncertain. Its naval wing, also weak, comprised five Soviet-built motor torpedo boats (MTBs) (a sixth had been sunk by the Turkish airforce off Kokkina in 1964) and one Canadian-built gunboat, named *Levantis*; by 1972 all were over 25 years old and of doubtful serviceability. This naval wing, which afforded no more than a limited coast patrolling capability to deter small scale infiltration and smuggling, also totalled about 300 men; most were Greek nationals, but a few Greek Cypriots were carried on board under training.

Since the civil police forces of each community were armed, they cannot be omitted from the reckoning. The 'Turkish Cypriot Police Element' (TCPE), as it was known in UN parlance, numbered about 800 men, most of whom had withdrawn from the Republic's integrated force at the time of the 1963–64 crisis. Since the Greeks held that they had done so voluntarily and therefore no longer had valid legal standing as policemen, the TCPE was unable to exercise authority outside Turkish-controlled areas. The police on the Greek side (known to UNFICYP as CYPOL) continued as the Government's recognized force, although unable in its turn to exercise authority in Turkish areas. The strength of CYPOL was about 4,100 men, with an additional 500 special constables with a limited role. The police of both communities were armed with small arms (mostly of older pattern) and were well disciplined and trained, many having undergone military service and some having served in the police under British rule. Both were regarded as efficient and generally un-corrupt, but there were doubts as to the loyalty of some members of CYPOL to Makarios and his government.[9] This lent significance to a special unit on the Greek side – the Police Tactical Reserve Unit (TRU) first formed in 1964 with a strength of 160 men. During 1972–74 the activities of EOKA-B led Makarios to expand the TRU and develop it as a hand-picked elite, 700 strong, loyal to him personally and under his direct operational control. Para-military in character, it was well equipped with modern weapons, vehicles and radios, which permitted rapid deployment. Except on one occasion in Limassol in January 1974 (described later), Makarios did not employ the TRU in the intercommunal context but only against armed anti- government groups in his own community. Nevertheless, the expansion of the TRU caused increasing anxiety and fears within the Turkish community, which obliged UNFICYP to keep its activities under observation.

The *Bozkurt* saw to it that there was no effective opposition to the Leadership within the Turkish community, any such manifestation receiving short shrift.[10] But growing violence during 1973–74 within the Greek community by anti-government armed factions (referred to in the local press as 'para-state groups') caused anxiety within the Turkish community, which necessitated UNFICYP monitoring these developments to ensure that Greek Cypriot quarrels did not spill over into the intercommunal sphere.

Given the size of the armed forces of each community (and armed factions within that of the Greeks), together with the national contingents of Greece and Turkey, the British forces in the SBAs and UNFICYP itself, a casual observer could be forgiven for thinking that the small island was all but sinking under the weight of arms. Disraeli can never have foreseen the extent to which his *place d'armes* was to become just that.

CHAPTER ELEVEN

THE NATIONAL CONTINGENTS OF GREECE AND TURKEY

> As is also the case with its Greek equivalent, the officers and men in the Turkish contingent
> are regular personnel of their national armies. They receive their early training and personal
> equipment before transfer to units in Cyprus. All weapons, equipment and other military
> support are furnished by the homeland army. Personnel are rotated twice a year; one-third to
> one-half of the contingent is relieved in each group transfer.
>
> Eugene K. Keefe *et al.*: *Area Handbook for Cyprus*, p. 214

Behind the armed forces of the two communities stood the national contingents of Greece
and Turkey, stationed in Cyprus in accordance with the Treaty of Alliance. Each contingent
consisted of an infantry battalion, limited by the treaty to a strength of 950 men in the case
of the Greeks and 650 men in that of the Turks. Location of cantonments and technical
details, such as scales of weapons and equipment, were specified in a Special Convention
associated with the treaty. The activities of the two contingents were not formally a concern
of UNFICYP, the Secretary General having failed in 1964 to bring them under the
command of the UN Force:

> The mandate of the United Nations Force in Cyprus . . . gives it no responsibility for matters
> relating to the Greek and Turkish Contingents in Cyprus. These Contingents are not part of
> UNFICYP, and, because the Government of Turkey would not agree it, they have never come
> under the over-all command of the Commander of UNFICYP as I had suggested at the time of
> the establishment of the Force.[1]

Nonetheless UNFICYP inevitably was obliged to remain cognizant of their presence because
this was liable to impinge on the intercommunal scene.

The cantonment of the Greek Contingent – ELDYK (*Elliniki Dynamis Kyprou*) – was situated on the north-western outskirts of Nicosia. Relations between it and the regular Greek
army officers who commanded the National Guard were close, but the contingent avoided
overt involvement in intercommunal matters and on that score gave UNFICYP little cause
for concern; for this reason UNFICYP's contacts with it tended to be few, limited generally
to routine liaison and military courtesies. The periodic rotations of its members between
Greece and Cyprus were monitored by UNFICYP, although the latter was not in a position

(nor did it have the authority) to check on quantities of arms and other military items imported then or at any other time. The Turks, who did not enjoy the advantage of control of any of the island's air or sea ports, resented this situation but were obliged to recognize that, so long as the Greeks refrained from any too blatant abuse, they had little alternative but to accept it.

The Turkish Contingent's situation was very different. Its authorized cantonment lay 500m north of that of the Greeks[2] but the bulk of the Contingent was actually stationed further north in consequence of its action in December 1963, when it had sallied out to support the Turkish Cypriot community and taken up positions astride the Kyrenia Road at the villages of Orta Keuy and Geunyeli in defence of the vulnerable narrow neck of the enclave. Here the Turks remained firmly esconced for the next ten years, rejecting all charges that in doing so they were in breach of the Treaty of Alliance. This gave the Cypriot Government ground for arguing that the treaty was no longer valid and that there was therefore no legal justification for the continued presence of the Turkish Contingent on the soil of the sovereign Republic of Cyprus. Since the Greeks were in no position to eject the Turks, the latter were unmoved by this argument.

It was this dispute that brought UNFICYP into close involvement with various aspects of the Turkish Contingent's presence. By deploying outside its authorized location the Turkish Contingent had secured control of virtually the whole length of the Kyrenia Road and, by using as its agents the TCF and TCPE, was denying its use to Greek Cypriots. This was an intolerable situation for the Government and, when a partial rotation of the Turkish Contingent became due in August 1964, it saw its opportunity to act. Smarting under Turkey's recent military action during the Tillyria incident and having renounced unilaterally the Treaty of Alliance, it declared that it would not permit the rotation to take place since the Contingent's presence in Cyprus now had no legality. The Turks maintained their right to rotate their men and made clear their intention to do so.[3] A dangerous crisis loomed.

Persuading Turkey to postpone the operation while he sought a way out, the UN Secretary General proposed not only that the incoming Turkish troops should be stationed within their authorized camp and not on the Kyrenia Road, but also that the road should become the exclusive responsibility of UNFICYP, who would open it to all civilians while denying its use to armed personnel of either side. The outcome was a compromise: the Turks accepted that the road should be opened under the exclusive control of the UN Force and that movement on it by unarmed Greeks should be permitted (albeit under circumscribed conditions), but were adamant in refusing to return all their troops to the authorized camp.

For their part the Greeks lifted objections to the impending troop rotation, which at the request of both sides was to be conducted under the good offices and with the practical assistance of UNFICYP. The Secretary General informed the Security Council of this outcome and arrangements accepted for the future control of the strategically important Kyrenia Road were published in an *Aide-Memoire*, to which the Turkish Government agreed. After delays due to the need to clarify certain points, the Kyrenia Road was opened at the end of October 1964 under UNFICYP's control and the rotation of the Turkish troops was carried out at the same time. Wording of the relevant documents had avoided linking these two matters, but the inference that each was a *quid pro quo* for the other was clear enough. This did not prevent the Turks in later years from denying any such linkage or from arguing that alleged breaches by them of the Kyrenia Road agreement were not grounds for hindering impending troop rotations – views that were inconsistent with the Secretary General's statement to the Security Council in September 1964, when he informed its members of

> the outcome of my continued search for a satisfactory solution of the problems concerning the projected rotation of the Turkish Contingent. I stated that the parties concerned had agreed in principle to the proposal which I had submitted to them whereby the Kyrenia Road, which was under the control of Turkish and Turkish Cypriot armed personnel, would be placed under the exclusive control of UNFICYP. . . . The Government of Cyprus, without prejudice to its position on the question of the Turkish Contingent's presence in Cyprus, would not interfere with the projected rotation of the Contingent.[4]

UNFICYP's relations with the Colonel commanding the Turkish National Contingent, invariably a high grade officer, and his subordinates were cordial and, for the reasons mentioned, closer than those with the Greek Contingent. But because UNFICYP's mandate did not extend over them, the Force's dealings with both contingents were a matter of some delicacy. Questions involving the Turkish Contingent had to be taken up through the Turkish Embassy, although some minor problems were dealt with pragmatically at lower level direct between Turkish officers and those of the Finnish Contingent, in whose operational area the Turks were stationed. Both Finns and Turks are proud, tough and uncompromising soldiers who respected each other's martial qualities. In the period 1972–74 occasions for friction were few and generally the two were on friendly terms, to the point even that Turkish officers were welcome guests at the Finns' sauna parties.

Such problems as did arise were usually caused by the Turks' construction of new or improved defences in the enclave or by surreptitious attempts to advance their positions in breach of the accepted military *status quo*. Finnish protests were met by bland denial of any Turkish Contingent involvement and recommendation that complaints be addressed to the Turkish Cypriot Leadership; the latter more often than not disclaimed responsibility so that stalemate was reached. The choice then facing UNFICYP was either to request the Secretary General to raise the matter with the Turkish Government (hardly warranted in the case of minor breaches) or to continue to press the matter in Nicosia. UNFICYP was not empowered to remedy matters by force and could only lean as heavily as it could on both the Turkish Embassy and the Leadership. Direct means of doing so were limited, but an indirect method was to draw attention in periodic Secretary General's Reports to the lack of co-operation which the UN Force felt itself to be receiving from the Turks. The Turks disliked public pressure of this kind, which was not conducive to smooth relations between them and UNFICYP. Since the UN Force had obligations to both sides to act impartially, it could not overlook even seemingly trivial matters – a point to which both Greeks and Turks sometimes appeared blind.

It was the six-monthly troop rotations of their contingent that brought UNFICYP into closest contact with the Turks. In consequence of the agreement reached in September 1964, and at the formal request on each occasion of the Turkish and Cyprus governments, the operation was conducted each January/February and August/September under the auspices of and with the considerable practical assistance of the UN Force. It was a unique business, in which sometimes there was an element of pantomime, but beneath the comic lay serious issues, taut tempers and risks of escalation into violence – aspects not readily deduced from the bland references to these rotations contained in the Secretary General's periodic Reports to the Security Council.[5] The operation, carried out in the course of a single day chosen by the Turks and notified to UNFICYP and the Government only a few days in advance, entailed a Turkish naval transport escorted by one or more destroyers entering the port of Famagusta soon after dawn to disembark incoming troops and stores, which, after checks by UNFICYP to verify that only numbers, quantities and types previously agreed with the Government had been landed, were then conveyed in UN vehicles and under UN protection to the Turkish Contingent camps in the Orta Keuy – Geunyeli area just north of Nicosia. Outgoing personnel and stores were then transported, again under UNFICYP escort, from Nicosia to Famagusta where after further UN checks they were loaded into the same vessel, which sailed for Turkey that evening.[6]

Thus summarized, these operations appear simple, but in practice they were fraught with complications and sensitivities that demanded delicacy and understanding on UNFICYP's part. Emotions and tempers among both Turks and Greek Cypriot officials were liable to come close to flash point and it was only UNFICYP's calming third-party presence, coupled with its efficient and business-like organization, that contained these during an invariably long and sometimes very hot day. As at last the Turkish ship sailed out into the gathering dusk, its decks lined with troops marking their departure for home in song (in contrast to glum faces seen on some of those disembarking earlier), all concerned within UNFICYP were able to look back on a difficult task well done.

The rotations entailed much preliminary work on UNFICYP's part. It mediated in long and tedious negotiations between the Turkish Embassy and the Government to reach agreement on detailed lists of items that might be imported. Arguments were many as the National Guard opposed the importation of anything that might conceivably improve the military capability of the Turkish Cypriot Fighters or the Turkish Contingent itself, while the Turkish Embassy resisted all demands to modify its catalogue of declared military needs. UN officers (exercising independent professional judgement) advised both as to what on military grounds should be accepted as reasonable and eventually an agreed list running to scores of pages was produced, sometimes only within hours of the start of the rotation.[7]

As this tedious bargaining went on, HQ UNFICYP geared up the Force for the many other aspects of its involvement in the rotation. A particular concern was the security of the Turkish incoming and outgoing personnel, who were carried between Nicosia and Famagusta in UN vehicles unarmed (their arms being retained in the Turkish Contingent's camps). UN picquets were required along the 50km length of the road which ran through Greek-controlled territory, with culverts and bridges inspected to ensure that they had not been mined; escorts found by scout cars of the Force Reserve squadron accompanied each convoy with air surveillance provided by Army Aviation Flight helicopters. At Famagusta docks a reception area, to which access was controlled by UN Military and Civilian Police and through which all men and stores passed for checking by UNFICYP personnel, had to be laid out in cooperation with the Harbour Master, and road transport for men and stores had to be organized. It was necessary to call on all UNFICYP Contingents for the provision of men and other resources to meet these needs, which afforded an opportunity for detachments of different contingents to work together under each other's command (the value of this was evident during the events of July-August 1974). To control operations on the day of the rotation a small Tactical Force HQ was deployed midway between Nicosia and Famagusta, allowing the JOC in Blue Beret Camp to continue without distraction to deal with the Force's activities elsewhere on the island.

With all preparations in place, the rotation duly proceeded, usually without disruption but not without minor pantomimes, especially at the dockside. In particular was a regular dispute occasioned by the landing of Turkish diplomatic bags. The Special Convention attached to the 1960 Treaty of Alliance contained certain provisions appertaining to the Turkish Contingent; these included agreement that at each rotation the Turks should be permitted to bring in sealed bags containing documents relating to personnel of the contingent and that these were not to be opened for inspection by Greek Cypriot officials, provided that they were accompanied by a Turkish Foreign Office certificate that they contained only such documents and the bags' seals were intact. Turks were wont to bring in three or four such sealed bags; since these were large and heavy (two men were needed to lift each), the Greeks suspected that besides documents they contained other items such as radios or weapons excluded from the agreed list. Tension rose as they were brought down the gangway and I would step forward to examine the certificate and the seals, which in turn were inspected by an official of the Greek Cypriot Foreign Ministry. Of course both certificates and seals would be in order and, when I declared this to be so, the official ritually objected to the size, weight and even number of the bags.[8] The pantomime was then acted out. The Greek official reported to his Ministry in Nicosia by telephone and asked for instructions. In the meantime the bags remained on the quayside with nervous Turks hovering over them, UN Military Police keeping others at bay, and the rotation operation halted. However, given the terms of the Special Convention there was little that the Government could do, and after a face-saving delay grudging consent came from Nicosia for the bags to be allowed through unopened. They were then hurriedly loaded into a Turkish Embassy vehicle to be whisked away to Nicosia and disembarkation of men and stores was resumed.

The incoming troops had to be counted by UNFICYP and were then required to undergo Greek Cypriot Customs examination; this, too, was something of a charade. The soldiers passed through a marquee where under the eyes of UNFICYP and by mutual agreement every tenth man (officers were exempted) was taken aside by a Greek official and made to turn out the contents of his personal pack – a mean business as each bewildered man's possessions were revealed to consist only of the barest necessities. It was also a futile procedure since it was all too easy for the Turks, had they so wished, to arrange for unauthorized items to be carried by one of the other nine. To UNFICYP observers it seemed no more than the Greek Cypriots' determination to demonstrate their authority, in reality empty, and thereby humiliate the Turks. It was an attitude that seemed to colour the Greeks' approach to these rotations and one that did nothing to improve relations between Ankara and Nicosia. The blame did not rest with one side alone – the Turkish Cypriots made maximum capital out of the rotations, partly to sustain their community's morale, partly to demonstrate gratitude to their mother-land and partly just to remind Greek Cypriots of the military strength and protection afforded to them by Turkey, the tangible demonstration of which was the presence in Cyprus of these Turkish soldiers. The incoming troops were given emotional welcomes as they passed through a Turkish Cypriot hamlet at the exit to the docks, with chickens killed in their honour, welcoming speeches, songs and cheers; similar scenes but on larger scale greeted their arrival in the Turkish quarter of Nicosia.

An exaggerated obsession with security caused the Greeks to insist that activities in the dock area should not be observed by TCF on the walls of the Old City, which overlooked the docks, and that photographs should not be taken from the ship of what was going on ashore. UNFICYP kept watch to check that neither happened, but from time to time the Greeks alleged that breaches were taking place; all operations were then halted while UNFICYP investigated and, if necessary, put matters right. During these long and usually tense days various other incidents were likely temporarily to halt the rotation, for example charges that Turkish warships were intruding into Cyprus waters, unexplained failures of the ship's derricks and arguments over the number or type of particular items being imported.[9]

Nonetheless, by evening all had usually been completed without serious incident. As the Turkish ship sailed out into the gathering darkness, the last Turks were escorted back to Nicosia, UNFICYP's quayside organization was dismantled, its protection parties along the route were stood down and the Force Commander informed New York that another rotation operation had been carried out successfully. Thorough planning and efficient execution had demonstrated yet again the value of a UN Force's third-party role in maintaining calm in a situation fraught with international friction and tension. As so often in UN peacekeeping, some of the tasks required of UNFICYP seemed trivial, if not actually absurd, but those who saw at first hand the underlying tensions that were liable suddenly to explode could be in no doubt as to the importance of the UN role. Indeed, it is difficult to see how these rotations could have been carried out without UNFICYP's good offices and practical assistance.

A curious secondary scene gave pause for thought on this account. While in Cyprus Turkish officers purchased various household goods not readily or cheaply available in Turkey, and these were transported from Famagusta in a small ship chartered privately by departing Turkish officers. The loading of this ship with crates containing refrigerators, cookers, washing machines, furniture and other goods could be seen taking place in a neighbouring berth and at the same time as the rotation operation, but outside UN arrangements. Turkish officers and Greek Cypriot merchants seemed to come and go freely without friction or difficulty and unhindered by Government officials. It was apparent to UNFICYP that political passions on both sides could be subordinated without difficulty where mutual commercial advantage was at stake.

Problems surrounding troop rotations of the Turkish Contingent were in marked contrast to the situation enjoyed by the Greek Contingent, which had no need to look to UNFICYP for assistance since all ports and access to them were under the Government's control. In its early days the UN Force had seen it as part of its task to monitor Greek rotations, which were carried out through Famagusta or Limassol, but the Government denied UNFICYP the right to enter the docks for this purpose. Unable on this account to check in detail the men and stores landed, it had become the practice by 1972 for UNFICYP to do no more than exercise a general oversight of the rotations. However, since most of the labour force in both ports was Turkish Cypriot, little could be imported without the knowledge of the Leadership, which then was able to make appropriate representations to UNFICYP. This served to some extent to prevent any too blatant breaches of treaty provisions, but the Turks nursed a lasting resentment that the Greek Contingent was spared procedures regarded as humiliating to Turkish national pride. The capture of Famagusta and Kyrenia by Turkish forces in July-August 1974 put an end to this situation.

CHAPTER TWELVE

UNFICYP'S *MODUS OPERANDI* 1972-1974

> No one can deny that the operational emphasis has changed radically from that which pertained in 1964, and that now it is primarily a political and reconciliation problem rather than one of violence control.
>
> Rikhye *et. al.*: *The Thin Blue Line*, p. 114.

The above observation related to the situation that prevailed in early 1974, before the intervention that summer of mainland Turkish forces and the *de facto* partition of Cyprus that resulted. This event imposed fundamental changes in the role of UNFICYP, which thereafter served as a buffer force deployed along a continuous line of military confrontation, on one side of which stood the Turkish army with Greek Cypriot forces on the other. Previously the diversity of intercommunal problems had required UNFICYP to be deployed throughout the island but, while complicating its operations, this also lent special interest to service in the UN Force during the first 10 years. The circumstances and difficulties varied as between each contingent but all required assiduous attention to and understanding of the problems. Some matters of dispute seemed trivial, if not ludicrous, but inherent in each was the ever-present risk that, unless settled or at least contained, it might spark an escalation to the point of intercommunal violence.

As the violence of 1964–67 gave way to the calmer and more stable situation that prevailed by 1972, UNFICYP had already made some changes, but the precedents and practices of the earlier years continued to a significant degree to govern its *modus operandi*. The general pattern established at the outset was explained by the Secretary General in September 1964:

> Deployed in sensitive areas throughout the country, the Force attempts to interpose itself between the Greek and Turkish Cypriot military positions, or, if this is not possible, to set up its own posts nearby so that its mere presence will constitute an effective deterrent to a recurrence of fighting. If, despite its precautionary measures, shooting incidents occur, the Force will immediately intervene and endeavour to end the fighting by persuasion and negotiation. In each case it will also carry out a thorough investigation of the incident. Frequent patrolling is organized whenever necessary to ensure safety on roads and in towns and villages in sensitive areas. . . .
>
> But the daily tasks of UNFICYP go far beyond the normal duties set forth above. A wide range of problems, large and small, are brought to the attention of UNFICYP for its urgent

action. In a Cyprus torn by internal strife the population of both communities lives in constant
fear and looks to UNFICYP for protection. Escorts are organized to protect persons of one
community who have to venture into the area occupied by the other. UNFICYP is frequently
called upon to deal with such problems as food supply, relief and refugees. The UNFICYP
Field Hospital, run by the Austrian medical unit, although primarily established for
UNFICYP personnel, also provides assistance to other patients on an emergency basis.[1]

There were changes of emphasis during the succeeding decade, but this remained the broad
framework within which UNFICYP's operations were conducted until July 1974.

In the same Report the Secretary General explained that problems and incidents were
dealt with at three levels in the Force – by troops deployed on the ground, by District (or
Zone or Sector) HQ, and by Force HQ. It was UNFICYP's policy to settle problems as
quickly as possible and at as low a level as possible, since experience showed that, if allowed
to escalate and spread, these were liable to become more explosive and difficult to defuse.
Nevertheless, because problems in one area could influence the situation in others, it was the
rule that all incidents and incipient problems, however trivial, should be reported at once to
Force HQ.

The tasks of troops on the ground were to know their areas intimately; to establish
personal liaison with local National Guard and TCF units and local civic leaders, such as
village *mukhtars*, with a view to ensuring that relevant agreements, arrangements and understandings[2] were observed; to anticipate intercommunal problems wherever possible and,
when these arose, to mediate and suggest solutions; and in the last resort to interpose themselves physically to prevent an armed clash. Importance was attached to rapid reaction in the
event of shooting incidents (which were rare in the period 1972–74) in order to prevent any
spread. In such cases the first need was to secure a cessation of the firing by making immediate contact with commanders on each side, after which the causes had to be investigated,
culprits identified and protests lodged. These tasks demanded constant vigilance and
thorough understanding of local issues and past history, and were carried out by means of a
network of permanently manned UN Observation Posts (OPs), of which in May 1972 there
were 55, augmented by patrols on foot, on bicycle (along parts of the Nicosia Green Line)
or in vehicles, and by helicopter observation.

Particular emphasis was laid on preserving the military *status quo ante* because any
change, however small, made by one side was likely to cause reaction by the other and lead
to escalation. 'Maintaining the *status quo*', even in such minor detail as the number of rows
of sandbags protecting a military post, became a constant UN preoccupation, experience
having proved this to be a valuable peacekeeping weapon. Problems of this nature had to be
thoroughly investigated and records checked before a conclusion was reached. UNFICYP
stressed the need for each side to accept its impartial judgement in these cases, and by 1972
there had been encouraging improvement in the degree to which both were willing to do so.
This required the maintenance of detailed records, a task made all the more important (but
also all the more difficult) by the frequent changes in the personnel of UNFICYP due to the
six-month tours of duty, but the need for them was evident in the readiness of both sides to
attempt on occasion to exploit any perceived lack of continuity within the UN Force.

UNFICYP's insistence on maintenance of the *status quo*, sometimes in matters of seeming triviality, irritated the Leadership, since most alleged breaches were on the Turkish side. The Leadership complained that the Force paid too much attention to such matters, which, it argued, were unimportant, while failing to give sufficient weight to its protests of discrimination by the Government against the Turkish community in the provision of public services. It was difficult not to sympathize with this view, but it was necessary constantly to remind the Leadership that the two matters were inextricably linked. Turkish breaches of the *status quo* were in military terms often pointless, but, trivial or not, they provoked Greek protests and acrimonious argument. This served only to sour intercommunal attitudes and was counter-productive to the UN Force's efforts to persuade the Government to improve its provision of those same public services that the Leadership was demanding.

Problems that could not be dealt with at once by troops on the ground were taken up at District HQ level, where commanders maintained close liaison and held frequent meetings with the District Officer on the Greek side, the local Turkish Cypriot leader and local commanders of the National Guard and TCF.[3] The many long-standing problems in each District usually gave rise to interminable discussion and progress towards a settlement was rare because what lay at their heart was the question of jurisdiction, a matter that was bound to remain unresolved without an overall settlement in Cyprus. Nonetheless two useful purposes were served: first, the meetings provided an opportunity for each side to 'let off steam' relatively harmlessly, often by transferring to UNFICYP's broad shoulders frustrations that might otherwise have been vented more destructively; second – and no less important, they afforded a channel of communication between the two communities and minimized risks of misunderstanding or worse. Some of UNFICYP's District Commanders grumbled that these long and inconclusive discussions were a worthless charade, but most came to see that they were an important ingredient of the peacekeeping game.

District Officers were officials of some local importance since they were appointed by the Ministry of the Interior to coordinate government activities within their District. After December 1963 all were Greek Cypriots but of a generation that had grown up with, knew personally and were accustomed to working with those Turkish Cypriots who assumed the local Turkish Cypriot Leadership. It was rarely possible for the two to meet formally or in public, but it was not uncommon for them to do so informally and privately, often on the initiative of the UN District Commander, who provided a suitably discreet venue on the neutral ground of a UN camp (and oiled the wheels by dispensation of whisky and soda). Such meetings away from the public eye offered better prospects for ironing out disagreements, since neither party felt the need to adopt postures calculated to satisfy those of their supporting staff present on formal occasions.

The UN Commander of Paphos District in 1974 has given a concise description of his role:

> At District level our task was to maintain a good relationship with the leaders of both communities at all levels in the two administrations. In Paphos the two local leaders [Mr C. Stephanides and Mr Fellaoglu] were well established in their appointments and had been the key men for some eight or nine years. They were also both local men and therefore had a genuine

love of the District. Unlike other Districts, we were fortunate here because these two men were quite definitely the bosses, and this was a great advantage when the situation got tricky, because they really could make decisions on behalf of their communities.

We held formal, but separate, meetings with both leaders and their senior officials monthly, which gave them the chance to pass on to us, the go-betweens, their feelings on the current problems in a semi-public forum. Minutes were taken at these meetings, and after we had approved them they were circulated far and wide by the respective leader, with the object of giving the current SITREP on all outstanding problems and showing all and sundry how good they were at maintaining the pressure on UNFICYP and the other side.

The problems that were discussed were very varied, ranging from disputed water rights, installations of telephones and electricity and the collection of debts and taxes, to hopelessly complicated land tenancy agreements, many of which were insoluble but had to remain in the minutes to keep the political pressure on the other side. One could sweat blood in the effort to solve problems and even get it agreed at the meetings that an item was closed, but this guaranteed the inclusion of a new item, and one was back to square one.

The meetings were the formal side of our work. Much more important was the constant contact at all levels, usually daily, with the officials of both administrations, and this was where most of the negotiating was done. It mattered a lot that we had the respect and friendship of our counterparts on both sides. We had sufficient time before the major troubles [of July – August 1974] to achieve this, get to know each other well and see through the man rather than his public facade. This to my mind was of critical importance.

One could quote many stories about day-to-day problems we faced, but out of context and away from the scene most of them seek farcical, as indeed they were. However, they were really a safety-valve, and we had to control the pressure; provided we gauged this right, both sides existed fairly happily.[4]

Matters requiring attention at UN Force HQ level were discussed with the parties through a variety of channels. Routine military problems were taken up by the UN LOs to National Guard HQ or the VPO. Questions of a primarily economic or social nature were dealt with in the Political Liaison Committee (PLC), chaired by UNFICYP's Deputy Chief of Staff, which met separately with representatives of each community every two weeks. Matters that were of particular urgency or not susceptible to constructive negotiation through those channels were taken up by UNFICYP's Chief of Staff, who, in company with the SPA had frequent meetings on an *ad hoc* basis with, on the Greek side, Government departments at Director General level and on the Turkish side with the VPO in the person of Mr Osman Orek (who retained the empty title of Minister of Defence). The Chief of Staff and SPA also maintained close contact at Counsellor level with the Turkish Embassy and other diplomatic missions, notably those of Greece, the UK, US and USSR. Where purely military matters were concerned, the Chief of Staff also had periodic meetings with the National Guard's Chief of Staff and maintained contacts with the Military Attachés of diplomatic missions, many of whom sought information on the UN Force's activities.

Policy questions, and problems of special importance, delicacy or urgency that could not be dealt with at lower level were taken up, often jointly, by the Force Commander and SRSG direct with President Makarios or appropriate Government Minister, or with the Turkish

Cypriot Leader, Vice President Kuchuk (succeeded in 1973 by Rauf Denktash). They, too, maintained formal and informal contacts at ambassador level with diplomatic missions in Nicosia, in particular the Ambassador of Turkey[5]. In the final resort, when negotiations through these channels failed to make progress, matters thought to warrant this were referred to the Secretary General in New York for action by him or his senior officials direct with governments concerned or, if need be, in the Security Council.

The daily round afforded the Force Commander, SRSG and their senior aides opportunities for wide contacts with Cypriots of both communities and others. The strategic location of Cyprus and its value as a listening-post for the region attracted a surprisingly large number of diplomatic missions to Nicosia. Invitations to attend their various social functions, such as those to celebrate national days, were numerous; since UNFICYP was an instrument of the United Nations it was not appropriate to decline these unless unavoidable. While taxing on the constitution of those concerned, these occasions were useful in maintaining contact with informed opinion, in gathering information and in providing opportunities to explain UNFICYP's activities and problems.

No account of UNFICYP's *modus operandi* at this period can be complete without mention of some operational practices, which experience had shown to be necessary, but which in varying degrees imposed constraints on how the Force went about its tasks. Of these the most important related to Military Intelligence, or in UN parlance 'Operations Information'. The operational performance of all military forces is related directly to the quality of information available to it and none can function to optimum effect without efficient arrangements for its timely collection, analysis and dissemination. UN peacekeeping Forces are no exception but, because they are not engaged in enforcement operations, their task is rendered difficult, even impossible, if by their activities they forfeit the confidence of the parties. Retention of that confidence is thus an overriding consideration and for this reason UN Forces do not indulge in covert intelligence-gathering activities, which the parties might see as being directed against them. Each side must be expected to be sensitive on this account, not least due to fear that information gained by the UN Force may be passed, intentionally or otherwise, to the other. Nonetheless UN Forces need information relating to the activities and intentions of the parties and thus are obliged to rely on overt means to secure this. The line is a fine one and in UNFICYP it was necessary sometimes to curb the zeal of some who overstepped it (in particular strict rules governed the use of cameras by UN personnel, since both sides were sensitive to photography to a degree that seemed ridiculous). However, much was possible by overt means, including vigilant observation from UN OPs, foot and vehicle patrols and helicopter sorties[6], to which was added the information gleaned from the various contacts already mentioned. (Diplomatic Missions had their own sources of information and, when they perceived this to be in their own interest, were usually ready to pass on relevant items to UNFICYP.)

The need to avoid compromising one side by disclosing information on its military activities to the other demanded special vigilance, especially since the UN Force might be used deliberately to this end. This might be attempted by concocting a protest alleging a breach of the *status quo*; UNFICYP would investigate and in conveying the outcome inadvertently give the protesting party information, whether positive or negative, which it was unable otherwise to obtain. There were other and sometimes subtle variants of this ploy and the UN peacekeepers needed to remain alert on this account. The Force also knew that both sides watched its own activities in case these provided a clue to some development of which they were not hitherto aware. This imposed two further constraints. The first concerned the Force's Alert States. There was a complaint in mid-1972 that UNFICYP itself was some-times creating tension by the too frequent adoption of a higher Alert State without proper justification – perhaps in over-reaction to cocktail-party gossip or bazaar rumours picked up by those at the top in Nicosia. Examination showed that existing Force Alert procedures did not provide for a low-profile State that could be adopted discreetly without alarming either party. Such a State was accordingly instituted which could be, and subsequently sometimes actually was, adopted quietly without raising tension on the island or causing alarm in New York.

The second related to the matter of training exercises by UN contingents, since these too were liable to misinterpretation by the parties. Although kept to a minimum, such exercises were necessary in order to maintain efficiency at both contingent and force levels – for example, in practising arrangements for bringing together a multi-national group to meet special contingencies.[7] Further, regular units of the British and Canadian Contingents could not be expected to forgo training to maintain operational standards appropriate to their task on leaving UNFICYP. While due allowance had to be made for this need, care was required in balancing it against possible adverse impact on the local situation.[8]

The primary language used in UN Forces is English. Those Greek and Turkish Cypriots with whom UNFICYP commonly dealt usually had good command of this, but not all members of UNFICYP were fluent in the language. This created the risk that written com-munications addressed by the latter to the former might be phrased in a manner open to misinterpretation and subsequent exploitation. For this reason, it was the practice that such communications should not be sent until first approved by UNFICYP HQ.

It is a common experience of UN peacekeepers to be confronted with threats made to them by one side against the other and a temptation for the peacekeepers to pass these on as they try to sort matters out. Experience in UNFICYP taught that it was counter-productive to do so, since threats served only to harden the threatened party's attitude and make it all the more intransigent. It was thus part of UNFICYP's operational doctrine not to transmit threats made by either side, although this did not inhibit the Force from giving its own warning advice where appropriate.

Last but by no means least was the need to respect the authority and sovereignty of the Greek Cypriot administration – recognized by the United Nations as the legitimate host government; sensitivity of its officials on this account was acute and any real or fancied trespass by members of UNFICYP was quickly brought to the Force's attention. This sensi-tivity extended even to such minor matters as a casual reference to 'a Turkish Cypriot District Officer', when no such person was recognized by the government, but was encountered more importantly in cases (by no means infrequent) where in the interests of preventing inter-communal incidents UNFICYP urged CYPOL not to enter a Turkish village – an action which the Greeks saw as entirely consistent with CYPOL's authority as the island's only legal police force. Situations such as these required UNFICYP to tread warily as it sought on the one hand to fulfil its mandate obligation to prevent intercommunal conflict and on the other not to infringe the government's authority.

The unique character of UN peacekeeping Forces and the essence of the manner in which they go about their tasks was well summarized by the spokesman for the Lebanon Force:

> UNIFIL is not an army of occupation. It is a peacekeeping Force. As such it will keep the peace using peaceful methods and exercising infinite patience. A greater discipline and ultimately a greater courage is demanded by UN peacekeeping Forces than in conventional military operations. The job is tedious. It is difficult. But the primary weapons remain negotiation and persuasion. Weapons will be used as a very, very last resort in self-defence and if force is used to prevent the mandate being fulfilled.[9]

It was in this spirit that UNFICYP's soldiers carried out their unaccustomed and sometimes dangerous mission.

CHAPTER THIRTEEN

UN CIVILIAN POLICE
AND ECONOMIC AFFAIRS

In a situation like Cyprus . . . the presence of an impartial police unit can reduce the sense of insecurity that obstructs any degree of reconciliation. The policeman is far better equipped, both mentally and by training, to fill this psychological vacuum than is the soldier, because he is dealing with a community problem that he has met many times in a different setting in his own home police force. . . . UNCIVPOL has more than proved its worth and has underlined the value of the role that a policeman can perform in a peacekeeping operation.

Rikhye *et al.*: *The Thin Blue Line*, p. 109.

UNFICYP's mandate required the Force to contribute to a return to normal conditions on the island and to this end there were two innovations in the Force's composition. First were the UN Civilian Police (UNCIVPOL) Contingents provided by Australia, Austria, Denmark, and Sweden[1]; second was the appointment of military officers at Force and District HQ levels as 'Economics Officers'. Both furthered this aspect of the mandate.

Although members of UNCIVPOL had none of the usual police powers of interrogation, search, detention or arrest and had no authority to compel movement, they earned the respect and trust of both communities. The Secretary General explained their role:

The United Nations civilian police . . . is principally concerned with incidents, offences and crimes simultaneously involving both Greek and Turkish Cypriots, which it investigates in liaison with both the Cyprus police and the Turkish Cypriot police elements. Generally speaking, the Cyprus police and the Turkish Cypriot police elements alike have shown great willingness to avail themselves of the help of the United Nations civilian police in such cases, although as might be expected there have been some cases with political overtones where its offers to render assistance and participate in inquiries have been turned down.

The duties of the United Nations civilian police also include the conduct of joint patrols with the Cyprus police in Nicosia and Ktima [Paphos], the maintenance of police posts in sensitive areas, observation at static and mobile Cyprus police check-points throughout the island, observation at Nicosia airport when Turkish Cypriots travel to or from Turkey, the marshalling and dispersal of the Kyrenia Road convoys, observation on the Kyrenia Road and security and traffic control in the Turkish Cypriot villages of Orta Keuy and Geunyeli at convoy times, and finally, investigations concerning the fate or whereabouts of missing persons.[2]

Small in number (174 in June 1972 and reduced to 152 during the next two years) these civilian policemen made a contribution to UNFICYP's task of maintaining a climate of intercommunal calm that was disproportionate to their numerical strength. Although responsible direct to the Force Commander through the Police Adviser, Dr Hans Wagner (Austria), who maintained personal liaison with the Chiefs of CYPOL and the TCPE, their activities were coordinated with those of their military colleagues through the JOCs at Force and District levels.

The varied matters with which UNCIVPOL dealt were sometimes seemingly trivial, but always important in their potential to spark worse problems and an escalation to violence. A detailed record is unnecessary, but the Secretary General's Report for the second half of 1972 provides typical example of the scope of UNCIVPOL activities:

> During the period under review UNCIVPOL has conducted about 690 investigations. These inquiries have dealt mainly with shooting incidents, accidents, assaults, the straying and theft of livestock, illegal cultivation of land, damage to crops and property, house-breaking, as well as illegal digging for antiquities. Allegations of restrictions on the freedom of movement of Greek and Turkish Cypriots have also been investigated.
>
> One of UNCIVPOL's inquiries concerned an incident that occurred near Kato Arodhes in Paphos District during the early hours of 20 August 1972, when a CYPOL patrol on the lookout for poachers intercepted a number of suspects. In the course of apprehending these men, subsequently identified as Turkish Cypriots, shots were fired, as a result of which one Turkish Cypriot was mortally wounded. UNCIVPOL's investigation indicated that the fatal injury was caused by a bullet fired from a CYPOL weapon. The accounts of the circumstances of the incident given by the CYPOL officers and the Turkish Cypriot concerned varied in some particulars, but UNCIVPOL concluded that in all probability the death had not been caused intentionally.[3]

The violence within the Greek community created by EOKA-B's anti-government activities during 1973–74 added to UNCIVPOL's tasks. There were numerous incidents involving the use of explosives and shooting, buildings and vehicles were destroyed, and police stations were raided for arms or blown up. These activities created alarm on the Turkish side and were monitored by UNCIVPOL in order to reassure Turkish Cypriots that they had no intercommunal significance. Other matters that required UNCIVPOL involvement included prosecutions of Turks in Greek courts for non-payment of radio and television licences; this raised the more general question of such licences which, it emerged, most Turkish Cypriots had not paid since the 1963 troubles.

Some activities of the TCPE gave cause for particular concern, as the Secretary General noted in May 1974:

> The Turkish Cypriot police element has continued to appear in uniform in the town of Limassol contrary to the *status quo*. Difficulties also developed when the Turkish Cypriot police element tried to exercise police powers with respect to Turkish Cypriots in Government-controlled areas of Paphos and Limassol Districts; CYPOL reacted by arresting members of the Turkish Cypriot police element. Those situations required intervention by UNFICYP in order to ease

the resulting tension. In this connexion, the Turkish Cypriot Leadership has given UNFICYP assurances that the Turkish Cypriot police element will not attempt to exercise authority in Government-controlled areas.[4]

UNCIVPOL's part in preventing the escalation of such incidents and problems and the more obvious peacekeeping activities of their military colleagues were but one facet of UNFICYP's mission to maintain a climate of intercommunal calm conducive to the search for a political settlement.

A second facet, which by 1972 had perhaps become the Force's principal pre-occupation, concerned the many economic and social problems that were causes for intercommunal friction and hampered that search. These included disputed grazing, water and agricultural rights, denial of educational facilities, withholding of public services and similar problems. It was part of UNFICYP's task to try to resolve such matters, or at least to devise a *modus vivendi* pending a general settlement, not only because this was a step towards a return to more normal conditions but also because it removed, if only for the time being, the danger of escalation to conflict. To deal with these matters a military officer was designated 'Economics Officer' in each District, and their activities were coordinated by the Force Economics Officer (FEO), also a military officer. The latter was a member of the Force HQ Operations Branch but in practice worked closely with the Senior Political Adviser (SPA), because most problems had political implications related to the central question of the Government's jurisdiction. The problems were manifold, ranging in nature from the parochial to the island-wide, but, as jurisdiction lay at the heart of most, few were susceptible to permanent solution.

This was especially evident in the increasing trend towards separate development of the economies of the two communities following the establishment of the 'Provisional Cyprus Turkish Administration' in December 1967. The Government protested that the Leadership had illegally established public services for its own community to provide for such matters as the distribution of mail, water supplies and the issue of various licences; for its part the Leadership argued that the Government's withholding of public services from the Turkish community had left it no alternative. UNFICYP's mediation rarely led to solutions fully acceptable to both sides, but usually the difficulties were alleviated temporarily and not allowed to fester to the point of violence.

Many disputes were pursued in fortnightly meetings of the Political Liaison Committee (PLC) which, with UNFICYP's DCOS in the chair and the SPA, Police Adviser and FEO present, met separately with the Liaison Officers of the two communities. This proved a cumbersome and unproductive procedure and in the latter part of 1972 HQ UNFICYP persuaded both sides that the time had come for all three to meet and talk together. Since neither Liaison Officer was prepared to recognize the other's official standing, it was agreed that they would meet jointly with the UNFICYP representatives on an *ad hoc* basis and in a personal capacity only. Two such meetings took place in 1972, when the atmosphere was cordial and constructive, but this early promise was not sustained; after a third meeting in 1973 the Committee was obliged to revert to earlier practice. The PLC was, nonetheless, a useful forum for the discussion of a wide range of problems and provided opportunities for UNFICYP to listen to grievances and exert some pressure on the parties.

UNFICYP was not the only United Nations body involved in economic matters, for the UN Development Programme (UNDP) maintained an office in Nicosia under a Resident Director to run various development projects, such as major irrigation schemes, technical training for Cypriots in a variety of fields and a livestock improvement programme (with which the UN Food and Agriculture Organization (FAO) was associated). These UNDP projects created valuable contacts between the two communities but also gave rise to Turkish complaints that their community was receiving a disproportionately small share of the benefits made available.

Other matters, the scope of which was wide, were of more direct concern to UNFICYP. By 1972 all the island's Greek villages had been connected to the electricity supply network, but over 100 Turkish villages were denied this service. UNFICYP saw this as a glaring case of discrimination against the minority community and exerted constant pressure on the Government to rectify the situation. As a result a plan was agreed for the stage-by-stage 'electrification' of the deprived villages. Although in UNFICYP's view this required too long a time for full implementation, it had to be recognized that the Government faced difficulties that were not easily surmounted. Some villages were without electricity in consequence of restrictions imposed by the Turks themselves on freedom of movement for Electricity Authority of Cyprus (EAC) workers (these being Greek Cypriots); in other cases the Government was wary of providing a supply because, where this was available, illegal connections had been made or electricity bills had not been paid.[5] The Leadership denied that there was any problem over freedom of movement for EAC technicians (insisting nonetheless on conditions that were unacceptable to the Government) and refused to acknowledge the Government's case with respect to outstanding charges on the grounds that these failed to take account of monies due to Turks who maintained the supply system within Turkish-controlled areas or of the subsidies due under the Constitution from the Government to the Turkish community for educational and other purposes.

There was some validity in the arguments of both sides, which occupied much of the time of the PLC and others in UNFICYP. Constant pressure on the Government (suspected by UNFICYP of deliberately dragging its feet in order to harass the minority) resulted late in 1973 in assurances from both sides, which should have allowed the electrification programme to proceed unhindered, but the question of jurisdiction obstructed yet again. The Turks required that EAC workers should give prior notice of entry into Turkish villages and, further, refused to accept that Turkish Cypriots who had failed to pay electricity bills or who had made illegal connections should be proceeded against in the Greek courts. In May 1974 the UN Secretary General had to report that in the preceding six months only limited progress had been made in the provision of electricity to Turkish villages.

An exceptionally severe drought prevailed in Cyprus during the winter of 1972–73 and throughout 1973.[6] Excessive pumping from existing wells (which in some areas led to saline intrusion) aggravated the situation and created serious shortages of water for agricultural, industrial and domestic purposes. Some villages had to be supplied by water-tanker and rationing was imposed in many areas, notably Nicosia, Famagusta and Larnaca.[7] Government measures to conserve supplies increased Turkish accusations of discrimination, requiring

UNFICYP's investigation and remedial action where possible. Although the winter rains of 1973–74 brought relief and assured the next cereal harvest, underground aquafers were not fully replenished and the Government was obliged to impose restrictions on the sinking of new bore-holes. This gave rise to yet more Turkish allegations of discrimination and need for UNFICYP mediation.

Arrangements for the compensation of farmers for losses suffered as a result of the drought included cash payments by the Government and distribution of grain either free or at subsidised prices. It was announced that these would be given to farmers of both communities, but there were many complaints that, while all Greek farmers had received due compensation by May 1974, many Turks had not. These complaints were aggravated by the Leadership's protests that in some cases deductions had been made in respect of debts allegedly owed to the Government. Again, UNFICYP's Economics Officers investigated with a view to settling such arguments.

Interminable negotiations between the Government and the Leadership concerning the complexities of reintegrating Turkish Cypriots into the national social insurance scheme were another of UNFICYP's concerns. The problem dated back to 1964 when the Government had ceased payments of various benefits such as old age pensions to members of the Turkish community. Due to UNFICYP initiatives some progress had been made by the end of 1973 for the resumption of payments in special cases, but none on the general principle. The situation was not improved by the Leadership's announcement of its intention to establish its own social security scheme if the Government persisted in its refusal to meet the Turkish community's demands. This served merely to harden Greek attitudes.

Given UNFICYP's mandate to work for a return to normal conditions, a major concern was the plight of the 25,000 Turkish Cypriots who had fled their villages in 1963–64 and were now displaced persons within the Turkish enclaves. The problems of returning them to their own homes were formidable. Foremost was the undeclared, but nonetheless evident, policy of the Leadership to use retention of these refugees as a stepping-stone to eventual *taksim*, but other obstacles stemmed from the Government's insistence that individuals it regarded as 'trouble-makers' be excluded from those allowed to return, a measure that the Leadership refused to accept. These and similar arguments (in which procrastination and little will to make progress were evident) concerning the practicalities of rebuilding and re-settling various villages abandoned by the Turks largely nullified UNFICYP's constant pressure on behalf of the Turkish refugees.[8]

A long-running dispute centred on the provision of postal services to besieged Turkish communities. *Ad hoc* arrangements had been agreed in 1966 to meet Turkish needs, but by 1973 the Leadership was finding these to be increasingly inadequate, as the Secretary General reported:

> In January 1973 the Cyprus Police stopped a Turkish Cypriot travelling in his car outside Nicosia and discovered that he was transporting a postal bag containing Turkish Cypriot mail. The Government impounded the mail-bag and charged that Turkish Cypriots were not observing the 1966 *ad hoc* arrangements on postal services but had established a separate service of their own.

The Turkish Cypriot leadership, while protesting this action, confirmed that postal services were being tendered to those Turkish Cypriot areas where no other postal services are available . . . . The leadership, however, . . . pointed out that all the above-mentioned measures had been undertaken solely to alleviate the hardship caused by the Government's failure to provide adequate services to the Turkish Cypriot community.

The mail-bag has been returned, and UNFICYP is continuing its efforts to normalise postal services throughout the island.[9]

But this was not to be. Six months later the Secretary General could only state: 'No progress has been made . . . . UNFICYP's efforts to bring about a meeting between the Postmaster-General and a representative of the Turkish Cypriot community . . . failed to materialize. A new attempt to resolve this long outstanding problem is being made by UNFICYP.'[10] Related to postal problems were those concerning the provision of public telephones in Turkish villages. UNFICYP secured some improvements, but the Government, while willing to talk, showed little inclination to act, citing arguments similar to those that bedevilled electricity supply disputes, and was influenced in this as in other matters by what it saw as the Turks' disposition always to want but never to give.

Numerous other matters within the general economic and social fields required UNFICYP's involvement with a view to finding a solution or devising a temporary *modus vivendi*. Turkish Cypriots born after 1963 were denied birth certificates; applications for passports encountered difficulties; there were arguments over deductions made by the Government from payments due to individual Turks on account of debts incurred by some Turkish villages collectively; the Turks complained of damage to some mosques and restrictions on the use of others, charges that in turn were met by Greek accusations of desecration of or denial of access to some churches; and when the Government announced its intention to issue new identity cards on which an individual's race or religion were not to be mentioned, the Turks protested this as deliberate discrimination against their community. The list was long and varied.

Many problems were exacerbated by restrictions on freedom of movement for members of both communities, especially Government officials denied entry to Turkish-controlled areas in pursuance of their duties. Sometimes UNFICYP's intervention, including provision of escorts, succeeded in overcoming the latter difficulty, but generally the Leadership's reluctance to display greater flexibility and cooperation on this account served merely to sour relations with the Government and render progress all the more difficult. This intransigence was frustrating, but UNFICYP believed firmly that it was incumbent on the stronger and economically more prosperous community – the Greek Cypriots – to show generosity and the flexibility which it was difficult for the weaker and poorer minority community to concede. This was a view which the Greek Cypriots, short-sightedly, seemed unable to recognize, blinded by their conviction that the strength of their position would ultimately bring the Turkish minority to its knees. The magnitude of this error of judgement was soon to be seen.

All these problems were emotive and UNFICYP's involvement was an important element in ensuring that they were addressed calmly. But progress towards a return to normal conditions as the mandate required was, even after ten years, not substantial, and the trend towards separate development of the two communities had accelerated. Only where it was perceived to be in their common interest was there a real degree of intercommunal co-operation. This was evident in the scheme initiated in 1974 to build a modern sewage system for the city of Nicosia (such a scheme could hardly take account of the vagaries of the Green Line) and in a major water development project in Paphos District begun the same year under UNDP auspices and funded by the International Bank for Reconstruction and Development.[11] Such projects helped to forge links between the two communities, but the imbalance in the economic circumstances of the two remained pronounced. The years of relative calm that had followed the Kophinou crisis of 1967 had allowed increased economic activity in both communities, but by far the greater share had been enjoyed by the Greeks. This was clearly evident by 1973 in unprecedented building activity, establishment of a record number of new businesses, increase and diversification of exports, and rapid expansion of the tourist industry (receipts from which had increased fourfold over ten years). However, the growing prosperity of the Greeks, among whom unemployment had all but ceased to exist, served only to widen the gap with the Turks, for whom it remained a serious problem.

It does not normally lie within the province of military officers to concern themselves with many of the foregoing matters, but UNFICYP's Economics Officers at all levels grappled with them with a competence and sympathetic understanding that was remarkable. Many in both communities who saw at first hand their activities would concede that they brought to their unaccustomed tasks a high degree of dedication and integrity. There can be no question but that they made an important contribution to what was achieved by UNFICYP in the ten years up to 1974.

CHAPTER FOURTEEN

THE PEACEKEEPERS' DAILY FARE, 1972-1974

All this I bear, for what I seek, I know:
Peace, peace is what I seek and public calm;
Endless extinction of unhappy hates . . . .

Matthew Arnold: *Merope.*

UNFICYP's low profile during the two years of intercommunal calm that preceded the storms of July and August 1974 blinded many to the value of the Force's presence on the island and its contribution to maintenance of that calm. Although unable altogether to extinguish the unhappy hates, its assiduous and patient attention to a plethora of problems and disputes was a major factor in containing intercommunal passions and sustaining the public calm essential to the search for a settlement of the Cypriots' difficulties. In particular, persistence was required to ensure maintenance of the military *status quo* and observance of current agreements, together with mediation to prevent fresh problems – or new twists to old ones – from escalating or spreading.

As in the case of economic matters, most of the disputes which at this period made up the Force's daily fare were of a long-standing nature and not susceptible to permanent solution without a settlement of the overall problem, since at their heart lay the question of jurisdiction – namely the Government's insistence on its right to exercise authority throughout the island, including those areas under *de facto* Turkish Cypriot control – a right the legality of which the Turkish Cypriots refused to recognize. This fundamental difference of view lay at the heart of most local incidents, raising the intercommunal temperature and requiring the UN peacekeepers' cooling hands to avert boiling point. Seen in isolation many disputes seemed petty, if not ludicrous, but all had to be judged against the risk that even the most minor squabble could flare rapidly where volatile tempers were involved.

The Green Line, which divided some 20,000 Turks from about twice as many Greeks in Nicosia, the island's capital and seat of government, was always a point of particular sensitivity. It ran in a deep curve from north-east to north-west through the heart of the city and in places was represented by no more than the width of a narrow back alley across which armed sentries of the two communities glared at each other. Friction was inherent in this situation which demanded vigilance and firm policing by men of the Canadian Contingent, whose operational responsibility it was. Violations of the Green Line Agreement, however trivial, had to be protested to the guilty party, not only in order to restore the *status quo* but

Cape Andreas

Rizokarpaso

Galinoporni

Yialousa

Platanisso

Leonarisso

Ephtakomi

Galatia

Komi Kebir

Ayios Andronicos
(Topsiou Keuy)

Ovgoros

Platani

Boghaz

Chatos

Knodhara

Lefkoniko

Trikomo

Famagusta

Petra tou Dihyeni

Psilatos

Marathovouno

Yenagra

Maratha

Bay

Angastina

Ayios Seryios

Prastio

FAMAGUSTA

Asha

Kouklia

Arsos

Athna

Famagusta

ousha

Tremetousha

**EASTERN
SBA**

Varosha

Athienou

Troulli

Pergamos

Pyla

Kellia

Goshi

alokhorio

Cape Greco

Larnaca

Klavdhia

Larnaca Bay

Kiti

Cape Kiti

zotos

Stazousa Point

Cyprus
showing
Civil Districts, Sovereign Base Areas
and
Places mentioned in this work

also to make clear that, although the UN had not been a party to that Agreement[1], it was UNFICYP's policy to maintain its integrity. Attempts were made by both sides to occupy empty buildings along the Line in contravention of the Agreement; patrols or sentries encroached on or over the Line itself[2]; fortifications were improved in breach of the *status quo*; tunnels were constructed clandestinely to gain positions further forward and disputes arose over occupation by one side or the other of property owned by the Greek Church or by EVKAF (the Turkish Religious Trust Council). Sometimes matters were settled quickly at low level through UNFICYP's mediation; more often weeks of tedious negotiation at levels right up to that of the Force Commander were required.

An especially sensitive area of the city was that comprising the Roccas Bastion (one of 11 strongpoints forming part of the massive Venetian walls surrounding the Old City), the Ledra Palace Hotel and Shakespeare Avenue situated behind it. The bastion faced the Cyprus Telecommunications Authority (CYTA) buildings and the Paphos Gate Police Station (the principal CYPOL station in the city), both only about 100m away, and also overlooked a football pitch in the dry moat surrounding the walled city. The Green Line ran along the moat immediately east of the hotel, then turned in a westerly direction across Shakespeare Avenue to the Pedhieos River (a dry water-course for most of the year) and thence northwards along its bed to the Irish Bridge (so named because it was not a bridge but a ford) and the Nicosia golf course. The Vice President's Office, the Turkish Embassy and the residences of leading Turkish Cypriots all lay just across the Line, close to the hotel and Shakespeare Avenue. Hence any military activity by either side in this general area was particularly sensitive.

Owned by the Church[3] and then the city's most prestigious, the Ledra Palace Hotel often featured in intercommunal events because its height dominated the adjacent Turkish quarter inside the the Old City walls. In order to deny its use to the National Guard, the Canadians maintained a presence inside the Ledra Palace Hotel (which until the events of July 1974 continued to function as a busy and prosperous establishment) and also manned a UN post on the Roccas Bastion itself.[4] Use by the Turks of the football pitch in the moat caused many arguments, leading to an agreement negotiated by UNFICYP governing the conditions and frequency of this use. The Turks nonetheless persisted in attempts to erode the agreement by, for example, arranging more games than allowed, flying Turkish flags provocatively, deploying excessive numbers of Turkish police (ostensibly to control spectators) and by attempts to hold military parades on the ground.

Other problems were created, particularly in Nicosia, when members of one community were arrested by the police of the other. Since 1968 Turkish civilians generally had been free to come and go to and from the Turkish quarter, to which on the other hand Greeks were denied entry; Greeks who did cross, inadvertently or not, were arrested. If they were not quickly released, tempers rose and the Government threatened action. Intervention by UN officers invariably secured release of those arrested, but usually only after a period of rising anger on the Greek side and a face-saving interval on that of the Turks. Although the degree to which the anger and threats were real or feigned could not easily be discerned, the UN peacekeepers could never afford to treat such incidents lightly.

An emotive issue, not confined to Nicosia, was the flying of national flags. The

Constitution provided for a Cyprus national flag (an outline of the island in gold on a white ground, surmounted by crossed olive branches in green) but also permitted unrestricted display of the flags of Greece and Turkey. The Cyprus flag was seldom to be seen except over CYPOL stations, the Greek side, especially the National Guard, flying the blue and white colours of Greece, while the Turks displayed only the white crescent and star on a red ground that was the national flag of Turkey. Routine daily hoisting of Greek or Turkish flags at various points around the island was accepted without demur, but where either was hoisted exceptionally in what was perceived as a calculated gesture, this was regarded by the other side as deliberately provocative and, incredibly, as a breach of the military *status quo* to be protested as such to UNFICYP.[5] The latter's suggestions that no flags be flown other than that of the Cyprus Republic were met by indignant protests by both Greeks and Turks, citing their constitutional right. The UN peacekeepers could only urge reason and restraint.

Although UN Contingents generally were faced with intercommunal problems peculiar to their own District, some of these were common to two or more. A recurrent cause of friction was attempts by CYPOL to patrol through, if not actually to exercise police functions in, Turkish villages. The Government justified this on the ground that its jurisdiction extended to all parts of the island, while the Leadership held that the Government had no legitimacy under the 1960 Constitution. Since the two positions were irreconcilable without a permanent settlement of the Cyprus problem, UNFICYP could do no more than propose temporary *modi vivendi* that saved face on both sides. Incidents of this nature were attributable to a variety of factors: sometimes it was excessive zeal on the part of local officials, sometimes local understandings that had been quietly observed for several years were broken on minor pretexts, and sometimes personal animosities were the cause. This problem was common in Famagusta and Limassol Districts, where respectively SWEDCON and BRITCON officers urged restraint and by patient mediation averted armed clashes. The name of the Turkish village of Ayios Andronikos in Famagusta District was engraved on the hearts of successive Swedes on this account, as were those of Alekhtora, Plataniskia and Ayios Thomas in Limassol District on those of many British.

A survey District by District indicates the variety of the problems requiring UNFICYP's involvement and demonstrates how UN peacekeeping Forces, by diligent attention to what may be relatively minor, if not trivial, causes of friction, manage to maintain the climate of calm essential for the peacemaking process.

Paphos District

Disputes facing the Austrians when they arrived in this District in 1972 were mostly long-standing. Their first priority was to monitor the line of demarcation in the town of Paphos-Ktima separating the Greeks from the Turkish quarter in which some 3,000 lived; this required a permanent UN OP and frequent patrols. Attention was also focused on the hamlet of Mavroli just to the north, where a CYPOL post provided observation over TCF buildings and a training area, but had no other plausible police function. A local agreement allowed the CYPOL men to go to and from the post past a group of Turkish houses, but required that, once at the post, they must not leave its immediate vicinity. Their movement to and fro sometimes provoked insults and hostile gestures by both sides – a typical situation requiring the presence of a few UN soldiers in a post established alongside to calm tempers. Other problems in the District were created in 1972 when the Greeks opened a new CYPOL station on the northern outskirts of Ktima clearly calculated to tighten the net around the Turkish quarter, and when the Turks established a new TCF post at an isolated café near the beach at Floria Bay south-west of the Turkish village of Mandria, thus extending the area under TCF control (and also, the Greeks suspected, affording a point of entry for the smuggling of weapons). Although the two problems were not directly related, both were settled after long weeks of UNFICYP's mediation. A face-saving formula was accepted, whereby the *status quo* was restored simultaneously at both places – a demonstration of how a UN Force as a third party can by quiet negotiation persuade the others to accept an honourable line of withdrawal, which, if left to themselves, neither could take the initiative in proposing.

The Turkish village of Mandria, 12km east of Paphos, with a population of about 400[6] was a point of special sensitivity due both to its proximity to the main Limassol- Paphos road and on account of the surrounding fertile land; a UN OP was located on Mandria Hill, which afforded observation over the village, the main road and the general area. In October 1972 a tangled agricultural dispute came to a head as leases to Turks of Greek-owned land in the vicinity became due for renewal. A tense confrontation developed between armed elements of the two communities, but, when a platoon of Austrians was interposed between them, both drew back and arguments were pursued by negotiation, not shooting.[7] Following some seemingly Byzantine bargaining (to which UNFICYP was not privy) between the Greek Church in the person of the Abbot of Kykko (some of the land was owned by this wealthy monastery) and EVKAF (the largest landowner on the Turkish side), an agreement was reached. The leases were renewed temporarily and further haggling resulted in exchanges of Church-owned land around Mandria for EVKAF-owned property elsewhere.

The Austrians kept watch over other potential flashpoints in Paphos District by a combination of permanent OPs and mobile patrols. These points included the large mixed village of Polis (on the north-west coast containing about 950 Greeks and 750 Turks), Stavrokono (a Turkish village of about 600 lying astride a road leading from the coastal plain up to the Troodos mountains) and Anadhiou (a small isolated Turkish village of about 350 situated in a predominantly Greek area in the western foothills of the Troodos).

(In November 1973, following the departure of the Irish to UNEF 2, the Austrians were moved to Larnaca District and the British took over Paphos District, which then became part of Limassol Zone.)

Lefka District

For the Danes a major commitment was to watch over the small Turkish coastal enclaves at Limnitis and Kokkina, the inhabitants of which lived with their backs to the sea and hemmed in by the National Guard on the surrounding hills. The Turks' interruption of Greek traffic using the coastal road through these enclaves (permitted under agreements reached following the 1964 Tillyria fighting) caused occasional disputes; others stemmed from

Turkish attempts to expand their enclaves and to improve conditions within them. A perennial problem was that of shepherds and their grazing flocks straying too close to the defence posts of one side or the other but, it was suspected, not always oblivious of the military sensitivities.

An example of the disputes that occupied so much of UNFICYP's attention at this period was provided by the small Turkish village of Selemani situated 3km south-west of Limnitis which, contrary to Turkish claims, did not lie within the limits of the recognized enclave. The Greeks constantly complained that the Turks were intent on establishing a TCF post in the village with a view to extending those limits and threatened action to prevent this. The Danes, who established an OP in the village, noted that TCF men wearing uniform and carrying arms were indeed entering the village from Limnitis in clear breach of the *status quo*. The Leadership justified this on the grounds that the men concerned were merely visiting their families and were obliged to go in uniform and take their weapons as they had nowhere to leave these. The problem was discussed *ad nauseam* over many months between UNFICYP and the Leadership, resulting eventually in the latter's reluctant agreement that a small 'armoury' should be built outside the village where TCF could deposit weapons and change out of uniform before entering, but the Leadership's procrastination and the events of July 1974 combined to frustrate its implementation.

Ever since the Tillyria fighting of 1964 the National Guard had suspected that the Turks were continuing to smuggle arms through the Kokkina coastal enclave and in 1973 the Government protested to UNFICYP that a new harbour was under construction there. This was improbable, the Danes observed nothing to substantiate such a charge and a UN helicopter reconnaissance found nothing more than a primitive breakwater capable of sheltering at most a couple of small dinghies. Nonetheless, Greek suspicions were not allayed that the clandestine landing of arms from ships off-shore was continuing.

Lefka town, home for about 4,000 Turks but only a handful of Greeks, was the focal point for Turkish interests in the District. During 1972–74 it posed few problems for the Danes in spite of several disputes of long-standing, such as Greek objections to Turkish plans to open a stone-crushing plant on the town's outskirts – needed, the Turks claimed, on economic grounds, but intended, the Greeks argued, for some obscure military purpose. Disputes of this nature tended to be passed to and fro between the District level and Nicosia without much heat being generated, so that those in UNFICYP could not help but wonder whether the true aim of the parties was merely to exert pressure on one another, or even on the UN Force, rather than to find a solution. A similar dispute over the re-opening by the Turks of a lime-kiln at the village of Ambelikou seemed a further example, for when a solution was in sight the Turks lost interest, declaring that the kiln no longer served a useful purpose.

Kyrenia District

The Finns were concerned primarily with observance of the Kyrenia Road Agreement (explained in the following chapter) and, like the Canadians, in maintaining the integrity of their section of the Nicosia Green Line that ran through the suburbs of Neapolis, Trakhonas and Omorphita. Finnish attention otherwise was focused on the northern part of their District, in particular their OPs sited on the peaks of the Pendadhaktylos mountains, where there was a tendency for National Guard and TCF posts, between which the Finns were interposed, to test each other's reactions, and the Finns' alertness, by minor provocations, such as improving defences in breach of the *status quo*, or by occasional random rifle shots. Other points of attention included the TCF stronghold in St Hilarion Castle (believed to house the main Turkish communications link with Turkey[8]), use by the National Guard of a forest track that led up to the Castle, and the small Turkish village of Temblos which lay below it a bare kilometre west of Kyrenia.[9]

Famagusta District

The whole of the eastern portion of the island, including its Panhandle, provided the Swedes with their fair share of problems due to the high proportion of Turkish villages it contained and the large Turkish community, numbering some 6,000, living within the walls of Old Famagusta – a Turkish stronghold ever since its capture from the Venetians following Lala Mustafa's bloody siege four centuries earlier. Disputes relating to the Old City, particularly those associated with construction of the (then) new harbour, had been settled in UNFICYP's earlier years by various agreements covering such matters as the appearance of armed and uniformed TCF on the massive Venetian walls, which dominated the harbour and surrounding areas, and any new construction that might have a military purpose. The Swedes devoted constant attention to ensuring observance of these agreements and mediated in cases of alleged or real breaches. For example, the National Guard protested against the erection by the Turks of a small kiosk and taxi-office just outside the Land Gate, arguing that this was no more than cover for a new TCF post, whereas the Turks claimed it was required to serve tourists.

The Chatos area, embracing a clutch of Turkish villages in the western part of the District, was under *de facto* Turkish control although not recognized as an 'enclave'. The Swedes maintained a platoon base near Chatos village itself with posts deployed to others. Their main concern was to ensure that procedures agreed after earlier disputes, centred on cultivation by Greek farmers of land contiguous to that of the Turks, were observed. These procedures, in which a SWEDCIVPOL detachment based in the village of Angastina played a key part, generally operated without friction. Another problem was a dispute arising from Turkish plans to construct a new road to provide better access to the small village of Platani in the southern foothills of the Pendadhaktylos, the Turks asserting that this was required to allow the transport of produce to market. The Government declared that it alone had the right to build roads but showed no inclination to take action to satisfy the Turks' need, and the temperature rose and fell as the Turks blew hot and cold over building it for themselves.

The problem of CYPOL attempting to exercise authority in Turkish villages has been mentioned already, with Ayios Andronikos 25km north of Famagusta cited in this context. In July 1973 armed TCF prevented CYPOL patrols from passing through the village on their way to or from two Greek villages, each of which could more easily be reached by more direct routes. The situation that developed necessitated the establishment of a UN post at the entrance to the village while protracted talks continued to reach a *modus vivendi*. Although a compromise was within reach, the Government was not willing to accept this and the dispute simmered on, a solution being unattainable without a settlement of the island's overall problem. However, the UN presence afforded a channel of communication between the parties, and constant UN pressure for restraint and commonsense prevented the quarrel from escalating to the point of shooting. Allied to this dispute was another: State-owned forest land lay adjacent to the village and the Turkish villagers laid claim to this on the grounds that the Turkish Cypriot community, as legal partner in the State, was entitled to its share of these lands.

The Panhandle, along the 70km length of which Greek, Turkish and mixed villages were scattered, was a rather remote and generally quiet area little touched by more dramatic events elsewhere. The Swedes maintained a Civilian Police detachment at Yialousa, a large Greek village of about 2,500 inhabitants, and carried out police and military patrols throughout the peninsula. Its proximity to mainland Turkey gave rise to periodic allegations of clandestine helicopter landings and the smuggling of arms by night.

Larnaca Sector

The problems of the Irish in this Sector (which formed the eastern part of the civil Larnaca District) lay mainly in and around the town of Larnaca itself with its population of some 20,000, of whom 4,000 were Turks living mostly in the Turkish quarters of Scala and Tuzla. There were three potential intercommunal flash-points. First was the Artemis Road, which runs south from the town to the large Salt Lake; this was a line of close military confrontation between TCF posts sited for the defence of Turkish Cypriots living in the 700m wide strip lying between it and the sea and National Guard posts on its other side, behind which lay one of that force's recruit training camps. The Turks could not afford to give any ground here and sought every opportunity to improve their positions with inevitable Greek reaction. This required Irish posts and patrols along the length of the road, for so sensitive was the area that any action, such as raising Greek or Turkish flags, shouted insults or even the appearance of shepherds with grazing flocks (a common sight) or of transient gypsies (suspected by each side as being armed members of the other) wandering forward of military positions, was liable to generate immediate tensions that demanded the cooling hand of the UN soldier on the spot.[10]

The second danger point was the Hala Sultan *tekke* (mosque) lying in a picturesque setting of palms, shrubs and fountains on the south-west shore of the Salt Lake; it was an important holy site in the Muslim world[11] and was visited by thousands of Muslim pilgrims. The Turks were angered by any action that impeded free access and were especially concerned by the presence of a National Guard post close to the track leading to the *tekke*. UNFICYP monitored the activities of this post to ensure that nothing was done to cause offence in the religious context and to ensure that Turkish access to the shrine was not hindered, especially on days of particular religious significance. The third point of concern was the Scala school, which in the past had catered for Turkish children but was now situated close to the line of confrontation. The building had been taken over by British troops during the troubles of early 1964 and had then been handed over to UNFICYP for use both as a military post and as accommodation. Lacking school premises, the Turks urgently needed its return, but negotiations over several years foundered on the Leadership's insistence, unacceptable to the Government, that, once returned, the Turkish flag should be flown over the school. When eventually the Turks dropped this demand, the Greeks objected to the re-opening of the school on the grounds that it was situated in an area of such sensitivity that it would alter the military *status quo* to Turkish advantage. In 1973 UNFICYP devised a solution, which entailed the construction of a new school for Turkish children at a less sensitive location, and the Leadership acquired a suitable site on the understanding that the costs of the new building would be found elsewhere. Dr Osorio-Tafall, the SRSG, wrung an undertaking from President Makarios to provide Government funding, but when by mid-1974 this still had not been backed by any show of cash Turkish patience was all but exhausted. The Leadership threatened that Turkish children would take matters into their own hands by marching into the school and re-occupying it, a move that would have faced the Austrians (who, following departure of the Irish to UNEF 2, had assumed responsibility in November 1973 for the whole of Larnaca District) with a delicate situation. What might have occurred remains a matter for speculation, for the problem was overtaken by the far more critical situation that erupted on the island that July.

Problems elsewhere in Larnaca Sector were similar to those in other Districts. They included disputes over water supplies (such as at the Greek-owned Troulli mine, water for which was drawn from Turkish-owned wells in a neighbouring village), land ownership (for example, requisition by the Government of Turkish-owned land for the extension of a Greek-owned factory at Vasilikos) and access to religious properties (as in the case of the Turks at the Hala Sultan *tekke* but also of Greeks to churches in Turkish controlled villages).

Kophinou Sector

The western part of the civil District of Larnaca – designated UNFICYP's Kophinou Sector – was the responsibility of BRITCON until handed over in November 1973 to the Austrians. UN posts were manned in and around Kophinou itself (a mainly Turkish village) and in the mixed village of Ayios Theodoros 3km to its south, both of which had been scenes of bitter fighting during the Kophinou incident of 1967. During 1972–74 problems in the area were few; although passions lay dormant, memories of the earlier events remained vivid and a small spark could have ignited a conflagration.

Limassol District/Zone

This District (from November 1973, Zone) was the operational responsibility of the British Contingent's battalion based in Polemidhia Camp 4km north of Limassol itself. The town had a population of about 31,000 Greek and 6,000 Turkish Cypriots, the latter resident in the Turkish quarter.[12] A permanent UN presence was maintained in the town in the form of a post known as Town OP, which served as both observation post and patrol base. As elsewhere on the island, various earlier agreements, arrangements and understandings remained extant in 1972, and problems in the town generally stemmed from Turkish attempts to erode the *status quo* as enshrined in these. Often this was done in a seemingly trivial manner (for example, UNFICYP was for ever refereeing a ludicrous dispute over the construction of a small wall in an insignificant earthen back alley which the Greeks asserted had some military purpose), but some other disputes were of more fundamental concern because they created risks of Greek retaliation against what were seen as challenges to the Government's authority. In this category fell arguments surrounding the increasing frequency with which uniformed TCF were conspicuous on streets in the Turkish quarter and the TCPE's practice of arresting Greek Cypriots for offences alleged to have been committed in that quarter.

The appearance of TCF in uniform illustrates the seemingly absurd situations with which UN Forces may find themselves obliged to deal. In UNFICYP's early days the TCF had possessed no uniforms except for military-type headgear; so long as they did not wear this, their unarmed presence on the street was not objected to by the Government. This situation persisted even after the TCF acquired other items of military uniform, so that the convention was established that, even if wearing a full outfit of uniform, its members were not held to be 'in uniform' unless sporting military head-dress. Since the martially inclined Turks considered it humiliating to have to appear thus improperly dressed, the convention was increasingly flouted. Each time this was observed – and by 1973 it was a regular occurrence – it was incumbent on UNFICYP to protest it as a breach of the *status quo*, even though such protests were merely shrugged off by the Leadership. This was UN peacekeeping at its lowest and exasperating in the extreme for professional soldiers obliged to practice it. Successive BRITCON commanders in Limassol were irritated by its futility and complained that it served only to undermine their authority where more important issues were at stake. General Prem Chand understood their irritation but was adamant, and rightly so, that protests, however ineffective, must be continued; the Leadership might otherwise conclude that UNFICYP could be induced just as easily to abandon its insistence on the maintenance of the *status quo* in other more important matters. Further, UNFICYP needed to balance the risk that failure on its part to resist changes in the *status quo*, especially one that the Government regarded as a challenge to its authority, against the danger that this would prejudice the Force's efforts to persuade the Government to display greater flexibility and cooperation in settling other more important, but possibly unrelated, intercommunal problems.

During 1972 the TCF in Limassol added insult to injury not only by appearing 'in uniform' but also by marching along the streets in formed bodies, usually in connection with flag-raising ceremonies instituted to bolster the Turkish community's morale. Protests against these breaches of the *status quo* were rejected by the Leadership, who argued that they were minor when compared with the gross breach represented by the Greeks' importation earlier in the year of a large consignment of arms from Czechoslovakia; they pointed out, further, that the prominence of uniformed National Guardsmen in and around Limassol caused apprehension within the local Turkish community, which needed the reassurance provided by the visible presence of their own uniformed Fighters. It was difficult not to sympathize with such arguments but the overriding importance of preventing erosion of the *status quo* generally left UNFICYP officers with no choice but to maintain pressure on the Leadership to mend its ways.

The problems caused by CYPOL attempts to patrol through the Turkish villages of Alekhtora, Plataniskia and Ayios Thomas have been mentioned already. UNFICYP's investigations disclosed that there had been an informal local arrangement whereby the Turks allowed the patrols to pass through unhindered provided that prior notice had been given and no attempt was made to exercise police powers in the villages. The Greek District Officer in Limassol, Mr P. Zachariades, denied knowledge of any such arrangement and threatened 'appropriate action' unless CYPOL was accorded access to these villages without let or hindrance from the Turks. With armed clashes in prospect, UNFICYP urged restraint while it sought a *modus vivendi* that would save face on both sides. As tedious talking continued over many months it became evident that, for all the threats and bravado, neither party really relished settling matters by force. Eventually each tacitly accepted UNFICYP's view of what it all along had judged to be the *status quo* – CYPOL would continue to give advance notice informally at low level of future patrols and the Turks would allow these to pass unhindered.

General Problems

The activities of the TCF not only in Limassol but also elsewhere on the island were a constant cause for protest by the Government. UNFICYP's attention was drawn to the steadily increasing military training carried out by the Fighters on the grounds that this improved their combat capability, was provocative and generated tension. The Leadership countered with protests against the growing capability of the National Guard which it saw as no less provocative and threatening to the security of the Turkish community. The charges of both were valid, but UNFICYP could do little other than to urge moderation, restraint and common sense, urgings that were reflected with monotonous regularity in the periodic reports of the Secretary General to the Security Council.

An important matter, not intercommunal in nature, that required constant vigilance concerned UNFICYP's right to freedom of movement, this being enshrined in the Status of Forces Agreement.[13] In its early days the Force had often found its movement restricted, especially by the National Guard under Grivas, who with the backing of Makarios argued that UN soldiers could not be permitted to enter areas considered by him as sensitive in relation to national defence and who designated numerous areas throughout the island as such. This was not acceptable to UNFICYP and after protracted argument a much-reduced number of these areas was formally recognized, which were to be entered by UN troops only when essential and then on a restricted basis.[14] From time to time each side attempted to limit UNFICYP's freedom of movement elsewhere, either through misunderstanding (in which language difficulties or inadequately briefed sentries played a part) or in deliberate attempts to establish new restricted areas. The UN Force accepted as a matter of practical common sense the need not to encroach close on the military positions of either side but stood firm in insisting that its right to freedom of movement must not be eroded. Whenever this right was challenged, if only in minor degree, UNFICYP invariably reacted promptly; during the period 1972–74 such cases were settled peacefully and to the UN Force's satisfaction.

It was matters such as these, some major but most minor, that constituted the Force's daily fare during these years. Time and again the value of UNFICYP's third-party presence was demonstrated by its patient and diligent mediation in diverse intercommunal quarrels, ensuring that tempers were contained in order that the search for a settlement of the island's fundamental problems might proceed in a climate of calm. It was ironic that this calm was to be shattered, not by a breakdown in intercommunal relations, but by reckless miscalculation on the part of the Greeks alone.

CHAPTER FIFTEEN

THE KYRENIA ROAD AND
ITS PROBLEMS

The continued presence of the Turkish contingent outside its camp, without due authorization, constitutes a grave violation of the Treaty [of Alliance] in that the forces stationed in
Cyprus by virtue of the Treaty have no right to move or deploy themselves in any part of the
territory of the Republic of Cyprus at will.

Letter from the Representative of Cyprus to the
President of the Security Council, (S/5674, 6 April 1964).

The Kyrenia Road, some 22km in length, was an all-weather two-lane highway of indifferent
quality linking Nicosia with the small north coast port of Kyrenia.[1] For the Turks it was a
jugular vein because it was the shortest and quickest route by which those living in the
capital's Turkish quarter could be reached by mainland Turkish forces landing from the sea.
Two alternative routes each entailed long detours – the first, westwards via Myrtou was 55km
long, and the second, eastwards on a new road (opened in 1973) via Kythrea and over a pass
through the Pendadhaktylos mountains involved a 40km drive. By 1973 the island's
economic prosperity had generated increased traffic on all three routes, but the Kyrenia Road
retained its advantage in terms of time and distance. However, Greek Cypriots wishing to
travel along it were faced with a major difficulty: for most of its length the road ran through
the Turkish main enclave.

Leaving Nicosia from the Kyrenia Gate in the heart of the Turkish quarter, the road ran
north-west through the Turkish villages of Orta Keuy, Geunyeli and Boghaz, the last-named
holding a strategic position at the southern approach to the vital Kyrenia Pass; between
Nicosia and that village the road winds through the undulating open, dry and rocky terrain
of the western Mesaoria. Above Boghaz it turns easterly as it climbs through the scrub of the
Pendadhaktylos to the head of the Pass at an altitude of 400m, at which point the island's
north coast, the sea and, on clear days, the mountains of Anatolia come into view. The road
then descends through olive and carob groves and a profusion of shrubs on the greener
northern slopes with at its end the picturesque port of Kyrenia, dominated by the massive
walls of the mellow Venetian castle guarding its entrance. At the head of the Pass a track leads
west to St Hilarion Castle and, just beyond, a narrow winding road, clinging to the steep
mountain-side and offering dramatic panoramic views of the coast below, leads east to the
village of Bellapais and its great Gothic abbey.[2] Until 1974 the whole length of the Kyrenia

Road between Nicosia and just short of the turn-off to Bellapais lay within the Turkish enclave.

The Turkish national contingent's action in December 1963 in moving out of its authorized camp and taking up positions astride the Kyrenia Road, denying its use to Greeks, and the problems that ensued when that contingent's routine troop rotations became due in the autumn of 1964 have already been mentioned. These problems had been resolved by negotiations conducted in New York by the UN Secretary General and in Cyprus by the SRSG and the UNFICYP Force Commander, resulting in October 1964 in agreement on the one hand for the re-opening of the road to Greeks and on the other for the rotation of the Turkish troops. The Kyrenia Road Agreement (as it was known) was incorporated in an *Aide-Memoire* dated 3 October 1964[3] presented by the Secretary General to and accepted by all the parties including the Turkish Government. It provided that control of the road would be vested exclusively in UNFICYP; that no armed personnel other than UN (and in defined and limited circumstances members of the Turkish contingent) were to use the road; and that UNFICYP alone was to be empowered to search those using it and deny its use for the movement of arms or warlike stores. The agreement also required removal of Turkish Cypriot police from the road and withdrawal of Turkish contingent troops from positions within 90m of it (although it was accepted that certain of the contingent's buildings close to the road in Geunyeli could be retained provided that doors onto it were closed and rear doors used instead). The Commander of the Turkish contingent undertook that his soldiers would not interfere with traffic on the road, and in return it was agreed that it might be used by his contingent for logistic purposes, subject to agreement with the UN Force commander. For its part the Leadership promised that TCF and inhabitants of villages along the road would not shoot at or in any way interfere with those travelling on it.

For the purposes of the Agreement the Kyrenia Road was defined as being the stretch running between a UN check-point on the north-western outskirts of Nicosia and another just south of Kyrenia; a further five UN posts were to be located at vulnerable points along the route. The movement of Greek vehicles on the road was to be organized in convoys under UNFICYP control and protection provided by mobile escorts, foot patrols and picquets. A convoy was to run in each direction each morning and each evening. These arrangements did not preclude use of the road at their own risk by non-Greek 'free runners' provided that they passed through the UN check-points and submitted to search by UN civilian police.

Acceptance of the *Aide-Memoire* by the Turkish government placed it in a different category from other agreements reached by UNFICYP with the two communities in Cyprus, and the UN Force's obligation to ensure that its provisions were observed was all the stronger on that account. However, both Cypriot communities harboured reservations – the Government doubted the effectiveness of UNFICYP's control of the road, while the Leadership feared that the Agreement might jeopardize the position of Turkish Cypriots vis-à-vis the Government. Such reservations were dispelled by the SRSG's assurances – first to the Government that:

> The Force Commander would take all possible measures to enforce the provisions of the *Aide-Memoire*, including the manning of check-points on a round-the-clock basis to the extent found

necessary, and the maintenance of frequent mobile patrols. Adequate measures would be taken, to the fullest possible extent, for the protection and security of the members of the public using the Road, as well as all possible precautions and measures to ensure effective control of the Road where it passes through villages,

and second to the Leadership that:

UNFICYP would take no action that would be unreasonable and vexatious or amount to an impairment of the rights and interests of the Turkish community. UNFICYP would not seek to assert its control over activities off the Road.[4]

In subsequent years neither side was slow to remind UNFICYP of these assurances.

The Kyrenia Road came under UNFICYP's exclusive control on 26 October 1964. In spite of initial difficulties and minor incidents the movement of the daily convoys, consisting sometimes of as many as 300 vehicles, settled into an established routine as all concerned became accustomed to the system. So well was it functioning a year later that control of the convoys was transferred from the soldiers of FINCON (through whose area the road ran) to the UN Civilian Police, who manned the check-points at each end, marshalled the vehicles and provided traffic control along the route. But during ensuing years, due in part to the lack of continuity inherent in the regular turn-over of men in UNFICYP, some erosion of the provisions of the Agreement took place imperceptibly so that by 1972 some encroachments on the road by TCF and the Turkish contingent were being allowed to pass without protest.

Matters came to a head in June that year when the TCF in Boghaz instituted the practice of marching in a formed body along the road, halting all traffic as they did so, in blatant breach of the Agreement. UNFICYP's determination to put an end to the practice was met by bland excuses on the part of Osman Orek of the Vice President's Office, and several weeks of inconclusive discussion ensued. It was the kind of problem which in earlier days UNFICYP might have settled by a show of force, but there was no call for this in the calmer climate prevailing in 1972. Moreover, it was apparent that in this as in so many other matters of a military nature Orek had little authority, being subject to the orders of the *Bozkurt*. This pointed the need to exert pressure directly on the Turks. A routine troop rotation of the Turkish contingent was scheduled for September and, while discussing the arrangements with Mr Karaca, the Turkish Embassy's Counsellor, I hinted that difficulties with the TCF at Boghaz might influence the degree of UNFICYP's cooperation to facilitate the rotation; his reaction was sharp, protesting that the two matters were not to be linked in this way. Formally he was correct, for care had been taken to avoid explicit linkage (although this was clearly inferred) when the twin problems had come before the Security Council in 1964, but Karaca knew as well as I did that the one had been a *quid pro quo* for the other. Although this ploy led to protest by the Turkish Government to the Secretary General, who instructed us not to link the two matters, it served to resolve the problem on the Kyrenia Road at Boghaz. Soon afterwards Orek made a face-saving proposal, suggesting that the road's wide verges (known locally as the berm) should not be regarded as part of the Kyrenia Road, and that the

TCF should be allowed to march to and fro using this. We agreed on condition that the Leadership erected a line of posts to separate this berm from the road itself, that the TCF did not encroach over that line and that traffic was not interfered with in any way. This arrangement was implemented to UNFICYP's satisfaction, Turkish face was saved and UNFICYP's control over the road itself was preserved.

The problem had coincided with a number of others involving breaches of the military *status quo* by the TCF, requiring UNFICYP pressure to be exerted repeatedly on the Turkish Cypriots, the sum effect of which was to create an impression in Turkish minds that the UN Force was leaning excessively hard on their community. Soon after the rotation of the Turkish contingent that September, for which (as was usual) the Cyprus Desk officer of the Foreign Ministry in Ankara came to Nicosia, I was approached to meet this individual for an off-the-record discussion of matters currently in dispute between UNFICYP and the Turkish Cypriot Leadership. We duly met privately and in the course of a long discussion the Turkish official complained that UNFICYP was bearing down unduly heavily on the minority community, that the Force was excessively preoccupied with what the Turks considered to be matters of minor importance, such as trivial breaches of the *status quo*, and that it was failing to give sufficient priority to more important issues, such as the need to exert pressure on the Government to improve the Turkish community's economic lot. Understandable though such complaints were, it was necessary to point out that provocative breaches of the *status quo* (whether or not thought by the Turks to be minor) and failure to observe agreements such as that relating to the Kyrenia Road served only to harden Greek attitudes and render it all the more difficult for UNFICYP to persuade the Government to respond more generously to calls for it to ameliorate the plight of the Turkish community. If only the military on the Turkish side would recognize the counter-productive effect of some of their actions (which rarely afforded any real military advantage), then perhaps UNFICYP's constant striving on the community's behalf would bear more fruit. The UN Force had responsibilities to both communities and exerted just as strong pressure on the Greek side in cases where the latter was judged to have breached the accepted *status quo*. Our discussion did little to change Turkish attitudes.

The Kyrenia Road remained a source of concern for UNFICYP throughout 1973 as breaches of the Agreement, often minor in themselves, by the Turks were observed. Minor or not, all had to be resisted by UNFICYP even though investigation sometimes showed that the practice of which we complained had been allowed in recent years to pass without protest. A comprehensive review of the 1964 Agreement to establish what erosions of its provisions had been allowed to creep in was carried out by HQ UNFICYP in late 1973; this showed that some erosion had indeed taken place, but also that it was unrealistic to suppose that the situation could be fully restored. Recognizing this reality, fresh guidance was issued within UNFICYP to ensure that no further erosion was permitted.

The brunt of implementing the Agreement (both before and after issue of this guidance) fell to the Finnish Contingent, then commanded by an able, experienced and robust UN peacekeeper, Lieut. Colonel Jorma Pullinen; it was liable to be a frustrating business in which not infrequently the Finns achieved only partial success. This led Pullinen to conclude that the 1964 Agreement was outdated and no longer appropriate to the situation nine years later.

His views were summarized in his own words on relinquishing his command in October 1975:

> Experience has shown that this kind of Agreement should be made to be valid only for a certain period of time and then re-studied with the parties concerned. Such matters as the normalisation of life for one party concerned should be taken into consideration as long as it does not cause any risk to the other party. All occurring changes to the previous situation should be accepted by UN as a basis for renewing an out-dated Agreement. At the time of the *coup* [against Makarios in July 1974] there existed some kind of "against the honour of the UN" policy ... Perhaps this fact was the reason why not a letter of the Agreement had been changed, and why FINCON had difficulties in implementing it.[5]

The fact of the matter was that the Kyrenia Road Agreement had been the outcome of negotiation by the Secretary General with the Cyprus and Turkish Governments and the Leadership and had the tacit endorsement of the Security Council. It laid specific obligations on UNFICYP which had been reinforced by explicit assurances given to the parties as to how the Force would implement these. It was not therefore just a matter of 'the honour of the UN' – if changes were to be made, this would require reopening negotiations with all the parties, a process which risked opening up many other matters of current dispute and which on this account was likely to be counter-productive.

Explaining considerations of this kind to UNFICYP's Contingent Commanders was not always easy and Pullinen's frustration was understandable. He felt that repeated protests to the Turkish side prejudiced his good relations both with officers of the Turkish contingent and with local TCF commanders and tended to diminish his authority, since it was rarely possible to obtain the satisfaction he sought. A minor incident illustrated the futility, as he saw it; when he protested a continuing minor breach of the *status quo* caused by the addition of some sandbags to a TCF position, the TCF commander sneered: 'You protested, HQ UNFICYP protested, and the matter was referred to New York and buried there. The sandbags are still in place and will remain there'. UN peacekeepers do indeed need a sense of humour.

CHAPTER SIXTEEN

THE CLANDESTINE
IMPORTATION OF ARMS

The process of reconciling acknowledgement of the sovereignty of the host state with fulfil-
ment of a mandate is never easy for a UN force. Throughout its long stay in Cyprus the
problem inevitably arose for UNFICYP in a variety of ways. One of the most important was
the importation of arms.

Rosalyn Higgins: *United Nations Peace-Keeping –*
Documents and Commentary, Vol. 4: Europe 1946–1979, p. 230.

Reporting to the Security Council in May 1974, the UN Secretary General, Dr Waldheim,
drew attention to the increase in combat effectiveness of the armed forces of both sides,
and added:

Recently there have been reports that additional weapons are being introduced into the island.
. . . UNFICYP has continued to exert its best efforts to investigate reports of such imports and
to take remedial action when necessary. Arrangements that were worked out in the past with
the agreement and cooperation of the parties concerned, under which the imported weapons
and equipment were placed under UNFICYP surveillance or control, have proved most satisfactory in reducing tension between the two communities . . . [1]

The problem was an old and recurrent one, dating back to UNFICYP's earliest days on the
island.

Successive Secretaries General had consistently held that the introduction of arms into
Cyprus, whether by Greek or Turkish Cypriots and whether or not held to be legal, was
strongly to be discouraged. UNFICYP's position was never easy because the Government
insisted on its right to import weapons it considered necessary for its own security and
regarded attempts to prevent this as an infringement of its sovereignty. This was made clear
as early as July 1964, when President Makarios (in response to representations made by the
Secretary General to him and to the Prime Ministers of Greece and Turkey) stated his
government's position uncompromisingly:

I share your anxiety about the accumulation of arms in Cyprus and your view that it does not
help in lowering tension. It has always been my firm belief that the Cyprus problem should be

solved by peaceful means and within the United Nations. But, on the other hand, I feel that so
long as the threat of a Turkish invasion continues, my Government has the responsibility and
the duty to build up its defences to protect the territorial integrity of the country.

My Government's action has been rendered inevitable by the overt threat of invasion from
Turkey . . . . Furthermore, it has been made necessary by Turkey's continuing smuggling of
arms and military personnel into Cyprus . . . . My Government has the primary responsibility
. . . to maintain law and order. In order to carry out this responsibility it must keep its forces
adequately strong. Consequently the build-up of our defence and security forces is being
effected in order to protect the country from threatened external invasion as well as from actual
internal subversion, and thus maintain peace.[2]

These words were written at a time when, with the assistance of the Greek Government,
Makarios was building up the National Guard under General Grivas, for which purpose arms
and equipment were being imported in considerable quantities. The anxiety this created in
the Turkish community was a matter of concern to UNFICYP, which sought to monitor
deliveries through the ports, citing to this end its right to freedom of movement. The
Government refused to accept that this right extended to entry to docks, ports or other
government premises. The outcome of the wrangle was a reluctant concession by the
Government that it would inform UNFICYP when imports of a military nature took place
through the ports of Famagusta and Limassol. This was less than satisfactory, not least
because UNFICYP then became aware that imports were also taking place secretly through
the Government's newly established naval depot at Boghaz (24km north of Famagusta – not
to be confused with another Boghaz at the foot of the Kyrenia Pass). The build-up of arms
on the Greek side brought inevitable reaction on the part of the Turks, who resorted to the
smuggling of weapons for their self-protection.

Since this escalation was a threat to the peace which it was UNFICYP's concern to maintain, it was the Force's policy to treat the acquisition, clandestinely or not, of new weapons
by either side as a change in the military *status quo* and, where there was incontrovertible
evidence that such acquisitions had taken place, to insist that the weapons be placed under
some form of UN custody, inspection or control. UNFICYP did its utmost to deal with cases
of this nature in impartial and even-handed fashion, but the Government's control of all sea
and air ports and its refusal to allow free entry to them by UN personnel gave it a major
advantage denied to the Turks. The Force's role in routine rotations of the Turkish contingent allowed it to scrutinize imports on those occasions, but comparable surveillance over
imports for the Greek contingent or for the National Guard was not possible, even when
these took place through the main ports of Famagusta and Limassol.[3]

Allegations of clandestine imports were common (although usually vague in detail) and it
was these that posed the most difficulty for UNFICYP; with hands tied by its lack of intelligence resources, thorough investigation was impossible. Consequently more often than not
the Force could only report that it was unable to establish the truth of the allegations.
Nonetheless, where a major clandestine import of arms had taken place, the secret could not
be kept for long on this small island of gossip-prone people – as an earlier UNFICYP Chief

of Staff once remarked: 'There are no secrets on this island – only doubts as to which secret to believe'.[4]

A prime example occurred in 1966 when the Government was obliged to admit that it had imported a quantity of weapons from Czechoslovakia, required (it asserted) for issue to CYPOL. No details were given other than that the consignment included 1,000 rifles, 1,000 sub-machine guns and some heavy machine guns, mortars and rocket launchers. Turkey protested strongly on the grounds that this was a major change in the military *status quo*. After prolonged UN pressure Makarios conceded that the weapons should be held in store, from which periodic small issues could be made either to meet normal wastage or for training purposes. This store was to be located in the Presidential Palace in Nicosia and open to inspection by UNFICYP's Commander personally. During the ensuing eight years (apart from one occasion in 1968, when some of the weapons were displayed on a public parade) these arrangements were implemented to the satisfaction of successive UN Force Commanders.[5]

A more serious repetition occurred in January 1972 when a large consignment of Czech armaments was landed clandestinely from a ship lying off the ore-loading terminal at Xeros on the island's north-west coast. The maladroitness with which the Greeks carried out the operation was matched only by the ineptness of its timing, for the incident brought an immediate halt to the new initiative then gathering momentum for a settlement of the Cyprus problem. There were rumours that the operation had been master-minded by Dr Lyssarides, Archbishop Makarios's personal physician and close confidant and leader of a left-of-centre political faction, acting on the personal authority of the Archbishop, who intended the arms for the Police Tactical Reserve Unit (his praetorian guard then being expanded and re-equipped to counter the increasingly unreliable Athens-dominated National Guard and the EOKA-B gangs it supported).[6]

The landing of a large number of crates at Xeros did not escape the notice of the Danes responsible for that area, nor were their suspicions allayed by Greek assurances that these contained 'mining equipment'; discreet observation revealed the crates being moved under CYPOL escort to the outskirts of Nicosia. Cypriot tongues soon wagged and within days reports appeared in the local anti-Makarios press purporting to give details of the consignment, alleged to comprise 10,000 boxes containing rifles, machine guns, mortars and pistols, together with large quantities of ammunition and grenades, at a total cost in the region of £1 million. These reports were met by indignant denials by the government spokesman, who declared the story to be a malicious fabrication, and Dr Osorio-Tafall and General Prem Chand were assured by Makarios personally that he had no knowledge of any such imports. However, the evidence soon proved too strong even for Makarios; as tension grew, he was obliged to retract and admit that a consignment of arms had indeed been received.

Believing this to be a serious threat to the Turkish Cypriot community, acute concern was expressed to the Secretary General both by the Turkish government and by Dr Kuchuk. There was anger, too, in Athens, with protests from the Greek junta, which feared that in the hands of Makarios's private army the weapons would be beyond the control of its own officers commanding the National Guard.[7] Dr Waldheim (who had recently succeeded U Thant as Secretary General) informed Makarios of his own deep concern. Discussions in

Nicosia between Osorio-Tafall and the Government led to agreement for inspection of the consignment by UNFICYP's Commander, and an exchange of letters in March set out arrangements for the storage and safe custody of the arms at CYPOL HQ (in the Nicosia suburb of Athalassa), the Government having confirmed that an inventory supplied to UNFICYP was complete and that all the arms were then held at Athalassa (the first UN inspection made there on 15 March confirmed that all tallied with the inventory). However, since neither Turkish anxieties nor the fears of the Athens junta and its officers in Cyprus were allayed so long as the arms remained in the physical possession of CYPOL, UNFICYP insisted on stronger safeguards.

The outcome was an agreement reached in April by which UNFICYP assumed physical custody of the weapons themselves and exercised close supervision over the large quantities of high explosives. The weapons were to be stored within a fenced area inside Camp UNFICYP (at Nicosia airport), while the various explosives remained at CYPOL HQ, in each case under a double lock and key system. The Secretary General explained:

> The fenced area where the arms will be stored will be in the charge of unarmed Cyprus Police personnel. Control of the camp perimeter and access to it will be the responsibility of UNFICYP. . . . The high explosive munitions will remain at Government Police Headquarters in Athalassa, but the fuses will be stored at the UNFICYP camp with the other weapons and ammunition. There will be a system of double locks and keys both at the storage area at the UNFICYP camp and at the Athalassa store. One set of keys will be kept by the Government, the other by UNFICYP.[8]

These arrangements demonstrated how UN peacekeeping Forces need to devise solutions that take due account of the sovereignty of the host government. The latter could claim that it retained custody and control of the arms within the compound guarded by the unarmed CYPOL, but in practice all comings and goings to or from that compound were effectively under UNFICYP's control.

Since the weapons presented a tempting target, a platoon of the Austrian Contingent was stationed in Camp UNFICYP as a 24-hour guard and the Camp's security procedures were tightened, with periodic practice alarms held to test their effectiveness and to serve as a deterrent.[9] Checks of the weapons and explosives, both in Camp UNFICYP and at Athalassa, were made at irregular intervals by the UN Force Commander or his Chief of Staff, assisted in each case by the Force EME, and in the presence of the CYPOL Quartermaster, Mr Phylactis, an efficient and courteous officer whose records were invariably immaculate and correct. Boxes were selected at random and contents checked; no discrepencies were found.[10]

While an importation of arms on this scale could not remain concealed for long, clandestine imports on a lesser scale were another matter, requiring constant vigilance on UNFICYP's part. This was rewarded late in 1972 when TCF parading in the Turkish quarter of Nicosia were seen – and photographed – carrying two types of weapons not previously possessed by them; these were identified as M72 anti-tank rocket launchers of US origin and RPG7 anti-tank grenade launchers of Soviet manufacture.[11] The Leadership was unable to produce evidence to show that they were not a new acquisition in breach of the military *status quo* and UNFICYP accordingly insisted that the weapons be brought under a form of UN custody, as had been done in the case of the Czech arms imported by the Greeks. It was agreed that those weapons seen and counted by UNFICYP during the TCF parade (the Force suspected, but could not prove, that there were also others) should be stored under double lock and key arrangement at the Saray Police Station in the Turkish quarter, with periodical inspections carried out by UNFICYP. Although not affording complete security, the arrangement was acceptable to UNFICYP because it placed a firm responsibility on the Leadership; if the weapons were removed without UNFICYP's prior agreement, the Leadership's good faith would have been shown to be lacking. The worth of the latter proved questionable for, when the first inspection was made by Prem Chand, the number of boxes was correct, but to the embarrassment of the Leadership several were found to be empty. A further inspection a few days later found all in order and subsequent checks found no discrepencies.

There was another curious saga, this time on the Greek side. It appeared that five used one-ton British-manufactured Humber wheeled APCs (known in the British army as 'Pigs') had been imported, reputedly privately, from Britain through the port of Famagusta in crates declared to contain 'agricultural machinery'. Rumour had it that the importation had been arranged by Polycarpos Georghadjis, the old EOKA henchman and one-time Minister of the Interior who had been found murdered after the shooting down in 1970 of the helicopter carrying Makarios. The true purpose for which the vehicles were destined was a matter for speculation, but it seemed that, following the murder of Georghadjis, they had remained for many months at Famagusta docks, with few aware of the contents of the crates and these in a quandary as to what to do with them.[12] It was unlikely, however, that at least some Turkish dockers were unaware of the contents, but the Leadership remained silent while the Greeks pondered what to do. Action came in November 1972 when a decision was made (possibly by the Ministry of the Interior, although denied by its Director General, Mr A. Anastassiou) to move the 'Pigs', still in their crates, to a private garage in Limassol where they were to be refurbished, ostensibly for agricultural use but more probably for use by CYPOL or the Police TRU. Their existence was revealed in a manner typical of the semi-farce that so often characterized events in Cyprus. One lorry, loaded with a 'Pig' still in its crate, was parked overnight outside the driver's house in Limassol where it caught fire, revealing a burnt-out but unmistakable military armoured vehicle. The cause of the fire was never established – gossip suggested that it was the work of a Turk or perhaps EOKA-B.

Together with John Miles, the SPA, I at once took up the matter with Anastassiou, pointing out that, once refurbished, these vehicles could be put to military use. He argued that they were private property imported legally for agricultural purposes and that the Government had no grounds for intervention. We could not accept his arguments and he agreed that the 'Pigs' should be immobilized and that UNFICYP should be accorded access to check progress on conversion for agricultural use and ensure that in the meantime they were not removed from the Limassol garage. Anastassiou also gave an undertaking that once the 'Pigs' had been made serviceable for agricultural use, the Government would require the importer to re-export them or else dismantle them. The BRITCON unit in Limassol, then 3rd Bn, The Queen's Regiment, was ordered in the meantime to maintain watch over the garage, despite protest from Anastassiou this was exceeding UNFICYP's authority. The reason for his protest was soon apparent. When four of the 'Pigs' had been made road-worthy (the fifth was too badly damaged by the fire), UN observers reported that the vehicles were being driven away under CYPOL escort. UNFICYP helicopter and ground surveillance revealed that they had been taken to the CYPOL HQ complex at Athalassa.

We lost no time in tackling Anastassiou and in the course of an acrimonious meeting upbraided him for this clear breach of his undertakings. His lame response was that it had been necessary to move the vehicles quickly to the security of Athalassa because of a fear that they might be seized from the insecure Limassol garage by anti-government elements. Refusing to accept his excuses, we insisted that more effective measures be now taken to prevent removal from the CYPOL premises; these entailed removal of the vehicles' control boxes and their storage at Athalassa under a double lock and key arrangement.[13] Anastassiou agreed and accepted that all the 'Pigs' (including the fifth, brought to Athalassa later) should be inspected periodically by UNFICYP. These arrangements were implemented to UNFICYP's satisfaction, but the Government never fulfilled its regularly reaffirmed undertaking to ensure that the vehicles would be either re-exported or dismantled. Although periodic UN inspections led to a suspicion that one vehicle at least had been used to a limited extent (possibly for driver training within the CYPOL complex), there was no evidence to substantiate occasional allegations in the local press that the 'Pigs' had been taken into use by CYPOL or the TRU.

No sooner was this matter settled than the Leadership protested against the Government's acquisition of what was alleged to be a 'motor torpedo boat'. UNFICYP's investigation showed that the craft in question was a second-hand unarmed fast patrol boat, which, once refurbished, was destined for use by CYPOL for coastal patrol duties. Given the Turks' concern, prompted no doubt by fears of the craft's potential to curb illegal immigration and arms smuggling, the Government undertook to inform UNFICYP when it was taken into service. Whatever the intention may have been, this vessel had made no such appearance up to July 1974.

Late in 1973 the UN Force's alertness led to yet another semi-farce. A patrol of the Canadian Contingent, diverted by road works from its usual route, passed behind the National Guard's camp at Lakatamia, 6km south of Nicosia. Through a screen of trees an observant member saw two trucks on which guided weapons appeared to be mounted. Since UNFICYP had no record of any such weapons in National Guard possession, the patrol was ordered to return to verify the sighting, if possible by means of a photograph; the result confirmed that what had been observed were two 'Snappers', the NATO nick-name for a Soviet-manufactured anti-tank guided missile system.[14] Since further investigation failed to reveal any evidence of previous possession of these weapons by the National Guard, it had to be concluded that they were a relatively recent clandestine acquisition in breach of the military *status quo*. General Prem Chand took the matter up with the Foreign Minister, Mr I.Cl. Christofides, who gave categorical assurances that the National Guard possessed no such weapons and I spoke similarly to the National Guard's recently promoted Chief of Staff, Major General P. Papadakis, with the same result. In the meantime we had informed New York of the discovery and had sent copies of the photographic evidence. Since this was incontrovertible, it was decided that I should tackle Papadakis again and, if he persisted in his denial, confront him with this evidence.

When we met he greeted me with the words, 'Brigadier, I am going to surprise you by telling you we have these weapons'. Any surprise I felt was confined to the fact that he had volunteered the admission so readily, offering no apology for his earlier denial. I kept the photographic evidence to myself and listened to see how he would brazen the matter out. His story was that the weapons had been in the National Guard's possession for many years, that this was public knowledge since they had been displayed on parades in Nicosia, and that in any case they were now no longer serviceable – it was for this last reason that he had indicated that the National Guard had no such weapons. I replied that it was UNFICYP's practice to monitor parades on both the Greek and Turkish sides (as our recent discovery of the TCF's M72 and RPG7 weapons had demonstrated) but had no record of the appearance of any 'Snappers'. If he would furnish me with the dates of such parades, I would re-check UNFICYP's records. In the meantime UNFICYP should be allowed to make a technical inspection to verify that the weapons were in fact unserviceable. Papadakis undertook to consider these points. What had brought about his volte-face? Probably knowledge of the photographic evidence supplied to New York had reached Greek ears, compelling realization that outright denial could not be sustained. An embarrassed Christofides apologized to Prem Chand and did not conceal his anger at having been deceived by the National Guard's Greek officers, a deceit that was indicative of the contempt displayed by these officers for the Makarios Government. Subsequent meetings with Papadakis failed to elicit information concerning past appearances on public parades. He procrastinated over requests for technical inspection by UNFICYP and resisted demands that, in the absence of proof that they were not a new acquisition, the weapons should be placed under joint UNFICYP – National Guard custody. (Discussions with Papadakis on this, as on other problems of concern to UNFICYP, were courteous and correct but achieved no real progress. It was evident that he was the National Guard's *eminence grise*, who had been heard to remark that he regarded UNFICYP as an interfering body which had no right to meddle in the affairs of the National Guard.)

Since the Makarios government had little effective control over the these mainland Greek officers, UNFICYP was all but powerless to bring the saga of the 'Snappers' to a satisfactory conclusion. Pressure on Papadakis was not relaxed, but no progress was made up to his departure in June 1974. In the meantime UNFICYP received reports of National Guard training with 'Snapper', including live firing. During the Turkish invasion in July the Finns observed that the National Guard had deployed eight 'Snapper' equipments and that despite poor tactical handling at least three Turkish tanks had been destroyed by five missiles. So much for Papadakis's protestations.

In the cases already described UNFICYP was able to establish beyond doubt the existence of the weapons in question, but often received allegations of other acquisitions, the truth of which could not easily be determined, as the Secretary General reported in May 1973:

> During the [six-month] period of the Report there have been allegations of the illegal or
> clandestine importation of arms by both sides. The Government reported to UNFICYP that

arms for the Turkish Cypriots had been illegally imported from a ship that anchored off Kokkina and from an unidentified helicopter that was alleged to have landed in daylight within the Turkish Cypriot enclave north of Nicosia. Careful investigations by UNFICYP personnel, who were in a position to maintain constant observation of the ship, led to the firm conclusion that no arms had been landed from it. Investigations by UNFICYP of the reported helicopter landing were inconclusive. On the other hand, the Leadership on several occasions drew the attention of UNFICYP to renewed press reports of clandestine importations of arms by illegal groups on the Greek Cypriot side . . . . UNFICYP once more was not able with the means at its disposal to substantiate these reports, although they cannot altogether be discounted.[15]

The incident of the ship anchored off Kokkina illustrated another of UNFICYP's operational handicaps. The New York view was was that the Security Council mandate gave no authority to interfere with coastal shipping, for example by boarding and searching vessels, and in any case UNFICYP lacked the naval resources to do so.

The case of the alleged helicopter landing gave rise to much speculation. The incident was said to have occurred on a Saturday afternoon, when the UN Force, in common with others, may not have been at its most vigilant. The National Guard claimed to have seen a Whirlwind helicopter (the type used by UNFICYP) bearing UN markings land at an isolated point within the Turkish enclave and to have observed stores being unloaded from it into a lorry which then drove away with the helicopter departing in a northerly direction. As soon as the National Guard's report was received, a check was made of UN helicopter operations, which showed that none had been near the area at the time, and a patrol sent to the scene found no evidence on the ground to support the National Guard report. Had this been a daring and successful landing by a Turkish aircraft disguised as a UN helicopter?

Greek Cypriot allegations of unidentified helicopter landings by night, in particular along the Panhandle, became common during the latter part of 1973 and early 1974. Temporary UN OPs were deployed and special patrols mounted, but no such landings were detected, possibly because their very presence, which it is not in the nature of UN peacekeeping to conceal, was a deterrent. It seemed that the National Guard's radar stations on the Pendadhaktylos were incapable of detecting clandestine flights, if any, for the Government never supported its protests with radar evidence. Informal enquiries to see if such flights might have been detected by British radars on Mount Olympus were met by bland statements that these radars were not programmed to look for low-level air activity in the vicinity of the Cyprus coast.

UNFICYP's apparent impotence in dealing effectively with matters such as these gave rise to local press criticism. For example, allegations appeared in anti-government newspapers that weapons held under double lock and key systems and subject to UN inspection had been taken into use by Makarios forces. UNFICYP invariably issued immediate denials and, when such criticisms impugned the personal integrity of General Prem Chand, the Secretary General intervened:

> In making these allegations the newspapers concerned have not hesitated to cast doubts on the personal integrity of my Special Representative and the Force Commander. While I do not find it necessary to respond to such unworthy aspersions, I can again state categorically that the

allegations are without any truth whatsoever. The agreed inspection and surveillance arrangements for these weapons have continued to be applied to the complete satisfaction of the Force
Commander.[16]

Such allegations may have derived from failure to understand that under the agreed
custodial arrangements the issue of some of the 1966 Czech weapons was allowed to meet
normal wastage or, temporarily, for training purposes. Prem Chand personally carried out
the checks on these weapons and ensured that there was no abuse of those provisions.
UNFICYP's inspections of the 1972 Czech arms, the M72s and RPG7s and the Humber
'pigs', made right up to the time of Turkey's military intervention in July 1974, never
disclosed any discrepencies.

CHAPTER SEVENTEEN

MILITARY CONFRONTATION AND UN FORCE REDUCTIONS

The desirability of bringing about deconfrontation and reductions in military strengths in the island has been emphasized by UNFICYP many times in the past. So long as armed forces confront each other in close proximity, tension will remain and, with it, the danger that fighting may break out at the slightest provocation from either side.

Report by the UN Secretary General (S/10842,
1 December 1972, para. 76)

From its peak of 6,400 men in 1964 the strength of UNFICYP had been reduced progressively to just over 3,000 by mid-1972. This had been made possible by a lowering of intercommunal tensions, but a decline in the Force's financial circumstances exerted its own pressure. Generally reductions had been achieved by changes in deployments, decreases in the number of permanently manned UN posts (offset by increased patrolling) and the transfer to UNCIVPOL of some tasks previously carried out by soldiers. At its much reduced 1972 strength the UN Force was faced with the first-line strengths of 12,000 Greek Cypriot National Guard and 4,500 Turkish Cypriot Fighters (with in addition the national contingents of Greece and Turkey). The Greek Cypriots manned about 215 permanent posts and the Turkish Cypriots some 290.

By late 1972 lack of progress in the intercommunal negotiations, compounded by an absence of any evident sense of urgency or will to compromise, was causing growing international impatience and calls for further troop reductions with consequential financial savings. The arguments were various: some believed that the situation no longer warranted a peacekeeping Force of the current size, some that the Force's presence and success in containing intercommunal tensions encouraged intransigence, others, notably the United States but also some troop-contributor governments, reinforced such arguments by complaints at the ever-growing financial burden they were being called to bear with no end in sight. For its part the British government as the major logistic provider had become increasingly restive at the costs of its support and suggested that an examination should be made of the Force's logistic arrangements to see what economies might be feasible. Since it was clear that in some respects logistic standards were already below what normally was acceptable and that worthwhile economies could only be achieved by reducing the numerical strength of UNFICYP, London did not press the matter. On the other hand the Americans, as the main financial contributors, believed that the time had come for fundamental change by the conversion of UNFICYP into a smaller Observer-type Mission and pressed for this both at UN Headquarters in New York and by lobbying by the US Embassy in Nicosia, to the irritation of General Prem Chand, who considered that the US diplomats underestimated the risks inherent in the current level of intercommunal military confrontation.

During the winter of 1972–73 at UNFICYP Headquarters we considered the options and were ready with proposals. When in the following spring Dr Waldheim set in hand studies to achieve substantial reductions in the size of UNFICYP, these proposals formed the basis for the plan adopted later entailing a two-phase reduction designed to achieve an overall saving of 25% (about 750 men). The ground was prepared by the Secretary General's announcement in May 1973:

> For some time now I and my colleagues both at Headquarters and in Cyprus have been studying ways and means of reducing the United Nations commitment in terms of both finance and manpower. . . . The feasibility of any such move will, of course, depend to a large extent on the progress of the intercommunal talks. Meantime, within the existing framework, I plan as soon as possible to make such economies as can be achieved without jeopardising the effectiveness of the operation.[1]

Changes in the force's *modus operandi* were not required, savings being achieved by the elimination of elements which, while desirable, could no longer be seen as essential. Small arbitrary cuts in the size of each contingent were entailed, the only obvious blow being the closure of the Austrian Field Hospital and its replacement by a small Medical Centre, located at Force HQ and staffed by the Austrians.[2] The plan for the first phase was accepted by all concerned on the assumption that the level of stability achieved during the preceding two or three years would improve further, and on Prem Chand's assurance that the reductions would not prejudice UNFICYP's effectiveness in discharging its mandate. This phase was duly implemented in October-December 1973; the reduction achieved was 440 men – over 14% of the total strength.

Although the first phase had been achieved relatively painlessly, it was clear that further reductions in the second phase, to be implemented in April-June 1974, would necessitate changes in UNFICYP's deployment and operational methods. It seemed opportune for a move to be made towards a gradual conversion of the Force into an Observer-type Mission and our proposals for this second phase envisaged a tentative step in that direction. These were incorporated in a working paper circulated in New York in September 1973, which explained that, although changes in deployments and in the *modus operandi* of UNFICYP would be required, we did not consider that the Force's effectiveness would be impaired, provided that certain prerequisites were met. The most important was a firm understanding that in cooperation with UNFICYP both communities would not only maintain but also strengthen the existing policy of preventing significant intercommunal clashes and that this policy would be underwritten by Greece and Turkey. With responsibility thus shared all would be expected to issue instructions to their military and civilian personnel to cooperate fully with the UN peacekeepers. The working paper concluded by stressing the desirability of both sides agreeing, if only on an initial trial basis, to proposals made to them three months earlier designed to achieve a measure of military deconfrontation.

General Prem Chand had long argued, not only that the existing degree of military confrontation was unnecessary in the prevailing climate of intercommunal calm, but also that it was counter-productive due to the friction it so easily generated. Earlier efforts to achieve a measure of deconfrontation had met with little success, as the Secretary General had reported in May 1973 when describing the difficulties:

> The Government has continued to assert its willingness to accept general island-wide military deconfrontation provided the Turkish Cypriot Leadership were willing to reciprocate. Since the Leadership has indicated its inability for the time being to accept a general deconfrontation, the agreement of both sides is being sought to a limited measure of deconfrontation. . . . UNFICYP is ready to negotiate appropriate limited agreements to this end and to provide a military presence to ensure that there is no increased risk to the security of either community as a result.[3]

The proposals pressed on both sides by UNFICYP that summer (and which Prem Chand expounded personally in New York in the autumn) were the outcome of a thorough study which indicated the vicious circle that needed to be broken. It showed how in some areas a military post on one side served only to counter a similar one on the other and that, if both were withdrawn simultaneously, neither side's security would be prejudiced. We indicated those localities where this situation prevailed and offered to maintain a UN post on the spot to provide reassurance following the withdrawal of the two sides' own posts. Further, we urged both sides to reduce their military posture by dismantling some defensive works and by arranging for sentries in others to keep weapons under cover. As encouragement, UNFICYP itself took the initiative in this direction by de-fortifying a number of its posts and creating the more pacific image of police posts in which the sentries were told to keep their weapons hidden.[4] This action proved in vain for, as so often in Cyprus, another factor intervened.

Increasing EOKA-B anti-government violence within the Greek community gave rise to mounting nervousness among the Turks, who judged the time not yet ripe to lower their guard, and the Greeks declined to make unilateral relaxations. Despite this setback, the New York working paper proposed that in future UNFICYP's role should lie mainly in preventative action in cooperation with both sides rather than in military interpositioning. Four options were considered to allow reductions while satisfying this change of emphasis: first, an across-the-board numerical cut in the strengths of UN contingents; second, dispensing altogether with some of the (in UN terms) more expensive contingents; third, alternating battalions of some of the latter by asking governments concerned to take turns in providing a unit for a six-month tour; and fourth, restructuring UNFICYP into an intermediate-sized mixed peacekeeping/observer-type operation. The first three options inevitably prejudiced the Force's flexibility and operational efficiency and two of them its multi-national character and political balance. The fourth option, which provided an effective means for fulfilling the proposed new role and achieved savings in manpower and costs (and constituted a first step towards the (unstated) goal of UNFICYP's eventual conversion to an observer role) was thus adopted.

It required one infantry company in each UN Contingent (one platoon in the case of the Irish) to be replaced by an 'observer/reconnaissance group' consisting of teams of four men carried in radio-equipped vehicles. Their tasks would be general patrolling, investigation of incidents and, where necessary, temporary deployment in static positions to monitor and assist in resolving particular disputes. Smaller in number than the infantry companies they replaced, these groups would provide significant manpower economies, while their mobility would offset consequential reductions in the number of permanently manned UN posts. The Austrian, Danish, Finnish and Swedish Contingents were to be reduced to 200 men each, organized as one infantry company, one observer/reconnaissance group and command and administrative elements, the Canadians to 450 men, including an observer/reconnaissance group, while the British Contingent would be cut to a total of 650 men. In the case of the latter, two infantry companies of its battalion would be withdrawn to the SBAs and cease to form part of UNFICYP, the Force Reserve armoured reconnaissance squadron would relinquish that role and (apart from one troop retained in Nicosia) move to join the battalion in Limassol as its observer/reconnaissance element. All these reductions were to be complemented by others in Force HQ, including the Signal Troop and Military Police Company, and in UNCIVPOL Contingents. Taken together, these measures provided a saving in this second phase of some 420 soldiers and 20 policemen – a total reduction after both phases of 750 men in the strength of UNFICYP as at May 1973.

Discussions on this basis proceeded satisfactorily in New York, although proposals for the second phase had to be modified in consequence of the despatch of UNFICYP contingents to Egypt in October 1973 in the wake of the Yom Kippur War.[5] All troop-contributor governments supported the plan for this second phase, albeit that most felt that satisfaction of the pre-requisites was essential. The Secretary General noted doubts on this score voiced in the Security Council's debate in December 1973, but indicated his intention nevertheless to pursue negotiations with all concerned with a view to implementing the second phase reductions in mid-1974. These further negotiations encountered fresh difficulties caused by events in Limassol in January, uncertainties following the death of Grivas that same month, but above all by a statement from Turkish Prime Minister Ecevit in March (advocating a federal solution for Cyprus) which brought an abrupt halt to the intercommunal talks. The Leadership and the Turkish government argued that, in the light of these developments, further reductions in the size of UNFICYP would be premature and some troop-contributor governments, notably those of Canada and Sweden, expressed similar doubts. Nonetheless, and despite an added complication – it had not proved possible to extract from the parties the assurances required to satisfy the stipulated prerequisites – the Secretary General was determined to press ahead. He informed all concerned that he 'assumed' that the parties would extend the degree of cooperation stated earlier as being a pre-requisite for further reductions, placing on them the onus of notifying him if they were not prepared to do so. When none did, he gave instructions for this second phase to be implemented during the routine troop rotations due in April – May 1974.

The changes required in UNFICYP's deployment and *modus operandi* were implemented in a gradual manner, calculated not to cause either side unfounded anxiety; in the few instances where they seemed genuinely to cause concern, minor adjustments were made. In the event it proved possible to un-man 15 UN posts – a 30% reduction – on the understanding that these would be visited regularly by the new observer/reconnaissance teams and be temporarily re-manned should the situation so demand. It was not the first time that UNFICYP had undergone a major reorganization and reduction, but it illustrated the lengthy process involved in making significant changes to a UN Force's composition and operating methods, in marked contrast to the speed with which these Forces are liable to be thrown together. In this case it had taken a full year from from initial planning to implementation.

The second phase was completed by the end of May 1974 without major problem and was shown to have been soundly conceived. But even as it was being implemented the Americans renewed pressure for further reductions and a move towards full conversion of the peacekeeping operation into an Observer-type Mission. Although the UNFICYP Special Account was in ever-increasing deficit and this was a factor, the Americans argued that further reductions (the US target was for a small UN Observer/Mediator Force of about 400–500 men) would induce a greater sense of responsibility on the part of both Cypriot communities. US diplomats lobbied energetically to this end both with HQ UNFICYP in Nicosia and with troop-contributor governments; the latter generally were not receptive, while Osorio-Tafall and Prem Chand were strongly opposed.

Apart from the fact that a pause was needed to digest the effects of the reductions already made, UNFICYP believed it would be a mistake to go further for the time being, given the anti-government violence within the Greek community and the new uncertainties created by Ecevit's recent pronouncement. Further, it was clear that the move advocated by the Americans would require modification of UNFICYP's mandate as contained in Resolution 186(1964), thus opening up wider contentious issues. Prem Chand was concerned, too, that some Contingent Commanders considered that the phase two reductions had already cut their contingent to the the point that its ability to carry out its operational tasks was prejudiced. In the face of this opposition the Americans did not to press their case. This was as well, for within two months the situation had changed so dramatically that it became necessary almost overnight to double the strength of UNFICYP to a new total of over 4,300 men. When the storm broke on 15 July 1974 the strength of UNFICYP stood at a mere 2,340 men, deployed all around the island in small detachments manning some 40 static OPs and supported by observer/reconnaissance patrols. There was no 'fat' in the Force and reserves at Force and District levels had been reduced to an absolute minimum. Well did the UN Secretary General report in the aftermath of the crisis of the summer of 1974:

> I believe that, in spite of its extremely small size – some 2,300 men at the beginning of the fighting – the Force displayed great devotion and ingenuity in its efforts to alleviate the appalling situation which prevailed in Cyprus during the latter half of July and in August 1974.[6]

CHAPTER EIGHTEEN

BLUE BERET LIFE

Service in the cause of peace with the United Nations in Cyprus has its ups and downs; its good times and its frustrations; its happy memories and bad memories of lonely hours away from loved ones. On balance, however, I believe the Cyprus tour is challenging, rewarding and a great opportunity to develop unit spirit and junior leadership.

Lieut. Colonel E.C. Quinn, 2nd Bn, The Royal Canadian Regt.:
2 RCR Cyprus Tour, October 1973 – April 1974.

Colonel Ed Quinn was the outstanding Commanding Officer of a first-class battalion. Most of those serving in UNFICYP at that time would endorse his verdict, but those who have never worn the UN's blue beret may wonder what service is really like for those carrying out the daily peacekeeping tasks. A British company commander has described how he and his men operated in mid-1974 in Paphos District:

The UN Force in Paphos District consisted of a rifle company [No. 4 Coy, 2nd Bn, Coldstream Guards], elements of Headquarters Company and an armoured recce troop, covering an area of about 570 square miles [1500 sq.km.] of the western end of Cyprus in a District which, because of its virtually total agrarian existence and remoteness from Nicosia, had a very unique flavour. We inherited five permanently manned OPs, which were all sited to discourage inter-communal problems in areas where these had occurred before, and out of a strength of about 100 this tied down 40-odd men. In addition we were required to keep a reserve platoon of up to 20 men available at any time and provide mobile patrols, who visited all villages in the District at regular intervals. We were a detached company in virtually every respect, and so our administrative overheads were high. By the time we had staffed a District Headquarters, MT, COMCEN, cookhouse, two messes and one canteen, there was virtually no fat. This was no problem in the routine days [before the events of July-August 1974], and helped to provide an interesting existence for everyone, together with a bit of time for recreation.

Life in the OPs and for our patrols was totally different to that which we had been used to in a Northern Ireland context. It was extremely pleasant to find that no one was "agin us"; this took some getting used to. It took a considerable readjustment of attitude for soldiers to change from being keyed-up fighting men, for which they had been trained, to being the equivalent of the respectable 'Bobby' on his beat in an English village. This was what was required, and included a detailed knowledge of the local problems and the history of the problem in a specific area. For this reason we rotated men as seldom as possible. A detailed knowledge of the local community and personalities was vital, and this all helped in gaining and maintaining the confidence of both sides by impartiality and apparent fair dealing with all routine grumps and grouses that permanently invaded us. Personal behaviour and example were of prime importance.

Patrolling from the OPs was again different. A man's eyes, ears and mouth were his weapons; force of any sort could only be used in the last resort in self-defence. Patrolling, one or two men, usually unarmed, would stroll through the area making their presence obvious, talking to all and sundry, stopping and having coffee with the locals in the coffee-shop, and doing anything to get to know the people and to hear the latest gossip. It would have been fatal to have been accused of spying, and all activity was strictly overt. As a basis for operating to achieve this, common sense and an understanding of the political situation, combined with inbred discipline, are the only requirements to make this type of situation work. I found that NCOs and soldiers reacted splendidly to the additional responsibility that they had been given by having to cope, in small detachments well separated from any support, with all sorts of odd problems.[1]

A Canadian officer has similarly described the UN soldier's task in the very different environment of the tortuous Green Line running through the built-up areas of old Nicosia:

The Canadian soldier is trained to be aggressive and to take action. Duty on the Observation Post is the opposite to all a soldier learned in his previous training. The job is frustrating since the soldier is required to stand and watch the world go by. He reports any incidents that occur between the two armed communities involved in the Cyprus confrontation. When he observes a Turkish or a Greek Cypriot soldier walking on the Green Line with his weapon or putting a magazine on his weapon, all he can do is diplomatically tell them to move back to their side of the Line and take off the magazine. Then the incident is reported. The majority of the time the antagonists comply and the incident is solved on the spot.

Sometimes, however, an incident such as this is blown out of proportion by the other side, and a series of bitter protests fly back and forth. The United Nations must stand in the middle and mediate. If the soldier cannot solve the problem on the spot, he reports it to his Company Command Post and the wheels of the next level of mediation start to move. . . . If the problem cannot be solved at this level, the incident is reported to the Battalion Joint Operations Centre and the Command elements of all sides negotiate. Finally, if all these attempts of mediation fail, the Force Headquarters and the politicians become involved. But normally the day-to-day problems continued. The soldier on the OP continued to observe and report, the negotiations at all levels went on, and the goats continued to wander. Who can tell a Turkish Cypriot goat that it is not supposed to graze on Greek Cypriot-controlled land?[2]

These two accounts convey the flavour of what peacekeeping in Cyprus during the period 1972 to mid-1974 entailed for those in close daily contact with both communities. They show, too, the psychological adjustments necessary for regular professional soldiers on joining a UN peacekeeping operation, a problem not encountered by those contingents composed mostly of non-professionals. The differences in skills and attitudes brought to the UN peacekeeping game by all-regular contingents on the one hand and by primarily non-regular contingents on the other have been commented on by some critics.[3] It suffices here to observe that in the years of relative calm that preceded the crisis of the summer of 1974 there was little to choose between contingents; each in its own way carried out its tasks effectively. But when UNFICYP was jolted out of its settled ways by the anti-Makarios *coup* in July 1974 and pitched into a war situation by the Turkish intervention that followed, differences were discernible, in the latter situation the discipline, training and quality of junior leadership in the all-regular contingents gave them a clear edge over the remainder.

Since the Kophinou crisis of November 1967 UNFICYP had enjoyed a calm and orderly way of life, notwithstanding the growing anti-government violence within the Greek community. On joining the Force in June 1972 it was my impression that it had settled into a well-worn rut, obsessed with time-consuming trivia of little obvious relevance to the fundamental problems and with little evident will to free itself from this depressing posture. It was dismaying to be confronted with a large body of accumulated 'folk-lore', governing, often in minute detail, what might or might not be done by armed forces on each side and, sometimes, even by UNFICYP itself. Did it really matter under what conditions the TCF might wear caps? Or whether armed men could walk on a particular stretch of road or only on its verge (or what constituted that verge)? Or where precisely a sentry might stand at different times of day to shelter from the hot sun? Or how many games of football might be played each week on a particular sports ground? However, the extent to which such trivia had become an inescapable part of the UN peacekeeping game as it had developed in Cyprus was soon apparent, as was realization that failure to accord such matters due attention was likely to destabilize situations at local levels, create obstacles to progress at higher levels, and ultimately to prejudice the peacemaking process, the furtherance of which lay at the heart of UNFICYP's mission. For all that, a personal feeling persisted that the Force was too set and inflexible in its ways, that its continued presence was taken too much for granted by Cypriots of both communities, and that there was a risk that some members of the Force, regulars and non-regulars alike, might treat their tasks too lightly, seeing their tour of duty under the blue beret merely as a pleasant interlude in the Cyprus sun.

General Prem Chand recognized this risk and the consequent need constantly to emphasize that UNFICYP was an emergency Force, temporary in character and with a mandate that ran for only six months at a time. To this end he refused to relax the requirement for members of the Force to wear uniform at all times both on and off duty and resisted pressure, notably from the New York-based civilians of the UN Secretariat, for adoption of a five-day working week instead of the six normally worked.[4] The rule that uniform was always to be worn (except when off duty within the confines of UN camps) had its origin in the need to ensure that members of UNFICYP were readily identifiable, so that neither side could ever claim mistaken identity in incidents involving UN soldiers or policemen.[5] Although some argued that the requirement, valid enough in earlier days, was less so in the more relaxed conditions prevailing by 1972, Prem Chand took a contrary view – the changed conditions rendered the requirement all the more necessary as a salutary and constant reminder of the operational nature of the Force's presence on the island. Some contingents took the requirement in their stride, but others, unaccustomed to wearing uniform except on duty, found it irksome.

The requirement had one unintended effect. UN soldiers, like any others, needed rest and recreation; the beaches were popular in summer, as were the Troodos ski-slopes in winter, while all year round men off duty patronized cafes, bars, hotels and restaurants, wandered through shopping streets and explored the island's monasteries, castles and sites of other antiquities. In this regard they were no different from the far more numerous British servicemen stationed in the SBAs, but, whereas the latter were free to do so in the anonymity of civilian dress, UN soldiers were conspicuous in uniform, giving rise to jibes such as 'UN tourists' or 'UN holiday army' and conveying to casual observers a wholly erroneous impression of UNFICYP's true activities.

The daily round could be monotonous for those engaged in the vital but usually tedious task of manning the OPs by day and night. How each contingent managed its deployments and logistic arrangements was a matter for the Contingent Commander concerned. The Canadian battalion in Nicosia maintained company and platoon bases where men were accommodated and fed, and from which they were sent out to man the OPs or patrol the Green Line; for this reason these OPs usually consisted of little more than a sentry-box. The three rifle platoons of a Canadian company worked a six-day cycle: two days manning OPs and patrolling, two days on stand-by and training, and two days free for other activities. In contrast the Danes deployed detachments of some six men to isolated OPs on the hills around Kokkina and Limnitis and elsewhere; these men lived sometimes for weeks at a time in these posts, where they cooked and otherwise looked after themselves, being supplied on foot, by vehicle or helicopter, and even in one case by means of a Greek and his donkey. The Finns did much the same in their OPs on the peaks of the Pendadhaktylos, while other contingents adopted other variations; the Swedes cooked meals centrally in their Carl Gustav Camp base and delivered these in insulated containers to outlying detachments.

Although such matters were left to the discretion of Contingent Commanders – for what might suit the temperament, training and circumstances of one contingent did not necessarily meet the needs of another – it was necessary for the Force Commander to keep a watchful eye on them. For example, while in terms of continuity there was advantage in not changing men around too frequently, there was also a risk that the contingent concerned might expose itself to the charge that its men were coming to identify themselves too closely with a particular local community to the prejudice of the Force's impartiality. (At one juncture the government complained that members of the Danish Contingent had become too sympathetic to the plight of Turkish refugees existing under harsh conditions in Kokkina, the implication being that they were turning a blind eye to Turkish activities such as arms smuggling. While refusing to accept such charges or to accede to government pressure for the Danes to be deployed elsewhere, Prem Chand decreed that no man was to serve for more than three months in the same post.)

Some UN OPs were too remote ever to be seen by the public at large[6], but these posts and the handful of men manning them by day and night were evidence of the Force's constant vigilance. Although the tasks might be monotonous, maintaining the smartness of the posts helped to pass the time, contributed to contingent *esprit de corps* and provided evidence of UNFICYP's discipline and military efficiency. Life for soldiers in the more remote OPs was largely what they themselves made of it. Detachments were too small for off-duty men to follow the usual sporting activities, but there was plenty to occupy those not actually on observation duty, such as operating radio communications, charging batteries, cooking, sanitation and general maintenance of the post's facilities and equipment. Personnel delivering rations, mail, pay and in some cases water were welcome regular visitors, and contingent commanders and others, such as medical officers, made frequent inspections, as did senior officers from Force HQ. There was much to keep the men on their toes.

For those not deployed in OPs or engaged on other operational or administrative tasks a variety of recreational activities was available. Football, tennis, squash, swimming, scuba-diving, water-skiing, rock-climbing, gliding, cross-country running, volley-ball, judo, horse riding and even polo were all popular[7], and for a few weeks it was possible to ski on Mount Olympus. Inter-contingent competitions were organized in many of these activities and a shooting competition with small arms always generated enthusiastic rivalry. Some competitions were organized by one contingent on behalf of UNFICYP as a whole, for example, Orienteering competitions in the Kantara Forest were run by the Finns; a novel 'Town Race' through the streets of Famagusta was organized by the Swedes, and keenly-contested Volley-Ball tournaments were arranged in Nicosia by the Canadians.

UNFICYP's operations were conducted on a 24-hour-seven-days-a-week basis, with all JOCs manned around the clock, and senior officers when off duty kept in touch by telephone or portable radio. But the normal working week for staff both military and civilian at Force HQ was limited to six days, with Sundays kept free.[8] Routine situation reports (SITREPS in military parlance) from District JOCs reached Force HQ during the night, as did code-cables and other communications from New York (the time differential working to mutual advantage). After consideration of these by the Force Commander, the necessary instructions were issued at a meeting of HQ staff officers chaired by the Chief of Staff at which the SPA, CAO and Police Adviser were also present. A fortnightly meeting was convened at Force HQ, attended by District Commanders and others, when briefings were given on developments, including those in the political sphere. Once a month this meeting was preceded by a 'Force Commander's Briefing', at which General Prem Chand was present (accompanied sometimes by Dr Osorio-Tafall). These gatherings provided opportunities for District Commanders to liaise personally not only with all branches of the HQ staff but also no less importantly with each other.

It was all too easy for those at the top to become immersed in routine business at the Force HQ, but it was these same individuals, holding the key posts and serving tours of duty of two years or longer, who provided the continuity that was so important in a Force most of whose men changed every six months. Prem Chand visited all contingents as frequently as his commitments in Nicosia allowed and it was my practice as Chief of Staff to set aside one day a week for similar visits, not only to units of the British Contingent (of which I was Commander) but also to all others; usually the SPA, John Miles, came with me and both the Contingents and I benefited from his wise advice. The visits were time-consuming and sometimes (especially in high summer) physically demanding, entailing climbing in and out of vehicles and helicopters, scrambling up rocky hills to reach OPs and touring base camps, but they provided a breath of fresh air away from the routine and pressures of Force HQ, valuable opportunities to monitor activities on the ground and the pleasure of meeting the men of the many different nations who comprised the Force.

The daily round at Force HQ did not make it easy to get away for these visits. Apart from routine staff business, operational, administrative and logistic, each week had its own full schedule. It included taking care of numerous official visitors of various nationalities, who had to be briefed and entertained; regular discussions with Prem Chand, Osorio-Tafall and Miles to review progress in the intercommunal talks and other matters; frequent (and sometimes lengthy) meetings with representatives of the Government, the National Guard, the Leadership, and diplomatic missions; briefings for foreign military attachés; attendance at Nicosia airport on the arrival or departure of VIPs; formal calls on the occasion of Greek or Turkish special anniversaries; periodic liaison visits to Commanders of British Forces in the SBAs; and, not least, attendance at numerous UNFICYP functions, such as briefings for incoming contingents and medal parades. This made for full days but was not all; a busy and obligatory evening social round followed. Invitations to attend Greek Cypriot, Turkish Cypriot and foreign diplomatic receptions, dinners and other occasions to mark national days or events, such as the arrival or departure of ambassadors and others were numerous; it was UNFICYP policy that, as a demonstration of the Force's impartiality, all such invitations should be accepted. To this diplomatic round were added UN Contingents' own social functions to mark national days, bid welcome or farewell to those being rotated, entertain ministers or senior officers visiting from home countries, or in celebration of medal parades.

After three months' service in UNFICYP its members qualified for the award of the UN Medal inscribed 'In the Service of Peace', presented on a ceremonial Contingent Medal Parade, normally by General Prem Chand personally.[9] These parades were a high spot in the tours of duty of contingents and high standards were the norm. Spectators were invited from other contingents and subsequent hospitality was generous. The form of parade was a matter for national preference or custom and ranged from a Swedish ceremony held in the amphitheatre of ancient Salamis to a British trooping-the-colour parade under floodlights with the firing of a *feu-de-joie* as its climax.

The multinational character of UNFICYP brought a large number of official visitors and, while welcome, these imposed a heavy load on the headquarters. They included Ministers, Members of Parliament, Chiefs of Staff and other senior officers, diplomats accredited to (but not necessarily resident in) Cyprus, and media correspondents from home countries. To these were added the Secretary General and senior members of the UN Secretariat, diplomats and service attachés from other countries, together with a variety of people, such as university research teams, interested in aspects of the UN operation in Cyprus. Most required the prior consent of New York, but few could be refused and the stream was constant. Protocol demanded that many be met at the airport and some had to be accorded the courtesy of a Guard of Honour; programmes had to be arranged and appropriate transport, hospitality and other facilities provided.

Those serving in the armies of most developed countries are accustomed to high standards of welfare amenities. New York provided no services comparable to those of the Navy, Army and Air Force Institute (NAAFI) in the British Services or the Post Exchange (PX) in the American, there were no UN-provided clubs, canteens, film services, concert parties or other entertainments for the troops, and no provision of sports facilities or equipment. All had to be provided by contingents themselves.[10] Members of the British Contingent (who saw the excellent facilities provided for the comfort and recreation of their comrades serving in the SBAs) could be forgiven for feeling somewhat neglected, but, paradoxically (as so often in the British army), the more they had to fend for themselves, the greater the initiative and satisfaction in organizing their own facilities.

UNFICYP HQ did not include a Chaplain; matters spiritual were a contingent responsibility. Each had its own padre (the Canadians had as many as four) and most established a small place of worship within their base camp. At Christmas each year groups from all contingents joined together in an UNFICYP Festival of Carols and Lessons held in the Garrison Church of St George in the Eastern SBA, accompanied by families and friends together with guests from the SBAs. General Prem Chand gave an introductory address and the congregation sang together the first and last carols. Other carols were chosen and sung by each contingent in turn and lessons, too, were read in turn by a member of each. Prayers were said by the different padres and at the end each pronounced a Blessing in his own tongue. Those present will not forget the Austrians' unaccompanied singing of Brahms's beautiful *Es ist ein Ros' Entsprungen*, the Canadians' robust *Go Tell it on the Mountain*, or the congregation rendering in unison the universally loved *Still the Night, Holy the Night*. As the congregation dispersed under the starlit sky of an island that lay so close to the Holy Land, few came away unmoved by a Service that rekindled a feeling of common purpose and unity in a Christian enterprise undertaken for the peace and good of mankind.

An important benefit of service in a UN Force is the opportunity it provides for soldiers to rub shoulders with, and thus better to understand, comrades from other countries. Sporting competitions were valuable in this respect and to these were added other non-competitive events that served to bring all ranks together. They included a run right around the island in which each contingent covered one section, with all coming together for a social gathering at the finish, and Contingent Marches in which parties from each marched together over set routes across country.

Grant of leave was a matter for Contingent Commanders. Each man was entitled (subject to operational requirements) to one period of two weeks away from the island during each six-month tour, although not all availed themselves of this; of those who did, some seized the opportunity to visit the Holy Land, Egypt, Lebanon and other countries in the region (visits to Greece or Turkey were forbidden, due to the risk that these might compromise impartiality), while others ventured further afield. Occasionally members of BRITCON were granted passage in RAF aircraft flying east or west from Akrotiri, and the Canadians made available to men of those contingents drawn from NATO countries seats on their weekly flight between Nicosia and Canada, flying via Lahr in West Germany.

While for the majority of UNFICYP's men the nature of society within both the Greek and the Turkish communities inhibited close social contacts with Cypriots, it would be misleading to conclude from this survey of blue beret life that the Force was introverted and concerned only with its own well-being, for wherever possible it responded quickly and generously to external calls on its resources. Requests for medical aid, whether for rapid evacuation of patients by helicopter to local hospitals or for treatment in the Austrian Field Hospital, were readily met without charge; help was given to fight forest fires and relief was provided in cases of disasters caused by severe storms; blood was donated to hospitals[11] and on their own initiative men of the Force gave unpublicized support to local charities. The variety of UNFICYP's activities both on and off duty was reflected in the Force's own weekly journal, *The Blue Beret*. Life in UNFICYP generally was active, interesting and rewarding for those with the initiative to make the best of it.

In 1974 General Prem Chand accorded me the honour of taking on his behalf the Medal Parade for the 5th Royal Inniskilling Dragoon Guards, a British cavalry regiment serving in UNFICYP in an infantry role. Addressing the parade, I referred to the regiment's many Battle Honours and proud record extending back to the Battle of Blenheim in 1704:

> Your predecessors who helped to win these many honours might find your present task in a United Nations peacekeeping Force a rather strange one. But it is a paradox not always understood that today a soldier's main task is directed towards the maintenance of peace. This is your task here, and this is the task to which you will soon be returning in Germany, where your military preparedness serves as a deterrent to those who might be tempted into armed aggression.

Turning to the regiment's successful military and sporting record while serving with UNFICYP, I concluded with these words:

> It is not only these successes that matter – what matter far more are the comradeship of the Force and the opportunity to be members of one international team working for one high ideal, the maintenance of peace. . . . You will, I am sure, be better soldiers for it, for your experience and humanity will have been widened. Not least, you can be proud to wear the United Nations medal awarded to you today 'In the Service of Peace'.

These words epitomized part of the intangible benefits which men (and now women) derive from participation in the peacekeeping operations of the United Nations.

PART THREE

YOM KIPPUR AND OPERATION 'DOVE'

The United Nations has shown that, by means of its peacekeeping machinery, it can sometimes play a significant and unique role in the strengthening of international peace and security. . . . This was particularly the case in the wake of the October conflict in the Middle East, when the Organisation was once again, in a situation of extreme urgency, called upon to set up a new peacekeeping Force.

UN Secretary General:
Report on the Work of the Organization, 1974.

1. General Prem Chand (India), the UN Force Commander, welcomes Brigadier Francis Henn (United Kingdom), his new Chief of Staff, June 1972.

2. Blue Beret Camp near Nicosia Airport, UNFICYP's Headquarters. *(UN/Nagata)*

3. *Right to left:* Lieutenant General G. Denizis (Commander National Guard, August 1973 – July 1974), Major E. Tsolakis (National Guard LO to UNFICYP), Captain T. Fredholm, (Sweden, ADC to General Prem Chand), General Prem Chand.

4. The author greeted by Colonel M. Fusunoglu, Commander Turkish National Contingent in 1973, and Asaf Inhan, Turkish Chargé d'Affaires, Nicosia.

5. Checking vehicles at the start of the daily UN-escorted Kyrenia Road convoys. *(UN/Nagata)*

6. Finnish soldiers climbing the Pendadhaktylos Mountains carrying supplies for OP Hilltop. *(UN/Nagata)*

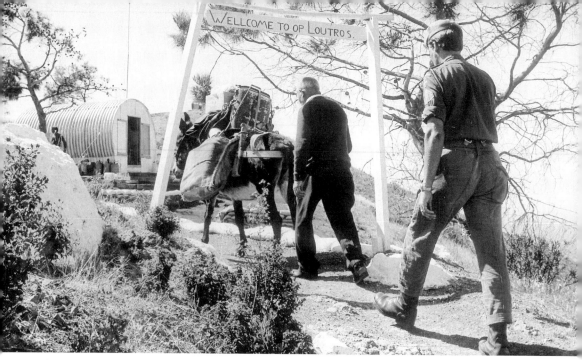

7. Supplies carried by donkey for the Danes' OP Loutros in the mountains overlooking the Limnitis enclave.
(UN/Nagata)

8. Routine briefing in May 1973 at UNFICYP HQ by the Chief Operations Officer, Lieutenant Colonel T.I. Kuosa (Finland). *In Front Row Right to Left:* Ramon Prieto (Spain) Legal Adviser, Hans Wagner (Austria) Police Adviser, John Miles (Australia) Senior Political Adviser, General Prem Chand, Bibiano Osorio-Tafall (Mexico) Special Representative of the Secretary General, George Ryder (USA) Chief Administrative Officer, Colonel C.E. Beattie (Canada) Deputy Chief of Staff; *Second Row:* UN District Commanders; *Third and Fourth Rows:* HQ staff and advisers. (Author in corner far left)
(UN/Nagata)

9. Colonel Georgitsis and Major Soulis, respectively Commander and Operations Officer of the National Guard's 3HTC Nicosia, with Lieutenant Colonel J. Pullinen (Finland) *centre*, Commander UNFICYP's Kyrenia District. These Greek officers were alleged to have master-minded the coup in Nicosia on 15 July 1974. Pullinen reported that both were tired and irritable immediately before-hand and that both disappeared from Cyprus when Turkish troops landed on 20 July.

10. After his escape from Nicosia, Archbishop Makarios, President of Cyprus, thanks Major Richard Macfarlane, Coldstream Guards, Paphos District Commander, for affording him and his party refuge in St Patrick's Camp, Paphos, before departing by helicopter for Akrotiri (and thence away from the island) on 16 July 1974.

11. The author is briefed by Major K.G. Hornung, Operations Officer, at the Danes' Headquarters in Viking Camp on the situation in Lefka District, July 1974. (*At left:* John Miles, Senior Political Adviser, and Lieutenant Colonel C.J.K. Severinson, District Commander).

12. The Danes dig in to defend Viking Camp, July 1974.

13. Nicosia Airport – plant and equipment deployed by UNFICYP on runways to prevent use of the airport, July 1974.
(*UN/Nagata*)

14. Saladin armoured cars and other vehicles of Regimental HQ 16th/5th Lancers established at the terminal building, Nicosia Airport, July 1974.
(*UN/Nagata*)

15. 100mm Howitzers of the National Guard, some of whose artillery was deployed close behind the Finns' Kykko and other UN camps, July 1974.

16. An officer of C Squadron, 4th/7th Dragoon Guards in observation from a Swingfire anti-tank guided weapon deployed at Nicosia airport, close under a bomb-damaged Cyprus Airways Trident aircraft, July 1974. *(UN/Nagata)*

17. *'What a noise! Better make sure the trousers stay up!'* General Prem Chand visits the Finns in Kykko Camp while under fire, July 1974.

18. The Danes' OP at Kokkina South.

19. Survivors from the Turkish destroyer *Kocatepe* sunk by the Turkish airforce are tended after rescue on board HMS *Andromeda*, 24 July 1974.

(Imperial War Museum)

20. The tripartite committee established by the Geneva Declaration to determine a security zone to be policed by UNFICY visits a forward UN post established by 16th/5th Lancers with a Saracen APC, August 1974. (Examining Turkish positions through binoculars is Colonel Hunter, Defence Adviser to the British High Commission, the Committee's Chairman).

(UN/Nagata)

21. The tripartite committee drafts its report at UNFICYP Headquarters, August 1974.
Left: Major E. Tsolakis (National Guard). *Centre:* Colonel C. Beattie (UNFICYP).
Right: Colonel N. Cakar (Turkish army). *Back to camera:* Colonel G. Hunter (UK).
(*UN/Nagata*)

22. Commandant J. Flynn, UNFICYP's LO to the National Guard, reports by radio from
outside the National Guard's Tactical Headquarters near Pyrga, August 1974.

23. A Danish casualty is evacuated by a Sioux helicopter of UNFICYP's Army Aviation Flight.

24. Turkish armour is greeted by local Turkish Cypriots as it reaches Lefka, August 1974.

25. A Swedish Skania APC at an OP overlooking Famagusta and Varosha.　　*(UN/Nagata)*

26. From his APC a Canadian observes the Greek Grammar School (middle distance), for the capture of which Turkish forces fought hard for three days, August 1974.　　*(UN/Nagata)*

27. Canadians, supported by a Lynx, discuss the situation with Turkish troops at a UN OP, August 1974. *(UN/Nagata)*

28. From the roof of the main terminal building on 25 August 1974 the situation leading to UNFICYP's take-over of Nicosia airport is described by the author to Kurt Waldheim, UN Secretary General (seen over author's right shoulder). (*On Right:* General Prem Chand with Brian Urquhart on his right). (*Behind, hand to head:* John Miles). *(UN/Nagata)*

29. The deserted Turkish Cypriot village of Maratha (Famagusta District) in which a massacre of villagers was alleged to have taken place in August 1974 by Greek Cypriots withdrawing in the face of the advancing Turkish army. (The minaret with aluminium painted top, identifying the village as Turkish, was typical). *(UN/Nagata)*

30. The body of the assassinated US Ambassador Rodger Davies, escorted by the Counsellor, Lindsey Grant, is placed aboard a UN Whirlwind helicopter at UNFICYP Headquarters to be flown to Akrotiri and thence to the US, 20th August 1974. *(UN/Nagata)*

31. Foreign nationals rescued from the north coast by the Royal Navy arrive by helicopter on the flight deck of HMS *Hermes*, 23 July 1974. *(Imperial War Museum)*

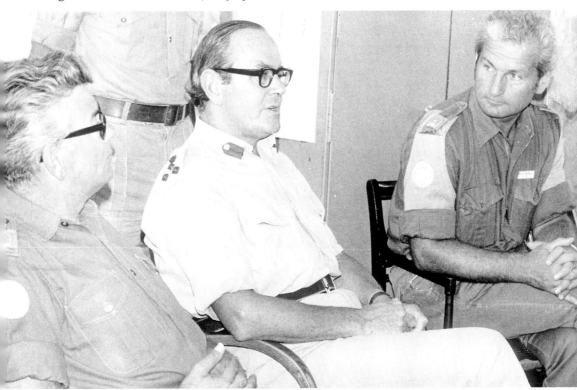

32. The author discusses problems in Larnaca District with *right*: Major L. Kremnitzer and *left*: Major H. Oberwinkler, UNFICYP's LO to the Vice President's Office, both of the Austrian contingent, August 1974.

33. Buffavento Castle, at a height of 954m in the Pendadhaktylos mountains, seized by Turkish troops, July 1974.

(UN/Nagata)

34. '*I found the Danes in good heart*'. The author is greeted by Lieutenant Colonel Severinson on landing in Viking Camp, Xeros, 24 July 1974.

35. M113 APCs of the Canadian Airborne Regiment patrol the ceasefire line north of Nicosia, September 1974.

(UN/Nagata)

CHAPTER NINETEEN

BOLT FROM THE UN BLUE

The conflict between Egypt and Israel was so involved and so complex that it was virtually impossible for any ceasefire to come about without outside assistance. . . . Thus, after three more days of fighting, the Security Council decided to set up UNEF II to interpose itself between the combatants. Using the resources of UNTSO and troops from the peacekeeping operation in Cyprus, it was possible to get the first units of the Force into the field within 24 hours of the Security Council decision, and their interposition between the armies of Egypt and Israel swiftly brought the very confused and bitter fighting to an end.

Brian E. Urquhart: *The World Today*, March 1980, p. 91.

In October 1973 the UN Force in Cyprus was rudely shaken from its ordered way of life by events unrelated to its mission on the island. That year Yom Kippur, the Hebrew Day of Atonement, fell on 6 October. The same afternoon Egyptian forces launched a massive assault across the Suez Canal against the Israeli army entrenched in the Bar Lev Line on its eastern bank, while Syrian troops simultaneously attacked the Golan Heights on Israel's northern flank. Both operations achieved surprise.

The Syrian action posed the more immediate threat and the Israelis gave priority to its early defeat, which allowed the Egyptian Second and Third Armies to gain initial success by breaching the Bar Lev Line, gaining a bridgehead on the eastern bank and throwing back an Israeli counter-attack. Early defeat of the Syrians in the north was followed by a rapid re-deployment of the Israeli forces and, as the Egyptians advanced east to a depth of some 10km from their bridgehead, they met the full strength of Israeli armoured and air forces. Now beyond the cover of their Soviet-supplied missile defences deployed west of the Canal, the Egyptians suffered a devastating defeat in a major armoured battle which left them with some 260 tanks destroyed to the Israelis' loss of a mere six.

With customary *élan* the Israelis quickly struck back across the Canal and by 22 October, when a ceasefire called for by the Security Council was due to take effect, their forces had fanned out to a depth of 25km beyond it, reaching the outskirts of Suez and Ismailia and cutting Egyptian communications with Cairo. As the fighting continued, with both sides seeking to improve their positions, a second call came from the Security Council for a cease-fire to take effect this time at noon on 24 October. It, too, went unheeded as the Israelis strengthened their grip on their bridgehead west of the Canal and the Egyptian Third Army tried desperately to break the stranglehold in which it now found itself. This situation caused mounting international concern, which a prospect of super-power intervention did nothing to reduce – seven Soviet airborne divisions together with a high-level military HQ were readied for action and US forces worldwide were placed on high alert.[1] Since neither the Americans nor the Soviets were prepared to see their own client-state defeated, super-power confrontation loomed close. There was even speculation that recourse might be had to the use of nuclear weapons.[2]

The immediate dangers and the prospect of wider conflict were averted by urgent dialogue between Washington and Moscow, but the situation on the Suez Canal remained confused and volatile as calls for a ceasefire went unheeded. Prompted by the two super-powers a consensus developed in New York for the interposition of a UN Force as a buffer between the two sides to halt the fighting and stabilize the situation while a settlement was sought, and the Security Council met on 25 October to consider a draft Resolution which called yet again for a ceasefire and for the immediate establishment of a UN Emergency Force to supervise it. The Secretary General was required to report within 24 hours on measures taken to this end.

Time was of the essence and Dr Waldheim had already concluded that the only way in which a UN Force could be produced on the ground in Egypt with the requisite speed was to draw on UNFICYP, accepting the risks this entailed.[3] The Cyprus Force was close in terms of time and distance and comprised troops experienced in the UN peacekeeping game, acclimatized to the Eastern Mediterranean and of nationalities likely to be acceptable to the parties. Having taken preliminary confidential soundings of the governments concerned, the Secretary General tabled a draft Resolution proposing the transfer of the bulk of the Austrian, Finnish and Swedish Contingents of UNFICYP to Cairo as the nucleus of the new UN Emergency Force (known as UNEF 2 to distinguish it from the earlier UNEF withdrawn in 1967). This Draft was adopted without dissent as Resolution 340(1973) at 1515hrs (New York time) on 25 October and Waldheim acted immediately to implement the plan. The speed with which troops were redeployed from Cyprus to Cairo exceeded all international expectations and excited admiration, not least in some hitherto critical of UN Forces. The manner in which it was accomplished demonstrated a new flexibility in the use of these forces and created an important precedent. The operation itself was a remarkable exercise in multi-national military cooperation, although it exposed some of the constraints and weaknesses that were a feature at that period of the UN's management of its peacekeeping operations.

A particular defect lay in the UN Secretariat's failure to disseminate to UN Commanders in the field regular confidential assessments of current events lying outside the sphere of responsibility of the Commander concerned. Thus at UNFICYP HQ we knew nothing of New York's thinking about events in the Middle East following the Yom Kippur offensive and depended on radio bulletins and press reports for information. These we followed with avid interest, speculating on the outcome as we watched a stream of Soviet Antonov transport aircraft pass high and silently in the clear blue sky over Cyprus carrying urgently needed supplies for the hard-pressed Egyptians. Those same reports indicated the pressures building in New York for the establishment of a UN Force in the Sinai, but, not being privy to the Secretary General's thinking, we had no inkling of UNFICYP's imminent involvement.

On the evening of 25 October the Cypriot League of Friends gave a dinner in Nicosia to mark United Nations Day the day before; those invited included the SRSG, Dr Osorio-Tafall, General Prem Chand and myself. The intercommunal situation was calm and UNFICYP (then embarked on the first phase of the planned reductions) was faced with no pressing problems, but, as so often, the intercommunal talks were in the doldrums. Progress was lamentably slow, political will for an early settlement was conspicuous by its absence and mistrust frustrated UN efforts to inject a spirit of compromise and greater sense of urgency. As we sat down to dine with our Cypriot hosts we could be forgiven if our thoughts were less on their tedious differences than on the dramatic events unfolding close across the sea. Nor were we surprised when Osorio-Tafall, responding to the toast 'The United Nations', chided those present for the lack of progress and urgency. UNFICYP, he observed, was now in its tenth year of duty in Cyprus and, with no end in sight, those who shouldered the burden of maintaining it there were becoming increasingly impatient. Who could object, he jocularly warned, if some might feel that their men would be better employed keeping the peace between Arab and Jew on the Suez Canal? Little did he know how prescient his words were soon to prove.

At home after the dinner my telephone rang at 2330hrs. It was Osorio-Tafall asking if I had yet seen a Most Immediate code-cable just received from New York and delivered in accordance with usual practice direct to him and Prem Chand; I had not, and he read its contents over to me. Originated in New York at lunchtime (about 2000hrs in Nicosia) on 25 October, it gave us our first warning of UNFICYP's involvement in the Middle East crisis. We were told that the Security Council was at that moment considering a proposal for the immediate establishment of a UN Force on the Suez Canal and that, should this be approved, the Secretary General intended to suggest that, as a first step and with the agreement of the governments concerned, the Austrian, Finnish and Swedish Contingents of UNFICYP should forthwith be transferred temporarily to Egypt. We were to take immediate steps to ensure that the three contingents were ready to move at very short notice, including making arrangements for the temporary redeployment of other contingents to fill the resultant gaps in Cyprus; logistic arrangements for the move would be notified to us as soon as possible. The cable added that the representatives in New York of Cyprus, Greece and Turkey had been consulted and the need stressed for them to cooperate in ensuring that this temporary reduction in the size of UNFICYP did not adversely affect the situation on the island, and that all three had indicated readiness to do so on the understanding that the three contingents would be replaced in UNFICYP as early as possible (this was to prove an important proviso). We were instructed to secure a similar assurance from the Turkish Cypriot Leadership as soon as the Security Council had formally approved Waldheim's plan, but were enjoined to keep any preliminary planning orders confidential until then.

This was a true bolt from the UN blue. UN Forces were not permitted to plan for contingencies unrelated to their own mandate[4] and no plans existed either in Nicosia or New York to cater for the prospect that now faced us; we had to start from cold. The urgent tone of the cable left no doubt that rapid action was required. My first question was to ask if Prem Chand knew of the cable and, if so, what his reaction had been (it was unusual for the SRSG rather than the Force Commander to communicate the contents of important code-cables to the

Chief of Staff). Osorio-Tafall replied that he had just discussed it with Prem Chand, who felt that action could be deferred until the Security Council's decision was known. I thought that the cable not only authorized but actually instructed us to take preparatory action so long as security was preserved. Conscious of the value of every minute gained for planning, I said that I intended to put this in hand at once. That, said Osorio-Tafall, was what he had hoped to hear.

Half an hour later I presided at a meeting at HQ UNFICYP attended by the Deputy Chief of Staff, Colonel Beattie (Canada), the Chief Operations Officer, Lieut. Colonel Clausen (Austria) and the Chief Personnel and Logistics Officer, Lieut. Colonel Pennell (UK). It was midnight and the aim was to have an outline plan that could be presented to Prem Chand as soon as the Security Council's decision was received. Action in four directions was required: first was the need to send early confidential warning to the three contingents concerned to allow them as much time as possible for their own planning; second, to propose how the remaining contingents might be redeployed to fill consequential gaps in Cyprus; third to consider how best to prepare the Austrians, Finns and Swedes for their rapid move and formulate a movement plan; lastly to decide how the operation, to which we gave the appropriate nickname Operation DOVE, should be handled within UNFICYP HQ. Warning to the three contingents was the least of these problems; at 0020hrs telephone messages were passed to each, security being preserved by using the appropriate national language – German, Finnish or Swedish.

An outline plan for redeployment of the remaining contingents was quickly formulated for Prem Chand's consideration. Preparation of the three contingents for the move would mainly be their own responsibility in accordance with such instructions as they might receive from their own governments, but there was much that UNFICYP could do to help. To handle Operation DOVE with minimum disruption to the control of continuing operations in Cyprus we decided to establish a small group at HQ UNFICYP under Clausen. Two BRITCON officers experienced in the techniques of emergency movement by air (experience that was lacking in the three contingents) were readily available; these were Major P. Wood, Parachute Regt (Force Operations Information Officer) and Major R. Scrimshaw-Wright, Royal Corps of Transport (Force Transport Officer); both joined Clausen's group without delay. An added bonus was the presence in UNFICYP of 1st Bn, Parachute Regt, a unit highly trained in these techniques and familiar with the Royal Air Force's movement procedures. The assistance of its members was to prove invaluable.

Formidable problems faced the Austrians, Finns and Swedes. Foremost was the timing, which scarcely could have been more difficult, for all were at the end of their six-month tour of duty and routine troop rotations were either imminent or already in train[5], but there were other complications. None of these contingents was constituted as a permanently established unit analogous to the regular battalions of Britain and Canada; each comprised a temporary unit formed specifically for the peacekeeping task in Cyprus and was neither organized nor trained to be ready to move to undertake operations elsewhere. Further, the majority of their men were not professional soldiers who could be sent wherever directed but volunteers contracted for UN duty solely in Cyprus. None could be sent to Egypt unless they so volunteered, and it was not reasonable to expect them to do this without knowing more about the conditions of service in the new UN Force, such as the length of tours of duty, pay and allowances, compensation for injury or death, and the safeguarding of civilian employment at home. These were all questions to which at that stage there were no ready answers and the uncertainties facing the men were not lessened by the prospect of finding themselves interposed on a desert battlefield between two large armies still clamped in combat, a prospect in sharp contrast to their current task on the agreeable island of Cyprus.[6]

To cap it all, the Austrians had an added difficulty; that very day, 26 October, being a national holiday to mark Austria's independence in 1955, various celebrations had been organized within the contingent and government offices were closed in Vienna. This latter was of serious concern because, irrespective of what instructions might arrive from New York, HQ UNFICYP had no authority to order contingents to undertake tasks outside the Republic of Cyprus. That authority rested solely with parent sovereign governments and the three Contingent Commanders needed to obtain instructions from their own capitals without delay.

CHAPTER TWENTY

PREPARATIONS IN CYPRUS

Some sophisticated professional military men might not be particularly impressed by the speed with which the operation got under way. Others more sceptical might claim that had the experts not been there to guide and lead, the move would not have happened. . . . For the operational organization to be effective and efficient, it is dependent upon every member of the staff at headquarters and in the unit.

Rikhye *et al.*: *The Thin Blue Line*, pp. 322–3.

The text of Resolution 340(1973) embodying the Security Council's decision to establish UNEF 2 reached HQ UNFICYP at 0215hrs on 26 October, and was followed 30 minutes later by confirmation that the Council had approved Waldheim's plan to send as its nucleus the Austrian, Finnish and Swedish Contingents from Cyprus. We were told that the UN Secretariat was arranging for their air-lift to Cairo and that the three contingents were to be held on stand-by from 26 October. I discussed this latest information at once with Prem Chand by telephone and told him of the action already set in hand. All concerned had already been warned of a likely Orders Group meeting[1] at HQ UNFICYP and he decided that this should be held at 0800hrs. Contingent and District Commanders were informed accordingly and helicopters tasked to bring in officers from the more distant locations.

Meanwhile Clausen's planning group was setting about its task with energy. Cables from New York at the administrative level flowed in, the first demand being for an estimate of the cubic footage and weight of stores to be moved on the basis that each contingent would take with it its normal contingent-owned equipment, rations for 30 days, tentage, a minimum number of vehicles and those radios necessary for internal communication. News quickly followed that Britain had undertaken to provide at no cost to the UN the required airlift from the RAF base at Akrotiri in the Western SBA[2] and that notification had been received from the Egyptians that the point of arrival was to be Cairo International Airport.

To assist the three contingents to comply with British air movement procedures BRITCON's parachute battalion was ordered to send a team of advisers to each to help over such matters as packing, marking and compilation of load tables; these teams remained with contingents until their departure from Akrotiri. HQ Near East Land Forces (NEARELF) was alerted to our need to draw heavily within the next few hours on depots in the Eastern SBA for a wide variety of stores, ranging from rations and medical equipment to tentage and packed petroleum. Also foreseen was the need for close liaison with the RAF movements organization and a helicopter was tasked to fetch the Near East Air Force's (NEAF) Command Movements Officer, Wing Commander C. Lim, from Episkopi to attend the 'O' Group at UNFICYP HQ at 0800 hrs. Aware of the likely logistic problems that flowed from New York's *ad hoc* approach to the mounting of UN peacekeeping operations, we had no illusions as to the bleak prospect sure to face the three contingents on arrival in Egypt: deployed in the Suez Canal area well before the establishment of any supporting logistic organization, they must expect to fend for themselves in most respects for weeks rather than days[3] in an inhospitable desert environment recently fought over by two large armies. We were determined to despatch them from Cyprus as well provided for as was feasible in the time. However, there were two limiting factors: first, UNFICYP could not be denuded of equipment to the point of prejudicing the continuing task in Cyprus; second, reserves held in British depots were limited and could be drawn on by UNFICYP only to the extent permitted by the British authorities in the light of their own national needs and contingency plans.

When the 'O' Group convened at 0800hrs General Prem Chand explained the instructions received from New York, issued orders for the redeployment in Cyprus and outlined the plan for Operation DOVE, the move to Cairo. On the island the Danes were to take over the northern part of Kyrenia District from the Finns, with the Canadians taking over its southern part. The latter were also to take over Famagusta District from the Swedes, while BRITCON's parachute battalion in Limassol was to extend west to take over Paphos District from the Austrians (this left the small Irish contingent undisturbed in Larnaca and the Force Reserve scout car squadron uncommitted). Members of the HQ staff elaborated details and the meeting concluded, as customary, with questions. Some could not be answered since they depended on action in New York or because they were matters for the home governments, some were resolved on the spot, while for the remainder only sensible guesses could be made. Little of what was decided at that meeting required modification later.

The immediate priority was to complete redeployment on the island as soon as possible. Skeleton advance parties from relieving contingents were despatched to begin the take-over of UN posts and the transfer of operational responsibility at District HQs. Briefings on the tasks in hand were essential and detailed records and instructions, usually in another language, had to be handed over. Since no UN post was to be left unmanned, even temporarily, men could not be withdrawn from them until relieved, although some 'thinning-out' was permitted. Movement of men to and from the more inaccessible posts was time-consuming; in the case of Finnish OPs on the mountains above Kyrenia helicopters were necessary to obviate slow and laborious climbs on foot. All ranks reacted with competence and speed so that by noon the necessary inter-contingent liaisons had been established and transfers of responsibility were proceeding. The Canadians had assumed control of Famagusta District by 1400hrs and of their sector of Kyrenia District soon afterwards; all the remainder had been completed by 1800 hrs. At some points the UNFICYP presence on the ground was thin, but at no stage had any UN post been left unmanned. The problem of maintaining continuity in dealing with current and sometimes complex local disputes, where intimate understanding of the past history was so important, was mitigated by the fact that no changes were made in the deployment of UNCIVPOL detachments (no UN Civilian

Police were required for UNEF 2), and their local knowledge and experience remained readily available to the newcomers.

The plan for Operation DOVE was relatively simple once the three contingents had shed operational responsibilities in Cyprus. Each was to move at a strength of 200 men[4]; an advance party of 35 under the Contingent Commander himself was to be ready to move at 1400hrs, with the main body on stand-by from 2030hrs. Those left behind were to form rear parties to look after base camps, vehicles and stores, pending the arrival of the expected replacements in Cyprus. Apart from a stipulated minimum number of vehicles to be left with the latter, Contingent Commanders were allowed discretion as to how many and what types of vehicles (subject to airportability limitations) they took to Cairo. This discretion was given on the assumption that replacements for UNFICYP would be readily forthcoming from British stocks in the SBAs; in the event, this was the only major matter that required subsequent modification.

For the rest, men were to move dressed in battle-order, carrying small arms and ready for immediate action; holdings of first line ammunition were to be taken, together with radios for internal contingent communication (but not those providing external links between District HQ and UNFICYP HQ) and batteries sufficient for the initial 48 hours (additional batteries were to be packed as unit freight); water needs were to be met by each man having a full water-bottle, by carriage of two full water cans on every vehicle and by issue of water sterilization outfits to individuals; petrol requirements were to be catered for by vehicles being emplaned with fuel tanks three-quarters full (the limit allowed by RAF regulations) and two additional jerricans carried on each. Further, men were to be given a hot meal before leaving bases in Cyprus, each was to carry rations sufficient for 48 hours, with a further 30 days' worth and field cookers despatched as unit freight.[5] Guidance was given, too, on diverse other matters, such as scales of tentage and bedding to be taken, medical items likely to be needed, and inoculations and anti-malarial precautions recommended, while such maps of the Suez Canal area as were available from local British stocks were obtained and issued. The CPLO, Lieut. Colonel Pennell, and his staff at UNFICYP HQ tried to anticipate every need and spared no effort to secure all that could be obtained within the few hours available.

This meticulous attention to matters that may seem mundane was critical because it was this that ensured that the three contingents were ready for immediate deployment on arrival in Cairo, in sharp contrast to the state of others that arrived from elsewhere in the ensuing weeks, as UNEF 2's Commander later observed:

> Fortunately the first contingents [*from Cyprus*] arrived with rations for 30 days and in many other respects were self-sufficient. . . . Unfortunately many contingents came [*direct from home countries*] poorly equipped, without tents and in some cases with no vehicles and no communications equipment. . . . For these reasons it took several months before some battalions were fully operational and this, of course, reduced the operational capability of the Force.[6]

UNFICYP's thoroughness was a key element in UNEF 2's immediate success (described later), but it must be conceded that the ready availability of the British army's resources was an exceptional circumstance. Prompt and efficient cooperation was received from British logistic units and depot staffs in the SBAs, including the latters' locally engaged Cypriot civilians; all worked cheerfully round the clock and through a weekend until UN needs were satisfied and Operation DOVE was concluded.

As they made their way back from HQ UNFICYP to their contingents the three Commanders, Lieut. Colonels Weingerl (Austria), Kemppainen (Finland) and Onfelt (Sweden), faced major problems demanding rapid action. While handing over operational responsibilities on the island and withdrawing men from scattered UN posts back to base, they had simultaneously to ascertain which individuals were willing to go to Egypt and which were not. Those volunteering to do so had to be organized into a unit that was viable both operationally and logistically, and then split into an advance party and main body, while those remaining had to be allowed sufficient resources to look after themselves and their camps, vehicles and stores. Individuals leaving for Egypt needed to pack their kits, settle personal affairs, receive inoculations and at the same time help in general preparations for this emergency move. Contingent Commanders also needed to consult urgently on many matters with their own government, a process made possible by the national radio links, which each of the three maintained with his own capital.

The speed with which governments concerned reacted was remarkable. As soon as the Security Council Resolution was adopted at 1515hrs (New York time) on 25 October the Secretary General had formally requested the governments of Austria, Finland and Sweden to make their battalion in UNFICYP available for the task in Egypt. This request was received, for example, in Stockholm at midnight (Swedish time), and on his own responsibility the Minister of Defence at once gave provisional agreement. Stockholm immediately issued instructions to Onfelt in Famagusta to prepare for the move and he received these shortly after the warning order telephoned from HQ UNFICYP at 0020hrs. This complementary action through UN and national chains of command dispelled any doubts as to the validity of the respective instructions and was an important element in ensuring that action went forward expeditiously and without misunderstanding. The Swedish Cabinet confirmed the Minister's provisional agreement in the morning; Waldheim in New York and Onfelt in Cyprus were immediately notified. The Austrian and Finnish governments took parallel action and Weingerl and Kemppainen received confirmatory national authority during the morning.

Britain's Ministry of Defence was no less slow to act. HQ BFNE at Episkopi was alerted and the RAF set in hand the concentration at Akrotiri of additional transport aircraft, the resources of the resident squadron, 70 Squadron RAF equipped with C130 Hercules and Argosy aircraft being insufficient to cater for the rapid airlift needed. To this end VC10, Belfast and further C130s of the RAF's 46 Group based in the UK were diverted from other tasks. HQ BFNE activated the RAF and Army Movements staffs in the Western SBA, warned RAF Akrotiri to be ready to sustain a high-intensity transport operation and ensured that army logistic units in the Eastern SBA were ready to meet UNFICYP's calls. The extent to which the latter might be met had to be cleared with London, while uncertainty as to facilities available at Cairo International required two RAF Mobile Air Movements Sections

(MAMS), with requisite cargo-handling equipment, to be readied to fly in with the leading aircraft to ensure rapid turn-round of subsequent arrivals.

In Nicosia Osorio-Tafall and Prem Chand called on Mr Denktash to explain UNFICYP's plans and to secure assurances that the Turkish community would refrain from any action that might disturb the military *status quo* while UNFICYP was at much reduced strength. These were readily forthcoming, possibly because coincidentally the community was celebrating the 50th anniversary of the founding of the Turkish Republic and the religious festival of *Ramadan Bairam*, with the period 26–31 October a holiday during which any deliberate disturbance of the prevailing intercommunal calm would in any case be unpopular. Next they visited Mr Christophides, Cyprus Foreign Minister, both to brief him on developments and to confirm that there was no government objection to the use of Akrotiri rather than Nicosia Airport for the move to Cairo. Christophides at once consulted Makarios who said that in view of the UN's need and the critical situation prevailing along the Suez Canal he would not object to the use of Akrotiri, but that this should not be seen as a precedent.[7] Christophides added that the Archbishop personally confirmed the assurances already given in New York of Greek Cypriot cooperation in avoiding any intercommunal incidents at this time of difficulty for UNFICYP. (The leaders of both communities proved to be as good as their word, demonstrating that they were well able to exercise effective control over their members when they so wished, and not least when they thought the UNFICYP umbrella might be leaky and they might get wet.)

Osorio-Tafall and Prem Chand then called in turn on the Greek and Turkish Ambassadors and briefed them similarly. On their return to UNFICYP HQ the Egyptian Ambassador arrived to stress his government's anxiety to see the earliest possible arrival of the UN troops. Prem Chand explained UNFICYP's plans and timings and the Ambassador expressed surprised delight at the speed with which the Force was acting. Arrangements were made to keep his Embassy informed of the progress of Operation DOVE and thereafter frequent reports were telephoned to it from the UNFICYP JOC. The US and Soviet Embassies and the British High Commission were kept similarly informed; the Israeli Embassy made no request for such reports.

Many other matters were keeping the staff of HQ UNFICYP busy. An early problem was the running of the Kyrenia Road convoys which were an operational commitment of the Finns. The morning convoys on 26 October were cancelled, traffic being diverted on to the long detour via Myrtou, while the afternoon convoys and those on succeeding days were made the responsibility of the Austrian UNCIVPOL[8]; the changes were accepted without demur by both Greek and Turkish authorities. It was necessary, too, to ensure that the Cyprus public as well as the armed forces on each side were left in no doubt as to the reasons for exceptional activity on UNFICYP's part. A Press Release was issued explaining this and LOs were despatched to brief the National Guard and the VPO and convey a personal message from Prem Chand inviting their cooperation to keep the peace 'as we will be quite busy in the next few days'.

Meanwhile the Austrian platoon in Camp UNFICYP had to be relieved of its task of guarding the Czech weapons held in the Camp's compound so that it might return to its Paphos base and prepare to move to Cairo (BRITCON logistic units formed an *ad hoc* platoon to replace it); helicopters had to be tasked for urgent missions connected with the redeployment; road transport to convey troops and stores to Akrotiri had to be organized; signal communications had to be rearranged and all the time a flow of questions and problems, some major and some minor but all of consequence for rapid implementation of our plans, had to be dealt with or resolved as quickly as possible. Finally, written Operation Orders in confirmation of those given orally at the 0800hrs 'O' Group had to be drafted and issued without delay. The multi-national staff of UNFICYP HQ handled all these matters with expedition and remarkable competence.

We had learnt that Lieut. General Ensio Siilasvuo of Finland[9] had been designated commander of the new UNEF, but due to communication difficulties between Cairo and New York he still did not know on the morning of 26 October the terms of the Security Council's mandate. He had no Force HQ, communications resources or supporting staff, apart from UNTSO's Senior Staff Officer, Colonel P. Hogan (Ireland), whom he appointed as UNEF 2's Chief of Staff, and a handful of other UNTSO officers of varying nationalities, whom he similarly pressed into service as staff officers. However, during the morning of 26 October Prem Chand succeeded in speaking by telephone to Siilasvuo in Cairo and told him of the planned despatch of troops from Cyprus. Siilasvuo was delighted to learn that he could expect the first of these that night and undertook to arrange for their reception at Cairo Airport.

This highlighted the need for reliable communications between UNFICYP's HQ and Siilasvuo's. Since the UN Radio system provided only intermittent service (due to atmospheric interference and the need to relay messages via Geneva or Jerusalem, there being no UN Radio direct Nicosia – Cairo link), we proposed that a direct military radio link be established, but this was not feasible due to the lack of resources at the as yet unestablished UNEF 2 Force HQ. Fortunately communications between Nicosia and New York posed no problem and at midday Prem Chand spoke by telephone to Urquhart at UN Headquarters to inform him of the progress of preparations in Cyprus and of his conversation with Siilasvuo. They agreed that a senior UNFICYP officer should fly to Cairo in the leading Operation DOVE aircraft to liaise personally with Siilasvuo before returning to Cyprus to report to us on the situation and UNEF 2's urgent needs. UNFICYP's Deputy Chief of Staff, Colonel Beattie (Canada), was nominated for this mission.

CHAPTER TWENTY-ONE

THE MOVE TO CAIRO

As darkness fell the area in rear of Alpha Dispersal at Akrotiri began to develop into a bedlam of lights, shouts in four languages, plus Scouse and Geordie *[slang terms for Liverpool and Tyneside dialects]*, the grind of vehicle engines, the roar of Hercules and Argosy turbo-fans running-up and the banshee screams of the jet engines of the VC10s. . . . 385 Air Despatch Troop opened up its Movement Control Check Point and Vehicle and Freight Preparation Area. It was now just a question of doing the job!

Major D.M. Bond: 'Friday, B . . . . . Friday', *The Waggoner*
(Journal of the Royal Corps of Transport), January 1974, p. 34.

Learning at 1300 hrs on 26 October, about four hours after the 'O' Group at HQ UNFICYP had dispersed, that the first Royal Air Force VC10 aircraft was due at Akrotiri at 1600hrs and would be followed soon afterwards by additional C130s, the three UNFICYP Contingent advance parties were ordered to leave base camps at 1400hrs for the airfield. They were already on their way when there came a set-back – the Senior Air Staff Officer (SASO) at HQ NEAF telephoned to ask at what time the first aircraft should be positioned at Nicosia Airport. This was an extraordinary question; clearly there was some misunderstanding.

I pointed out that UN Headquarters in New York had told us that Akrotiri was to be the departure airfield (which could not have been done without the British Government's prior consent), that all planning had proceeded on this assumption (as his Command Movements Officer was aware, having attended HQ UNFICYP's 'O' Group), and that the Cyprus government in the person of Makarios himself had no objection to the UN's use of Akrotiri. I added that the resources available at Nicosia Airport to cope with an emergency military move of this nature were altogether inadequate and that, in any case, the advance parties were already on the road to Akrotiri. The SASO agreed to consult the Ministry of Defence in London immediately, while somewhat to their mystification orders were given for the Austrians, Finns and Swedes to halt temporarily at the roadside. At the same time the British High Commission was urged to press the Foreign Office in London for a rapid decision in the light of Makarios's consent for the use of Akrotiri.

This unexpected development was worrying. If RAF Akrotiri and its excellent movements organization were not to be made available, a rapid and difficult switch of plans would be necessary with a serious consequential slowing down of Operation DOVE, for there was no military air movements organization at Nicosia and HQ UNFICYP's small Movement

Control cell did not have the resources to cope. I discussed the problems with General Prem Chand as we waited anxiously for a decision from London. By now it was 1500hrs in Cyprus but only 1300hrs in London and, when HQ BFNE and the High Commission were further pressed, we were told that it was 'lunchtime in Whitehall' with consequential difficulty in reaching the appropriate individuals. As time slipped by our anxiety mounted to the point where there was a temptation, despite the problems, to opt for the use of Nicosia. I advised strongly against this, since there was no doubt that the operation would then quickly become bogged down, even if the first aircraft was despatched with minimal delay. In any case I was convinced that there had been a misunderstanding somewhere and that consent for the use of Akrotiri would be received as soon as Whitehall had recovered from its luncheon interlude. This came at 1600hrs (1400hrs in London), and movement of the three advance parties was resumed at once. The incident had imposed a delay of about one and a half hours, but, had it been necessary to switch to use of Nicosia Airport, the cumulative delay for the whole operation would have been a matter of days, not hours.

On the British side the airlift was directed by HQ BFNE through its Air Transport Operations Centre (ATOC) at Episkopi, where the army representative, Major D.M. Bond, worked hand-in-glove with his RAF colleague, Wing Commander Lim, who, having attended the 'O' Group at HQ UNFICYP, was conversant with our plans. Akrotiri's Station Commander was responsible for implementing the flying operations and for the smooth movement of UN troops through the Station, coordinated by the RAF Movements Squadron assisted by the army's 385 Air Despatch Troop and an Army Air Transport Liaison (ATL) Section. This Section's role was to organize the UN Contingents and their impedimenta into appropriate aircraft loads – vehicles and freight had to be sorted into required priorities, correctly packed, checked for safety, weighed and entered on the manifest, while the men and their personal kit had to be split into 'chalks'[1] and manifests prepared for them too. The hub of this activity was the office of the ATL officer, Captain J.D. Fielden, alongside which an UNFICYP cell manned by Major K.R. Maddocks (Canada) and Major J. Dobie (UK) was established. Loading the aircraft was the RAF's responsibility, with assistance given by the army Air Despatch Troop. As the tempo of Operation DOVE increased additional help for baggage-handling became necessary and UNFICYP's Force Reserve, A Sqn, 16/5th Lancers, was detailed for the task. Meanwhile RAF Akrotiri's full logistic resources were brought into play; incoming UN troops were met and guided to a transit mess where meals were provided, while vehicles, baggage and freight were assembled in marshalling areas. It would have been far beyond the resources of UNFICYP to have provided at Nicosia Airport an organization of comparable professional competence.

The air movement plan required the three advance parties to fly out in the first three available aircraft with main bodies following in the order FINCON, AUSCON, SWEDCON,[2] this order being determined by UNFICYP's limited transport resources for movement to Akrotiri. This task, to which was added that of delivering stores from the Dekhelia depots direct to Akrotiri, required UNFICYP's transport unit, 65 Sqn, Royal Corps of Transport, to be augmented by an *ad hoc* transport platoon found by 2nd Bn, Royal Canadian Regt and assistance by 58 Sqn, Royal Corps of Transport, a non-UN unit stationed in the SBAs. To facilitate road movement UN Military Police signed routes and UNCIVPOL liaised with

CYPOL to ensure unimpeded passage through towns and provided a radio-car to travel with each convoy to maintain contact with HQ UNFICYP.

With the question of the departure airfield resolved and advance parties preparing to emplane, the three main bodies were ordered to move to Akrotiri. The Finnish advance party under Lieut. Colonel Kemppainen was expected to take off at 1915hrs, to be followed at 30 minute intervals by the Swedes and the Austrians. General Prem Chand arrived by helicopter at Akrotiri to bid them farewell only to learn of another set-back – NEARELF's commander, Major General Hew Butler, arrived to say that owing to a shortage of vehicles in British army depots it was unlikely that any vehicles of British origin taken to Cairo could be replaced from British stocks in the short term.[3]

This was a shock because it meant that the incoming UNFICYP reinforcements would find themselves without vehicles, other than the few left with rear parties, unless they brought their own vehicles with them (which was unlikely and in any case contrary to UN policy for standardization in the interests of economy). Since maintenance of UNFICYP's operational capability was a prime concern, Prem Chand immediately decided to reduce from over 100 to 45 the number of vehicles of various types scheduled to be taken to Cairo and the three Contingent Commanders were obliged to make rapid and vexatious changes of plans. Nonetheless, the first C130 aircraft took off from Akrotiri at 2020hrs on 26 October – a mere 18 hours after the Security Council's decision was received by UNFICYP. In it went Kemppainen and his Finns, together with Beattie and the first RAF MAMS; the Swedes and Austrians followed close behind.

As the airlift got under way the British movements staffs found themselves dealing with unaccustomed problems:

> How do you explain to a non-English speaking Finnish volunteer that he has 200lbs too much kit and that his *(radio)* battery requires UK 6TN vent breathers? How can you tell six residents of Kitzbuhel or Salzburg or any alpine village, who only recognize English sufficiently well to hire you a pair of skis, that an armchair is not a tactical load and that a packing case, one of several which it takes 12 men to lift, is not airportable . . . ? Anyway, what is the Tie-Down Scheme number for Haflinger jeeps, a Scania APC, a Volkswagon Minibus, a 'civilian radio-car', a Saab van or any of an assorted number of types of nationally-owned load carriers? How do you talk to three contingents . . . about hazardous cargo when the first time they ever heard of airportability – in any language – was eight minutes ago? How do you make out 18 copies of F/Mov/236 [*passenger manifest*] in Finnish?[4]

Another reported:

> The only common factor amongst the three contingents apart from the blue beret was their lack of previous experience in carrying out a unit air move. . . . Despite this, patience, fortitude and good humour abounded throughout. Long discussions were held over the airportability of the Mess sofas and armchairs of the Swedish Contingent – the ATLO prevailed and they remained in Cyprus; but crates of pickled herring and other northern delicacies, too large and heavy to be manhandled, were included as combat rations.[5]

However, not all the UN troops were as inexperienced in these matters as these accounts imply and it was not surprising that some felt that British organization, procedures and paper-work were excessively elaborate and calculated as much to baffle as to ensure an orderly move to Cairo. The amusing stories that filtered back to HQ UNFICYP were not confined to one side; the UN Contingents could be forgiven if sometimes they thought the British lacking in understanding when they failed to appreciate the place of pickled herring in Nordic diets or the need for items such as armchairs when about to embark on a new UN operation in the Sinai desert where the logistic organization (if it existed at all) was unlikely to produce furniture of any kind for many months. These contingents, all old hands in UN service, had learnt the hard way that it paid to look after yourself.[6] Points of difficulty and potential friction exacerbated by language problems were many and it was to the credit of both the UN troops and the British movements staffs that problems were resolved with good humour in practical and sensible fashion. The flexibility displayed by the RAF in applying its normally strict airportability rules made its own helpful contribution. The Parachute Regiment's teams sent to assist each contingent also played a crucial part:

> They were invaluable, tireless and without exception first class. . . . The operation would have been very difficult without them.[7]

Although a cable had been received during the evening from the Egyptians notifying the flight path into Cairo and giving radio and other technical information, the pilot of the leading C130 aircraft with the Finns and Beattie on board was heading into an uncertain situation, for Cairo International Airport had been closed for some time (except for Soviet aircraft flying in at a rate of up to 100 a day) and a black-out was in force. Nevertheless, he made a safe landing at 2225hrs and was followed within 50 minutes by the two aircraft carrying the Swedish and Austrian advance parties. Beattie described the scene that greeted them:

> As the aircraft doors opened and I went out, I was met by a large group of civilians and military officials and a Press Corps who broke the black-out with their TV lights and flash-bulbs. The message I received was one of great urgency – their strong representation that UN Forces should head for Suez immediately. I replied that time was required to organize the remainder of the aircraft loads, to re-form the contingents in Egypt and to receive orders for their deployment from General Siilasvuo. . . . I then instructed Lieut. Colonel Kemppainen, the Finnish Contingent Commander, to gather his troops as they arrived and to form a secure base in the area which had been allotted to us at a nearby race-track.[8]

Having checked that UNTSO officers would assist in the reception of the incoming UNFICYP troops, Beattie then made for UNTSO Headquarters in Cairo where he met Colonel Hogan, recently appointed by Siilasvuo to be UNEF 2's Chief of Staff. While awaiting the arrival of Siilasvuo (who was telephoning New York from the office of the Egyptian Foreign Minister – the only way he could reach UN Headquarters), they discussed the help that would be arriving from Cyprus and UNEF 2's likely future needs. In the early hours of 27 October Siilasvuo himself arrived and briefed Beattie on the latest developments and the further help that he hoped UNFICYP would provide. Beattie returned to Akrotiri in the first available aircraft and on reaching HQ UNFICYP reported accordingly.

In the meantime the Operation DOVE airlift had proceeded steadily, the main body of the Finns having reached Cairo soon after 0100hrs on 27 October and those of the Swedes and Austrians by 0745hrs. The airlift of men was complemented by sorties carrying vehicles and freight, so that by 2030hrs that day, less than 48 hours after the first warning was received at HQ UNFICYP, some 460 men, 44 vehicles and 44 tons of freight had been delivered to Cairo from Cyprus and UNEF 2 had already achieved initial success. The move of the Finns with all their vehicles and the bulk of their freight had been completed that afternoon, and some had already set out for Suez to interpose themselves between Arab and Jew. Soon afterwards the Swedes headed for Ismailia on a similar mission, while the Austrians were held in reserve in Cairo to carry out essential supporting tasks. The airlift was completed early on 29 October, when a total of some 575 men, 45 vehicles and 170 tons of freight had been delivered from Akrotiri to Cairo. This, however, was to prove only the first phase of Operation DOVE.

During the afternoon of 26 October we had informed New York of UNFICYP's redeployment plan and the action taken to transfer the Austrians, Finns and Swedes to Cairo. We had also raised the problems created with respect to current or imminent troop rotations and suggested that the incoming men for these three contingents be diverted direct to Cairo. New York's reply received early next day, while expressing much satisfaction with UNFICYP's speed of reaction and 'fully approving' the redeployment plan (by then already implemented), stated that some Swedes were already on their way to Cyprus and that the Swedish government wanted these men retained in UNFICYP.[9] It added that the Finns also intended prompt replacement of their men in Cyprus and that the UN Secretariat was discussing with the Austrians what was to be done in respect of their contingent. Of more immediate concern was a warning that, in view of pressure for the early reinforcement of UNEF 2, Waldheim was considering sending UNFICYP's Irish Contingent; our views on this were sought as a matter of urgency.

Having already given thought to the implications of these developments for UNFICYP in both the short and long term and how the situation might be turned to advantage in the context of current plans for reductions in the size and costs of the Force, we pointed out that the small Irish Contingent (only some 140 men strong) would add little in military terms to the capability of UNEF 2, while further reducing operational continuity in UNFICYP. Further, since the Irish was a 'low cost' contingent[10], there was advantage, we suggested, in retaining it in UNFICYP and expanding it to a total of 220 men, while sending to UNEF 2 those Swedes – a 'high cost' contingent – that had remained in Cyprus together with those due shortly. Further, we proposed that the Austrian and Finnish Contingents (also 'high cost') should also not be replaced in UNFICYP and that, instead, the Canadians ('low cost') should be allowed an additional two rifle companies (about 250 more men). UNFICYP would then comprise only four military contingents – Canadian, Danish, Irish and British – of which only the Danes were 'high cost'. This would cut logistic overheads and allow an overall saving of 500–600 men and achieve at a stroke the Phase 2 goal of a 25% reduction in the size of UNFICYP, together with significant savings in its costs. We appreciated the political implications of our proposals, which changed the international balance within UNFICYP, and New York's reaction came as little surprise. There were overriding reasons, we were told, for sending the Irish to join UNEF 2 without delay and the decision could not be reversed; indeed, Waldheim had already informed the Security Council that he was seeking the Irish government's agreement. Pending this, the Contingent was to stand by to move at short notice and the Swedish replacements were to be expected in Cyprus shortly.

A warning order was sent at once to Lieut. Colonel Allen, Commander of the newly arrived Irish 25th Infantry Group, and Phase 2 of Operation DOVE began. With staffs at Force HQ and Akrotiri now well run-in, few problems were anticipated. A Sqn, 16th/5th Lancers, the Force Reserve, was ordered to take over operational responsibility for Larnaca Sector and its Commander, Major A.J. Durie, was sent to liaise with Allen. As before, 1st Bn, Parachute Regt provided advisers to assist the Irish, while the UNFICYP HQ Logistics Staff set about obtaining the necessary additional stores from British stocks in the SBAs. A coordinating meeting was held at HQ UNFICYP at 0830hrs the same morning (28 October), and the ATOC at Episkopi was alerted to the need for the requisite airlift to be available at Akrotiri from 1400hrs. Road transport was put at notice to ferry the Irish from Larnaca to Akrotiri at midday, although it was appreciated that movement could not take place until formal approval was received from Dublin. The hand-over of operational responsibility proceeded in the meantime and at 1400hrs Durie reported that this was complete. HQ BFNE stated that the airlift could begin as soon as UNFICYP wished but, since Dublin's consent was still awaited, it was agreed that aircraft should be held at five hours notice, with the Irish at two hours' notice to leave Larnaca. Urgency gave way to anticlimax when it was learnt that the Irish government required the approval of the Dail (Irish Parliament), which was not due to meet until 30 October – a further 48 hours. So, with Phase 1 of the Operation completed early on 29 October, a pause in the activity at Akrotiri ensued.

On the afternoon of 30 October HQ UNFICYP was informed that the Dail had met and consented to the despatch of the Irish Group to Egypt and its move was set in train at once. The advance party left at 1830hrs, the main body followed at 0100hrs, and all the men, vehicles and freight had arrived in Cairo by afternoon. During the two phases of Operation DOVE the RAF had flown a total of 43 sorties, carrying 730 men, 55 vehicles and 214 tons of freight – all within a period of 70 hours (excluding the pause between phases). The operation had been completed in under six days from the moment that the Security Council had taken its decision to deploy a second UN Emergency Force on the Suez Canal.

CHAPTER TWENTY-TWO

UNEF 2 ESTABLISHED

It was almost a miracle to see how the presence of United Nations troops lessened tension, and the firing, which had continued day and night, suddenly stopped. The number of troops was small but, as so often in a United Nations peacekeeping operation, the numbers were not decisive but the quick deployment, the symbolic presence of the UN flag, the courage and enthusiasm of the troops and the determination of their Commanders have an immediate effect.

Lieut. General E. Siilasvuo, speaking to the Seminar for Nordic UN Personnel, Gurrehus, Denmark, February 1977.

United Nations records confirm that an almost complete ceasefire prevailed from 1300hrs on 27 October 1973, the time at which the first Finns were deployed forward from Cairo. This dramatic change in the situation was wholly due to the speed and efficiency with which troops had been transferred from Cyprus. General Siilasvuo was in no doubt as to the advantages, both operational and logistic, gained by drawing on UNFICYP's resources:

Bringing the troops from nearby Cyprus was, of course, an excellent idea. Had the contingents arrived from far-away home countries, it would have taken several days, maybe a week, before UNEF could have been operational, and in the meantime the military situation would have worsened considerably, making UNEF's task still more difficult. . . .

My instructions to the Contingent Commanders were very short indeed. The basic order given, for instance, to the Commander of the Finnish Contingent was: "Go to Suez and make peace" – nothing else. Fortunately all three Commanders were experienced United Nations officers who knew exactly what they were supposed to do.[1]

Although the number of troops available to him was small[2], Siilasvuo was obliged to retain the Austrians in Cairo to carry out essential supporting tasks until such time as these could be handed over to others; since UNEF 2 still lacked a proper Force HQ, these tasks included the provision of clerks, messengers, signallers, guards and escorts. The Austrians also satisfied other demands such as the provision of road convoys and escorts for the International Red Cross.

The parlous state of the Egyptian Third Army encircled east of Suez and the Canal gave cause for acute concern, especially to the Soviet Union which pressed for immediate action to ease its plight.[3] At a meeting in the early hours of 28 October between Egyptian and Israeli commanders, with Lieut. Colonel Kemppainen present as UNEF 2's representative, a plan was agreed for delivery of urgently needed non-military supplies through Israeli lines to the Egyptians isolated on the Canal's east bank. Since the Israelis would not allow Egyptian truck-drivers to go forward of Egyptian positions west of Suez, UNEF 2 agreed to provide 75 drivers to take over the trucks at that point and drive them through Israeli lines to the Canal's west bank. There, under UN and Red Cross observation, they were to be unloaded for inspection by Israelis to ensure that no warlike material was included before being re-loaded and ferried across the Canal for onward delivery to the beleaguered Egyptians. The first truck, carrying fresh water, crossed the Canal under these ponderous arrangements the same evening and was followed early next morning by others carrying emergency food supplies. It was essential to maintain this flow of relief so long as the Egyptian Third Army remained isolated, but the commitment soon proved too great a drain on UNEF 2's limited resources. In response to a call for help received on 15 November, UNFICYP appealed for volunteers from the Finns and Swedes who had recently reached Cyprus (Britons, Canadians and Danes were ineligible and the Austrian replacements were due in Cyprus only that day). The response was immediate; 40 Finns and 21 Swedes left for Cairo on 17 November and eight Austrians followed; the arrival of these 69 drivers greatly eased UNEF 2's task. (All returned to UNFICYP some two months later, their services by then being no longer needed.[4])

Although the contingents from UNFICYP had been despatched in great haste and with spartan scales of vehicles and equipment, the thorough action taken in the few hours available to ensure that, as far as possible, they would be self-supporting during their first few weeks in Egypt was of critical importance, as Siilasvuo subsequently made clear in an account which military men saw as a telling indictment of the consequences of the *ad hoc* philosophy which for so long was the hallmark of the UN Secretariat's approach to the mounting of peacekeeping operations:

> Improvisation was the only way to arrange in the early days the administrative and logistic support of the Force. Everything had to be started from scratch, makeshift arrangements had to be made for housing and supplying UNEF troops as there was no logistic unit. Communications between Force HQ and the contingents had to be borrowed from Israel and Egypt. . . .
>
> One of the great shortcomings of the early days of UNEF was the lack of preparation by the United Nations for the launching of a new peacekeeping mission and for giving it administrative support. . . . We knew that the UN had a central stores in Pisa but we learned it was empty. . . . The only way to solve the problem was to strip UNTSO and UNFICYP as far as possible. I am afraid we did it so thoroughly that both had difficulties in carrying out their functions.[5]

Indeed, completion of Operation DOVE on 31 October did not bring an end to appeals for further assistance from UNFICYP, whose CAO, George Ryder, working hand-in-glove with the Force's CPLO, Lieut. Colonel Pennell, maintained close touch with his opposite number in Cairo. Requests ranged from medical stores and radio batteries to blankets, camp beds, cookers, UN insignia, maps and additional vehicles and radios; also needed were fresh fruit and vegetables, purchased on the island and flown to Cairo for issue to the men in the desert.

This raised a new question: the future relationship between the two UN Forces and the degree, if any, to which UNFICYP should provide support to UNEF 2. The proximity of Cyprus and the excellence of the British military infrastructure in the SBAs caused apprehension in London that the UK might become inextricably caught up in an open-ended commitment to provide logistic support to UNEF 2. Reflecting these fears, the British authorities at Episkopi made clear that such a commitment could not be accepted. UNFICYP itself had only limited logistic capabilities and it was out of the question for it, too, to shoulder responsibilities in the longer term for the support of UNEF 2. Nonetheless, we appreciated the severe problems facing the latter and were determined to do our utmost to help until such time as the new Force had established its own logistic organization. UNEF 2 achieved its full operational strength of about 7,000 men in February 1974 and, as its logistic organization was built up, calls on UNFICYP's help all but ceased (although it continued to make use from time to time of some facilities in Cyprus, such as the British Service hospitals in the SBAs).

Establishing a new UN Peacekeeping Force is never easy (and UNEF 2 was no exception), but the termination of an operation is usually far more difficult. In this respect UNEF 2 was a notable exception. Its success in bringing peace and stability to the Sinai was such that, after nearly six years of patient duty, its mandate was terminated by common consent on 24 July 1979. Dr Waldheim bestowed this valedictory accolade:

> It was set up urgently in a time of intense international tension and was deployed in a confused and still violent conflict situation. It was remarkably successful in stabilising the ceasefire and implementing successive disengagement agreements. It has assisted the transition from conditions of war to a peace treaty in its area of operations. The Force has been an outstanding peacekeeping operation.[6]

Operation DOVE laid the foundation for this successful outcome. All concerned in the the British Services in the SBAs deserved credit for their part, but UNFICYP's contribution drew the particular admiration of three military critics:

> The results of this crash-action UN operation do great credit to the professionals and non-professionals alike in UNFICYP, from the Force Commander and his senior staff officers down to the junior leaders in the contingents. It is doubtful if it could have gone much better had it been a straightforward move involving a single unit trained for the task. Bearing in mind the circumstances, the limited experience and the extraordinary complications of which the planners had to take account, Operation DOVE does represent a remarkably impressive performance on the part of UNFICYP as a whole, and opens one's eyes to the future potential of UN Forces in terms of quick action deployment and redeployment of resources.[7]

The operation was not especially remarkable in terms of the size of the airlift involved – what distinguished it was the speed and efficiency with which, as a multi-national operation lacking any prior contingency planning, it was organized and implemented. Even the sternest critics of UN Forces were compelled to recognize that a new and valuable flexibility in the employment of these Forces had been demonstrated.

CHAPTER TWENTY-THREE

AFTERMATH IN CYPRUS

Replacements for the Austrian, Finnish and Swedish personnel transferred to UNEF were sent to Cyprus by the governments concerned. . . . As regards the Irish personnel, I have requested the government of Ireland to dispatch additional available troops to the Middle East for service with UNEF rather than to Cyprus. Consequently the Irish infantry group will not be replaced in UNFICYP for the time being.

Report by the UN Secretary General (S/11137, 1 December 1973).

The intercommunal situation in Cyprus remained calm during Operation DOVE, although an anonymous bomb threat telephoned to HQ UNFICYP on 27 October caused mild excitement, and the Turks' disposition to fire guns to mark the start of *Ramadan Bairam* early next morning caused momentary anxiety to those not familiar with the custom. But the sudden and drastic reduction in UNFICYP's front-line strength was a matter for concern and on 27 October, the airlift now well under way, Prem Chand and I each visited different areas of the island to check that the Force's operations were being maintained at an adequate level of efficiency. Although it was clear that troops on the ground were stretched to the limit, no major problems were evident. There was, however, a lack of a local reserve within Paphos District where time, distance and the remoteness of some UN posts did not allow quick reinforcement from elsewhere. The Austrians' rear party in Paphos was instructed to provide an *ad hoc* platoon as a reserve for the new District Commander, Major M.P. Ryan (1st Bn, Parachute Regt.). The problem of a Force Reserve arose on 28 October when A Sqn, 16th/5th Lancers had been ordered to take over Larnaca Sector from the Irish. This was solved by the formation of a second *ad hoc* platoon found by the Finns' rear party located in Kykko Camp, adjacent to Force HQ.

With Operation DOVE completed, attention turned to the composition, organization and deployment of UNFICYP in the longer term. Our initial proposals made on 26 October had been rejected not only because these would have altered the international balance of the Force but, more particularly, because the Secretary General's plan to transfer three contingents to UNEF 2 had been accepted by the governments of Cyprus, Greece and Turkey on his undertaking[1] that all three would be replaced in Cyprus as soon as possible. In the case of the Irish, however, the position was different – the decision to send that contingent had been taken later and was not subject to that undertaking. On 5 November we were informed that, since the Irish Government preferred to provide one full contingent for UNEF

2 rather than a small one in each Force, the Irish Group would not be replaced in UNFICYP 'for the time being' (in the event it was never so replaced), although the Irish LO was to be retained at UNFICYP HQ as a token of continuing Irish participation in the Cyprus operation.

In the meantime replacement of the other three contingents proceeded. The Swedish Contingent was quickly restored to full strength and under its new Commander, Lieut. Colonel B. Medin, reassumed operational responsibility for Famagusta District on 30 October, only four days after the Canadians had taken over temporary control. In the case of the Finns 75 men arrived from Finland on 7/8 November, but some exchanges and adjustments with the Contingent in Egypt were required before Lieut. Colonel Kemppainen and a party of his men were able to return to Cyprus on 11 November (having been relieved by a stand-by battalion sent to Cairo direct from Finland). The Finns resumed operational responsibility for Kyrenia District at once, but the Contingent remained at reduced strength until a further 150 of the original volunteers returned from Egypt on 6 December. That same afternoon, only a few hours after arriving direct from six weeks' arduous duty in the desert, the Finnish Contingent mounted an impeccable parade to mark Finnish Independence Day. Presenting its members with their UN Medals well earned 'In the Service of Peace', General Prem Chand congratulated them on their outstanding contribution to the tasks of the United Nations, both in Cyprus and in Egypt. Those present could not but admire these stalwart men of Finland.

On 15 November the first replacements arrived for the Austrian Contingent, which was restored to full strength a fortnight later, but the future deployment and responsibilities of the the Austrians were settled only after prolonged and tiresome argument. The saga is told here because it illustrates the kind of problems that are liable to beset a UN Force Commander to the detriment of efficient conduct of operations. The difficulties were a consequence of the departure of the Irish, which left a gap to be filled in Larnaca Sector, now looked after temporarily by A Sqn, 16th/5th Lancers, which was required to resume its role as the Force Reserve. Prem Chand had considered for some time that the Austrian Contingent of 275 men was larger than the tasks in Paphos District warranted; further, the location of the Austrians' HQ at Paphos entailed wasted time and expense in travel between it and Force HQ at Nicosia.[2] He accordingly decided to redeploy the Austrians and make them responsible for the whole of Larnaca District. This would relieve the BRITCON battalion of responsibility for the District's Kophinou Sector and allow it instead to take over Paphos District, which together with Limassol District would then become Limassol Zone under overall command of the British battalion commander at Polemidhia Camp, Limassol. This plan had two merits: first, the boundaries of the civil District of Larnaca would then coincide with those of the UN operational District, thus obviating the need for the District's civil authorities to deal with two different UN Contingents; and second, no increases would be required in the strength of any Contingent.

On 7 November the Secretary General cabled his approval of this plan, but this was followed next day by an ominous warning that the Austrian Mission in New York was concerned at the standard of the camp in Larnaca to be taken over from the Irish. For some years the Irish had been housed in the dilapidated Wolfe Tone Camp (originally a chicken farm) on the northern outskirts of Larnaca. Pressure by HQ UNFICYP in 1972 had obliged the Cyprus government to provide a site for a new camp situated south of the town, close to the Salt Lake. Although by no means ideal – it was located on a bare and dusty hill – it was well situated from an operational point of view and accepted by HQ UNFICYP. The government undertook to build a brand-new hutted camp on this site and work began early in 1973. However, progress was slow and by October (in spite, ironically, of help provided by a party of Austrian engineers) the camp, named Innisfree[3] by the Irish, still lacked all but the essentials. It had to be admitted that, perched on its bare hill between the Salt Lake and the sea, exposed to wind and dust and as yet deficient of the trees and shrubs planted later, the camp presented a less than inviting prospect. In sharp contrast the Austrians, who had provided a battalion to UNFICYP for the first time in April 1972, enjoyed occupation of the recently rebuilt Duke Leopold V Camp at Paphos, on which they had lavished time, energy and money in transforming it into something of a showpiece; huts had been turned into comfortable quarters in the Austrian style and the site had been extensively planted with trees and shrubs.[4] The Austrians had seemingly assumed that their battalion could expect to enjoy permanent residence in Paphos District. The decision to move it to Larnaca came as an unwelcome shock.[5]

Their dismay was not lessened when they saw the contrast presented by Innisfree Camp and dissatisfaction was increased when they saw, too, the spartan accommodation which they were to take over from the British unit in the Kophinou Sector of the District.[6] The Austrian Contingent Commander complained to Vienna and the Austrian Minister of Defence, Brig. General Karl Lutgendorf, instructed the Austrian Mission in New York to request Dr Waldheim to reverse Prem Chand's decision. Although this pressure could not be ignored (not least because it was being exerted on an Austrian Secretary General whose known aspiration was to seek election as President of Austria), Waldheim had little choice but to uphold the Force Commander's authority in the matter, since this was clearly stated in Force Regulations:

> The Commander exercises in the field full command authority of the Force. He is operationally responsible for the performance of all functions assigned to the Force by the United Nations, and for the deployment and assignment of troops at the disposal of the Force.[7]

Nonetheless he instructed Prem Chand to defer implementation of the plan until agreement had been obtained from Lutgendorf. We then learnt that Lutgendorf 'was on holiday' and that it would not be possible to secure his agreement for a further two weeks. The situation was ludicrous, but illustrated how a UN Force Commander, notwithstanding the powers formally delegated to him, can be obstructed by troop-contributor governments.

There was no sense in handing back operational responsibility for Paphos District to the Austrian Contingent (now restored to almost full strength) and its men remained inactive in their camps until the pleasure of the Austrian minister was known. Operational tasks were carried out by BRITCON's 5th Royal Inniskilling Dragoon Guards (nicknamed 'The

Skins'), an armoured unit which had taken over in a dismounted infantry role from 1st Bn, Parachute Regt early in November. During this period The Skins had also to take care of the Kophinou Sector and the whole of Limassol District, while A Sqn, 16th/5th Lancers was obliged to remain in Larnaca at the expense of its proper role as the Force Reserve. In due course Lutgendorf's reluctant agreement was given and at the end of November the Austrians left the comforts of Paphos and assumed responsibility for the whole of Larnaca District. The episode had imposed a vexatious and unnecessary delay in the redeployment of UNFICYP, had given rise to some unhappy inter-contingent strains and had demonstrated how narrow national self-interest can hamper efficient conduct of UN peacekeeping operations.

By early December all elements of UNFICYP had settled into their new tasks and the 16th/5th Lancers squadron had resumed its role as the Force Reserve (in which it was relieved on rotation soon afterwards by B Sqn, 4th/7th Dragoon Guards). The first phase of the UNFICYP reduction plan, modified in consequence of Operation DOVE, had been implemented and at the end of 1973 the Force consisted of 2,730 men (including 173 Civilian Police) deployed as follows:

At Nicosia Airport
In Blue Beret Camp
UNFICYP Force HQ – Military Staff (drawn from all contingents).
UN Civilian Staff – SRSG, SPA, Legal Adviser, CAO, Secretariat and UN Radio.
Military Signals (BRITCON and CANCON)
Military Police Company (drawn from all contingents)
BRITCON HQ
CANCON HQ and CANCON logistic base
UNFICYP Medical Centre (AUSCON)

In Camp UNFICYP
Force Logistic Units (BRITCON)

In Gleneagles Camp
Force Reserve – B Sqn, 4th/7th Dragoon Guards, less one troop (BRITCON)

Accommodated with RAF Nicosia
Army Aviation Flight (Sioux helicopters) (BRITCON)
Detachment 84 Sqn, RAF (Whirlwind helicopters) (from NEAF)

Nicosia District
(CANCON) (HQ: Wolseley Barracks, Nicosia)
   2nd Bn, Royal Canadian Regt
   Austrian Civilian Police

Famagusta District
(SWEDCON) (HQ: Carl Gustav Camp, Famagusta)
   51st Swedish UN Battalion
   Swedish Civilian Police

Larnaca District
 (AUSCON) (HQ: Duke Leopold V Camp*, Larnaca)
    4th Austrian UN Battalion
    Swedish Civilian Police (in Larnaca Sector)
    Danish Civilian Police (in Kophinou Sector)

Limassol Zone
(BRITCON) (Zone HQ and District HQ: Polemidhia Camp, Limassol)
    (Paphos District HQ: St Patrick's Camp⁺, Paphos)
    5th Royal Inniskilling Dragoon Guards
    One troop, B Sqn, 4th/7th Dragoon Guards
    Australian Civilian Police

Lefka District
(DANCON) (HQ: Viking Camp, Xeros)
    20th Danish UN Battalion
    Danish Civilian Police

Kyrenia District
(FINCON) (HQ: Kykko Camp, Nicosia)
    20th Finnish UN Battalion
    Austrian Civilian Police

Although by then the second phase of the UNFICYP reduction plan was already under way, the above was the Force's general deployment when crisis erupted in the summer of 1974.

* Name transferred from camp in Paphos to Innisfree Camp
+ Reverted to earlier name on departure of Austrians

PART FOUR

FOOLS BY HEAVENLY COMPULSION

'We make guilty of our disasters the sun, the moon and the stars; as if we were villains by necessity, fools by heavenly compulsion.'

William Shakespeare: *King Lear.*

CHAPTER TWENTY-FOUR

THE TALKING RESUMES

Rightly or wrongly, the Turks are convinced that the Greeks want to achieve *enosis*, and the Greeks on their part are convinced that the desire of the Turks is to ensure *taksim* – partition. These convictions are so strong that they are rapidly transformed into a 'complex', the substance of which is composed of fear, doubt and reciprocal suspicion. It ensures that the smallest and most benign act of State is transformed into an element of *enosis*, and that premises of *taksim* could be found in the most innocent request.

Professor Orhan Aldikacti: *Analysis of the First Phase of the Expanded Intercommunal Talks*, 4 October 1972.

The intercommunal talks, launched in June 1968 in the wake of the Kophinou crisis, had petered out in September 1971, their momentum lost. Positions on some issues had been clarified, but deep divisions, symptomatic of fundamentally different concepts for the nature of the future Cyprus State, remained. Turkish attitudes were dominated by implacable opposition to any proposal that might serve as a springboard to *enosis*, which the Turks were convinced was the Greeks' ultimate target, as the Turkish Cypriot interlocutor, Rauf Denktash, made clear:

> For us the retention of this balance *[assured by the 1960 Constitution]* which gave the Cyprus State its Cypriot character by providing for the cooperation in partnership of the two ethnic communities is, and always has been, very important, because without this balance the Cyprus State becomes, not a Cypriot State, as it should be, but a Greek Cypriot State with the door wide open to *enosis*.[1]

Fear of *enosis*, which the Turkish Cypriots' recent experiences at the hands of the Greeks had done nothing to allay, gave rise to two cardinal demands. First, there must be a degree of physical separation between the two communities, each living in its own designated areas administered autonomously in so far as local government was concerned, a form of what was termed 'functional federation'; otherwise, Denktash argued, continuation of intercommunal friction was inevitable. He was willing to concede (in somewhat vague terms) that at some future date circumstances might allow some unscrambling of the separation of the two communities, but claimed that events had demonstrated that for the time being Greeks and Turks could not live together in either harmony or security. The second demand reflected the Turkish community's even deeper anxiety as to its very existence in the future and its suspicion that the Greek side was not negotiating in good faith for a settlement that would preserve the island's sovereign independence. With Ankara's firm backing, Denktash was adamant that the external guarantees embodied in the 1960 treaties, which Makarios had sought to abrogate, must be retained; it was only these, the Turks believed, that had held the Greeks back from declaration of *enosis* long ago.

Growing dissension within the Greek Cypriot community generated by the anti-Government violence of EOKA-B under Grivas (described in the following chapter) hardened the Turks' attitudes, in particular their claim that the 1960 Constitution had embodied the concept of functional federation. However, Dr Galo Plaza had pointed out in his 1965 Report that, while a federal régime would, indeed, require separation of the communities on a territorial basis, such a basis did not exist, despite the creation of Turkish Cypriot enclaves. The Greeks feared that the Turks' pursuit of a cantonal solution would bring this about.

Faced with these uncompromising attitudes, Glafkos Clerides, the Greek Cypriot negotiator, sought to convince the Turkish side that *enosis* was no longer the objective of Greek Cypriot policy and that his side was committed to a solution of the constitutional problems on the basis of an independent and united Republic of Cyprus. It was the other side, by its demand for the separation of the two communities, that was seeking the destruction of the State and eventual partition of the island; indeed, Clerides charged, the action already taken by the Leadership in creating enclaves was proof positive of the true Turkish purpose. That action, and insistence on future separation under autonomous local authorities, served only as obstacles to realization of an independent sovereign State in which both communities could live together in peace and prosperity.

The kernel of the problem, Clerides declared, lay in the unworkable 1960 Constitution, which by its extreme bi-communal provisions perpetuated and even increased divisions between Greek and Turkish Cypriots, preventing progress towards the truly Cypriot State and nation that should be their common aim. The Treaties of Alliance and Guarantee, he added, had served to exacerbate the situation by affording Turkey a military foothold on the island and a potential cloak of respectability for future intervention in pursuit of partition. Moreover, the demand for autonomous Turkish areas was calculated, he said, to establish a separate Turkish Cypriot identity with a view to bringing about a total divorce between the two communities in anticipation of partition. An independent sovereign Cyprus could only be ensured by the full integration of Greek and Turkish Cypriots under a modified Constitution which, while providing adequate safeguards for the minority, was not rendered unworkable by the excessive entrenched rights imposed on Cyprus at Zurich and in London.

It was deadlock over such fundamental opposing views that had caused the talks to grind to a halt in September 1971. The danger inherent in allowing a vacuum to prevail pointed the need to bring the parties back to the conference table and give the talks fresh impetus. The difficulties encountered (in particular the delay imposed by the discovery of Makarios's clandestine import of Czech weapons early in 1972) frustrated early efforts to this end, so that it was not until June 1972 that talking was resumed under a new formula embodied in an *aide-memoire* put forward the previous October by U Thant (then nearing the end of his tenure as UN Secretary General). With a view to widening participation, U Thant proposed not only that Dr Osorio-Tafall, his Special Representative, should become a participant but also that the Greek and Turkish governments should each appoint a constitutional expert to attend in an advisory capacity.[2] (Their presence could be expected, he thought, to induce less rigidity in the positions of the two Cypriot negotiators and oblige them to re-examine old arguments and justify these before two fresh minds). After lengthy consultations, Dr Waldheim, the new UN Secretary General, informed the Security Council in May 1972 that all the parties, including Greece and Turkey, had agreed to the reactivation of the inter-communal talks on this basis.

After a petty squabble as to whether the venue should be in the Greek or the Turkish quarter of Nicosia, the inaugural session took place on 8 June 1972 on the neutral premises of a UN Other Ranks Club situated on the Green Line.[3] An air of optimism was evident, even if some old Cyprus hands were less than sanguine that the two sides were willing to shift from entrenched positions. Waldheim attended in person and in opening the proceedings reminded those present that the United Nations had been closely involved in the island's problems for more than eight years and that it had a strong interest in carrying its peace-keeping function forward to a settlement of the long-standing differences. His appeal that they should display

> a spirit of forward looking conciliation, a readiness to compromise, and a clear realization that any agreed, peaceful, lasting and just settlement is not only feasible but essential to the welfare of all concerned[4]

was to prove in vain. His sentiments were echoed by Clerides in an anodyne opening state-ment, but the occasion was soured by Denktash, who, disregarding an understanding that known points of controversy were not to be raised at this inaugural session, spoke in terms that provoked sharp Greek Cypriot protest.

This initial bickering did not prevent the talks from proceeding in a generally construc-tive and harmonious fashion. Letters, documents and proposals were exchanged, and the work done by Clerides and Denktash in the earlier talks was scrutinized to identify points of agreement, where these existed, and causes for disagreement where they did not. The presence of the two constitutional experts, who on some matters were able to present a joint opinion, proved valuable. Progress was such that on 1 December 1972 a moderately optimistic Waldheim reported:

> The assistance given by my Special Representative and the two constitutional experts . . . has been constructive and has injected new life into these discussions. Limited progress has been achieved in some areas. Although a number of important issues are still unresolved, the existing difficulties are being approached in a reasonable and earnest manner. It must be realized that it will not be an easy task to find a solution to the long-standing problems of Cyprus, and there are as yet many obstacles on the road to a settlement, not all of them of an intercommunal character. . . . But at least the impasse that had paralysed the talks until last June has been over-come, and both sides have shown a genuine desire to settle their differences through peaceful negotiations.[5]

The rock upon which the earlier talks had foundered – the degree of local autonomy to be allowed to the Turks – remained the major obstacle, it having been accepted that the question of external guarantees would not be a matter for these talks. Since it was understood by both sides that, even where agreement was reached on a specific issue, this would not be binding until such time as agreement was reached on the package as a whole, a settlement continued to be elusive.

It was only later that Clerides disclosed that in his view a settlement had been within reach in December 1972 and that failure to grasp that opportunity had been due to intransigence on the part of Makarios. Clerides believed that the Turkish side had given sufficient ground on the question of local government as to allow the Greek side, without prejudice to its own interests, to compromise on this thorny problem. He had sought to persuade the Archbishop to this view:

> The most important and fatal meeting I had with Makarios occurred on 12th December 1972. It was fatal because had I succeeded in convincing Makarios to accept my point of view, events in Cyprus would have taken an entirely different course. The *coup* would have been avoided, the invasion of Cyprus would not have taken place, and Cyprus would have been spared its devastating effects.[6]

Clerides' advice had the support of both the Greek government and Osorio-Tafall (in the Secretary General's name), but Makarios refused to let him seek a settlement on its basis. This stand strengthened the Athens junta's mistrust of the Archbishop and reinforced not only its view but also that of others in Washington and other Western capitals, that it was Makarios personally that was the obstacle to a settlement in Cyprus. Clerides has written bitterly:

> The decision of Makarios of 12th December 1972 not to compromise, after the concessions the Turkish side had made, sealed his fate and that of Cyprus. The die was cast and the worst followed.[7]

The talks were adjourned between mid-January and mid-March 1973 on account of elections for the offices of President and Vice President,[8] but when they were resumed two fresh complications cast their shadow. First, Clerides sought to resign as Greek Cypriot negotiator, dismayed by the EOKA-B anti-government campaign and the reaction it was provoking within his own community which, he said, was undermining his authority at the conference table. He gave his reasons at a meeting with Makarios in April:

> I emphasized to him that if the violence in the Greek community between EOKA-B and his armed supporters went on, and if the pro-Makarios police elements continued to use violence to contain the violence of EOKA-B, as well as other illegal interrogation methods, the image of Cyprus would be so tarnished internationally that the Turkish demand for separate administration and security would be both understood and supported.[9]

Makarios and Waldheim both appealed to him not to resign and, following a statement from the Greek government reaffirming its policy of securing a peaceful solution of the Cyprus problem through the intercommunal talks, Clerides agreed to continue for the time being.

Controversy concerning the basis upon which agreement for reactivation of the talks had been reached gave rise to the second new complication. It was centred on application of the term 'unitary' to the nature of the future Cyprus State. Waldheim explained:

> It may be recalled that when the intercommunal talks began under the auspices of the Secretary General in the spring of 1968, the Secretary General indicated his understanding, which at the time seemed generally acceptable, that the search for an agreed solution of the Cyprus problem would be based on the concept of an independent, sovereign and unitary State of Cyprus. However, after various problems had arisen in the talks, especially over the issue of local government, certain reservations were voiced by the Turkish Cypriot side concerning the use of the term 'unitary', on the grounds that the parties attached different interpretations to it and that it could therefore lend itself to misunderstanding and even prejudge the nature of the ultimate settlement. In this connection, the Greek Cypriot side continues to regard the idea of a 'unitary' State of Cyprus as essential for the success of the intercommunal talks.[10]

Disappointed that progress was being frustrated by argument on this matter, Waldheim commented with resignation that it was not only the complexity of the problems but also that the words used to define them that served to generate long and difficult debate. The talks made some progress during the second part of 1973, but the degree of local autonomy to be allowed to the Turkish Cypriots remained the main stumbling-block. Waldheim (who had visited Nicosia briefly in August) reported cautiously at the end of the year:

> The success of the intercommunal talks cannot as yet be taken for granted, although at the present juncture the Special Representative *[Osorio-Tafall]* feels that there are no insurmountable obstacles which would prevent a constitutional accommodation from being reached between the Greek Cypriots and the Turkish Cypriots. One of the main difficulties would still appear to be the mutual suspicion and mistrust of the two communities.[11]

Meanwhile, as it became ever more apparent that the Makarios administration no longer enjoyed the support of Athens, so did the Turks become ever more intransigent, as demonstrated by Denktash's tendency to shift his ground, to reopen old arguments and generally to prevaricate. This lack of progress and a seeming absence of political will to compromise gave rise to cynicism in Cyprus and to irritation abroad, not least among those who bore the burden of maintaining UNFICYP and who after ten years could still detect no light at the end of the tunnel.

(At informal 'in-house' reviews of the situation Osorio-Tafall, Prem Chand, Miles and I, impatient at the lack of vision being displayed, sometimes speculated that partition might be the only solution. However, when tempted in that direction, we had to remind ourselves that this would necessitate an exchange of populations, with the transfer, possibly forcibly, of some 200,000 Greek Cypriots to make way for less than half that number of Turkish Cypriots in an area of their own in the island's north. Of course, we said, this could never seriously be considered, not least because it would constitute an outrageous violation of all for which the United Nations stood. Ironically this was to be the very solution imposed within months under the military boot of Turkey.)

The talks continued in desultory fashion into 1974 with no settlement imminent, although not without some optimism that a package might eventually be agreed allowing the Turks a degree of local autonomy in exchange for surrender of some of their entrenched constitutional rights. The optimism was not long-lasting; a new and serious set-back occurred when Turkey announced an apparent major change of policy by declaring that a federal solution was best for Cyprus. In March Prime Minister Ecevit stated unequivocally:

> The Turkish government will exert every effort to secure a peaceful and lasting solution to the problem within the framework of an independent and federal State. On this issue there is no reason for people of goodwill to have any suspicion about our intentions.[12]

The effect, however, was exactly that: Greek Cypriot reaction was angry and immediate. The statement was seen as a volte-face by the Turks and on 2 April 1974 the talks were abruptly adjourned *sine die*. Declaring that Ecevit's statement cut the ground from under the talks, Clerides demanded clarification from Denktash. For good measure he affirmed that on no account would the Greek Cypriots accept partitionist, federalist, cantonal or other solutions which constituted the creation of a State within a State. Denktash replied that there was no change in Turkish policy, it was merely that in a State like Cyprus, where the nationalism of the two communities was so deep but the need for coexistence unavoidable, the concept of federalism was consistent with progress towards the eventual realization of a common Cypriot nation. Turkey believed that this was the sensible direction in which to proceed and (as Ecevit had stated) did not involve a physical division of the island. In the exercise of his good offices once again, Waldheim despatched his Under-Secretary-General for Special Political Affairs, Dr Roberto Guyer, to Nicosia, Ankara and Athens to overcome the impasse. With all professing support for early resumption of the talks, Osorio-Tafall was instructed to explore how this might be achieved. His skill was demonstrated by an announcement that the talks would be reconvened in early June on precisely the same basis that had governed them before abrupt adjournment two months earlier. In reality the problem had merely been swept under the carpet: the Greek Cypriots and Athens held that the talks were continuing on an agreed understanding that a settlement was being sought within the concept of an independent, sovereign and unitary State, whereas the Turkish Cypriots and Ankara remained insistent that a unitary State, as understood by the Greek side, had never been an agreed basis for reactivation of the talks. A main prop of the negotiations had been knocked away.

Osorio-Tafall's success in bringing the parties back to the table marked the end of his term as Special Representative. Now past his 70th birthday, he retired from UN service begun some 26 years earlier. In his seven years in Cyprus he had made an outstanding contribution to the UN's perseverance in seeking a solution to the island's complex problems, making many friends in the process and winning wide respect. A ceremonial Guard of Honour, drawn from all UN Contingents, was paraded for his departure on 26 June 1974. His wise counsel, long experience and robust commonsense, not to mention his energy, humour and shrewd judgement, were to be greatly missed, especially at the UN Force's Headquarters, when Nemesis struck Cyprus only three weeks later. His successor, Mr Luis Weckman-Munoz of Mexico (who remained in the post until October 1975) arrived in Nicosia on 1 July, which did not allow him to play any substantial part in the intercommunal talks before these withered in the events of the next few weeks. There had been two meetings during June, when the two constitutional advisers had been asked to continue to wrestle with the intractable problem of local government but at which no new momentum was evident. Weckman-Munoz attended a third on 9 July which proved to be the last; the next, scheduled for 16 July, was overtaken by events.

Was there ever any real prospect that the reactivated talks might succeed? Agreement had been reached during the two years on a majority of points – the obstacle to an overall settlement had been the question of local government. It has become clear since that, so long as Makarios adamantly refused to contemplate a compromise on this crucial issue as advocated by Clerides in December 1972, a successful outcome was unlikely. At heart lay the deep lack of trust between the communities. It was all very well, the Turks argued, for Clerides and Athens to protest that it was Greek policy to achieve a sovereign and independent Cyprus, but such protestations rang hollow against Makarios's frequent declarations of his adherence to the dream of *enosis*. Even as the reactivated talks were proceeding the Archbishop had declared,

> I have struggled for the union of Cyprus with Greece and *enosis* will always be my deep national aspiration, as it is the aspiration of all Greek Cypriots. My national creed has never changed and my career as a national leader has shown no inconsistency or contradiction . . . .[13]

No matter that Makarios had been compelled by the 1967 Kophinou crisis to recognize that, so long as the Turks were opposed, *enosis* was unattainable without risk of simultaneous *taksim*, or that he was known to have little taste for the military dictatorship in Athens – his statements served only to fuel Turkish mistrust. For their part the Greek Cypriots were convinced that the Turks remained intent on a settlement that would open the way to eventual partition, a belief that was given new force by Ecevit's advocacy of a federal solution. In the face of such deep-seated suspicions on both sides reconciliation of the opposing positions was all but impossible. With hindsight, Cypriots of both communities were soon to regret the lost opportunity, fleeting though it may have been.

Outside Cyprus there was general support for direct negotiations between the island's two communities, even though there were few illusions as to the degree to which Ankara called the Turkish Cypriot tune. Notwithstanding a disposition to abstain from obvious meddling, external pressures were not absent, especially where the two superpowers were concerned. The United States was anxious to secure a settlement that would afford stability and cohesion to NATO's southern flank and it was no secret that the Americans came increasingly to see the Archbishop as an obstacle; few tears were likely to be shed in Washington were he to go. The Soviet Union, on the other hand, was bent on a settlement that would ensure an independent non-aligned Cyprus[14] and prevent annexation by either Greece or Turkey, thus incorporating the island into the NATO camp. Otherwise neither the

Americans nor the Russians seemed much concerned with the complexities of the Cypriots' constitutional quarrels. While the cohesion of NATO's southern flank was a prime interest for Britain, too, there was an added national concern: the security and proper functioning of its two SBAs. British policy was governed by the need not to prejudice the latter by antagonizing any of the parties, while supporting the Secretary General in his pursuit of a settlement through the medium of the intercommunal talks.

For his part Waldheim saw the intercommunal process as the only practicable way to a settlement and he and his senior officials in New York, ably assisted by Osorio-Tafall in Nicosia, worked with persistence and patience to help it forward. Although adhering to the understanding that had prevailed at the outset that a solution was to be sought on the basis of an independent, sovereign and unitary State, both Waldheim and Osorio-Tafall realized the need for some flexibility in the application of this formula. It was their general view that the basis for a future constitution should be:

> A unitary State with bi-communal participation and a degree of communal local government and autonomy not incompatible with the concept of a unitary State.[15]

Osorio-Tafall's fertile mind had been active in devising compromises that both sides might have accepted but for their mutual mistrust. His impartiality was not doubted but he made little secret that in his view it was for the Greek Cypriots, as the stronger and more prosperous majority, to display the generosity and flexibility that it was difficult for the weaker Turkish Cypriot minority to show. This was not an argument that commended itself to the Greeks, who, lacking his wisdom and breadth of vision, adhered stubbornly to their conviction that democracy required that the minority should not dictate to the majority. Since the Turks never accepted that this argument was relevant to the Cyprus situation, the Greek attitude was both futile and counter-productive. In July 1974 it became irrelevant.

CHAPTER TWENTY-FIVE

GRIVAS – THE THIRD AND FINAL ROUND

Nobody can deprive General Grivas of the right to offer his services to Cyprus. But he has no right to resort to lawlessness.

President Makarios, 29 October 1971.[1]

Now aged 72, Lieut. General Georgios Grivas had languished under house-arrest in Athens ever since his expulsion from Cyprus in November 1967. He returned to the island at the end of August 1971 to make his third and final bid to win *enosis*. Accompanied by his second-in-command, Major George Karousos, he landed clandestinely from a fishing boat and went into hiding. It was put about that he had 'escaped', but at the time few believed that he could have returned without the connivance, at least, of the Athens Colonels. Whether true or not[2], the return of Grivas gave a malign new twist to the situation by creating dissension and violence within the Greek Cypriot community, which in turn caused rising concern among the Turkish Cypriots and hindered progress towards a settlement through the intercommunal talks.

His years of exile in Athens had enhanced the legendary standing of Grivas among Greek Cypriots of all political leanings, and the Archbishop understood well that it was necessary to treat his old comrade-in-arms with a degree of respect and restraint. For his part, steeped as he was in his EOKA past and belief in the success achieved then by resort to violence, Grivas was ready to adopt similar tactics again, not recognizing that a very different situation confronted him; then it had been a fight against an alien colonial power, now it was a struggle against a popularly elected and charismatic Greek Cypriot leader who enjoyed over-whelming support within his community. There was, nevertheless, no dearth of former members of the old EOKA gangs and other malcontents (mostly on the extreme right) who remained obdurately set on winning *enosis* – the goal of their hero Grivas. They were angered by what they saw as Makarios's betrayal of Hellenism, demonstrated in his failure, despite fine words, actively to pursue *enosis*, and his ill-concealed antipathy to 'the national centre', Athens and its military dictatorship. It was these sympathizers who rallied to Grivas' banner and whom he recruited into a second clandestine terror organization, known as EOKA-B.

In Cyprus little remains secret for long, and the activities of Grivas and his henchmen were soon known to the Archbishop, who as early as October 1971 warned:

The Government has enough information and knows many details about this illegal activity, which can serve no national purpose except the partitionist plans of the Turks. Those who believe that it is possible to carry out a national struggle for the achievement of *enosis* through armed groups and hide-outs by far exceed all limits of seriousness. Against whom will the groups being formed in the name of General Grivas turn their weapons? Against the government or organs of the State or Greek citizens. And probably against Turks. But no matter what their targets will be, in the final analysis the grim reality will be this: Cyprus will suffer the blows. The national cause of the Greek Cypriot people will receive the injuries. The armed groups will become allies of the enemies of Cyprus. Those plotting against the territorial integrity of our island will find an unexpected ally.[3]

Adding that, if Grivas wished to pursue *enosis*, he should do so through the accepted democratic process by openly seeking the electorate's mandate, Makarios concluded:

The armed groups being formed in the name of the General can only cause national damage. And I am very much afraid that illegal activity may result *inter alia* in illegal reactions. Where then are we leading to? To civil strife and self-destruction. And the enemies of Cyprus will rejoice, because in this way their sinister plans against the island will be promoted towards their implementation.[4]

Prophetic words, indeed!

In December 1971 Grivas demanded that Clerides acknowledge that *enosis* was the only solution for Cyprus and resign as negotiator, because the talks were not being conducted to that end. Clerides refused to do so (pointing out that continuation of the talks had the formal support of the Athens government). Three months later Makarios met Grivas in person in an attempt to convince him that the policy of the Athens junta would lead only to a settlement that was contrary to the Greek Cypriot interest. In this he failed and Grivas then demanded that Makarios resign as President and retire from the political scene, a demand the Archbishop dismissed with disdain. Twice rebuffed and realizing that Makarios had no intention of yielding to the threat posed by EOKA-B, Grivas resorted to violence. This grew in intensity throughout 1972 and reached a peak the following year. Attacks were made on police stations (some were destroyed and the weapons in them stolen), pro-government newspaper offices were bombed, cars were set alight and other acts of intimidation against government supporters were carried out. Further, some government employees, in particular schoolteachers and policemen, were suborned. This latter action was shrewdly calculated, for CYPOL became demoralized and ineffective in countering EOKA-B's terror tactics. Not willing to remain passive, some government supporters took matters into their own hands by banding together to take retaliatory action. These people, dubbed 'para-State groups' by the local press, were drawn from the ranks of AKEL and supporters of Dr Vassos Lyssarides.[5] Between them these groups and EOKA-B created what Makarios euphemistically termed 'a situation of anomaly'. The result was mounting anxiety on the Turkish side and a hardening of its stand in the intercommunal negotiations.

Although not intercommunal in nature, the violence was of concern to UNFICYP, not only because of the sense of insecurity that it generated among the Turkish community but also on other counts. It was an obstacle to progress in securing military deconfrontation and UN Force reductions, caused both communities to strengthen their military and police forces, and led to changes in the military *status quo* more generally. UNFICYP accordingly monitored events within the Greek community closely[6] and quickly investigated reports of bombing, shooting or other violent incidents in order to establish that there were no direct intercommunal implications. CYPOL sometimes resented what they saw as interference in incidents that they claimed had nothing to do with the UN Force's mandate, but tactful investigation by UNCIVPOL officers usually elicited the confirmation required and allowed reassurances to be conveyed to the Leadership without delay.

Makarios was not slow to organize counter-measures. Policemen and other government servants whose loyalty was suspect or who were thought to have been intimidated were dismissed. More importantly, having long recognized that in the last resort he could not rely on the loyalty of the Athens-dominated National Guard, he gave priority to building up a well-armed para-military counter-force loyal to him personally, with the mobility and communications necessary to ensure rapid reaction to information gained by his own formidably effective intelligence network. It was to this end that he had organized the clandestine import of weapons in early 1972, the quantity and variety of which had so alarmed not only the Turks but also the Athens junta and its officers in the National Guard. The taking into UNFICYP custody of these weapons had been a set-back for the Archbishop, but he did not allow it to frustrate his plans for long. Evidently other sources of supply were not difficult to find, and he set about the expansion of the small 160 man Police Tactical Reserve Unit (TRU)[7] and its conversion into an elite paramilitary unit of about 600 men under his personal operational control. Recruits were selected with care, emphasis being placed less on educational standards normally demanded for entry to the police service than on loyalty to the Archbishop personally. These men were tough, well able to stand up to the EOKA-B fanatics and play them at their own game; they wore military-style uniform, possessed modern small arms and support weapons, had good radio communications and were equipped with appropriate vehicles.[8] The unit was commanded by Major Pantazis Pandelakis who was answerable, not to Mr Antoniou, the CYPOL commander, but direct to the Archbishop and officers of his personal guard.

The TRU soon proved an effective response to EOKA-B, against which it scored increasing success, but its overt military character gave much concern to the Leadership, which protested that expansion and re-equipment of the TRU constituted a serious breach of the military *status quo*. In its turn UNFICYP expressed concern to the government, on whose behalf Mr Anastassiou, Director General of the Ministry of the Interior, gave repeated assurances that the Turks had nothing to fear from the TRU since its activities were directed exclusively against anti-government factions within the Greek community. The expansion and re-equipment of the TRU nonetheless posed a dilemma for UNFICYP. It could not be denied that they constituted a change in the military *status quo*, to which in normal circumstances UNFICYP would have strongly opposed, but circumstances were not normal; the government was confronted by a serious internal challenge to its authority, which neither the National Guard nor the ordinary police force could be relied upon to meet. The government could not be expected to remain passive or to surrender its only effective counter, the TRU, merely because in the intercommunal context its existence breached the military *status quo*.[9] We appreciated the Government's problems, but were obliged to point out that, so long as the TRU was retained in its enlarged para-military form, it was difficult for us to persuade the Turks for their part to refrain from changes in the *status quo* to which the Greeks objected.

As the violence within the Greek community escalated during 1973, we kept the balance as best we could by urging the government to reduce the TRU to its former state at the earliest opportunity while doing our utmost to reassure the Leadership and discourage any action that might give the government an excuse for not doing so. A setback occurred in January 1974 when the TRU was deployed in an intercommunal situation in Limassol. Anastassiou conceded that an error had been made and assured UNFICYP that it would not be repeated; this assurance was honoured. (The government's undertaking that the TRU would be re-absorbed into the ordinary police force as soon as the security situation allowed was overtaken by events.)

An election for the office of President became due in February 1973 and Makarios challenged Grivas to stand for office against him. It was a challenge that Grivas declined, recognizing that the outcome would be public and humiliating defeat, stripping his campaign of all credibility. Makarios proved to be the sole candidate and, accepting re-election at a mass rally in Nicosia, he voiced scathing criticism of Grivas' fear of the democratic process:

> Those disagreeing with the handling of the problem ought to have asked the people to entrust to them the responsibilities, and the Presidential election provided this opportunity. Their non-participation in the election betrays weakness. They know that they do not enjoy the people's confidence. . . . The people speak today and give their verdict. They condemn violence and terrorism. They condemn the unlawful armed men, the bomb-throwers, the masked men, those unconsciously working for fratricidal disaster. But the people express their will in a positive manner also. The people desire concord, coordination of forces, smooth political developments. The people desire, particularly in the present conditions, a solid internal front. And unity of the internal front does not mean absence of opposition. Opposition is desirable. But an opposition following democratic principles and not a catalytic policy.[10]

Nonetheless Makarios extended peace-feelers to Grivas (while at the same time quietly purging CYPOL of some 100 officers). He knew the general's whereabouts in Limassol but made no attempt to apprehend him, appreciating that this would merely create new problems. Grivas, for his part, eschewed the use of violence against the person of the Archbishop, much as he had come to dislike and distrust him. Innate respect for the Church, grudging admiration for Makarios's stand against the Athens junta in its apparent readiness to sacrifice the unity of Cyprus in order to achieve an agreement with Turkey and a first-hand awareness of the Archbishop's place in the hearts of most Greek Cypriots restrained him from going that far. He was ready to harass Makarios to the limit but not to sanction action against his person that might precipitate a collapse within the Greek Cypriot community at a time when it was facing the Turkish challenge.[11]

Grivas and his EOKA-B groups were dependent for much of their practical support on mainland Greek officers in the National Guard (which was subjected to an overdue shake-up to improve training and discipline following the arrival in August 1973 of a new Commander, Lieut. General G. Denizis). The Greek officers under the overall control of KYP , the Greek Central Intelligence Agency, were the channel through which arms, money and advice on organization and training reached EOKA-B. Liaison officers were provided to the Grivas gangs in each District and members of the latter were reportedly sometimes given safe refuge in National Guard camps. Nevertheless the old general tended to be his own man and was not disposed blindly to follow the dictates of others. As realization grew of the junta's true purpose, a settlement with Turkey at Cyprus's expense, he became increasingly wary of orders emanating from Athens. It was yet another paradox, such as only Cyprus provides, that so long as he was alive on the island Grivas served as a brake on more extreme measures sought by the Greek Colonels to further their own designs.

Meanwhile events were not standing still in Athens. Colonel Papadopoulos, now President of the Greek Republic, advocated moderation towards Makarios by appealing to Grivas to call off the violence and lend support for the intercommunal talks. His appeal did not altogether ring true (the more militant members of the junta were not pleased) and student riots in Athens in November 1973, which were suppressed with utmost severity, put paid to the moderation represented by Papadopoulos. He was ousted and his place taken by General Phaedon Gizikis who proved to be little more than a figurehead; real power rested with an even more extreme and politically inexperienced group of officers dominated by Brig. General Demetrios Ioannides, a sinister *eminence grise* who derived his hold over others from his nominal post as head of the military police. In Cyprus EOKA-B's campaign was achieving wide publicity but when the smoke of bombings and other incidents drifted clear its impact was seen to be more dramatic than real. Ioannides and his colleagues in Athens, impatient of Grivas' lack of success, looked for more ruthless action to bring Makarios to heel.

During the first half of 1973 UNFICYP had recorded over 100 incidents involving the use of explosives and some 35 in which shooting had taken place. Buildings and vehicles were destroyed and 59 police stations were either raided or blown up, although surprisingly few personal injuries were inflicted. The violence abated somewhat during the second half of the year, but in December and in January 1974 there was a marked resurgence, reflecting the advent of the more extreme régime in Athens. However, the EOKA-B campaign was making little impression on Makarios, whose resolve was undiminished and who was hitting back with increasing success through the TRU and by other measures. Ioannides and his colleagues, who had not shrunk from brutal repressive measures at home, were unlikely to be inhibited in the methods they adopted to rid themselves of the unyielding Archbishop. Grivas was seen as a brake on extreme action to this end, but he did not remain so for long.

The general was now 75 years old and not in good health. The Athens junta can have shed few tears on learning that he had died in Cyprus on 28 January 1974 (rumours that he was poisoned by Greek officers seem untrue[12]). His funeral took place in Limassol two days later after unseemly wrangles as to whether or not his corpse should be returned to the mother-land for interment. The Archbishop offered to officiate, but the offer was angrily rejected by EOKA-B. The ceremony was an emotional occasion attended by a large crowd that included EOKA-B men in uniform, two of the unfrocked Bishops and even a smattering of government officials. Nicos Sampson, proprietor of the anti-Government newspaper *Makhi* (*Combat*) and a notorious killer of the earlier EOKA days (and who within six months was to spring into momentary prominence in the improbable role of President of Cyprus), draped himself in a Greek flag and, springing to the platform, promised to keep alive 'the pure flame of *enosis*' and cried, 'We will avenge you, Dighenis!'

In pursuit of his dream of *enosis* Georgios Grivas had three times inflicted violence and death on the peoples of Cyprus. He failed each time to achieve that dream yet, paradoxically, he remains a hero in the Greek popular mind. How will history judge him? A fellow country-man has given this verdict:

> In reality Grivas's political influence in both Greece and Cyprus was nil. He was a great organ-izer, a most skilled guerilla fighter, but politically he was always unsuccessful or, at least, negative. The record of his last years in Cyprus shows that he was incapable of achieving anything, and all he could do was to prevent and delay. It is still premature in the circumstances to prejudge the career and achievement of George Grivas. It can be said only that he was a single-minded, ruthless and honest patriot.[13]

His death brought a lull in the violence while a struggle for future control of EOKA-B took place, but the respite was only temporary. The departure of Grivas from the Cyprus stage began the final countdown in the bitter battle of wills between Makarios and the hostile Colonels in Athens:

> That funeral rally was to become a green light for both the régime in Athens and agents in Cyprus to plot the downfall of Makarios. It would culminate in a stunning series of events which plunged not only Cyprus, Greece and Turkey but also the United States, Great Britain and the Soviet Union into a serious crisis in the Eastern Mediterranean.[14]

CHAPTER TWENTY-SIX

TO LABOUR AND TO WAIT

Let us, then, be up and doing,
With a heart for any fate;
Still achieving, still pursuing,
Learn to labour and to wait.
H.W. Longfellow: *A Psalm of Life*.

The reactivated intercommunal talks and EOKA-B's anti-government campaign formed the backdrop for UNFICYP's peacekeeping between June 1972 and July 1974. In December 1972 the Secretary General informed the Security Council that

> UNFICYP will continue to exert its best efforts to assist in the maintenance of quiet in the island and to promote deconfrontation and normalisation of conditions wherever possible. While the intercommunal talks are in progress, UNFICYP will have special responsibility to assist in finding peaceful solutions to the problems that may affect intercommunal relationships and, in particular, to ensure that the military *status quo* is maintained and that neither side gains a unilateral advantage over the other.[1]

Preoccupation with the minutiae of the Force's day-to-day activities sometimes made it difficult to see the wood for the trees, but none in UNFICYP was in doubt that the overriding priority was to maintain a climate of intercommunal calm conducive to progress in the talks. Arguments over the military *status quo*, economic, agricultural and water disputes, Turkish troop rotations, Operation DOVE, UN Force reductions, de-confrontation, clandestine arms imports and all the other matters already described ensured that all ranks were kept fully occupied. It was a period that was coloured by two further factors – the steadily rising tide of economic prosperity, especially evident on the Greek side, and the severe drought that prevailed during the winter of 1972 and throughout the following year.

Now and again other unexpected events added to the load. One such was the tragedy of a civil aircraft disaster on 29 January 1973 when just after dark an Ilyushin of Egyptian Airways on a flight from Cairo to Nicosia crashed high on the Pendadhaktylos mountains as it made its final approach; all 38 persons on board were killed. As radio contact with the aircraft was lost and a crash suspected, the JOC at HQ UNFICYP was alerted. The National Guard and CYPOL were trying to find the site of the crash, presumed to be in the mountains, and a Finnish search party led by Lieut. Colonel Kallio, the Contingent Commander, set out to help. In spite of darkness and difficult terrain they reached the scene, where daylight revealed the full horror – bodies had been hurled over a wide area and the aircraft wreckage was a tangled burnt-out mass lying at the foot of the sheer rock face into which it had flown. UNFICYP helped in the grim task of recovering corpses and bringing them to Nicosia for the difficult task of identification. The disaster touched the UN Force closely, for three of the dead were its members returning from a few days leave in Egypt.

It also touched UNFICYP in a quite different way. As Kallio and his Finns were struggling to reach the scene, I had gone to the JOC to monitor developments and was dismayed by the sight that met me. The room was full of people, some trying to make themselves heard on radios or telephones in a variety of languages above a babble of conversation, and some just curious spectators; no one seemed in overall control, radio and telephone hand-sets were being passed to and fro in a tangle of cables and papers were strewn about in disorder. Messages and requests for information were coming in from all sides: the Joint Air Traffic Control (JATC) at the airport, the National Guard and CYPOL, Kallio's search party, UN OPs, diplomats in Nicosia, HQ BFNE at Episkopi and press correspondents. The JOC seemed overwhelmed by the pace and pressure and it was difficult to elicit any coherent picture of what was happening. This state of affairs prevailed only for a relatively brief period in the immediate aftermath of the disaster, but was enough to cause serious concern. It was the first time since joining the Force six months earlier that I had seen the JOC, UNFICYP's nerve centre, under such pressure. That it had been found wanting was all too apparent and I was far from confident of its ability to handle an acute operational crisis, should this come.

The need for a radical reorganization was clear. An elaborate and expensively equipped Operations Centre could not be contemplated, not only because the necessary funds were not available but also because such a Centre was inconsistent with the temporary nature of the UNFICYP and the limitation of its six-month mandate. Nevertheless a pragmatic plan was worked out and implemented at minimum expense under the direction of a new Chief Operations Officer (COO), Lieut. Colonel Clausen (Austria), with expert advice from the Force Signals Officer (FSO), Major Cathcart (UK). But for this, it is difficult to see how UNFICYP HQ could have coped under the extreme operational pressures which prevailed for weeks, not hours, during the crisis of July and August 1974. A lesson from the disaster had been learnt just in time.

During the 1970s Arab terrorism directed against Israeli interests was endemic in some countries and it was remarkable that Cyprus, situated so close to the Middle East and so readily accessible, seemed generally to be immune; there was, perhaps, a tacit understanding that the Cypriots had troubles enough of their own and should be spared the quarrels of others. For its part the Cyprus government tolerated the presence of Arabs and Israelis so long as they abstained from terrorist activity against each other, but there were exceptions. In January 1973 an Arab 'businessman' was killed by an 'accidental' explosion under his bed in a Nicosia hotel[2] and three months later an attempt was made on the life of the Israeli Ambassador, Mr Rahamin Timor. Serious though it was, the latter incident was not lacking in a degree of farce. Four Arabs had driven to the block of flats in Nicosia housing the Ambassador on the second floor, shot the guard and placed an explosive charge that damaged the ground-floor flats. Mr Timor had left a few minutes earlier and the flat was only slightly damaged, but the explosion had severely damaged the Arabs' getaway car and alerted CYPOL, who after a brief gunfight arrested all four. Meanwhile another Arab group mounted in two vehicles was attempting to hijack an Israeli aircraft at the airport. The alert CYPOL opened fire and an Israeli security guard on the aircraft joined in, hitting all three Arabs in the first vehicle; the second crashed into a set of gates and its two occupants were captured by CYPOL. A total of nine Arabs had taken part in the venture; one was killed and the other eight were arrested, tried and subsequently convicted.

The incident had demonstrated that for all EOKA-B's campaign of intimidation there were still efficient and determined elements in CYPOL. Other points of interest emerged: some 22 kilos of explosives found in one of the vehicles proved to have been stolen from a Yugoslav firm then building the new harbour at Limassol, disposing of earlier suspicions that EOKA-B had been responsible for the theft. Makarios publicly deplored the incident and urged both Arabs and Israelis not to spread their fight to the island; his words were heeded and there were no repetitions.[3] For UNFICYP it had been a matter of monitoring events in order to be able to reassure Turkish Cypriots that there were no intercommunal implications. On an island where rumour flourished, this was of no small importance.

The intercommunal calm prevailing at this period allowed UNFICYP to devote increased attention to the third of its tasks – to contribute to a return to normal conditions. Problems related to the construction of new buildings in the vicinity of the Green Line in Nicosia offered scope in this respect. So long as buildings were not on the very Line itself or did not have an obvious military purpose, UNFICYP adopted a relaxed attitude, in the belief that capital investments of this nature were a disincentive to renewed intercommunal violence in which the buildings concerned might be damaged or destroyed. But the Leadership objected to the addition of further floors to the Ledra Palace Hotel overlooking the Turkish quarter and counter-protests came from the government concerning new buildings on the Turkish side, such as a block of apartments overlooking the Green Line near the Irish Bridge across the Pedhieos River. Each alleged that the other's buildings had a military purpose and breached the military *status quo*, while denying any such purpose in respect of its own; UNFICYP's response was that, if building on one side was to be halted, so then must that on the other. Neither accepted this proposition and work continued without convincing evidence of genuine concern on the part of either. It was difficult not to suspect that each was intent merely on using UNFICYP to obstruct the other's economic progress.

The need for physical intervention by UNFICYP in such cases was rare, but one such occasion arose in September 1973, when a Turkish Cypriot bank manager decided to build himself a house right on the Green Line. This was at a sensitive and disputed point on the Line and the National Guard protested that it was a Turkish ruse to move the Line forward and establish a military strongpoint on it. The matter gave rise to mounting tension and a threat of action by the National Guard. When the the Leadership professed not to have the authority to halt construction UNFICYP decided to intervene. Under cover of darkness a small UN post, found by the Finns in whose operational area it lay, was deployed right on the spot where the foundations were being prepared, a UN flag was hoisted and the post was surrounded with barbed wire. When Turks turned up in the morning to resume work, they were told politely that this was a UN post (nicknamed 'Piknik 2' – a reference to a nearby restaurant of that name) to which entry was not permitted. Both sides accepted without demur what UNFICYP had done, there were no protests and a potentially explosive situation had been peacefully defused.[4] It had been a demonstration of how loss of face prevented the Turks from climbing down and how a UN Force can break the deadlock.

Typical of other potentially serious incidents defused by UNFICYP at this time was that which occurred in Paphos District in February 1973, when the TCF detained two members of CYPOL who had entered Ayios Nikolaos, a remote Turkish village in the Troodos some 14km SW of Mount Olympus, their detention being seen by the government as a direct challenge to its jurisdiction. Although the two were soon released, the Turks retained their weapons, adding to the government's wrath. When a few weeks later CYPOL arrested one of the Turks alleged to have been involved, it was the turn for the Leadership's anger and intercommunal tension rose. UNFICYP's mediation settled the matter to the satisfaction of both; the weapons were returned and the Turk was released.

The Limassol Incident in January 1974, when elements of the TRU were for the first time deployed in an intercommunal situation, was potentially more dangerous. From 4–7 January the Turkish Cypriots were celebrating *Qurban Bairam*, while for the Greeks 6 January was the Feast of the Epiphany. For no apparent reason and without warning the Turks took unusual military precautions, including the erection of barriers to close roads into their quarter of the town, the posting of additional sentries and the siting of more weapons, all in breach of the accepted military *status quo*. Greek reaction was immediate: in an angry telephone call to the UN District HQ Mr Zachariades (District Officer) demanded that the barriers be removed at once and the *status quo* fully restored, otherwise CYPOL and the National Guard would be ordered to do this by force. Operational responsibility at the time rested with BRITCON's 5th Royal Inniskilling Dragoon Guards ('The Skins') whose District Commander, Major Crowdy, persuaded Zachariades to hold his hand to allow UNFICYP to sort matters out. Crowdy lost no time in contacting the local Turkish leader, Mr Ustun, who claimed that the actions were no more than a routine exercise and undertook to do his best to restore the situation. Although Ustun was known to have little real authority and would have to refer to the undercover mainland Turk in command of the TCF in Limassol, he achieved partial success; just before a deadline agreed with Zachariades the barriers were dragged aside, but otherwise the *status quo* was not fully restored.

At Force HQ we had not been unduly worried up to this point since it appeared to be a relatively minor local problem and we were content to let Crowdy sort matters out at his level (for all the fighting talk from Zachariades, we were well accustomed to cries of 'Wolf!' from one side or the other). But during the night of 7 January the situation took a distinct turn for the worse as the Turks re-positioned the barriers and began to erect new defences. Crowdy was unable to contact Ustun, who was said 'to be away', and tension rose rapidly when in retaliation the Greeks sealed off the Turkish quarter and denied entry to all, including British personnel from the adjacent SBA. National Guard units were placed on alert and, to our dismay, elements of the TRU appeared on the scene. It was time for prompt action on UNFICYP's part at both local and Force HQ level.

In Limassol the acting Zone Commander, Major Rucker, deployed patrols to monitor events at the road barriers and placed his reserve squadron at immediate readiness to be interposed if necessary. At the same time he went to see Zachariades (whose two Doberman Pinschers, he said, nearly ate him) and, after numerous cups of coffee and a long homily from Zachariades on the *status quo,* persuaded the latter to defer further action. Meanwhile in Nicosia we urged restraint on both sides and pressed the Leadership to instruct the TCF in Limassol to restore fully the *status quo* without delay. The situation appeared genuinely to be worrying the Leadership as much as it did us. (We suspected that the cause of the trouble was an over-enthusiastic mainland Turkish officer in Limassol acting without the consent and perhaps even without the knowledge of the Leadership and the *Bozkurt* himself; if this was indeed the case, it was disturbing evidence of a lack of effective control on the Turkish Cypriot side.) UNFICYP pressure had the desired effect: after the ritual face-saving interval all barriers were removed, the new defences were dismantled and the *status quo* was restored to UNFICYP's satisfaction. At the same time the Greeks held back from any more drastic action, although the blockade of the Turkish quarter was maintained until all was back to normal. In spite of threats and hot tempers not a shot had been fired and no one was hurt. Would this have been the case but for UNFICYP's presence and mediation?

(The Commander of British Forces in the SBAs, Air Marshal Aiken, had been worried by these developments both because his personnel were being prevented from free movement through the Turkish quarter and because an outbreak of intercommunal fighting would endanger some of the many British service and civilian families who lived in Limassol. I had discussed the situation with him and Mr Olver, the British High Commissioner, in Nicosia on the afternoon of 8 January. I was reasonably confident that UNFICYP would be able to defuse the crisis without an outbreak of fighting and persuaded Aiken to refrain from any action that might make our task more difficult. In the event no harm came to any of those for whom he was responsible.)

The incident had wider repercussions. It reinforced doubts in the minds of some UN troop-contributor governments as to the wisdom of proceeding with the second phase of the plan to reduce the size of UNFICYP, since it demonstrated (they argued) that the prerequisites envisaged for further reductions were lacking. Moreover, the appearance of the TRU had cast doubt on the government's good faith, and the general climate was further soured by Prime Minister Ecevit's declaration soon afterwards, advocating a federal solution to the island's constitutional problems. All in all, the Limassol Incident, the death of Grivas three weeks later, the worsening of relations between Makarios and the junta that followed, the Ecevit bombshell and the adjournment *sine die* of the intercommunal talks combined to create fresh uncertainties and a renewed feeling of inherent instability in Cyprus.

In late April and early May 1974 public demonstrations took place in Nicosia and Limassol. These were EOKA-B-inspired and primarily anti-Government in nature, but an anti-Turkish element was also evident – a disturbing development deplored by the more responsible sections of the local press. More disturbing for UNFICYP was a series of incidents that occurred in Ayia Irini and other mixed villages north of Morphou provoked by National Guard officers and members of EOKA-B or their sympathizers. Young Greeks took to driving through the villages shouting insults at Turks and matters came to a head when a body of 150 National Guardsmen marched into Ayia Irini and halted in the Turkish quarter.

The Turks alleged that they were threatened by the soldiers, while the latter counter-charged that they had been provoked by the Turks. To prevent escalation the Finns increased patrols in the area and an undertaking was secured from National Guard HQ that in future its troops would not halt in the village. But such were the fears created by incidents of this kind that Turkish Cypriots in these villages were unwilling to travel to work in Nicosia and it became necessary for the Finns to deliver food to them. For some time thereafter the Finns maintained a standing patrol in the area, which demonstrated the validity of the observer/reconnaissance team operational concept introduced under the UN Force's reduction plan.

Cyprus had been relatively free of incidents of this nature for some time and their recurrence did not bode well. Indeed, the first five months of 1974 (which had opened on a note of optimism) had brought a distinct turn for the worse. Reporting to the Security Council at the end of May, the Secretary General morosely observed:

> More than ten years have passed since the Security Council established the United Nations Peacekeeping Force in Cyprus. Thanks in great part to the presence of the Force, the situation in the island has remained quiet in recent years, but some of the basic objectives of the United Nations operation have yet to be achieved. . . . The relations between the two communities are still marred by mutual fear and distrust. . . . Despite the present quiet, the situation in the island is still tense and potentially dangerous.[5]

Heavy winter rains and snow (which for a time closed the Kyrenia Pass, a rare event) signalled the end of the long drought and the spring of 1974 brought a blaze of colour to the island as a profusion of wild flowers, some of which had been dormant for years, burst into bloom in banks of brilliant hues all over the island. As these began to fade and die with the onset of summer's heat, everyday life for the majority continued in a seeming carefree way. The economy boomed, building activity was intense, tourists flooded in and Cypriots of both communities went about their daily tasks or gossiped in the coffee shops in apparent unconcern for constitutional or other intercommunal arguments, much less care for the blue beret soldiers whose presence in their midst was taken for granted.

Most in the UN Force served only for a brief six-month tour of duty and for these the outward and visible signs tended to convey a deceptive impression of stability and calm; even at Force HQ the sinister undercurrents were not readily perceptible. But those with longer experience in the Force were wary of outward appearances and could not escape an uneasy feeling that beneath it all events were moving towards a climax, the nature of which could not be guessed. We could but learn to labour and to wait.

CHAPTER TWENTY-SEVEN

WITHIN GUNSIGHT OF THE JUNTA

> Now persuaded that a major assault against him was being organized by the Greek officers and EOKA-B forces, he decided to take an audacious gamble.
>
> Laurence Stern, *Foreign Affairs*, Summer 1975, p. 53.

The death of Grivas in January 1974 brought a lull in EOKA-B activity as a struggle developed for control of the organization. His designated successor, Karousos, who had returned with him in 1971, advocated a return to political action to achieve *enosis*, a change of tactic welcomed by Makarios who extended an olive branch by offering amnesty to members of EOKA-B. But the Athens Colonels were determined that neither Karousos nor this offer should deflect them from their aim of ridding Cyprus of the Archbishop. Karousos was removed from the island and, with Grivas buried, the junta was in undisputed control of EOKA-B through KYP and the National Guard's mainland Greek officers. Nothing now stood in the way of more extreme action.

Makarios had no illusions as to the attitude of the Athens régime. Asked in 1974 why it should have wanted to get rid of him, he replied:

> General Ioannides personally has been angry with me ever since 1963–64, when he was serving as a member of the Greek contingent in Cyprus. . . . *[At a secret meeting]* he put to me a plan involving a general attack against the Turkish community on the island, with a view to achieving *enosis*. I rejected his idea indignantly. . . . The Athens generals had several reasons for getting rid of me. They wanted to extend to Cyprus their own order of dictatorship; they considered that the government in Nicosia ought to take its instructions from 'the ethnic centre' – Athens; and they were intent on undermining the intercommunal negotiations because of their fear that these might result in an agreement consolidating our autonomy vis-à-vis Greece. But they were not able to achieve any of these objectives without first doing away with the obstacle which in their eyes I constituted.[1]

But, he was asked, had not Athens – and Washington, too – taken exception to his non-aligned foreign policy and his relations with the communist party, AKEL? He answered:

> Yes – certain foreign powers judged that Cyprus was sliding to the left. The Greek leaders complained of my attitude with respect to AKEL. I repeatedly explained that I did not back the party but that I benefited from its support. As for my foreign policy, no one ever made a specific complaint.[2]

Following the return of Grivas money had flowed steadily into the coffers of EOKA-B and to the local anti-Makarios press from outside Cyprus. The main source was reputed to be a wealthy Athens ship-owner, but it was not the sole one. The Athens Colonels also contributed directly or indirectly and there was talk, too, of American CIA involvement. The part played by the United States in events in Greece and Cyprus during the years 1972–74 is not examined here, but circumstantial evidence pointing to a CIA hand is not lacking.[3] It suffices to observe that it has been suggested not only that officials in the State Department in Washington and its diplomats in Athens and Nicosia were not made privy to the precise nature of CIA activities in Greece and Cyprus, but also that the CIA through its own 'back channel' to the junta gave encouragement to plans aimed at toppling the Archbishop.

By its very nature the Athens dictatorship was repugnant to American public opinion, but at senior government level repugnance was tempered by *realpolitik*, notably the strategic importance of preserving the cohesion of NATO's southern flank; a settlement in Cyprus was necessary to this end and Makarios was seen as the obstacle. The Archbishop himself detected deeper motives in the American attitude. Two months after the *coup* that unseated him it was put to him that the US government considered that his stand had exacerbated Graeco-Turkish relations. He replied:

> On this point Mr Kissinger has told me that any solution acceptable to the parties concerned was equally acceptable to his Government. But I suppose that in reality the Americans preferred the partition of the island, a double *enosis*, which would tie the two parts of my country to Greece and to Turkey. This would make Cyprus an integral part of NATO. The United States would then be able to establish their own bases on the island. In this connection Washington also feared that at some future date Britain might decide, whether for financial or other reasons, to abandon its own bases, which *[under the Treaty of Establishment]* cannot be transferred to a third power.[4]

With EOKA-B now firmly under their thumb, the National Guard's Greek officers became ever more blatant in anti-Makarios activities and contempt for Cypriot ministers. Youths conscripted into the National Guard were subjected to pro-Athens indoctrination (any conscript rash enough to show pro-Makarios leanings was dealt with in harshest fashion); the flag of Greece was flown over the force's camps, which were plastered with the Phoenix badge and slogans extolling the Athens coup of 21 April 1967; the camps were used to provide asylum to EOKA-B terrorists under hot pursuit by the TRU and purported 'raids' on their armouries were staged deliberately as cover for the supply of weapons to EOKA-B.[5] However, Makarios's intelligence network had penetrated the organization and the TRU was hitting back with growing success. This unexpectedly robust response spurred the junta to more desperate measures, not least perhaps in order to distract public attention in Greece, where repression, corruption, inflation and general government incompetence were causing mounting domestic discontent.

In this climate rumours of plots and impending *coups* flourished. Denied the intelligence resources to evaluate these properly, UNFICYP could only remain watchful (and not a little sceptical) as a flood of flowery rhetoric flowed from all sides. Vernacular newspapers referred incessantly to 'fighting on the bastions', 'the thunderous voice of the people', 'standing upright on the ramparts' and 'the noble ideal of Hellenism', while opposition organs, such as Sampson's *Makhi*, wrote disparagingly of the President as 'the Pope-Caesar of Cyprus' or merely used of him the dismissive patronymic 'Mr Mouskos'. The Turkish community, too, watched and waited, and prevaricated at the conference table. The Leadership saw in these events not only plausible grounds for declining to institute the measure of military de-confrontation consistently urged on both sides by UNFICYP, but also justification for changes in the military *status quo*. (On the basis of documents said to have been seized by Turkish forces in July-August 1974, some Turkish Cypriots have asserted since that in April 1974 the National Guard had drawn up a plan (on the model of the Akritas plan) for the extermination of their community, and have even advanced the absurd notion that the conflict between Makarios and the junta was no more than a smoke-screen to conceal this plan, the purpose of which was to pave the way for the annexation of Cyprus as part of a 'Greater Greece'.)

The lull of January 1974 was followed by a resurgence of EOKA-B activity, and rumours circulated that another attempt on the life of Makarios was to be made before Easter, which fell on 14 April, just a week before 'Junta Day', the anniversary of the Athens *coup*. The countdown gathered pace with the abduction of the Minister of Justice, Mr Christos Vakis (he was released later unharmed in unexplained circumstances), the assassination of Makarios supporters, the proscription of EOKA-B (following rejection of the offer of amnesty) and the dismissal in growing numbers of its sympathizers in the police, civil service and teaching profession. The TRU stepped up its pressure and scored a major success on 18 June when, hot on the trail of Eleftheros Papadopolis, the EOKA-B 'Coordinator' (the post that since the death of Grivas had replaced that of commander), it raided an apartment in Nicosia. The quarry escaped, but left behind incriminating documents that established beyond doubt the direct hand of the junta and the Greek officers in EOKA-B activities. The documents were said to include details of a plan to assassinate Makarios and replace him by a puppet figure obedient to Athens.[6] EOKA-B's response was a week-long wave of violence, in which five people were killed and several others wounded.[7]

The gloves were now off. Speaking to supporters, the Archbishop described EOKA-B as 'a bunch of hideous murderers and an organized crime syndicate bent on destroying Cyprus'. The increasing subversion of the National Guard caused him deep concern because of the realization that, if the point came where the force was used against the government, the TRU could not provide an effective counter. His repeated complaints to Athens were met by equivocal denials and bland assurances that the activity of the Greek officers was designed solely to inculcate the spirit of Hellenism in the Greek youth of Cyprus. Makarios was especially incensed that with unconcealed contempt for the government the Greek officers denied his ministers a proper say in the selection of cadets sent to Greece for training as officers. This flagrant infringement of the government's authority, coupled with the clear evidence now in his hands of the Greek officers' complicity in EOKA-B, persuaded him that the mainland Greek officers must go:

> Previously I had complained several times to Athens about the subversive intrigues of the Greek officers. Each time, however, General Gizikis replied that without proof he could take no action. Now I was in possession of proof and I was not going to deny myself of its use.[8]

The domestic situation in Greece may have influenced his reasoning and the timing, but the decision was to prove a miscalculation of epic proportion. It ignited a chain of events which not only compelled Makarios to flee the island but also led to Turkey's military intervention, *de facto* partition and hardship and misery for tens of thousands of Cypriots of all communities.

In spite of an inherent preference for the oblique the Archbishop decided to meet the situation head-on, throwing down the gauntlet in a long letter dated 2 July 1974 to President Gizikis of Greece. Makarios did not mince his words. He explicitly accused the National Guard's Greek officers of giving active support to EOKA-B and charged that this was being done with the backing of Athens:

> I am sorry to say, Mr President, that the root of the evil is very deep, reaching as far as Athens. It is from there that the tree of evil, the bitter fruits of which the Greek Cypriot people are tasting today, is being fed and maintained and helped to grow and spread. In order to be absolutely clear, I say that cadres of the military régime of Greece support and direct the activity of the EOKA-B terrorist organization.

No less explicit was his accusation that the junta was intent on his life:

> I have more than once so far felt and in some cases I have almost touched a hand invisibly extending from Athens and seeking to liquidate my human existence.

His earlier protests concerning the selection and training of Greek Cypriot cadets as officers were reiterated, as were his complaints of other 'inadmissible' conduct by the Greek officers.

He went on to refer to the government's decision announced the previous day to reduce the period of conscription from 24 to 14 months (the effect of which would be to reduce the size of the National Guard to about 6,000 men with consequential reduction in the number of officers needed) and rejected criticisms that this would render the National Guard less able to resist an external threat to Cyprus. The crunch lay in his unequivocal demand that all the present Greek officers, totalling some 600, be recalled to Greece, although this bitter pill was sweetened somewhat by a proposal that they be replaced by about 100 others who would serve only as instructors and advisers with no power of executive command. Couched throughout in terms that clearly were intended to be challenging, if not actually insulting, to the military dictatorship, the letter concluded with barbed sarcasm:

> I am not an appointed prefect or *locum tenens* of the Greek Government in Cyprus, but an elected leader of a large section of Hellenism, and I demand an appropriate conduct by the National Centre towards me.

A final sting was the statement that 'the content of this letter is not confidential'.[9]

On the day the letter was despatched the plan for a *coup* (contained in the documents captured by the TRU on 18 June) was leaked in Nicosia and on 6 July the letter itself was made public, Makarios letting it be known that he had set 20 July as the date by which he expected to receive the agreement of the Athens Colonels for the removal of their officers from Cyprus. While there was grudging admiration for his audacity, this was tempered by doubt as to the wisdom of provoking the notoriously unpredictable Colonels in such public and humiliating fashion. Breaths were held in Nicosia and elsewhere as their reaction was awaited. Publication of the letter added to a feeling of apprehension that pervaded the island as events moved with gathering momentum towards a climax, the nature of which remained unclear. The key lay in Athens and all eyes were turned on Ioannides and his politically ingenuous colleagues. Would they withdraw their officers? Would they merely ignore the letter? Or would they grasp the nettle and rid themselves of the Archbishop once and for all? With the letter made public it seemed improbable that the Colonels would opt for either of the first two courses, but few thought that they would elect for physical intervention, since this would be certain to provoke a response by Turkey. Makarios himself did not believe that even the Athens Colonels could be so stupid as not to recognize this danger.

At UNFICYP Headquarters, as with Nicosia's embassies and the Leadership, we could but speculate. Rumours, much embroidered by the local press, were rife. As the days passed in silence from Athens, the UN Force was prudently placed at the first level of Alert with 'Increased Vigilance' discreetly implemented. UN District Commanders were warned that the period leading up to 20 July was likely to be especially delicate, and a contingency plan was implemented for special patrols in Nicosia briefed to watch for unusual activity that might presage unforeseen developments. During the week up to 15 July these patrols reported nothing untoward[10], but UNFICYP's helicopter pilots noted unusual tank training activity on the barren plateau north of the National Guard camp at Kokkini Trimithia (6km west of the airport) housing most of the obsolescent T-34 tanks with which the 23rd Medium Tank Battalion was equipped (the tanks were of uncertain serviceability and rarely seen outside the camp); further, there were unsubstantiated reports of members of ELDYK (the Greek National Contingent) receiving instruction on them. There were rumours, too, of groups of men in civilian dress arriving at the airport on flights from Athens, only then to be spirited away in military vehicles, and reports that the Greek officers were checking equipment and holding secret meetings.[11] There may even have been a rehearsal on Friday 12 July for an attack on the Presidential Palace:

> On the morning of that day National Guard tanks came up Severis Avenue and passed in front of the Presidential Palace; it appeared that they were engaged on a routine exercise. President Makarios telephoned the Commander of the National Guard to advise that tanks should not pass in front of the Palace in order to avoid the risk of any misunderstanding or undesirable consequences with the Presidential Guard in view of the uneasy atmosphere that prevailed. . . . The tanks had not been on exercises – they were timing the distances and rehearsing their attack against "the enemy target".[12]

With benefit of hindsight all these activities can be seen to have been intelligence indicators to which UNFICYP (in so far as it was aware of them) and others in Nicosia should have attached greater significance, but the Cypriots' addiction to rumour and cries of 'Wolf!' gave rise to caution and scepticism within the Force, lacking as it did the means to garner its own intelligence upon which a more perceptive assessment might have been made. In any case,

UNFICYP's attention was focused primarily on matters of more obvious and immediate intercommunal concern, and events within the Greek Cypriot community were not accorded the notice which they could subsequently be seen to have merited.

There were pointers outside the island, too, as to what was afoot. In Athens Foreign Minister Tetenes, unable to deflect Ioannides and his colleagues from what he perceived to be an ill-advised adventure, resigned. In Washington the Americans received unambiguous signals from the junta that it was contemplating ousting Makarios, and Ambassador Tasca in Athens was instructed to urge caution on Ioannides. He spoke instead to Prime Minister Androutsopoulos (who was little more than a figurehead) and there has been controversy since as to whether Washington's warning ever reached Ioannides himself. Some suspect that it did not, leading the Greek dictator to assume that the Americans were ready to turn a blind eye to his intended action. When later the hapless Tasca was criticized for not conveying the message to Ioannides in person, he replied that 'it was not the Ambassador's role to make diplomatic *démarches* to a cop'.

In Cyprus the US Military Attaché, Colonel Maurice Jessup, sought to discover National Guard intentions following the Makarios letter to Gizikis:

> I talked in the next two days to Jerry Hunter *[Defence Adviser, British High Commission]*, UN people, Tomas (KYP) and Athos Mirianthopoulos (Cyprus Army). There was a consensus that a *coup* was possible but not probable. Athos went so far as to say that the Cypriot members of the National Guard would probably kill any Greek officers who ordered such a thing, or at least fight to the last to protect the Archbishop. On the 4th July, it being our Independence Day, we had a rather large reception . . . and the subject was further pursued with various guests. Again the consensus was that the Archbishop was too strong for Ioannides and, besides, the Turks would react to such an event.[13]

Jessup, who was about to leave to attend a meeting in London (followed by a period of leave), called on the National Guard's Chief of Staff, Brig. General Yiannikodemos, on 5 July:

> The interview with the Chief of Staff was not very productive, but before leaving I expressed our concern about the unanswered letter, mentioned that I was going to England for a few weeks and said "Not to do anything stupid while I was gone". On leaving the building escorted by the Liaison Officer he asked me in a light manner what I had meant in saying "don't do anything stupid". I elaborated by saying we had in mind the possibility of a *coup* attempt or something equally stupid. He laughed and said "You can trust the Greek Army".[14]

With his Ambassador's approval, Jessup left for London next day, suspicious of the assurances of these two Greek officers and with an uncomfortable feeling that with each passing day the silence of Athens was ever more ominous.

Britain, concerned for the security of the SBAs, also monitored events closely. In spite of the rumours that abounded, the view prevailed in official circles that a *coup* against Makarios could not succeed and, ergo, was unlikely. The caveat of a senior Whitehall official that the Athens junta consisted of men who were politically ignorant, dangerous and stupidly blind to the logical consequences of their actions went unheeded. Like his American counterpart,

Colonel Jerry Hunter, Defence Adviser to the British High Commission, was also allowed to leave Nicosia for the meeting in London.

Questioned in 1975 by the House of Commons Select Committee on Cyprus, Foreign Secretary James Callaghan denied that Her Majesty's Government had had any advance intelligence of a coup being imminent.[15] Many thought this an astonishing admission which disclosed not only a notable failure of British intelligence but also a remarkable lapse in the exchange of information between Washington and London. Callaghan had actually met Henry Kissinger, US Secretary of State, in London in early July, when they discussed the SALT talks, NATO problems, the Middle East, oil supplies and other matters, but:

> At no time in our long discussions did either of us speak of the Cyprus situation, and I can only conclude that we had no inkling that the ten thousand-strong Greek National Guard would launch a *coup d'état* against their own President within the next seven days.[16]

Later Kissinger himself admitted that his own eye had not then been on the Cyprus ball.[17]

What of others? The Russians were as uncommunicative as ever, although the Soviet Ambassador in Ankara told Turkish Foreign Minister Gunes that the USSR was aware of the rumours and had warned the Greek Government against any action to overthrow Makarios. However, the Russians seemed as lacking in hard information as others. On the morning of 13 July their Military Attaché called on me at UNFICYP HQ, clearly fishing for information. We reviewed events together but neither, I think, gained much in the process, and I reported to Prem Chand that the Soviet Embassy appeared to be as much in the dark as we were. In Ankara the Turks appeared not over-concerned, reassured perhaps by what the Russians had told Gunes and content that Makarios and the junta should be at each other's throat.[18] In Nicosia the Leadership was watchful but evidently unaware of the moves being prepared under its nose by the Greek officers. In NATO circles there were uneasy stirrings and in Brussels restraint was being urged on both Greece and Turkey. But from UN Headquarters in New York there was silence, even though tongues must have been wagging. At UNFICYP HQ we received nothing from our masters on the 38th Floor: no appreciation of the situation, no warnings and no guidance as to our action should the rumours prove true.

It was the Americans who, through their close contacts with the military régime in Athens, were the best informed. Despite Kissinger's failure to focus fully on the Cyprus situation, there was growing apprehension in Washington that the junta remained set on action to overthrow Makarios and on 12 July Ambassador Davies in Nicosia was instructed to warn the Archbishop of the danger in which he stood. Makarios has described their meeting and a later conversation with Kissinger himself:

> During our talk the American Ambassador asked me if I shared the opinion being expressed by many that the situation in Cyprus was dangerous. I do not know whether Mr Davies's question implied information about a *coup*. I know only that after our meeting he sent a telex to the US State Department to the effect that to the relevant question I had answered him with a smile, saying that I had no fears of anything serious happening.
>
> The US Secretary of State, Dr Kissinger, told me about the telex during the first meeting I had with him in Washington after the *coup*. Commenting on it, Dr Kissinger told me that when

he read the telex he had enquired whether the information which his government had received from the US Information Service in Athens about an impending *coup* was correct, since apparently I was not worried about such an event. Dr Kissinger also told me that his information was that the *coup* could not be prevented and that it might take place at any moment. However he added that his government had no positive information as to the exact date when the *coup* was to take place.

I cannot say for sure that the Americans knew about the *coup* and did nothing to prevent it, nor can I say that they encouraged it. I can only say that Dr Kissinger assured me to the contrary, saying that the US government had no reason for wanting me to be overthrown. What I do know, however, is that a telex had been sent from the US Information Service in Athens to the State Department in Washington saying that assurances had been received from the leader of the military régime in Greece that there would not be a *coup*. Apart from the above information about the possibility of a *coup*, I repeat that for my part I did not lend credence to rumours about a *coup*.[19]

In the aftermath of the *coup* rumours of American CIA complicity were rife, but this has been firmly denied by a US State Department official.[20] Makarios himself remained sceptical:

> I have no formal proof as to the active participation of the CIA in the plot. But of this I am sure . . . that the CIA were perfectly well aware of what was being plotted. How could it have been otherwise when General Ioannides, the "brain" behind the conspiracy, collaborated closely with the American intelligence services? Moreover, EOKA-B maintained direct connections with the CIA. We intercepted, for example, a cheque for US $33,000 issued in the United States in favour of Mr Dimitrios Chacoliades, a leading member of EOKA-B, who could not give any satisfactory explanation of this mysterious payment.[21]

As Ambassador Davies reported to Washington on his conversation with the Archbishop, the Greek Ambassador in Nicosia, the well-respected Mr E. Lagacos, and the National Guard's commander, Lieut. General Denizis[22], were on their way to Athens; both had been summoned by the junta to a meeting on 13 July convened ostensibly to review the situation created by the Makarios letter of 2 July. It was public knowledge that this meeting was taking place and that it was expected to continue on Monday 15 July, fostering an assumption that no dramatic developments were likely in the meantime. It seems that at that point the junta had succeeded in duping Makarios into thinking that a peaceful solution to the differences between Athens and Nicosia was in sight:

> I would say that, on the basis of certain developments, some optimism for the settlement of the crisis was justified. On Saturday 13 July they assured us that all would be straightforward and that the special meeting that day in Athens would be continued on the morning of Monday 15 July. . . . They not only cheated us but did so in a sly and dishonest manner.[23]

In Cyprus the weekend of 13–14 July saw UNFICYP maintaining its Alert State of 'Increased Vigilance', but despite the spate of rumours we still had no firm grounds for thinking that the island's history was nearing an abrupt and bloody change of course; routine troop rotations in the Austrian and Finnish contingents due the following week were not postponed. The

French Embassy prepared to celebrate Bastille Day with its customary reception (to be held this year on 15 July because the 14th fell on a Sunday) and others went about their normal summer weekend activities in seeming unconcern. The Archbishop forsook the heat of Nicosia for the Presidential Lodge in the cool forests of the Troodos mountains, and the Commander BFNE, Air Marshal Aiken, was at his bungalow nearby. I and my family were at our weekend retreat in the Greek village of Bellapais high above Kyrenia and spent Sunday in a relaxed launch picnic with John Miles, family and friends. All was peaceful as we cruised out of Kyrenia harbour past the massive Venetian castle and two nondescript motor torpedo boats of the Cyprus navy made fast beneath its mellow walls, the sentry barely glancing at the Sunday procession of launches, ski-boats and other craft passing in and out of the narrow entrance. We anchored a few miles to the east, swam in the crystal-clear warm sea, enjoyed a picnic luncheon and soporific local wine, and lazily speculated about events on the island. From time to time I called the JOC at UNFICYP HQ by hand-portable radio; each time the Duty Officer replied 'Nan Tare Roger' (Nothing To Report).

That Sunday evening, for what was to be the last time, we watched from a vine-covered verandah in Bellapais the glowing sun sink slowly into the sea and the twinkling lights of Kyrenia far below assert themselves in the gathering summer night. There was still no inkling within UNFICYP or among the diplomats in Nicosia, much less in the Troodos mountain retreats, that the old order was about to be shattered in a crisis of international proportions. Even in Washington the Americans were lulled:

> On the morning of July 14, the day before the *coup*, a message flashed into Washington from the CIA backchannel in Athens indicating that Ioannides was cooling off on his *coup* intentions. He was impressed, the cable suggested, by the arguments against violence. At that point there could have been only one purpose for the general's piece of disinformation: preventing any advance warning by the Americans, as had happened before, of the junta's intentions. Makarios was now within gunsight of the junta.[24]

CHAPTER TWENTY-EIGHT

COUP D'ÉTAT

I cannot think of any single act which has caused more suffering and more prospect of continuing misery than the crazy assault that Monday morning.

Lord Caradon: 'Cyprus – The Drift to Disaster',
World View, December 1974.

'That Monday' was 15 July 1974. The clear early morning held promise of a hot summer's day as I walked down the steep narrow lane to the Tree of Idleness in the centre of Bellapais, where driver and car were waiting in the square beside the great Gothic Abbey to take me back to Nicosia. The time was 0630hrs and Greek villagers already going about their business greeted me with a friendly *kalle meira* as I passed. From Bellapais we followed the narrow winding road, closed to the public, that hugged the mountainside before joining the main Kyrenia Road just north of the Pass. As the barrier was lifted at the National Guard RFU camp at its Bellapais end I received a smart salute from these disciplined troops; within their camp all appeared normal. We aimed to reach the Kyrenia Road ahead of the UN-escorted convoy scheduled to leave the Kyrenia check-point at 0700hrs – a call on the radio confirmed that we had done so – and we motored on south through the Turkish enclave and the villages of Boghaz, Geunyeli and Orta Keuy, where we turned off to follow the road running round the western outskirts of Nicosia to reach UNFICYP HQ near the airport at 0715hrs. As was my practice, I had watched for breaches of the Kyrenia Road Agreement but saw none, nor was any unusual activity evident either within or outside the enclave; the military and police forces of both communities were going about their duties with no sign of impending crisis.

Archbishop Makarios, too, had left early by car from his Troodos Lodge to return to Nicosia. Escorted by the Presidential Guard, his route took him past the camp of the Greek National Contingent, ELDYK, near Wayne's Keep west of the city and on through the suburbs to the Presidential Palace at Strovolos on the south-western outskirts. By 0740hrs he was at his desk and embarking on a busy Monday morning schedule. An early engagement was to receive a party of school children visiting from Egypt; it was to prove his last before compelled to flee the palace for his life.

At UNFICYP HQ General Prem Chand and I discussed the overnight cables from New York and situation reports from our District Commanders; none contained anything of special significance and it seemed we could anticipate a normal Monday's business. At

0815hrs I chaired my routine meeting with the Force HQ staff officers when the weekend's events were reviewed; it had been uneventful generally and the meeting was brief. At about 0830hrs, as we were about to disperse, explosions were heard from the direction of the airport 1km away. There had been recent blasting there during work to extend the main runway but this was more like gunfire. Had the National Guard given notice of practice firing, I asked? 'No,' replied Commandant Flynn (Ireland), LO to that Force. Had the Turks done so then? 'No' too said Major Oberwinkler (Austria), LO to the Vice President's Office. Alarmed, I went at once to Prem Chand's office, from which the unmistakable sounds of automatic small arms fire, punctuated by gunfire, could clearly be heard. We were in no doubt as to the significance – this was the junta's reply to Makarios: a *coup d'état*. Although not primarily an intercommunal matter, there was clear need for UNFICYP to monitor events and to prevent intercommunal incidents. As a first step the code-word 'INDIAN' ordering 'Blue Alert' was flashed throughout the Force. This required, *inter alia*, the cessation of training, the recall to camp of off-duty personnel, the doubling of sentries and the strengthening of local defence measures.

Plans for the *coup* had followed classic pattern: rapid action, initially in Nicosia but soon afterwards elsewhere throughout the island, to seize control of key points, such as the airport, broadcasting station, telecommunications centres and important road junctions, to neutralize the TRU and 'para-state' groups, to disarm CYPOL and take over their HQ, barracks, police stations and the Central Prison, and, above all, to assault the Presidential Palace and kill the Archbishop. If the pattern was predictable, the timing, which achieved complete surprise, was not, as Makarios himself acknowledged:

> In spite of the fact that I did not believe there would be a *coup*, men of the Presidential Guard kept watch on the *[ELDYK]* camp. I was informed later that they had kept the camp under observation throughout the night of 14 July, but with the coming of daylight they had left. From what I know, *coups* usually take place during the night, but ours took place at a time when nobody could have expected it. And the people who observed the tanks leaving the camp in the early morning thought they were leaving on normal exercises. It was only realized that something was afoot when they entered the Palace grounds.[1]

Every effort was made from the outset to portray the *coup* as the Cypriot National Guard's spontaneous reaction against the Makarios régime, but few were duped by the Athens junta's claim that the hand of Greece was not involved, for it was common knowledge that the National Guard was under the unfettered control of the mainland Greek officers.[2] Ample evidence quickly came to light to show that ELDYK played a key part, assisted by men of the Hellenic navy in technical tasks such as the take-over of CYTA telephone exchanges.

Security had been preserved by ensuring that knowledge of the plan was confined to a select few officers in Nicosia and it was not until after the signal for its implementation was given at 0800hrs on 15 July that National Guard commanders elsewhere received orders for complementary action. As soon as word spread from Nicosia, National Guard troops were joined by EOKA-B men and sympathizers, some in uniform but most not, armed with a variety of weapons ancient and modern, who sprang into excited action. Bands of these 'cowboys', subject to no apparent discipline or control, commandeered cars and were soon careering through the streets of all the main towns, firing weapons indiscriminately with bravado and stupendous waste of ammunition and generally flaunting their new-found importance. Members of the TRU and CYPOL, together with the Archbishop's active supporters, such as those recruited by Dr Lyssarides[3], were hunted down and in the ensuing few days some old, and sometimes private, scores were settled.

As soon as word came that Makarios had reached the Presidential Palace[4], the National Guard began to set up road-blocks to seal off the capital, while tanks and infantry left their camps to mount assaults on the airport and the palace and other groups moved to seize key points and installations elsewhere in Nicosia. Capture of the airport, where a strong TRU guard was maintained, was a high priority and its proximity to the National Guard camp at Kokkini Trimithia and the ELDYK camp near Wayne's Keep made it the earliest target. Men of the TRU put up a prolonged and determined resistance[5], but, although some shooting continued for much of the day, they were no match for the tanks and ELDYK's men.

Meanwhile National Guard tanks and infantry in APCs advanced into the city. The Presidential Palace came under attack and was soon in flames and its approaches blocked; a battle was in progress at the Kykko Monastery annex (a Makarios supporters' stronghold on the Nicosia bypass) which was being pounded by tank guns; the Archbishopric (within the walls of the Old City) was under fire; fighting was in progress to capture the TRU and CYPOL HQ at Athalassa and main police stations; an attempt was being made to seize the Central Prison, where EOKA-B and other anti-Makarios convicts were incarcerated; the Cyprus Broadcasting Corporation (CBC) building at Athalassa was taken over and normal programmes were replaced by martial music; roadblocks were in place on all main approaches to Nicosia and prisoners, arrested civilians and casualties were to be seen at various places, with many calls for ambulances. At about 1000hrs CBC radio announced:

> The National Guard has intervened today to stop internecine war between Greeks. The main purpose of the National Guard is to maintain order. The matter is an internal one among Greeks alone. The National Guard at this moment is in control of the situation and Makarios is dead. Anyone who puts up resistance will be executed at once.

Adding that an immediate island-wide 24-hour curfew had been imposed, a proclamation to the people of Cyprus was read out, the evident purpose of which was to persuade a wider international audience that the coup was an internal matter that did not warrant external intervention. The claim that Makarios was dead was a shock to the Greek community, but a consequence was that the Greek officers' fears that the TRU might be reinforced by Lyssarides groups and members of AKEL taking to the streets in opposition to their action were diminished. Shooting continued, nonetheless, as Makarios supporters were hunted down.

Events outside Nicosia followed similar pattern. In Limassol the town's two CYPOL stations came under National Guard attack and heavy firing continued throughout the morning. Most Greek Cypriots remained indoors as bands of indisciplined 'cowboys' roamed the streets firing weapons in wild excitement. In Paphos District, where pro-

Makarios support was strong, news of the *coup* caused bewilderment and confusion. There was feverish activity in the CYPOL and National Guard barracks, where the Greek officers had the tables turned on them and were placed in the cells. Although initially stunned by the report that Makarios was dead, the morale of Paphiot Greeks surged when later in the day they learnt that he was alive and on his way to join them.

In Famagusta the National Guard's attack on the local CYPOL and TRU HQ was watched by the Swedes' Commanding Officer, Lieut. Colonel Kristensson, then visiting his contingent's OP on the Land Gate of the Old City:

> The force consisted of three T-34 tanks and 4–5 lorries carrying infantry in steel helmets. . . . When the attack started there was enormous shooting. As we were situated on Land Gate in the extension of fire, we at first took cover; and then we were amused that there were so few bullets or ricochets against us – only from time to time during this fantastic fire-storm did the bullets come up to Land Gate. The tanks were only shooting with machine-guns, not with their heavy guns. . . . The scene was very astonishing.[6]

It was not until 1800hrs that evening that Famagusta's CYPOL and TRU HQ was reported to have succumbed to the hail of fire brought to bear by the National Guard, whose men (like those elsewhere) showed marked disinclination to close physically with the objective. (Next morning Kristensson was surprised to find the CYPOL commander, Chief Superintendent K. Phesas, reinstated in his post, apparently none the worse for the battle.) Larnaca witnessed similar scenes with shooting throughout the morning in the vicinity of the District Office and the CYPOL station, which continued into the late afternoon. In Lefka District (where there was no large town with a predominantly Greek population) the situation generally was calm, apart from some shooting between pro- and anti-Makarios elements in the National Guard at the village of Pakyammos on the coast road. In Kyrenia District National Guard troops erected road-blocks at several points and firing broke out in Kyrenia itself as they, too, attacked the police station and took over control of the town.

It had been a day of many surprises, but one that none can have anticipated came with the CBC's broadcast announcement at about 1500hrs that Nicos Sampson had been appointed the new President to head a 'Government of National Salvation'. Most who heard it were appalled:

> No more disastrous step could be imagined. Sampson was one of Grivas's most effective assassins during the EOKA campaign. He was distrusted by his colleagues because he appeared to enjoy the job. Personally charming and capable of rallying the innocent, he had become a newspaper editor, family man and race-horse owner, but to those who knew him he remained foolish, ignorant and a psychopathic killer. He had received "revelations from God", participated in massacres of Turks in the intercommunal fighting and loyally followed each twist and turn of the Athens line. He was a person of little substance – chosen by the junta to serve their purpose.[7]

How could such an inept choice have been made? The Constitution provided that in the event of the death or incapacity of the President the office was to devolve temporarily on the President of the House of Representatives, at that time Glafkos Clerides. The *coup* planners, it seems, expected that, if Makarios was toppled, Clerides would be willing to step into his shoes, but he was not, and the news that Makarios was alive and still in Cyprus stripped such an appointment of all vestige of constitutional validity. The plotters' second choice was said to be the President of the Supreme Court, Mr M. Triantafyllides, but he was found to be absent from the island. The third choice was Mr Z. Severis, honorary Consul General of Finland, but he sent Sampson packing when he arrived to offer the post. The Greek officers, in desperation, then told Sampson to take on the task himself. He was clearly no more than the Greek officers' puppet and few gave his 'government' much more than a week in office.[8]

By evening on that Monday, 15 July, it seemed that the *coup* had achieved a wide measure of success in Nicosia and elsewhere, except in Paphos. However, a curfew remained in force, sporadic shooting was commonplace in most towns, and news that the Archbishop had survived gave fresh heart to his supporters. For UNFICYP the main concern had been to ensure that events did not take an intercommunal turn. Actions to this end are described in the chapter that follows.

CHAPTER TWENTY-NINE

PRESERVING INTERCOMMUNAL CALM AND OTHER TASKS

At 1715 hours local time on 15 July the Senior Political Adviser and the Chief of Staff of UNFICYP visited Mr Orek, who agreed to do his best to keep the Turkish Cypriot community calm. He added, however, that the community was deeply concerned at developments and was preoccupied that an attack might be made on it.

UN Secretary General: *Statement to Security Council*, 16 July 1974.

Two Sioux helicopters of UNFICYP's Army Aviation Flight were already airborne when the *coup* was launched, one tasked for a surveillance mission over Kyrenia District and the other for routine reconnaissance over Nicosia. Passing over the Morphou Road just north of the airport soon after 0810 hrs, the pilot of the first observed what he took to be a road accident. Making an orbit to see if help might be required, he noted that troops were present from the nearby Greek camp and, judging that matters were under control, continued on his mission; in fact he had seen the first roadblock being established to seal off the city. At about 0830hrs the pilot of the second and his two Canadian observers saw smoke rising from the Presidential Palace and National Guard troops and vehicles deployed around it. Minutes later both pilots picked up confused radio traffic on the civil Air Traffic Control net and reports on UNFICYP's own Command net of shooting in the city. An agitated and peremptory 'We are forced to close – No more traffic!' quickly followed from the airport local control.

With initial action confined to Nicosia, UNFICYP's Commanders elsewhere were puzzled at first to receive the codeword 'INDIAN' placing the Force on Blue Alert, but were quickly enlightened by a message confirming that a National Guard *coup* against the Makarios government was in train, together with instructions for local leaders of both communities to be contacted at once and the need impressed on them to ensure that all under their control exercised the utmost restraint. Orders were also issued for UN flags to be displayed on UN vehicles and flown over UN premises in order to minimize risks of mistaken identities.[1] The Secretary General was informed by cable via the UN Radio that, while the situation was confused, our preliminary assessment indicated that a *coup* was in progress and that a CBC radio report, which we could not confirm, stated that Makarios was dead.

As soon as the Turks heard the sound of shooting the TCF fully manned all its positions, work was begun to improve defences, reserves were mobilized and the Turkish National contingent was placed on alert. Entry to the Turkish quarter of Nicosia was sealed off and

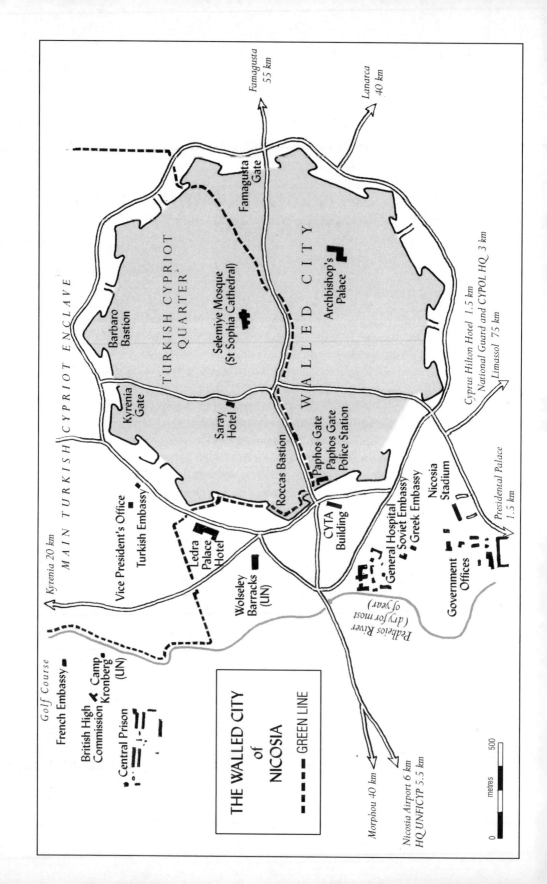

THE WALLED CITY
of
NICOSIA

GREEN LINE

metres
0   500

Golf Course
French Embassy
British High
Commission
Camp
Kronberg
(UN)
Central Prison

Kyrenia 20 km
MAIN TURKISH CYPRIOT ENCLAVE

Vice President's Office
Turkish Embassy

Ledra
Palace
Hotel

Wolseley
Barracks
(UN)

Morphou 40 km

Nicosia Airport 6 km
HQ UNFICYP 5.5 km

Pedheios River
(dry for most
of year)

CYTA
Building

General Hospital
Soviet Embassy
Greek Embassy

Nicosia
Stadium

Government
Offices

Presidental Palace
1.5 km

Limassol 75 km

Cyprus Hilton Hotel 1.5 km
National Guard and CYPOL HQ 3 km

Larnaca
40 km

Famagusta
55 km

Barbaro Bastion

TURKISH CYPRIOT QUARTER

Selemiye Mosque
(St Sophia Cathedral)

Famagusta
Gate

WALLED CITY

Archbishop's
Palace

Kyrenia
Gate

Saray
Hotel

Roccas Bastion

Paphos Gate
Paphos Gate
Police Station

movement in or out forbidden, as much to safeguard the Turkish community as to prevent Greeks seeking asylum. Denktash realized that events were primarily an internal Greek community concern and urged his own community to remain calm and not to respond to occasional stray shots that might come their way from the Greek side. Turkish discipline and restraint prevailed, and UNFICYP received no reports of shooting from that side. The Leadership, nonetheless, was apprehensive of future developments.

As reports poured in to the JOC at UNFICYP HQ of shooting at the airport and tanks on the runways, of more tanks and APCs on the move into Nicosia, of firing at the Presidential Palace and near the Archbishopric as well as at various other points on the Greek side of the city, it became imperative for UNFICYP to establish close contact with National Guard HQ on the one hand and the Turkish Cypriot Leadership on the other. All civil telephone lines had been cut when the CYTA main exchange was seized, which posed a serious problem since UNFICYP relied on the civil system for telephonic communication with the Government, National Guard Commander, the Leadership and diplomatic missions; for the time being the Force was thrown back on its own radio links and a few military lines.[2] These provided a rapidly developing picture of events as information flowed in from the Sioux helicopters, CANCON posts and patrols in the city, and individual members of the Force going about their normal duties around Nicosia, but there was, nonetheless, an urgent need to establish direct and reliable communications with both the Leadership and the Commander of the National Guard. Immediate deployment of UNFICYP's accredited LOs was prevented by National Guard roadblocks supported by T-34 tanks established at various key road junctions, and protests to those manning them, citing UNFICYP's right to freedom of movement, were unavailing. Since a way through could not be forced, UNFICYP's LO to the Leadership, Major Oberwinkler (Austria), was sent by Sioux helicopter; equipped with a hand-portable radio, he was landed in the dry moat beneath the Barbaro Bastion in the Turkish quarter soon after 0930hrs and was taken immediately to the Vice President, Rauf Denktash, to whom he remained close throughout succeeding days. Using his radio nickname 'CRESCENT', his voice was to be heard on UNFICYP's radio net throughout the crisis of the following weeks, providing an invaluable link between Force HQ and the Leadership.

The confused situation on the Greek side, including reports of fighting in the vicinity of National Guard HQ at Athalassa, where the TRU barracks was under attack, made it imprudent to send in Commandant Flynn (Ireland), LO to the National Guard, by similar means; instead he prepared to get through by road once the situation became clearer. Leaving for Athalassa soon after midday, he was instructed to obtain freedom of movement for all UN flag cars and patrols, to arrange a meeting as early as possible between General Prem Chand and the National Guard acting Commander and to seek agreement for he himself to remain at the latter's HQ to provide a radio link with UNFICYP HQ. Flynn successfully negotiated his way through various roadblocks and eventually reached National Guard HQ just after 1400hrs – the usual 20-minute journey had taken two hours. Catching sight of Colonel Constantinos Kombokis, Commander of the RFU, he approached and asked to see the Commander of the National Guard:

[Kombokis] said: "The Commander is in Greece", so I asked to see the Acting Commander or the Chief of Staff, Brig. General Yiannikodemos. . . . To my surprise he then escorted me himself into the HQ, saying: "This is nothing to do with the UN or the Turkish Cypriots. Everything is under control". He took me to the Chief of Staff's office where I met Brig. General Yiannikodemos, and then Major Tsolakis, the National Guard LO to UNFICYP, arrived.[3]

Flynn at once requested a meeting between the Acting Commander and Prem Chand, restoration of telephone communications between their two HQ and freedom of movement for UN troops.

Stressing that the National Guard was not seeking a fight with the Turkish Cypriots, but, rather, would respect all agreements and resume the intercommunal talks shortly, Yiannikodemos regretted that neither a meeting with Prem Chand nor restoration of telephone communications were possible that day. Further, freedom of movement could not be accorded to UNFICYP troops because (he lamely explained) he could not guarantee their safety in the existing situation. Although unwilling to allow Flynn to remain at his HQ, the latter convinced him of the need for a radio link between the two HQs so long as telephone lines were cut, and, having obtained a National Guard pass, Flynn left for HQ UNFICYP to report. He encountered no difficulties on his return journey, but came across a party of 48 schoolchildren from RAF Nicosia who had been abandoned by their Cypriot bus driver; Flynn had them loaded onto UN lorries halted nearby and led them safely back to Blue Beret camp.[4] After de-briefing, Flynn returned to National Guard HQ at Athalassa and thereafter played a key part in the conduct of UNFICYP's operations throughout the following critical days. Using the radio nickname 'SOCRATES', his voice became as familiar on UNFICYP's radio net as that of Oberwinkler's 'CRESCENT'. At times both were exposed to acute personal danger, but in this they were not alone.

As the BRITCON camp adjutant, Major D. Miles, was leaving Camp UNFICYP at about 0830hrs firing erupted at the airport passenger terminal only 300m from the camp's main gate and, with his driver, Trooper Sykes, he went to investigate. Military vehicles were parked nearby and explosions and the fire of automatic weapons could be heard. When a burst was directed over their Land Rover they went forward on foot only to be met by another burst. Two wounded soldiers ran towards them and Miles told Sykes to take them to the Austrian Medical Centre in Blue Beret Camp. Miles himself managed to enter the terminal building to find the ground floor a mass of spent rounds, broken glass and water, and was joined there by Major J. Ottesen (Denmark), HQ UNFICYP Operations Staff Officer. The two then made their way to the upper floors where they found frightened tourists, whom they calmed down and gathered together out of the line of fire.

Fighting continued at the airport for much of the day and casualties were brought in to the Austrian Medical Centre in Blue Beret Camp, where its Commander, Colonel Dr Josef Meyer, ensured that they received prompt attention. They included four seriously wounded soldiers who were then evacuated to the British Military Hospital at Dhekelia, where one at least was identified as a member of ELDYK. In addition to the wounded, some members of the airport's TRU and CYPOL detachments sought sanctuary in Camp UNFICYP or Blue Beret Camp and as a humanitarian measure they were disarmed and taken in. Later, as others elsewhere sought asylum under the UN flag, Prem Chand consulted New York on the policy to be adopted in such cases, since giving asylum might be seen as an infringement of the host government's authority and might even expose UN camps to attack. Dr Waldheim's guidance was clear and humane – UNFICYP was to discourage people from seeking such asylum, but, where it was judged that their lives might be at stake, this should be granted. Those to whom UNFICYP subsequently gave this protection included Makarios himself and, after Turkey's intervention, some Turkish Cypriot Fighters and a few mainland Turkish officers.

At this time the Canadians responsible for Nicosia comprised the high-grade 1st Commando Group, commanded by Lieut. Colonel D. Manuel (which formed part of the Canadian Airborne Regt, the balance of which remained in Canada). Their first indication of trouble came at 0830hrs, when explosions and heavy firing were heard in the vicinity of the Paphos Gate (only 300m distant from Manuel's District HQ in Wolseley Barracks), followed quickly by more explosions and shooting elsewhere. As reports flowed in from his OPs, patrols and the Austrian UNCIVPOL (who supported the Canadians), Manuel realized that a well-coordinated military *coup* was in train and that the National Guard was moving fast to seize control of key points and to seal off the city. As soon as the codeword 'INDIAN' was received, he placed his reconnaissance platoon on standby and the reserve platoon of his Observation Company (which manned the OPs) at 15 minutes' readiness.[5] His Operations Officer, Capt. I. Nicol, then airborne in the Sioux helicopter over the city, provided a commentary on the movement of troops and vehicles.[6] Restricting movement outside Canadian bases to men in radio-equipped vehicles, Manuel sent a patrol to investigate events in the vicinity of the Paphos Gate, where to its surprise it found some civilian traffic still circulating in spite of the shooting and confusion. He had been obliged to find this patrol from within his own HQ, illustrating the degree to which his contingent, like others, was short of men in consequence of the recent Force reductions. This was highlighted when soon after 0900hrs he requested the Force Reserve armoured reconnaissance troop and reserves from the Finnish and Swedish battalions to be sent to assist in maintaining the integrity of the Green Line. With the island-wide situation too unclear at that stage to justify commitment of UNFICYP's slender resources in this way his request had to be refused. Nonetheless the Canadians were successful in preventing serious intercommunal incidents along the Green Line.

Manuel maintained close touch with the Turkish side through Mr Meri Hassan, the Political Liaison Officer at the VPO. A military telephone line was still available and this was supplemented by a Canadian LO at the VPO, who was joined there by an Austrian UNCIVPOL member equipped with radio. Coupled with the presence of Oberwinkler at Denktash's side, these officers ensured that the Leadership was kept well informed from the outset of events on the Greek side.[7] Hassan stated that the Turks would refuse to accord asylum to any Greeks and asked that the Green Line be secured to prevent any from attempting to gain this. Manuel's response was to institute roving patrols along the Line and to establish additional UN posts. Hassan confirmed that it was Turkish policy to remain aloof from the quarrel and to react only if directly threatened. That the Turks were taking no risks was evident by the double and even treble manning of TCF posts along the Line, action that was reciprocated by the National Guard.

The patrol sent to investigate the situation at the Paphos Gate gave a vivid account of the fight as two T-34 tanks engaged the adjacent police station with machine-gun and main armament, supported by intense small arms fire from three platoons of RFU (later seen carrying corpses from the police station). When a tank trained its gun on the Canadian patrol and two soldiers made towards it, its commander judged that discretion was the better part of valour and the patrol withdrew. Other Canadians also faced dangers; one making a routine check of the CYTA building was beaten up by four men and his rifle stolen[8], while sentries manning the unprotected UN posts at Paphos Gate itself and on the adjacent Roccas Bastion had to be withdrawn due to the intensity of fire to which they were exposed (45 minutes later the latter was re-established on the Bastion and the former re-located in a less vulnerable position).

Meanwhile information was flowing in unabated to the JOC at Force HQ. In Nicosia shooting was continuing in the Paphos Gate area and at the Presidential Palace from which smoke was pouring to the sky; more troops had moved into the airport where the Air Traffic Centre had been taken over by armed men; there was confusion at the Central Prison where two T-34 tanks were to be seen and some prisoners were being released and others put inside; at Athalassa the TRU appeared to have surrendered, some 200 men being visible spreadeagled on the ground; elsewhere throughout Nicosia there were frequent outbreaks of firing for which there was no apparent cause. On the Turkish side reserves had been called up and a force of some 100 TCF, armed mostly with Thompson-type machine-guns, was standing ready near the Quirini Bastion.

Reports also flowed in from other UN Districts. In Limassol the Zone Commander, Lieut. Colonel Christopher Willoughby (Commanding Officer, 2nd Bn, Coldstream Guards) was holding a meeting when the codeword 'INDIAN' was received:

> The news of the *coup* broke on on Monday 15th July as a complete surprise. I was planning a parade for the presentation of UN medals and was trying extremely hard to be tactful in my efforts to get members of the Royal Corps of Transport Squadron to take part in a drive past and not try to march past as they wished to do. This important matter was solved by the Greek-officered National Guard attack on the Presidential Palace in Nicosia . . . .[9]

Weightier matters soon demanded his attention. Within half an hour shooting broke out in Limassol town as the two CYPOL stations came under attack and heavy firing continued throughout the morning. His first concern was to maintain close touch with leaders of each community but this was easier said than done. On the Turkish side Mr Ustun was well known to him, but (as usual) direct contact with the Turkish officers who exercised the real power was impossible. There were problems, too, in dealing with the Greek side:

> Maintaining contact with the Greek officers and the Greek Cypriot government officials was complicated by excessive and completely wild shooting, by the arrest of Greek colonels by Greek policemen, by the attacks of the National Guard on the Police, and by remarkable flexibility of mind which allowed the local government officials to support first one régime and then the other.[10]

The Parachute Sqn RAC (the armoured reconnaissance unit which, except for one troop located in Nicosia, was part of Willoughby's command in Limassol Zone) was quick off the mark. The Squadron Leader, Major P. Bentley, and his Sergeant Major set off into the town to see what was happening; they reported much firing and confusion and came across a number of distressed wives of British men serving in the SBAs. The safety of these families was not UNFICYP's responsibility, but they took it upon themselves (as Flynn had done in Nicosia) to carry out several mercy missions, such as helping to find lost children and restoring a measure of calm.

The TCF in Limassol adopted a high alert as soon as shooting was heard and barricaded themselves in the Turkish quarter behind buses, cars and barrels, from which they looked on nervously (and with a certain satisfaction) as Greek fought Greek. Willoughby's men watched over the Turkish quarter while monitoring and reporting events on the Greek side. During the morning a cry for help came from the latter – Limassol hospital was in dire need of blood plasma. Willoughby arranged for two of his guardsmen to fetch this from the RAF Hospital at Akrotiri in the SBA and to deliver it to the Greek hospital, where they learnt that there were four dead and three wounded from the fighting at the police station.

In Paphos, too, the TCF went on full alert, but there were no intercommunal incidents. Although stunned initially by the claim that the Archbishop was dead, the morale of the Paphos Greeks surged when reports spread that he had survived and was on his way to them. The latter news first reached the Paphos District Commander, Major Richard Macfarlane (Coldstream Guards), when the District Officer, Mr Stephanides, and the Mayor turned up at his HQ in St Patrick's Camp to say that the Bishop of Paphos had received information by radio that Makarios was alive and requested that a message to be passed by UNFICYP to New York calling for a meeting of the Security Council. Macfarlane's initial reaction was one of scepticism, but, persuaded by them that the information was correct, he undertook to pass the Archbishop's request to UNFICYP HQ; this he immediately did.[11] During the ensuing 24 hours events in Paphos District were to occupy much of UNFICYP's attention.

Like UN Contingents elsewhere, the Swedes in Famagusta District were quick to respond to the new situation. Their commander, Lieut. Colonel Svante Kristensson, then enjoying a few days' local leave, returned to his HQ in Carl Gustav Camp as soon as the codeword 'INDIAN' was received.[12] His OP on the Othello Tower of the Old City reported that the TCF were strengthening defences on the walls and shooting was reported in the vicinity of the CYPOL and TRU HQ. When a Swedish patrol sent to investigate was turned back Kristensson reinforced a nearby OP and established a new post on the Land Gate; he also cancelled planned patrols by his detachment at Chatos (in the west of the District) and ordered the re-manning of the post at Bey Keuy (recently unmanned as part of UNFICYP's reduction measures). The Swedish UNCIVPOL were also alerted, leading to a plaintive call from a lone policeman left at the sub-station at Leonarisso (on the Panhandle) while his colleagues returned to Famagusta for routine purposes, wanting to know what was happening. During the morning the Swedes in OP Othello Tower reported more shooting and that work in the docks had stopped.

In Larnaca District, where the pattern of events was similar, the Austrians' Commander, Lieut. Colonel Franz Rieger, deployed an LO to the Turkish side while personally maintaining close touch with the local National Guard commander. Implementing UNFICYP's Blue Alert, the Danes in Lefka District re-manned their recently unmanned OPs and Lieut. Colonel Carl Severinson, too, maintained close contact with leaders of both local communities. Generally the Danes were less touched by events at this time than UN Contingents elsewhere, but during the morning there was a curious incident (described in the following chapter) when a Danish UNCIVPOL patrol was temporarily detained near the village of Evrykhou.[13]

In Kyrenia District the Finns were closer to the action. As soon as 'INDIAN' was received Lieut. Colonel Jorma Pullinen ordered four unmanned OPs around the main enclave to be re-manned. He also increased patrolling along the Finnish sector of the Green Line and moved his reserve platoon from Tjiklos (at the head of the Kyrenia Pass) to reinforce his posts in the Nicosia suburbs of Omorphita and Trakhonas. Other patrols were sent to Turkish and mixed villages in the western area of the District and local leaders were contacted and urged to remain calm. Pullinen also deployed an LO to the commander of the Turkish National contingent, Colonel Mustafa Katircioglu; the only person available for this task was his padre who played an important part in dampening down tension in the Turkish contingent, especially when later in the day some mortar rounds fell near its camp in Orta Keuy.

The many foreign tourists in the Kyrenia area remained unharmed in their hotels and apartments, but there were some individuals who were anxious to return to Nicosia. These were gathered together in the town by Colonel C.E. Beattie, UNFICYP's Deputy Chief of Staff (then on leave in the area) and in a convoy of some 20 cars were shepherded under the UN flag to the Finns' camp at Tjiklos. With the assistance of British residents in neighbouring houses, the Finns took this group of men, women and children under their wing until they were conducted under UN escort back to Nicosia next day.

At a staff meeting at Force HQ in mid-morning we took stock of the situation. Since it was clear that Nicosia had been sealed off apart from the Larnaca road (which, due perhaps to a National Guard oversight, was still open) and in view of the imposition of an island-wide curfew, the Kyrenia Road convoys were cancelled until further notice and UN District Commanders were summoned to a meeting at Force HQ at 1600hrs in order to hear their latest reports and assessments; helicopters were tasked to bring them in.

It was not until 1230hrs that we learnt that traffic on the CYPOL radio net was indicating that Makarios was not dead and that a call had gone out to CYPOL stations everywhere to rally support for him. We treated this information with reserve, but it was soon followed by the message from Macfarlane which gave credibility to the news that somehow the Archbishop had survived the onslaught on the Presidential Palace. We immediately informed the Secretary General:

At about noon *[New York time]* on 15 July I received a further message from my Special Representative informing me that the UNFICYP Zone Commander in Limassol had reported that the Bishop of Paphos had informed him that he had received a radio message from President Makarios asking him to send a message to the Permanent Representative of Cyprus to the United Nations requesting him to call forthwith a meeting of the Security Council of the United Nations. My Special Representative added that he was not able to verify the authenticity of this message and in particular whether it emanated from Archbishop Makarios. In the circumstances I considered it my duty to communicate this message to the Permanent Representative of Cyprus, at the same time mentioning the inability of UNFICYP to verify its authenticity.[14]

The survival of Makarios, if true, injected a new factor into the situation and gave the prospect of continuing conflict between his supporters and the *coup* perpetrators.

After a busy morning at Force HQ, I set out to see for myself the situation in Nicosia. Suspicious National Guardsmen and the crews of two T-34 tanks eyed my car with its UN flag at roadblocks but did not stop me. Driving on through streets that were deserted except for nondescript men in commandeered cars driving around and flourishing weapons, I made for the District JOC in Wolseley Barracks. Here Manuel briefed me on the latest reports and the measures successfully taken to maintain the integrity of the Green Line and pre-empt intercommunal incidents along it.

At 1600hrs UNFICYP's senior Commanders assembled in Blue Beret Camp, not without incident in some cases. The RAF Whirlwind helicopter bringing Kristensson from Famagusta and Rieger from Larnaca was fired upon with small arms as it passed over Strovolos and was struck by two rounds; fortunately the damage was minor and the aircraft landed with its passengers unscathed. After a review of the day's events, General Prem Chand stressed that the overriding priority was for UNFICYP to do its utmost to prevent intercommunal incidents, with restraint urged on leaders at all levels in both communities. He emphasized the need to preserve the Force's freedom of movement and asked all to render whatever assistance they could in the humanitarian field, suggesting, in particular, that contingent medical officers should offer their services to local civil hospitals. In the meantime UNFICYP was to remain at Blue Alert.

Reports that small arms, mortar and even tank fire was falling on Turkish areas in and around Nicosia gave cause for growing concern. It was unlikely that this was deliberate and so far incidents had been minor with no casualties reported, but it was giving rise to Turkish anger and risk of retaliation. The Canadians acted quickly to stop such firing whenever they could pinpoint its source[15], but, as further incidents were reported, Orek asked for a meeting with me to discuss these and other problems. Given possible difficulty in crossing the Green Line into the Turkish quarter, I decided to go by Sioux helicopter and John Miles agreed to accompany me. We landed in the dry moat beside the Barbaro Bastion and immediately went to Orek at the VPO, where we gave him an account of the day's events and informed him of UNFICYP's measures to prevent intercommunal incidents. Orek undertook to do his best to keep Turkish Cypriots calm, but said that they were deeply concerned at developments on the Greek side and anxious lest they came under attack. Emphasis was given to his words when, even as we spoke in his office a mere 100m from the Green Line, small arms fire could be heard in the vicinity and two mortar rounds fell close by. Miles and I then walked across to the Turkish Embassy to see the Counsellor, Mr Karaca. We briefed him, too, on the day's events and UNFICYP's reactions. He made two complaints: first, that heavy weapons including mortars had been fired in the direction of Turkey's National contingent, and second, that electric power to its camp had been cut off. We undertook to do our best to remedy both matters.

On our return to Force HQ General Prem Chand and Mr Weckman-Munoz decided to follow up our visits by going themselves to see Mr Denktash and the Turkish Ambassador, Mr Inhan. The latter protested strongly that five artillery rounds had fallen in the area of the Turkish contingent's camp and pressed Prem Chand to intervene without delay with the National Guard commander to stop all such firing. Appreciating the serious implications of this complaint, Prem Chand decided to tackle the National Guard personally, not-withstanding that Flynn had been told earlier that a meeting between the two Force Commanders was not possible. Escorted by UN Military Police, he drove straight to Athalassa, where at 2030hrs he insisted on a face-to-face meeting with the Acting Commander of the National Guard, Brig. General Georgitsis, erstwhile Commander of 3rd Higher Military Command.[16] Also present at their meeting was Yiannikodimos (Chief of Staff), Kombokis (Commander of the RFU) and Tsolakis (LO), as well as Flynn, now estab-lished at Athalassa with his radio link.

Prem Chand protested, first, at the fire that had been falling on the Turkish side, stressing the danger inherent in this. Replying, Georgitsis said that the Turks had nothing to fear from the *coup*, which was an internal matter of concern to the Greek community alone, and that the National Guard was under strict orders not to fire at Turkish areas – any such fire must have come from the TRU. When Prem Chand then complained that a UN helicopter had been fired on over Strovolos, Georgitsis pointed out that at the time the National Guard was continuing to meet resistance at the Presidential Palace and again suggested that the TRU had been responsible. He undertook to give instructions for the safety of UN heli-copters to be respected but asked that these should not fly at low levels where mistakes might occur; Prem Chand agreed.

Next, Prem Chand emphasized the UN troops' entitlement to freedom of movement in accordance with the Status of Forces Agreement and demanded that they should not be obstructed while engaged on their intercommunal responsibilities as set out in the Security Council mandate. The Greeks replied that the situation was still tense, that sporadic sniper fire was to be expected and that this might be directed at UNFICYP personnel by people other than the National Guard in order to foment trouble and discredit the latter. Prem Chand gave no ground on this fundamental matter and Georgitsis undertook to issue instruc-tions to ensure that UNFICYP's right to freedom of movement was respected. Finally, Prem Chand sought and obtained Georgitsis's assurance that the National Guard would not create any trouble that night in so far as the Turkish community was concerned and, as he left, he stressed the mutual benefit of Flynn's continuing presence at National Guard HQ to provide a reliable communication link between them.[17]

UNFICYP did not possess a radio intercept service but throughout the day useful infor-mation gleaned by casual listeners to the CYPOL radio net (also used by the Presidential Guard and the TRU) was passed to the JOC. This had given the first indication that the Archbishop had escaped from Nicosia and as the day wore on added to our knowledge of other developments. During the afternoon there were reports on the situation at Troodos, Morphou and Larnaca, of an ambush of a CYPOL patrol at Kokopetria (all escaped), and of prisoners being released from the Central Prison. At about 1700hrs Major Pandelakis, the TRU's commander, was heard calling on those of his men still holding out to surrender in order to avoid further bloodshed[18], but at the Archbishopric resistance continued. Firing in its vicinity intensified when an appeal to its Presidential Guard defenders to surrender was rejected (going to investigate, a Canadian officer climbed the bell-tower of the nearby Church of Ayios Antonios for a better view but was ordered down by members of the National Guard; when he moved to another vantage point two bursts of fire hit the wall beside his vehicle and he reported: 'I decided to postpone the recce until a quieter period'). Shooting and explosions reached a climax at about 1900hrs and continued sporadically until about 2100hrs, when the Archbishopric fell to the National Guard; daylight showed it to have suffered extensive damage.

As the long hot day drew to a close it seemed that the *coup* had achieved substantial success and a curfew was in force throughout the island. In Nicosia sporadic shooting continued at many places in the Greek sector (some designed, perhaps, to ensure compliance with the curfew). Occasional stray rounds impacted close to TCF posts on the Green Line and at least six mortar rounds had fallen inside the Turkish quarter but no casualties were caused. At the airport there was constant activity accompanied by occasional shooting (a group of the TRU held out on the terminal's top floor for several hours), some prisoners were taken away, and UN observers reported troops breaking into shops and other parts of the terminal and other buildings. The airport had been closed to traffic since the morning, but at 2200hrs a Boeing 707 aircraft of Olympic Airways was seen to land and disembark men in civilian clothes before leaving 20 minutes later.

Famagusta was under National Guard control, the CYPOL station having fallen after its battering and loud-speaker calls on its defenders to surrender, but there was sporadic shooting elsewhere and the telephone exchange was in the hands of Greek naval personnel. No intercommunal incidents had occurred although the TCF had been strengthening the Old City's defences. In Larnaca, where by nightfall the main CYPOL station had fallen, some shooting continued, but all was quiet in the Turkish quarter where the TCF stood mobilized; at Kophinou (22km to the west) the Austrians were trying to persuade the TCF to halt the construction of new fortifications. The Danes in Lefka District reported that Morphou was under control of the National Guard, who had declared that UN vehicles would not be permitted on the roads after dark – a ruling that the Danes rejected. From Kyrenia District the Finns reported that, apart from occasional rounds that had landed in the Turkish enclave, the situation along their sectors of the Green Line was calm although the TCF remained on high alert; that the Kyrenia Road was closed; and that there was sporadic' shooting in Kyrenia itself. In the mountains a forest fire, described by a British tourist as 'pure Hieronymous Bosch'[19] was blazing out of control near Karmi just west of St Hilarion Castle. This was threatening the Finns in nearby OP Pileri but there was a temporary respite when the fire turned east; when at around midnight the fire turned again, the Finns had to abandon the OP for the time being.

UNFICYP had been unable to establish with any degree of certainty what the day's events had cost in terms of human lives on the Greek side, but reported to New York that at a conservative estimate some 20–30 had been killed and more than 100 wounded in Nicosia alone[20]; although a few Turks had received minor injuries from stray rounds, no fatalities were reported. Several requests were received during the day from the Turkish side for escorts for various purposes but were refused because in no case was the urgency judged sufficient to warrant these.

Reviewing the day's events at Force HQ, we felt reasonably satisfied that within the limits of its resources UNFICYP had discharged its responsibilities under the mandate positively and constructively, while recognizing that the Turkish community had displayed commendable discipline and restraint. We were thankful, too, that in spite of incidents where members of the Force had been exposed to fire there had been no UN casualties. As we reflected on what the day had brought, it was the situation in the south-west of the island, where the presence of a defiant Archbishop Makarios was now public knowledge, that gave most cause for concern. There was little doubt but that the leaders of the *coup* would not tolerate a situation in which Greek Cypriots might rally around him to oppose the new 'Government of National Salvation' under their puppet, Nicos Sampson. How, we wondered, would they deal with Makarios now that he had escaped their clutches?

CHAPTER THIRTY

ESCAPE FROM THE CLUTCHES
OF THE JUNTA

Greek people of Cyprus – the voice you hear is familiar. You know who is addressing you. It is I, Makarios! I am not dead as the Athens junta and its local representatives would wish – I am alive. And I am with you, struggling with you and bearing the banner of the common struggle. The junta's *coup* has failed. I was the target of the junta, and while I am alive the junta will not pass in Cyprus.

> Archbishop Makarios, Broadcast from 'Radio Free Paphos',
> evening of 15 July 1974.

How had Makarios escaped? There were elements of both luck and farce in the story. On Saturday 13 July, the day after he had received (but discounted) US Ambassador Davies's warning, he left Nicosia for his Troodos mountain lodge. There he received a telephone call from a Greek Cypriot recently returned from Athens who asked to see him to impart what he said was 'very serious information' from a reliable source. The Archbishop replied that he was tired and that the matter could await his return to Nicosia after the weekend. Early on the morning of Monday 15 July he left by car for the capital, little suspecting what was to meet him there.

The Presidential Palace, which he reached at 0740hrs, stands on a low hill surrounded by its own grounds in which were situated a police post, a radio station and a small barracks for the Presidential Guard. His first business was with the Under Secretary to the President, Mr Patroclos Stavrou; next, he saw the Attorney-General, Mr C. Tornaritis, before receiving some villagers and listening to their problems. At 0815hrs he left his office for the reception hall to greet a party of school children visiting from Egypt; as he was doing so the sound of gunfire was heard. Stavrou has described events:

> It must have been about 8.20am when we heard gunshots. . . . I went outside immediately to see what was going on. The gunfire increased. I hurried back to Makarios and told him that we must be under attack. . . . Our impression was that the illegal EOKA-B was making a display of strength at the Presidential Palace and that either it would be withdrawn immediately or it would be repelled. The Archbishop even told me to telephone the police but the line buzzed and seemed to be cut off. Meanwhile the few men of the Presidential Guard at the Palace started to fire back, and a sergeant informed the President that tanks and armoured vehicles of the

National Guard were in front of the Palace. The President told me to telephone the Cyprus Broadcasting Authority to ask them to appeal to the nation to organize speeches and rallies. We dialled the number . . . it kept ringing but there was no answer. . . . Meanwhile the Presidential Guard continued its defence. There were not many of them as the majority were on guard all night and so in the morning they went home to rest.[1]

The reception hall being very exposed, the Archbishop ushered the children into an adjoining corridor where those taking shelter included the Minister of Justice, Mr C. Vakis, who was awaiting an audience. The next minutes have been described by Makarios himself:

> We stood in the corridor for about 15 minutes. . . . My Under-Secretary and members of my staff told me to leave because I was the target of the attackers and I would not survive if the coupists were to come into the building. Finally I decided to leave the Palace, the east side of which had already caught fire. Looking out of the windows of my office I saw that the Palace was not completely surrounded and that there was an exit towards the west side of the building. I left from the west door of my office and followed a downhill path which led to the bed of the [*dry Pedhieos*] river. I crossed to the opposite bank and after a small hill reached the road. . . . Generally, I was not at all frightened.[2]

He was accompanied by Nicos Thrasivoulou (Chief of the Presidential Guard and his personal bodyguard), Andreas Neophytou (Captain in the National Guard and his nephew), Andreas Potamaris (officer in the Presidential Guard) and a young policeman. The remainder stayed behind in the Palace so that the escape of the Archbishop might go unnoticed.[3]

Once across the dry river bed Makarios decided to make for the Kykko *Metohi* (Monastery annex) about one kilometre to the north. A passing car was waved down and its driver agreed to lend it, though warning that it was almost out of petrol; with nephew at the wheel they set off only to halt after a short distance, the fuel exhausted. Another car then approached and its owner, too, agreed to its use, notwithstanding that it was an invalid's car, the owner having two wooden legs, and in this they continued on towards the *Metohi*. When about 400m short of it they spotted an officer of the National Guard reserve, Nicos Pastelopoulos, who was known to be loyal to the Archbishop. He warned that tanks were approaching, whereupon the whole party, including Pastelopoulos, hurriedly turned about in order to get clear of Nicosia before all escape routes were sealed. Pastelopoulos led the way, driving some 200m ahead to give warning of any roadblocks and, if need be, to create a diversion to allow Makarios to get away. In this order, His Beatitude still in the invalid's car, they headed out of the capital along a minor road to the village of Klirou, 20km to the south-west. Luck had played a major part in his escape, although, as befitting an Archbishop, Makarios later ascribed his good fortune elsewhere:

> My escape and survival were due to a miracle. Had I left the Palace a few minutes earlier, I would have gone to the *Metohi* before the tanks appeared on the road causing me to reverse direction. In the *Metohi* I would have been surrounded and there would have been no escape. . . . On the

other hand if I had been a few minutes later, they would have completed the ring around the Palace and my escape would have been cut off.[4]

At Klirou they halted at the house of Neoclis Malekos, an off-duty member of the Presidential Guard, while deciding on the next move. Makarios was persuaded of the need to put as much distance as possible between himself and Nicosia and, changing to Malekos's car, he headed on up through the mountains to Troodos itself, a further 25km along a very winding road. The others followed and all reached Troodos without incident ; there the party halted. A group went on to the Presidential Lodge one kilometre further south to tell its guards that the Archbishop was alive, to collect weapons, to warn them of the danger they were in and to advise them to follow His Beatitude to Kykko Monastery, a further 24km of tortuous mountain road to the west. Meanwhile Makarios, Thrasivoulou, Neophytou and Potamaris drove on to a point from which the Monastery could be observed, and here they rested while awaiting the others. It was now mid-morning.

When the others arrived, Makarios learnt that the CBC radio had been announcing his death. Noticing that one of the CYPOL vehicles from the Lodge was equipped with radio, he tried to contact the Presidential Guard at the Palace. There was no reply, so he called the Archbishopric using the call-sign 'Acropolis Ena (One)', which identified him personally. He was answered by the astonished commander of the Archbishopric guard:

> "The Archbishop is speaking", I said; immediately I heard voices and shouts which I did not understand. The explanation was that they thought that I was dead. And yet now they could hear my voice – I was alive. . . . I told them to ring the church bells and to tell the people to go out into the streets to foil the *coup* forces of the National Guard.[5]

A message was also passed by this CYPOL radio to the Bishop of Paphos, telling him that the Archbishop was alive and asking him to request through UNFICYP a meeting of the Security Council to condemn the action being taken in Cyprus by the Greek junta.

These radio exchanges were the first indications that Makarios had survived the onslaught on the Palace. Misinterpretation of them gave rise to a remarkable notion entertained at high level at HQ BFNE that in reality he had not been in Nicosia at all that morning.[6] They may also have been the reason behind an incident during late morning when two Danish UNCIVPOL on routine patrol were halted near Evrykou by CYPOL officers, who demanded that they hand over the vehicle and their uniforms on promise that these would be returned within a few hours. The Danes refused to hand over their uniforms, but their vehicle was commandeered and they were detained in the police station, where they over-heard telephone conversations in Greek from which they deduced (wrongly) that Makarios himself was the speaker at the other end and that their vehicle was being used to help his escape. At about 1300hrs the two Danes were released and, with their vehicle handed back, they returned to their HQ at Xeros, bringing with them news that Makarios had survived and a message from the Bishop of Paphos similar to that already transmitted to UNFICYP HQ by Major Macfarlane.

While still halted within sight of Kykko Monastery Makarios learnt that a radio station calling itself 'Radio Free Paphos' was broadcasting calls for Greek Cypriots to disregard CBC radio announcements and to resist 'the coupists'. He decided to send Pastelopoulos straight to Paphos to contact this station while he and the remainder went on to the Monastery, regarded as a sanctuary since medieval times. It was reached at about 1300hrs and the Archbishop went into its church to pray before the golden ikon of the Virgin, held by tradition to be one of three painted by St Luke. Makarios recalled:

> It was with feelings of great emotion that I arrived at the Monastery. I was reminded of my years there, first as a novice and later as a deacon. There, in peace and serenity, I had prepared myself for my difficult march into the future.[7]

News of his presence quickly spread locally and people, some armed, gathered from nearby villages to resist any attempt by anti-Makarios forces to reach him in this remote mountain sanctuary.

As he rested in a cell after a meal with the monks, word came that Pastelopoulos had reached Radio Free Paphos, which was announcing that His Beatitude had survived and would shortly speak to the people. Realizing that the road was open, Makarios decided to make for Paphos at once. Borrowing a cassock and hat (the former threadbare and the latter a little small)[8], he and his party set off along more winding mountain roads to reach the Paphos Bishopric at about 1830hrs. When, soon afterwards, he was heard speaking in Greek to the people of Cyprus through Radio Free Paphos, CBC announcements that he was dead ceased and the National Guard gave up raking over the ashes of the Presidential Palace in futile search for his corpse. The *coup* leaders were now confronted with a new and pressing problem: how to get at the Archbishop now that he was at a point on the island that they could not quickly reach. However, if he had escaped the trap set for him in Nicosia, he was not yet altogether beyond their grasp.

Meanwhile Mr Stephanides, the Paphos District Officer, was despatched hot-foot to St Patrick's Camp on the town outskirts to tell Macfarlane of the Archbishop's presence in the Bishopric. A sceptical Macfarlane asked to meet Makarios in person in order to satisfy himself as to the truth of this and at about 1930hrs was invited to the Bishopric where he met Makarios, dignified, composed and proud of his escape. The Archbishop was anxious for news of the situation in Limassol, saying that he had it in mind to go there next day since he thought that it was there that the key lay to the success or failure of the *coup*; if a *coup* was to succeed, he said, it must do so within eight hours. Since that limit had already expired with the outcome in Limassol still uncertain, he was hopeful that the *coup* could be defeated. Makarios also read out the text of a second broadcast (this time in English), which was to be recorded for transmission by Radio Free Paphos, and gave Macfarlane the text of a second message to be passed by UNFICYP to New York without delay:

> To Mr Zeno Rossides, Head of Cyprus Delegation, United Nations. Please ask for an urgent meeting of Security Council to condemn the Greek 'Junta' for trying to liquidate by force the independence [*sic*] State of Cyprus. Archbishop Makarios.

Finally, he asked Macfarlane to convey an invitation to Mr Weckman-Munoz and General Prem Chand to visit him in Paphos next day. Macfarlane carried out these requests at once and the Archbishop's message was transmitted to New York that night.

Loyalists had already placed Greek officers of the National Guard in Paphos under arrest and during the afternoon, in response to the urging of Radio Free Paphos, Greek Cypriot villagers converged on the town by car, lorry, bicycle and even donkey in their naive enthusiasm to take up arms against their Archbishop's enemies:

> In the town centre anyone who turned up was issued with a weapon. We were amazed at the arsenal that was produced and at the number of men and boys who appeared from throughout the District to go to war for Makarios. Many of them had never handled a weapon before, and a combination of this and the issue of masses of ammunition . . . produced firework displays that gave the Turkish community only a matter of yards away sufficient grounds to come to full alert and improve their defences, which for the past ten years the UN Force had worked hard to prevent.[9]

At that stage Macfarlane and his men concentrated on monitoring the intercommunal situation, constantly passing assurances by the Greeks that this quarrel was not with the Turkish community.

By mid-afternoon it was apparent that Nicosia had fallen, but that the fight for Limassol was continuing and the Archbishop's supporters in Paphos decided to throw their weight behind those loyal to him in Limassol:

> So this rapidly recruited army, if one can call it such, set off to fight in Limassol. It was really a tragedy, because somewhere between two and five thousand men and boys set off in any available transport to Limassol with no idea of what was happening there and with absolutely no leadership except from the men who could shout the loudest. There was no question of a plan except "to go to Limassol". It was the most misguided display of enthusiasm that one could ever witness.[10]

This rag-tag army (which observers in the SBA estimated to number only between one and two thousand) reached the Western SBA at about 1730hrs and was allowed to pass through[11] to the village of Episkopi where a pause ensued, perhaps to formulate a plan. The aim, it seemed, was to raise the siege of the Limassol police stations, to rout the anti-Makarios forces and to declare the town for the Archbishop. It was a forlorn hope.

As darkness fell the motley army moved on towards Kolossi where a brief firefight took place.[12] On the outskirts of Limassol it split into two, one group turning off to follow the coast road that led through the Turkish quarter, to the immediate concern of Lieut. Colonel Willoughby, the UN Zone Commander:

> It was all too clear that at any minute a battle would break out between the Turks shooting up the Paphians and vice-versa, and the Paphians shooting up the Limassol anti-Makarios National Guard, who in turn would belt hell out of the Turks. . . . The Turkish leader was rung up and

told not to shoot, but he replied that there was no bother – the Paphos posse had already passed through without hindrance![13]

During the night there was much wild small arms firing in the town, punctuated by sounds of mortars, rocket-launchers and grenades. The Coldstream Guards reported 'a major battle at Ayios Ioannis (on the western outskirts) with thousands of rounds fired', but it was impossible to determine precisely what was happening. Occasionally, when stray rounds struck their positions, the TCF responded with warning shots, but no serious intercommunal incidents occurred. Although the Australian UNCIVPOL HQ in the town was hit by stray rounds, and in spite of the prodigious expenditure of ammunition, UNFICYP sustained no casualties; indeed casualties seemed to have been remarkably light among the combatants themselves. With the coming of dawn the Makarios supporters accepted defeat and a retreat towards Paphos began. Some 70 vehicles, crammed with disconsolate men in every kind of dress, straggled back west through Episkopi at about 0700hrs.

Thus on the morning of 16 July the only resistance on the island yet to be overcome was centred on Paphos where the presence of Makarios served as a rallying point. The National Guard needed to move fast against him if the *coup* was fully to succeed. Soon there were reports of its forces heading for Paphos on two axes, one from Nicosia through the Troodos mountains and the other along the coastal road from Limassol. Meanwhile loyalists in Paphos and those drifting back from Limassol were taking up defensive positions to halt them.

During the night of 15/16 July we had kept the UN Secretary General informed of developments and he had authorized UNFICYP to extend on humanitarian grounds its protection to the Archbishop, should this be sought. Weckman-Munoz and Prem Chand flew by helicopter to Paphos on the morning of 16 July and met Makarios in the Bishopric. They reviewed the situation with him and asked if he wished any help from UNFICYP with respect to his personal security; he declined the offer and discussion turned to his future movements. The possibility of seeking refuge in the British SBAs was touched on, but Makarios said that his own preference was to take to the mountains and remain with his people. Bishop Chrysostomos and some of his advisers argued against this, urging him instead to seek safety for the time being away from the island. No decisions were reached and Weckman-Munoz and Prem Chand returned to Nicosia unsure of the course that the Archbishop would adopt.

Meanwhile the National Guard's advance towards Paphos was proceeding with truckloads of troops, artillery, armoured cars and APCs observed on the move on both axes; a column of 40 vehicles had reached Troodos village by 0930hrs. As the net tightened, Makarios (whose second broadcast, this time in English and directed at the world at large, had now been made from Radio Free Paphos[14]) was tempted to take refuge in Panayia, his native village high in the hills north-east of Paphos:

> I thought that the *coup* tanks would not get that far. But the Bishop, the Members of Parliament and the Mayor thought otherwise. They advised me to leave Cyprus. . . . I could not reconcile myself with such a thought. The people would say that I, who had invited them to resist, had abandoned them and left to save my own life. . . . In the end, however, I came to see that the arguments for my departure were not without merit. It was . . . a question of avoidance of blood-

shed. The putchists were remorseless, and they had already killed very many. Persuaded, I decided to leave Cyprus.[15]

A new development had perhaps served to concentrate his mind. The Coldstream Guards had observed the Cypriot gunboat *Levantis* and two MTBs sailing past Floria Bay (10km south-east of Paphos) and reported at 1215hrs that the gunboat had opened fire on the Paphos Bishopric. There were claims that the building, situated on a bluff 1600m inland, was hit, but UN observers only saw rounds falling short of the bluff and believed that the Bishopric was beyond the range of the *Levantis* guns. Makarios had now to make up his mind how to escape:

> There was a way – from the British base a few miles distant from Limassol. But to get there by car would mean running a serious risk of interception, and the only safe mode of transport was by helicopter. Once I got to the base I could send a message to President Al Assad of Syria or to President Sadat of Egypt requesting an aeroplane. Thus my destination would depend on the country of origin of the aircraft. Had I taken the decision to leave earlier, I could have requested the use of a helicopter from Mr Weckman and General Chand when they came to see me in Paphos.[16]

As he had not done so, he sent an urgent message to Macfarlane requesting UNFICYP to arrange for a helicopter to take him and his immediate entourage to the British base at Akrotiri, from whence he might then leave the island by air. Macfarlane passed this request to me at 1235hrs, and I spoke at once to Mr Derek Day, Counsellor at the British High Commission, who undertook to consult the High Commissioner, Mr Olver. As these conversations were taking place, Makarios and his entourage presented themselves at St Patrick's Camp[17] and *Levantis* sailed on to silence the CBC relay station at Coral Bay (10km further north) from which the Radio Free Paphos broadcasts were being made.

Losing no time, Olver telephoned to say that the Archbishop's request was receiving urgent and sympathetic consideration and that a decision was expected within half an hour. However, as a precondition to meeting his request, Makarios was required to accept that he would not remain in the SBA but be flown from Akrotiri to the UK; Olver asked me to obtain Makarios's acceptance of this condition. He also sought my view on the use of one of UNFICYP's RAF Whirlwind helicopters for the evacuation from Paphos to Akrotiri. I replied that I saw two objections. The first was practical: the distance from Nicosia, where these aircraft were based, to Paphos was some 90km and the flight time would be signifi-cantly increased by the need to climb over the Troodos mountains, whereas the distance from Akrotiri, where NEAF helicopters were based, was less than 60km, all of which could be covered quickly at low level along the coast. The second was more serious: I pointed out that when it became known that a UN helicopter had been used for the escape, this was likely to prejudice UNFICYP's relations with the National Guard and might endanger UN heli-copters on missions elsewhere on the island. For these reasons I urged that one of the NEAF helicopters based at Akrotiri be used for the task.

Olver noted my views and I undertook to obtain the Archbishop's acceptance of the precondition as quickly as possible. The need to preserve a degree of security imposed some unavoidable delay, but confirmation duly came from Macfarlane that Makarios accepted the precondition; the British High Commission was notified accordingly. In the meantime Olver had telephoned again to say that CBFNE, Air Marshal Aiken, wished a UN helicopter to be used for the task because those at Akrotiri were painted yellow (their primary task being Search and Rescue) and would therefore be too conspicuous, an argument that I found unconvincing. However, since the helicopters serving UNFICYP were formally under CBFNE's and not the UN Force's command (*see Chapter 7*), we had no choice but to comply. Stipulating that all UN distinguishing marks were to be removed from both aircraft and crew before despatch to Paphos, I gave orders for one of the Whirlwind helicopters to be flown forthwith to Akrotiri, where it arrived at 1445hrs. During the next hour tension mounted as the National Guard closed in and London's decision was awaited. To the relief of all, authority came from London at 1545hrs for the operation to proceed, and the Whirlwind, all UN identification removed, landed in St Patrick's Camp, Paphos at 1615hrs.[18]

Throughout his wait of nearly four hours in the camp Makarios remained dignified and composed and regaled Macfarlane with an account of his escape from Nicosia. For his part Macfarlane, who kept the Archbishop's presence a close secret locally, handled matters with calm competence, correctly extending to him the courtesy due to the President. With Makarios and his entourage of Thrasivoulou, Neophytou and Potamaris as passengers, the helicopter reached Akrotiri at 1650hrs. There were media reports that the aircraft was fired on en route, but neither its crew nor UNFICYP observers on the ground were aware of any such shooting. Nonetheless it had been a close-run thing.[19]

With their Archbishop flown, the Paphiot Greeks saw the futility of further resistance and bloodshed, and Macfarlane reported a rapid volte-face:

> As soon as he had gone, I went to see the District Officer [*Stephanides*], who told me that Paphos now supported the Sampson régime and that he would remain as District Officer. Various Greek officers reappeared from the cells, in which they had been locked for the past 36 hours, to take command of local forces, and our full attention returned to the intercommunal front, which was now building up to a crescendo of activity.[20]

On their arrival at Akrotiri no time was lost in transferring Makarios and his three companions to CBFNE's Argosy aircraft and within 15 minutes they were on their way to London with an overnight refuelling stop in Malta. The party flew on next morning, 17 July, to England, where in London Makarios was received as Head of State and treated as a guest of the British government. He described later his emotions as he embarked on the first stage of this journey:

> Words cannot express how terrible I felt as I boarded the helicopter. The harsh reality finally hit me. When we took off, I looked down at Cyprus from the little window and a terrible feeling of grief filled my heart. . . . For a quarter of a century it was my life and I lived for the good fortune and future of Cyprus. I had known struggles, humiliations, exile, attempts on my life and many other hardships for the sake of the people of Cyprus, who loved me and whom I loved.

And now I was obliged to leave. They had thrown me out of Cyprus. . . . I was thinking also about the consequences of the *coup*. I had no doubt that Turkey would use it as a pretext to invade.[21]

How right he proved to be! Subsequently the Archbishop was wont to remark contemptuously that the Athens junta could not even mount a successful *coup*; all they had succeeded in doing was to ensure the partition of Cyprus by the Turks.

CHAPTER THIRTY-ONE

PUPPET PRESIDENCY

The various organs of the United Nations never wavered from the view that the Makarios government was still the legitimate government of Cyprus.

Rosalyn Higgins: *United Nations Peacekeeping – Documents and Commentary*, Vol. 4, p. 240.

The *coup d'état* did not change the status or role of UNFICYP. The Force continued to be engaged in a UN peacekeeping operation established by the Security Council and conducted with the consent of the Cyprus government. But what now was to be recognized as that government? The Force, which had continued to treat Makarios as President right up to his departure from Paphos on the afternoon of 16 July, was faced with this dilemma that same evening, when an invitation came from the Cypriot Ministry of Foreign Affairs for the SRSG, Weckman-Munoz, to call upon the new (Sampson-appointed) Foreign Minister, Dimis Dimitriou. Informed of this, Dr Waldheim instructed that, pending further consideration, UNFICYP was to have no formal contacts with the Sampson régime.[1] The Ministry was accordingly told that such a call was not appropriate, but that one of its officials would be received in a personal capacity by UNFICYP's Senior Political Adviser, John Miles. In consequence Vanias Markides, a senior official well known to UNFICYP for his integrity and courtesy, called on Miles in Blue Beret Camp on 17 July, when UNFICYP's position was explained to him.

Waldheim had realized the wider implications of the *coup* as soon as news of it reached him on 15 July and in telegrams couched in identical terms had expressed concern to the Prime Ministers of Greece and Turkey, urging maximum restraint in order not to exacerbate the situation. On 16 July he convened a meeting of the Security Council to report and it met again on 19 July; on each occasion Rossides, the Government's Permanent Representative in New York, was accepted as the legitimate representative of Cyprus and spoke in support of the Makarios government. The reaction of the Sampson régime was to declare that Rossides had been dismissed and that Mr L. Papaphilipou was being sent to New York in his place. Turkey refused to recognize the legitimacy of these actions, but Papaphilipou nonetheless cabled a request to present his letters of credence to the Secretary General on 20 July; this request was firmly rejected by the UN Legal Counsel on Waldheim's behalf. Welcoming this stand, Denktash declared not only that the appointment of Papaphilipou was unconstitutional[2] but also that the Leadership did not recognize the Sampson régime either. Thus the Sampson government was recognized by neither UNFICYP nor the Leadership, much less the international community. Nonetheless there was a pragmatic need, in so far as its mandate was concerned, for UNFICYP to deal with those in control on the Greek Cypriot side. It was clear that these were not Sampson and his so-called ministers, but the Greek officers in the National Guard. During the eight days of the puppet presidency it was with the latter that UNFICYP dealt, declining direct contact with Sampson or those appointed by him.

With Makarios gone there was a general acceptance that the *coup* had succeeded, albeit that few believed the Sampson government could survive for long. The security situation gradually returned to one approaching normality, although all resistance had not ceased and sporadic firing was common during the next few days and nights as Makarios loyalists were hunted down, some old scores settled and the curfew enforced. However, the Turkish community became increasingly restive and critical, drawing no comfort from Sampson's declarations that it had nothing to fear from him; his past record belied his words. The opportunity to improve military defences in clear breach of the military *status quo* was seized by the Turks with consequential National Guard protests. UNFICYP's efforts to secure a return to that *status quo* met with little success because the sounds of sporadic shooting and the activities of indisciplined National Guard and EOKA-B 'cowboys' served only to increase Turkish Cypriot anxieties.[3] Such problems and a spate of others kept UNFICYP, still at Blue Alert, exceptionally busy in the days up to 19 July, unaware that they were but a precursor to far more critical days.

As a measure of calm was restored, the 24-hour curfew was progressively lifted but remained in force from dusk to dawn. Shops, businesses and government offices reopened and, within curfew limits, civil activity all but resumed normal pattern. Prevention of inter-communal incidents remained UNFICYP's first priority and every effort was made to ensure that the Greeks exercised utmost restraint *vis-à-vis* the Turks, and to persuade the latter not to exploit the situation by provocative changes of a military nature. The situation in Limassol was typical. Meeting the Greek Colonel in charge in the town on 16 July, Lieut. Colonel Willoughby, the UN Zone Commander, not only learnt that the town's police had now changed sides but also secured the Colonel's guarantee of freedom of movement for UN vehicles and an undertaking that he (Willoughby) would be consulted on any matter impinging on the Turkish community. The meeting was not without its lighter moments:

> The interview was difficult, the Colonel having virtually no English and his interpreter little more. Excited Greeks kept running in, shouting to each other, and a tiresome major kept showing me swathes of bandages covering a wound to his shoulder inflicted "in cool" (presumably in cold blood) by some wicked policeman who had captured him. When it looked as if some progress was being made with the Colonel, the same major returned with his jacket which had a hole in it and some bloodstains. I think he wanted me to get a new one for him – or give him my own shirt, but I did not make an offer.[4]

Touring the town with his District Commander, Major M. Frisby, Willoughby noted little serious damage: even the police stations, the primary targets, were relatively unscathed.

They found the Turks relaxed about events on the Greek side, complaining only of a shortage of flour (which Willoughby arranged to remedy). He conveyed to them the National Guard's assurances with respect to their community, but his request that recently erected barricades be dismantled went unheeded. Returning to their HQ in Polemidhia Camp, the two encountered a National Guard convoy of troops and artillery heading for Paphos where Makarios then still survived. Its approach was accompanied by sounds of small arms fire; Willoughby wrote: 'I waved my stick in a jolly way as each truck passed. . . . They replied with a jolly wave back and bursts of fire into the air'.

Next morning, 17 July, Willoughby flew to Paphos to check with his District Commander, Major Macfarlane, how matters stood following the flight of Makarios the previous evening, and to meet the Greek Colonel now in control:

> The District Officer Mr Stephanides, was back in office having changed his allegiance – luckily from our point of view. He knows the people, both Greek and Turkish, and is far better employed in helping to keep things quiet than hiding up in the hills and waiting for Makarios's return. The Colonel was well turned out, unlike his Limassol equivalent, and again guaranteed cooperation with us and professed no evil designs against the Turkish community.[5]

The *coup* had given the Turks of Paphos an ideal excuse to improve their military defences and during the ensuing days Macfarlane was much involved in dealing with this problem as the National Guard's new area commander, Colonel Gravenes, pressed for the changes to the *status quo* made by the Turks to be reversed:

> [In the Turkish quarter of Paphos] they included new machine-gun positions, explosive charges in most houses along the [intercommunal] interface, explosive charges under access roads, 60mm mortar positions and a considerably increased manning of all recognized and new posts. The pattern was the same throughout the District in all Turkish enclaves.[6]

In Lefka District Lieut. Colonel Severinson's Danes faced a potentially serious situation on 17 July, when a group of 25 armed pro-Makarios members of the National Guard sought asylum in the Turkish town of Lefka. The local Turkish Leadership refused to grant this, whereupon the Makarios loyalists settled down to camp within the recognized limit of the Turkish area, creating the risk that the National Guard might go in to bring them out or that the Turks might evict them by force. Severinson solved matters by securing a written guarantee that the 25 would be humanely treated if they surrendered to the National Guard; this they did.[7] The Danes also grappled with problems stemming from Turkish violations of the long-standing agreements that provided for free passage of Greek traffic on the coast road through the Kokkina and Limnitis enclaves. Additional problems were caused by a serious forest fire which broke out on 18 July, damaging Selemani village and its UN OP (from which the Danes were obliged temporarily to withdraw) and threatening Limnitis and the adjacent Danish camp. Greeks and Turks, together with all available Danish soldiers, worked closely and amicably together to bring the fire under control that same night: demonstration of how the common interest could, when necessary, override intercommunal differences.

In the south of the island the Austrians in Larnaca District reported increased tension along the Artemis Road (the area of close confrontation south of Larnaca town) and around Kophinou as both sides improved their defences. Nerves were not calmed by the practice of men in National Guard vehicles loosing off volleys of small arms fire as they passed various posts along the main Nicosia – Limassol road. Lieut. Colonel Rieger did his best to discourage provocative actions by both sides and by the evening of 18 July was able to report some lessening of the earlier tension.[8]

The safety of some 5,000 Swedish tourists in the Famagusta area was a particular national concern for the Swedish Contingent. Lieut. Colonel Kristensson, appreciating the need to keep them informed of what was happening, arranged for bulletins to be posted each day in some 50 hotels and in the offices of travel agents. (In the event none of these tourists came to any harm and most had been able to leave Cyprus by 20 July, although about 1,000 still remained in Famagusta when Turkish forces landed that same day). Kristensson had the first of many meetings with the new National Guard local commander on 16 July; this proved to be Lieut. Colonel Kostas, who had arrived from Greece only shortly before (whether with prior knowledge of the impending *coup* was not clear). Kostas was friendly and helpful and it was clear that it was the military who gave the orders.[9] Discussions with him centred on the TCF's improvements of defences, especially those on the walls of the Old City in breach of the Famagusta Agreement. As this Turkish activity continued and Kostas threatened to halt it by force, General Prem Chand intervened with the Leadership in Nicosia with the result that the Famagusta Turks were ordered to halt further improvements (although those already made were not dismantled). Tension was further lowered by Kristensson's success in persuading the Turks to reduce the presence of TCF on the Old City's walls and to order their dock labourers back to work. These actions, and the institution of UN-escorted convoys for the conveyance of Turks between their villages and the Old City, strengthened relations between the Swedish Contingent and both communities. An important consequence was the readiness with which both accepted the presence of a Swedish LO during the fighting of succeeding days.

There was much speculation at this time that Turkey might intervene militarily and Kristensson discussed the rumours with Mr Vryonides (a local hotelier and honorary Swedish Consul), who thought intervention probable. Although Kristensson doubted the Turkish capability to mount an amphibious operation on the scale required, he judged it prudent to order shelter trenches to be dug in Carl Gustav Camp, the Swedish base near Salamis. Thanks to his foresight, this protection for his men was ready by 20 July.

Throughout the island an early action of the National Guard had been to order all privately held weapons to be surrendered by 17 July on pain of court martial. The response proved mixed, whereupon CYPOL began to search houses for arms. In some villages where Greek policemen entered the houses of Turkish Cypriots, UNFICYP intervened to stop their action and ensure that confiscated weapons were handed back. These CYPOL searches gave rise to tension, particularly in the western part of Kyrenia District, and Lieut. Colonel Pullinen stepped up Finnish patrolling in the area to bolster Turkish confidence in the mixed villages.

For the Canadians in Nicosia the first priority was maintenance of the integrity of the Green Line. Static OPs were augmented by frequent patrols and close liaison was maintained with both sides. Visits were paid to all TCF company commanders, but Lieut. Colonel Manuel, the District Commander, encountered reluctance at the HQ of the National Guard's 3rd HMC to deal with him direct rather than through National Guard Force HQ at Athalassa. The Canadians also found that movement in and around the city was not without its problems:

> There was not too much danger on the Green Line itself. The danger lay in driving around the Greek sector . . . . Everywhere EOKA-B types were driving around in their cars with an AK-47 sticking out of each window. The new régime had little respect for the UN, and our soldiers continually had cocked weapons stuck in their faces at various road-blocks.[10]

The Canadians' actions during 15 and 16 July gradually reduced intercommunal tensions in the city, but in the early hours of 17 July Manuel was alarmed by a Turkish report that an attack was imminent on the CYPOL station at Omorphita in which some pro-Makarios policemen were said to be holding out; the building was situated right on the Green Line with a UN OP located on its roof. Manuel immediately pressed the National Guard not to take any such action and warned the occupants of their danger. A Canadian reserve platoon was stood ready to intervene and those in the UN OP on the roof prepared for hasty evacuation. In the event the policemen in the building declared their support for Sampson, the National Guard disclaimed any intention to attack and the Canadian post remained *in situ*. Had it been a false alarm or another demonstration of successful peacekeeping? UNFICYP was not to know. The Canadians' efforts to halt TCF breaches of the laboriously constructed military *status quo* were less successful: new bunkers were built and heavy and light machine guns mounted. Both sides maintained double manning of their posts and serious incidents would have been inevitable but for UNFICYP's vigilance. For example, when the Turks complained that they were receiving tank fire from the direction of Omorphita:

> Major K.C. Eyre went up with his driver in the middle of the night to investigate. They found a lone T-34 shelling an abandoned ice-cream factory, and when the tank missed the rounds were falling in the Turkish enclave. Major Eyre explained the problem and suggested that the tank move to the other side of the building. The tank commander was very cooperative. He promptly moved his tank to the new position, and continued shelling the factory from the other side.[11]

Canadian responsibilities were not limited to the city of Nicosia and Manuel's patrols visited Turkish and mixed villages throughout the District. Other tasks undertaken by the Canadians included rectifying an interruption of water supplies to Nicosia's Turkish quarter and keeping a discreet eye on the houses of Glafkos Clerides and erstwhile Foreign Minister Christofides.[12]

The competence of UNFICYP's District Commanders in dealing with unexpected new problems and in preventing these from escalation to the point of intercommunal conflict gave cause for satisfaction at UNFICYP HQ, where the flow of information into the JOC not only provided a good picture of developments across the island but also ensured that New York was kept well informed. Sundry calls for help came from the Turkish community, now hemmed in by National Guard road-blocks and its own policy of maintaining tight control over its own people; assistance was sought in the provision of grain for its main flour mill in Nicosia, the distribution of flour and other necessities to its communities elsewhere, the conveyance of sick from outlying villages to the Turkish hospital in the capital, the safe carriage of cash between banks, and checks on the condition of Turkish convicts in the Central Prison.[13] UNFICYP responded to such calls in so far as resources allowed; helicopters were tasked to bring the seriously ill to hospital and escorts were provided for the protection of movement by road. (Demands for the latter were such that on 18 July the Parachute Sqn, RAC was ordered to re-deploy its 1st Troop of scout cars from Paphos to join its 2nd Troop based in Camp UNFICYP adjacent to Nicosia airport.) Calls for assistance also came from others – the British High Commission sought help in tracing two British nationals rumoured to have been killed; others requested checks on the safety or whereabouts of other individuals; a plea for asylum came from an ousted Makarios minister (this was refused after reference to New York because his life was not judged to be at risk); tourists caught on the island clamoured for information, in particular as to when Nicosia airport would be reopened and civil flights resumed.

Late on the night of 17 July the National Guard announced that the airport would be opened for civil traffic at 0500hrs next morning and on 18 and 19 July incoming and outgoing aircraft were frequent, allowing most of those whose departure had been delayed to leave Cyprus before the airport was closed again following Turkey's military intervention on 20 July. UNFICYP assisted by establishing a small air movements cell in the main terminal to give help and advice to all comers. These UN officers noted that the usual customs, immigration and airport control officials were back in post, that portraits of Makarios were conspicuous by their absence and that, apart from much broken glass, the terminal generally had reverted to its normal state. However, the airport was under military control with a Major Papadopoulos (with whom UNFICYP was later to have close dealings) in local command.

Incoming Greek aircraft arriving before the airport was reopened to general traffic gave UNFICYP cause for concern. On 16 July one was observed to disembark about 20 men and a number of boxes before departing with some wounded Greek soldiers; two more on 18 July brought in some men in military uniform and an exceptionally high proportion of other young men among its passengers. These arrivals did not escape the notice of the Leadership, which protested to UNFICYP that the National Guard was being clandestinely reinforced. It complained, too, that Turkish Cypriots were being prevented from leaving through the airport, unless in possession of a special permit issued by the Sampson government, which it did not recognize; both complaints were well founded but UNFICYP was unable to remedy either before disaster struck on 20 July.

The *coup* had attracted worldwide attention and representatives of the international media headed for Nicosia. Some of the more enterprising reached the island quickly by boat, but as soon as the airport was reopened the number of press, radio and TV correspondents increased to an eventual total of about 350. Their demands for information placed a heavy burden on UNFICYP's meagre PR resources, the civilian post of Force PIO having been vacant for 18 months. The Force's MPIO, Major I. McK. Robertson (UK), advised by the SPA, John Miles, filled the gap as best he could, but inevitably some correspondents approached UN Contingents direct. Contingent Commanders had to be reminded that UNFICYP Standing Orders required all contacts with the media to be channelled through Force HQ and they were instructed not to transmit press copy via the contingent's military communications. For years the customary meeting point for the international press in Nicosia had been the bar of the Ledra Palace Hotel and this now became the *rendez-vous* where news and rumour were bandied to and fro. On 19 July UNFICYP arranged a tour of the Green Line so that correspondents might see for themselves the intercommunal situation along it.

For UNFICYP an unwelcome consequence of the *coup* was the attention focused on the large store of Czech weapons held since 1972 in Camp UNFICYP; these, together with the associated ammunition held at Athalassa under parallel arrangements, were a tempting prize. The first inkling that others might have designs on them came on the afternoon of the *coup*, when a Greek officer arrived at the main gate of Camp UNFICYP demanding to inspect them, only to be refused admission. Next day, 16 July, an individual of foreign nationality but married to a Cypriot asked the British High Commission for its assistance in persuading the UN Force to hand over the arms to an anonymous group loyal to Makarios, which, he said, intended to mount a counter-*coup* in support of the Archbishop, then still in Paphos. A parallel approach was made by him to the US Embassy. He received short shrift from both. It was, perhaps, no coincidence that next day (17 July) the National Guard appeared to turn its attention to these weapons. Early that morning a T-34 tank was positioned at the airport terminal with its gun trained on Camp UNFICYP and a machine-gun post was sited on the terminal's roof from which fire could be brought to bear on the camp. Disquiet gave way to alarm when some 200 men of the National Guard's elite RFU were to be seen near the camp, seemingly being briefed by an individual in civilian dress, and alarm increased as some 50 then deployed in extended line facing the camp's western fence. An immediate 'stand-to' was ordered in both Camp UNFICYP and Blue Beret Camp, and, since troops in the former numbered no more than 200, all of whom (except for one platoon of Coldstream Guards) were members of BRITCON logistic units, reserve platoons from the Canadian and Finnish contingents were at once despatched. These reactions may have given the National Guard cause for second thoughts.

Soon afterwards a Greek Lieut. Colonel presented himself at the entrance to Force HQ in Blue Beret Camp demanding that the weapons be handed over. He was told firmly that the matter could be discussed only with National Guard HQ. I drove at once to Athalassa to confront the National Guard's Chief of Staff, Brig. General Yiannikodemos, to whom I protested strongly both the presence of his men in close proximity to the Czech weapons store and the Lieut. Colonel's demand. I stated that in no circumstances would UNFICYP surrender the weapons without the Secretary General's express authority and that any attempt to seize them would be met by force. Yiannikodemos, who appeared taken aback, evidently had little knowledge of the circumstances governing custody of the arms and lamely excused the presence of his troops with the explanation that they had been on the move past the UN camp and had merely halted there temporarily. As to the Colonel's demand, he said that there must be some misunderstanding – the National Guard had no need of more weapons – and he would clarify matters with the officer at once. I stressed the risk of misunderstandings in present circumstances if sizable bodies of his men moved close to, much less halted alongside, UN camps and he said that this would be avoided in future. (On my return to Blue Beret Camp, the UN troops were stood down and the Canadians and Finns returned to their contingents.)

Our meeting had been amicable, but in view of his evident ignorance as to the status of these weapons I arranged that we should meet again two days later so that I might brief him fully on the subject and discuss other matters of mutual interest. I did so on the afternoon of 19 July, when Yiannikodemos assured me that he now understood the position regarding the Czech arms and that the National Guard was content that these should remain in UNFICYP's custody. However, the incident had pointed the need to strengthen defences in Camp UNFICYP and measures taken to this end included the deployment of a Canadian 106mm RCL anti-tank detachment. The incident had also indicated the need to make an early check on the security of the ammunition held under parallel arrangements within the CYPOL compound at Athalassa and I was to have carried this out on the morning of 20 July had not more momentous events intervened.[14]

With the situation on the island now calmer, the Force Chief Medical Officer, Colonel O'Carrol-Fitzpatrick (UK), reminded contingent medical officers of the need to offer assistance to local hospitals. For the most part these offers were declined, incidentally rendering it impossible for UNFICYP to establish with any degree of certainty the casualties, fatal or otherwise, suffered during and in the immediate aftermath of the *coup*.[15]

On the morning of 18 July John Miles and I set out to find how the Ministry of Foreign Affairs and certain diplomatic missions were faring. At the Ministry we met Markides, the official who had called on Miles the previous day and who clearly was embarrassed by the situation; we reiterated the UN's continuing recognition of Makarios as President and stressed the delicacy of the new situation *vis-à-vis* the Turkish community. Our arrival at the Soviet Embassy, situated near the Paphos Gate (the scene of some of the heaviest shooting three days earlier) proved both timely and welcome. The anti-communist *coup* forces had surrounded the Embassy at the outset and confined the staff within it; to their anger and discomfort they were still so confined. Moscow had appealed to Waldheim for help and his instructions to UNFICYP to have this restriction lifted had reached Force HQ just as Miles and I were leaving; our rapid response impressed the Russians. We were greeted by the Counsellor, Mr Belaiev, who showed us a hole in the windscreen of his car, made by a bullet that had only just missed him and the military attaché.[16] Promising to have the troops surrounding the Embassy withdrawn as soon as possible, we took up the matter with the National Guard, who said that the cordon had been put in place for the Russians' own protection and that it would be lifted soon. Calling next at the Embassy of Greece, we found the curtains drawn and the building seemingly closed and deserted, but our knock on the door was answered by the Counsellor, Mr Serbos, who was subdued and nervous. The Ambassador, Mr Lagacos, had not returned from the meeting in Athens the previous weekend and Serbos had little knowledge of what was happening, since the Greek officers in Nicosia were ignoring him and his Embassy. He said he was not in need of help and thanked us for calling and for the information we had imparted.

On the afternoon of 18 July Nicos Sampson staged a bizarre press conference, which:

was a frightening experience, as the hall was jam-packed with at least six groups of armed men, not all of whom seemed to be in agreement, and all were negligent and careless in the way in which they carried their assorted arms. At one point there was a stand-up shouting match between an EOKA-B captain standing in the aisle and Nicos Sampson on the platform. It was at this conference that all the "victims" of Makarios's secret police torture, etc. were paraded to show the ill-treatment they allegedly had suffered, plus the various instruments of torture used. Altogether a very gruesome business.[17]

Little of substance emerged. Sampson claimed that casualties during the *coup*, both dead and wounded, numbered only 'some dozens'; he promised a return to normality as soon as possible, that Makarios 'torturers' would be brought to trial and that the actions of the former Ministers of the Interior (G.K. Ioannides) and of Justice (Chr. Vakis) would be investigated; he dismissed assertions that the *coup* was the work of the Athens junta or that its purpose was to secure *enosis* and he declared that the intercommunal talks would continue with Clerides as the Greek Cypriot negotiator.

Challenged with regard to international reactions, Sampson conceded that 'no government has recognized us so far nor have we asked for anybody's recognition'. As to reports of troop mobilization in southern Turkey he declared:

> I see no reason why Turkey should intervene militarily in Cyprus in view of the fact that the Turkish community is in no danger whatsoever. We have declared that our aim is to find a peaceful solution through the enlarged intercommunal talks.[18]

Questioned further, he said that clashes on the Greek side had not affected the Turks at all; that aircraft arriving before the reopening of the airport had brought only much needed medical supplies; that telephonic communications would soon be restored; that some hundreds of illegally held arms had been found and that those civil servants and teachers dismissed by Makarios had already been reinstated. Taunted as to why the Greek officers should have appointed him as President, he countered that it was not those officers but the Cypriot youth of the National Guard who had turned to him. As to the Archbishop's escape and possible eventual return he declared:

> To us Makarios is dead as a leader. He has abandoned those who believe in him. He has betrayed them and proved to be a person caring only for himself. He has chosen exile. If he repents, let him apply to my government.[19]

Sampson concluded this extraordinary press conference by announcing that parliamentary elections would be held within one year. For all his bluster, few present were deceived that he was any more than a puppet in the hands of the Greek military.

This tallied with the observations of UNFICYP's LOs at National Guard HQ, who reported that little respect was shown to Sampson, who was 'always looking very worried and in terrible need of sleep'. They described the situation at Athalassa on the afternoon of 17 July as 'a complete mess – Greek officers, EOKA-B people, members of the government and soldiers have all been mixed up in discussions, conferences and giving of orders'.

Reservists were being issued with a rudimentary uniform and brand new Czech automatic rifles seized from those stored at the Presidential Palace since 1966; after minimal instruction they were turned loose to drive around the city in commandeered cars and under no apparent control. Through it all the Greek officers at the HQ nonetheless remained calm and sure of success. The police, too, were under the close control of these officers, one of whom was always at the side of the new Chief of CYPOL, Mr P. Andreou (hitherto deputy to Mr Antoniou, now under arrest). CYPOL officers seemed embarrassed by their situation and remained unarmed until 17 July, when some were seen with old rifles while others in uniform but without cap badges were armed with new automatic weapons. (Asked what the distinction might be, UNFICYP's LO was told there was none; those without a badge had merely lost it!)

Throughout the week UNFICYP's primary purpose had been to prevent events from taking an intercommunal turn. We realized, nonetheless, that the real decisions governing the future of Cyprus were being taken outside the island. The horizon was darkening; a straw in the wind was a reconnaissance flight by six Turkish F84s over the north of the island on 18 July.

CHAPTER THIRTY-TWO

THE GUARANTOR POWERS AND
INTERNATIONAL REACTION

As far as world opinion was concerned the last straw was the man whom the conspirators installed in Makarios's place: Nicos Sampson, former EOKA terrorist and leader of the 1963 assault on the Turks of Omorphita. If Turkey ever wanted to establish herself on Cyprus, she would never have such a favourable opportunity again – the legal grounds of the Treaty of Guarantee, . . . the transparent intervention of the Greek Government, . . . the insult of "President" Sampson.

Keith Kyle: Minority Rights Group Report No. 30: Cyprus,p.14.

When news of the *coup* reached London and Ankara on the morning of 15 July both were taken by surprise. In the House of Commons that afternoon the British Foreign Secretary, James Callaghan, expressed 'very deep dismay and regret' at the reported death of Makarios and said that Britain had drawn the attention of the Greek and Turkish governments to the provisions of the Treaty of Guarantee governing maintenance of the independence, territorial integrity and security of Cyprus. Stressing the need for restraint on all sides, he added that he was in touch with the UN Secretary General and other interested governments.

Speaking for the Conservative Opposition, Sir Alec Douglas-Home associated himself with these remarks and hoped that the UN Force would be able to keep order. This prompted an exchange between a Labour back-bencher and Callaghan that was indicative of the misconceptions then surrounding UN peacekeeping operations:

Mr Norman Atkinson: Does he recognize also that this situation raises one of the important questions in foreign politics throughout the world, namely the purpose of UN troops? Is it not the purpose of UN occupancy by troops to prevent a change of government or Head of State by methods other than those approved by the UN?

Mr James Callaghan: I am not sure what obligations were laid on the UN troops, but my recollection is that they were introduced to ensure that there would be no outbreak of violence between the Turkish and Greek Cypriot communities. As to their effectiveness in preventing a bloody *coup* . . . my information is that there are 2,400 *[UN]* troops of various nationalities and that the National Guard alone is over 10,000 strong.[1]

Replying to a further question, Callaghan made clear that Britain had no responsibility for internal security in the Republic of Cyprus and added:

> We have a right to consult the other governments who are signatories of the Treaty of Guarantee. That is what I have set in motion today to ensure that security is maintained in the island and that there is no attack from outside.[2]

Ankara's reaction was one of alarm. Convinced that the *coup* was no less than disguised *enosis*, Prime Minister Ecevit judged that Turkish military intervention was imperative to foil this. Breaking off from his visit to Afyon to return to Ankara, he declared:

> Let no one try to profit from the chaotic situation in Cyprus to infringe upon the rights of the Turks. We will never accept a *fait accompli*. We will let no one trample on the rights of the Turks.[3]

Nervous of world opinion should Turkey invade and unsure of the ability of Turkish armed forces to execute such an operation, some colleagues urged caution. During 15 July a series of meetings was held in Ankara, culminating in a midnight session of the National Security Council:

> Ecevit once more stressed the serious implications of the Sampson *coup* for the security of Turkey. He reviewed the situation in the Aegean. He pointed out that it would now be a simple matter for the Greeks to proclaim *enosis* and thus create a Hellenic island base from which, for the first time, central and south-eastern Turkey would come within range of Greek airforce bombers. Finally he expressed concern that oppression and even massacre of Turkish Cypriots might follow the *coup*.[4]

(This account is revealing of the extent to which strategic considerations, rather than concern for the plight of Turkish Cypriots, were foremost in Turkish minds.) The Council endorsed Ecevit's view that the *coup* was the work of Athens, that Sampson was committed to *enosis* and that preemptive action was essential. The Armed Services Chiefs expressed confidence in the ability and readiness of their forces to intervene and said that such an operation could be launched five days later – that is, on 20 July. The Council decided that preparations to that end should proceed and instructions were issued accordingly in the early hours of 16 July to General Staff HQ in Ankara. A member of the headquarters commented later:

> All Ecevit wanted of us was the securing of a bridgehead which would give the Turkish Cypriots an outlet to the sea and establish a balance of power. He impressed on us that, once this was achieved, further action would be in accordance with developments. It was, therefore, a two-stage plan based on the Sahin and Attila lines.[5]

He added that, while it was not considered that the operation posed any major risk since Greece could offer little, if any, opposition in or around Cyprus, the main Turkish concern was the Greek threat in the Aegean, which required the retention of a substantial proportion of the Turkish forces in western Turkey.

Ankara was now the focus of international attention and pleas for restraint flowed in from the UN Secretary General, NATO, Britain, France and others. The Soviet Union, suspicious as ever of a NATO stratagem to secure the island to the Western Alliance, was vociferous in its criticism of Greece, but, significantly, the voice of the United States was ambivalent and muted:

> When the news of the *coup* in Cyprus first reached Washington shortly after midnight, there was an initial spasm of indecision and confusion. The first reports of the death of Makarios did not bring unalloyed grief to Foggy Bottom *[US State Department]*. One official, on hearing the news . . . that the Archbishop had survived, remarked in a telephone conversation with a colleague "How inconvenient".[6]

Dr Kissinger announced that the US government was awaiting further news of the situation, but it did not escape notice that he neither criticized the all too obvious hand of Athens nor expressed regret at the reported death of Makarios, creating an impression that he was inclining towards acceptance of the new order in Cyprus. Turkish anxiety was thus increased and was not allayed by a later announcement, after it was known that the Archbishop had survived, that the US continued to recognize him as Head of State.

In Athens the junta attempted to shrug off developments in Cyprus in a show of studied indifference:

> The Greek régime today went about its business as if nothing had happened. A government spokesman warned newspaper editors that they would be allowed to publish nothing about the *coup* except for this item: "It was learnt from Nicosia that the President of Cyprus was overthrown by the Cyprus armed forces. They are in full control of the situation in Cyprus". Greek army generals, who attended the French Embassy reception for Bastille Day in Athens today, insisted that the *coup* in Cyprus was an independent action by units of the Cyprus National Guard without the knowledge or consent of Athens or the Greek commander.[7]

Reporting to the House of Commons again on 16 July, Callaghan confirmed that Makarios had survived and said that, following his request to do so, action was in hand to facilitate his entry to the SBAs. He also said that the Athens junta had confirmed to the British Ambassador its intention to honour its international obligations in relation to Cyprus and added that, in the interests of reducing tension, he was pressing the junta to replace its officers in the National Guard as soon as possible. Callaghan further stated that Britain was maintaining close touch with her allies in NATO and with others and that the UK continued to recognize Makarios as Head of State. Finally, he warned that, although the Turkish Cypriots seemed not to have become involved in the continuing Greek Cypriot internecine violence, the situation contained grave risks. It was, he said, of great importance that peace should be restored without delay.

The UN Security Council met in New York at 1500hrs (2100hrs in Cyprus) that afternoon (16 July), by which time it was known that Makarios had reached Malta *en route* to

London and New York. In an opening statement Waldheim reported on the situation on the island and concluded:

> I have followed the recent developments in Cyprus with the deepest concern. While the mandate of the United Nations Peacekeeping Force in Cyprus is specifically related to the conflict between the two communities in Cyprus and the Force cannot therefore be involved in the internal affairs of one of the communities, the repercussions of violent disturbances such as those of the past two days can very easily extend beyond the confines of one community. When this happens the matter becomes one of direct concern to UNFICYP under its mandate. ... UNFICYP has been doing all it can to prevent the present violence from causing renewed intercommunal strife. Moreover, in the context of the Cyprus problem such events carry a serious risk of a threat to international peace and security in a much wider framework.[8]

Speaking next, Rossides, the Greek Cypriot representative, commended UNFICYP's past peacekeeping success and urged that it had a duty now to act to prevent a deterioration in the situation, implying that it should intervene in what so far had been an internal problem of the Greek community. More importantly, he pressed the Council to adopt a resolution that would prevent outside intervention.

The Soviet representative condemned 'the flagrant intervention by outside forces', while Osman Olcay for Turkey said that his country had had the sad satisfaction of seeing confirmed its most pessimistic predictions with regard to Greek intentions *vis-à-vis* Cyprus. He declared that by instigating the *coup* Greece had violated the treaties to which it had subscribed jointly with Britain and Turkey, and he spoke of 'the fratricidal fury' of Greek against Greek and the sense of insecurity that this induced in the Turkish community (although, significantly in view of later allegations, he made no complaint of any harm suffered by the latter). Like Rossides, he urged that UNFICYP should act 'to re-establish the balance of force' in Cyprus, adding that the UN Force should prevent a routine troop rotation within ELDYK due that day from being exploited to Greek advantage.[9]

The French representative (also representing the EEC, of which at the time France held the Presidency) expressed the concern of The Nine (as they then were) and was followed by Ivor Richard for Britain, who thought it advisable for the Council to defer action until it had heard from Makarios in person; he added that, while the situation was highly explosive both for Cyprus and for peace in the Mediterranean, he saw no point in trying to apportion blame at this stage. For Greece, Constantine Panayotacos refuted 'vehemently and categorically' allegations of Athens's complicity in the *coup*, denied any involvement of the Greek officers and repeated the absurd myth that the National Guard was under the exclusive authority of the Cyprus government. The US representative confined himself to an anodyne declaration deploring the violence which, he said, had upset the delicate balance on the island.

Winding up the discussion, Rossides spoke again to expose the absurdity of Panayotacos's claim that the Cyprus government controlled the National Guard, and he appealed to the Council to call for an immediate ceasefire, for (he said) 'tanks are moving towards Paphos'. The Security Council adjourned after two and a half hours of debate that had resulted in no such call; no decisions had been reached and none of the Council's permanent members had shown any inclination to make the running.

At NATO Headquarters near Brussels news of the *coup* and its implications for the cohesion of the Alliance's southern flank gave rise to immediate disquiet. There were no illusions that the *coup* was anything but the work of Athens, and the Greek representative, the hapless Mr Chorofas, came under the concerted fire of his colleagues, who rejected his defence of the junta and called for the withdrawal of all Greek officers from Cyprus and the restoration of Makarios as President. Throughout the traumatic weeks of July and August both the NATO Council and its Military Committee exerted pressures to avert armed conflict between Greece and Turkey to a degree not generally recognized; this was due in part to the advantage enjoyed by those at the top, who had access to the most reliable intelligence available with respect to developments in Greece, Turkey and the Alliance's southern region generally. That NATO did not succeed in averting Turkey's military intervention, which seriously weakened the Alliance's southern flank by causing the withdrawal for over six years of Greece from its military command, was not for want of effort.[10]

Meanwhile in Ankara Ecevit turned his attention to preparing international opinion for the military action now being readied. Worldwide condemnation of the Greek action gave the Turks encouragement, but Ecevit appreciated the need to be seen to be observing the procedure stipulated in the Treaty of Guarantee. A note was accordingly delivered to the British government on 16 July containing a formal request for immediate joint consultations in accordance with Article IV of the Treaty[11] and asking for a reply within 24 hours; since the Greek government was seen as instigator of the *coup*, the Turks held that these consultations were a matter for Ankara and London alone. The British government acceded 'in principle' to the request, but Ecevit detected no sense of urgency in London's reply. In the light of Callaghan's statements to the House of Commons he concluded that Britain was dragging its feet, creating a risk that a *fait accompli* in Cyprus would pass into acceptance. This risk and the need to be seen to be acting urgently to concert action with Britain as a co-guarantor persuaded Ecevit that he should go to London in person at once. Brooking no delay, he arrived uninvited on the evening of 17 July, accompanied by Hasan Isik, Defence Minister and acting Foreign Minister.[12] He was preceded by Makarios who had reached London from Malta that afternoon for talks with British ministers before going on to the UN in New York.

Ecevit's arrival coincided with press reports of troops, tanks and artillery being concentrated in southern Turkish ports, their purpose no secret:

> "WE ARE MAKING AN INVASION OF CYPRUS", *Gunaydin*, Turkey's second largest newspaper, said in red banner headlines.[13]

Officers were recalled from leave, reservists were mobilized, merchant ships were requisitioned and these, together with amphibious and other naval units, were converging on the ports of Mersin and Iskenderun, while the airforce was concentrating aircraft at its bases at Adana and Antalya, both within 300km of Cyprus. The Turkish army's main formation involved was its 39th Division, which had long been held ready for this contingency, and the press reported its troops driving through Adana to a concentration area at Mersin, the convoys being urged on by cries of 'To Cyprus! To Cyprus!'

On the afternoon of 17 July Callaghan told the House of Commons that Makarios was even then closeted with Prime Minister Wilson and that he himself would be meeting the Archbishop shortly. Reporting Ecevit's imminent arrival, he added that he and Wilson would be conferring with the Turks that night, their purpose being to coordinate views on action to be taken and to gain Turkish support for the convening of a tripartite meeting with the Greeks. Callaghan reported that fighting in Cyprus had died down and the situation generally calm. To a question, he replied that British forces in the SBAs had 'no duty to sally forth', either to help UNFICYP or to restore order or legitimacy in Cyprus, words that can have given only cold comfort to the visiting Turks.

In their talks with Makarios, Wilson and Callaghan gave assurances of continuing British recognition of him as President of Cyprus and said that Britain was doing its utmost to resolve the situation peacefully by diplomacy; as he left for New York that evening, the Archbishop declared that he had been 'fully satisfied' by these talks.[14] In London Makarios had been accommodated as guest of the government at Claridge's Hotel where a crowd of Greek Cypriot well-wishers had greeted him. Once in his suite, he had turned to reading messages of condolence on his reported death received by the Cyprus High Commission and obituaries printed in the newspapers:

> They really were wonderful obituaries. Perhaps I am the only man who has read what others have said of him after his "death". I do not know when I will die or if they will say again the same good words of me.[15]

Wilson's and Callaghan's meeting with Ecevit and Isik extended into the early hours of 18 July; both sides described it and another meeting later that day as 'abortive'. Reporting to the House of Commons, Roy Hattersley (Callaghan's Minister of State) confined himself to a bland statement to the effect that the British side had explored the situation, while urging restraint on the Turks and stressing the need to allow time for negotiation.[16] A later Turkish account was less reticent:

> Mr Ecevit put Turkey's case clearly before the British leaders, emphasizing that Turkey could not remain passive in its attitude to the *coup*. In the course of his remarks he said: "If you want to avoid bloodshed and irreparable harm to NATO, let us undertake joint action, permitting the Turkish armed forces to operate from British bases. I call upon you to fulfil your obligations under the Treaty of Guarantee". Replying, Wilson assured him that Britain was well aware of the sort of man Sampson was and shared Turkey's anxieties. "But," he said, "it is not too late to restore the old régime."
>
> Ecevit answered: "With every hour that passes the situation becomes more difficult. It is imperative that Sampson should quickly be forced to step down and a new order established. The balance has been completely upset and we are determined to safeguard the Turkish community."
>
> Wilson: "Let us invite Greece to London for a tripartite conference; Kissinger is continuing his efforts and the United Nations is in session, so there is no call for military action."

Ecevit: "Greece is responsible for the *coup* and therefore cannot be considered a party to the talks. Nor will the situation be improved by academic speeches and resolutions."[17]

With discussion continuing in this vein, neither side made much impression on the other. It has been asserted since that, in private, Ecevit gave assurances that Turkey would not invade and that military preparations were going forward only in order to exert pressure on the junta. Ecevit has denied this:

> I did not give any assurance either to Mr Wilson or to Mr Callaghan that Turkey would not take military action in Cyprus. On the contrary, I made it sufficiently clear that Turkey could not stand by as the virtual annexation of the island to Greece was being manufactured and the lives of Turks seriously threatened. I also made it clear that if Great Britain, as one of the guarantor powers, did not cooperate, Turkey would have to take the initiative in accordance with her treaty rights and duties.[18]

What had all too clearly emerged was that Britain would neither join with Turkey in military intervention nor permit Turkish use of the SBAs for unilateral action. The latter had been an unexpected demand:

> I had not been prepared for this direct request to use British bases, but it was an impossible proposition. The island needed fewer Greek, not more Turkish troops, and we had called on the Greek government to withdraw their National Guard officers. Both the Prime Minister and I emphasized that the legal status of the bases was different from the rest of the island and that to permit them to be used for a third country's troops to enter Cyprus would certainly give rise at some stage to a direct challenge to their status by the government of Cyprus.[19]

Explaining Britain's position under Article IV of the Treaty of Guarantee, the British ministers stressed that, while there was an obligation to consult and a right to take action, there was no obligation in respect of the latter. Britain would fulfil the former but chose not to exercise the latter in so far as military action was entailed.

Three factors influenced the British position. First, it was argued that the state of affairs which the treaty was intended to preserve had in practice long since ceased to exist and that it was unrealistic to suppose that it could be restored now – the sole justification for action under Article IV. Second, it was considered that in any case British forces garrisoning the SBAs were insufficient for military intervention.[20] And third, it was held that such intervention would bring greater hardship than benefit to the people of Cyprus. (This last reflected views expressed earlier to Wilson and Callaghan by Makarios and by messages from Nicosia reporting that Greek Cypriots would regard British intervention as unwarranted interference in their internal affairs, and that British expatriates were nervous lest such action might bring retaliation upon them.) Two further considerations exerted a less apparent influence on British thinking. One was a lack of political will bred of an aversion to seeing British servicemen embroiled yet again in the Cypriots' intractable quarrels. The other was the realization, which had haunted British governments since the Anglo-French *débâcle* at Suez in 1956, that it would be folly to embark on military action without US approval, if not actual support. As the situation then stood, it was clear that Kissinger was unlikely to offer either.

It was an unhappy coincidence that the Cyprus crisis was gathering momentum and finally erupted at a time when Kissinger was preoccupied with more pressing concerns. Immersed in the search for a settlement in the Middle East in the aftermath of the Yom Kippur War, which had posed serious problems for East-West relations, he had been engaged since the spring of 1974 in vigorous 'shuttle diplomacy', which had culminated in a visit in the company of President Nixon to the Middle East in June. Both had then gone to Yalta for a summit meeting with the Russians and had not returned to Washington until six days before the Cyprus *coup*. Small wonder if Kissinger had little time, or inclination, to ponder the significance of events on the small island.[21] No less distracting was the American domestic scene: the Nixon Administration was nearing the final throes of the Watergate disaster and had only three more weeks of life when the Cyprus crisis erupted. Kissinger later lamented[22] that for the United States government the crisis could not have come at a worse moment.

It was not until 17 July that Kissinger, alarmed by Turkish statements and reported military preparations, stirred himself to action. He despatched Joseph Sisco, his Under-Secretary of State for Political Affairs, an expert on Cyprus and an experienced Middle East trouble-shooter, to London, Athens and Ankara. In the expectation that the Sampson régime would soon crumble, Sisco's instructions were to support Britain in negotiations to avert Turkish military intervention. Informed opinion in Washington judged it to be an impossible mission.

Ecevit was persuaded to delay his departure from London to allow a meeting with Sisco on 18 July, but insisted that their discussion must be on a bilateral basis, the US not being a guarantor power. The two met at the Turkish Embassy that afternoon:

> It was at this meeting that the United States came to appreciate the strength of Turkey's determination. In the strongest terms Sisco urged Turkey to abandon her decision. He had brought an equally strongly worded message from Dr Kissinger: "The United States is opposed to intervention using the *coup* as vindication. We believe that such action may lead to war between two NATO allies." In reply Ecevit emphasized that Turkey had no intention of provoking war with Greece. "But," he replied, "it is impossible for us to overlook any more *faits accomplis* in Cyprus."
>
> Sisco expressed the opinion that war between Greece and Turkey would be a disaster for the whole area and that it would impair relations between Turkey and the US. Ecevit agreed on the importance of Turkey's relations with the United States, but pointed out that American attempts to hinder Turkey might be just as damaging. "In the past the United States has repeatedly obstructed Turkey's efforts, and this has had a hardening effect on Turkish public opinion. If the US attempts once more to stand in the way, the reaction in Turkey might get out of hand".[23]

His arguments having made little impression, Sisco said that he was going on at once to Athens and offered to convey to the Greeks the conditions upon which Turkey would stay its hand. Ecevit replied that the Greek officers must be withdrawn from Cyprus and Sampson replaced without delay. Further, he demanded that the presence of Turkish troops on the island to ensure the security of the Turkish community must be accepted, that the community be given an outlet to the sea and that there must be an equality of rights and facilities with those enjoyed by the Greeks. Undertaking to deliver this message to the Athens junta, Sisco urged that Turkey should refrain from action until he could notify Ecevit of the Greeks' response; he anticipated delivering this in Ankara two days later, that is on Saturday 20 July. This was not good enough for Ecevit:

> Saturday is too late. We have no time to waste. With every hour that passes Greece is massing troops in Cyprus. Try to be in Ankara early on Friday. On Saturday the Grand National Assembly is convening and your presence in Turkey on that day might be taken in some circles as evidence of American pressure.[24]

It was an ingenious reply; the true reason why Ecevit did not want the embarrassment of Sisco's presence that Saturday was that this was the day set for the initial Turkish landings on Cyprus.

Before leaving for Athens Sisco met Callaghan. They agreed that, for all Ecevit's words, Turkish military action was not imminent, but Callaghan emphasized the need for a common US-British policy in order to avert a war between Greece and Turkey. However, their interests did not otherwise exactly coincide:

> Britain felt a special obligation to Cyprus as a member of the Commonwealth and to her people because of our past links, as well as responsibility under the 1960 Treaty. The United States had neither a similar background of history nor a similar treaty relationship. Their principal concern was to avoid an extension of Soviet influence in the Middle East, and to the extent that this meant preventing Turkey and Greece from getting at each others's throats, British and American policy coincided. But it also resulted in the United States being less willing to antagonize either the Greek Colonels in the early stages of the conflict or the Turks after their invasion. I felt fewer inhibitions.[25]

Ecevit had a final meeting with Callaghan before leaving London on the night of 18 July. His position now hardened, he insisted that a physical Turkish presence on the island was a prerequisite to a settlement. Offering nothing new, Callaghan reiterated his proposals for the removal of Sampson and the restoration of Makarios (or perhaps Clerides), the withdrawal of all Greek troops from the island and an invitation to the Greeks to a tripartite meeting of the guarantor powers. Ecevit saw all this as temporizing and declared that time was of the essence: Greece was landing more troops, while Turkey was not enabled to do the same; it was essential for Turkey to gain access by sea and air to the Turkish Cypriot community without delay. With Ecevit regretting that Britain declined to act jointly with Turkey under the Treaty of Guarantee and Callaghan remaining adamant that the use of the SBAs by Turkey was out of the question, they parted with positions far apart.

At a press conference before his departure Ecevit complained that Greek aircraft were continuing to arrive at Nicosia bringing reinforcements for the National Guard and that this amounted to a Greek invasion. Turkey, he said, could never accept the rule of Greece over Cyprus and its Turks and could not tolerate the Sampson régime, which had no constitutional legality. He and his team left London in a mood of some disgust at the British attitude but satisfied that the letter of the Treaty of Guarantee had been observed, thus opening the way for unilateral action. Reporting to Ankara, Ecevit gave the signal for military action to proceed as planned. General Staff HQ issued orders for the embarkation of troops and initial movements to commence at 0830hrs on Friday 19 July.

Meanwhile, with a prudence born of experience, Britain took its own precautionary military measures against the contingency that diplomacy might fail. In the Cyprus SBAs the garrison had been placed on alert as soon as news of the *coup* was received; operations rooms were activated, restrictions were imposed on movement outside the bases and those living in the dormitory towns of Famagusta, Larnaca and Limassol were advised to remain at home until further notice.[26] Forces in the bases relied on locally engaged civilians for many day-to-day chores, but a contingency plan (Operation PLATYPUS) provided for replacement of the more essential in time of crisis by servicemen from the UK; on 15 July certain of these were placed at short notice to fly to Cyprus. HQ BFNE also activated Kingsfield airstrip in the Eastern SBA (normally maintained in reserve) and adjusted local troop dispositions. The HQ of 19 Brigade, then on exercise from the UK in the Akamas training area (in the extreme north-west of the island), was recalled to Episkopi, where it was to be retained temporarily, together with a battery of 12 Light Air Defence Regt also then exercising on the island.

On 16 July HMS *Hermes*, a helicopter commando ship on passage from New York to Malta, where it was to disembark the 700 men of 41 Royal Marine Commando, was ordered to retain the marines on board and to proceed to a position from which they could readily be put ashore in Cyprus. The frigate *Andromeda*, already at Malta, was sailed for Cyprus the same day and the guided missile destroyer *Devonshire* and a second frigate, *Rhyl*, both on passage from Gibraltar to Livorno, were also diverted to the eastern Mediterranean. This Royal Navy group of four warships was augmented on 19 July by the submarine *Onslaught*, then carrying out trials in the area.[27]

These precautionary moves, especially the sailing of the warships towards Cyprus, coupled with London's pressure on Athens for the withdrawal of the Greek officers, disturbed Mr Olver, British High Commissioner in Nicosia. The puppet Foreign Minister, Dimis Dimitriou, had cautioned against any British intervention and Olver was worried lest the naval moves might be construed as a sign of impending British action. He advised that *Hermes* should not show herself above the horizon and warned London that Callaghan's pressure for removal of the Greek officers was being seen by the Sampson régime as unwarranted interference in Cypriot affairs. Taken together, these British actions created the risk of an anti-British reaction on the island.

The Royal Navy was not alone in deploying to the eastern Mediterranean. On 17 July a Pentagon spokesman announced that the Soviet navy was moving ships east too and that the US Sixth Fleet was remaining at sea instead of putting into port as scheduled. Steaming south of Crete, *Hermes* encountered a reconnaissance aircraft of a US amphibious force and early on 18 July passed a Soviet tanker lying stopped. A few hours later *Hermes* came up on the USS *Forrestal's* task group (itself shadowed by a Soviet *Kotlin* class destroyer) and then met the USS *Little Rock* and its task group, with the US amphibious group now positioned to the south-west. As the three navies watched each other, all were avid to know the intentions of the Turkish forces now gathered off the coast of Anatolia.

PART FIVE

A WANT OF HUMAN WISDOM

If therefore war should come . . . it will not, I think, be due to irresistible natural laws, it will be due to the want of human wisdom.

Bonar Law, House of Commons, 1911

CHAPTER THIRTY-THREE

THE DIE IS CAST

Last July the quiet which had prevailed for many years, thanks in large measure to the presence of UNFICYP, was suddenly shattered as a consequence of events which were clearly outside the purview of the United Nations Force.

Report of the UN Secretary General
(S/11568, 6 December 1974, para. 75)

Prime Minister Ecevit arrived back in Ankara in the early hours of Friday 19 July, and at once confirmed to his Service Chiefs that Turkey was to go it alone – there would be no drawing back, Turkey was not bluffing this time. They told him that the naval forces would have to sail that morning in order to arrive off the north coast of Cyprus in time to permit a landing at 0630hrs next day, Saturday 20 July, as planned. The embarkation of some 3000 soldiers and loading of 30 tanks and stores were quickly completed and by mid-morning these forces had put to sea in two groups – a main amphibious force of some 14 ships and 25 smaller craft, which sailed from Mersin, and a secondary group of seven ships, which left from Iskenderun.[1] A screen of five destroyers provided protection against any interference by the Hellenic navy.

Meanwhile Sisco had arrived in Athens to deliver the Turks' demands. He encountered the utmost difficulty in reaching members of the junta but eventually met Ioannides, General Bonanos (Chief of Staff) and Prime Minister Androutsopoulos, who offered no constructive response to the Turks' demands. A pessimistic Sisco left for Ankara that evening (19 July) empty handed. Nonetheless, he pressed Ecevit to allow time for further negotiation but the latter held out little hope that this would prove possible. (Sisco was given Ecevit's reply in the early hours of 20 July, when the Turkish forces, by then poised off Kyrenia, were about to strike.)

In Cyprus UNFICYP was continuing efforts to promote a return to pre-*coup* normality. It was decided that the Kyrenia road convoys, suspended on 15 July, should be resumed on 20 July and in anticipation of this, the Finns were pressing Colonel Katircioglu, commanding the Turkish national contingent, to dismantle military posts recently established along the road in contravention of the 1964 agreement (he declined to do so, and the matter was referred to UNFICYP HQ). The reopening of Nicosia airport on 18 July had led to a stream of charter aircraft of various nationalities arriving to take off those tourists whose departure had been delayed. Many had left by the early hours of 20 July, but a substantial number of others, their holidays not yet over, chose to remain (mostly in Famagusta and on the north coast around Kyrenia). Those stranded at the airport during curfew hours were escorted to hotels by UN Military Police, one of the services rendered by the Force Provost Marshal, Major J.L. Cullen (Canada), who had established a UN MP post in the terminal building. By monitoring the movements of aircraft this UN post also served an operational purpose in ensuring that HQ UNFICYP was able to answer protests by the Leadership that Greek military reinforcements were continuing to arrive by air.

Advice offered to foreign tourists at this stage varied. On 19 July the British High Commission complained to UNFICYP that the Swedish contingent was advising Swedish tourists in Famagusta to leave and that this was causing unnecessary alarm; a check showed that a representative of the Swedish Foreign Ministry now in Nicosia was advising its nationals to leave while the going was good, and that SWEDCON was merely assisting by notifying individuals regarding departing flights. Similar arrangements were being made for Canadians, who were being urged to contact a member of the Canadian Department of External Affairs, also now in Nicosia. British policy was different. Although the Foreign Office announced in London on 19 July that those intending to visit Cyprus should postpone doing so for the time being, the British High Commission was not encouraging British holiday-makers (estimated to number about 2,000) to leave. Indeed, at its behest a message was broadcast by the BFBS appealing to British residents and tourists to remain calm and not to worry. There were no grounds (the announcement declared) for rumours that Turkey was about to invade, this at a time when it was known that Turkish forces were putting to sea. Some who heeded this advice, only to be caught up in the subsequent fighting, were bitter in their criticism.[2]

In the days following the *coup* the Turks became increasingly concerned that Greek reinforcements might reach Cyprus not only by air but also by sea. A routine troop rotation in ELDYK had been scheduled for 17 July, but UNFICYP established that the landing ship *Lesbos*, usually used for the purpose, was not expected at either Limassol or Famagusta and that there was no sign of it in the sea approaches. Enquiries failed to elicit Greek intentions with respect to the rotation and this uncertainty bred fear on the Turkish side, already deeply suspicious of movements through the airport, that rotation plans were being revised with a view to bringing in substantial reinforcements for the Greek national contingent. As explained earlier, UNFICYP was not normally able to exercise the close supervision of Greek rotations that was required of Turkish rotations, but in the current situation there was a clear need to ensure that this particular troop rotation was not exploited to Greek military advantage.

On 18 July UNFICYP learnt that *Lesbos* was due at Famagusta at 0600hrs next morning and the National Guard confirmed that the rotation was to be carried out that day. The Swedes were ordered to monitor the operation closely and ELDYK's commander agreed to the presence of two UN officers on the quayside for this purpose. By the time that *Lesbos* berthed in Famagusta a convoy of some 80 vehicles carrying ELDYK soldiers was to be seen heading east on the Nicosia – Famagusta road. No time was lost in disembarkation and the first of the new arrivals had left for Nicosia by 0730hrs in blissful ignorance of what was to face them within 24 hours. *Lesbos* was guarded by National Guardsmen and by sailors from the nearby naval establishment at Boghaz, but difficulties arose when the latter began to patrol the general dock area; Turkish dock labourers downed tools and men of the TCF showed themselves on the walls of the Old City overlooking the port. The Swedes' Commander, Lieut. Colonel Kristensson, quickly intervened, persuading the Greeks to stop their patrols, the TCF to withdraw their visible presence on the walls and the dockers to resume work. Throughout the day HQ UNFICYP kept the Leadership informed of the progress of the rotation and confirmed that when *Lesbos* sailed that evening it had brought in 410 men and 11 vehicles and taken out 422 men and 10 vehicles, figures that were consistent with earlier rotations. It had been yet another demonstration of how, in a situation of mutual suspicion and potential friction, a calm and even small third-party UN presence serves to cool tempers and prevent rumour and misunderstanding. However, no sooner had *Lesbos* put to sea than events took a more ominous turn. Two Turkish F100 aircraft overflew Boghaz, Famagusta, Larnaca, Nicosia and Kyrenia in what evidently was another reconnaissance mission. As they did so, reports were circulating of the two Turkish naval groups steaming slowly towards the island.

In spite of a return to a semblance of normality, Friday 19 July was an anxious day for all on the island. Optimism that Turkey might be restrained from military intervention was tempered by reports of activity to this end. When news came that the Turkish fleet had put to sea speculation and rumour became rife to the point that some believed that the Turks had already landed at Famagusta. A degree of panic was evident in Nicosia, with shouting, closure of many shops and traffic jams, as people took to cars to escape from the city and seek refuge in the villages or mountains. So deserted had the streets become by mid-afternoon that Lieut. Colonel Manuel, the UN District Commander, asked if a new curfew had been imposed. Nervousness was apparent within the Turkish quarter too, and tension was not diminished by Denktash's demands for the removal of Sampson and for joint Turkish-British intervention, and by his warning of possible conflagration unless the situation was speedily resolved. UNFICYP pressures had imposed some restraint on Turkish action to improve defences in breach of the *status quo*, but the TCF remained on high alert, reservists had been called up and the level of manning of most posts had been increased. However, UNFICYP observed nothing during daylight hours on 19 July to suggest that the Turkish community was anticipating Turkey's military intervention next morning.

National Guard reservists, too, were being called up and on 19 July some reorganization to meet possible Turkish landings by sea or air was evident. Those T-34 tanks still on the streets of Nicosia and Famagusta were withdrawn in readiness for other tasks, and troops and artillery were redeployed towards the north coast and in and around Nicosia and the airport. On the lines of intercommunal confrontation the National Guard matched the TCF's alert state and between them stood the men of UNFICYP, still at Blue Alert. Recent alarms over the Czech weapons held in Camp UNFICYP pointed the need to review arrangements for their security. A rudimentary plan for their destruction to ensure that, come what may, they did not fall into unauthorized hands was devised by the Camp Commandant, Major M. Barker (UK); thanks to his steadfastness and that of others under his command it never had to be put to the test

In London Roy Hattersley, Minister of State, reported to Parliament on 19 July on the talks which Wilson and Callaghan had had with Makarios, Ecevit and Sisco. He said that the British ministers had urged restraint on the Turks to allow time for negotiation and added that the Security Council was to meet later that day, that the NATO Council had been playing a helpful part and that, with fighting in Cyprus now ceased, Nicosia airport had reopened, allowing a substantial number of British tourists to leave. He stated, further, that the Greek government had notified its intention to begin replacing its officers in Cyprus within the next few days and that Britain had invited the Greeks to come at once to London for talks. Britain's aim, he said, was to discuss how the National Guard should be officered in future and whether arrangements for security in Cyprus should be modified. A back-bencher pointed out that with every day that passed the new régime was consolidating its position. Could not, he asked, UN officers take over the National Guard temporarily? Hattersley thought this a valuable idea, while observing that the National Guard was only part of the problem.[3] Replying to another question implying that Britain had an obligation to take military action to restore the *status quo* on the island, Hattersley said:

> I do not believe that it is the will of this House, nor do I believe that it would be in the interests of Cyprus, were our obligations to be discharged in that way at this stage.[4]

His words can only have reinforced the Turks' conviction that they were going to have to go it alone and the sooner the better.

The British government's apparent reluctance to take more positive action did not halt military measures to ensure the security of the SBAs. On 19 July HQ BFNE called for certain of the PLATYPUS logistic personnel to be sent to Cyprus and requested the Ministry of Defence to place at short notice other troops required under a second contingency plan, Operation ABLAUT, which provided for reinforcement of the operational strength of the SBA garrison.[5] All the while *Hermes*, escorted by *Rhyl* and tailed at close quarters by a Soviet surveillance vessel, was closing Cyprus, followed by the other RN ships and fleet auxiliaries. Captain C.R.P.G. Branson RN in *Hermes* sought permission to send an officer ahead to Episkopi by helicopter to discuss command, control and administrative arrangements for the naval task group now assembling[6], but his request was refused by Air Marshal Aiken, CBFNE, who feared that the arrival of such an officer might increase speculation that intervention by Britain was imminent. Fortunately Branson's concerns had been anticipated by the First Sea Lord in London: Rear Admiral D. Cassidi, Flag Officer Carriers and Amphibious Ships (FOCAS) was ordered to fly to Cyprus on 19 July to assume control of the RN force as Naval Deputy to Aiken. Accompanied by a small staff, he reached Akrotiri on the morning of 20 July to be greeted with the news that Turkish forces were now landing on Cyprus. Such was Aiken's continuing caution that even then Cassidi and his party were instructed to remain in civilian dress.

Still concerned about the security of the Czech arms and ammunition, I had returned to National Guard HQ on the afternoon of Friday 19 July to pursue my discussion with the Chief of Staff, Brig. General Yiannikodemos. We agreed that I would inspect the stores in both Camp UNFICYP and in the police barracks at Athalassa next morning. As we talked I was handed a message inviting me to attend a meeting to be held at CBFNE's Command Post at Episkopi at 1800hrs to review the situation. Confirming with General Prem Chand that it would be useful for me to do so, I left at once by helicopter for Episkopi, where I found Major General Butler, the Army commander, and senior Army and RAF officers together with others assembled in the Command Post. Here I inspected the maritime plot and was able to see the dispositions not only of British, US and Soviet naval forces in the eastern Mediterranean but also of the two Turkish groups now hovering to the north and east of Cape Andreas, their intentions a matter for speculation.[7]

At the meeting the situation was reviewed (primarily as it bore on the SBAs) and assessments were made of Turkish capabilities and likely intentions. Asked about the situation in Nicosia, I said that the forces of both communities remained at high alert but that UNFICYP had not detected any indications that a Turkish landing was imminent. I added that the near panic in Nicosia during the afternoon had been due to unfounded rumours that the Turks had already come ashore at Famagusta. Summing up, Aiken said that the situation was very uncertain. In view of the meeting of the Security Council that was about to convene in New York and international pressures being exerted on the Turks elsewhere, it seemed likely that they would stay their hand for at least a further 24 hours with ships held off Cyprus as a threat. If the Turkish moves were not a bluff (as had been the case on previous occasions), then in his view a landing might be expected on the morning of Sunday 21 July, for which the beaches north of Famagusta appeared the likely point.[8] On my return to Nicosia at 2045hrs I reported this view to Prem Chand. Aware that sources of information available to Aiken were far more extensive than those enjoyed by UNFICYP, we were inclined to accept his judgement and decided not to place UNFICYP at a higher state of alert, not least because this might create unnecessary alarm in the already nervous civil population. In view of the uncertainties, I told Prem Chand that during the night I would maintain close touch with the British and let him know at once of any significant change in the situation.

At 1530hrs that afternoon (by then 2130hrs in Cyprus) the Security Council resumed consideration of the problem, while in Ankara (and unknown to UNFICYP[9]) Sisco was playing out the final act of his hopeless mission. Having decided that he should be received as President of Cyprus, the Council invited Makarios (recently arrived from London) to address it. He summarized the events that had culminated in his letter of 2 July to President Gizikis and reiterated that the *coup* had been the work of the Athens junta, with ELDYK playing a leading role. He also described how he had escaped (thanking the British government, Prem Chand and Weckman-Munoz 'for the interest which they showed in my safety') and said that the appointment of Sampson, 'a well known gunman', as President and of known EOKA-B adherents as ministers offered no prospect of progress in the intercommunal negotiations. He concluded with an appeal to the Council to end 'the anomalous situation' created by the *coup* and to restore constitutional order and democratic rights in Cyprus. It was not, he declared, an internal matter solely for the Greeks of the island; its Turks, too, were affected. The Security Council should insist on the recall to Greece of the Greek officers so that UNFICYP might be free to fulfil its mandate. The Archbishop then withdrew and the Council turned to discussion of his statement and a draft resolution.

The Greek representative, Panayotacos, 'flatly and unreservedly' rejected Makarios's 'vicious' charge of Greece's involvement and defended the services rendered to Cyprus by the Greek officers. He went on to attack the Soviet Union for its earlier criticisms, pointing to Russian action in Czechoslovakia, and then turned on the Turkish representative, Olcay, reminding the Council of the Turkish airstrikes on Cyprus in 1964 and referring to the 'hundreds, if not thousands' of Turkish mainland officers training the TCF and 'neutralizing all political opponents to Denktash'. Panayotacos ended with a tirade against Makarios personally, accusing him of ambivalence and insincerity in supporting simultaneously both *enosis* and the independence of Cyprus: it was the Archbishop, he asserted, who in February 1972 had turned a deaf ear to the call of Athens for a government of national unity.

Olcay replied that it needed all his self-control not to say 'I told you so'. Turkey considered the present situation to be very grave. The world community had a duty to restore the *status quo* in Cyprus, but Turkey had a particular obligation to this end enshrined in an international treaty. He endorsed Makarios's call for withdrawal of the Greek officers; it was not sufficient merely for them to be replaced. (It was not without interest that Olcay, prompted no doubt by the Turkish General Staff, drew special attention to the need to ensure the security of the Czech weapons entrusted to UNFICYP's safe-keeping.)

The representatives of Australia, Austria, China, India, Romania, the Soviet Union and Yugoslavia (the last speaking also for 'the Coordinating Bureau of the Non-Aligned Countries in New York') all added their condemnation of the Athens junta and declared support for Makarios. The Russian, Safronchuk, specifically accused ELDYK of having stormed the Presidential Palace and seized the airport and described the *coup* as 'a fascist *putsch*'; he did not let slip the opportunity of a side-swipe at the West, charging that 'certain circles in NATO' had participated in its planning. For the United States Mr Scali affirmed his government's support for the independence, sovereignty and territorial integrity of Cyprus and for the 1960 constitutional arrangements. With the mission of Sisco, then in Ankara, much in mind, he urged all to exercise maximum restraint:

> In particular the US Government is firmly opposed to any attempt to bring about a military solution to the present problem. . . . We most earnestly appeal to all the governments concerned to resist the temptation to settle this issue by force.[10]

Declaring that it would be a serious error to rush into judgements on an issue of this gravity, he expressed understanding of the pressures on Turkey, and some detected in this a lack of American firmness. Speaking for Britain, Ivor Richard ridiculed the Soviet charge of NATO involvement in the *coup*, pointing out that it was Britain, a NATO power, that had made it possible for Makarios to address their meeting. He reported on the discussions with the Turks in London and said that the Greeks had been invited to come to London for the same purpose in two days time, that is on Sunday 21 July, when Britain intended to discuss future arrangements for officering the National Guard. The junta's announcement that the Greek officers were to be replaced was helpful, but this should be seen only as a first step towards a solution of the problem. Like others, he affirmed British recognition of Makarios as President.

The Security Council meeting ended with an arid exchange between Rossides (for Cyprus) and Olcay, the latter declaring that 'today we are living through what might seriously be called a Greek tragedy – a drama of Greeks, not a word being said about the plight of the Turks' (he was not quite right, for ironically it had been Makarios who had pointed out that the Turks of Cyprus, too, were affected by what had happened). After more than three hours of debate the Council rose at 1850hrs, by then 0050hrs on Saturday 20 July in Cyprus. As before, no decisions had been taken. A draft resolution[11] had been tabled, but a vote on this was deferred until the Council's next meeting (which suited Turkey well and saved it from acute embarrassment). In the event the terms of this draft resolution were overtaken by the developments in the next few hours. Indeed, the meeting had been something of an irrelevance: Turkey had made up its mind and, regardless of international opinion, the die was already cast.

Late on the night of 19 July, after reporting the outcome of my visit to Episkopi to Prem Chand, I went to the British High Commission to talk over the day's events with the duty officer, Julian Mersey. We noted reports that the TCF were putting out coloured ground-to-air recognition panels to mark forward positions in Nicosia and around the edges of the main Turkish enclave and had little doubt but that Episkopi's estimate was wrong; with daylight we could expect to see Turkish forces landing on the island, most probably in the north. The National Guard appeared to be of the same opinion, for during the evening and night there was increasing military movement towards the north coast and reinforcement of the defences at Nicosia airport. I left Mersey at about midnight with the promise that we would let each other know at once of any developments of importance.

We were not to know at that time of an added pointer to what was impending. UNFICYP's LO, Major Oberwinkler, had been at Denktash's side since the morning of 15 July and was accommodated in the latter's own residence, but late that Friday night he had been required to move (for greater safety, he was told) with Denktash to the cellars of the EVKAF Bank in the Turkish quarter of the Old City. Oberwinkler realized that momentous events were about to unfold, but was told that until further notice he was on no account to use his radio or disclose his location to anyone; he had no alternative but to comply:

> I felt that something very important must be going on during the night or in the hours to come. Mr Denktash's closest associates were now permanently around him and the whole situation was very tense and nervous. Dr Unel, the chief medical officer of the Red Crescent Hospital, turned up in Fighter's uniform (I had never seen him in uniform before), as well as a number of medical personnel. Denktash had various conferences during the night and messengers were coming and going all the time. Fighter sentries outside and inside the Bank building were set up – the situation was definitely escalating. . . . I did not get much sleep that night.[12]

Oberwinkler was not alone in this respect. For me, as for so many others, it had been a long and gruelling day at the end of an exceptionally busy and eventful week not made any more tolerable by unusually hot weather: the thermometer touched 42^0C in Nicosia that day (with similar high values prevailing throughout the week that followed). I retired to bed in my house situated right on the Nicosia Green Line with relief but little expectation of an undisturbed night's rest.[13]

CHAPTER THIRTY-FOUR

NOT BOMBS BUT MESSAGES
OF GOODWILL

The Turkish Armed Forces have started a peace operation in Cyprus this morning . . . [they] are not going to open fire unless they are fired at. The Turkish planes are throwing not bombs but messages of goodwill to all the people of Cyprus.

Public Announcement by Bulent Ecevit,
Turkish Prime Minister, 20 July 1974.

In the early hours of Saturday 20 July there was a flurry in UNFICYP's Danish Contingent in the north-west of the island when the sound of aircraft and a report of an unidentified warship off the coast alarmed the local National Guard. But nothing further transpired and it was not until 0320hrs that I was awoken to learn that maritime reconnaissance reported the main group of Turkish ships to be approaching the island on a course and at a speed that suggested a touchdown on beaches east of Kyrenia at first light (about 0415hrs at that time of year in Cyprus).[1] Anticipating the effect that news of a Turkish landing was sure to have along the Nicosia Green Line, I immediately warned Lieut. Colonel Manuel, the Canadian Commander of Nicosia District (whose HQ in Wolseley Barracks was close to my house on the Green Line itself), to expect an outbreak of shooting along the Line; he lost no time in placing his men of 1st Commando Group on full alert.

I then drove to UNFICYP HQ some 10 minutes away near the airport, having asked Lieut. Colonel Pullinen, the Finnish Commander of Kyrenia District, to join me there from his own HQ in the adjacent Kykko Camp. On meeting, I told him that a Turkish landing was likely in his operational area within the next hour or two and to alert his OPs on the heights of the Pendhadaktylos mountains, which provided good observation seawards, as well as those along his sector of the Green Line and around the main enclave. I stressed that the most useful service that they could render at this stage was to provide information. In the meantime I had reported developments to General Prem Chand, who agreed that UNFICYP island-wide should be placed on the next higher State of Alert, and the code-word TULIP, denoting Orange Alert, was issued at 0400hrs.[2] I also gave instructions for a Sioux helicopter of the Army Aviation Flight to make a reconnaissance as soon as it was light enough of the coast around Kyrenia, but stipulated that its pilot, Sergeant Woodhall, was to keep clear of the Turkish forces and to return to base if there was any risk of becoming caught up in their operations.

As dawn broke Finns in OP Hill Top reported ships and aircraft far out to sea, with three warships heading west (bent, perhaps, on guarding against any interference by the Hellenic navy). Then came news that when some 10km from the shore the whole force had carried out a curious manoeuvre, turning to steam away from the island on a north-westerly course. Were the Turks engaged in a game of bluff as had proved to be the case in earlier crises? As we pondered this question it became clear that the manoeuvre had been either an ineffective feint or a navigational error, for soon afterwards the ships turned back onto a bearing that suggested a landing west, not east, of Kyrenia. As they did so, Turkish combat aircraft were reported to be lifting off from bases at Adana and Antalya. There was no doubt now that the invasion was on.

Little did UNFICYP know that this had already been made clear in Ankara to Mr Sisco, who had been doing his utmost at a meeting in the early hours of that Saturday to persuade Prime Minister Ecevit that the situation in Cyprus presented no threat to the Turkish community. Warning of the likely dire consequences for both Turkey and NATO of Turkish military action, he said that the Athens junta was willing to replace the Greek officers involved in the *coup* and, after a suitable interval, to replace Sampson by a more acceptable leader. Moved neither by Sisco's warning nor by the junta's offers, Ecevit was adamant that the presence of his troops on the island was essential to safeguard Turkey's strategic interest, protect Turkish Cypriots and ensure ready access to them by sea or air. If this meant war with Greece, so be it; Turkey was not seeking this but, if war was declared, responsibility would rest with Greece alone. Sisco pressed Ecevit to allow a further 48 hours in which to work out a solution acceptable to Ankara, but Ecevit replied that it was too late; Turkish troops were about to set foot on Cyprus. A shaken Sisco hurried to the airport and left for Athens just before Turkish air space was closed to civil traffic.

The Turks had planned a two phase operation – the first to secure a substantial lodgement area and the second to extend this area to include the whole of northern Cyprus and the port of Famagusta. The first phase was to be achieved in three days: on the first, seaborne troops were to establish a bridgehead and seize the port of Kyrenia, while airborne troops were to reinforce the main enclave and protect the Turkish quarter of Nicosia; on the second, a link-up over the Kyrenia Pass was to be effected; and on the third, the airport was to be captured. All the while the enclave was to be expanded to strengthen its defence against counter-attack and, in particular, to reduce the vulnerability of its villages to the National Guard's artillery.

The topography presented problems. Several possible beaches for amphibious landings lay east and west of Kyrenia and afforded access on to the coast road, but (unlike those north of Famagusta) they were small and restricted, depths of water offshore were not great and in places rocky reefs were obstacles. Kyrenia's port, also small and little used except by fishing boats and pleasure craft, was not a good natural harbour and lacked both a deep-water approach and deep-water berths. A narrow coastal strip varying from one to three kilometres in width lay between the sea and the mountains. A network of minor roads and tracks served the score of villages that lay among its olive and carob groves, vineyards and orchards. Only one village (Temblos, 3km west of Kyrenia) was Turkish; the rest were Greek, although some had a small Turkish element, as did Kyrenia itself. The area attracted many foreign holiday-makers and in mid-July hotels and apartments scattered along the coast were generally full.

Others attracted to this north coast were expatriates of various nationalities, mostly British, who had retired to live in its congenial climate and surroundings. Also in the area was an important radio station of the US Foreign Broadcast Information Service located near Karavas.[3]

The Pendhadaktylos mountain range constituted a formidable barrier to movement south. Narrow in width, it extended 40km east from Kyrenia and 20km west, rising generally to a height of 600m with some peaks of over 900m. A single indifferent track ran along the top of the range and roads across it were few. The most important was the Kyrenia road which afforded the shortest route between Kyrenia and Nicosia. This climbed over the Kyrenia Pass, the summit of which lay just inside the main Turkish enclave (situated on a 700m peak west of the Pass was the Turkish stronghold and communications centre of St Hilarion Castle overlooking Kyrenia). On their southern side the mountains fell away steeply to the plain of the Mesaoria, which extended east and west in an undulating, open, dry and often rocky vista. Although the cross-country going was difficult, there were few major obstacles and the many minor and several major roads or tracks made movement on the plain relatively easy. Within the Turkish enclave the Mesaoria provided areas suitable for landings by parachute or helicopter and the disused airstrip at Aghirda, 3km south-west of the Kyrenia Pass, was suitable for transport aircraft of the C130 type. For troops landing from the sea the going in the coastal strip was generally good, although room for manoeuvre, especially by armoured units, was restricted. In the mountains movement was difficult for all except infantry, but, once through these, an advance south towards Nicosia and its airport presented few topographical problems. A major advantage for the Turks was that the entire area lay within the range of aircraft and helicopters operating from bases in Turkey.

The Order of Battle of the Turkish ground forces, referred to by Ankara as its 'Peace Force', is shown at Annex 6. The field commander was Lieut. General Nurettin Ersin, Commander of 6th Corps, whose HQ remained at Adana (Turkey) until transferred to Aghirda. The main element for the initial intervention comprised 39th Infantry Division (long earmarked for the task) under Maj. General Bedrettin Demirel.[4] Other elements in the first phase included the Turkish Airborne Brigade of three battalions and the smaller Commando Brigade. Support was provided by some 30 strike and 35 transport aircraft and a fleet of 80–100 helicopters, all operating from bases in southern Turkey, and by Turkish warships. (The additional troops required for the second phase did not begin to arrive in Cyprus until after the ceasefire marking the end of the first phase. The main element of these was 28th Infantry Division, commanded by Maj. General Fasil Polat, which had begun to move south from the Ankara area on 20 July.)

Turkish plans entailed initial airstrikes on National Guard HQs and camps in the Nicosia – Kyrenia sector to deter reaction, and further strikes on Nicosia airport and the airstrips at Tymbou and Lakatamia to prevent use by the Greek airforce, should it attempt to intervene. Concurrently warships and other aircraft were to engage National Guard defences and radar stations along the north coast and in the mountains in order to suppress resistance to the seaborne operation. Only after this preparatory action were troops to land on the north coast from the sea and into the enclave from the air. The seaborne operation was the task of 39th Infantry Division, its 50th Infantry Regt landing on a beach near Ayios Yeorios (3km west of Kyrenia) but with one battalion going for a second beach near Karakoumi (2km east of Kyrenia Castle).[5] Once ashore 39th Division was to capture Kyrenia, open the road over the Pass to effect a link-up with the enclave and expand the bridgehead in order to prevent any interference from east or west by the National Guard.

Meanwhile men of the Airborne and Commando Brigades were to be dropped by parachute into two Dropping Zones (DZs) inside the enclave, one near Aghirda airstrip and the other 4km north of Nicosia, near Mandres Hamid. Their first tasks were to secure the airstrip and Landing Zones (LZs) for follow-up helicopter-borne units of the Airborne Brigade, which was then to protect the western flank of the enclave, the eastern flank being the responsibility of the Commando Brigade. As the operation proceeded, the Turkish national contingent was to defend the vulnerable narrow neck of the enclave in the Geunyeli-Orta Keuy area, where in breach of the Treaty of Alliance the contingent had been stationed for the past ten years. The Turks expected that by the third day, with their first two aims achieved and heavy weapons including artillery and tanks landed by then, they would be able to turn their attention to the capture of the airport.

The TCF was to render all possible assistance in and around the enclave and, in particular, to hold firm along the Green Line. Elsewhere, away from the area of operations of the mainland forces, the TCF's role was to defend isolated Turkish communities as best it could until such time as a ceasefire was declared or mainland troops could reach them. This action would serve also to tie down National Guard units that otherwise might be redeployed to oppose the Turkish intervention.

The National Guard's contingency plan to defeat a Turkish attack from the north was code-named APHRODITE. It provided for the defence of the beaches and the port of Kyrenia by infantry and artillery units stationed in the coastal strip and in the mountains above, with concurrent action by RFU troops to destroy the TCF HQ at Boghaz (close to the Pass) and the Turkish communications centre in St Hilarion Castle. In the open going of the plain south of the mountains armoured/infantry thrusts were to be launched from east and west against the enclave to cut it in two and sever communication between the Turkish quarter of Nicosia and the coast. Meanwhile other units, including anti-aircraft batteries, were to defend the airport against airborne attack and prevent any Turkish incursion across the Green Line in Nicosia. In other parts of the island National Guard units were to contain local Turkish communities and compel the surrender of their TCF defenders.

Confirmation that Turkish military intervention was imminent reached UNFICYP HQ at 0450hrs on Saturday 20 July, when Ambassador Inhan telephoned General Prem Chand to inform him that his government, invoking the provisions of the Treaty of Guarantee, would be landing military forces on the island very shortly. The Turkish government, he added, gave its assurances that these forces would not open fire unless fired upon first. Prem Chand recognized that UNFICYP had no authority to oppose the Turkish action, for Turkey was a sovereign state, a member of the UN and a signatory of the internationally recognized treaty it now invoked. For this reason and in the light of Inhan's assurances, orders were issued that, so long as they were not in danger, UN posts were to remain in position and to observe and report, without interfering with the Turkish operations.

The situation that now confronted UNFICYP had been neither foreseen nor provided for in the mandate approved by the Security Council ten years earlier. In the days following the *coup* the probability of Turkish intervention must have become ever more apparent in New York and it was surprising that the Force had received no advance guidance from the Secretary General as to the policy it should adopt in such a contingency. Even when it was known in New York that Turkish landings had been made: 'All we could do was to tell Prem Chand to "play it by ear" and do his best to limit violence and protect civilians.'[6] Throughout the days that followed Prem Chand and those under his command did so with energy, courage and a degree of success that generally went unrecognized by many on the island. The fact was that UNFICYP was on the spot, a disciplined international Force present in Cyprus as an instrument of the Security Council, and it was unthinkable that, despite its small size, it should stand by doing nothing. We took the view, rather, that in the absence of more specific instructions we would be failing in our duty if we did not do our utmost at least to limit the fighting, even if it was beyond our power to halt it, and to render assistance to all on the island, regardless of community, race or creed, in any way that seemed appropriate and consistent with the Charter of the United Nations. It was in this spirit that all ranks in the UN Force acted throughout the traumatic weeks that followed.

For Prem Chand the immediate problem was to decide how UNFICYP should react in those areas where it was brought into direct contact with mainland Turkish forces. Elsewhere the mandate remained valid, that is to say, the prevention of conflict between Greek and Turkish Cypriot communities. The most pressing need was to avert fighting as the Turks came ashore. To this end Inhan's message and his government's assurance that it contained were passed immediately to Brig. General Georgitsis, acting Commander of the National Guard, urging him to issue orders to his own men to withhold fire. He agreed to do so, but demanded clarification of the intention and full scope of the imminent Turkish operation. This we sought from Inhan, who professed himself unable to enlighten us, but in any case the matter was soon overtaken by events.

At 0500hrs the Canadian OP on the roof of the Flour Mill in north Nicosia reported Turkish jet aircraft over the mountains to the north. Minutes later the Finns in their mountain OPs heard firing in the area of 6½ Mile Beach (west of Kyrenia) and saw two Greek Cypriot MTBs heading out from Kyrenia towards the Turkish ships. Next, Pullinen reported that shooting had broken out along the Pedhieos River in northern Nicosia and that he had had to withdraw two OPs situated on exposed observation towers in that area. Another report followed quickly from the Austrian UNCIVPOL post in Kyrenia of a Turkish airstrike, the first of many, on the National Guard camp just west of the town that housed the HQ of 3rd Tactical Group and one of its infantry battalions[7], but that no seaborne landings had yet been observed. Meanwhile Sergeant Woodhall in his Sioux helicopter had been recalled to base after reporting the Turkish shipping off the coast, some naval gunfire and considerable air activity. The pilot of a second Sioux, Warrant Officer Green, carrying out a reconnaissance for the Canadians confirmed that red recognition panels were visible on the roofs of buildings along the Green Line; his aircraft was fired at (but not hit) as he came in to land at the Canadian HQ in Wolseley Barracks. On the ground the Canadians reported a proliferation of Turkish flags hoisted to mark forward positions and intense Turkish activity along the Green Line. When Manuel asked the VPO what was going on, he was told that Denktash had just announced that Turkey was coming to liberate the island.

By 0530hrs, when Radio Ankara broadcast to the world that Turkish troops were now landing in Cyprus, reports of shooting, airstrikes, naval bombardments and other activity were flooding in to the JOC at UNFICYP HQ. As they did so, the National Guard angrily protested that the TCF had opened fire in the Nicosia suburbs of Neapolis and Trakhonas and moved forward along the line of the Artemis Road in Larnaca, that Turkish air and naval forces were violating Cypriot airspace and waters, that Turkish aircraft had attacked the camp near Kyrenia and that the two MTBs sent out to investigate the approaching Turkish ships had been fired on (one being set ablaze and the other sunk). Georgitsis warned that, unless these actions were halted immediately, he would order his men to open fire. Inevitably they did not wait for any such orders.

If the arrival of mainland Turkish forces in Cyprus confronted UNFICYP with an entirely new situation not provided for in its mandate, the presence of the UN Force constituted in its turn a complication for the Turks. The situation was unique; never before had an invading army had to contend with the presence in its path of a neutral third party in the form of an international peacekeeping force. How UNFICYP, the Turkish army and the National Guard acted in this situation is described in the chapters that follow.

CHAPTER THIRTY-FIVE

THE TURKISH LANDINGS

Turkey, which has the obligation under the Treaty of Guarantee of 1960 to safeguard the independence, territorial integrity and security of the Republic of Cyprus, has endeavoured to fulfil this obligation in concert with the other Guarantor powers. You are no doubt aware that these endeavours have unfortunately been inconclusive.

Letter from Turkish Prime Minister to UN Secretary General
(S/11356, 22 July 1974).

The ferocity of the Turks' unprovoked airstrikes and naval bombardment, unleashed before their troops had even set foot on Cyprus, suggested that the Turkish purpose was to cow the Greek Cypriots into early submission by use of overwhelming force. Not only were these actions manifestly premeditated, they also made a mockery of Ecevit's public declaration that his forces would not open fire unless fired upon first. The duplicity of the assurances conveyed by Inhan and passed on to the National Guard in good faith by UNFICYP gave rise to the suspicion that it had been a deliberate Turkish ploy to use the UN Force to delay the National Guard's reaction. Whether or not it succeeded in this is unclear; certainly that reaction was not rapid, but the National Guard had been caught partly off balance in consequence of the *coup* five days earlier. The supremacy enjoyed by the Turks in the air and at sea and their massive superiority in men and equipment on land must have dismayed the Greek Cypriots, for whom there was scant hope of early or decisive military support from the mother-land. But, if outnumbered and out-gunned in all three elements, they were not wanting in courage or patriotic resolve to oppose the invaders of their small and sovereign island. Unequal though the struggle was and its outcome never in doubt, the Turks were by no means to have matters all their own way.

The hot July morning had dawned clear and free from haze, and from Blue Beret Camp Turkish airstrikes on nearby targets were clearly visible, as were transport aircraft spilling out parachute troops into the enclave. The first airstrikes, carried out by F84 Thunderflash, F100 Super Sabre and F104 Starfighter aircraft using a mixture of 750lb bombs, 2.75in rockets, 20mm cannon and napalm, took place soon after 0500hrs and continued for about one hour. Most, regardless of range, were met by a hail of light AA and small arms fire from any weapons that could be brought to bear. The waste of ammunition was prodigious, for generally the fire was ineffective except as a boost to the morale of the National Guard and civilians alike, for whom these intimidating airstrikes were a grim foretaste of what was yet to come.[1]

The Turkish national contingent was alerted at 0200hrs to the impending operation and at once fully manned defences in the critical Orta Keuy – Geunyeli sector; it did not have long to wait before it was reinforced. Just before 0600hrs 27 troop-carrying aircraft, a mixture of C130 Hercules, C160 Transall and DC3 Dakotas, arrived over the enclave, escorted by five fighter aircraft and disgorged about 1000 paratroops in two groups. The first (the aircraft of which turned close over Nicosia airport, sparking speculation that the airport was the objective) was dropped between Geunyeli and Aghirda; the second, which came down near the northern suburbs of Nicosia, evidently landed further south than intended, for Canadian observers reported that the men were then moving off north towards Mandres Hamid. The troop-carrying aircraft were followed by a further seven C130s dropping equipment and supplies. All were watched, as if part of a peacetime exercise, not only by UNFICYP observers but also by enterprising international media representatives, who had driven out in anticipation to vantage points along the Kyrenia road. At about 1030hrs a second wave of 25 aircraft made further drops of men and equipment in the Aghirda, Geunyeli and Mandres Hamid areas. A final drop took place over Aghirda at 1845hrs, with unconfirmed reports of further small paratroop drops near Lapithos and Bey Keuy east of the enclave.

Since DZs were already under Turkish Cypriot control, no opposition was encountered on landing even though the aircraft and the figures floating down attracted optimistic fire from National Guard positions that generally were out of range. Nonetheless later reports indicated that the Turks suffered about 150 casualties, half of them fatal, during the operation. Since this was carried out in ideal weather conditions such a high casualty rate, if true, may have been due to inadequate training (it was said that for some men it had been their first drop) and because some drops has been made from too low an altitude on to the hard rocky ground. The speed with which the Turks gathered themselves together once on the ground did not impress UNFICYP observers, but this was partly remedied by help received from Turkish Cypriots, who gave them an emotional welcome and guided them to their intended positions.[2]

After the disappointments of earlier years the prospect of Turkey's imminent intervention had galvanized the Turkish Cypriot Fighters into excited action. Victor Mills, UNFICYP's CAO, recalled to HQ UNFICYP from Kyrenia soon after Orange Alert was declared, described the scene as he drove south over the Pass and down the Kyrenia road:

> As I moved down through Boghaz mobilization was already under way in a very confused and hurried manner. Soldiers were running about in all states of uniform and in all directions, obviously trying to get to their duty stations as quickly as possible. Some even tried to hitchhike rides from me; I did not stop to ask questions.[3]

There was no less excitement in the Turkish quarter of the capital. Major Oberwinkler described the scene that met him on emerging from his cellar:

> I went upstairs intending to report over radio to HQ UNFICYP . . . Already outside the building were Mr Denktash and his colleagues. One could clearly hear the noise of planes and ack-ack fire. Looking towards the Kyrenia mountains I saw some 10 to 15 Hercules transport aircraft

dropping paratroopers. This part of the sky appeared to be full of parachutes. Everybody was cheering and some of the people even had tears in their eyes. At this very moving moment I must have been overwhelmed by emotion. I remember that I turned to Mr Denktash . . . and said to him: "Congratulations – now you are truly saved".[4]

About an hour after the first parachute drops the air-landed troops arrived, carried in waves of Iroquois and Augusta Bell 205 helicopters and landing either in the Aghirda LZ (the main LZ) or that at Mandres Hamid; four such waves (the first at 0715hrs, followed at 3–4-hour intervals by the remainder), totalling some 280 helicopter sorties in all, were observed during the day. UNFICYP estimated that by nightfall the Turks had delivered into the enclave about 5300 men by parachute or air-landing, consisting of the Airborne and Commando Brigades and elements of 39th Division, the HQ of which was established at Boghaz. However, although one drop of heavy equipment from a C130 was seen in the evening, within the enclave the Turks as yet had no armour and little, if any, artillery; such support evidently depended on a rapid link-up with the seaborne elements.

Things had not been going so well for the Turks on the north coast, where the operation appeared from the outset to be running behind schedule. Perhaps the curious manoeuvre observed earlier (when the ships were seen to turn away from the island only to turn back onto a new course) had indeed been due to a navigation error, throwing out the planned timings (which were thought to require the initial assault at 0630hrs). Whatever the reason, the first party of Turks, about 30 strong and including frogmen tasked to check for mines and underwater obstacles, did not land on a beach near Ayios Yeorios until 0700hrs and a further hour elapsed before the first wave of assaulting troops came ashore. This consisted of two infantry companies carried in seven landing craft and was followed by a second wave in some 20 landing craft. At least two were reported grounded short of the beach, but nevertheless there was then a steady but slow build-up throughout the day as men, tanks, guns, vehicles and stores were ferried ashore.

The narrow and constricted nature of the selected beach led to congestion and delay. Small arms fire from the National Guard 251st Infantry Bn[5] (whose men had had time to recover from the earlier airstrike on the camp they shared with HQ 3TG) and artillery fire from guns in the mountains compounded the Turks' problems; among their casualties was the 50th Infantry Regt's commander, whose death may have contributed to a lack of drive on the part of those ashore. Although the bulk of 50th Infantry Regt, together with about 30 tanks and some artillery, was thought to have landed by nightfall, the Turks by then had reached only the outskirts of Kyrenia and, in spite of supporting airstrikes and naval gunfire, had yet to capture its port and castle.

The Turkish airforce and navy kept up their attacks throughout the day. From early morning Nicosia airport and Greek camps in its vicinity, including that of ELDYK, were targets for repeated airstrikes. The pattern quickly became familiar: operating in pairs, the FGA aircraft circled at altitude identifying targets, then came in low for an initial bombing pass, followed by further passes firing rockets and cannon and in some cases dropping napalm. Some aircraft passed close over Blue Beret Camp and even closer over Camp UNFICYP situated only 100m from the airport's main terminal. Although the Greek camps suffered severely, it was apparent that in the case of the airport the Turkish purpose was to neutralize its air and ground defences and to crater the runways rather than to destroy buildings and installations. The aim, it seemed, was to deny use of the airport to the Greek airforce should Greece attempt to intervene, while facilitating its capture and subsequent use by Turkish forces. Targets elsewhere in the Nicosia area included the National Guard HQ at Athalassa[6], where no time was lost in implementing a contingency plan to move the HQ to an alternative location near the village of Malounda in the foothills of the Troodos[7]; its first elements began to leave early in the morning, but Georgitsis and the remainder of his staff did not do so until 1330hrs, when they departed at breakneck speed after suffering a third airstrike.

In the north targets for airstrikes and naval gunfire included Kyrenia and its castle, the RFU camps at Bellapais and Ayios Chrysostomos monastery (situated below Buffavento Castle), the barracks of 361st Infantry Bn at Kato Dhikomo, the radar stations at Cape Kormakiti, Orga and Kandara, and artillery and infantry OPs and positions in the mountains, especially those overlooking the landing beach. These attacks inflicted heavy damage on the National Guard; five of its meagre force of T34 tanks were destroyed west of Kyrenia, while a column of 183rd Artillery Bn near Kondemenos (west of the enclave) and another of 140th Artillery Bn on the coast road 5km east of Kyrenia both suffered heavily when caught on the move. Turkish naval bombardments became intense during the afternoon; these and air attacks set fire to several areas of the tinder-dry mountains, parts of which were obliterated by drifting smoke.

Preoccupied as they had been during the preceding days with the *coup* and its aftermath, it had not been until 19 July that the National Guard's Greek officers had begun to take seriously the prospect of Turkish military intervention and had started to redeploy troops to meet this threat.[8] Only then had tanks been withdrawn from the streets and infantry and artillery dispositions strengthened on the north coast, around the main enclave and at the airport. And only then were the junior Greek Cypriot officers, who had been sent on leave or summoned to the Nicosia HQ before the *coup*, ordered to return to their units. The speed with which the National Guard recovered from this initial unpreparedness was remarkable. As soon as Georgitsis had seen his men, camps and HQ come under air and naval attack and observed the first parachute drops, he realized that the Turkish assurances conveyed to him by Prem Chand were worthless. He decided that all-out resistance must be the order. Cyprus Radio announced the imposition of an island-wide curfew and broadcast a general call for Greek Cypriots to take up arms against the Turkish invader. Reservists were instructed to report for duty and these instructions were repeatedly broadcast throughout the day. In Nicosia the reporting centre was the Central Stadium, HQ of 3HMC, to which men flocked to be equipped before being sent out to join the fight. A Canadian LO who went to the stadium at 0545hrs (only to be turned away) noted that 'everyone was loading weapons and some NCOs were giving crash courses on weapon handling to recruits'.

Georgitsis ordered the implementation of Operation APHRODITE, the National Guard's plan to meet a Turkish attack from the north; only the Turkish quarter of Nicosia was to be excluded from offensive action. Execution of the plan was slow and poorly coordinated, with the result that attacks against the enclave on 20 July lacked momentum and soon petered out. Artillery batteries west of the enclave did not begin to engage targets (mainly in the area of Geunyeli and along the Kyrenia road) until about 0800hrs, which allowed the first Turkish parachute and helicopter landings to be made virtually unmolested. As the day wore on infantry units and the elite RFUs mounted attacks on the northern part of the enclave intended to close the Kyrenia pass, destroy the St Hilarion Castle communications centre and capture the TCF HQ in Boghaz.[9] These attacks were made from east and west along the mountains and from Kato Dhikomo below, where some of the Greeks' ancient Marmon Harrington armoured cars were seen in action. Some fierce fighting ensued in which the village of Pano Dhikomo was set ablaze, but by nightfall the National Guard had failed (apart from the raid on St Hilarion Castle described later) to make any significant inroad against the enclave. On the coast, however, its 251st Infantry Bn, supported by 140th and 183rd Artillery Bns, had succeeded in delaying the Turks' advance on Kyrenia. A British holidaymaker sheltering with others in their hotel close to the Turkish landings admired the valour of the Greek gunners:

> The Greeks fought hard on the *[coastal]* plain, mostly with small arms, but the core of the resistance was a few Greek guns on the mountains, apparently mobile. From our hotel we had a grandstand view of the continuing efforts of the Turks to silence these guns, shelling from warships, bombing and cannonading from aircraft, setting the hill-forests alight with napalm. I gathered later that they had destroyed one of the guns but the others continued firing. Much credit to the gun-crews – it must have been desperate work, moving and firing in the heat under constant attack from dawn to dusk.[10]

The National Guard stepped up its attacks, including a determined attempt, in which ELDYK took part with artillery, tank and APC-mounted infantry support, to break through to Geunyeli from the direction of Yerolakkos. This was halted by the Turks about 2km short of Geunyeli, although Greek artillery harassing fire continued throughout the night.[11] It was the National Guard's 33rd RFU that seemingly scored the most notable success; the Greeks claimed later that, attacking in the late evening from their camp at Bellapais, men of this RFU had succeeded in destroying the Turks' vital communications centre in St Hilarion Castle, killing most of the Turks within, although not capturing the castle itself. The price was heavy; only 10–15 men out of a 100 strong RFU group were said to have returned alive.

Turkish air power had been telling, but as darkness fell air activity ceased. The Greeks took fresh heart – as a Greek officer remarked to a UN officer 'the day is theirs but the night is ours' – and the Turks felt far from secure:

> With darkness approaching the jets suspended their attacks, leaving large stretches of the mountain sides ablaze. An eerie silence broken only by the crackling of burning trees settled over the hills, bringing a disquieting feeling of isolation to the Mehmetciks *[Turkish soldiers]*. . . . Where were the Greeks and what were they up to? Why had there been so little resistance? Were they being lured into some unforeseen disaster? Similar thoughts were worrying the General Staff in Ankara. The first and most difficult step, the landing of troops from the sea and from the air, had taken rather longer than expected, mainly because of the

restricted space on the beach; but a bridgehead had been established and that with but few casualties and no unpleasant surprises.

The ships were now on their way back to Mersin for the next shipment. Reports confirmed that units detailed to take Kyrenia were slowly making their way along the mountain slopes, hoping to link up with the paratroops dropped at Boghaz. All the same, this seeming inactivity of the enemy was disturbing. To add to their anxiety communications between HQ and commanders in the field had not been satisfactory and at around 1700hrs had almost completely broken down *[in consequence of the RFU raid on St Hilarion Castle]*. There were reports that units of the Cypriot National Guard were advancing in directions not clearly established; that troop concentrations had been observed near caves in the mountains; but no clear picture emerged.[12]

As the night wore on and reports of the National Guard's activities filtered through to Ankara, Turkish unease grew:

> The High Command in Ankara had much to worry over and sleep was out of the question. The bridgehead . . . was now seriously threatened, with infantry hanging on grimly to their positions after their commander, Colonel Karaoglanoglou, had been killed by a mortar shell. Everywhere the Turkish troops were under relentless pressure and for a time it looked as though the Greeks were winning. By 0200hrs the Adana Control Centre was being flooded with desperate requests for help from the battle zone – requests that could not be met. Only 6000 troops had been landed so far and the second *[seaborne]* wave could not reach the island before the morning of July 22nd. The situation was well nigh intolerable and it became clear that the Intelligence Service reports had been lamentably inaccurate.
>
> The commanders worked through the night reviewing their plans in the light of the latest information. Without waiting for the outcome General Akinci, Land Forces Commander, in the realization that more tanks were essential, had ordered the 39th Tank Division to proceed from Osmaniye to Mersin and place themselves under the orders of General Bedrettin Demirel. In the early hours of the morning *[21 July]* the plans for what Ecevit had hopefully termed "a peace operation" were amended to include the destructive bombing of military targets, and the destroyers *Tinaztepe, Adatepe* and *Kocatepe*, now on their way to Mersin, were ordered to return to Cyprus immediately to help in carrying out his decision. It was hoped that this action would relieve the pressure sufficiently to permit the dropping of much-needed supplies to the Turkish soldiers and also to the beleaguered Turkish Cypriot villages.
>
> With seemingly inexhaustible resources, the Greeks were launching attack after attack upon the greatly outnumbered Turks, who each time managed to ward them off whilst praying for the dawn so that the jets could come to their aid. At the focal point of the battle *[the Greek thrust towards Geunyeli]* the Greek Military Contingent *[ELDYK]* found itself unable to crush its Turkish counterpart . . . . The effects of this dogged and unyielding resistance became apparent around 0300hrs, when the pressure started to relax. The Turkish Commandos and the Turkish Cypriot Fighters had put up an almost superhuman resistance and their losses were high. No official figures have so far been issued but the first day's fighting is believed to have cost the Turkish Cypriot Fighters alone some 2000 men.[13]

If the Turkish airforce was intent on denying use of Nicosia airport to the Greek airforce, the National Guard was no less determined to prevent its use by the Turks. From early morning on 20 July the airport had been the scene of constant activity as AA and ground defences were strengthened. Runways were partially obstructed by heavy airport equipment and even by the positioning of Cyprus Airways aircraft on them.[14] The close proximity of the adjacent Camp UNFICYP exposed those within it to special danger and action to mini-mize this had its lighter moments, as Major Herbert (UK), the Force Transport Officer, described:

> Our first problem was a Greek armoured car . . . which took up a firing position against the perimeter fence . . . . The Camp Commandant asked me to persuade the crew to move off as their position would endanger the United Nations personnel if the vehicle was attacked by the Turkish airforce. . . . I explained to the crew that their position was unacceptable to the UN. To our surprise they drove away without argument. But this was a short-lived victory, for on walking round to the other side of the hangar we discovered the main gate was blocked by a lorry-mounted anti-aircraft gun, which was promptly joined by a Bofors *[AA gun]*. Persuading the Bofors crew to move away proved extremely difficult, and the excited Greek driver made much ado about cocking his sub-machine gun and waving it about dangerously. Meanwhile the sergeant in charge of the Bofors became so agitated that he accidentally pulled the Bofors trigger and the resulting din so startled the driver that he put his vehicle into gear. As the vehicle moved off, albeit unintentionally, the other Greeks decided to go with it.[15]

During this and subsequent days the Force's logistic and supporting units based in Camp UNFICYP found themselves right in the firing line, but were not alone in this respect.

CHAPTER THIRTY-SIX

UNFICYP'S REACTIONS
–NICOSIA AND THE NORTH

The arrival in its area of a large fighting army which it is neither equipped nor authorized to resist creates an impossible situation for a peacekeeping force.

Brian Urquhart: *A Life in Peace and War,* p.256.

Impossible though the situation may have been, UNFICYP was determined to do its utmost to mitigate its consequences. The Force was confronted by two distinct but inextricably linked predicaments: the first was where (in direct reaction to the second) Greek and Turkish Cypriots were turning on each other; here it remained UNFICYP's clear duty under its mandate to halt the intercommunal violence. The second was where Turkey's mainland forces were engaging the Greek Cypriot National Guard and ELDYK, a development never envisaged in the mandate. Nonetheless, whether covered by the mandate or not, General Prem Chand was never in doubt of the need to limit this second conflict, although well aware that with a mere 2340 lightly armed men and these spread throughout the island UNFICYP had neither the military resources nor (as the Turks were not slow to emphasize) the authority to attempt to halt Turkey's action. Common to both situations were calls for the UN Force in accordance with honoured UN peacekeeping custom to do all it could to succour civilians of all communities suffering as a result of the fighting.

Saturday 20 July and subsequent days brought momentous developments and a multitude of incidents throughout Cyprus; within the limits of this work it is not possible to record them all. UNFICYP was closely involved at many points and in many ways, striving always to play a constructive role. The unprovoked airstrikes and naval bombardments, which had followed within half an hour of the spurious assurances conveyed by Ambassador Inhan, brought rapid realization that UNFICYP was powerless to halt Turkey's operation: responsibility for this must rest with the UN Security Council and, possibly, NATO. In Cyprus the immediate need was to dampen down outbreaks of intercommunal fighting as far as might be possible in the passions of the moment. UNFICYP's actions in and around Nicosia and further north – that is, in those areas most immediately experiencing the impact of Turkey's action – are described in this chapter; its actions elsewhere are told in those that follow.

The city of Nicosia gave cause for particular concern on account of its population of some 110,000 Greeks, Turks and others who lived in densely built-up areas such as those

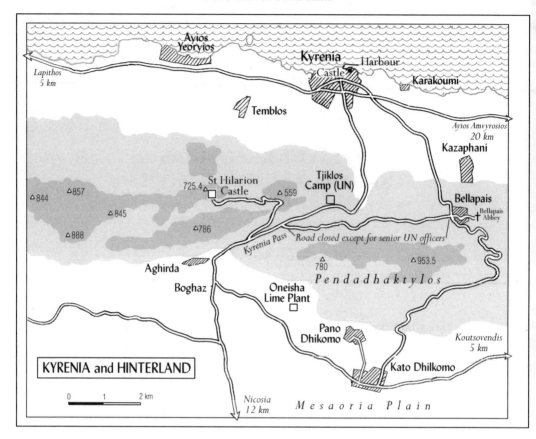

within the walls of the Old City. There was wide recognition that a Greek attack on the Turkish quarter was likely to result in escalation with the use of heavy weapons, retaliatory Turkish airstrikes and consequential heavy casualties and damage. Turkish Cypriots, cooped up in their quarter, appreciated their vulnerability only too well and Greek Cypriots had no illusions as to the effects of bombing on their own sectors. Prem Chand was quick to recognize the dangers and the common interest in averting any general battle for Nicosia. Although UNFICYP's efforts to stop the shooting along the Green Line met with only limited success, it was largely due to untiring exertions by Prem Chand personally and his local commanders that there were few civilian casualties and only minor damage in the city.

An urgent need was for UNFICYP to establish reliable communications with the leaders of both Cypriot communities and with the Commander of the intervening Turkish forces (whose identity and location were unknown to UNFICYP). Major Oberwinkler (Austria) was already at Denktash's side in the Turkish quarter where he also had access to Inhan[1]. Since it was clear that Sampson exercised no control over the National Guard, it was with the latter's Greek officers that communication was essential. Soon after the declaration of Orange Alert Commandant Flynn (Ireland) had returned to the National Guard HQ at Athalassa where he was to do sterling work, at times in circumstances of acute danger[2]; in this he received the ready cooperation of Major Tsolakis, the National Guard's LO to UNFICYP.[3] But it was not until six days later (and then only after Waldheim's personal intervention) that a liaison link was established between Prem Chand and Lieut. General Ersin, the Turkish Force Commander, with whom in the meantime the only means of communication was through Inhan, who professed to be able only to pass messages via the Foreign Ministry in Ankara.[4] This was both slow and unsatisfactory because UNFICYP could never be certain that these had been passed correctly.

As soon as fighting had erupted Prem Chand had pressed both Cypriot communities through UNFICYP's LOs and in personal telephone calls to Denktash, Inhan and Georgitsis to exercise the utmost restraint, but, as the Turkish onslaught developed ever more fiercely, UNFICYP's hopes on this account quickly faded. Shooting became constant along Nicosia's Green Line and reports flowed in of violent Greek reaction elsewhere as news of Turkey's offensive actions spread. The UN Force nonetheless made clear that it stood ready to give whatever assistance that might be required to bring a quick end to the fighting. With the support of diplomatic missions, Prem Chand proposed as early as 0800hrs that Nicosia should be declared an 'open city' with military forces of both sides withdrawn and intercommunal security entrusted to UN troops. He urged that, failing this, both sides should undertake not to deploy or use heavy weapons within Nicosia, and that the Turks should agree not to mount airstrikes on it; he further proposed that the National Guard should reciprocate by refraining from any attacks on the Turkish quarter, the Turkish enclave and Turkish communities elsewhere. Inhan undertook to pass these proposals to Ersin on condition that the National Guard gave prior assurance through UNFICYP with respect to the latter. (For the Leadership Orek said that the TCF would fire only in self-defence, but pointed out that he exercised no control over the mainland forces; since in practice he exercised no control over the TCF either, his words carried little weight.)

Georgitsis, however, was adamant – the National Guard would agree to the proposals only on condition that Turkey ceased its aggression immediately. Faced by this impasse, Prem Chand despatched Colonel Beattie (Canada), UNFICYP's Deputy Chief of Staff, to Athalassa at 0815hrs with instructions to press Georgitsis personally for agreement to a general ceasefire and declaration of Nicosia as an open city, and for an assurance that the National Guard would respect the safety of Turkish Cypriots throughout the island. Beattie was to tell Georgitsis that, if he accepted these proposals without unrealistic conditions, then UNFICYP would press the Turks for parallel undertakings. Surrounded by excited members of the National Guard and amidst general pandemonium, Beattie did his utmost for the next 90 minutes to convince Georgitsis of the need to accept, but the latter refused to budge from his insistence that the Turks must first agree to halt offensive operations and withdraw all their forces from the island. With progress impossible, Beattie was told to return to Blue Beret Camp as soon as it was safe to do so.[5] Despite this set-back, UNFICYP at all levels redoubled efforts to secure ceasefires not only in Nicosia but also in all other areas where fighting had broken out.

The Canadians in Nicosia District

Lieut. Colonel Manuel, Nicosia District Commander, had lost no time in establishing his own liaison links with both sides. Canadian LOs were sent to the Leadership at the VPO and to the HQ of the National Guard's 3HMC located in the Nicosia stadium. Captain Mathieu, the LO turned away earlier, returned to HQ 3HMC and others were deployed to two TCF companies manning the Green Line.[6] Manuel himself had gone to the Leadership to urge restraint and was told that the TCF were firing only in self-defence and that mainland forces now arriving intended to defend Turkish Cypriot areas. His LOs reported that local TCF commanders were critical of what appeared to them to be one-sided pressure on them by UNFICYP, which pointed the need to broker an agreement for both sides to stop firing at a mutually agreed time; Manuel proposed that this should be at 1000hrs. It was the first of several such attempts made by UNFICYP during 20 July but, like those that followed, it met with little success. Each side was willing in principle to accept a ceasefire along the intercommunal divide, but neither proved able to exercise the necessary control over its own men to ensure it was effective. Mathieu's experiences illustrated the difficulties:

> I was ushered into the office of the commander of 3HMC . . . . I said that the fighting along the Green Line had to stop as soon as possible and that we, the UN, had LOs with the TCF who were trying to do the same thing. I was informed that the commander had not received any instructions concerning a ceasefire and that only the National Guard HQ *[at Athalassa]* could make that decision. I asked that he get that permission and that a local ceasefire for 1000hrs be arranged. . . . After 20 minutes I was informed that no local ceasefire could be arranged and that all contact was to be made with National Guard HQ.
>
> A civilian was also at 3HMC, a Mr Myrianthopoulos; he appeared to have a great deal of influence over the senior officers . . . . During the next couple of hours I went to this civilian to pass on any protests or communications from the *[Nicosia District]* JOC. The answer however was always the same – decisions could not be made by 3HMC . . .
>
> After an 'O' Group I was told my presence at 3HMC was no longer required as a decision had been made to fight the Turks. I said that I should remain to provide an important link between the National Guard and the UN locally . . . . The commander of 3HMC agreed that it was better that I leave as they could not guarantee my safety. Some of the National Guard said that they were ready to go into the Enclave and fight the Turks, who had started the fighting. Also some said that the Greek Cypriot people might turn against the UN as a sort of convenient scapegoat, even though they realized that the UN's job was making peace. . . . I left 3HMC at 1100hrs.[7]

Manuel's efforts to halt the fighting in the city were complemented at Force HQ, where Prem Chand was indefatigable in exerting pressure on both sides. At midday, following the 1000hrs failure, the Leadership agreed to call a halt to shooting along the Green Line provided that the National Guard reciprocated; an hour later Georgitsis accepted that this should take place at 1400hrs on the understanding that UNFICYP would ensure that the TCF did not use this to its advantage. Denktash agreed, but hopes were dashed at about 1330hrs by a Turkish airstrike on the National Guard's Athalassa HQ. Heavy firing ensued along the Green Line, while Georgitsis and his immediate entourage departed at high speed for the alternative HQ at Malounda, declaring as they left that the withdrawal of all Turkish forces from the island was now a pre-condition for any future ceasefire agreement.[8] Soon after 1400hrs Oberwinkler reported that, in spite of heavy firing opened on the Turkish quarter, the TCF were not responding, in the hope that the ceasefire agreed for that time would take effect. They hoped in vain.

By now both sides were alarmed by the growing scale of the fighting and more amenable to UNFICYP's pressures for a ceasefire. From Malounda came the National Guard's agreement for a ceasefire along the Green Line to take effect at 1700hrs and, informed of this, Denktash also agreed. For the first time on this long hot day the UN Force's perseverance was rewarded: a degree of calm prevailed along the Green Line for some two hours that evening, but, as time passed and the Greeks saw that there was no let-up in the operations of the Turkish forces further north, sporadic outbreaks of firing occurred. By 1930hrs, when darkness fell, the ceasefire along the Line had broken down altogether.

Many members of the UN Force were exposed to danger in the fighting. For reasons already explained, most UN posts had been de-fortified as a matter of deliberate policy, leaving the men in them with protection from the elements but little else. In this new situation those exposed to the shooting from either side had to be withdrawn. The first Canadian post so withdrawn was OP Golfcourse on the city's northern outskirts, where as early as 0545hrs the TCF had moved forward to the OP itself, drawing National Guard fire. By 0700hrs OPs Hermes 2 and Constantine 2 (both inside the walled city) had had to be withdrawn (although re-established later). Elsewhere the OPs on Roccas Bastion and on the tall Flour Mill (in the northern suburbs) received close mortar and small arms fire, and most other Canadian posts had similar experiences. There had been no Canadian casualties so far, but at midday the Canadian HQ in Wolseley Barracks was hit by three mortar rounds (from which side was uncertain), wounding four men (a fifth was hit by shrapnel soon afterwards), damaging vehicles and causing a fire. The situation of the Canadian OPs constantly changed; OP Roccas Bastion had to be withdrawn, as was Constantine 2 (for the second time) and withdrawal of OPs Clinic and Chimo followed. When Paphos 2 reported a fire out of control in the building on which it was situated, its men were ordered to abandon the post and to take with them some civilians caught in the blaze. However, the Canadians continued to man OPs at Omorphita Police Station, Red Line 2 and on the Flour Mill, the last especially providing useful reports.

The National Guard's increasing use of mortars gave rise to Turkish protests to UNFICYP, including complaints that the Red Crescent hospital had been hit and that an elderly Turkish woman had been killed in Orta Keuy. Manuel made every effort to find the base-plate positions of these mortars and sent officers to stop their firing. This was often haphazard, as Colonel Hunter, Defence Adviser to the British High Commission, noted from the roof of its Chancery building:

> The Greek Cypriots had set up a 3inch mortar position inside the prison wall about 40 yards from the Chancery building. They opened up on the Turkish quarter completely blind, because they had no possible OP except my roof, over which they were lobbing their bombs. The Turks

very quickly appreciated the source and I retired below. The Chancery building suffered surprisingly little damage, and the mortar position was maintained in action until the ceasefire. My own house was similarly placed. The National Guard set up another mortar and a LMG in the shell of a partly built house about 200 yards the other side of my house. When the Turks replied, the National Guard firing became a bit erratic and rounds aimed at the Turks ended up through our windows and in our walls. . . . Throughout that day firing by both sides increased in intensity. It was a fantastic waste of ammunition.[9]

The proposed 1400hrs ceasefire having failed to materialize, the Canadians continued to contend with shooting and outbreaks of fire along the Green Line. Those in Camp Kronborg (on the west bank of the dry Pedhieos river) experienced constant firing throughout the afternoon and a mortar bomb exploded in the camp (others fell close by), fortunately without causing casualties. But a sixth Canadian was wounded by small arms fire, the JOC suffered a near-miss when another mortar round struck Wolseley Barracks, and a seventh Canadian was wounded while patrolling on the Green Line. Casualties were evacuated to Blue Beret Camp under escort by Ferret scout cars of the Parachute Squadron RAC. On one such run the escort was fired upon by small arms (which hit) and a rocket launcher (which missed). A single round fired in response from a Ferret had the desired effect. Although shooting along the Green Line generally died down as the 1700hrs ceasefire took effect, it applied only to the city of Nicosia. National Guard artillery continued to shell targets inside the Turkish enclave and the VPO warned that airstrikes would be called for unless this shelling was halted; as darkness fell flames could be seen in the enclave. UNFICYP's Camp Kronborg came under fire again and (as described later) increased activity in the vicinity of the Ledra Palace Hotel caused mounting concern.

Darkness and the confused situation both in Nicosia and elsewhere pointed the need to minimize risks to UN troops, and District Commanders were authorized at their discretion to withdraw men from OPs into base camps. Manuel decided to maintain in being OPs Flour Mill and Red Line 2 (despite its sentry's complaint that a sniper was shooting out the light that illuminated it) and to retain men in two bases within the walled city as well as in the Neapolis clinic (in the northern suburbs) and in Camp Kronborg. During the night the Canadians suffered their eighth casualty when their LO to the TCF's 22nd Company was wounded by a bullet.

The predicament of some 385 civilians, mostly foreign nationals (including women and children and a large contingent of international media representatives), who were trapped in the Ledra Palace Hotel, had given cause for much concern since early morning, when a group of national guardsmen had moved into it:

> First the Greeks raised their flag on the roof and set up sniping positions at the four corners of the five-storey building. The first casualty came at 8am. A mortar bomb fired from the Turkish lines hit one of the sniping points. One man was killed and another badly hurt. The incident obviously had a tremendous effect on the young part-time soldiers who had been up all night expecting an invasion. As photographers clustered round to take pictures of the wounded man one of them lashed out hysterically at a TV crew and brandished a drawn revolver. The soldiers abandoned their roof-top positions and moved down to the foyer

which was packed with a 200-strong international press corps confined to the hotel by the island's 24-hour curfew. A few remaining tourists, including women, had by this time taken refuge in the basement.[10]

This shooting only 200m from his own HQ in Wolseley Barracks prompted Manuel to take swift action. Pressing both sides to stop shooting at or from the hotel, he sent a patrol to investigate:

> At this point two French Canadian soldiers . . . ran into the hotel after their Landrover had been fired on. They failed to persuade the Greeks not to fire from inside the hotel. After a lengthy conversation with their headquarters over the radio they left. The Greeks then took up - positions at the front and rear of the hotel and started firing. Half a dozen men took cover behind the hotel's musical equipment . . . from where they blazed away in the general direction of the Turkish lines. . . .
> The first contingent of Greek troops had come from a small police station opposite the hotel. . . . Some of the soldiers escaped from there into the Ledra Palace. . . . By 11.30am the original group had been joined by a brigandish-looking band of militia men who came weaving through the olive trees in the garden at the rear of the hotel. . . . At 2.10pm the second soldier was hit in the wrist as a salvo of bullets came straight through the plate-glass sliding doors at the back of the hotel.[11]

Manuel realized that the civilians must somehow be got out of the hotel but that it would be too dangerous to attempt this while shooting continued. Although he secured the agreement of both sides for a ceasefire at midday in the hotel's vicinity, this was not honoured; indeed, the situation worsened when the TCF threatened to eject the National Guard from the hotel by force. When the wider ceasefire due to take effect all along the Green Line at 1400hrs also failed to materialize, Manuel decided on radical action: the hotel would be declared a 'UN-protected area' from which both sides would be excluded. To this end a ten-strong party of Canadians entered the hotel. However, the National Guard contested this action and it was not until 2000hrs that Manuel was able to report that the hotel was effectively under UN control.

Darkness, sporadic shooting and mortar fire prevented evacuation of the civilians, who were obliged to spend the night under trying conditions. Women and children sheltered in the basement, water was cut off, food was short and there was no electric power for lighting, air-conditioning or refrigerators, all this at the end of a day when temperatures had reached 40°C. Moreover, these were not the only anxieties; Manuel had to deploy further men to ensure the removal of a National Guard mortar post in the vicinity and the sounds of continuing mortar and small arms fire allowed little rest (at one stage the hotel became the target for Turkish machine-gun fire and soon after dawn it was hit by two mortar rounds). How the civilians were rescued from the hotel is described later.

The sole Canadian post outside Nicosia was at the Turkish village of Louroujina, 18km to the south-east, where its role was to maintain peace between it and the neighbouring Greek village of Lymbia. At 1000hrs the TCF had forced a way into the post, replaced the UN flag by a Turkish flag and taken up position on a hill dominating Lymbia. Manuel ordered his men to stay where they were and maintain observation, but in early afternoon, when shooting erupted between the two villages, radio contact was suddenly lost. Concern for the safety of the Canadians grew with reports that Louroujina was coming under mortar fire, but next morning, when radio communications were restored and the UN flag re-hoisted, they were all found to be unharmed.

The Finns in Kyrenia District

Deployed as they were around the main Turkish enclave and in the mountains above Kyrenia, it was the Finns who were the best placed to observe and report on the progress of the Turkish air and seaborne operations. Their OPs closest to the fighting were at Temblos (a small Turkish village just west of Kyrenia), another near the Turkish hamlet of Pileri (west of Aghirda and its airstrip), three on the mountain peaks (OPs Saddle, King's Nest and Hill Top) and two on the eastern flank of the enclave, one at the Oneisha lime plant 3km north-west of Kato Dhikomo and the other on Martin's Mound, a bare rocky feature 3km south of that village. All these posts were manned by the Finnish company based in Tjiklos camp at the head of the Kyrenia pass. Other Finnish posts were situated in the Trakhonas and Omorphita suburbs of northern Nicosia (one of which was the appropriately named OP Crazy Corner at a convoluted point on the enclave's southern limit). They had all been alerted by Lieut. Colonel Pullinen following his meeting with me in Blue Beret Camp at 0330hrs and, despite the dangers, most remained in position all day providing a valuable flow of information.

UNFICYP HQ was kept informed not only of the naval activity off the north coast, the seaborne landings west of Kyrenia, the airstrikes and naval bombardments, and the parachute and helicopter landings, but also the movement of National Guard armoured, infantry and artillery units towards Nicosia airport and Yerolakkos (to its north), where Greek forces were being concentrated for the APHRODITE operation against the Turkish enclave. Although fighting had broken out at about 0830hrs within 100m of their OP, the Finns at Martin's Mound stayed put and succeeded temporarily in halting further shooting near Kato Dhikomo. Further north, where the National Guard was reported to be withdrawing along the coast towards Kyrenia, fires in the mountains hampered observation and endangered some UN posts; those in OP Saddle had to vacate it temporarily. As morning wore on Turkish airstrikes were mounted on Kato Dhikomo and the National Guard's camp below Buffavento, and heavy shooting developed close to Finnish posts in the area, but it was in Kykko Camp (the Finnish Contingent's base close to HQ UNFICYP) that the Finns suffered their first casualty, an officer being wounded by a bomb that struck the camp at about 0900hrs. It was here too that in the early afternoon Pullinen had to contend with a new danger to which there was no ready peacekeeper's text-book answer. National Guard artillery batteries were being deployed close to some UN camps (in his case the dead ground behind Kykko camp), attracting Turkish airstrikes and (later) counter-battery fire.

That evening men of the National Guard 33rd RFU set out from their Bellapais camp for a raid on St Hilarion Castle and its vital Turkish communications centre. In their path lay Boghazi Farm situated on a prominent hill overlooking Kyrenia and the home of a retired British expatriate, Lieut. Colonel Simonds. On reaching it some threatened to shoot him and a guest 'because all the British are pro-Turk'[12], whereupon Simonds telephoned another retired British officer, Major A. Napier (who house was adjacent to Tjiklos camp) asking him to obtain UNFICYP's help. Napier at once contacted Captain Ekku Lenck, the Finns' Company Commander in the camp, who sent a patrol of four men in a radio-equipped Land Rover to investigate (Napier volunteered to go with them but Lenck would not permit this). By now it was dark. The patrol reported that it had been stopped near Boghazi Farm and then radio contact abruptly ceased. Anxious for the safety of his men and those in the farm, Lenck sent out a second patrol, with the same result. He then sent a third, but this time with a concealed radio with its 'send' button taped down so that it transmitted continuously; it too was stopped and (as proved to have been the case with the others) its four men were overpowered and disarmed. All 12 Finns were then taken on foot to an unknown destination, which the concealed radio revealed to be Bellapais. After urgent protests by HQ UNFICYP, all 12 were released unharmed next afternoon, together with their vehicles (which had been observed during the morning withdrawing east still flying UN flags). Simonds and his guest were held unharmed as prisoners in the farm until the following day when they made their way to Tjiklos camp. Soon afterwards the house was shelled and set on fire with all contents destroyed. Napier (an ex-Coldstream Guards officer), wrote of this incident:

> The action of the Finns on the night of 20th July was very courageous and instrumental in causing the Greeks not to shoot Colonel Simonds and Miss Lowe *[his guest]*. I have the greatest admiration for Captain Lenck and his Finnish company.[13]

This was not Lenck's sole worry. As Turkish forces closed on Kyrenia the Austrian UNCIVPOL detachment in the town was authorized to withdraw to Tjiklos and did so in the late evening, taking with it about 150 civilians of a score of different nationalities, all of whom were given shelter in the Finns' camp.[14] Lenck and his men had already had experience in coping with such an influx, having cared for other civilians at the time of the *coup* five days earlier, but this time the problems and dangers were far more acute. Food and water were short, and on this and succeeding days the camp came under mortar and small arms fire and was in danger of attack by Turkish troops who were oblivious of its status as a UN camp:

> Once, for instance, a Finnish officer, Lieutenant Markupiitari, with his small pistol and ten men armed with assault rifles had to face three tanks and a platoon of Turkish soldiers at the main gate of the camp, saying, "This a UN area – you are not allowed to come inside. If you come, I have to open fire at you".[15]

This was typical of the Finns' robust attitude. Although their situation at Tjiklos was at times precarious, Pullinen rightly insisted on retention of this important UNFICYP foothold in the island's north.

Nightfall on 20 July found the Finns still holding OPs Saddle, Hill Top and Martin's Mound in the north, together with OPs Omorphita 2, Crazy Corner and Trakhonas in the south, but Pullinen had withdrawn his men from all others, either on account of forest fires or because they no longer served a useful purpose.

The Airport, Czech Weapons and Force HQ

Those in the UN camps close to the airport did not lack excitement or danger either. The Military Police Company's base at the entrance to Blue Beret Camp afforded excellent observation and its members maintained a flow of reports to the Force JOC on the repeated Turkish airstrikes and parachute and helicopter landings, the movement of National Guard reinforcements towards the airport, the mortar fire (which at times came close to the RAF married quarters and Blue Beret Camp itself; two rounds fell inside it), and the many fires burning in the tinder-dry scrub all around. Problems in Camp UNFICYP were aggravated by an influx of civilian workers and stranded passengers fleeing from the airport; the latter included an officer of the Guyana army engineers attending a course in Cyprus:

> He wanted to don his uniform and join the war but was firmly demoted to civilian refugee status by RSM Birch [Camp Regimental Sergeant Major]. . . . We put these refugees into the International Club [the camp canteen], appropriately since they included many nationalities with a number of children and even a Cypriot who said he was the Swedish consul. We fixed them up as comfortably as possible and they stayed until the convoy took them to Dhekelia next day.[16]

The Camp Commandant, Major Barker (UK), established an OP on the water tower from which the whole airport, part of Nicosia and much of the enclave were visible; in spite of its exposed position there was never a lack of volunteers to man it, and their reports confirmed that the Greeks were working energetically to strengthen the airport defences. In view of its close proximity to the airport, Barker took steps to ensure the ready identification of the camp as UN premises, but, although the Turkish pilots appeared to be recognizing this, some mistakes inevitably were made, the first soon after 1000hrs when a rocket hit the camp, fortunately without causing casualties. Some 90 minutes later bombs and cannon fire damaged two vehicles, while in the early afternoon air-dropped napalm started a fire and a bomb hit the Force's REME Workshop, wounding a British sergeant. Although troops in the UN camp suffered no further casualties that day, civilian wounded were brought into the camp and given first aid before transfer to the Austrian Medical Centre in Blue Beret Camp.

During the morning the commander of the Greek troops defending the airport asked for a UN officer to meet him and Barker sent Major J. Herbert (UK), OC of the Force Transport Squadron, who described his experience:

> It was to be the first of many meetings with Major Papadopoulos, a middle-aged officer already exhausted from the strain of commanding the airport since the coup d'état five days earlier. His throat was wrapped in a white cloth and he had difficulty in speaking. His agitation and excessive perspiration did little to inspire confidence. He made a passionate statement to the effect that the Greek people had been done a great wrong that morning by the Turks, who had

without cause invaded the island of Cyprus, and that all the Greek people of the island and the mainland would fight to the last man and to the last drop of blood to preserve their Hellenic heritage. I replied in rather lower key that the United Nations would remain impartial, that he must respect the United Nations position at the airport, and finally that he must not endanger UN soldiers by placing his troops any closer than 50m from the camp perimeter. He gave me this assurance and I returned to camp.[17]

The relationship established by Herbert with Papadopoulos was soon to prove valuable, but this was only the first of several occasions on which Herbert played a notable part.

The next occurred the same afternoon when he handled an ugly situation with firmness and courage. A group of armed Greeks, who by their demeanour and dress appeared to Herbert to be terrorists, arrived in several cars at Camp UNFICYP's main gate. Their leader proved to be a police inspector (colonel) who demanded that the large cache of Czech weapons stored in the camp be handed over within five minutes, arguing that UNFICYP should help them as Greek Cypriots fighting for their homeland. Herbert (to whom Barker had delegated responsibility for controlling entry to the camp) explained that the weapons were held in trust by the UN and that the demand would have to be addressed to the UN Force Commander. A heated altercation followed, but Herbert was adamant:

> Our position was quite clear and the Colonel, realizing this, challenged it by threatening to walk in. His men emphasized this threat by cocking their weapons. I had already called out the reserve section of the Coldstream Guards platoon and they, together with a number of 7 Squadron RCT *[Herbert's own unit]* stood in line at the ready facing the intruders. I responded to the Colonel's challenge by informing him that we would have no hesitation in opening fire should they attempt to move forward. The Colonel queried whether the English would spill their blood with the Greeks and I replied that we would. I asked him to consider the situation carefully and suggested that he would be best advised to withdraw and raise the matter with the Chief of Staff at UN Headquarters. The Colonel gave an order in Greek and he and his men fell back, except for one "civilian" who stepped forward and, addressing me by name, threatened my life and those of my family if the weapons were not handed over. After repeating this threat and saying they would be back, he left with the rest of the party.[18]

Soon afterwards the group arrived at the entrance to Blue Beret Camp demanding to see the Force Commander. I gave orders for four to be admitted and, after temporarily surrendering their weapons to the Military Police, to be escorted to my office. The leader and three others, all clearly under emotional strain, duly entered. Seating them on sofas and offering coffee, my purpose was to calm them down and play for time while Camp UNFICYP's defences were reinforced. I explained the history of the weapons and the agreements reached for their custody, and made plain that there was no question of releasing them to anyone without a formal approach by the Cyprus government to the UN Secretary General. Whom, I asked did they represent, the Cyprus government? In spite of repeated questioning they refused to identify themselves or say on whose behalf they were acting. We talked in circles for some 45 minutes and, as I repeatedly brought them back to the fundamental point, their tempers grew ever shorter. Their leader angrily declared that they were wasting their time (as indeed

they were) and made to leave. To gain more time and drive home the points already repeatedly made, I took them in to see General Prem Chand himself, who made no less clear that
UNFICYP was inflexible in its determination not to release the weapons without the formal
agreement of all concerned. After about an hour the four departed, glowering, but
empty-handed. As this small drama was being played out, defences at Camp UNFICYP had
been strengthened against the possibility that the group might carry out the threat to return
and, as darkness fell, I visited the camp to brief Barker and Herbert on action to be taken in
the event of any further attempt on the weapons: force was to be met by force and, if there
was any danger of the weapons being lost, a contingency plan for their destruction was to be
implemented without further orders.[19]

Domestic problems were making life increasingly difficult in UN camps. In many areas
electricity supplies ceased, causing lighting and air-conditioning failures in operations rooms
and medical centres and, more seriously, water shortages due to dependence on electrically
powered pumps. All base camps, but especially Blue Beret Camp, relied on locally engaged
civilians for many day-to-day chores, including the staffing of messes. These civilians
absented themselves as soon as fighting began, so that essential domestic tasks had to be
undertaken by soldiers who could ill be spared. Problems were aggravated by an influx of
the 40-strong UN civilian Secretariat and their families, normally accommodated in apartments scattered around Nicosia, as well as sundry other foreign nationals with dubious
claims on the UN Force's hospitality. The desirability of evacuating as many as possible to
a safer area, such as one of the British SBAs, was clear, but General Prem Chand judged that
an evacuation at that stage might spark a panic amongst Cypriots generally; in spite of the
difficulties caused by their presence and the risks to which all in the camps were exposed,
they were to remain for the time being.

The dangers from misdirected airstrikes, artillery, mortar and small-arms fire were real,
but protection within Blue Beret Camp was minimal, the experiences of the previous ten
years having never pointed the need for shelters to be built. To construct them now was
impracticable, for the camp stood on hard rocky ground, defence stores such as sandbags
were few and neither the necessary manpower nor mechanical plant were available. When
airstrikes developed close overhead, those in the camp could only take cover in the stone-
built huts and hope for the best.

Unlike an army field HQ such as that of a brigade or division, UNFICYP HQ was a static
establishment neither organized nor equipped for mobile operations, but it became prudent
to examine the feasibility of an emergency move of essential command and logistic elements
to an alternative location should fighting in the vicinity render the present camps untenable.
The English School situated on the southern outskirts of Nicosia offered a possible location,
but a reconnaissance party sent to examine this discovered that the school was already
occupied by the National Guard (who apologized after firing at the party). Further consideration led to the conclusion that a move in present circumstances was not practicable; a
small tactical HQ could be deployed away from Blue Beret Camp, but the vital communications link with New York provided by the UN Radio could not. There was no practical
choice but to remain in Blue Beret Camp and trust that it would be possible to continue exercising effective command from it.

Those caught up in the fighting included the Austrian UN Civilian Police whose base, known as Blue Danube Camp (in which some of their families also resided), was situated on the Turkish side in the northern suburbs of Nicosia. Some of the earliest shooting had erupted here with occasional rounds passing through the camp and, as the day passed without let-up, Colonel H. Fuchs, the Austrian police commander, pressed for his men and families to be evacuated to safety. This was not feasible while the fighting continued, but, when the 1700hrs ceasefire in Nicosia began to take effect, UNFICYP's Police Adviser, Dr Hans Wagner (himself an Austrian), authorized Fuchs to take his men and their dependants to the safety of the Saray Hotel in the Turkish quarter. Agreement for this move was obtained from both sides and escorts were provided by the Parachute Squadron RAC, but to general astonishment Fuchs instead brought his whole party, vehicles weighed down with personal effects, to Blue Beret Camp where it was not only at risk from airstrikes on the airport area but also a severe embarrassment in the already overcrowded Force HQ camp.

Throughout 20 July the JOC at Force HQ had been the focal point for a flood of reports. With its Contingents, OPs and patrols deployed throughout the island, efficient radio communications, liaison links with both sides and contacts with diplomatic missions and others, none was better placed than UNFICYP to gain an up-to-date and balanced view of the rapidly changing situation. The need for full and timely reports to New York had been appreciated at the outset and to this end a small cell under the SPA, John Miles, assisted by an officer of BRITCON HQ, was established with the sole task of drafting these. They were despatched via the UN Radio at frequent intervals (sometimes every 15 minutes) and many were then circulated in New York to members of the Security Council. It was said later that never before had a UN Secretary General been kept so well informed in time of crisis. No less important, these factual and unbiased reports served also to counter some of the wilder claims and counter-claims that circulated on this and succeeding days.

For everyone in UNFICYP it had been a long hot day but the cool evening breeze, characteristic of summer in Nicosia, brought some relief. As darkness fell those in the UN camps settled down to an uneasy night that was illuminated by spectacular fires burning in the mountains and punctuated by the sounds of artillery, mortar and small arms fire, sometimes uncomfortably close. Few had much optimism that daybreak would bring any improvement in the situation.

CHAPTER THIRTY-SEVEN

UNFICYP'S REACTIONS –FAMAGUSTA AND LARNACA DISTRICTS

I hardly recommend international peacekeeping as a tranquil occupation.

General Carl von Horn: *Soldiering for Peace,* p.2.

Airstrikes apart, UNFICYP's contingents other than in Nicosia and the north were not at first brought into direct contact with the mainland Turkish forces. Their tasks remained primarily intercommunal in character, but to these were added numerous cries for help of a humanitarian nature. Whether professional soldiers or not, all reacted with energy to halt the bitter fighting and to succour those caught up in it. Cypriots of all communities, and many foreign nationals, too, had cause for gratitude for the numerous selfless and often courageous actions of these men in the UN's blue beret, too many for all to be recorded here.

The Swedes in Famagusta District

There was no better example than that set by the Swedes, few of whom would have dissented from the verdict of their distinguished UN peacekeeper compatriot, General Carl von Horn. For Swedish UN Battalion 53C under Lieut. Colonel Svante Kristensson there were two main areas of special concern: first, the Turkish-controlled area of Chatos (30km west of Famagusta) where about 4,000 Turkish Cypriots inhabited a group of villages; second, the old walled city of Famagusta itself, which, together with three small hamlets situated close to its north and west, held some 6,000 Turkish Cypriots.

In the early hours of 20 July Lieutenant Hansson, commanding the platoon based at Chatos, reported sounds of shooting further north, but otherwise the day began quietly for the contingent, in which Orange Alert was implemented soon after 0400hrs. An hour later Hansson reported an airstrike on the National Guard's radio relay station at Halevga, in the mountains to the north, and this was followed by reports from OP Othello Tower in Famagusta that the TCF was reinforcing its posts on the walls of the old city. Greek reaction was swift; the commander of 1 HMC, Colonel Kostas, warned that unless the TCF left the walls at once the National Guard would open fire. Reports from other OPs soon followed: Turks inside the walls were taking to recently opened air raid shelters[1]; Greeks in the Pilot Tower had trained a heavy machine gun on the Swedes' adjacent OP Othello Tower and the

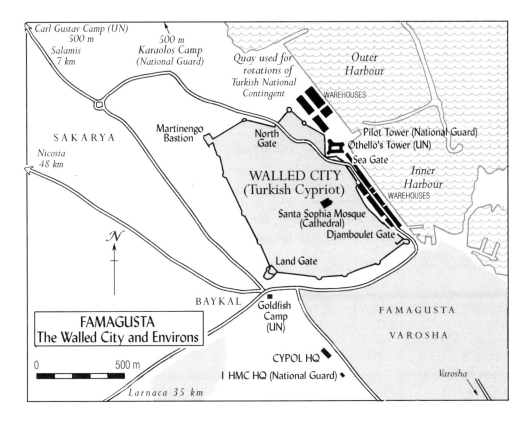

Carl Gustav Camp (UN)
500 m
Salamis
7 km

500 m
Karaolos Camp
(National Guard)

Quay used for
rotations of
Turkish National
Contingent

WAREHOUSES

Outer
Harbour

Martinengo
Bastion

SAKARYA

Nicosia
48 km

North
Gate

Pilot Tower (National Guard)
Othello's Tower (UN)
Sea Gate

WALLED CITY
(Turkish Cypriot)

Inner
Harbour
WAREHOUSES

Santa Sophia Mosque
(Cathedral)

Djamboulet Gate

Land Gate

N

BAYKAL
Goldfish
Camp
(UN)

FAMAGUSTA

VAROSHA

FAMAGUSTA
The Walled City and Environs

0   500 m

CYPOL HQ
I HMC HQ (National Guard) ◆

Varosha

Larnaca 35 km

National Guard in Karaolos Camp (500m east of the Swedes' HQ in Carl Gustav Camp) were forming up with the engines of T-34 tanks running.

Military reasoning suggested to Kristensson that the National Guard would exploit its advantage of mobility by concentrating its forces to meet the Turks landings on the north coast and in the main enclave, leaving minimum elements to contain the TCF elsewhere, for it was the invading Turks, not the local TCF, who threatened the very existence of the Cyprus state. If this proved to be the National Guard's strategy[2], then Kristensson reasoned that it should not be too difficult to stop fighting between Greeks and Turks within his District, and this he was determined to do.

At about 0600hrs he sent his Operations Information Officer, Captain Krister Lindholm, to carry out a reconnaissance of the old city and neighbourhood. Finding a TCF roadblock near the hamlet of Sakharya, where Greeks were being halted in order to obstruct the National Guard's mobilization in Karaolos Camp, Lindholm pointed out the vulnerability of the three nearby Turkish hamlets; the TCF commander smiled – all would be well he said. Claiming that he was on his way to contact Mr Hilmi, the Turks' LO to the Swedes, Lindholm was allowed to enter the old city through its North Gate. First he went to the Swedish OP Othello Tower, then past the Sea Gate to the Djamboulat Gate (at the south-east corner) where he found the TCF being briefed and in good heart; next to the Land Gate, where a TCF company was receiving orders, and on along the western walls to the massive

Martinengo Bastion at the north-west corner. Leaving through the North Gate, he reported that everywhere within the walls the Turks were preparing for the worst.

Reviewing the situation at 0700hrs, Kristensson ordered all OPs to remain in position, observing and reporting, while ready to move quickly should their position become untenable. He also deployed LOs to the HQ of the National Guard's 1 HMC located near the police station 500m south of the old city, and to the local Turkish Cypriot leadership within its walls; Captain Bengt Holmberg was assigned to the former and Lindholm to the latter. In spite of radio reports of Turkey's fierce onslaught in the north, the situation in Famagusta, although tense, remained calm during the next three hours. However, there was feverish activity on both sides: reservists were streaming in to the National Guard camp at Karaolos; the TCF in the old city was hastily improving defences close to and on the walls; and from Chatos, over which aircraft frequently passed, Hansson reported rapid mobilization of TCF in the vicinity, with new defences dug, mortar posts set up and Turkish flags much in evidence.[3] Red sheets and Turkish flags were also being displayed in the old city and, when Turkish aircraft appeared over Famagusta at 0825hrs ('bringing tears to the eyes of some Turks', Lindholm reported), pandemonium reigned in the harbour as shipping began to leave.[4] At 0950hrs the TCF forced its way into OP Othello Tower and refused to leave. Nonetheless, at this juncture Kristensson, who reported that both sides had ordered their men to hold their fire, remained hopeful that intercommunal fighting might be averted.

Suddenly the situation changed: '1008hrs: Hell begins around Carl Gustav Camp. Firing begins from both sides – the war had begun!'[5] The spark was a single shot from the direction of Sakharya. It was answered by a burst of automatic fire and then all restraint was thrown to the wind; firing became general, with mortars, tanks and artillery included. When Sakharya came under concentrated Greek fire, the Swedes in its OP had to take shelter in a cellar until brought back in an APC to Carl Gustav Camp two and a half hours later.[6] The three Swedes in OP Karaolos also came under fire and had to take cover; by midday the National Guard, advancing cautiously, had reached the OP with a T-34 tank drawn up on each side, their thirsty crews demanding water. Since the OP now no longer served a useful purpose, Kristensson ordered its withdrawal; brandishing a UN flag the three men left on foot across country to reach Carl Gustav Camp at 1300hrs. The eight-man detachment in the Swedes' Goldfish Camp, where another APC was stationed, suffered similarly; withdrawal of this detachment was impossible while fighting raged in the close vicinity and its men remained pinned down for the next six hours. They were to play a key part later in trying to establish a ceasefire. While the predicament of those in these UN posts was dangerous enough, Carl Gustav Camp itself also came under crossfire as National Guard troops and tanks moved behind it to outflank the Turks in the hamlets of Sakharya and Karaolos. Kristensson's foresight in having shelters prepared in the camp during preceding days was instrumental in saving Swedish lives.[7] No less perilous were the situations of those manning OPs Othello Tower and Land Gate in the old city, or the Swedish Military Police based in a villa just outside the walls. None of these could be extricated while fighting continued.

The TCF, who had broken into OP Othello Tower and forcibly disarmed its Swedes, opened fire on the Greeks in the Pilot Tower only 100m away. When TCF elsewhere opened mortar fire on Greek positions near the hospital outside the walls, which drew National

Guard retaliatory artillery fire, the Swedes manning OP Land Gate were also obliged to take cover in a shelter built into the massive old walls. Here they found civilians and members of the TCF, the latter insisting that the Swedes hand over their weapons: the firing mechanism was surreptitiously removed from a rocket launcher. Using personal medical dressings, the UN soldiers gave first aid to some wounded Turks and also rounded up some foreign tourists trapped in the old city, all of whom were subsequently escorted to safety.

Lindholm had returned to the old city soon after 0700hrs, only to find that the Turks' Command Post near the police station had been moved to a shelter in the walls between the Djamboulat and Land Gates to which he was not allowed to go, being allotted instead a room at the police station. With calm still prevailing, he decided to visit the OPs at Othello Tower and the Land Gate and it was as he was passing the latter that the single shot was heard that at once caused firing to break out all around. Returning to the police station he reported to Kristensson that Hilmi was protesting that the National Guard was firing on the old city from the nearby hospital. Kristensson instructed Holmberg at the National Guard HQ to persuade the Greeks to halt this shooting.

As firing continued, Kristensson sought agreement for a ceasefire at 1230hrs. Lindholm reported that the Turks would accept this, provided that the Greeks stopped firing from the hospital and withdrew from the ground to which they had advanced near Karaolos. Holmberg said that the Greeks too were ready to accept, but on condition that the Turks withdrew from the hamlets of Karaolos, Sakharya and Baykal (an unrealistic demand since all three were Turkish). With neither side willing to compromise, fighting continued. As it did so, a shell landed close to Lindholm's radio vehicle, causing all to dive for cover. Realizing that the National Guard was targeting the old city's police station[8], Lindholm set out, despite the shelling, to establish personal contact with the local TCF commander in his new CP. Although compelled from time to time to take cover from rounds falling in the deserted streets, he reached the CP just as heavy firing was resumed and was invited inside by Hilmi. Further heavy shelling then compelled all to take cover within an inner sanctum, where Lindholm found about 15 members of the TCF grouped round a table strewn with papers; all except one were in uniform; he proved to be the commander, a mainland Turkish colonel who was unperturbed by Lindholm's presence, although Hilmi was agitated that the Swede had penetrated the inner sanctum. Lindholm explained that UNFICYP was doing its utmost to secure a ceasefire, while Hilmi protested that it was all the fault of the Greeks, who had been planning to attack for years; the Turks were only defending themselves, he said, and, if the Greeks stopped, so would they. Lindholm won the confidence of the Turks and his continued presence in the CP was accepted.

Kristensson meanwhile redoubled his efforts to secure a ceasefire; protracted negotiations were conducted through the two LOs as each side sought to impose its own conditions, but as the afternoon wore on he detected a readiness on the part of both to end the senseless fighting. On learning that agreement had been reached for a ceasefire at 1700hrs along the Green Line in Nicosia, he proposed a concurrent cessation in Famagusta. Both sides agreed on the understanding that the Turks would withdraw from Sakharya and Karaolos and the Greeks from two Turkish buildings just outside the walls, from which fire was being brought to bear on the old city[9]; this success was short-lived. Due to communication difficulties, orders to withdraw had not reached the Turks in the two hamlets by 1700hrs, whereupon the National Guard resumed its attacks and firing intensified, several rounds falling in Carl Gustav Camp and wounding two Swedes. Lindholm pressed Hilmi to ensure that his Turks left Sakharya and Karaolos without further delay, but the latter said that they would only do so under UN protection. Kristensson thereupon arranged for written orders from the TCF commander to be delivered to those in the two Turkish hamlets, telling them to withdraw under UN supervision and to enter the old city through the Land Gate; the Greeks agreed to hold their fire while this was done.

Sergeant Antonsson, commanding the Swedes' Goldfish Camp detachment, took his APC to the Land Gate to receive these written orders but by the time they were handed over it was dark and the APC came under Greek fire as it drove north towards Sakharya; a wounded Turk who ran forward was hauled inside and given first aid. The orders delivered, the Swedes drove on to Karaolos where they were halted by a road-block and again came under fire, this time from the TCF. Kristensson decided that withdrawal under UN protection during darkness was not feasible and ordered his men to make for Carl Gustav Camp with a view to carrying out the operation at first light. However, as the APC was turning, some TCF ran forward and apologized for opening fire; they had mistaken the APC for a Greek vehicle. The orders and the wounded Turk were handed over and the Swedes returned to Goldfish Camp, where they spent an uncomfortable night sheltering in their APC. Antonsson remarked later that at times he had felt as though he had been sitting in a tea-strainer.

Captain Holmberg's experiences on the Greek side were no less stirring. On arrival at the HQ of the National Guard's 1 HMC situated about 700m south of the Land Gate he had been well received by the commander, Colonel Kostas, and his officers. He reported that it was the scene of great activity as reservists reported for duty, but he was unimpressed by their low standard of training. The sudden eruption of shooting just after 1000hrs found him standing beside his vehicle outside the HQ, at which Turkish fire was immediately directed; diving for cover, he saw a young girl sheltering close by and gave her his helmet (he did not see it again). He crawled away from the Turks' field of fire and went to the nearby Swedish CIVPOL base in Varosha to report to Kristensson, returning to Kostas's HQ when it moved to a less exposed location. Throughout the morning and afternoon he acted in parallel with Lindholm in attempts to secure ceasefires, with each side's bargaining demands passed to and fro by radio. As the shooting was going on, Holmberg could hear the Greek artillery's fire orders and then Lindholm's radio reports of the fall of shot – it was, he said, a curious experience. When the ceasefire accepted for 1700hrs failed and the operation to escort the Turks out of Sakharya and Karaolos had to be postponed until daylight, there was little more that Holmberg could do and at midnight he snatched a brief rest with the SWEDCIVPOL in Varosha.

Swedes elsewhere were not without problems. During the late morning Hansson reported from Chatos that the National Guard was attacking the small village of Kourou Monastir (6km south-west of Chatos) and that he had been asked to provide an escort to bring out one dead and one wounded Turk, but as he was speaking the TCF could be seen withdrawing from both that village and the nearby Petra tou Dhiyeni. As the fighting drew closer to Chatos itself, Hansson readied his men to leave their small camp, now caught between the two sides. It was clear that the Swedish detachment was powerless to halt the fighting and, as this worsened, Kristensson ordered its withdrawal to Carl Gustav Camp. Leaving in Land Rovers as shells fell on Chatos, and after negotiating a way through road-blocks, the men were welcomed back into the Swedes' base camp just before dark. The Swedish Military Police detachment was pinned down by cross-fire all day in its villa near the walls of Famagusta (at one stage Greek tanks positioned only 50m away were drawing Turkish fire), but, though food and water were short, Kristensson judged it to be too dangerous for it to withdraw while firing continued. Thus, as darkness fell, Kristensson still had soldiers stationed inside the old city, in Goldfish Camp and in the MP villa, as well as his LOs with the two sides. The rest of his Contingent was back in Carl Gustav Camp.

There was little that the Swedish Civilian Police could usefully do while fighting went on. The detachment in the Greek village of Angastina (6km south of Chatos) was withdrawn to the Varosha base during the morning. Since the detachment at Leonarisso, on the Panhandle, was in no immediate danger, the SWEDCIVPOL Commander, Superintendent Ake Ekström, deferred until next day a decision about its withdrawal. His third detachment, deployed in support of the Austrians in Larnaca, was withdrawn into the latters' base camp during the morning.

The Austrians in Larnaca District

Lieut. Colonel Franz Rieger's Austrian 5th UN Battalion watched over two areas of special concern: firstly, in and around the town of Larnaca, itself inhabited by 13,000 Greeks and 4,000 Turks, as well as sundry others, including British families from the adjacent SBA; and secondly, in the District's west around Kophinou, Ayios Theodoros and other mainly Turkish villages, holding between them some 3,500 Turks.

Orange Alert was implemented in the Contingent at 0400hrs on 20 July without incident, but an hour later sirens were sounded in Larnaca's Turkish quarter, ground-to-air recognition panels were laid out and, simultaneously, the National Guard reinforced its posts along the sensitive intercommunal divide of the Artemis Road. When soon afterwards the Turks demanded that the Austrian post in the Scala school be withdrawn, Rieger instead reinforced it. He also deployed LOs to Colonel Zioubos, commander of the National Guard's 6TG and to the local Turkish Leadership in the person of Mr Mehmet.[10] Although the sounds of bombing and gunfire came from the direction of Nicosia some 30km distant, intercommunal calm prevailed throughout the District due in no small part to Rieger's urging restraint on both communities. Hopes that fighting between them might be averted were raised when the Greek Mayor of Larnaca, Dr Francis, agreed to go under Austrian escort to an exposed point to turn on a valve supplying drinking water to the Turks in the Scala area; optimism was further increased when the Austrians persuaded technicians of both communities to work together to repair the electricity supply to the Turkish quarter of the town. The situation looked even brighter when at about 1100hrs the leaders on both sides assured Rieger that, although fighting had already erupted in other Districts, their own men would not be the first to open fire.

These hopes were dashed two hours later when, as in Famagusta, a single shot rang out – from which side was uncertain – and shooting quickly spread. It was especially heavy along the Artemis Road, close to the Scala school and in the vicinity of the old Turkish fort and mosque on the seafront. Calling at once on both sides to stop, Rieger warned the Turks of the weakness of their situation given their constricted areas, limited resources, isolation from external reinforcement and vulnerability to mortar and artillery fire; to the Greeks he pointed out that the small and poorly equipped local Turkish community posed little threat – the National Guard would be better advised, he suggested, to conserve its resources to counter the far more grave threat that was developing in consequence of Turkey's action in the island's north. Neither side disputed his arguments, but the fighting continued nonetheless, and the Austrian OPs along the Artemis Road and the men in the Scala school were caught in cross-fire for several hours as these messages were passed to and fro.[11] When the National Guard asked the Austrians to rescue a wounded man left in the open, Rieger proposed a ceasefire to permit this, but then the man was reported dead and the opportunity was lost. As the shooting intensified, and in the face of Austrian protests, Tuzla (the smaller of Larnaca's two Turkish quarters) came under the fire of the National Guard's mortars and recoilless rifles.

Rieger's determination to halt the fighting was rewarded at 1500hrs when both sides agreed to a temporary ceasefire to permit a meeting half an hour later to discuss terms for a permanent one. The meeting was to be held between the two front lines on the Artemis Road, but Rieger and his party setting out from Duke Leopold V Camp, at the southern end of the road, were twice compelled by continuing heavy shooting to turn back. The meeting was then re-arranged for 1600hrs, but by then shooting had become so intense all around the Austrians' camp that it was impossible for them to leave. There was now no longer any operational justification for keeping his men in exposed posts between two combatants, neither of which showed any readiness to stop fighting, and Rieger decided to withdraw those along the Artemis Road and those in the Scala school. Lacking APCs, protection was improvised, using sandbags on an unarmoured truck, and by this means all were safely withdrawn, Rieger having warned both sides that his men would reply if fired upon.

Nonetheless, his redoubled efforts gave some hope for a ceasefire to take effect at 1700hrs. This was honoured by the TCF, for whom the effect of Greek mortar fire on the confined areas in which their families lived was proving especially traumatic, but not by the National Guard. Rieger urged that the Greeks should at least stop mortaring Turkish civilian areas, which prompted a new demand. Rumours were rife that mainland Turkish forces were poised to make further landings on the island's south coast. Zioubos demanded, as a condition for a ceasefire, an assurance from the Turks that no such landing would be made in the Larnaca area. Further ceasefire negotiations carried out under Austrian auspices during the night were frustrated by this demand, for the local Turkish Cypriot leadership was in no position to give any such assurance.[12] Although the shooting died down during darkness, daylight saw an early resumption.

Meanwhile, further west, the Austrian rifle company under Captain Brell based at Zyyi and its platoon under Captain Bauer at Kophinou had problems too. At about 0545hrs the TCF had taken up positions near Mari, Kophinou and Ayios Theodoros in breach of earlier agreements. Although shooting was heard during the morning from the direction of Larnaca 25km away, both sides heeded the Austrians' calls for restraint and, as in Larnaca, declared their intention not to be the first to open fire. It was not until mid-afternoon that events took an ominous turn: Bauer reported that National Guard troops were advancing on the Turks in the mixed village of Alaminos and that he was unable to halt them. Soon afterwards heavy fire was opened on these Turks who quickly surrendered and were made prisoner. In response the TCF opened fire on Greek positions around Kophinou and nearby Skarinou and, bringing mortars into play, on the Greek part of Alaminos; the angry National Guard threatened to kill their prisoners unless this fire was halted. In Larnaca Rieger pressed Mehmet, the local Turkish leader, to issue orders accordingly, but the latter said he had no means of communicating with the Kophinou TCF: he could only refer the matter to the Leadership in Nicosia. Evidently the latter was unable to communicate with Kophinou either, for at 2045hrs the VPO asked HQ UNFICYP to instruct the Kophinou fighters on the Leadership's behalf to stop shooting in order to save the lives of the prisoners; this message was passed at once by the Austrians to the local TCF commander. Twenty minutes later the mortar fire on Alaminos was lifted, but the National Guard was reported to be looting Turkish property in the village and still to be holding the prisoners.[13]

When shooting had erupted in this area the TCF in Mari had moved onto Crown Hill, a feature that dominates the main Nicosia – Limassol road, and it became necessary to withdraw the unprotected Austrian OP on the hill. The general deterioration of the situation in the west of the District gave Rieger mounting concern for the safety of his men. When authority came from General Prem Chand at 2215hrs for men to be withdrawn to base camps at the discretion of District Commanders, Rieger warned Bauer's platoon to be ready to leave Kophinou and rejoin its company in the Zyyi camp; if this was not possible, then outlying OPs were to be brought back to the Kophinou base located inside the police compound. In the event Bauer's men were able to retain possession of their Kophinou base with some OPs, including that at Ayios Theodoros, still manned. Reporting to HQ UNFICYP at 2240hrs on this first day of Turkey's military intervention, Rieger said that, except for some sporadic shooting, Larnaca District generally was quiet and that negotiations for a District-wide cease-fire were continuing, although agreement was not expected before morning.

CHAPTER THIRTY-EIGHT

UNFICYP'S REACTIONS –LIMASSOL, PAPHOS AND LEFKA DISTRICTS

> With the advantage of hindsight it was quite obvious that the National Guard had orders to mobilize and attack the Turkish quarter, but we had to accept the local Greek Colonel's assurances that this was not the case.
>
> Major J.R. Macfarlane, speaking to the Army Staff College,
> Camberley, 21 July 1975.

The British in Limassol Zone

Limassol and Paphos Districts together formed UNFICYP's Limassol Zone under the overall command of Lieut. Colonel The Hon. Christopher Willoughby, whose 2nd Battalion Coldstream Guards provided its main military element. However, in consequence of the recently implemented UNFICYP reductions only about half the battalion was available to him, the remainder being stationed in the Eastern SBA under British national and not UNFICYP command.[1] The Zone HQ was co-located with the Limassol District HQ in Polemidhia Camp, 3km north of the town, which was the battalion's UN base and that of the Parachute Squadron, RAC,[2] led by Major Peter Bentley (also under Willoughby's command).

Limassol District

The District was commanded by Major Myles Frisby, with under him the battalion's No. 1 Company, less one platoon detached to guard the Czech weapons in Camp UNFICYP, Nicosia. The only permanently manned UN post was Town OP in Limassol itself, which served as the base for patrolling and surveillance of the Turkish quarter and neighbourhood; patrols from Polemidhia monitored mixed and Turkish villages elsewhere in the District. Australian CIVPOL, whose main station was in the town, supported the guardsmen.

With Orange Alert implemented soon after 0400hrs, Willoughby and Frisby went together into Limassol to contact the leader of each community and urge restraint:

> We found the Turks all cock-a-hoop, marching around the streets with their weapons to martial music played over their transistor radios. Mr Ustun, the Turkish leader, was in his office

wearing a new suit of khaki drill, and he assured us that he would keep his Turkish Cypriot fighters in control and not allow them to attack the Greek Cypriot community – unless they themselves were fired on. We went from the Turkish quarter, which was still barricaded in with cars and buses, to the headquarters of the Greek National Guard, which was surrounded by a milling mass of excited Greek Cypriots anxious to draw a gun and shoot a Turk. We caught the Greek Colonel just as he was leaving, and he explained he was off to fight the war against the Turkish invaders and that the National Guard had no intention of interfering with the Turkish Cypriot community – unless they themselves attacked the Greeks. I passed on his assurances to the Turkish leader and we went our separate ways.[3]

The Greek officer to whom they had spoken was Colonel Sirmopoulos, Commander of 4 HMC, which controlled the National Guard throughout Limassol District; also present was his designated successor, Colonel Rossis, and during subsequent events it was not always clear which was in effective command.[4]

The town remained quiet though tense for the next few hours and there was guarded optimism that the assurances received from both sides would be observed. But anxiety grew as Coldstream Guards observers and the Parachute Squadron, RAC, whose 3rd and 5th Troops were patrolling the interface between the Greek and Turkish quarters, reported that both sides were mobilizing and strengthening their defences, and, more ominously, that the National Guard was deploying additional forces around the Turkish quarter. The reason for this soon became clear: at 1015hrs, without apparent cause, fire was opened on the hemmed-in Turks, who at once replied. Shooting quickly became general with small arms, machine guns and mortars brought into play. Willoughby was in no doubt that the Greek action was pre-planned and deliberate, in direct breach of the assurance so glibly given by Sirmopoulos.

Frisby at once went to tackle Sirmopoulos, whom he reached only after making his way past National Guardsmen who attempted to hold him up at gunpoint. The Greek agreed to order a ceasefire at 1130hrs, provided that the Turkish side agreed to do so too. Lieutenant Critchley-Salmonson in Town OP was ordered to deliver this message to Ustun, now barricaded in the Turkish quarter:

> This required him *[Critchley-Salmonson]* to run across open ground which was being liberally sprinkled with fire of all kinds. Ferret scout cars *[of the Parachute Sqn RAC]* were locating National Guard positions and passed messages to them, as if coming from the National Guard commander, that they were to stop shooting.[5]

However, both sides lacked adequate communications with their men on the ground and no sooner had one group stopped firing than another opened up.

Bentley had deployed his Squadron HQ close to the Turkish quarter to observe, control his two scout car troops and provide a radio link with the JOC in Polemidhia, with which radio communication from within the town was not always satisfactory. While trying to halt the firing, Lance Corporal Butler's scout car of 3rd Troop, led by Lieutenant R.C. Leigh, was hit several times by small arms and a mortar bomb damaged all four tyres; it was fired on again as it withdrew. Learning this, Willoughby ordered that, if engaged, troops were to return fire and no sooner had he done so than Leigh's own scout car came under automatic fire from a

Greek post; six rounds were fired in reply. Next it was the turn of Corporal Wilding's Ferret, mortar and small arms fire puncturing a tyre. Nonetheless Leigh's 3rd Troop and Staff Sergeant Broomfield's 5th Troop both did valiant work by patrolling and maintaining a UN buffer between the combatants; thanks to their armoured protection, none was injured.

As firing continued past the proposed 1130hrs deadline, a new factor gave fresh urgency for a ceasefire. The Commander of the British forces, Air Marshal Aiken, had ordered the withdrawal into the security of the Western SBA of all British families, numbering some 10,000 individuals, living in the dormitory areas of Limassol but the operation had had to be suspended on account of the fighting. A temporary ceasefire of at least three and a half hours was required to allow it to proceed and Major General Butler, the Army Commander in the SBAs, had asked Willoughby to secure agreement for this, for which the time proposed was 1300hrs.[6] Willoughby decided to go in person to the HQ of 4HMC:

> I was met at the gate *[of Ayia Phyla camp, to which HQ 4 HMC had moved from the town]* by a bandit who stood in front of the car pointing his rifle at me – except when he had to lower it to light another cigarette. Finally word came that the colonel had consented to see me. The meeting that followed started off in a friendly but disjointed way with constant interruptions from excited Greeks rushing in and shouting. When I stressed the importance of his orders to cease fire reaching all his wild and woollies, the colonel assured me that his men were fully under control. This was immediately followed by bursts of firing from woollies in his own camp, surprisingly described as "anti-aircraft fire". After this had happened about six times the poor colonel lost his temper, rushed to a loudspeaker and treated the whole area to a tirade of abuse . . .
>
> I then asked him if he would extend the ceasefire *[for the British evacuation]*, which he had guaranteed as long as there was still a British family on the road, to the Turkish quarter, provided that I could get the Turks to stop firing meanwhile. He then got very stroppy and said that, if the Turks did not stop shooting within 30 minutes from that moment, he would order an immediate attack. I could only reply that it would take me longer than that to reach the Turks because his gangs were holding up UN vehicles at gun point and shooting at them frequently. We parted on cool terms.[7]

With the time now about 1300hrs, Willoughby instructed Critchley-Salmonson to pass the Greek's warning to the Turks; he did so at once, making another dangerous run to reach Ustun.

At their meeting Sirmopoulos had alleged that Turks wearing blue berets had been firing at his men; the National Guard, he said, would not hesitate to reply in kind at men thus dressed. Willoughby saw this as an excuse for shooting at UN troops, which added to his mounting concern for the safety of his men. After discussing with me the dangerous situation of Town OP, I agreed that it should be withdrawn when the situation allowed, but so heavy was the shooting in its vicinity that this was not possible until the late afternoon, when the six men in the post were brought out under the protection of Leigh's scout car troop.[8]

Greek mortar fire was having a devastating effect on the morale of the TCF, surrounded as they were by their womenfolk and children within the confines of the Turkish quarter. This induced a sudden change of heart; just before 1330hrs (the Greek deadline) the Turks said that they wished to surrender on terms to be negotiated through UNFICYP. Willoughby lost no time in convening a meeting to this end at the District Office, to which he went to notify the District Officer, Mr Zachariades, and a major who was the National Guard's representative. Although at times under fire, Frisby brought in a chastened Ustun from the Turkish quarter. Willoughby noted that the Turk had exchanged his smart khaki drill uniform for civilian clothes. Under Willoughby's mediation, the following terms were agreed:

- the TCF would lay down their weapons in the street and march out of the Turkish quarter under a white flag.

- they would then be taken under National Guard escort, but under UN observation, to the sports stadium near the sea front.

- the National Guard would then enter the Turkish quarter, again under UN observation, to collect the weapons.

- this done, the TCF would be returned from the stadium to their quarter, still under UN observation.

No timetable was stipulated, but it was understood that the first step would be implemented without delay. This was easier said than done.

Escorted back to the Turkish quarter by Frisby with mortar and other fire still continuing, Ustun had difficulty in convincing the TCF that they could safely place themselves in the hands of the National Guard.[9] Both Frisby and Leigh, who, with another scout car of his troop, made several sorties under fire into the Turkish quarter, pressed the TCF to accept and implement the agreed terms. When the Turks demanded additional guarantees, Willoughby intervened:

I went down and explained to them that they were in no position to argue or haggle and that, if they did not get out quickly as agreed, I would not be able to prevent the National Guard from coming in. I then went back to the Greeks and told them to be patient. As time went on and still no sign of a Turk, first Myles *[Frisby]* and then *[Lieutenant]* Shane Alabaster went in to get them to get a move on. At about 1740hrs the National Guard commander said that 1800hrs was the deadline, after which he would come in shooting. Myles, Shane and I all went in again to the Turks, who by now were milling around in Ataturk Square, arguing. We found one sensible Turk and, after some cajoling, managed to round up 21 men who were prepared to march out, which they did at 1759hrs![10]

This meagre bag did not satisfy the National Guard, who had expected at least 100 TCF to emerge, but Willoughby persuaded them to proceed nonetheless with the collection of the weapons now strewn on the pavements. As encouragement, he said he would accompany them:

They were very reluctant but eventually agreed to come with us. The Greek major was convinced that his duty lay elsewhere but we persuaded him to come too with an interpreter. We then had the rather odd situation of more UN than National Guard going in to do the National Guard's job. In fact we did not get very far before a different lot of National Guard opened fire on us with mortars and machine guns. Having extracted the major from under a table in a house and a very frightened interpreter from under the staircase, we told them that they had better think up a new plan and see if they could not better control their own people. The poor major was almost shedding tears of mortification, but walked back in quite a dignified manner until he reached his own people when he went berserk, yelling abuse at them. He then recovered somewhat and came back to me and apologized handsomely for his soldiers and thanked me effusively for our efforts.

I then went with Myles to Zachariades to tell him of the recent events and to let him know that I was not prepared to risk another UN soldier doing the National Guard's job for them. After a long telephone conversation with the Greek colonel, Zachariades announced that he had the colonel's "assurances" that we would not be fired on by the National Guard, and would we please have another go. I refused. Zachariades implored, begged, besought, but having seen the effect of Greek "assurances" throughout the rather long day, I did not give way, even when Zachariades half climbed through the window of my car in a final effort to persuade me that I was effectively signing the death warrant of hundreds of innocent lives. I suggested that another approach might be for him to persuade the National Guard not to attack the Turks, but he did not seem to consider that relevant.[11]

In spite of this setback the surrender process proceeded, albeit slowly. At 2100hrs Willoughby reported that the first 21 men had reached the stadium and that further groups of unarmed Turks were on their way under the watchful eyes of men of the Coldstream Guards and Parachute Squadron RAC. A situation report two hours later stated that there were about 150 male prisoners in the stadium and that another 1000 Turks had been gathered together at National Guard HQ in the town; they would be allowed to return to the Turkish quarter as soon as all weapons had been collected, but the Greeks were either confused or seeking deliberately to mislead Willoughby:

> At 2330hrs a Greek major and his interpreter came to our camp with a frightened looking Turk. As only 25–30 Turks had surrendered – so they said – they wished me to escort the National Guard into the Turkish quarter to recover the weapons. When I questioned their figure, they admitted that there might be up to 100, but alleged that most were women and that no fighters at all had come out. I got through to my patrol in the stadium who confirmed that at least 500 people were there, all of them men. Once again the Greek looked rather stupid and went home.[12]

By the end of this long hot day intercommunal fighting in the town was at an end. Elsewhere in Limassol District no fighting had been reported, although a UN patrol passing through the Turkish village of Kandou, 10km west of Limassol, found it deserted.

Paphos District

Willoughby's troops in this District, commanded by Major Richard Macfarlane, consisted of the Coldstream Guards' No. 4 Company and one (Land Rover-equipped) troop of the Parachute Squadron, RAC. There were two permanently manned posts in the town of Paphos (Villa OP in the Turkish quarter and Mavroli OP on its northern outskirts); OPs elsewhere were on Mandria Hill (overlooking the Turkish village of Mandria), at the Turkish village of Stavrokono and at the large mixed village of Polis. District HQ was in St Patrick's Camp, just north of Paphos town. Australian CIVPOL detachments were located in the town and at Polis.

Following receipt of Orange Alert, Macfarlane reported a hurried mobilization of the National Guard and similar activity on the part of the TCF. At 0530hrs three Greeks manning the small CYPOL post at Mavroli bolted from it, alleging that they had been threatened by the Turks, and it was clear that a National Guard build-up around Turkish areas was taking place. Macfarlane urged the District Officer, Mr Stephanides, the Greek commander, Colonel Gravenes (whose HQ 5 HMC was located in Paphos) and the local Turkish leader, Mr Fellahoglu, to impose maximum restraint on their men. Although concerned lest poor discipline[13] might at any moment ignite a general intercommunal conflagration, Macfarlane was not unhopeful that this might yet be avoided:

> Throughout this period, because of the assurances we were being given by the National Guard and the District Officer, we really believed that they had no intention of aggressive action, but were genuinely only taking precautionary measures. However, the situation had become incredibly tense and the National Guard commander had become almost hysterical, which resulted in great difficulties while negotiating.
>
> In our opinion at this time he was a mentally sick, warmongering fanatic, who despite his assurances was following an aggressive course of action that would lead to inevitable confrontation. With the benefit of hindsight it is quite clear that his orders were to attack the Turkish areas, and that he was hiding this from us while we were so desperately trying to negotiate a more stable situation. However, we did not realize this at the time and many attempts to control him and his temper were frustratingly thwarted.[14]

There had been occasional, possibly accidental, bursts of fire both in Paphos and at Mandria, but at 0940hrs events took a serious turn. Lance Sergeant Smith reported from Mandria Hill OP that National Guard troops with mortars had deployed in fire positions round the OP and that TCF had moved forward to take up defensive positions facing the hill, which dominates the village. Smith mediated between the two sides with a view to defusing a rapidly deteriorating situation, but the National Guard claimed to be under orders to open fire if the Turks were seen outside the village and at 1050hrs threatened to do so unless the TCF withdrew immediately. Smith urged restraint to allow the matter to be taken up by Macfarlane with Gravenes in Paphos. Macfarlane was already pressing both sides on three counts: first, he repeatedly reminded them of their assurances that their men would not be the first to open fire; second, he urged that the TCF be ordered to withdraw into Mandria village, and that in parallel the Greeks should withdraw from Mandria Hill and from around the Turkish quarter of Paphos; and third, he proposed that the three members of CYPOL should return to their Mavroli post. There was no Turkish objection to this last, but the CYPOL men were reluctant to do so.

At Mandria the National Guard commander had agreed to hold fire, but declared at 1145hrs that he would only continue to do so provided that a decision was reached within ten minutes. It was no empty threat, but his action took unexpected form: his men forced their way into the UN OP, took two guardsmen hostage at gunpoint and said that they would not be released until the TCF withdrew back into Mandria village. Macfarlane immediately protested to Gravenes and I did likewise to the Commander of the National Guard in Nicosia, demanding immediate release of the two. Half an hour later both were set free by the surly local commander. By midday, with intercommunal tension growing, Macfarlane had gathered into St Patrick's Camp those of his men's families temporarily present in Paphos town and the Australian CIVPOL detachment based on its eastern outskirts; an increasing number of others also sought refuge in the UN camp. Since telephone communications with the Turkish quarter had been cut, he also arranged for Inspector Hill of the Australian police to go to the Turks' HQ with a radio to ensure communication with Fellahoglu.[15]

The true worth of the Greek assurances was seen at 1220hrs, when fire was opened on the Turkish quarter and National Guard troops formed up east of Mavroli ready to attack. Twenty minutes later shooting erupted at Mandria; the UN OP was caught in the crossfire and its hut set ablaze, compelling Smith to lead his men to a safer position 200m north. For the next hour Macfarlane strived to avert further escalation, but at 1320hrs the National Guard shattered all hope of this by launching an attack with machine guns and mortars in the Mavroli area. With battle joined and firing across the town's intercommunal interface general, Macfarlane's calls for both sides to stop and for the Greeks to pull back fell on deaf ears. Concerned for the safety of his men in Villa and Mavroli OPs and of Inspector Hill in the Turkish quarter and, after consulting HQ UNFICYP, Macfarlane ordered all to withdraw to St Patrick's Camp if safe to do so; otherwise they were to take cover and remain in position. Mavroli OP lay in the line of the National Guard attack, but Lance Corporal White and his men courageously remained in the post, providing a flow of valuable reports and taking in four wounded Turks, to whom they rendered first aid. Guardsman Gain of Villa OP, observing alone at the nearby mosque, was pinned down by shooting, but managed to withdraw to the OP after firing several rounds at Greeks shooting at him. Lance Sergeant Thompson, in command of Villa OP, had recalled his men from other observation or patrol tasks. All remained in the OP, as did Inspector Hill at the Turkish HQ, while intense firing continued all around.

After some two hours Stephanides telephoned Macfarlane to say that the National Guard intended to stop shooting from 1445–1500hrs to give the Turks an opportunity to surrender; informed accordingly, the Turks said that they had no intention of doing so. During the lull and in spite of continuing sporadic shooting, Macfarlane seized the opportunity to extricate his men from Villa and Mavroli OPs and Hill from the Turkish quarter; when fighting resumed at 1500hrs all were safely back in St Patrick's Camp. Shooting continued for the rest of the afternoon, fire on the Turkish quarter being added to at one stage by an unidentified naval ship.[16] As in Limassol, Greek mortar fire had a telling effect on the Turks confined with their families in the small area and at about 1730hrs Fellahoglu requested Macfarlane to arrange a temporary ceasefire to allow the removal of women and children from the by now badly damaged quarter. Macfarlane pressed the National Guard to agree on humanitarian grounds, but the Greeks refused in the knowledge that the predicament of the women and children was an inducement for early Turkish capitulation. In this callous attitude they were proved right.

An hour later Fellahoglu announced that the TCF were ready to surrender and hand over their weapons to UNFICYP, but not to the National Guard. However, before doing so they needed to consult their Leadership in Nicosia and Fellahoglu asked for a message to be passed requesting Denktash to contact him accordingly. HQ UNFICYP did so, but a reply was not received until just after 2000hrs, when the Leadership, whose own communications had evidently broken down, merely stated that it wished UNFICYP to arrange a ceasefire in Paphos, seemingly oblivious that Macfarlane had been trying to do so all afternoon. The question of surrender was not addressed. Since the Greeks were adamant that a TCF surrender to UNFICYP was not acceptable (they did not object to weapons being handed over initially to Macfarlane's men), agreement proved impossible. At about 2030hrs Fellahoglu stated that the TCF would never surrender to the National Guard; they would rather die on their weapons. Brave words! Sporadic shooting ensued throughout the night, with a National Guard assault on the Turkish quarter expected in the morning.

As darkness gathered, Smith and his men on Mandria Hill (they had re-occupied their OP during the afternoon only to find their personal possessions and rations looted by the Greeks) reported that the National Guard was preparing a pincer attack on the Turkish village and that this was likely to materialize soon after dawn.[17] At the mixed village of Polis in the District's north the UN detachment commander, 2nd Lieutenant Style, reported that the Greeks had surrounded the Turkish quarter, but that both sides had promised not to start fighting; these promises were holding and the night found Polis tense but quiet with the Coldstream OP in place and Australian CIVPOL present in support. An uneasy calm also prevailed at Stavrokono; the National Guard had made no attempt to open the road through the village and the Coldstream OP continued to monitor events.

Macfarlane was anxious as to what the morning might bring, but he also had more immediate domestic concerns:

> Nearly 100 refugees were in St Patrick's Camp being cared for admirably by anyone with a spare hand. . . . But there was an uneasy atmosphere because on many occasions during the day the camp was in line of fire from the Turkish quarter and received a fair amount of "overs". Several windows were broken, there were some good thuds into several huts and bursts of fire kicked up the dust around the camp on a number of occasions. A radio aerial from the top of our mast was severed. It was not pleasant with so many civilians, including our own families, in the camp.[18]

The Danes in Lefka District

UNFICYP's Lefka District was the responsibility of the Danish 21st UN Battalion commanded by Lieut. Colonel Carl Severinson. As elsewhere, Orange Alert was implemented without incident and the intercommunal situation remained calm, despite a mortar round fired, possibly accidentally, at a nearby Greek post by the TCF in Limnitis. However, Turkish civilians began leaving the Limnitis enclave for the Turkish town of Lefka, Turkish aircraft were seen further west over Kokkina and the situation became increasingly uneasy as news spread of Turkey's air, sea and land operations in the Kyrenia – Nicosia sector. Mobilization of National Guard units was hurriedly taking place as reservists reported for duty in response to CBC radio appeals. These units were controlled by 2 HMC under Colonel Chios Charalambous, whose HQ was in Morphou[19] and with whom Danish relations were good. Similar good relations prevailed with the local Turkish leader in Lefka, Mr Erol Bayram, and the Danes were hopeful that their calls for restraint would be heeded by both sides.

It was the Turkish Cypriots who made the first provocative moves. Just after midday, in breach of a long-standing agreement, the TCF moved onto Ambelikou Hill, on which an unmanned UN OP, its flag still flying, was sited; Danish demands for withdrawal were ignored. Next the TCF cratered the main coast road between Limnitis and Kato Pyrgos, isolating National Guard troops in the latter. Both actions were evidently part of a contingency plan, but the National Guard did not react and the uneasy calm continued into late afternoon. Since Danish posts on the hills around the Kokkina and Limnitis enclaves were isolated and difficult to reach, General Prem Chand authorized Severinson to withdraw any that he considered to be in danger. However, when intercommunal fighting broke out in Lefka District, it was not around these enclaves but further east at the Turkish village of Ghaziveran, the scene of a bitter intercommunal incident ten years earlier. Shooting erupted here at about 1700hrs and became so intense that it was necessary temporarily to withdraw the Danes from its OP. At about the same time brush fires threatened OP Limekiln near Ambelikou and Severinson told his men to be ready to evacuate it. Fires and shooting soon spread to other points in the District, including Limnitis, where mortar rounds fell close to the Danish company's camp.

Severinson pressed the National Guard to halt its attacks on the Turks besieged at Kokkina and Limnitis, but Charalambous would undertake only to respect the neutrality of UN posts in these areas, which he urged should be withdrawn into the Danes' camp at Limnitis. This undertaking had not been given until after it was dark and, since withdrawal then was not feasible, the Danes continued to man eight posts around the two enclaves. (Severinson reported that these posts were not in immediate danger, the intensity of the shooting having diminished, and that any withdrawals considered necessary would be made after first light next morning.) As darkness fell, the Danes also reported that Limnitis was under heavy Greek fire but that as yet the UN camp had escaped damage; that fighting had now broken out around Kokkina, which was suffering heavy National Guard mortar and small arms fire; that OP Mosquito[20] on the eastern side of the Kokkina enclave had been evacuated owing to fires, its men making their way to OP Mansoura 1km away; that OP Limekiln too had now been evacuated on account of fires and that, except for a few old people, the Turkish village of Selemani had been abandoned. Severinson also reported that he had been asked to evacuate Turkish women and children from Lefka town, but, lacking the resources (some 50 foreign nationals had already taken refuge in the Danes' Viking base camp at Xeros), he had had to decline; just as these reports were being passed, the sounds of mortar and small-arms fire from the direction of Lefka town were heard. What had sparked this outbreak was uncertain, but an uneasy calm had returned to the town by midnight and, apart from occasional bursts of fire and an unexplained explosion near Viking Camp, this prevailed for the rest of the night, which was illuminated by fires blazing out of control on tinder-dry hills.

UNFICYP Signallers at Troodos

For almost everyone in the UN Force it had been a long and exceptionally hot day. Only one group had respite from the heat, the small team of British and Canadian signallers who manned UNFICYP's radio relay station 1800m high in the mountains near Troodos village. Throughout the day the team had tirelessly and efficiently maintained communication between HQ UNFICYP and District HQs all around the island, relaying voice messages under the call-sign 'Zero One'. But it, too, was exposed to danger when in the early afternoon a forest fire swept close and Forestry Department officials warned the team to be ready to leave. This fire was brought under control, but then another much larger blaze was observed spreading rapidly and there were fears that this might engulf Troodos village during the night. Fortunately for UNFICYP, which depended on the station for efficient island-wide radio communications, it did not do so, but the threat caused anxiety at Force HQ that night.

Summary of UNFICYP's Response

What had UNFICYP achieved during this first day of Turkey's military intervention? Pressure had been exerted at once and at all levels on leaders of both communities to exercise utmost restraint in the new situation created by the landing of mainland Turkish forces. When, nonetheless, intercommunal fighting of the fiercest nature erupted, members of the Force, often in circumstances of acute personal danger, had acted energetically to arrange local ceasefires. Messages were carried to and fro between the two sides, conditions for surrender were negotiated and these were subsequently monitored. Efforts had been made to establish effective liaison with the intervening Turkish forces, whose operations UNFICYP had neither the authority nor the military means to halt. The UN Secretary General, and through him the Security Council and the world at large, had received full, timely and impartial reports on what was happening on the island. Finally, and by no means least, humanitarian assistance had been rendered to many, irrespective of community or nationality. This last was soon to become a major commitment, gladly undertaken in the well-established tradition of UN Forces. The response of all ranks in UNFICYP throughout this momentous day had given confidence for whatever lay in store.

CHAPTER THIRTY-NINE

BRITISH FORCES NEAR EAST
AND THE SOVEREIGN BASE AREAS

At no stage during the events of July and August 1974 were British troops involved in military action; their role was limited to evacuating large numbers of people, including British subjects, who had been caught up in the fighting and to assisting the United Nations.

Report from the Select Committee on Cyprus, Session 1975-76, para. 10.

Whether Britain could or should have intervened militarily under the Treaty of Guarantee either at the time of the anti-Makarios *coup* or subsequently in cooperation with, or even in opposition to, the Turks are questions much debated at the time and since. The fact is that it was the British Government's firm policy not to become directly embroiled again in events in the Republic of Cyprus, but, rather, to look to Kissinger and the United States and to the UN Security Council and its Force on the island to halt the fighting and secure a permanent ceasefire. While continuing to provide vital logistic support for the UN Force, the main concern of the Commander British Forces, Air Marshal Aiken, was to maintain the security of the SBAs and safeguard both those stationed within them and their families quartered in towns outside.[1] Additionally there were calls to help other British nationals caught up in the fighting; in the event that help was also extended to thousands of foreign nationals and to tens of thousands of Greek and Turkish Cypriots who fled to the sanctuary of the SBAs. Following the *coup* on 15 July Royal Navy ships, including HMS *Hermes* with No. 41 Royal Marine Commando embarked, were converging on Cyprus and Operation PLATYPUS, the provision from the UK of army logistic reinforcements, had been implemented. Operational reinforcements required by Operation ABLAUT had been placed at short notice but had not yet been despatched, not only because Turkey's intentions were unclear but more particularly because of fears that their arrival might be taken by the Greeks to presage joint British-Turkish intervention.

Considering a Turkish landing unlikely before 21 July, Aiken had decided at his meeting on the evening of 19 July to defer until next morning any decision to withdraw into the SBAs those families living outside the two base areas. When it became clear early on 20 July that Turkish military intervention was imminent, warning orders for withdrawal were issued and a BFBS broadcast at 0530hrs advised families to remain in their homes and to listen for further instructions. Soon after 0600hrs, with Turkish airstrikes and landings in the north confirmed, Aiken ordered plans for withdrawal of families to be implemented, called for the

ABLAUT reinforcements to be sent from Britain and warned HMS *Hermes* to be prepared to disembark her Royal Marines at Dhekelia, where their primary task would be to protect the important communications unit at Ayios Nikolaos.[2] Anxious to refute an allegation by Dimitriou (Sampson's 'foreign minister') that Britain was aiding the Turks, Aiken also broadcast a declaration that Britain was not involved in Turkey's action.

Withdrawal of the British families from the dormitory towns (Limassol, Larnaca and Famagusta) by means of either private cars or army transport was coordinated by a Control Post established in each town. In Limassol this was the responsibility of the Command Provost and Security Officer, Wing Commander M.I. David RAF, who had already secured an assurance from the local National Guard commander that, should withdrawal be ordered, free movement of the British convoys would be allowed. For the task David had the support of 1st Battalion, The Royal Scots (the Western SBA resident battalion), and men of the RAF Provost Branch. With some 10,000 dependants to be moved, their task was formidable:

> They *[the families]* lived in hirings throughout the town among the Cypriot population, and in areas where there was clearly a steady build-up of fighting. The policy of non-involvement remained, which precluded the showing, let alone the use, of force. The only means of communication with families was through British Forces Broadcasting Service and a small number of Royal Air Force Police patrols. The transport to lift families was limited to normal administrative transport, bearing in mind that much of this was normally driven by local employees who were not available or by service drivers who were cut off in Limassol.[3]

Although intercommunal fighting had not yet erupted when the first convoy left the SBA for Limassol, the British troops encountered obstruction at road-blocks manned by excited and ill-disciplined Greeks then assembling to attack the Turkish quarter. Reminded by David of his earlier assurances, the National Guard commander declared at 1030hrs that the problems had been sorted out and that it was now safe for the British families to move (although warning that elements not under his control might still cause difficulties). His duplicity was quickly apparent, for the signal for the National Guard's attack on the Turkish quarter immediately followed and the furious shooting that then erupted compelled suspension of the withdrawal operation.

During the next two hours David and his team, sometimes pinned down by small arms fire, tried to obtain guarantees for the safe passage of British convoys. A convoy of 60 vehicles already lined up and a group of about 600 dependants gathered at another point gave cause for anxiety, not only because some women and children were suffering in the heat but also because there had been warning of possible Turkish retaliatory airstrikes on the town. The prospect of the latter so alarmed Aiken that he asked me to pass a personal message from him to the Turkish forces warning that, if any such action was contemplated, RAF Lightning aircraft from Akrotiri might have to intervene. I instructed Major Oberwinkler, UNFICYP's LO with the Leadership in Nicosia, to pass this message to Mr Inhan, the Turkish Ambassador, but had no way of knowing whether or when it might reach the Turkish force commander, with whom UNFICYP at that stage had no direct liaison link.[4] No reply was received, but no air attacks were mounted on Limassol then or later. When the ceasefire secured by Lieut. Colonel Willoughby, the UN Zone Commander, took effect at 1300hrs, the withdrawal of the Limassol families proceeded:

> Throughout the afternoon we were concerned with an enormous movement and traffic control problem, but by 1730hrs . . . we had succeeded in moving all the families and a number of tourists into the security of the Sovereign Base Area. They were met on arrival by a piper who by all accounts did much to revive spirits and morale after a day which certainly most families would prefer not to endure again.[5]

Meanwhile parallel action was being taken in the Eastern SBA, where the main concern of its commander, Brigadier W.P.W. Robertson, also was the security of the base and the safety of those within it and their dependants living outside. The latter numbered some 1500 in Famagusta and 400 in Larnaca, but there was also the prospect of an influx of other foreign nationals and Greek or Turkish Cypriots seeking refuge, the numbers of whom were unpredictable. Planned arrangements for withdrawal of the dependants were implemented as soon as the order came from HQ BFNE at 0600hrs. The troops available to Robertson were: B Squadron, 16/5th Lancers (armoured reconnaissance); Nos 2 (Support) and 3 Companies, 2nd Battalion, Coldstream Guards; an Army Aviation helicopter flight; and miscellaneous logistic units; also available was a UK-based battery of 12 Light Air Defence Regt RA, recalled from a training exercise in the Akamas training area in the island's remote north-west. Withdrawal of the Larnaca dependants was achieved with little difficulty under the protection of a Coldstream Guards platoon and all were safely back within the SBA by midday. Withdrawal of those in Famagusta proved a different matter. Control here was exercised by the Station Staff Officer in the town, to whom two troops of Lancers and ten lorries of 58 Squadron, Royal Corps of Transport, were sent; additional assistance was provided by a platoon of No. 3 Company of the Coldstream, which under Major J.R.G. Crisp had been sent to bolster the security of the communications unit in the SBA salient at Ayios Nikolaos.

When fighting first broke out in Famagusta on the morning of 20 July it was thought inadvisable to proceed with the operation but, as the situation deteriorated, Robertson decided that there must be no further delay. At 1030hrs he sent Major P.E.W. Gibbs, Second-in-Command of the Coldstream battalion, together with two further troops of Lancers, to take over control in the town, with orders to evacuate British families as rapidly as possible, using force if necessary. Gibbs lost no time:

> The first sector to be attempted not only had in it the base plate position of a Greek National Guard mortar which was being counter-mortared by the Turks in the walled city, but the road had an eight-foot trench down the middle . . . . It was therefore impossible to get the trucks along and the evacuation of the first 120 people had to be carried out on foot with No. 10 Platoon being used as a shield on either side of the road with the evacuees in the centre. This took nearly two hours to complete, largely due to the length of time it took the sector warden to find all his charges in the cellars and other safe places, and also the transportation of budgies, dogs, and the odd Aunt Gladys out from England on holiday, and pregnant ladies in abundance slowed up the crocodile trudging back to the transport at Lion House [Station HQ]. As soon as this sector was

completed the first convoy ran the gauntlet through the town back to Ayios Nikolaos with an escort of Landrovers and two Ferrets covered in Union Jacks and arrived without incident.[6]

The operation continued methodically but slowly due to the continuing fighting in the northern part of Famagusta. By 1830hrs, when darkness was falling, about 740 people had been extricated but a further 760 dependants, as well as numerous British and other foreign holiday-makers, many of whom had pleaded to be taken to safety, still remained. Robertson decided that to continue the operation in darkness posed unacceptable risks and suspended it until daylight; he was influenced in this decision by the possibility that by then UNFICYP's Swedish Contingent might have secured a firm local ceasefire, but this was not to be.

Apart from SBA dependants in the three main dormitory towns there were others elsewhere, including a small number in the mountains at Troodos and Platres, all of whom were safely escorted into the Western SBA during the day. However, still present in quarters within the British-retained site at Nicosia airport were not only families of members of RAF Nicosia but also families of those of UNFICYP's British Contingent serving on an accompanied basis. The plight of these, as well as that of numerous other British and foreign nationals elsewhere, including Nicosia and along the north coast, gave cause for concern. As night approached on 20 July the British High Commissioner, Mr Olver, discussed with the US Ambassador, Mr Davies, diplomatic colleagues and Aiken the possibility of organizing the evacuation from Cyprus via the SBAs of all such people who might wish to leave. Since evacuation by road of those isolated along the north coast was not feasible so long as fighting continued, it was agreed that the consent of Greece and Turkey should be sought for a British-conducted naval operation to be mounted on 22 July. For those in the Nicosia area, it was decided to carry out an evacuation by road to the Eastern SBA next morning, 21 July, provided that a local ceasefire could be arranged. Both operations were to be conducted by Aiken using British forces under his command, UNFICYP's assistance being assumed. During the night planning to this end took place in Nicosia, Episkopi and London.

An important element in this planning was the Royal Navy force now gathering off Cyprus. Captain C.R.P.C. Branson RN in command of HMS *Hermes* and Lieut. Colonel M. Marchant, Commanding Officer of the embarked RM Commando, had been following events closely. Branson was relieved to learn of the arrival early on 20 July of Rear Admiral D. Cassidi at the Episkopi HQ, having found himself hitherto dealing with a multiplicity of authorities – CBFNE, HQ NEARELF, HQ NEAF and 'RN ONE' (until then the Royal Navy's sole representative at the HQ):

> The command and control situation quickly resolved itself with the arrival . . . of Rear Admiral Cassidi. He generously assigned part of his operational staff to me . . . and shortly afterwards these officers arrived on board by helicopter, together with staff officers from the Headquarters, who came to brief us on the situation ashore. FOCAS became CTF 321 and I was assigned Flagship Command as CTG 321.1.[7]

Warned by Aiken to be prepared to land the RM Commando at Dhekelia, *Hermes* made for Larnaca Bay, but Branson was not pleased to be ordered to respect war danger zones declared by Turkey. (A Turkish Notice, repeatedly broadcast from early on 20 July, proclaimed the limits of these zones all around the island; a second Notice defined corridors to the ports of Limassol and Larnaca open only to the UN, UK and US. Shipping was advised to use these only if essential and then with great caution. A further Notice issued on 21 July revised the sea danger areas and extended them to the airspace above 'from sea level to any altitude without limit'.) Thus obliged to steer a course less direct than otherwise would have been possible, it was late afternoon before *Hermes* approached Dhekelia; Marchant and other officers were at once put ashore to work out with Robertson details for the landing of the RM Commando, which Aiken had now ordered to be made next morning, 21 July.

While on passage to Dhekelia Branson and his staff gave thought to the feasibility of withdrawing RAF personnel and their families from the Nicosia airport area by means of the ship's helicopters, should a break in the fighting allow, but the operation was judged too risky and the idea was abandoned. However, the likely need for a naval operation to rescue civilians isolated on the north coast became ever more apparent. These and other matters exercised naval minds as darkness came:

> That evening I decided to effect surveillance of the two sea corridors by stationing *Hermes* and *Rhyl* in the one to Larnaca and *Andromeda* in that to Limassol, with Nimrod and helicopter patrols to the south of us. I got all the other Commanding Officers on board for briefing and the general posture we should adopt. It was very hot and sticky at this time but, what with the Danger Areas declared by the Turks and the general uncertainty of the situation, we maintained a high degree of readiness (Defence Watches), which inevitably made conditions much more unpleasant . . . .[8]

As Branson's Task Group stood by off the island's south coast, two Task Groups of the US Sixth Fleet, one of which carried a force of US Marines, were also closing on this part of the Eastern Mediterranean.

The arrival of Rear Admiral Cassidi gave better tri-Service balance to the Joint HQ, in which he became the Naval Commander, with Major General H.D.G. Butler (GOC NEARELF) and Air Vice Marshal R.D. Roe (SASO HQ NEAF), respectively, Army and Air Commander, all under the overall command of Air Marshal Aiken as CBFNE. Cassidi considered exercising his command afloat in *Hermes,* but appreciated the need for his presence ashore to ensure close personal liaison with his Army and RAF colleagues. He was surprised to find that there was no tri-Service Operations Centre and that he had to contact the separate NEOC(Land) or NEOC(Air) when he needed information; he established his own naval cell in the RAF section of the HQ.

Coping with the influx of large numbers of service dependants created difficult problems in both SBAs, but willing help was offered to ease their lot; most of the new arrivals were given shelter in existing quarters in the bases, with hosts in some cases accommodating as many as four or five families. In the Western SBA problems were aggravated when fighting broke out in the mixed village of Episkopi (not to be confused with the nearby British cantonment of Episkopi), where some Greek Cypriots turned on their Turkish neighbours, who fled into the SBA. Action was taken to build a camp for them in Happy Valley (the SBA's main sports field complex), and within a few days over 5,000 Turkish refugees were housed in it as others from nearby villages also sought refuge.

In the Eastern SBA plans provided for temporary accommodation under austerity conditions of up to 2000 foreign nationals (other than Cypriots) until such time as their onward movement away from Cyprus could be arranged. Greek and Turkish Cypriot refugees were to be segregated in separate areas within the SBA and provided with basic food, essential sanitation and health support; Athna Forest, a wooded area on the edge of the SBA which afforded some shelter from the elements, was earmarked for Greeks, and another area close to the Turkish village of Pergamos was designated for Turks. In the ensuing days the number of foreign nationals and Cypriots that had to be catered for far exceeded the most pessimistic predictions.

The first of the ABLAUT reinforcements from the UK arrived at Akrotiri during the night of 20 July. With them came the Under Secretary of State for the Royal Air Force, Mr Brynmore John MP, sent to serve as a ministerial link between Aiken and the government in London. His visit was brief and he returned to the UK on 24 July full of praise for the manner in which all ranks of the British forces were meeting the challenges facing them. Soon after arriving in Cyprus he had made a broadcast over BFBS, and on his return to Britain he was quoted as having claimed: 'People who were having a hard time . . . said that their morale was boosted when they heard the broadcast.'[9] An elderly British expatriate, confined in his house near Kyrenia while fighting raged all around, took a somewhat different view, confiding to his diary on 21 July:

2015hrs: Heard a truly dreadful speech by the RAF Minister of Defence who has been in Cyprus for ten hours and claims credit for everything the Military have carried out. . . . The Military have been first class and have 12,500 extra bodies in the SBAs.[10]

CHAPTER FORTY

THE ALARMING PROSPECT

The prospect of a general Graeco-Turkish war is extremely alarming for the world at large including the super-Powers. There is very little possibility of the Turkish invasion bringing the swift and clean return to legitimate government in Cyprus which early Turkish statements claimed as its objective.

The Sunday Times, London, 21 July 1974.

Having failed to dissuade the Turks from military intervention, Dr Kissinger's envoy, Joseph Sisco, had hurriedly left Ankara early on 20 July and arrived back in Athens soon afterwards. The prospect of imminent war between Greece and Turkey and consequential catastrophe for the cohesion of NATO's southern flank rendered a ceasefire in Cyprus an urgent necessity. The prospects were not good. The Athens junta, having ordered general mobilization, affected an air of outward confidence which belied its internal anger that the US had not prevented Turkey's action as the Colonels had too readily assumed it would do. Sisco met the junta's leading members at midday; it was not an easy occasion.[1] Threats were made to leave NATO and the sinister Brig. General Ioannides went further, declaring that the US had betrayed Greece and that he would order an attack on Turkey. His more realistic, and more senior, colleagues, who as the formal heads of the armed services knew only too well their unpreparedness for such rash action, were more cautious. Detecting the first signs of a crack in the junta, Sisco warned sternly against any such precipitate action, for which (he said) Greece could expect no US support. He proposed instead, as a first step, the immediate recall of those Greek officers implicated in the anti-Makarios *coup* five days earlier, on the understanding that for its part the US would press the Turks to halt their operation and give support for a conference to sort out the situation. Action on these lines, Sisco suggested, might be acceptable to the Turks. The junta was non-committal.

In Washington (where the Watergate affair was moving inexorably to its climax) Kissinger, dismayed by the failure of Sisco's mission to Ankara and the unpredictability of the Athens colonels, prompted President Nixon to address a personal message to Prime Minister Ecevit warning of the dangers created by Turkey's action.[2] Kissinger also urged NATO governments to press Turkey to accept an immediate ceasefire and he asked the British Foreign Secretary, Mr Callaghan, to convene a meeting of the three guarantor powers as soon as possible. Kissinger was quick, too, to establish close contact with his Soviet counterpart to ensure that the crisis did not escalate into super-Power confrontation on account of Russian fears that Cyprus might cease to be an independent non-aligned state and brought instead into the NATO orbit.

Turkey's Foreign Minister, Mr Gunes, sought with ingenious argument to reassure the Soviet Ambassador, Mr Grubyakov, on this point when they met in Ankara on 20 July. It was a mistake, Gunes suggested, for the Soviet Union to pin its faith on Makarios and AKEL (the Cypriot communists) to preserve the island from western domination; Makarios was mortal and AKEL was not strong enough to prevent a future referendum resulting in a vote for *enosis*. Russia would then be powerless to stop Cyprus from falling under US influence in the NATO camp unless prepared to prevent this by military means. Turkey, which had the right to safeguard the Turkish Cypriots, was the only power, Gunes argued, that was in a position to prevent *enosis*. Its current operation, in which (he asserted) territorial ambitions played no part, could therefore well serve the interests of the Soviet Union. Whether or not this argument had made any impression, there was tacit Soviet acquiescence in Turkey's action, albeit accompanied by ostensible support for the call for a ceasefire and the withdrawal of all foreign troops from Cyprus (for so long a familiar Soviet cry). As in the past the Soviet Union position was ambivalent.

In Brussels the Turkish landings caused alarm, and meetings of the NATO Council and its Military Committee were hastily convened. There was no evidence of Soviet involvement (as some suspected) and a general disposition to see Turkey's reaction as understandable and even justified in the light of the Greek junta's instigation of the *coup*. The NATO Council was anxious, nonetheless, for the fighting to be halted as soon as possible and for Turkey to disclaim any intention of seizing the whole island. The only dissenting voice was that of the Greek representative who demanded NATO condemnation of Turkey's action. Britain's representative reported the UK's invitation for Greece and Turkey to attend a meeting of the guarantor powers in London as soon as possible and his US colleague informed the Council of Nixon's message to Ecevit. The Council's meeting concluded with a call for an end to the fighting and for Greece and Turkey to accept the British invitation, but there was no condemnation of Turkey's action and no call for the withdrawal of its forces from Cyprus. For the Turks this outcome was not discouraging.

The European Community added its voice. Acting for The Nine (as they then were) France made clear to Ankara and Athens that the Community supported Britain's call for an immediate meeting of the guarantor powers. The Nine, too, called on Turkey to halt its operation and accept a ceasefire, and on Greece not to exacerbate the crisis by its own military intervention. Support was declared for the restoration of constitutional order in Cyprus, with which the Nicos Sampson régime was inconsistent, and the Greek and Turkish governments were urged to declare similar support.

In London Callaghan was woken early on 20 July with the news that the Turks had begun landing in Cyprus and at about 0500hrs (then 0700hrs in Cyprus) went to the Foreign Office[3], to which the Turkish Ambassador and the Greek Chargé were summoned. Both were asked to arrange for their governments to send to London without delay representatives empowered to make decisions. He also expressed strong disapproval of Turkey's action, while making clear the British view that the situation was the direct consequence of the actions of Greek officers in Cyprus and that an early return to constitutional government was essential. On learning later in the morning of Greece's decision to mobilize, Callaghan summoned the Greek diplomat again to warn against any intemperate action. However, behind his words was the clear realization that the only power in a position to exert effective pressure on Greece and Turkey was the United States. Callaghan was never in doubt of the need to avoid any initiative that might conflict with US policy and to this end he maintained close personal touch with Kissinger throughout the crisis.

A meeting presided over by Prime Minister Wilson and attended by Callaghan and Mr Roy Mason, Defence Secretary, endorsed the Foreign Secretary's actions and approved the British military measures already described, including orders for despatch to Cyprus of the ABLAUT reinforcements. After the meeting a spokesman explained that Britain's aims were to:

- protect British lives and property
- ensure the security of the two SBAs
- press the Turks to stop the fighting and establish a ceasefire as soon as possible
- prevent the Greeks from escalating the situation
- arrange early talks in London between the guarantor powers
- reduce international tension and work for a return to constitutional rule on the island.

It was emphasized that the British reinforcements now being sent were not intended to become involved in the fighting between Greeks and Turks.

In New York urgent consultations took place all day at UN Headquarters with a view to agreeing the terms of a draft resolution to be tabled at a meeting of the Security Council called by Greece. The meeting was not brought to order until 1650hrs on 20 July (by then 2250hrs in Nicosia) and was conducted against a background of sympathy for Turkey's action and condemnation of the Greek junta. The draft resolution was immediately put to the vote and approved unanimously; the clearly perceived threat to international peace and security had served to concentrate minds in the common interest. The operative parts of the resolution[4] were summarized by Mr Ivor Richard, the British representative:

> What we have done is to call yet again . . . upon all States to respect the sovereignty, the inde-
> pendence and the territorial integrity of Cyprus – all States, not just one. Secondly, we, as the
> supreme forum of the world community concerned with peace and security, have called upon
> all parties to the present fighting as a first step to cease all firing – all parties, not just one.
> Thirdly, we have demanded an immediate end to foreign military intervention in the Republic
> of Cyprus. We have requested the withdrawal without delay from the Republic of Cyprus of
> foreign military personnel. We have called upon Greece, Turkey and the United Kingdom to
> enter into negotiations. We have called upon all parties to cooperate fully with UNFICYP, and
> we have decide to keep the situation under constant review. It is a comprehensive resolution
> and it is one which, if it is accepted by those nations most intimately concerned with Cyprus,
> hopefully will bring peace to the area.[5]

The hope was to prove in vain.

The Secretary General, Kurt Waldheim, then reported on the day's events in Cyprus, which had included the first UN casualties – six men wounded in the Canadian Contingent. He concluded:

> We are faced with an appalling and extremely dangerous situation. The fighting in Cyprus, with the arrival of the Turkish forces, has reached a new level of violence and bitterness. The dangers of a wider conflict . . . have now become a tragic reality. A major breakdown of international peace and security has occurred, despite all bilateral efforts to avoid it. An enormous responsibility has now fallen on the Security Council – the responsibility for putting a halt to the fighting, for preventing further escalation and for finding a way in which we can begin to restore peace.

There was general condemnation in the debate that followed of the Greek junta, but only muted criticism of Turkey's action. For Britain Richard announced that Greece had accepted the invitation for talks between the guarantor powers proposed for next day in London, but that as yet there had been no response from Ankara. He also made clear that there should be no fear that these talks would be conducted over the heads of the Cypriots, since there was no question of attempting to settle the island's internal problems without their participation. To this end the British government would keep in close touch with Makarios, whom it recognized as the legitimate Head of State.

The contribution of Mr Scali for the US was surprisingly brief. He regretted that Turkey had not allowed the diplomatic process to run its course, but it was on Greece that he heaped his main criticism. The most constructive role for the Security Council now, he said, was to press Greece and Turkey to accept immediately the UK's invitation to talks. Mr Guiringaud (France) complained, as did others, that in the five days since the *coup* on 15 July the Security Council had failed to take firm action:

> We cannot but deplore the delays which took place and which prevented concerted action on the part of the Council, and which incited one of the parties to violate one of the provisions of the Treaty of Guarantee and resort to force in order to preserve interests which should have been preserved by peaceful means.

Speaking next, Mr Safronchuk (USSR) reiterated support for Makarios and criticized what he saw as the hypocrisy of the Greeks in calling for the Council to meet when the need for this was the direct consequence of action in Cyprus instigated by the Athens government itself. Later in the debate he read out a long statement just received from Moscow, which was notable for its charge that the US government had failed to utter any word in support of the Archbishop; added to it was the customary sideswipe at NATO:

> Certain members of NATO, instead of adding their voices to the defence of the sole lawful government of Cyprus, the government of Makarios, have in fact taken the course of supporting the *putchists*. This is shown by the very fact that not a word has been said in support of the lawful government of Cyprus and its President, President Makarios, in the capital of this country *[Washington]* while lavish praise is heard of those who are flagrantly flouting the sovereign rights of the Cypriot people.[6]

But, like the Americans, the Russians were noticeably muted in their criticism of the Turks.

Mr Rossides – still recognized as the representative of Cyprus (Waldheim having refused to accept the credentials of the Sampson-appointed Papaphilipou), pointed to yet another of the paradoxes so characteristic of Cyprus: that the two countries which had violated its independence and territorial integrity were two of those which had undertaken by treaty to guarantee both. Recalling the island's past vicissitudes, Rossides said that it had survived and recovered from these because it had never before been partitioned. But now:

> The threat to our territorial integrity is the greatest of threats, because even if you lose your independence you may regain it; but if you lose the wholeness of your country by its being cut in two, it is lost for ever.

Subsequent decades have demonstrated the prescience of this observation.

The tactic of Mr Panayotacos for Greece, heard with little sympathy, was to stress the danger of war between his country and Turkey: 'We are,' he said, 'faced with a very grave, really explosive situation.' Rejecting the Turkish charge that the rights of the Turkish Cypriot minority had been endangered by the *coup*, he argued that this charge was merely a cloak to conceal an action to achieve Turkey's long-standing goal. Its policy of creating and gradually expanding its enclaves on the island, together with its recent demands for federation, were preludes to the partition that was Ankara's ultimate aim. He also repeated his earlier criticism of Makarios (especially 'his treacherous assertion that he felt more threatened by the Greeks than by Ankara') and condemned Turkey's violent action which, he said, included the use of napalm against ELDYK, the Greek national contingent. His anger, reflecting that of the junta, was clear:

> Greece, all its margins of patience exhausted by the uninterrupted Turkish provocations that culminated in the dastardly bombardment of the camp of the Greek contingent in Nicosia, feels obliged to its great regret to take in turn appropriate counter-measures in exercise of its inherent right of self-defence provided by the Charter and in order to safeguard its national interests. To that end, and considering the camp of the Greek contingent in Nicosia to be Greek territory, the Ambassador of Turkey in Athens was today summoned to the Foreign Ministry and instructed to convey urgently to Ankara the demand of the Greek government that . . . the invading Turkish forces should immediately be confined to the limits of the Turkish enclaves pending a final settlement of the matter. Furthermore, it was made clear that in the event of Turkey's failure to comply Greece would consider itself the victim of aggression, reserving for itself full liberty of appropriate action as a guarantor State by virtue of Article 4, paragraph 2, of the same Treaty of Guarantee invoked by Turkey.

Concluding, Panayotacos said that the Sampson 'government' had granted amnesty to pro-Makarios paramilitary forces imprisoned at the time of the *coup* and that all Greek Cypriots were now united in opposition to the Turkish invaders. This demonstrated, he declared, that for Cypriots at least the isolation of Makarios was complete. His bluster had made little impression on the Council, while events were soon to prove that the isolation of the Archbishop from his people was only temporary.

Mr Olcay, for Turkey, confined himself to explaining the political objective of the Turkish military action:

> When the takeover by the Nicos Sampson administration took place with the dramatic ousting of Archbishop Makarios, and when it became clear that the invasion by Greece – and "invasion" is not my word, it is the word used by Archbishop Makarios to describe what Greece was doing – would not cease despite protracted negotiations in various capitals and in this Council, Turkey exercised its legal rights under the Treaty of Guarantee with the sole aim of returning the island as a whole to constitutional rule and protecting the Turkish community's rights within that framework.

Continuing, he criticized the resolution just adopted (since Turkey was not a current member of the Security Council its vote was not involved) on the grounds that it left unresolved the *fait accompli* of the Sampson *coup* while calling for an end to Turkey's action, which was its direct consequence. (Although he did not say so, the resolution was also unwelcome to the Turks in its call for a ceasefire, for which they were not yet militarily ready.) Further, he complained that Britain's promise to maintain close contact with Makarios ignored the need for similar close contact with Turkish Cypriots. Nor did the Americans escape his strictures: he hinted with little finesse that Washington had been guilty of covert action of dubious legitimacy in both Greece and Cyprus. Finally, he rejected Panayotacos's charges of Turkey's intentions, dismissing these as as a paranoid attitude typical of a fascist government.

Speaking for a second time, Rossides disputed the Turks' interpretation of the Treaty of Guarantee, arguing that its terms did not authorize military action:

> Those words "concerted action" mean lawful action, peaceful action, through measures of representation, through the Security Council and through other means – not through aggression, which under the Charter of the United Nations is forbidden. There should be no use of force except in self-defence.

It was an argument that not only has been much debated ever since but also one that irritated Council members, who were intent on dealing with the situation as it was. Discussion was brought sharply back to the terms of the resolution by Richard, who asked:

> Does the representative of Turkey accept the need for a ceasefire? Is his government prepared at this stage to respond to the unanimous wish of the Security Council in that respect? Secondly, may I ask both him and his colleague from Greece whether they will accept, either or both of them, the necessity for the negotiations which we hope will soon take place?

From Panayotacos came silence. An urbane Olcay replied blandly that the only thing that any representative around the table could say at that stage was that he had transmitted faithfully the text of the resolution to his government. The Security Council rose at 2005hrs (then 0205hrs on 21 July in Cyprus) after three and a half hours of debate. The fighting on the island continued and the alarming prospect remained.

CHAPTER FORTY-ONE

TURKEY'S OPERATION CONTINUES

Reports reaching me from Cyprus indicate that the fighting is extremely violent and bitter, and that the civilian population in many parts of the island is living in grave danger, fear and great suffering. As long as the Council's demand for a ceasefire is not complied with and the fighting continues, the situation remains extremely serious.

UN Secretary General, 21 July 1974 (*S/11353*, para. 13).

Daylight on 21 July found the Turks' foothold on the island tenuous and, with all three of their initial military objectives still to be achieved, they were not yet ready to accept a cease-fire. The Secretary General informed the Security Council that, although fighting had died down during the night, it had grown in intensity during the morning, that there were reports of atrocities, and that the UK and US authorities in cooperation with UNFICYP were acting to evacuate foreign nationals to the British SBAs.

With the pattern of events on this second day following that of the first, the UN Force renewed its efforts to secure local ceasefires, to limit the extent of the fighting and to render assistance to those caught up in it. UNFICYP's HQ received a multitude of reports and appeals for help from all around the island and responded to these as far as the Force's limited resources allowed. By no means the least valuable of its functions was to provide a channel of communication between the combatants at all levels (albeit that it still lacked a direct liaison link with the commander of the mainland Turkish force).

Their first night ashore had been an anxious one for the Turkish troops, but morale rose with daylight and the reappearance of the Turkish airforce, as (with some licence) a Turkish journalist has recorded:

Day was just breaking as the jets began a shuttle-service between their bases and Cyprus. Gone was the peaceful – or at least restrained – approach of the previous day. Throughout Sunday *[21 July]* death rained from the sky and Cyprus was turned into a hell. The Greek military contingent camp was reduced to ashes, while the National Guard bases were system-atically wiped off the map. Other targets were dealt with on request from the ground forces. For the Turkish troops the danger was over. Now all that remained to be done was to clear the pockets of resistance in the mountains and create a firm link between Kyrenia and Nicosia.[1]

But the capture of Kyrenia was to prove a slower business than the Turks had planned and, until it was in their hands and a secure link established between it and the Turkish quarter of Nicosia, the danger remained.

Turkish airstrikes and the build-up by air of troops in the enclave continued all day. A wave of 65 helicopters landed troops and stores near the Aghirda airstrip at 0830hrs and a similar wave followed three and a half hours later. UNFICYP estimated that a full battalion was brought in on each occasion, but smoke drifting from numerous brush fires obscured the subsequent movement of these troops. A similar number of helicopters formed a third wave that came in to the same area at about 1700hrs and this was followed by a force of 15 C130 aircraft dropping supplies. The build-up by air was not complemented by seaborne reinforcement since the ships had returned to Turkey to embark follow-up units and were not due back off Kyrenia until next morning, 22 July. However, warships gave gunfire support to the troops already ashore, now struggling along the coastal strip and in the mountains above, towards Kyrenia and the Pass; their progress was slow and throughout 21 July the port remained in Greek hands.[2] South of the mountains the air-landed Turks, confined within the enclave by National Guard forces and under fire from well-handled Greek artillery, were able to make only limited progress in expanding outwards. The pressing need was for an early link-up over the Kyrenia Pass with the seaborne elements, especially the tank and artillery support currently lacking.

In the absence of an effective Turkish counter-battery capability, the Greek gunners enjoyed free rein, the principal targets being Turkish positions and command posts in Orta Keuy, Geunyeli and Boghaz along the Kyrenia road. This artillery fire and that of mortars inflicted considerable damage and ignited further brush fires, but drifting smoke hampered observation. Later the Turks claimed that the inaccuracy of the Greek gunners had minimized casualties. The Turks relied on close air support to silence the Greek artillery, but UNFICYP observers thought their procedures to call for this slow and inefficient. Greek batteries, whose concealment techniques were rudimentary, were able to change positions at will and keep up their fire with little interruption. More serious for the National Guard was the realization that, following the failure of their Operation APHRODITE counter-attack, there was little prospect, bar major reinforcement from Greece, of being able to do more than contain the invading Turks within their lodgement areas.

The Finns continued to be the only UN Contingent caught up directly in the fighting between mainland Turkish troops and the National Guard. The morning of 21 July found them still holding their camp at Tjiklos at the head of the Kyrenia Pass and their OPs at Hilltop (in the mountains), Martin's Mound (on the eastern flank of the enclave) and three others in Nicosia's northern suburbs; their HQ remained in Kykko Camp, the Finnish base just east of Force HQ. When fighting flared again in the area of the Pass with the coming of daylight, Lieut. Colonel Pullinen, the Finns' Commander, was much concerned for the safety of his men and the civilians sheltering in Tjiklos Camp. There was also an upsurge of fighting east of Boghaz. The Greek village of Dhikomo was attacked by three aircraft (one of which was reported shot down), and OP Hilltop, which looked down on that village, came under Turkish small-arms fire and, later, under Greek fire; the plight of its Finns became acute when during the afternoon the Turks mounted an attack through the OP onto Greek positions beyond, obliging the Finns to take cover. Pullinen reported later that none was harmed, that the situation in the vicinity was now calm, that his men had supplies for three days and that they would continue to man the post for as long as possible. Heavy fighting elsewhere in the mountains was reported during the morning and an airstrike, in which napalm was used, was made on the National Guard's RFU camp just west of Bellapais. Later a degree of calm returned in the area of the Pass as Greek troops withdrew eastwards after their raid on the Turks' communications centre in St Hilarion Castle and their attempt to seize the Pass and destroy the TCF IIQ in Boghaz. (This fighting had been fierce with some 75 men of the TCF said to have been killed; Greek casualties were not known.) On the enclave's eastern flank Finnish observers in OP Martin's Mound reported sporadic shooting throughout the day. Further south, along the Finns' sections of the Green Line in Nicosia's northern suburbs, heavy shooting broke out at 0630hrs and those in OP Omorphita 2 experienced near-misses during a Turkish airstrike. When his men in OP Crazy Corner came under crossfire, Pullinen decided to withdraw them on the grounds that they could no longer serve a useful purpose, but, when the Turks protested that this would create a vacuum at a sensitive point on the Green Line, Pullinen agreed to retain the post in place for as long as possible.

As the day wore on a different problem caused him mounting anxiety – the danger for his men created by the deployment of a Greek battery of six 100mm guns only 150m south of his contingent's base in Kykko Camp. Emphasizing the danger for UN troops of such deployments, HQ UNFICYP pressed HQ National Guard to move the battery away and in future not to allow gun positions within 2000m of any UN camp. There was no immediate response and in the early afternoon the battery was still firing from the same position, giving rise to fears of a Turkish airstrike. In view of this danger, Pullinen asked permission to send some of those in Kykko Camp to the nearby Blue Beret Camp for greater, safety but was told that they were unlikely to be any safer there and that in any case that camp was already over-crowded.[3]

When darkness fell on this second day Pullinen reported that firing continued to be heavy along his sector of the Green Line and that there was fighting in the north round Bellapais; other areas were relatively quiet. OPs Hilltop, Martin's Mound, Omorphita 2 and Crazy Corner were still held, as were Tjiklos and Kykko Camps. Brush fires and fighting in the close vicinity of Tjiklos Camp, which was sheltering some 150 civilians of 16 different nationalities, had led to suggestions that it should be evacuated and its occupants withdrawn to Nicosia. Pullinen had discussed the situation with me and we were agreed that there should be no withdrawal. We were determined to retain UNFICYP's presence at this tactically important point; in any case the Kyrenia road, along which a withdrawal would have had to be made, was under Greek artillery fire. Pullinen accordingly ordered the civilians to be gathered for greater safety into a gravel pit within the camp area, and there they remained until it became possible later to evacuate them.

In Nicosia throughout the night of 20 July the Canadian 1st Commando Group under Lieut. Colonel Manuel had manned its OPs at Flour Mill and Red Line 2 and retained its presence in the Ledra Palace Hotel, in which some 350 men, women and children of assorted nationalities were still trapped; Canadians had been withdrawn into company and platoon bases from all other OPs in the city. The early hours of 21 July had seen only sporadic shooting along the Green Line (each side claiming that the other was responsible), but dawn brought reports of MG and mortar fire in the area of the Ledra Palace Hotel, two mortar rounds hitting the hotel, fortunately without causing casualties.[4] The reappearance of Turkish aircraft over the city led to a more general exchange of fire, requiring the withdrawal of OP Red Line 2. This resurgence of fighting increased concern not only for those in the hotel but also for the Canadians in their HQ in Wolseley Barracks, only 200m away. With need to secure a fresh local ceasefire clear, UNFICYP proposed this for 0600hrs, and both sides agreed. Shooting in the vicinity of the hotel died down soon after 0600hrs, but Turkish air activity continued, drawing the fire of Greek AA guns, one of which was sited virtually on the Green Line. When the TCF threatened to resume shooting all along the Line unless this gun ceased firing, the Canadians persuaded the Greeks to comply, but the fragile cease-fire that followed was shattered some three hours later when three rockets from a Turkish aircraft struck the Greek suburb of Trakhonas.[5] Firing broke out again all along the Green Line and in view of the danger to his men in Wolseley Barracks Manuel evacuated as many as possible to Camp Kronborg some 600m away across the dry bed of the Pedhieos River.[6]

During the morning HQ UNFICYP was informed by Inhan, the Turkish Chargé, that intelligence indicated that the National Guard was intending to attack the Turkish quarter that afternoon or evening. He warned that, if this was attempted, mainland Turkish forces would attack Nicosia and other areas of the island in retaliation. HQ UNFICYP pressed both sides not to take any such actions, not only because of the major escalation that would result but also because of the decision to mount a British-conducted operation (described later) to evacuate foreign nationals from Nicosia to the Eastern SBA. (This was to start at midday and a local ceasefire, at least, was essential to allow it to proceed.) The Turks then demanded that the National Guard withdraw all its field and AA artillery from the city on pain of attack by the Turkish airforce; the National Guard was sufficiently alarmed to agree to do so by 1345hrs. When told this by Prem Chand, Inhan asked if this information was sufficiently reliable for him to pass to Ankara. Prem Chand confirmed that it was, but Inhan then said that removal of the guns from Nicosia would not halt the operations of the Turkish forces; it would serve only to preserve the city itself from air attack. This was clear indication that Turkey was not yet ready to accept a general ceasefire.

These exchanges were complemented by pressure exerted on both sides by the British High Commissioner, the US Ambassador and other diplomats for a halt to the fighting in the city to allow the evacuation of foreign nationals. Although there was no formal agreement to this effect, there was a tacit understanding that, in view of its humanitarian nature, the evacuation should be allowed to proceed without hindrance. In the course of the evacuation operation it had been possible to rescue those trapped in the Ledra Palace Hotel, so that by early afternoon its only occupants were a small detachment of Canadians and a demoralized 40-strong platoon of the National Guard. (The hotel had been under effective UN control since the previous evening, but the latter still had to be persuaded to leave so that the hotel might be declared a UN-protected area.) The Turks, who protested that Greeks on the hotel's upper floors were sniping with silenced weapons at the Turkish quarter, refused to accept Manuel's assurance that the only Greeks were sheltering on the ground floor. Turkish fire was opened on the hotel in the early afternoon and for the next two hours became intermittent along the Green Line in this vicinity.

So acute was the Turks' anxiety with respect to the hotel that Inhan himself then protested to Prem Chand, demanding that UNFICYP forcibly evict the National Guard platoon. He was mollified by assurances that the Canadians were doing their utmost to persuade the Greeks to leave so that the hotel might then be declared a UN-protected area, a move which Inhan supported. At about 1700hrs Manuel reported that the Greeks were at last leaving; his own men were assuming full control of the building and its immediate surroundings, with an OP established in the hotel, a UN flag hoisted and patrols maintained all night to ensure that no Greeks returned. No sooner had it seemed that this vexed problem had been settled than a new crisis developed. Dismissing repeated Canadian assurances to the contrary, Inhan insisted that some Greeks were still in the hotel sniping with silenced weapons, and at 1745hrs he warned Oberwinkler, UNFICYP's LO, that an airstrike would be made in five minutes' time. The latter immediately radioed HQ UNFICYP: *'Order people out of the Ledra Palace Hotel at once – Air attack on way!'* but was told to assure Inhan that the hotel's only occupants were UN troops and demand that the airstrike be called off immediately. Inhan replied was that it was too late – the aircraft could only be contacted via Ankara and were already airborne. I spoke immediately to Inhan saying that we did not believe that it was impossible to abort the mission and stressing that, in view of our repeated assurances to him that the hotel was under full UN control, a most serious view would be taken by us, the Secretary General and the Security Council of a deliberate attack on UN troops.

Adding a national voice, Colonel Beattie, UNFICYP's DCOS and Commander of the Canadian Contingent, assured Inhan that the hotel was harbouring no Greeks. When Inhan said that he accepted this assurance but that there was little he could do to stop the airstrike, Beattie pointed out that such a strike required a Forward Air Controller (FAC) to be in visual range of the target in order to direct the aircraft onto it and that such an officer would have the means to abort the mission right up to the last moment[7]; Inhan replied that he would do what he could. Ten minutes later a pair of ground attack aircraft came in; although no bombs were dropped (possibly because of the close proximity of the Turkish Embassy), the hotel and adjacent areas were subjected to cannon fire. Minutes earlier the Canadians had hastily withdrawn under cover of Ferret scout cars of the Parachute Squadron, RAC, and suffered no casualties; as soon as the attack was over they re-occupied the building. Only minor damage had been caused, but immediate protests came from the Counsellor of the Greek Embassy and the Soviet Military Attaché that their respective buildings nearby had been hit; the Russian added that ground fire was still taking place within 100m of his Embassy. I informed Inhan of these protests and told him that they were being passed to New York, but privately we had some sympathy for his predicament; it was evident that slow and inefficient communications between him and the Turkish military command prevented him from keeping the latter abreast of the rapidly changing situation. (UNFICYP had greater success in averting an airstrike on the Nicosia General Hospital after a Turkish warning that this was planned because National Guard guns were sited on the hospital roof. Discovering that there were two .50 calibre MGs so sited, the Canadians persuaded the National Guard to remove them and the hospital was spared.)

The numerous airstrikes of the previous day brought a strong National Guard protest early on this second day that the Turks were indiscriminately bombing the civilian population and targets such as hospitals: unless such attacks ceased, the National Guard threatened to retaliate with much loss of blood (the implication was clear: isolated Turkish Cypriot communities scattered throughout the island would suffer). Inhan shrugged off the threat with the comment that a war was going on, that such attacks were accidental and that in any case the National Guard never abided by its agreements. From dawn to dusk the Turkish airforce continued to make its presence felt across the island. Its targets lay in the Pendhadaktylos mountains, around the main enclave, and in Famagusta, Paphos and the eastern outskirts of Nicosia, but its main weight was concentrated on Greek camps and gun positions west of the city in the area of the airport. Here the pattern followed that of the previous day and, as then, the nearby UN camps, although not deliberately attacked, were in jeopardy.

Airstrikes on the airport itself seemed designed to avoid major damage to buildings and installations while cratering the runways sufficiently to prevent use by the Greeks; the National Guard, on the other hand, was determined to prevent its capture or use by the Turks. An airstrike at about 0500hrs was the first of many on this second day and constant National Guard activity could be seen as defences were strengthened and troops, guns and armoured vehicles were deployed and re-deployed. In late afternoon a mechanized road-roller, together with truck-loads of asphalt, arrived and, as soon as it was dark, hurried repair of the cratered runways began, lending credence to a report that the arrival by air of reinforcements from Greece was imminent.

At about midday there was an unforeseen and unwelcome development of immediate concern to UNFICYP. Led by the Station Commander himself, all male RAF personnel manning the British Retained Site, known as RAF Nicosia[8], were observed hastily abandoning it and joining a convoy formed up outside UNFICYP HQ to take women and children under UN escort to the Hilton Hotel on the southern side of Nicosia, where they were to join the long column of civilian refugees fleeing to the Eastern SBA under the British-mounted evacuation operation. It emerged that Air Marshal Aiken, commanding British Forces in the SBAs, had authorized the abandonment of RAF Nicosia, but neither he nor the Station Commander consulted, warned or even informed General Prem Chand (or me, as Commander of UNFICYP's British Contingent) of this decision.[9] Abandonment of RAF Nicosia in this precipitate manner had immediate adverse consequences for the UN Force. The premises of RAF Nicosia were situated among the complex of UN camps at the airport and, with the RAF occupants gone, an awkward vacuum was created which the National Guard lost no time in trying to fill, thus seriously prejudicing the security of the UN camps. No sooner had the RAF personnel gone than reports came of National Guard soldiers entering their premises, of fires in the vicinity, of failure of RAF Nicosia's electricity generators (upon which the UN camps also depended for power and the pumping of water supplies), and of the RAF communications centre (COMCEN), through which some of UNFICYP's line communications ran, being left unmanned. At a time when the UN Force's meagre resources were already over-stretched, it became necessary to send men to eject any National Guard found in the RAF premises, secure unlocked buildings, check on and attempt to deal with several fires (the fire-fighting back-up hitherto supplied by the RAF no longer being available) and restore essential signal communications. Further, escorts had to be found for Cypriot government technicians sent to repair power and other services in the airport area.

Turkish airforce activity had necessitated the grounding of UNFICYP's four Army Sioux and four RAF Whirlwind helicopters. All were based in an area of the airport forming part of RAF Nicosia, on which they depended for various technical facilities; following the abrupt departure of RAF Nicosia personnel (but not the men of the Whirlwind detachment) they were left isolated and vulnerable. On the afternoon of 21 July, on the initiative of Major P. Gill, the Army Flight Commander, and between Turkish airstrikes, the four Sioux were manhandled by his men over rough ground into the security of Blue Beret Camp 1000m away. Squadron Leader Barrell's Whirlwind detachment, attempting to follow suit, encountered National Guard opposition, but this was overcome by negotiation, and the more difficult task of also bringing these larger aircraft into Blue Beret Camp began at dusk and was completed by next morning. This was none too soon, for later that day the hangars of both the Army Flight and the RAF Detachment were damaged by Turkish cannon and rocket attacks and any aircraft in them would have been destroyed.

As the operations to evacuate foreign nationals from Famagusta and Nicosia were proceeding on this second day, planning was in train for the Royal Navy's operation to rescue those caught up in the fighting along the north coast. The British High Commission informed HQ UNFICYP[10] that an announcement was to be broadcast by BFBS that a frigate would patrol east of Kyrenia from dawn next morning, 22 July, to take off British nationals, who were to be advised to gather on the beaches. UNFICYP informed the National Guard and Turkish Ambassador accordingly, requesting the cooperation of both sides in this humanitarian action. The National Guard's response was to warn that beaches were mined and that the safety of civilians using them could not be guaranteed; this information was passed at once to the British High Commission, who then suggested that the National Guard should be asked to provide guides through the minefields. The latter replied that this would not be possible and advised that British civilians should be instructed instead to move along the coast road to Kyrenia for embarkation from the harbour. Inhan's reaction was less helpful: he protested at the lack of consultation with regard to the proposed British operation and warned that Ankara was likely to tell London that Turkish consent for it was withheld.

Although darkness on this second day brought a reduction in the tempo of the Turks' military activity, they were not yet ready for a ceasefire. None of their three initial aims had been achieved: Kyrenia was still in Greek hands, seaborne units had not yet linked up effectively with the airborne units in the enclave and capture of the airport had not yet been attempted. Further, protection of scattered and isolated Turkish Cypriot communities elsewhere around the island had yet to be ensured.

CHAPTER FORTY-TWO

TURKISH CYPRIOT SURRENDERS

None of us had ever had any training in arranging surrenders.

Lieut. Colonel The Hon. H.E.C., Willoughby,
Speaking to the Army Staff College, Camberley, 21 July 1975.

Larnaca District

Early on 21 July Lieut. Colonel Rieger reported that, apart from sporadic shooting, the night had been quiet in Larnaca town, although agreement for a local ceasefire was not yet possible. The Turkish Cypriots, confined with their backs to the sea in the Scala and Tuzla quarters of the town, appeared ready for this, but the National Guard was demanding an assurance that mainland Turkish forces would not attack Larnaca from either air or sea, adding that in any case any order to stop fighting must come from its HQ in Nicosia. It was thus no surprise that daylight brought a sharp resumption, with the Greeks raining down telling mortar fire on the Turkish quarters. Rieger exerted renewed pressure on Colonel Zioubos, National Guard commander, Dr Francis, the Greek mayor, and Mr Mehmet, the local Turkish leader, for a ceasefire to take effect at 0600hrs. Sensing victory, Zioubos refused, declaring that nothing less than full Turkish surrender was acceptable; unless the Turks did so immediately he would mount an all-out assault at 0800hrs. He was restrained in this by his superiors in Nicosia following pressure by HQ UNFICYP.

A lull at about 0730hrs led the Austrians to suspect that both sides might be running short of ammunition, but Greek mortar fire had already had a devastating effect on the Turkish quarters in which the womenfolk and children were huddled. The TCF were compelled to recognize that, if heavy casualties were to be avoided, they would have to lay down their arms. Accepting the inevitable, Mehmet informed Rieger soon after 0800hrs that the TCF in Larnaca were ready to surrender on terms to be agreed through the Austrians. Rieger lost no time in arranging telephonic communication between Mehmet and Francis, during which terms proposed by him were accepted. These required white flags to be displayed at TCF posts to denote surrender, the handing in of weapons to the Austrians and the assembly of the TCF at designated points for movement to and detention under UN protection in a school in the Turkish quarter. Rieger's purpose was to secure UN control of the weapons and to keep the disarmed Turks well away from the Greeks; in this he was to prove only partially successful.

As the first white flag was raised in the Scala quarter the Greek mortar fire was lifted, but it was only a temporary respite: the impatient National Guard resumed firing within minutes, claiming that no further surrender signals could be seen. The Turks complained to the Austrians not only that they did not have enough white flags (a barely visible pocket hand-kerchief was used at the police station) but also that Greek fire was preventing them from being hoisted. Sending them some white bedsheets with instructions to display these without delay, Rieger sent patrols to notify men in TCF posts that they were to move at once to the designated assembly points and there hand in weapons and come under UN protection.[1] Duke Leopold V Camp at the southern end of the Artemis Road was one such point and by 0900hrs the first TCF had made their way there and were awaiting onward movement to the Turkish school. Soon afterwards the National Guard alleged that the Turks were firing with mortars from within the UN camp and threatened to retaliate. Rieger immediately refuted the allegation, but the National Guard then claimed that some TCF were using the protec-tion of UNFICYP and white flags to fire on its men.

Trigger-happy men on both sides made the task of the Austrian patrols dangerous, some coming under fire from men not yet aware of what their superiors had agreed. One Austrian patrol succeeded in having a large white flag raised over the Turkish police station, at which Greek fire then ceased, and another persuaded a TCF platoon still showing fight at the old fort on the sea-front to do the same.[2] By about 1100hrs the display of white flags was wide-spread, but the National Guard, impatient at the seeming slow progress in disarming the Turks, then demanded that all the latter be handed over to it, threatening that, unless this was done and the surrender process expedited, fire would be opened on Duke Leopold V Camp where many of the surrendered Turks were gathered. On instructions from HQ UNFICYP Rieger immediately went to see Zioubos and firmly rejected the demand. Tension remained high, but the Greeks did not make good their threat. Instead Zioubos demanded that the surrendered Turks should be held, not in the Turkish quarter, but in the Greek-controlled area. To avert a total breakdown of the ceasefire, Rieger agreed that the TCF should be held in Larnaca Stadium (on the Greek side) subject to the following conditions, which Zioubos accepted: all surrendered TCF would remain under UNFICYP protection; the stadium would be a UN-controlled area, from which the National Guard would be excluded; the National Guard would supply food rations on the same scale as for its own men, these to be issued to the TCF by the Austrians; and UNFICYP would provide to the National Guard a list of the surrendered TCF and of weapons handed in. Rieger also obtained an assurance from Zioubos that, should there be any isolated shooting incidents from within the Turkish quarter, the National Guard would not reply but allow the Austrians to investigate. Lastly, the two agreed that, as soon as the Austrians had installed security lighting and erected barbed-wire fencing, the detained Turks (still under UN protection) would be transferred from the stadium to the Gaza school in the Turkish quarter, this offering better facilities. Rieger anticipated that this would be done the same evening.

By evening some 200 disarmed TCF had reached the stadium and their transfer to the Gaza school, meanwhile hastily prepared by the Austrians, then began.[3] As this was taking place a fresh problem was caused by the National Guard siting machine guns on the roof of houses around the school. Fearing that this might presage a National Guard attack, Rieger demanded their withdrawal, only to be met by increasing Greek hostility, whereupon he deployed his own machine guns. In the face of this firm Austrian response, Zioubos withdrew his men on the understanding that responsibility for external security of the school would be assumed by CYPOL, while UNFICYP exercised exclusive control within it. The Greeks were as good as their word in providing food on the agreed scale, and during the next few days the Austrians succeeded in negotiating various alleviations for the detained Turks: families were allowed to talk to them across the wire fence and to pass to them additional food to supplement the Greek rations.[4] In spite of the surrenders then taking place, Zioubos demanded that his men be allowed to search the Turkish quarters for weapons before darkness fell; Rieger would not agree, but as a compromise proposed that searches should be conducted by teams consisting of Austrians, CYPOL and the Turkish Police Element, but not the National Guard. This was agreed and (despite an initial marked reluctance on the part of CYPOL to participate) the searches began; they could not be completed before dark and it was decided to resume the task next morning. Thus on this second night of Turkey's intervention a degree of intercommunal calm prevailed in Larnaca town.

In the western sector of the District the Austrian company under Captain Brell based at Zyyi and its platoon under Captain Bauer at Kophinou both had their own problems. Shooting had broken out around Kophinou soon after dawn on 21 July and the Austrian OPs at Ayios Theodoros and Skarinou, isolated and powerless to halt it, were withdrawn to Zyyi. At 0645hrs Bauer reported agreement for a local ceasefire in his area and, four hours later, that the area was quiet. Reporting again at 1430hrs he said that the TCF in both Ayios Theodoros and Kophinou had given up the fight; by late afternoon 102 members of the TCF had been disarmed and were being held under UN protection in the Austrians' Kophinou compound. From Zyyi Brell reported that Greeks were attacking the Turks in the mixed village of Tokhni (6km north of Zyyi) and that the latter were on the point of surrender. In early afternoon a National Guard company was seen advancing on the mainly Turkish village of Mari (3km north-west of Zyyi) and nearby Crown Hill, on which the TCF had reinforced their post overlooking the main Nicosia – Limassol road (and from which the Austrian OP had been withdrawn the previous day). The Greek company commander, Major Gregoriou, said he was under orders to attack Mari; if the Austrians wished to avert this, then Mari's Turks, some 700, must be persuaded to capitulate, hand over their weapons, allow all adult males to be made prisoner and permit a house-to-house search of the village.

Recognizing that he could not prevent an attack if the Greeks were intent on it, Brell persuaded Gregoriou to agree that, if the Turks surrendered, weapons would be collected by the Austrians, adult males would be detained under UNFICYP control and house searches would be conducted by not more than two Greeks and with Austrians present. When these terms were put to Mari's TCF commander, Sergeant Ekrem, he asked for a UN guarantee that they would be observed. Gregoriou told Brell that he gave 'his word of honour as a Greek officer' that the stated terms would be fulfilled by his men; when told of this assurance, Ekrem said that the Turks of Mari would surrender. The Austrians prepared to collect their arms, only to encounter a change of heart: the TCF on Crown Hill refused to leave or to hand over their weapons, declaring their intention to continue fighting. On hearing this, those in Mari itself decided to follow suit. Resigned to the likelihood of a Greek assault on the village, the Austrians withdrew after persuading Gregoriou to defer any such action until at least the following day, 22 July. In order to avert this potential bloodshed, HQ UNFICYP urged the Leadership in Nicosia to advise the Turks in the village to surrender; the VPO replied that this decision must be left to the TCF commander on the spot. It seemed that the National Guard, too, hoped to avoid a battle for Mari, for during the night Gregoriou's superior in Limassol proposed that a meeting be held at 0700hrs next morning near Zyyi to negotiate the village's surrender. The Turks showed no interest, evidently determined to fight on. Thus, although intercommunal fighting in this area had subsided by nightfall on 21 July, the prospects for the Turks in Mari and other villages which had not yet surrendered were not encouraging.

Limassol District

The TCF in Limassol town having surrendered, been disarmed and detained in the stadium under National Guard control (but subject to UN surveillance) the previous day, 21 July was a relatively uneventful day for the Coldstream Guards. Lieut. Colonel Willoughby reported early in the morning that the town was quiet and, later, that women and children (many frightened and distressed) were being allowed to return to their houses in the Turkish quarter, now patrolled by his own soldiers to provide a sense of security and to deter any Greek excesses. The quarter had suffered considerable damage and there had been some looting during the National Guard's search for arms. The morale of the returning Turkish families was not improved, Willoughby said, by bullying behaviour on the part of some Greek soldiers.

The National Guard, aided by irregular elements, was now turning its attention on the Turkish inhabitants of the many scattered villages elsewhere in the District, for the protection of which at that time UNFICYP lacked the resources. The consequence was a growing influx of Turkish refugees into the Western SBA. Automatic small arms and mortar fire was heard soon after dawn at the mixed village of Episkopi, just outside the SBA boundary, and about two hours later came the news that its Turks had surrendered. The Turkish village of Kandou (3km further north) was next to suffer, and then in turn Evdhimou, Ayios Thomas, Plataniskia and Alekhtora, all Turkish villages situated west of the SBA. In each case the TCF were made to surrender their weapons to the Greeks before fleeing with their families to seek asylum in the SBA. Events at Evdhimou were typical: the Turks were given an ultimatum to surrender or face their village being attacked and destroyed, whereupon women and children fled to safety in the SBA 4km away. A member of 1st Bn, The Royal Scots, which, as part of the SBA garrison, guarded its entry points, described subsequent events:

> A United Nations patrol under command of Sergeant Deakin, Parachute Squadron, Royal Armoured Corps was sent to negotiate a truce with the Greeks. There then began a long period of negotiations during which Major Ashmore [Royal Scots Company Commander] was escorted to the Greek positions . . . to arrange the truce. The escort consisted of a hard-line EOKA

terrorist in the back of the Landrover holding a grenade in front of the car in which Major Ashmore was travelling! Accompanying the Company Commander were two Turkish negotiators. After an hour . . . terms were agreed that, if the Turks laid down their weapons and withdrew from the village and the arms collected were handed over to the United Nations, no further action would be taken by the Greeks. These negotiations were carried out brigand fashion with a band of EOKA and resulted in Sergeant Deakin and a Turk remaining as hostages until the terms had been carried out. Once negotiations were completed the Turks moved unmolested from the village which was then occupied by EOKA.[5]

It was no part of UNFICYP's mission to garrison abandoned villages, even if resources had permitted, and most were looted, wantonly damaged and even put to the torch by in-disciplined Greek soldiers or irregulars. By the evening of 21 July virtually all the TCF in Limassol District had capitulated and surrendered their weapons, and were either detained under UN surveillance or refugees with their families in the Western SBA.

Paphos District

On 21 July the Coldstream Guards company under Major Macfarlane continued to be faced with severe intercommunal problems. There had been sporadic shooting throughout the night in Paphos town and daylight brought a sharp upsurge with machine guns and mortars; the telling effect of the latter was soon evident. Just before 0500hrs the local Turkish Cypriot leader, Mr Fellahoglu, told Macfarlane that he was ready to discuss surrender on the terms suggested, but not accepted, the previous evening. The National Guard agreed to stop shooting at once, but action to negotiate terms had to be aborted when firing, especially of mortars, continued, due (it seemed) to difficulties in passing ceasefire orders to men on the ground. The UN team preparing to enter the Turkish quarter was obliged to wait outside the National Guard HQ while Macfarlane pressed the Greek commander, Colonel Gravenes, to stop the firing:

It finished up with the only amusing incident of the whole story when the Colonel jumped into a tattered pick-up truck with a loudspeaker on it. The loudspeaker would not work, the van would not start and it was last seen being pushed by two hairy youths down hill. It still wouldn't start and later we found it abandoned, having last seen it trickling out of sight with an irate Colonel gesticulating furiously.[6]

When the mortar fire stopped and other firing died down, Macfarlane and his party moved to the edge of the Turkish quarter where they discovered that the TCF were not quite as ready to give up as Fellahoglu had led them to believe. Shooting was still continuing in the northern part of the quarter, so Macfarlane, taking Fellahoglu with him and escorted by two of his own men, courageously toured the Turkish posts and persuaded the TCF in them to cease firing. He then escorted Fellahoglu out of the quarter to the local CYPOL station, where surrender terms were agreed and embodied in a hastily drafted document typed by the Greeks in English and signed at 0645hrs by the two sides and witnessed by Macfarlane. It was quite simple:

AGREEMENT BETWEEN THE TURKISH LEADER AND THE AREA COMMANDER OF THE
NATIONAL GUARD AND THE AREA COMMANDER OF THE UNITED NATIONS FORCE IN CYPRUS

1. Turkish Cypriot Fighters to come to UN for handing in arms and ammunition.
2. All defence works in the Turkish quarter should be demolished. Turkish Cypriot
    Fighters weapons to UN, then to a place where UN and National Guard can each hold a
    key.
3. Patrols of Turkish quarter of Paphos to be done jointly with representatives from:
    a. UN (armed).
    b. Two police constables (armed) *[CYPOL]*
    c. Turkish representative to act as interpreter. Weapons should not be displayed.
4. No National Guard or Police other than patrols will enter the Turkish quarter. Times of
    patrols will be four times a day with two cars, one Police car and one UN car.
5. The delivery of the arms should take place at about 8.00 am.
(signed)   Fellahoglu – Turkish Representative
                 Gravenes – Area Commander National Guard
                 Macfarlane – Area Commander UN
21st July 1974.

The 0800hrs deadline left little time for collection of the arms and ammunition and for their
transport to CYPOL HQ (the agreed point), but Macfarlane was determined to do his best.
The fragility of the situation was clear: if the deadline was not met, there was a risk that the
impatient National Guard might open fire just when the TCF were at their most vulnerable.

> To avoid this possibility a small group of five UN members went to the Turkish Headquarters
> and arranged for the fighters to pile their weapons. If it looked as though we could get sufficient
> weapons handed over and if the Greeks kept the ceasefire, we would call in a truck to collect at
> the last possible minute. If it did not work, the five could pull out and leave the piles of weapons
> for the fighters to use again. It did work. By 0750hrs there was a substantial pile and the first
> 4-tonner was called to collect. The weapons were of many types from Brownings to
> Thompsons, bazookas and a variety of automatic weapons.[7]

It was impossible in the time to check each weapon to ensure that it was not loaded and many
were in a dangerous state when surrendered, as was only too soon demonstrated when one
was accidentally fired, killing Guardsman G. Lawson; he was the first fatal casualty suffered
by UNFICYP during this 1974 crisis but sadly not the last. For the TCF the surrender of
their weapons was a traumatic experience:

> It was a sight that those who witnessed it will never forget. It was a picture of total misery. Many
> fighters were crying loudly – they ripped off their uniforms and flung them away – they lay on
> the streets beating the ground – they even threw themselves through windows. Most of them
> did as much damage to their weapons as they could and beat them against walls or on the
> ground. Some had last minute thoughts and re-took their weapons, threatening to fire at anyone
> who came near. Others were holding grenades and threatening to pull pins. They were
> eventually restrained by their comrades. It was an extremely tense and heart-breaking scene.[8]

As the ceasefire held and additional weapons were collected in, both sides observed the agreement. (Later in the morning Gravenes complained that the tally of surrendered arms fell short of Greek expectations and, fearing that this might afford the National Guard a pretext to search the Turkish quarter, Macfarlane persuaded the Turks to produce a few more.) Meanwhile his men had collected a group of foreign nationals who had been in the Turkish quarter and took them to St Patrick's Camp on the town's northern outskirts for subsequent evacuation[9], and Coldstream patrols were sent out to assess damage and wherever possible to give help to all and sundry. (One such patrol led by Company Sergeant Major Robinson had the unpleasant task of removing dead Turks from the old UN OP at Mavroli and delivering the corpses to the Turkish hospital.) For its part, the National Guard lost no time in demolishing TCF fortifications.

By early afternoon on 21 July the situation in the town of Paphos was calm and, with tele- phonic communication cut, Inspector Hill of the Australian Police had returned to the Turkish quarter to provide a liaison link between Macfarlane and the now disarmed Turks. The Coldstream Guards were busily engaged in humanitarian tasks such as burying the dead, conveying wounded to hospital, comforting hysterical women, clearing debris and generally helping to relieve suffering in both communities, when suddenly events took a grave and unexpected turn: five Turkish F104 Starfighters were seen out to sea and five minutes later unleashed a fierce airstrike (including napalm) on the harbour and Greek part of Paphos. Their purpose was unclear; initially their targets had been seen to include ship- ping far out to sea.[10] Whatever their intention, the strikes on Paphos did no service to its Turkish inhabitants:

> They were terrifying and provided the National Guard with the excuse they had wanted all day
> to enter the Turkish quarter. . . . The Turks were rounded up by the National Guard and
> herded into the main square with the threat that, if there was another airstrike, they would all
> be shot. The only UN person actually at the square at this time was an Australian policeman
> [Inspector Hill] who with considerable calm used a stick to tap up the muzzles of the National
> Guard. His display of calmness took the initial heat out of the situation until others arrived.[11]

These latter included Macfarlane himself, who pacified the angry and excited Greeks and, with the Turkish aircraft gone, persuaded the National Guard to leave the Turkish quarter. A protest by the VPO in Nicosia that the withdrawing Greeks had taken 60 hostages with them proved unfounded. No sooner had Macfarlane and his guardsmen restored a measure of calm than the Turkish airforce attacked for a second time, starting at about 1800hrs and continuing for nearly an hour in the gathering gloom, causing considerable damage. The National Guard immediately re-entered the Turkish quarter and this time seized hostages whom they threatened to shoot unless the attacks were called off. Macfarlane's men once more did their utmost to restrain the Greeks, now more angry than ever:

> It became our task to ensure that they behaved themselves and respected life and property. To
> a large extent we were able to do this by keeping constant vigil on all their activities and protesting
> strongly when they stepped out of line, which they frequently did. We were gradually accepted
> as the umpires and most of our protests produced action that prevented a recurrence.[12]

As the surrender in Paphos was proceeding Lance Sergeant Smith and his men in their post overlooking the Turkish village of Mandria could only watch as the predicted National Guard attack developed soon after dawn. Smith's repeated efforts to persuade the Greeks to stop firing to allow him to negotiate with the Turks were to no avail: the National Guard was intent on total defeat of the Turks in this village which for so long had been a thorn in the Greek side. Soon after midday Mandria was overrun, although some sporadic shooting could still be heard, and by nightfall it was reported burnt to the ground.[13] Macfarlane withdrew Smith and his men to St Patrick's Camp, having decided to watch over the area in future with patrols.

After a night of uneasy calm, tension had built up during the morning of 21 July at the mixed village of Polis, 30km north of Paphos. 2nd Lieutenant Style, commanding the Coldstream detachment, talked to both sides with a view to averting bloodshed, but at 1230hrs the local TCF commander told him that the Turks were determined to fight.[14] Since there was little more that his men could do, Macfarlane ordered the detachment back to St Patrick's Camp and the six men of the Australian UNCIVPOL post came with them. Turkish determination not to submit was evident, too, at Stavrokono, situated 18km east of Paphos astride a road leading up to the Troodos (its TCF commander enjoyed an especially tough reputation); here the Coldstream OP under Lance Sergeant Denton remained in position, monitoring events closely. There had been no fighting in the vicinity so far, but during the night of 21 July Denton reported rumours that TCF from neighbouring villages, together with others said to have escaped from Limassol, intended to make a stand at Stavrokono. Macfarlane impressed on Denton the need to do all he could to prevent a tragedy such as had befallen the Turks of Mandria. (In the event the National Guard showed no inclination to take on the Stavrokono Turks, which proved to be one of the few Turkish villages that never capitulated.)

The Turkish airstrikes on Paphos and the sight of a naval ship on fire on the horizon, coupled with BBC and Radio Ankara reports of a likely seaborne intervention by Greece, gave Macfarlane an anxious night as he speculated on what the morning might bring – a Greek landing in the Paphos area? If so, further Turkish airstrikes would surely follow and St Patrick's Camp would be exposed to these. Or did the Turks' air action presage a Turkish landing in the area? In this event St Patrick's Camp might find itself in the battle area and suffer bombardment from the sea. With either on the cards, he set in hand protective measures in the camp. Meanwhile a degree of quiet returned to the town of Paphos.

Lefka District

Here, too, the power of the Turkish airforce was experienced. After a quiet night illuminated by brush fires and disturbed only by sounds of occasional small arms and mortar fire and an unexplained explosion close to Viking Camp (the Danes' main base at Xeros), attention on the morning of 21 July was focused on the small Turkish town of Lefka, on which the National Guard opened artillery, mortar and heavy machine-gun fire just after dawn. The TCF replied as best it could and intermittent exchanges continued all day as the National Guard adopted the tactic (seen elsewhere) of pounding the Turks from a distance to induce surrender while shrinking from actual assault. Here, however, the Greeks did not have matters all their own way; responding to an appeal for support, Turkish aircraft mounted a strike on a hill north of the town from which Greek artillery fire was being directed.

The two small Turkish coastal enclaves at Kokkina and Limnitis came under fire from the ring of National Guard posts which hemmed them in. During this and subsequent days the three Danish OPs watching over the Limnitis enclave were withdrawn and then re-established as the situation, including brush fire dangers, dictated. (Later a new fourth OP was deployed.) But the situation of the five Danish posts around the Kokkina enclave, all exposed to cross-fire and powerless to halt it, became impossible, and Lieut. Colonel Severinson, the Danish Battalion Commander, ordered their withdrawal to the platoon base in Kokkina. This was achieved during lulls in the shooting, although not without casualty – Private B. Skett was seriously wounded by fire from the National Guard.[15] Greek pressure on the two small enclaves was relieved during the early afternoon by Turkish airstrikes which included napalm that ignited fresh fires in the tinder-dry hills. Since his men in the Kokkina platoon base could no longer serve a useful purpose Severinson ordered them to rejoin their company in the less exposed camp just outside Limnitis. They did so after a difficult 15km drive along the tortuous coast road, cratered in places by the TCF. As night fell on 21 July the Danish contingent was thus concentrated within its main base at Xeros, with one company holding the Limnitis camp; most OPs had been withdrawn.

Throughout the day Severinson and his officers had been energetic in mediating between Colonel Charalambous, commander of 2 HMC at Morphou, and local Turkish leaders in Lefka, Kokkina and Limnitis in attempts to halt the fighting. Danish patrols checked the situation in those Turkish and mixed villages throughout the District which had not yet come under National Guard attack, but from which some Turks were fleeing to what they believed to be their stronghold in Lefka town. At Ghaziveran some 60 Turks were reported to be planning to seek refuge in the nearby Cyprus Mines Corporation (CMC) hospital on the coast at Pendayia, and Mr Erol, the Turkish leader in Lefka, told the Danes that he was fearful for the safety of 100 Turks said to be held prisoner in the Greek village of Prastio; Danish investigation showed the latter to be unharmed (Erol was informed accordingly).

The presence in Viking Camp on the night of 21 July of some 50 foreign nationals[16] gave cause for concern because the National Guard had occupied the CMC premises immediately adjoining the camp and were attracting Turkish fire. Instructed by HQ UNFICYP to organize their evacuation under Danish escort to safety further south, Severinson despatched all from Xeros soon after 0900hrs on 22 July; they reached the Western SBA safely that evening after a 12-hour journey over the Troodos mountains. Severinson's further anxieties during the night of 21 July included the possibility of Turkish airstrikes on the adjacent CMC premises next morning and realization that his Xeros base and the Limnitis camp both lay uncomfortably close to the coast within an area of likely ground action by mainland Turkish forces. He warned HQ UNFICYP of the possible need for DANCON to abandon both camps and to establish new bases in the mountains further south. In the event, although the Turkish army later overran the area, the Danes remained esconced in both camps.

Famagusta District

The night of 20/21 July had been uneasy in Famagusta, where sporadic shooting continued. Under cover of darkness the TCF had left the hamlets of Karaolos and Sakharya for the Old City, where the Swedes observed constant activity on the massive Venetian walls. Captain Lindholm, kept busy all night passing messages to and fro between Mr Hilmi and the Swedish HQ in Carl Gustav Camp, reported that morale within the Old City had received a major boost when Turkish aircraft were sighted over Famagusta soon after dawn on 21 July. Daylight also brought a resumption of heavy firing. Some rounds struck the Swedes' OP Goldfish near the Landgate, compelling its men to shelter inside their APC; hearing a cry nearby, they dragged a wounded Turkish fighter to safety inside the vehicle and gave him first aid. As they did so, six Turkish aircraft using bombs, rockets, cannon and napalm attacked Greeks in the area of the harbour and the Landgate, Karaolos camp, National Guard artillery and AA batteries, and the HQ of 1 HMC and the adjacent CYPOL station (which was set ablaze and destroyed); both Carl Gustav Camp and OP Goldfish suffered near misses. Since the latter was no longer serving a useful purpose, Lieut. Colonel Kristensson ordered its men to withdraw; despite coming under National Guard fire, the team reached Carl Gustav Camp unharmed (and delivered the wounded Turk to its medical centre).

At this time the 15 Swedes from OPs Landgate and Othello Tower were still sheltering in the Old City and the MP detachment was still pinned down in its villa just outside. Kristensson decided that all these, too, should be brought back into Carl Gustav Camp. The MPs were rescued in two APCs (at some risk since National Guard tanks sited close to the villa were drawing mortar fire from within the Old City) and were safely back in Carl Gustav Camp by about by about 0730hrs, where they were joined by their CIVPOL colleagues who had been withdrawn without incident from Leonarisso.

Extracting the 15 men from the Old City proved more difficult. Kristensson had decided that APCs should be reversed up to the Landgate to allow the men to clamber inside with a minimum of exposure, but just as the first APC was backing onto the bridge over the dry moat Lindholm was alarmed by sudden frantic TCF activity: their commander was ordering every man up onto the walls and a mainland Turkish officer ran towards the Landgate shouting for demolition charges to be inserted in chambers previously prepared in the walls each side of the Landgate. Apparently a Greek attack was thought to be imminent, in which event the charges were to be detonated and the bridge demolished. Lindholm immediately warned the JOC in Carl Gustav Camp and the APCs were at once withdrawn. Lindholm was no less concerned for the safety of civilians, mostly women and children, in the shelters built into the walls immediately adjacent to where the demolition charges had been placed; pointing out their peril to the Turkish officer, he succeeded in having them moved away. Fortunately it was a false alarm: no Greek attack materialized and demolition of the Landgate and bridge did not take place. The situation continued tense nonetheless; withdrawal of the Swedes through the Landgate was now out of the question, but, a ceasefire having been achieved later, the Swedes marched out through the North Gate (guided by a Turkish fighter through a minefield) carrying their weapons and equipment now recovered as a result of

Lindholm's negotiations. They were met by two APCs, which brought them safely into Carl Gustav Camp.

Earlier Kristensson had secured agreement for a local ceasefire at 1400hrs, but this did not stop the shooting altogether, not least because of the National Guard's difficulty in passing orders to some of its men; to overcome this problem two of his officers, Major A. Wendelberg and Major A. Rosen, donned flak-jackets and delivered the ceasefire orders to front line Greek posts.[17] At about 1500hrs Kristensson informed HQ UNFICYP that there was now only sporadic firing in Famagusta, that airstrikes had ceased and that he had been asked to evacuate the wounded from Karaolos and Sakharya to hospital. In a further report that evening he said that both sides had been busy collecting their dead and wounded under UN supervision. As darkness came to Famagusta and the uneasy ceasefire prevailed, the Swedes could see fires burning to their north in the vicinities of Ephtakomi, Komi Kebir and Trikomo, and at midnight another fierce blaze lit the sky to their west. Anxious to ensure that the ceasefire continued to hold next day, Kristensson asked how best to ensure this; we could only tell him to maintain pressure on both sides locally until such time as agreement was reached for an island-wide ceasefire, action to which end was in train in New York and elsewhere.[18]

Throughout the day Kristensson had been much preoccupied by another concern – the safety of some 800 Scandinavian (mostly Swedish) tourists still in Famagusta and not evacuated under the British operation the previous day. Asked in mid-morning by Stockholm how they might be brought to safety, he had recommended that they should be evacuated by his contingent to the Eastern SBA and flown from there to Beirut under Swedish government arrangements. Brigadier Robertson, the SBA Commander, whom Kristensson consulted, welcomed the suggestion since it was likely to reduce calls on his own men already fully stretched in handling British and other nationals. Stockholm approved and when Kristensson informed me accordingly I gave HQ UNFICYP's blessing, while cautioning that action must not be at the expense of his contingent's obligations under the Security Council mandate. He assured me that this would not be the case and events proved him as good as his word; the operation was to begin at 0600hrs next morning, 22 July.

CHAPTER FORTY-THREE

EVACUATION OF FOREIGN NATIONALS FROM FAMAGUSTA AND NICOSIA

There were not many countries, I said to an American colleague, that could mount such a rescue operation. Still fewer, he replied, who would have bothered to take the trouble and responsibility. And he was right. The United States took off its own citizens plus the Canadians. The Russians and French looked after their own. Britain took everyone else. My anti-colonialist colleagues confessed that they would never again be able to look coldly at a Union Jack.

Levant Correspondent, The Economist, London.

The evacuation of British families from Famagusta, suspended when darkness fell on 20 July, was resumed next morning in spite of the fighting that had erupted again around the Old City and accompanying airstrikes. The return of Major Gibbs and his evacuation team drawn from British units in the Eastern SBA was delayed until 0600hrs by the air action and the risk that Turkish pilots might mistake the British vehicles for a reinforcing Greek convoy. Nonetheless Brigadier Robertson, the SBA Commander, anticipated that by about noon all remaining British service families would have been rescued and a start made on evacuating other foreign nationals, estimated to number as many as 7,000.

Gibbs described how his men went about their task while exposed to small arms, mortar and artillery fire and the threat of further airstrikes:

The first convoy of families moved out at 0730hrs, but after a recce of the sector next to the walled city it was discovered that a small triangle of this, where 69 service personnel lived, was occupied by a large force of National Guard and that this area was under continuous fire from the walled city. It had also been severely damaged in the Turkish airstrike earlier in the morning. It was decided . . . that the only way to get in and out would be in armoured vehicles. Four Saracens *[APCs]* of B Sqn, 16th/5th Lancers . . . with hatches closed down but covered in Union Jacks like mobile coffins, went in and carried these unfortunate families out. Some of them were in a very distressed state as they had been fought over and attacked from the air for 30 hours. On the third run-in one of them reported that about half an hour earlier there had been screams for help in English from the road nearest the ramparts to the walled city, so the ambulance and Medical Officer accompanied the Saracens on the fourth and last run-in. The particular street was a shambles and the unfortunate family was quickly identified. The house had been hit many times and some explosive projectile had exploded in the living room, where there were the mother and her four children. Miraculously the only serious injury was to the 10-year- old son, who, despite the efforts of the Medical Officer, died shortly afterwards.[1]

During the morning those foreign nationals with their own cars were formed into groups and moved into the SBA under British escort. The rescue of the remainder then began – hotels were methodically visited and people without cars were ferried in military vehicles to the SBA until darkness again intervened:

> At 1815hrs the last convoy pulled out amidst some understandably hysterical scenes from the ones who were faced with another night of fear.[2]

(Those obliged to suffer for a second night included some 800 Scandinavians for whom Lieut. Colonel Kristensson, the SWEDCON Commander, had accepted responsibility; all these were brought out safely next day.)

The British-conducted operation for the evacuation of foreign nationals from Nicosia was mounted on the morning of 21 July in cooperation with UNFICYP[3], the decision to do so having been made at about 0900hrs by Air Marshal Aiken, CBFNE, notwithstanding that the overnight ceasefire had been less than complete and shooting and Turkish airstrikes had been resumed at dawn. The plan provided for evacuees to be conveyed to Dhekelia in the Eastern SBA for onward movement away from Cyprus. To this end a British convoy of 40 army lorries and buses, escorted by armoured cars and infantry, was to be sent to Nicosia under the command of Major J.A. Wright, 16th/5th Lancers. For its part, UNFICYP undertook to provide a further 12 army lorries, assist with marshalling arrangements at the Hilton Hotel on the capital's southern outskirts (which was to be the assembly point) and provide guides and escorts within the city.

A statement broadcast by BFBS made clear that the operation was being mounted in order to help foreign nationals caught up in the conflict (Cypriots were not included), and Greek and Turkish commanders were urged to respect this humanitarian purpose by not impeding it. It was also announced that escorting vehicles would display British flags and that the troops concerned would open fire only if directly fired at.[4] Those wishing to avail themselves of this opportunity to escape from Nicosia were told to assemble at the Hilton Hotel at 1200hrs, carrying no more than one small suitcase and with sufficient food and water for immediate needs (temperatures were in the region of 38°C). HQ UNFICYP notified both sides of the impending operation and gave them notice of routes and timings. Diplomatic missions in the city were also informed so that they might warn their own nationals.

Although his men in the SBA were placed at short notice for the operation at about 0730hrs, Wright was less than happy at what he perceived to be an air of vagueness surrounding his mission and it was not until 1000hrs that he received more detailed orders. He was told that he could expect to evacuate about 600 people, some of whom would wish to use their own cars, and that his convoy was required to reach Nicosia 55km away within the hour. This was not feasible (vehicles had yet to be marshalled, men briefed, flags provided and communication arrangements coordinated), but, with Wright determined to do his best, the convoy set off just before 1100hrs. With him went Major P.E. Wood

(Parachute Regt.), who until recently had been HQ UNFICYP's Operations Information Officer and whose local knowledge of the Nicosia area was to prove valuable. British army pickets were established along the road between the SBA and Nicosia and the convoy was met short of the capital by UN Military Police who guided it to the Hilton Hotel, reached at 1230hrs. The sight that greeted Wright was not of 600 people and a few cars, but of thousands, most with their own cars; the whole area was congested and more were arriving by the minute. UNFICYP's Provost Marshal, Major J.R. Cullen (Canada), and some of his Military Police were already on the spot trying to instil some order and Wright made immediate contact with him and with Mr J. Cheeseman of the British High Commission, who had been deputed to establish a British control point at the hotel.[5]

Dependants of UN servicemen and UN civilians in quarters at RAF Nicosia or in Blue Beret Camp were also to be evacuated under the British arrangements, both because they were at risk from ground fire and airstrikes in the vicinity[6] and because their presence imposed a severe strain on already overstretched logistic resources. No sooner had they been formed up in a convoy of vehicles at the entrance to Blue Beret Camp than they had to be dispersed on account of renewed artillery and mortar fire and an airstrike. The convoy was re-formed during a lull and left under UN escort for the Hilton Hotel, reached at about 1400hrs. The convoy included the families of RAF Nicosia personnel and of the Austrian UNCIVPOL who unexpectedly had sought shelter in Blue Beret Camp the previous evening, but as it moved off there was astonishment that among the women and children were not only the male uniformed men of RAF Nicosia (as already described) but also the male Austrian UN policemen themselves. The sight of all these able-bodied men leaving without warning (or, in the case of the Austrian police, General Prem Chand's authority) was one that those who witnessed it could scarcely believe. (The immediate consequences of the British abandonment of RAF Nicosia have been mentioned already, but there were more serious consequences for the UN Force later.)

Meanwhile a group of vehicles escorted by a troop of UNFICYP's Parachute Sqn, RAC, was sent from the Hilton Hotel to rescue the 350 people trapped in the Ledra Palace Hotel and another went to collect others from the British High Commission building where 40 people had gathered:

> The Canadians rescued my family in two jeeps driving straight between the contestants, flying UN flags and shouting through bullhorns. The families immediately adjacent to the High Commission were rescued in a foray led by the Counsellor, Derek Day.[7]

These 40 were taken unharmed to the Hilton Hotel assembly point, but at the Ledra Palace Hotel unexpected difficulties were encountered. A National Guard platoon was still in the hotel and its officer, described as small and nervous, was refusing to allow foreign nationals to leave, as the Italian Ambassador, Signor V. Manfredi, discovered when, following an appeal for help from a group of Italian correspondents trapped in the hotel, he went there himself:

> At around 1230hrs I drove my official car to the hotel followed by two other Italian Embassy cars. We managed to reach the hotel, thanks to a short ceasefire locally arranged by UNFICYP

but which was due to expire at 1500hrs. At the entrance to the hotel . . . I was met by the entire group of my nationals who received me as though I was a saviour sent from above. But they had to go through some other emotions because a National Guard officer . . . wanted to get authorization from the Ministry of Foreign Affairs. He arranged for a telephone communication to the new *[Sampson-appointed]* Minister, Mr Dimitriou, to whom I spoke and who . . . authorized the officer to let me take my men to safety, which I did right away. The men were supposed to be eight in all, but when I checked the three cars I discovered nine; a Japanese reporter had managed to sneak into the group of Italians, and so I took him too.[8]

On reaching the hotel the British rescue mission faced with the same problem:

The worst moment came after the rescuing convoy, British vehicles under the UN flag, arrived in the forecourt. Then, at the last minute, we were refused permission to board because the National Guard would not allow people of several nationalities to leave until their embassies had received permission from the Cyprus foreign ministry. This was apparently an attempt to enforce recognition of the Sampson régime – and to compel those embassies which had given asylum to its opponents to hand them over. The UN, in the person of a young British lieutenant, said firmly that it either evacuated all civilians or none.[9]

Informed of this difficulty, the British High Commissioner, Mr Olver, prevailed on Dimitriou to order the National Guard to allow all foreign nationals to leave the hotel and at 1430hrs the Canadians reported that they had done so; soon afterwards the convoy reached the Hilton Hotel with all its people unharmed.

Here Cheeseman and Wright, supported by Cullen and his Military Police, had established a degree of order and the first 40–50 assorted vehicles had already been despatched under escort, reaching the SBA at 1450hrs. Cypriots had been specifically excluded from the operation, but many held British passports and arguments arose as some attempted to join the convoy. Matters were not made easier by National Guard checkpoints seeking to ensure that no one of Turkish origin was escaping:

At one point they stopped a car, holding up the whole convoy, because they believed that one of the occupants, an old woman, was Turkish. I was sent to the check-point to get the convoy moving again. There were nine or ten Greeks shouting and waving weapons around and looking very trigger-happy. To add to the confusion all six people in the car were in tears and making a great deal of unintelligible noise. The normal British officer manner failed to have much effect on the situation and I was extremely relieved when a very large and ferocious Canadian Military Policeman waded into the argument. Within seconds the convoy was on the move again.[10]

Major Wood devised his own way of solving similar situations:

Wood was used as a trouble-shooter whenever the National Guard road-block stopped the convoy because of suspected Turkish Cypriots. . . . He was marvellous – just took them out of the convoy packet without arguing and then fed them back into a later one.[11]

The mass of people and vehicles at the Hilton Hotel was steadily reduced as successive packets were sent on their way to the SBA (for most it proved a clear non-stop run). At 1600hrs Cullen informed HQ UNFICYP that all those wishing to leave had done so and the last British military vehicles, some empty, made their way out of Nicosia. A Lancer officer described the journey:

> By now it was approximately 1615hrs, after the promised armistice time given by the Turks. Every now and again aircraft flying very high would pass over the city. The sight of these was enough to send the Greek soldiers sprinting for the nearest ditch and the convoy would proceed more quickly. At last, long after the deadline, everyone had left and I tagged onto the back of the convoy. All the way back to the SBA cars would come roaring up behind me, flashing lights and sounding horns, and relieved late-comers would slot into the convoy ahead of my Ferret scout car.[12]

UNFICYP's British families had been escorted to the SBA by an officer of HQ BRITCON, who likened the scene on arrival at Dhekelia to a popular race-meeting as hundreds of cars were lined up on the playing fields and more arrived throughout the afternoon:

> Reception for the [British] Service families was pre-planned and excellent, and all were under cover within a short time . . . . It was sad to hear the carping of some non-British civilians (for whom after all the Base had no responsibility), who once they had recovered from their fright complained of the arrangements for them. These were a minority – most were very grateful.[13]

It had been a highly successful operation in which no casualties had been suffered. Counting exact numbers was impossible, but it was estimated that about 4500 people and over 1000 private cars had been escorted to the SBA, these being additional to those evacuated from Famagusta and, earlier, from Larnaca. The numbers, far in excess of those provided for in contingency plans, faced Brigadier Robertson and the SBA garrison with formidable problems: many were frightened, some had suffered traumatic experiences and all were hot, tired, hungry and thirsty, while a few were in need of medical attention.

During 21 July 41 RM Commando had disembarked from HMS *Hermes* at Dhekelia; one of its troops was deployed to reinforce the defence of the Ayios Nikolaos communications unit and another was employed in protecting other parts of the SBA. The remainder, together with other troops of the garrison, were engaged in caring for the vast influx of civilian refugees. This was a mammoth task and everyone, not just the servicemen but also wives, schoolteachers and other civilians, rallied round to help, many working for 72 hours with little sleep. Conditions were spartan, but over 2000 people were accommodated in a barracks, and marquees were erected to shelter others, food was provided throughout the day and night, and each family was allowed to send a telegram notifying safe arrival in the British base.

It was British policy to evacuate away from the island as soon as possible all foreign nationals who arrived in the SBAs. For most this was to be done under a plan nicknamed Operation FALLACY, using RAF aircraft flying from Akrotiri, to which those in the Eastern SBA were to be ferried in Hercules and Argosy aircraft from Kingsfield airstrip near

Dhekelia. At Akrotiri they were to be transferred to VC10 and Britannia aircraft for onward movement to RAF airfields in the UK, from where foreigners could then travel on to whatever destination they wished. For a minority their own government made other arrangements; some Americans and Canadians were taken by helicopter to ships of the US 6th Fleet; the French took off some of their nationals by sea and Soviet and Eastern bloc nationals were embarked in a merchant vessel at Larnaca. (The families of British servicemen generally were to remain in the SBAs pending a decision as to whether or not the situation might allow them to return to their quarters in the island's various dormitory towns.[14])

Action proceeded accordingly. Passports were checked, each passenger was documented[15], and the various categories of refugees were organized into separate groups – those for onward movement by RAF transport to Akrotiri and the UK, those to be lifted off by helicopter to the US 6th Fleet, those to be embarked on French or Soviet ships at Larnaca, and those who were to remain in the SBA until such time as the situation in the Republic became clearer. (It greatly helped that the 800 Scandinavians now in the SBA were efficiently cared for by SWEDCON and evacuated by air under Swedish government arrangements.) For some it seemed a long wait in uncomfortable conditions, but RAF aircraft took off from the Kingsfield airstrip hourly for three days and it was only a question of patience before all had been called forward to emplane. By the evening of 24 July the onward movement had been completed of all those who had opted to go to the UK; left in the SBA were about 500 people who either were ineligible to go or who wished to stay until the situation became clearer. Altogether over 7,500 passengers of 46 different nationalities were flown out from the two SBAs. When the last had left Kingsfield in the Eastern SBA:

> There was only a barracks that looked as if it had been hit by a tornado, rows of empty marquees and some 600 cars abandoned in the base to show what had happened. The car owners left their keys and . . . in the ensuing months the cars were either reclaimed or shipped out by their owners. By Christmas the number was down to less than 100; of these 60 were British-registered and half of these eventually proved to have been stolen in the UK.[16]

Admiration for the skill with which the Nicosia evacuation had been conducted prompted a message of congratulation from the British Prime Minister to Air Marshal Aiken. It made no mention of UNFICYP's part, but amends were made next day when the Security Council was informed by the British representative that:

> some 4,500 foreign nationals, including many British subjects, were evacuated from Nicosia, and we are extremely grateful to UNFICYP for facilitating that. It was not a solely British affair.[17]

Brigadier Robertson remarked later that, considering that many had abandoned homes, property and cars and that tourists had had an end to their holiday that they could never have dreamt of, the morale of all was amazingly high and the gratitude expressed overwhelming; for weeks afterwards letters of thanks arrived at his Headquarters from all over the world. (An exception was a German lady who was indignant on being told that the RAF could fly her to the UK, but not Dusseldorf).

CHAPTER FORTY-FOUR

TURKISH AND GREEK 'OWN GOALS'

In Ankara there was rejoicing in the corridor of the Prime Minister's office on receipt of a report that the convoy taking reinforcements to Paphos had been attacked and stopped and that an enemy destroyer had been sunk. In the Navy operations room there was a deathly silence . . . .

M.A. Birand: *30 Hot Days*, p. 43.

Joseph Sisco, Dr Kissinger's envoy, returned from Athens to Ankara on the morning of 21 July bearing proposals for a ceasefire. The junta, he said, was ready to accept that Turkish troops now on the island should remain for the protection of Turkish Cypriot communities and was willing also to replace Sampson as President, to withdraw those Greek officers implicated in the *coup* and to attend a conference in London to work out a settlement. When the Turks replied that a ceasefire was out of the question until their operation had achieved its military objectives, Sisco warned that, if a ceasefire on the basis suggested was not accepted, then Athens seemed set on war with Turkey.[1] The Turks shrugged off this risk but this attitude concealed real anxiety; from the outset they had been nervous of a military reaction by Greece, perhaps in Thrace or the Aegean or by landing troops in Cyprus itself. Sufficient forces had been retained in Turkey to meet any threats in Thrace or the Aegean[2], and a watch was kept on any movements that might portend a Greek landing in Cyprus. Turkish fear on the latter score was such as to induce an almost paranoid disposition to believe any rumour that such a landing might be imminent.

During 20 July Ankara had received a report suggesting that Greece was assembling a convoy of ships off Rhodes (400km west of Cyprus). Due to failing light Turkish air reconnaissance that evening had been unable to verify the type or nationality of shipping in the area, but a sortie next morning reported 8–11 ships in the vicinity, apparently heading for Cyprus. This was said to have been confirmed by radar surveillance, while a report from Rhodes suggested that the ships were carrying vehicles and arms. When an intercept of Greek communications revealed an army warning order for units to prepare for embarkation, those in Ankara, taking counsel of their fears, jumped to the conclusion that military intervention by Greece in Cyprus was imminent, which seemed to them consistent with the warning just delivered by Sisco. Air surveillance of the 'convoy' (which in Turkish minds it had now become) was maintained, but so inept was this that positive identification of the ships was still lacking and Ankara assumed them to be Greek. Even when during the morning the shadowing aircraft reported that the convoy appeared to be no more than a chance grouping of ships, none of which had as yet entered the declared exclusion zone[3], Ankara remained apprehensive and unconvinced. The decision was made to attack and sink the ships should they enter the zone.

This decision was notified to Sisco who, resuming his shuttle mission, returned to Athens with the information that Ankara had rejected the Greeks' proposals for a ceasefire. The Turks, he added, insisted that, if war between their two countries was to be averted, the 'convoy' must be recalled, the National Guard must withdraw from all Turkish Cypriot areas and any ceasefire on the island must be accepted and declared by both their governments; as for a conference, the Turks would go to Vienna but not London. The most pressing problem, it seemed to Sisco, was the convoy, but the Greeks denied its existence[4]; when so informed, Kissinger telephoned Prime Minister Ecevit to say that the Greeks insisted that there was no such convoy and had added that, if the Turks could find one, they were at liberty to sink it.[5]

However, two further reports from shadowing aircraft did nothing to allay Turkish anxiety. The first stated that several destroyers of a type provided by the Americans to both the Greek and Turkish navies had been sighted, while the second said that there were nine ships in the convoy. Ankara was now in no doubt that a Greek military convoy was heading under destroyer escort for a landing in the Paphos area. Orders, said to read as follows, were issued:

Instructions are hereby issued for an attack on a convoy of 11 landing craft and transport ships, escorted by five destroyers, which is now 15 miles off the Paphos coast. The following units will take part: the 181st Squadron from Antalya, the 141st Squadron from Murted, and the 111th Squadron from Eskisehir. The landing craft will be attacked first. . . . it is reported that the Greek destroyers lack adequate anti-aircraft defences . . . .[6]

The destroyers *Adatepe, Kocatepe* and *Cakmak* were detached from their role off the north coast of Cyprus with instructions to intercept the convoy and sink any vessels flying the Greek flag that entered the exclusion zone. After a minor skirmish at about noon off the Akamas peninsula with three Greek MTBs (one of which was believed to have been sunk), the three destroyers were informed that Turkish airstrikes on the convoy and its escorts were to be made soon after 1500hrs. An extraordinary sequence of events then unfolded.

The information given in the orders for attack was at variance with what reconnaissance aircraft had reported and, coupled with apparently confident Greek disclaimers as to the existence of any convoy, there were now doubts in Ankara. A further air reconnaissance was ordered and those in the Turkish destroyers below heard the pilot reporting that he was flying over two ships; they were flying no flags but *'Line Messina'* was clearly visible on the side of one and the only cargo to be seen was a motor car; all appeared normal. He also reported that the three Turkish destroyers, but no others, were in sight. This information mystified the commander of the Turkish naval group and his perplexity was increased when radio operators in the two merchant ships were overheard conversing in Italian. But, fatally, this latest air reconnaissance report apparently did not reach those concerned in Ankara. A further problem arose when the pilot of the reconnaissance aircraft challenged the Turkish ships with the identifying codeword for that day; this was unknown to the latter and when they failed to reply the scene was set for tragedy.

The Turkish airforce squadrons arrived over the area at 1500hrs, saw only the three destroyers, assumed these to be their target and dived to make repeated attacks. For their part the Turkish sailors assumed them to be enemy aircraft and opened fire; they were unable, it seems, to identify the aircraft, while pilots of the latter, observing that all three destroyers were flying Turkish ensigns, assumed in their turn that this must be a Greek ruse, both navies having ships of the same type. *Kocatepe* was set ablaze by a bomb down its funnel and sank after being abandoned by its crew; the other two suffered less severe damage and withdrew to the north as the air attacks ceased. Some 25 of *Kocatepe*'s company had been killed and about 205 survivors in life rafts were swept south in rising seas as a northerly wind freshened. It now dawned on those in Ankara that a dreadful mistake had been made.

Initially the tragedy remained unknown outside Turkey[7]; only when reports began to filter through some 24 hours later of Turkish survivors being picked up did the story begin to emerge. The first to be rescued were 42 men found next day on life rafts west of Cyprus by an Israeli naval vessel and taken to Haifa. Realizing that others might still be adrift, the Turkish navy asked HQ BFNE on 23 July, 48 hours after the event, to assist in a search and rescue operation. A reconnaissance that evening by an RAF Nimrod reported debris in the indicated search area but no survivors. Search of a wider area was resumed next morning and was joined by a Turkish aircraft and the Turkish destroyer *Berk*. At this time the British frigate *Andromeda* was replenishing at sea south of Akrotiri from RFA *Gold Rover*, and on learning that a search and rescue operation was in progress 20 miles to his west, her Commanding Officer, Captain R.W.F. Gerken RN, broke off the evolution and with *Gold Rover* following went to investigate:

> On closing the search area I saw a Royal Air Force Nimrod, who was the commander of the operation, supported by two RAF launches, two of HMS *Hermes*'s Sea King helicopters and a yellow RAF Whirlwind helicopter. I imagined that an aircraft had crashed and was surprised to see another warship which turned out to be the Turkish frigate *Berk*, a recent addition to the Turkish navy. However, two life rafts were sighted and I closed them to recover the occupants who turned out to be Turkish naval personnel from the destroyer *Kocatepe* who told us that the ship had been sunk by Greek gunboats on the previous Saturday, 20th July *[sic]*. The few men who spoke some English were engine-room personnel who had been below decks during the action and therefore were unable to give much information of where, why or how their ship had been sunk. There were 37 of them and some had minor injuries and nearly all were badly sunburned since they had little clothing and the canopies of the life rafts were not inflated. However they had survived nearly four days and many were able to climb unaided up the scrambling net and over *Andromeda*'s guard rail.[8]

Berk was seen to pick up 38 men so that between them 75 survivors had been rescued.[9]

Gerken proposed that those picked up by *Andromeda* should be transferred to *Berk*, but was informed by HQ BFNE that all the survivors were to be taken instead by the Sea King helicopters to the RAF hospital at Akrotiri; 72 were so transferred. But there had been confusion at HQ BFNE, and on learning that the RAF hospital was harbouring Turkish naval personnel Air Marshal Aiken, fearful of the Greek reaction if this became known, ordered them to be removed at once. The 72 were embarked in the RFA *Olna*, then close by, and Gerken was instructed to arrange their transfer to *Berk*, being left in no doubt of the urgency:

> From the tone of my orders from Admiral Cassidi *[Aiken's naval deputy]* I knew that there was a pressing need to remove them from the SBA, get them into *Berk* and the least said the better![10]

Assuming control, Gerken told *Berk* to await *Andromeda's* return while he gathered *Olna* under his wing. He proposed to effect the transfer outside the 12-mile limit during darkness, with *Olna* stopped beam on to wind and sea to allow *Berk* in her lee to take off the survivors by boat. *Berk* and *Olna* both judged the sea too rough, whereupon Gerken took *Andromeda* under *Olna's* lee to demonstrate that boatwork was feasible, but *Berk* still would not agree. Gerken then proposed that the transfer be effected by jackstay, but this too was rejected by *Berk* because its engines would not permit accurate station keeping. Since it was now well into the night and no progress had been made, Gerken considered taking the three ships east to calmer waters in the lee of the island, although this would not allow completion of the transfer before dawn.

But Lieutenant I. McKechnie RN, senior pilot of *Andromeda's* Wasp helicopter flight, had seen that *Berk* was fitted with a helicopter platform and proposed that the survivors should be transferred from *Olna* to the Turkish ship by means of the Wasp, even though only three men could be carried at a time. Gerken agreed and a remarkable operation ensued:

> My next orders to *Olna* and *Berk* were that the Wasp would transfer the survivors using the flight decks of the two ships and that the Wasp would return periodically to *Andromeda* to refuel. *Olna* pointed out that she was not cleared for night flying, having only just completed a refit, and had no qualified helicopter controller or flight deck crew. With these reservations she was all for having a go. *Berk* found even greater reservations in that she was a new ship, had never operated a helicopter, had no night landing lights and generally had no wish to start her experience of matters aeronautical that particular evening.
>
> A few minutes of enthusiastic planning by my operations and flight deck team, fired by determination to beat this problem, came up with a solution. *Olna* would be provided with a flight deck officer and skeleton flight deck crew from our own resources and positioned by the Wasp before the transfer started. All radar control would be vested in my controller in *Andromeda* and with this assistance *Olna* was very happy to go ahead. I told *Berk* that I would send over my senior flight deck officer and a second pilot with a supporting crew to conduct operations and that some lighting should be provided to illuminate the deck without shining in the direction of the aircraft – the deck to be cleared of obstructions and fire-fighting gear laid out ready for emergencies. *Berk* sounded less than happy but agreed to receive the aircraft.[11]

Gerken manoeuvred the three ships into suitable formation and the operation began. It was to prove a gruelling test of McKechnie's skill and endurance. Flying for a period of four hours and twenty minutes (the normal maximum for a helicopter pilot flying at night in one operation was one hour), he made 55 deck landings, and by 0415hrs on 25 July had delivered the 72 Turkish sailors, some of them stretcher cases, to *Berk* and had recovered *Andromeda's* own men. Gerken and his ship's company had displayed outstanding initiative and professional competence and before parting company *Berk* expressed the Turks' deep appreciation. The part played by McKechnie came in for special recognition by the government of Turkey, which awarded him its Distinguished Service Medal, only the 75th to have been awarded and the first ever bestowed on a foreigner.

If the Turks' determination to sink a non-existent convoy had ended in tragic fiasco, their fears of attempts by Greece to reinforce Cyprus were not altogether unfounded, as a second tragic fiasco demonstrated within hours; this time it was the Greeks who scored an 'own goal'. In Athens during the morning of 21 July there had been acrimonious argument amongst the junta following Brig. General Ioannides's insistence that the decision (taken the previous day by President Gizikis and himself without consulting the commanders of the armed services) to declare war on Turkey and to launch an immediate attack in Thrace be implemented. The three Service commanders dissented, not only because they considered that such action would not have international support, but also because their forces were not ready for such an operation: while able to defend Greece, to launch an offensive was out of the question. Frustrated, Ioannides demanded some form of military action to demonstrate that Greece was not sitting idly by and to show the Greek Cypriots that they had not been deserted by the motherland. As a compromise and somewhat forlorn gesture it was agreed that a force of 200 Commando troops together with ammunition, medical and other urgently needed supplies should be flown in to Nicosia under cover of darkness that night. That it was seen as a desperate mission was evidenced by the aircraft to be used – 15 elderly Noratlas transports of uncertain reliability.

On the evening of 21 July UNFICYP had observed activity at Nicosia airport suggesting that the arrival of aircraft from Greece was expected. That this was imminent became apparent just before 0100hrs on 22 July when the runway lights were tested and a convoy of some 70 assorted National Guard vehicles was seen approaching. The 15 Noratlas took off from Greece after dark and were refuelled in Crete before flying on the further 750km to Cyprus. They approached the island from the south and, without warning or permission, entered the air corridor reserved for aircraft using the RAF airfield at Akrotiri[12] before heading for Nicosia to land on the short secondary east/west runway (an approach which brought them in at roof-top height over Blue Beret Camp). The first aircraft came in at 0200hrs and the remainder followed at three-minute intervals. All were greeted by a hail of small-arms and AA gunfire from the National Guard, who assumed them to be Turkish. One was brought down just short of Blue Beret Camp (rumour had it that it fell on the Greek AA gun responsible) and others were seen to have been hit and landing with smoke streaming; of these, three were so badly damaged that they could not take off again.

Unloading was hampered by Turkish mortar fire, but as soon as it was completed the troops and some stores were driven away towards Nicosia, the bulk of the ammunition was stacked in a hastily camouflaged dump on the edge of the airport and the surviving 11 aircraft took off to return to Greece, some carrying Greek wounded; the last was gone just before the coming of dawn allowed a resumption of Turkish airstrikes. Their return route took them west over Morphou Bay and away from Cyprus towards Rhodes. Two of the three damaged aircraft left behind were beyond repair and were deliberately set on fire by the National Guard before dawn; the third was towed into a Cyprus Airways hangar situated within a few metres of Camp UNFICYP, presumably for repair.[13] Greek casualties in consequence of the National Guard's fire were not known.

It had been a brave but foolhardy undertaking, demonstrating to the Greeks, if demonstration was needed, the futility of attempting to fight a war with Turkey in Cyprus. And NATO allies were little impressed by the want of professional competence shown by the armed services of Greece and Turkey in the course of these two 'own goals'.

CHAPTER FORTY-FIVE

TOWARDS A GENERAL CEASEFIRE

Turkey, who considers respect for the United Nations as the most essential element of its foreign policy, decided to respond positively to the appeal for cease-fire that you conveyed to me in accordance with the Security Council resolution adopted on 20 July 1974. Accordingly, necessary instructions are issued to the Turkish troops to ceasefire, effective from 1400hrs GMT *[1600hrs Cyprus time]* on 22 July.

Letter from Prime Minister of Turkey to UN Secretary General,
22 July 1974 (*S/11356*).

International pressure for an island-wide ceasefire, called for by Security Council Resolution 353(1974) adopted on 20 July, continued to increase. France (holding the Presidency of the EEC) urged Greece and Turkey to heed the call, NATO's Secretary General expressed the Alliance's deep concern, and Britain as a guarantor power made its own representations to Ankara, which clearly held the key. For the United States Kissinger was in frequent contact with Ecevit by telephone throughout 21 July. A Turkish officer, said to have been present during these exchanges, has been quoted as saying:

> Kissinger has a tremendous grasp of military affairs. . . . He was aware that the Turkish armed forces had secured their bridgehead, that the second wave of troops was on the way and argued that they were now secure enough to agree a ceasefire. At times he went so far as to suggest that, even after the ceasefire, further reinforcements could be sent to Cyprus and minor territorial adjustments made to consolidate their position. In short, he was being extremely realistic.[1]

Kissinger himself has stated[2] that US pressure during the night of 21 July (which included a threat to withdraw nuclear weapons from positions where they might have been vulnerable in any clash with Greece) induced Turkey to halt its operations in Cyprus while its forces were still confined to a limited enclave.

Bowing to these pressures, Ecevit accepted Kissinger's proposal for a ceasefire to take effect at 1600hrs (Cyprus time) on 22 July, his generals having assured him that by then Turkish forces on the island would have achieved adequate security. Sisco, now back in Athens, was told to wring parallel acceptance from the junta. This proved no easy task (ministers were not to be found) but Admiral Arapakis, the Navy's Chief, gave an assurance that the Greek government also accepted the proposal. (Arapakis said that Ioannides had agreed, but this was not the case; this marked the end of the power of Ioannides and the impending collapse of the junta.) Rumours that Greece and Turkey had accepted a ceasefire reached HQ UNFICYP in the early hours of 22 July. These were confirmed by a BBC World Service bulletin at 0600hrs and an official announcement in Ankara at 1000hrs. UNFICYP's District Commanders were informed at once and instructed to use this information in support of efforts to secure local ceasefires in the meantime. The prospect of a general cease-fire later in the day otherwise made little impact on the Force's immediate problems.

The situation in Nicosia continued to give cause for particular concern. At about midnight on 21 July the Turkish Chargé, Asaf Inhan, had informed General Prem Chand that the possibility of further airstrikes, such as that already made in the vicinity of the Ledra Palace Hotel, would depend on developments during the night; he intended to review the situation at 0400hrs and, provided that there had been no attacks on the Turkish quarter, he thought further airstrikes on the city unlikely. In the event the night passed relatively quietly with only sporadic firing in north-western suburbs and, determined to preempt any excuse for a resumption of airstrikes after dawn, HQ UNFICYP sought the agreement of both sides for a complete cessation of all shooting in Nicosia as from 0500hrs. The National Guard agreed on condition that Turkish air attacks ceased, but Inhan replied that he had no authority to give such an undertaking; he could only refer the matter to Ankara. He added that, since the word of the National Guard was not to be trusted, agreement for a full ceasefire within the city should be committed to a written document signed by the commander of the National Guard and endorsed by UNFICYP.[3] There was thus no formal agreement for a local cease-fire at 0500hrs, but a marked improvement all along the Green Line suggested tacit acceptance by both sides; indeed, at 0515hrs the Canadians reported that there had been no shooting whatsoever during the previous 45 minutes. When, soon afterwards an airstrike was made on the airport, sparking fears that firing would erupt again in the city, HQ UNFICYP stressed to HQ National Guard that this strike had not been against the city and should not be seen as grounds for a resumption of fighting in Nicosia itself. With one exception, and in spite of occasional minor breaches, calm reigned along the Green Line until the general ceasefire took effect at 1600hrs; the exception, described later, was at the Ledra Palace Hotel.

Inhan repeated his demand for a written ceasefire agreement from the National Guard, which the latter's commander said he was willing to sign. Informed of this, Inhan then demanded that the agreement be underwritten by UNFICYP (which lay outside the UN Force's authority) and that, as soon as the ceasefire took effect, the Force visit all parts of the island to maintain the ceasefire and examine all areas 'to see what atrocities were committed by National Guard against Turkish Cypriots'.[4] Inhan was told that a UN officer was already at National Guard HQ securing a written agreement and that the document would be delivered to the Turkish Embassy as soon as possible. Captain Bruno Granlund (Sweden), accompanied by Warrant Officer J.T. McCowat (UK) and with an escort from the Parachute Squadron, RAC, had been sent to Malounda, the National Guard's secret emergency HQ, with a brief document drafted by HQ UNFICYP for signature by Brig. General Georgitsis, the Greek commander. There they met Commandant Flynn, UNFICYP's LO, and together (outside the subterranean HQ) they presented it to Georgitsis, who was accompanied by his

LO to UNFICYP, Major Tsolakis, acting as interpreter. Georgitsis was unwilling to sign without two additions to the draft:

> I then radioed UNFICYP HQ for permission to include these two paragraphs *[incorporated as paras. 2 and 3 of the following document]* . . . and when this was given WO McCowat set up his typewriter on the chopping block of the village butcher's shop and typed a new ceasefire document . . . . Tsolakis read it, spoke to the General who signed it, then Bruno, Tsolakis and myself signed, and Bruno left with the document and his Ferret escort.[5]

The document read as follows:

Headquarters National Guard 22 July 1974

The ceasefire has been arranged for 1600hrs local time (Cyprus), 1400hrs GMT. This has been broadcast by the British Broadcasting Service who have confirmed that Greece and Turkey have accepted this. The following conditions will obtain:

1. A document of similar content to be signed by the Turkish Ambassador to Cyprus, Mr Inhan.

2. The ceasefire will include no crossing of lines as they existed at 1600hrs by either side.

3. No reinforcements to be brought into Cyprus after 1600hrs local time, 22 July 1974.

As Commander of the National Guard I confirm that I have received this instruction and that I shall comply with this instruction.

(signed) Brig. General Georgitsis, Commander National Guard.

Witnessed by: James J. Flynn, Commandant.

Bruno Granlund, Captain.

Evangalos Tsolakis, Major.

22 July 1974.

If the precise wording left room for improvement, the document's spirit and intention were clear enough. It was delivered by Granlund to the Turkish Embassy at 1730hrs, but, in spite of a personal appeal by Prem Chand, Inhan refused to sign a parallel agreement on the grounds that he was not empowered to do so. Granlund returned to UNFICYP HQ without any written Turkish acceptance of the conditions to which Georgitsis had subscribed. It was not an auspicious start to what soon became a fragile general ceasefire.

It had been apparent all day that the Turkish forces were intent on gaining maximum advantage before the 1600hrs deadline and their build-up on the island had continued apace. The Finns reported four warships off Kyrenia at dawn and, soon afterwards, that troops, tanks and artillery were coming ashore under cover of naval gunfire; the seaborne follow-up echelon of the Turkish 'Peace Force' had reached the island. Ship-to-shore movement continued throughout the day and was complemented by further airborne reinforcements landed in the enclave. Three waves, each of between 55 and 60 helicopters, landed during daylight hours and further sorties by C130 Hercules and DC10 Dakotas made airdrops of men, light vehicles, guns and stores, with some aircraft landing on the Aghirda airstrip. UNFICYP estimated that by the evening of this third day and with the general ceasefire now formally in force, the bulk of the Turks' 39th Division, Airborne Brigade and Commando Brigade had landed on the island, providing a total of about 16,000 men with some 50 tanks and some artillery. It was a formidable force, equipped with modern weapons and enjoying powerful close air and naval gunfire support, but a lack of drive was apparent. Confined within the enclave and the northern coastal strip, its tactical situation would have placed it in severe difficulty in the face of any opposition stronger than that offered by the gallant but inadequately equipped Greek Cypriot National Guard.

During the morning the Finns' Commander, Lieut. Colonel Pullinen, reported much activity in northern parts of Kyrenia District: targets in the mountains were being bombarded, there was shooting around Kyrenia, Bellapais and Dhikomo, and Turkish troops were advancing east through the mountains beyond OP Hilltop; in northern Nicosia in the early afternoon the TCF was attacking across the Green Line in the Trakhonas sector. As the 1600hrs deadline neared there was no discernible lessening of such activity and by evening Turkish troops had entered but not yet captured the town of Kyrenia. Throughout 22 July the situation of the Finns in Tjiklos Camp on the Kyrenia Pass gave cause for concern. With the coming of daylight Turkish troops resumed their cautious advance towards the Pass, drawing Greek mortar fire which fell close to the UN camp. When they reached it in mid-morning the camp came under small-arms fire, some Turkish soldiers entered it and a fire was started close to the ammunition store. Captain Lenck, the Finnish company commander, persuaded a Turkish officer to withdraw his men who then moved away towards Kyrenia, but within half an hour there was another outbreak of firing with shells and bullets striking the camp. HQ UNFICYP's urgent protests to both sides led only to promises by each to stop shooting provided that the other side also did so, a common experience for UN Forces. A wounded Turkish soldier was tended by the Finns, who also found the corpses of two others killed by the fires burning all around. These fires spread rapidly to engulf much of the camp, compelling the Finns and the Austrian UNCIVPOL (withdrawn from Kyrenia) to take refuge in the gravel pit where the 150 foreign nationals (two of whom had sustained minor wounds) were already sheltering. It was too dangerous to attempt to evacuate this large group of foreign nationals so long as the fighting continued, but Pullinen succeeded in evacuating to Nicosia by ambulance one of his officers wounded the previous day and whose condition had deteriorated.

In Nicosia District Lieut. Colonel Manuel's immediate concern was to maintain the tacitly accepted 0500hrs ceasefire. To improve surveillance of the Green Line, from which most of his OPs had been withdrawn, he decided to institute patrols along the Line by scout cars of the Parachute Squadron, RAC, but could not do so immediately because the only two scout cars available to him[6] had been sent to cover the withdrawal of the Canadian detachment from the Turkish village of Louroujina, 28km south of Nicosia, currently threatened by a Greek attack. When the situation at Louroujina took a turn for the better, the two scout cars returned to Nicosia and, supplemented by Canadian patrols, monitored the Green Line throughout the day. The situation in the city nonetheless continued tense and Turkish air activity at the airport drew wild fire from Greek troops in the western suburbs. There were

Turkish protests that the water supply to their quarter had been turned off (UNFICYP had it restored), that UN patrols refused to halt at TCF checkpoints and that the National Guard had advanced to occupy premises from which the Canadians had withdrawn. These and many other protests flowed in to HQ UNFICYP from one side or the other throughout the day, suggesting that each side was staking claims to new positions before the 1600hrs cease-fire took effect.

Once again it was the Ledra Palace Hotel that was the focus of attention. The Leadership was fearful that the National Guard might try to re-occupy the building and warned that, if it did so, the TCF would open fire. Repeated assurances that the hotel was now a UN-controlled area from which the Greeks were excluded failed to satisfy the Turks, who continued to assert that snipers were firing from it into the Turkish quarter. In spite of Manuel's personal assurance (given after a floor-by-floor search of the building to ensure that not a single Greek was left in it) that no fire had come from the hotel, Turkish fears, indicative of the climate of nervousness and insecurity prevailing within the Turkish quarter, were not entirely allayed.

In Famagusta a major concern for Lieut. Colonel Kristensson on this third morning of the Turkish action was the need to evacuate those Scandinavian tourists still in the city, esti-mated to number about 800 scattered between 50 different hotels. The plan, devised in consultation with Brigadier Robertson, Commander of the Eastern SBA, was for the evacu-ation to be carried out by road, starting at 0600hrs, to the sanctuary of the SBA where they would be looked after by men of the Swedish Contingent. Onward movement was to be in aircraft provided by the Swedish government, but at this stage Kristensson did not know when, where or in what numbers these aircraft would be made available. He appointed Captain A. Wendelberg to be in charge of the operation with Captain A. Rosen responsible for caring for the tourists once they reached the SBA. A party of 35 Swedish soldiers and 17 lorries were allotted for the operation. After some 48 hours exposed to the dangers of fighting and airstrikes many of the tourists were shocked, nervous and clamouring to leave, but their morale was much raised by the cheerful and disciplined bearing of Kristensson's men as they loaded people and baggage into the lorries to be transported to Rosen's care in the SBA.[7]

The lack of information concerning onward movement and the prospect of possibly being required to look after these 800 people for a prolonged period worried Kristensson, but, seeing the distress of many of them, he was in no doubt of the need to press ahead with the operation. This was as well for towards midday, as Wendelberg and his men were on their way back for a third lift, they were halted at a British checkpoint and advised to go no further on account of Turkish airstrikes; he courageously said that they would go on at their own risk. These airstrikes had been concentrated on the northern part of Famagusta, severely damaging and causing the partial collapse of some high-rise hotels. Fortunately tourists had already been taken from these, but such was the consternation and panic among civilians generally in the town that the Swedes were met by hundreds pleading to be rescued. Wendelberg was firm: his plan for systematic clearance of the town from north to south would be adhered to.[8] Turkish air activity continued overhead, requiring those already in the lorries to dismount twice and take cover. The Swedes worked quickly southwards, clearing as they went many other hotels which stretched for more than 2km along the seafront. Their task was made no easier by the National Guard, some of whom in angry reaction to the Turkish air action were firing weapons indiscriminately; some rounds struck Swedish vehicles, happily without causing casualties.

When all lorries of this third lift had been filled to capacity, about 40 Scandinavians still remained, some of whom verged on panic at the prospect of being left behind. The Swedish UN Civilian Police came to the rescue and picked them up in their own vehicles, so that in the final lift just over 200 were rescued.[9] No foreign tourists were thought now to remain in Famagusta, but there was anxiety as to what might have become of about 320 Scandinavians not accounted for. Investigation revealed that they had availed themselves of the British operation the previous day and they, too, were taken under Rosen's care. In spite of airstrikes and wild shooting in the town, all the Scandinavians had been safely evacuated.[10]

In reaction to the airstrikes on Famagusta the National Guard had opened fire on the Turks in the Old City, bringing in turn threats of further airstrikes. Pressed by UNFICYP, Colonel Kostas, the National Guard commander, agreed to halt this fire, but the Turks protested that it was continuing nonetheless. After numerous exchanges between UNFICYP and the two sides, Kostas announced in the early afternoon that his troops had ceased firing but that the Turks were mortaring civilian areas of the town; unless this stopped, he would order artillery fire onto the Old City.[11] The situation had been exacerbated by a Turkish airstrike at about 1330hrs on the National Guard camp at Karaolos, just north of the Old City and within 1000m of Carl Gustav Camp (which also was hit, although without casualties to the Swedes in their shelters), and Turkish aircraft came over the city again 90 minutes later when severe damage was inflicted on high-rise hotels along the seafront and casualties were caused to Greek Cypriot civilians.

There were problems for UNFICYP elsewhere in Famagusta District. Just after midday Inhan protested strongly that atrocities, including the hanging of a Turk, were being committed against Turkish Cypriots at Chatos (in the west of the District), from which the Swedish detachment had been withdrawn two days earlier. He threatened that, unless these ceased immediately, the Turkish airforce would strike throughout Cyprus (a threat that by now had become routine). The National Guard commander's personal assurance, conveyed through UNFICYP, that such reports were untrue failed to mollify Inhan, who demanded confirmation by the UN Force itself, failing which, he reiterated, airstrikes would be ordered. The National Guard gave clearance for a UN patrol to go to Chatos to verify the situation and Inhan was persuaded to hold his hand while it did so. But these three-sided exchanges relayed through UNFICYP's LOs had taken some time and it was now about 1530hrs, with a general ceasefire due to take effect 30 minutes later. Since a ground patrol could not quickly reach Chatos, it was decided to await the ceasefire, when hopefully UN helicopter operations could be resumed and a patrol sent by this means. In the event the Turkish airforce's failure to observe the agreed ceasefire prevented this, so that it was not until later that UNFICYP was able to assure the Turks that there had been no Greek atrocities at Chatos.[12]

In Larnaca District Lieut. Colonel Rieger, the Austrians' Commander, reported on the morning of 22 July that the District generally had been quiet during the night. The 600 surrendered TCF were being held under UN protection in Larnaca town and a further 100 were similarly held at Kophinou, while white flags had been raised by Turks in the villages of Kellia and Klavdhia. But at Mari, which had refused to surrender the previous day, an attack by the National Guard now surrounding the village was to be expected. The situation here caused UNFICYP concern throughout the day and involved Captain Brell, the local Austrian commander, in constant mediation between the two sides as he tried to avert bloodshed. Since the course of events at Mari illustrates well how UN peacekeepers go about their task, it is worth recording in some detail.

At Brell's 0700hrs meeting with both sides (arranged the previous evening) to discuss terms for the surrender of the village he informed them of the Greek and Turkish governments' agreement for a general ceasefire at 1600hrs, which made further fighting pointless. The Turks replied that any surrender decision must rest with the village committee, which included Sergeant Ekrem (the local TCF commander) and the *mukhtar*; on meeting the committee decided to surrender on the terms proposed the previous day, provided that Ekrem was allowed first to see for himself that the TCF in nearby Kophinou had already surrendered (as Brell had stated). By now a force of 400 men of the National Guard was surrounding Mari, and at another meeting with its commander, Major Najatou, Brell secured agreement that, if Mari surrendered, arms would be collected by the Austrians for handing over to the National Guard, that no Turks would be made prisoner and that house searches would be carried out by the Austrians with a Greek officer present only as an observer. (As they talked, Ekrem was taken by the Austrians to Kophinou, where he saw that white flags were flying over the village, with the TCF held under UN protection in the police compound and all weapons handed in.)

On his return to Mari Ekrem was told of the agreement Brell had reached with Najatou, but then both Ekrem and the *mukhtar* said that the village had changed its mind: it would not surrender. By now it was about 0930hrs and Brell urged both sides to exercise maximum restraint, sensing that the Turks were disposed to surrender, but were being held back by an undercover mainland Turk in the village. Half an hour later the threatened National Guard attack was launched. HQ UNFICYP instructed Lieut. Colonel Willoughby, Commander of the adjacent Limassol Zone, to contact Colonel Sirmopoulos at 4 HMC (which controlled National Guard units in the Mari area) and press for the attack to be halted; Sirmopoulos was unhelpful. Simultaneously HQ UNFICYP pressed the Leadership in Nicosia to authorize those in Mari to surrender in order to avoid needless casualties; the Leadership gave this authority soon after midday on the understanding that the village surrendered, not to the National Guard, but to UNFICYP. Rieger asked HQ UNFICYP to secure the agreement of both sides for a 30-minute truce to allow Brell to re-open negotiations.

Although the National Guard's attack had obliged the Austrians to withdraw, Brell and others often came under fire as they did their utmost to bring an end to the fight. The Company War Diary records their actions:

1155: UN again contacts Major Najatou to arrange a ceasefire. Meanwhile a 106mm recoilless gun with 12 rounds takes up position on the main road near the crossroads to Zyyi. Major Najatou states that Major Gregoriou commands the attack on Mari and therefore only he can order a ceasefire.

<u>1220</u>: Further contact with a National Guard major from Limassol HQ. He is only willing to order a ceasefire if an officer from his HQ can check that Kophinou has surrendered *[evidently the Greeks, too, doubted UNFICYP's word to this effect]*. A medical officer of the major's staff was then taken in a UN vehicle towards Kophinou. Following the explosion of an anti-tank grenade, he asked the driver to stop the vehicle at Major Najatou's HQ near Zyyi crossroads. He seems to press for a ceasefire. After the major received further orders from the National Guard at Skarinou *[west of Kophinou]* he is willing to ceasefire if Major Gregoriou agrees.

<u>1400</u>: Major Gregoriou was contacted and agreed to a ceasefire if all Turkish flags are taken down and white flags are hoisted. The Turks will have to stand up in their positions, holding their weapons above their heads. Major Gregoriou then wants to talk to the Turkish Cypriot leader. UN then contacts the Turkish Cypriot leader.

<u>1415</u>: The school at Mari has already hoisted a white flag. The village committee agrees to capitulate. Sergeant Ekrem and Mr Erzen *[committee member]* are taken to the National Guard major from Limassol in a UN vehicle. The following agreement was reached:
1.   Weapons will be handed in to UN, who will hand them over to National Guard at the crossroads on the main road.
2.   National Guard will be permitted to search houses for further weapons under UN supervision.
3.   After search in Mari the National Guard is allowed to check Turkish positions on Crown Hill *[the nearby feature dominating the main road]* for arms.
4.   National Guard troops will not enter the village, the only exception being the search party.
5.   After all these procedures the National Guard will leave the area of Mari.

<u>1500</u>: The attack on Mari is finally halted and fire ceases. UN re-occupies OP Mari and OP Crown Hill.'[13]

By 1615hrs the TCF's weapons had been collected by the Austrians, but, as darkness approached, a National Guard platoon took up position overlooking the village on the flimsy pretext that an unexploded mortar bomb there had to be guarded. Brell's response was to interpose a small Austrian detachment and for the time being Mari remained calm.[14]

In the town of Larnaca the situation was mostly calm throughout 22 July, but tension rose when the National Guard, in breach of the previous day's agreement, began to search the Scala Turkish quarter; some shooting (the Greeks alleging that they were firing at fleeing members of the TCF) and some looting of Turkish property took place. Rieger at once protested the action, but the National Guard's response was to demand entry to the Gaza school to interrogate the Turks held there under UN protection. HQ UNFICYP warned HQ National Guard that under no circumstances would this be permitted. Meanwhile Rieger's Medical Officer, Major Kurz, arranged for Larnaca's Greek hospital to provide care for the TCF in the school and for a Turkish doctor to attend to Turkish patients.

UNFICYP's concerns at this time extended also to the plight of Turkish Cypriots in Turkish and mixed villages elsewhere in Larnaca District. The local Turkish Cypriot leader, Mr Mehmet, wished to encourage these small, isolated and vulnerable communities to capitulate in order to avoid bloodshed and to this end Rieger sent patrols to the villages concerned, with a view to negotiating surrender terms. The reception encountered by his patrols was mixed: at Kellia the TCF refused to consider surrender, at Goshi civilians were fleeing, and at Klavdhia the Turks did not want to fight but feared ill-treatment if they surrendered; Pergamos and Pyla, both situated on the Eastern SBA's convoluted boundary, were reported invested by the National Guard but with their Turkish inhabitants unharmed. After pressure by Mehmet the Turks of Kellia, Kalokhorio and Klavdhia (from which the TCF had vanished) agreed to surrender and the Austrians informed the National Guard accordingly. At Goshi negotiations were inconclusive, but no Greek attack materialized, and at Tokhni the village surrendered after some shooting in the early afternoon. (Since its arms could not be collected before dark, an Austrian patrol remained in the village overnight.) The Turks of Kivisil gave in after lengthy negotiations and here all arms had been collected by 1845hrs, when both the Austrians and the National Guard withdrew from the village. Thus, when the island-wide ceasefire formally came into force at 1600hrs, calm prevailed in Larnaca District.

From Limassol Lieut. Colonel Willoughby reported early on 22 July that the town was quiet, and so it remained throughout the day. (There had been momentary concern during the night when a single shot was heard from the stadium in which the surrendered TCF were held; it had not been possible to ascertain whether or not a Turk had been shot; if one had been, then this was the only casualty suffered by the TCF throughout their detention in the stadium.[15]) During the afternoon there was some anxiety as rumour spread of an imminent Turkish airstrike on Limassol, but this proved unfounded. (Air activity observed out to sea may have been associated with the search for survivors of the *Kocatepe* sunk the previous day.) Throughout 22 July the Coldstream Guards and troops of the Parachute Squadron RAC patrolled outlying areas of Limassol District paying particular attention to Turkish and mixed villages. At this juncture concern was caused by the activities of roving bands of Greek Cypriot irregulars which were venting their anger on Turkish property and terrorizing those Turks who had not yet fled to the Western SBA. These activities had serious implications for maintenance of the general ceasefire.

Overnight the town of Paphos had been a quiet and so it remained throughout the morning of 22 July, even though the National Guard under the close eye of Major Macfarlane's guardsmen had started to dismantle the barriers surrounding the Turkish quarter. However, during the afternoon the Turkish airforce again attacked the town; the reason was obscure since Paphos was calm and the surrendered Turks were under no imminent or particular threat. HQ UNFICYP warned Inhan that, while the Greeks in Paphos were currently behaving correctly, any further airstrikes would be sure to exacerbate intercommunal relations. At Mandria village Macfarlane's men were rendering assistance to Turkish wounded, while at Stavrokono the reputedly tough local TCF gave no signs of surrender: indeed, TCF from other villages were reported by Lance Sergeant Denton in the UN OP to be reinforcing it. Macfarlane warned that it might become necessary to withdraw the OP because the Turks were ignoring Denton's advice to halt construction of new fortifications which was likely to provoke a National Guard attack. In the event the Greeks showed marked reluctance to take on the defenders of Stavrokono and Denton and his men were able to remain in position.

However, the large mixed village of Polis (30km north of Paphos), from which the Coldstream Guards detachment had been withdrawn the day before in consequence of the local TCF's decision to fight on, gave continuing concern. Having been told early on 22 July by the District Officer, Mr Stephanides, that the Turks of Polis had indicated a desire to surrender but only in the presence of UN troops, Macfarlane ordered his Coldstream detachment under 2nd Lieutenant Style and a troop of the Parachute Squadron RAC to return to the village to arrange the surrender. As Brell and his Austrians had found at Mari, it was no easy task:

> It became a protracted performance and was not as straightforward as first appeared. Discussions became inflamed by the news that a ceasefire had been agreed island-wide as from 1600hrs. This made the Turks play for time and eventually to cancel their original agreement to surrender. At 1040hrs the National Guard issued an ultimatum that the TCF had 30 minutes to surrender or the assault would start. 2nd Lieutenant Style continued to protract negotiations and gained considerable amount of time by getting continued periods of 15 minutes extensions to the ultimatum. At 1200hrs he could do no more and the firing started. It continued throughout the afternoon, observed from a nearby hill by the UN party. The battle at Polis continued until 1920hrs despite the agreed ceasefire at 1600hrs. All efforts at District and local level failed to implement the ceasefire. The National Guard case was that the Turks had surrendered and stalled when they heard about the ceasefire for 1600hrs. They therefore considered they had the right to continue their operation. They occupied the Turkish quarter at 1920hrs.[16]

The fighting was finally ended, but the National Guard prevented Style and his men from returning into Polis and they withdrew for the night to the Limni mine 5km away. Next morning they re-established the UN post in Polis and thereafter maintained watch over the surrendered Turks.

For the Danes in Lefka District the day had started uneventfully, but in mid-morning fighting erupted when the National Guard attacked the coastal village of Limnitis and opened artillery and mortar fire on Lefka town. Both developments caused Lieut. Colonel Severinson particular concern: at Limnitis because the National Guard was firing on the village from positions behind his company's camp[17], and at Lefka because the fire was being answered by Turkish fire that came close to Viking Camp, the Danes' main base at Xeros. His representations to Colonel Charalambous, commander of 2 HMC at Morphou, to halt both actions was ignored and parallel pressure by HQ UNFICYP on HQ National Guard in Nicosia proved no more successful. At Limnitis the Turkish response was inevitable: just before the 1600hrs ceasefire deadline aircraft attacked Greek positions on the surrounding hills and Limnitis remained in Turkish possession.

In Lefka town the outcome was different: Greek artillery and mortar fire continued into the afternoon with such telling effect that the local Turkish leader, Mr Erol, announced that his community was ready to surrender, but only through UNFICYP's agency. A local ceasefire at 1530hrs was agreed and the National Guard entered the town without resistance. Severinson convened a meeting between both sides to agree surrender terms attended by Erol and a mainland Turkish officer (hitherto under cover) and by Charalambous and several of his officers. After difficult and sometimes heated discussion and with Severinson's mediation, terms were agreed, committed to paper, signed by both sides and endorsed by him on UNFICYP's behalf. These terms, to be overseen by the Danes, provided for correct treatment of the town's Turkish Cypriots, a prohibition on the taking of prisoners (the mainland Turk and his subordinate were excepted), and a procedure for the handing in of weapons. Severinson quickly established a Danish OP in the town. (Later a full company was based in its technical school.) The National Guard deployed a full battalion in and around Lefka and generally behaved correctly. Within days the Turkish Cypriots were able to move freely within the town and, with special permission, outside it, although this latter freedom was withdrawn later on account of alleged abuse.

The plethora and variety of problems in all parts of the island that flowed in to Force Headquarters located in Blue Beret Camp close to Nicosia airport strained the multi-national staff to the limit. Although tired, over-stretched and under constant threat of misdirected ground fire or airstrikes (Turkish aircraft coming in low to strike targets at the airport were a frequent reminder of the dangers) all responded valiantly. Particularly important was the need to keep the UN Secretary General closely informed by means of frequent situation reports cabled to New York by the UN Radio, these being amplified from time to time by telephone conversations between Prem Chand and Brian Urquhart and others in New York. Intense pressure on the capacity of the UN Radio, whose civilian operators handled not only a large volume of Force HQ traffic but also much increased traffic on behalf of those contingents, notably the Canadians, which lacked a national radio link with their own government, necessitated the imposition of strict traffic priorities.[18]

A further concern was the predicament of foreign nationals still cut off by fighting along the north coast. The British plan to rescue them by sea, starting at dawn on 22 July, had to be deferred due to Turkey's refusal to consent to the operation while its forces were still heavily engaged in the area. It was now hoped to carry it out on the morning of 23 July and planning to this end gathered momentum during 22 July, involving HQ UNFICYP in discussions with the British High Commission and the US and other diplomatic missions, as well as with the Turkish and Greek authorities.

The pattern of Turkish airstrikes on the airport on this third day suggested a Turkish determination to make certain before the 1600hrs ceasefire deadline that it could not be used for a repeat of the previous night's attempt by Greece to land reinforcements. A strike made at exceptionally low level at about 1500hrs scored nine hits on the runways, but evidently this did not satisfy the Turks, for the airport continued to receive their airforce's attention well after the time agreed by Ankara for a general ceasefire. Nevertheless, as that hour neared there was a feeling of cautious optimism in UNFICYP that the senseless fighting was about to end. General Prem Chand issued orders to UN District Commanders, who during these three days had without exception displayed admirable initiative, to exert the utmost pressure on military commanders on both sides to respect the ceasefire accepted by the two mother-countries. The need now, he said, was for UNFICYP to re-establish effective observation and to record and report all violations.

PART SIX

CUSTODIAN OF THE ORPHAN CHILD

It was at this juncture that the United Nations found itself confirmed, more or less by default, as the custodian of the orphan child. In my discussions with the representatives of Britain, France and the US it became clear to me that they had no intention whatsoever of taking serious action to stop the Turkish offensive. Without their leadership very little could be done.

Kurt Waldheim: *In the Eye of the Storm*, p. 85.

CHAPTER FORTY-SIX

THE FRAGILE CEASEFIRE

During the hours that followed the entry into force of the ceasefire there were numerous violations of the ceasefire agreement. . . . In an effort to head off the potential danger of a breakdown of the ceasefire agreement, the Special Representative and the Force Commander were in constant contact with the National Guard Headquarters and with the Chargé d'Affaires of Turkey.

UN Secretary General, 23 July 1974 (*S/11353/ADD. 4*)[1]

By 1600hrs on 22 July, when the agreed ceasefire formally came into being, Turkish troops landed from the sea had reached Kyrenia, although not yet in control of the town, and had all but secured the Pass in order to link up with those landed by air into the main enclave. Although those in the Turkish quarter of Nicosia were thus about to gain direct access to the north coast so long denied, the Turkish forces were contained within a relatively constricted area that gave little room for manoeuvre. Their vulnerability, especially to National Guard artillery deployed around the enclave, led the Turks in the days that followed to press ever more outwards in disregard of the ceasefire. Elsewhere the situation on the evening of 22 July was as already described: the Turkish Cypriots of Limassol, Larnaca, Paphos, Lefka and some Turkish villages had surrendered to the National Guard and were under the watchful eye of UNFICYP; others, notably those behind the Green Line in Nicosia, those within the walls of Old Famagusta, those in the small coastal enclaves at Kokkina and Limnitis, and those in a few other Turkish villages, still remained defiant, while others further south had fled from Turkish and mixed villages to seek protection in the British SBAs.

In New York the Security Council met at 1215hrs (1815hrs in Cyprus, some two hours after the ceasefire), when discussion was marked by two features: first, a disposition to claim for the Council, on the basis of its call two days earlier, the credit for achieving a ceasefire, whereas that credit was due in the main to Kissinger's pressure; second, the familiar but sterile exchanges between the Greek and Cypriot representatives on the one hand and the Turkish representative on the other (which did nothing to promote a settlement of the immediate problems and dismayed their colleagues around the table). Nevertheless, important points emerged, notably that Greece and Turkey had agreed to Britain's proposal for an early meeting of the guarantor powers in Geneva to begin negotiations for the restoration of peace in the area and constitutional government in Cyprus.

Of immediate concern was criticism of UNFICYP voiced by the Turkish representative, Mr Olcay:

> I am speaking of the present moment, and I am referring to the towns of Famagusta (called Magosa in Turkish), Paphos (called Baf in Turkish) and a place of which I know only the Turkish name, Serdali *[Chatos]* where, even as I address the Council, Turks are being massacred – and the massacres could not be prevented by the United Nations Force, whose sole purpose in Cyprus, to the best of my knowledge, was to interpose itself between the two parties precisely to avoid what is happening now.
>
> As far as I am aware the United Nations Force . . . has, regrettably, not succeeded in preventing the massacre of Turks by Greeks. Those *[UN]* troops, whether because they are too few in number or because they are unskilled or because they cannot be everywhere at once – and I must recognize that there are difficulties – have not succeeded in carrying out their task.[2]

Both Olcay (whose criticism was based on reports that were either erroneous or exaggerated) and other Turks seemed blind, both at this juncture and later, to the fact that it was Turkey's resort to military intervention that had created the current perils for Turkish Cypriot communities scattered around the island. UNFICYP had been, and still was, doing its utmost to halt intercommunal violence, but it was unrealistic to expect that, as a lightly armed force of a mere 2,200 men, it could achieve complete success in the highly charged situation created by the Turkish action.

A more realistic note had been struck by Dr Waldheim in an opening statement. Reporting that the ceasefire had not yet taken full effect, he stressed the need for this to be made effective in order to allow negotiations for a peaceful settlement to proceed with the utmost speed, adding:

> The United Nations peacekeeping Force in Cyprus (UNFICYP), although very small in numbers, has during the past tragic days been doing its utmost to limit the fighting and to protect the civilian population, and I wish here to pay tribute to the courage and devotion of all the personnel of UNFICYP for their exemplary conduct during this very grave crisis.
>
> However, during the fighting UNFICYP has received requests for assistance from all sides which have been manifestly beyond its present capability. As we are well aware, after a bitter conflict a ceasefire is virtually impossible to maintain without the assistance and supervision of some impartial but generally acceptable agency, especially in a situation as complicated as that which exists in Cyprus at present. It is obvious that the present strength of UNFICYP is not sufficient for it effectively to ensure the maintenance of the ceasefire. I have the intention, therefore, in compliance with Resolution 186 (1964), as a first step, to ask the troop-contributor countries urgently to reinforce their contingents which are already serving with UNFICYP.[3]

Speaking again later in the meeting, he commented:

> I have listened with interest to . . . the remarks of the representative of Turkey concerning the role of UNFICYP. . . . The requests for assistance received from all sides during the recent fighting were manifestly beyond the present capabilities of UNFICYP. This applies particularly to the role of UNFICYP in preventing the recurrence of intercommunal strife. It

was precisely for that reason that I informed the Council of my intention to reinforce UNFICYP.[4]

It was after 2000hrs in Cyprus when the Council rose and the Secretary General cabled instructions to General Prem Chand setting out UNFICYP's tasks in the new situation that now prevailed. The UN Force was to make every effort to restore order, to implement the ceasefire and, where possible, to interpose itself in crucial areas on ceasefire lines. Waldheim added that he was aware of the difficulties, but stressed the need to establish efficient control of the ceasefire and to strengthen this as reinforcements were received. Further, he emphasized that UNFICYP was to continue to act in the spirit of its existing mandate as set out in Resolution 186 (1964), paying particular regard to the intercommunal situation. Lastly, he reminded Prem Chand that, in accordance with established UN practice, UNFICYP should assist in humanitarian matters, provided that this could be done without prejudice to its operational tasks.

The Secretariat in New York had lost no time in requesting reinforcements from the troop-contributor governments. Although details had yet to be confirmed, HQ UNFICYP was informed that the following were to be expected shortly:

Austria – 60 men, comprising one infantry company.

Canada – 460 men, including a mechanized infantry company and an armoured reconnaissance troop.

Denmark – 200 men, comprising one infantry company.

Finland – 400 men, comprising two infantry companies (the first to arrive on 25 July and the second about 4 August).

Sweden – 200 men, comprising one infantry company.

United Kingdom – 610 men, including a Regimental HQ, two armoured reconnaissance squadrons and two infantry companies.

(Ireland, which since November 1973 had maintained only a token presence in UNFICYP, had not been asked for further troops.)

These planned reinforcements almost doubled the operational strength of UNFICYP. Especially welcome was the proposed increase in armoured capability represented by the Saladin armoured cars and Ferret scout cars of the two British armoured reconnaissance squadrons and the M113 APCs and Lynx tracked vehicles of the Canadian mechanized infantry company and armoured reconnaissance troop.[5]

Some fighting continued at several points around the island after 1600hrs, but the first major breach took place at 1645hrs. Its significance lay in the fact that it could not be attributed to lack of effective control by either side in Cyprus, but could only have been the result of a deliberate decision taken at senior military, if not political, level in Turkey. Six F104 Starfighters, followed by two F100 Super Sabres, attacked Nicosia airport and Greek artillery positions near Yerolakkos (about 1500m to its north) using bombs, rockets, cannon and napalm. It was a devastating and spectacular action, some 20 bombs striking the runways and damaging two aircraft of Cyprus Airways. Two bombs and napalm fell short on Camp UNFICYP, wounding a British soldier and starting a fire:

> Two aircraft dived low and the *[napalm]* tanks struck the store's perimeter fence, bursting into a sheet of flame . . . . The burning patch was backed by the Czech arms store, flanked by our own magazine and the guardroom containing some 20 men of the Coldstream Guards. A young REME soldier let off a burst of fire at the offending aircraft . . . . He was duly charged with "Conduct to the prejudice of good order and military discipline, in that he did, without authority, open fire on a Turkish aircraft engaged in dropping bombs on him". His excuse was that when the tanks burst into flames someone had shouted "Fire! Fire!", so he did.[6]

This attack took place just as the Turkish Chargé, Inhan, was engaged in acrimonious exchanges with the SRSG, Weckman, using UNFICYP's main radio net (their conversation being heard by many). Inhan was demanding urgent UNFICYP investigation into alleged atrocities against Turks at Chatos and Polis, but his increasingly emotional and strident outbursts (which contrasted sharply with Weckman's calm argument) suggested that he was under such strain as to cast doubt on his rationality. It had already been decided to send a UN patrol by helicopter to investigate the situation at Chatos as soon as the 1600hrs cease-fire took effect, but, since Turkish air and ground action was continuing, to send a patrol by either air or road entailed an unacceptable risk. Weckman patiently explained this to Inhan, stressing that the Turkish airforce was not observing the ceasefire agreed by his government; if Inhan gave his assurance that there would be no action by Turkish air or ground forces for at least three hours, a UN patrol would be sent at once to carry out the investigation he was demanding. For good measure, Weckman urged that the Turks should accept and observe the ceasefire provisions (contained in the document delivered to Inhan by Captain Granlund) already accepted by the National Guard, namely that there should be no crossing of ceasefire lines and no reinforcement from outside Cyprus.

Inhan's response was a tirade delivered in increasingly excited voice. Stating that he was tape-recording the conversation, which would be reported 'word for word' to Ankara, which in turn would 'place them in front of the world', he declared that he could not discuss cease-fire conditions: these were a matter for his government.[7] He brushed aside the dangers caused by continuing Turkish air action, insisted that UNFICYP must use all its resources 'immediately! immediately!' to stop the massacres that he claimed were taking place not only at Chatos but also at Polis, and declared that 'all responsibility will fall on UNFICYP if these massacres continue'. With ever-rising agitation he said that, regardless of all difficulties, UNFICYP must act at once: a UN helicopter could reach Chatos within ten minutes. Weckman calmly replied that within the last few minutes the Turkish airforce had attacked Nicosia airport, hitting Camp UNFICYP and wounding a British UN soldier; so long as such action continued it was out of the question for UNFICYP to resume helicopter operations. If Inhan was not able to give the assurance requested for a cessation of at least three hours of action by the Turkish forces, then, Weckman robustly told him, responsibility for preventing action by the UN Force would rest squarely with him. Inhan lamely claimed that he had 'no means whatsoever' of communication with the Turkish force commander and, addressing Weckman and Prem Chand personally, warned that time had run out and that further retaliation 'could come within minutes'.

Prem Chand was firm: first, Inhan should reconsider his refusal to subscribe to the reasonable ceasefire provisions accepted by the National Guard; second, airstrikes at various points since 1600hrs were clear violations of the agreed ceasefire; third, allegations of atrocities at Chatos and elsewhere would be investigated by UNFICYP at once, provided that Inhan gave his personal assurance that Turkish forces would observe the ceasefire for at least three hours. He was not prepared, he said, to risk the lives of UN soldiers while the Turks failed to respect the ceasefire accepted by Ankara; he added that, so long as the Turks persisted in doing so, responsibility for any slaughter of Turkish Cypriots would rest with the Turks themselves. The reaction of an emotional Inhan was to break off the conversation abruptly, but in a message passed subsequently through UNFICYP's LO a cooler Inhan stated that the Turks were ready to observe the ceasefire; their airstrikes had been in retaliation for attacks on Turkish villages all over the island, which, he alleged, had continued after 1600hrs.

These exchanges had done little to enhance relations between the Turkish side and the UN Force and nothing to ameliorate the plight of isolated Turkish communities beyond the areas of the mainland Turks' landings. However, they had further highlighted the need for a rapid and reliable means of direct communication between the UN Force commander and the Turkish field commander. The Turks declined to accept an exchange of LOs for which HQ UNFICYP had already been pressing and it was not until 26 July, nearly a week after the first Turkish landings and then only after pressure exerted on Ecevit by Waldheim, that adequate arrangements for future liaison between the two were agreed.

UNFICYP had not expected all fighting suddenly to stop at 1600hrs – ceasefires rarely work that way – and the airstrike on the airport, a clear and deliberate violation, was not the only case of fighting continuing after the stipulated time.[8] The Finns' Commander, Lieut. Colonel Pullinen, reported heavy fighting on the Kyrenia Pass as Turkish troops inched forward to link up with the main enclave, that shooting was continuing near Martin's Mound, on the enclave's eastern flank, and along the Finns' sector of the Green Line, and that four Turkish aircraft had attacked the village of Mia Milea 3km north-east of Nicosia. At about 1700hrs Pullinen added that a Turkish tank column had broken through the Pass to reach Boghaz and that tanks had joined an attack near Dhikomo. It was clear that, notwithstanding the agreed ceasefire, the Turks were determined to expand the enclave, especially in the east in the area of Dhikomo and Martin's Mound. More welcome was Pullinen's news that soon after dark his men at Tjiklos and the Austrian UNCIVPOL detachment had been able to move back into their camp which they had been obliged to leave earlier on account of fierce fires.

The situation in Famagusta District was calmer. There was some shooting at the small and remote Turkish village of Platanisso on the Panhandle, due, it appeared, to ceasefire orders not reaching the local National Guard; the Swedes brought this to a halt. Lieut. Colonel Kristensson also reported shooting at Karaolos, close to the UN camp, which may have been sparked by TCF attempts to return to that hamlet. A more serious problem arose when the

Greeks cut off water supplies to the Turks crowded within the walls of old Famagusta. HQ UNFICYP pressed HQ National Guard to order these to be restored at once, but the latter replied that there were communication problems with its commander at Famagusta and asked UNFICYP to deal with him direct. This Kristensson immediately did and reported at 2145hrs that the water was flowing again and that there was no fighting in the area. Other problems to occupy him included the temporary detention of a Swedish UNCIVPOL patrol by TCF at Kouklia in the west of his District and an appeal from a group of women claiming to be British subjects[9] for evacuation from the Turkish village of Psilatos near Chatos; he decided to send a patrol at first light to investigate and, if necessary, evacuate the women.

Larnaca District, too, was generally quiet as from 1600hrs. The Austrians had no reports of shooting, in spite of the National Guard's action in breaching the agreement not to move forward on to Forbidden Hill (a dominating feature between the villages of Kophinou and Ayios Theodoros), declaring that it had done so because the TCF had failed to surrender all their weapons.

The Coldstream Guards reported that all was quiet in Limassol, that there was no shooting in the town and that the TCF detained in the stadium were being correctly treated. In Paphos District it was events at Polis culminating in the surrender of the TCF in the evening that was the focus of attention in the immediate wake of the ceasefire. As darkness fell the District otherwise was calm, the Coldstream Guards still manning posts on the interface between the Greek and Turkish quarters of Paphos and at the defiant Turkish village of Stavrokono. But a few hours later calm was broken when fighting was reported at the remote Turkish village of Vrecha on the western slopes of the Troodos, said to be surrounded by the National Guard. Major Macfarlane sent a patrol to investigate and, with the coming of daylight, it reported that fighting was still in progress with six dead and six wounded. The National Guard disclaimed responsibility and suggested that the action may have been that of EOKA-type irregulars who were not under its control.

In spite of the fiasco which had led to the sinking of the *Kocatepe* the previous afternoon (but which was unknown to UNFICYP and the world at large until 48 hours later), the Turks remained apprehensive of a possible Greek operation to land troops on the island's west coast. This led Inhan during the evening to demand that UNFICYP immediately investigate, and either confirm or refute, reports of such landings in Khrysokhou Bay near Polis and further south near Paphos. Checks by the Coldstream Guards confirmed that such reports were false,[10] but after dark lights were observed out at sea, two unidentified vessels were seen off Paphos and an unidentified destroyer off Polis (activity that no doubt was associated with the sinking of the *Kocatepe*).

Some problems continued for the Danes in the west of Lefka District. The Leadership protested to HQ UNFICYP that after dark the National Guard had opened fire on and set ablaze some houses in the village of Kokkina, where Turkish Cypriots were pinned down with their backs to the sea. The Danes in Limnitis Camp, to which their Kokkina detachment had withdrawn the previous day, heard firing to their west, but were unable to contact either side to establish the cause. HQ UNFICYP reported matters to HQ National Guard, demanding that any offensive action against Kokkina be halted at once, while Lieut. Colonel Severinson sent a patrol to the area, which reported only sporadic shooting.

In Nicosia the Canadians under Lieut. Colonel Manuel did their utmost to consolidate the ceasefire along the Green Line, but the task proved difficult. A Turkish airstrike soon after the 1600hrs deadline on the Trakhonas area, where the TCF moved forward, brought bitter protest from the National Guard, which threatened counter-action unless the TCF withdrew. Pressure on the Leadership to this end had no effect; indeed, the situation was made worse by further TCF violations of the Green Line. Fear of another Turkish airstrike no doubt played a part, but it was to the National Guard's credit that, in spite of these provocations, it observed the ceasefire along the Green Line. The TCF, its morale boosted by events, caused further problems when it attempted, without success, to detain two patrolling scout cars of the Parachute Squadron, RAC. As darkness fell the Green Line was once again quiet, but towards midnight the Turkish Embassy complained (yet again) of Greeks firing with silenced weapons into the Turkish quarter from high buildings in the vicinity of the Ledra Palace Hotel, possibly from the hotel itself; some bullets, it was alleged, were impacting close to the Embassy; immediate retaliation was threatened unless this shooting was halted. Simultaneous investigation by the Canadians and the National Guard, to whom the complaint was passed, failed to reveal any evidence of such shooting and the Turkish Embassy was informed accordingly.

Throughout this third day of the Turkish operation Nicosia airport remained a focus of activity. The National Guard continued after the 1600hrs deadline to reinforce its defences, and other troops including two T-34 tanks, were deployed at the Greek grammar school which occupied a tactically dominating position on the western outskirts of Nicosia 2km east of the airport. When, after 1600hrs, Turkish troops were observed advancing south towards the airport, automatic small arms, mortar and artillery fire were opened on them from the school. The National Guard was clearly determined to maintain sole possession of the airport, to the point that a UN patrol was refused entry to that part which constituted RAF Nicosia (abandoned by the RAF) on the grounds that it now was under the jurisdiction of the Cyprus government; the patrol would have to obtain permission to enter from the local Greek commander established in the terminal building.[11] The National Guard also occupied Gleneagles Camp, a small UN camp sandwiched between HQ UNFICYP and the airport which had been left vacant by the move a few weeks earlier of the Force Reserve squadron to Limassol but retained against possible future need. When a patrol was sent to insist that the Greek soldiers withdraw from it, they did so without demur. Some 24 hours later the camp was indeed needed as a base for UNFICYP reinforcements.

An immediate concern for UNFICYP following the ceasefire was a humanitarian one – the rescue of the 150 civilians of various nationalities sheltering with the Finns at the burnt-out camp at Tjiklos. Pullinen despatched a convoy of vehicles from Nicosia up the Kyrenia road for this purpose soon after 1600hrs, ignoring the Leadership's stipulation that no more than one vehicle and two Finnish soldiers were to be sent. With some difficulty it reached Tjiklos at 1730hrs, having reported that Turkish troops were still attacking south from Orta Keuy, the action that was drawing Greek fire from the grammar school east of the airport. When HQ UNFICYP sought clearance for the convoy's return journey with the civilians, the Turks would give no guarantee of safe conduct. As by then it was dark and the convoy was already on its way but out of touch by radio, the Turks were told that the safety of the civilians rested with them. Radio contact was regained when the convoy reached the village of Geunyeli, where Turkish troops refused to allow it to go further, seemingly on account of suspicion that some of the families of mainland Greek officers were among those carried. Pullinen had no option but to order the convoy to return to Tjiklos, where the civilians were obliged to spend yet another night huddled together in the open under Finnish protection. There they awaited rescue in the British naval operation planned for the following morning.

CHAPTER FORTY-SEVEN

RESCUES ALONG THE NORTH COAST

He strolled casually through the rubble-strewn streets in the town where the night before Turkish tanks had been rolling by, firing as they went. He was immaculate in spotless white ducks with the insignia of a Commander of the British Navy on his shoulders. "My God – is he real?" cried one of the dozens of dirty and dishevelled holidaymakers who had spent four days huddled under mattresses as the battle raged around them. All he said was: "Good Morning! Sorry we're a bit late – we got delayed".

Angus Macpherson, *The Daily Mail*, London, 27 July 1974.

While foreign nationals were being evacuated from Nicosia and Famagusta by road, the Royal Navy frigates *Andromeda* and *Rhyl* were despatched to a position off Cape Andreas, the north-east tip of Cyprus, in anticipation of evacuating from north coast beaches on the morning of 22 July those who, due to the fighting, could not be reached by road; with them went the RFA *Olna*. Notice that the operation would start at first light on 22 July was broadcast by the BFBS during 21 July, but to the Royal Navy's chagrin discouragement then came from the British Embassy in Ankara, which reported strong Turkish objections and advised against proceeding in the face of these. When it was learnt that a general ceasefire was to take effect on the afternoon of 22 July, it was decided to postpone the operation until next morning. An announcement to this effect was broadcast by BFBS, which advised all concerned to remain where they were pending further instructions.

This-24 hour delay gave more time for planning and for the assistance of UNFICYP to be enlisted. The danger of mines on the beaches caused concern, but the National Guard stated that it was unable to provide guides through these (UNFICYP's later experience showed that no proper records had been kept of the location of minefields) and advised that foreign nationals should move along the coast road to Kyrenia for embarkation from the harbour, then still in Greek hands. HQ UNFICYP urged the National Guard to ensure that its troops afforded safe-conduct to those seeking evacuation and explained that it was British policy to exclude Cypriots of all communities from the operation. Appropriate assurances were received, although the National Guard would not permit civilians to move while fighting continued in the vicinity of Kyrenia.

For Captain C.R.P.C. Branson RN, Commander of the British naval Task Group and Commanding Officer of the helicopter commando carrier HMS *Hermes*, then stationed off the island's south coast, 22 July was a busy day:

The course of this day was marked by the extensive exchange of signals arising from grotesque Greek accusations to the effect that *Hermes* was assisting the Turks at Kyrenia and much else along these lines; that Greek submarines were in the area, for whose conduct the Greek staff could not hold themselves responsible, etc. – all quite hysterical, it seemed, and requiring lengthy replies as to past and present dispositions of British ships and meticulous denials of all these nonsensical Greek statements. It was a remarkable insight into the atmosphere prevailing in Athens! In the late afternoon I was ordered to land four Wessex helicopters for deployment in support of 40 Commando RM ashore *[in the Western SBA]*.

The situation now developed fast. . . . *Hermes* was ordered to proceed with HMS *Devonshire* *[guided missile destroyer]* to join the frigates already south of Cape Andreas, the aim being, once clearance had been given for the operation, that all ships should arrive off Kyrenia at first light on Tuesday 23rd to effect the evacuation. . . . At about 2100 *Hermes* and *Devonshire* proceeded at 25 knots to rendezvous with the frigates south of Cape Andreas . . . .

This was naturally a period of intense activity. Firstly, press representatives came on board by Sea King helicopter and had to be given a briefing. We then immediately got down to planning . . . in order to have an operation order out for all ships as soon as we could, working through the night. Much of the detailed administration required in *Hermes* *[for reception and care on board of evacuees]* had already been organized in anticipation and merely required final touches. I snatched a quick hour's rest en route between Cape Greco and Cape Andreas.[1]

Meanwhile appeals for help were reaching HQ UNFICYP from groups of foreign nationals cut off along the north coast, many of whom were suffering acutely following destruction of their hotels, lack of shelter in the blazing sun and shortages of food and water, not to mention fighting close by. There was little that UNFICYP could do except to advise them to stay put, listen to BFBS radio announcements and prepare for evacuation by sea next day. One such group, consisting of about 130 men, women and children, was being held under the wing of the Turkish army close to Five Mile Beach, where the main Turkish landing was in progress. During the morning a Turkish major telephoned[2] HQ UNFICYP requesting that they be taken off his hands. He spoke to Major D. Bamford (Canada), Operations Officer, who said he would investigate the situation and call back: when he did so, for whom should he ask? 'Tarzan,' replied the Turk, drawing Bamford's inevitable rejoinder 'Me Jane'. Exchanges between 'Tarzan' and 'Jane' continued at intervals throughout the day, the former pressing for the early removal of his charges and the latter explaining the need to await the British naval operation next morning. This group, whose number grew to over 200, reported later that it was well treated by the Turks, but suffered four wounded caused by Greek artillery fire. Others awaiting evacuation as night fell included isolated groups at Karavas and Ayios Yeorios (both west of Five Mile Beach) and those now returned to and sheltering with the Finns in Tjiklos camp; some wounded were reported at each location.

It was estimated that as many as 2000 foreign nationals might still be awaiting rescue along the north coast, most of whom were holiday-makers of sundry nationalities scattered in hotels, apartments and villas on the coast or in the mountains above. There was also a significant number of resident expatriates, nearly all elderly, who by now were suffering acute hardship with no electricity, refrigerated food rotting, and supplies including water lacking; added stresses were imposed by fighting in the close vicinity, airstrikes, naval bombardments, forest fires and the activities of trigger-happy men on both sides intent on food, water or loot: all this while exceptionally hot weather prevailed. Typical were the experiences recorded by an expatriate in his diary as night fell on 22 July:

2010 Have now emptied fridge of all food except eggs and bacon. It was smelling to high heaven. Will have a biscuit and cheese and coffee (less milk). Firing now stopped – forest fires burning on lower mountain slopes. . . . Wind now dropped and hot as hell.

2045 In fact had a water biscuit and butter for dinner – cheese was bad. Have not much food left . . . – no electricity – no water. . . . Vilely hot and no wind. Fires burning and small arms fire broken out all around. . . .³

With cries for help flowing in from many directions it became clear that the Royal Navy would need assistance ashore in organizing evacuees, advising them of boat or helicopter pick-up points and guiding and escorting them to these, as well as in dealing with any difficulties caused by Greek or Turkish forces. It was no less clear that, given its local knowledge, good communications and links with both sides, UNFICYP alone was in a position to render this. When towards evening the British High Commission asked me to organize this (and General Prem Chand immediately gave his consent), I decided to form a small team for the purpose under Major P.N. Gill (UK), the able artillery officer commanding UNFICYP's currently grounded Army Aviation Flight; it proved a happy choice. Given free rein to select for his team any available men he chose and warned to be ready to leave for Kyrenia at first light next morning, he lost no time in getting together a multi-national team, soon known as 'GILLFORCE', consisting of a troop of four Ferret scout cars of the Parachute Squadron RAC, five radio-equipped Land Rovers and an ambulance, a total of 26 men.

Meanwhile BFBS broadcasts advised those wishing to be evacuated by the Royal Navy to gather next morning (23 July) near beaches (Six Mile Beach east of Kyrenia in particular) or in the port itself; baggage was to be limited to one suitcase each. During the night the British Defence Adviser, Colonel Hunter, provided UNFICYP with information covering such matters as radio frequencies and call-signs for communication with the naval Task Group. Informed that no evacuation by either boat or helicopter would start before 0700hrs on 23 July, HQ UNFICYP notified HQ National Guard accordingly and warned of the move of GILLFORCE from Nicosia at dawn.

Uncertainty persisted as to whether Ankara's agreement would be forthcoming, but after consulting the British High Commission (which stated that London had given approval for the operation to proceed), I ordered Gill and his team to leave for Tjiklos at 0530hrs, calling en route at the British High Commission for up-to-date briefing:

At the High Commission I met Colonel Hunter and the High Commissioner, Mr Olver, who told me that we still had not got clearance from either the Greeks or the Turks, but that he felt that we should make a move towards Kyrenia to evacuate the tourists. . . . With a certain amount of trepidation we left the High Commission building and moved through the battle zone. . . . However, without incident we arrived at Tjiklos Camp to find approximately 200 tourists already waiting to move in convoy to either Kyrenia or Nicosia. The majority of these people were Greek nationals and my brief had been that neither Greek nationals, Turkish nationals nor any Cypriots would be allowed to be evacuated *[by the Royal Navy]*. So I had to tell them to wait and only those other nationals in the immediate area of Tjiklos were allowed to move down to Six Mile Beach.[4]

The Task Group had assembled off Cape Andreas at about 0200hrs and Branson was given authority to sail on west, only to encounter further frustration:

Even now I received a further injunction not to proceed beyond 33° 30' West *[16km east of Kyrenia]*, no doubt all part of the business of awaiting Turkish agreement. The ships had all to be very clearly identifiable – great Union flags and ensigns spread on sides and decks – to avoid any false moves by the Turks . . . and all the while pumping out the message on voice radio that this was a British force on an errand of mercy. As I recall, we even had the formation we should adopt suggested by the Embassy in Ankara in order to look the least warlike possible. However, I swallowed all this, realizing that it was well meant, however inappropriate.[5]

The Turkish government was still objecting and had declared that it would not accept responsibility for the safety of any British ships or aircraft that entered the previously notified exclusion zone, but, in spite of further warnings from an apprehensive British Embassy in Ankara, London authorized the operation to proceed.

Instructed to keep the main elements of his Task Group some 16km off the coast, Branson sent helicopters to reconnoitre beaches between Kyrenia and Stazousa Point (26km to its east). These reported that the main concentration of people awaiting evacuation was at Six Mile Beach, with smaller groups gathered elsewhere. He also ordered *Andromeda* to investigate the situation in Kyrenia itself, as her Commanding Officer, Captain R.W.F. Gerken RN, has described:

I was delighted to be ordered to proceed to Kyrenia and as *Andromeda* made best speed towards the port I decided that my aim would be to anchor close off the harbour entrance so that the ship's boats could be employed ferrying off evacuees, and that an urgent first step was to speak to both the UN personnel and those wishing to escape. I had no knowledge of the situation in Kyrenia but put full trust in the announced ceasefire. . . . I decided to go ashore myself, taking with me a radio operator to maintain the link with my First Lieutenant, Lieut. Commander M.S. Pringle, who took over the direction of affairs on board. . . . As the ship closed the shore just before seven o'clock the first thing which was noticed was a throng of people on an open space close by the shore and on what proved to be the verandah of the Dome Hotel. Many were waving and a large Union flag was held up.[6]

No sooner was *Andromeda* lying to anchor off the port than Gerken was ordered to weigh immediately and rejoin *Hermes* out at sea:

My own view of the people thronging the hotel verandah and the apparent peaceful air of the place led me to make a signal to Peter Branson asking for permission to land but this was refused, and with thoughts of the virtues of the blind eye and a telescope to put to it, I ordered . . . the anchor to be weighed. On board we could sense the disappointment of the crowd ashore, and as *Andromeda* gathered speed a heliograph started flashing from the balcony of the hotel but the message could not be read.[7]

The problem had been caused by a warning sent by the Turkish High Command direct to HQ BFNE not to proceed with the operation, obliging Aiken to suspend action while matters were sorted out between London and Ankara. Branson was as vexed as Gerken by what he saw as further vacillation:

> This was, to say the least, embarrassing on three counts: firstly, *Andromeda* had encouraged people to come down to the jetty to be taken off by boat; secondly, people on Six Mile Beach had seen ships and helicopters and now expected prompt action; and finally, we were enjoying a calm spell ashore with no firing evident and therefore were wasting time. However, retire we duly did – shamefacedly and not without violent protests from Captain Bob Gerken in *Andromeda*.[8]

Meanwhile liaison had been established between the Task Group and GILLFORCE. At UNFICYP's request an RN officer, Commander A. Hutton (*Hermes* Executive Officer, whom Branson had earmarked to act as Beachmaster at Six Mile Beach), flew by helicopter to Tjiklos Camp, where he met Gill just as *Andromeda* was heading out to sea again. Quickly agreeing a plan for the role of GILLFORCE, they flew together to *Hermes*, where this was discussed with and confirmed by Branson:

> Commander Hutton, initially stuck ashore, was soon brought off by helicopter with the UN officer, Major Gill (a British officer of the Army Air Corps), who impressed me in every way. We now went over the plan they had both agreed, which was to concentrate on Six Mile Beach, bringing people there by road convoys, as this seemed clear of trouble and offered good pick-up points for helicopters on the coastal road. The beach itself was rather liberally marked with signs announcing "Danger – Mines" . . .
>
>   Major Gill was not keen that we should extend operations westward at first, though he appreciated that many people including a number of casualties were congregated there. His own idea was to send UN people there, establish liaison with whatever military forces controlled those areas and then effect withdrawal of evacuees to Six Mile Beach by road convoy under UN flag. All very elaborate and time-consuming, especially when helicopters could very easily go in and pluck people out from most places where they had assembled. Major Gill was also rather hesitant about any operations in Kyrenia itself, despite *Andromeda's* report that all was quiet there. But I went along with his concept initially to save further time-wasting.[9]

They agreed that evacuation from Six Mile Beach should be by helicopter rather than boat, both on account of the mine danger and because the existing sea state was likely to make boat-work difficult.

After urgent exchanges between London and Ankara, stressing the essentially humanitarian nature of the operation, Branson was given clearance at about 0800hrs to resume his mission. Gill returned to Tjiklos accompanied by *Rhyl's* Gunnery Officer who remained in the Finnish camp for the rest of the operation, providing a radio link between GILLFORCE and the Task Group. (Gill himself spent the day moving around throughout the area, leaving at Tjiklos another member of his team, Captain N.R. Pullman (UK), commander of UNFICYP's Signals Troop, as his link with both the RN officer and HQ UNFICYP.)

Civilians gathered at Tjiklos and eligible for evacuation by the Royal Navy were escorted by the Finns to Six Mile Beach to join others already gathered there. A Finnish officer, who kept HQ UNFICYP informed of progress, marshalled them all on the coast road, from which they were ferried out to *Hermes* in Wessex helicopters. On board they were greeted with kindness and efficiency:

> *Hermes* produced heart-warming stories – of tables with food and coffee stuck among parked helicopters; of tough sailors who admitted to a lump in the throat as holiday-makers were whisked on board after huddling on beaches with battle raging around them; of the playroom for children with toys seemingly plucked from a magician's hat; of comforting survivors, young and old, frail and infirm, with frightening stories to tell.
>
> Ship's doctor Surgeon Commander Peter Bond said: "We had three to four nurses who offered help. We couldn't have got by without them. We had pregnant ladies, a two-day-old baby, three women in their 90s and one who had had a heart attack that morning, a man recovering from a stroke, 20 to 30 with minor flesh wounds, plus three major cases, two of which were operated on that afternoon". Commander Bond added laconically: "It's not often a naval doctor at sea gets so much to do".
>
> The Second-in-Command of *Hermes*, Commander Anthony Hutton, said that there were lots of tears and emotion. Cabins were turned over to families and the cafeteria worked non-stop dispensing hot coffee. "There was an unceasing flow of questions. Bottles, nappies and nippers suddenly became our lot for 36 hours. I have never known the sailors in this ship to be more warm-hearted, more hospitable and more determined to go out of their way to help".[10]

It was a story that was repeated in all the other ships of the British Task Group.

Retaining *Hermes, Devonshire* and *Olna* off Six Mile Beach, Branson sent *Andromeda* back to Kyrenia to begin evacuation, using ship's boats, and *Rhyl* was ordered further west in support of her helicopter reconnoitring that area. Meanwhile Gill had gone to Kyrenia where he found about 300 holiday-makers (including five wounded) gathered at the Dome Hotel, another 70 at a second hotel and a further group that included 40 members of a Ukrainian dance troupe at a third.[11] Those at the Dome Hotel, looking tired and dirty, though cheerful at the prospect of rescue at last, had been organized into a convoy of cars ready to leave for Six Mile Beach as Gerken came ashore from *Andromeda*:

> Once back in the anchorage – it was 0910 by then – I immediately embarked in the boats with the landing party and we made for the harbour. No arms were carried and I had ordered all hands to be dressed in white uniforms, since this seemed appropriate during a ceasefire and I wanted no possible mis-identification between my people and the Greek or Turkish factions ashore. For my own part I had custody of an ebony cane with a silver knob which my pre-decessor as Captain F6 had left behind when I relieved him. This item seemed the perfect accoutrement to lend authority in any parley with the Turkish army or Greek Cypriot militia, and whilst holding the cane I could not be suspected of being about to brandish a fire arm. . . .
> On into the main harbour where yachts, motor boats and local fishing craft lay alongside the jetties, silent, no soul aboard and in all the buildings the shutters hid their interiors, nobody

looked out – all was still. My first objective was the Dome Hotel, and as we moved across the open space towards the building we saw people and cars and a comforting blue beret of the UN Force amongst them all.[12]

This was Gill. They agreed that those not in the convoy about to leave should be embarked in *Andromeda*. Gerken wasted no time: with his landing party acting as porters, people were shepherded down to the jetty and into the boats to be ferried to the ship. In mid-morning, with the task at Six Mile Beach progressing well, Branson sent *Olna* to join *Andromeda* and took *Hermes* inshore to launch her landing craft (LCVP) to augment the lift provided by *Andromeda*'s boats. All the while helicopters continued the shuttle service onto *Hermes, Devonshire* and *Olna* from Six Mile Beach and, later, from landing points marked out at hotels in Kyrenia itself.

The Finns monitored the military situation in Kyrenia District, kept local Greek and Turkish forces informed of what was happening and assisted in the evacuation operation by providing escorts and guides. Their Commander, Lieut. Colonel Pullinen, and his Medical Officer, Major J. Sorasto, together with an ambulance, made their way from Nicosia to Tjiklos to see the situation for themselves and render medical aid. He arranged for those civilians still at Tjiklos, who either were ineligible for evacuation by the Royal Navy or who did not wish to avail themselves of this, to be escorted back to Nicosia by road. After attending to casualties in the camp Sorasto set off along the coast road west of Kyrenia to give aid to any in need. (He reached the Mare Monte Hotel 10km west of Kyrenia before Turks at a field medical post deprived him of his medical supplies and he was obliged to turn back.)

Turkish forces had succeeded in penetrating the outskirts of Kyrenia the previous evening, but were not yet in control of the town or its castle, where some National Guard were still holding out. The Finns reported at 0835hrs that six Turkish tanks were at Tjiklos and that their commander had stated that he intended to attack the castle. Pullinen persuaded him not to enter the town, much less mount such an attack, but evidently the Turk then received further orders. At 1115hrs the tanks and a company of infantry were reported to be advancing into Kyrenia and towards noon the Turkish tank commander issued an ultimatum: he would open fire on the castle in 20 minutes time unless UNFICYP persuaded its garrison to surrender.

Since *Andromeda* and *Olna* were anchored in the tanks' field of fire beyond the castle and ship's boats were passing to and fro close beneath its walls, this caused alarm. Branson took *Hermes* further out to sea and ordered *Andromeda* and *Olna* to follow. *Olna* complied, but, when Gerken replied that he thought it safe for *Andromeda* to continue as a UN officer appeared to have the situation under control Branson gave him discretion to do so.[13] The UN officer who defused this dangerous situation was Pullinen himself; as soon as he learnt of the Turk's ultimatum he went to the castle and, displaying great courage, entered it alone only to find it deserted, its Greek defenders having fled. The Turkish troops were reluctant to accept his word to this effect, but, after some persuasion and nervously keeping their distance, they followed him into the castle, where a Turkish flag was then raised without a shot being fired.

As this drama was acted out, Branson took *Hermes* back to join *Devonshire* off Six Mile

Beach, where evacuees were arriving in reduced numbers. With the task here nearing its end (Gill reported at 1400hrs that all evacuation east of Kyrenia had been completed), Branson turned attention to the area west of Kyrenia, where helicopter reconnaissance had disclosed groups of people gathered near several large, but now burnt-out, hotels. *Rhyl* had been working back eastward from Vavilas (18km west of Kyrenia) picking up some people in her Wasp helicopter and reporting the locations of others; these were plotted in *Hermes's* operations centre, which then tasked Wessex helicopters to pick them up. It was, Branson commented, rather like a Commando landing operation in reverse.

In spite of a rising sea *Andromeda* and *Olna* were continuing to embark people from Kyrenia by boat and helicopter. By early afternoon when the last evacuees had been taken off, *Andromeda* had a full complement of some 200.[14] All were made to feel at home with a shower, a meal and a rest in the bunks of their hosts. (Gerken's own cabin was made over to a member of the French Embassy and his wife and five children, one born only three days earlier as fighting raged.) *Andromeda* was ordered to sail west-about to deliver her charges to Akrotiri and Gerken prepared to leave:

> With Kyrenia clear of evacuees the place had a desolate look and it was impossible to tell whether the houses and shops contained any inhabitants or not. Shutters were up everywhere, though where shop windows were not covered the glass was in good shape and unbroken with the goods all on display. I bade farewell to the UN Force's people and our embarkation party returned to the ship.[15]

The remainder of the Task Group worked westwards, the evacuation operation proceeding methodically by the use of helicopters. At some points difficulties were experienced with Turkish troops, but Branson found a Turkish-speaker among the evacuees who volunteered to help sort out the problems:

> A most impressive figure of a man came forward . . . and this did the trick, though not before our helicopter pilots had had some quite unpleasant experience of interference from Turkish soldiers.[16]

For the holiday-makers, many by now in dire straits, there could not have been a more welcome sight than the Royal Navy's helicopters overhead:

> Then a helicopter came over us, counting. More waves and cheers. More helicopters and a small naval landing party, including a UN officer, appeared and evacuation began. One of the smartest bits of taxi-work I have ever seen – as soon as one helicopter lifted off another was there. Some sixty of us, with a case apiece, were lifted off in what seemed a matter of minutes. Yet there was no impression of hurry or strain.[17]

Helped by the Finns, GILLFORCE scoured the area for further evacuees whose locations were then passed to *Hermes* for helicopters to be tasked to collect them. Gill ensured that wherever possible there was a UN presence at pick-up points to deal with problems like those encountered by some pilots and his team marked out suitable landing sites:

Everything went very well and my only complaint was that on occasions an enthusiastic pilot would ignore or fail to see our marker panels, indicating a relatively dust-free pick-up point, and fly to a point as near the tourists as possible, sometimes on the side of a cliff, and invariably cover us all in sand and muck.[18]

The problem of Greek or Turkish Cypriots (especially those who held British passports) and Greek nationals, all of whom as a matter of British policy were ineligible for evacuation, often reared its head.[19] At the Dome Hotel Gerken had had to refuse the pleas of Cypriot hotel staff to be taken off and GILLFORCE, faced with similar entreaties elsewhere, sometimes had to turn a blind eye in order not to slow down the operation while arguments over eligibility took place. A particular problem was posed by the US Radio Station at Karavas, the staff of which included Cypriots, all of whom the US Embassy wished evacuated. Finding about 40 employees ready to leave, Gill called for helicopters and explained to the Station Chief the restriction on those ineligible to be picked up. The latter became agitated, but Gill calmed him by remarking that probably all were already on their way even as they spoke. He was right; the Station Chief barely had time to gather his own possessions and clamber aboard the last aircraft.

As the evacuation operation neared completion in mid-afternoon Branson ordered *Olna* to sail east-about to disembark her Ukrainians at Dhekelia (the Soviet Embassy having arranged for Eastern bloc nationals to be embarked at nearby Larnaca in a Soviet ship, *Baskira*, due to sail for Odessa next morning), but when a Turkish naval group was detected approaching Cyprus from the north-east *Olna* was ordered to turn about and follow *Andromeda* west-about. *Devonshire*, now also with a full complement of evacuees embarked, was also sailed for Akrotiri west-about. Branson then was requested to check areas bordering on Morphou Bay, in particular the CMC hospital at Pendayia, for foreign nationals in need of rescue; *Andromeda's* and *Devonshire's* helicopters did so, the former's drawing a blank and the latter's landing at the hospital, only to be told by the staff that they were determined to stay. A final sweep back towards Kyrenia was made by *Hermes* and *Rhyl*, the latter recovering her Gunnery Officer who throughout had played a key part at Tjiklos as the link between the Task Group and GILLFORCE.

The Turkish naval group detected earlier appeared unwilling to become entangled with the Royal Navy Task Group, for when *Hermes* signalled her identity, it had turned away to the north. Comprising the frigate *Berk* (which was to join *Andromeda* next day in the rescue of the *Kocatepe* survivors), two other escorts, a tank landing ship and a transport, this Turkish group now hove into sight, believing, perhaps, that the westward movement of British ships indicated that the evacuation operation had been completed:

The presence of *Hermes* and *Rhyl* still there before the old town of Kyrenia must have startled them. I therefore felt that this was the moment to call it a day, and we made off westwards ourselves. In doing so I had to cancel arrangements for the recovery of four wounded National Guard soldiers whom the UN officer ashore was particularly anxious we should take off on humanitarian grounds *[HQ National Guard had requested HQ UNFICYP to arrange this]*. As the ships moved slowly along the coast, helicopters continued to look carefully for stragglers and found a few. By 1730 the evacuation was completed and I now detached *Rhyl* to go ahead, with the Press party also embarked. Some 1530 people had been evacuated, of many nationalities.[20]

Some expatriate residents along the north coast, most of whom were elderly and retired, decided to remain, for Cyprus was their only home; they preferred, they said, the uncertainties of life under the Turks to the prospect of becoming refugees. For those who did leave, expatriates and others alike, pathos and problems were all too evident — the elderly abandoning their home and possessions of a lifetime save what could be carried in a single suitcase; women and children separated from their menfolk, as the former were taken off first, and household pets abandoned to their fate.

In ships of the Task Group sick bays and medical staffs were busy dealing with many cases of shock, the very elderly and the wounded, but a calm and uneventful passage round Cape Kormakiti and the Akamas peninsula, past Paphos and on to the anchorage off Akrotiri (reached by *Andromeda* at about 2100hrs and by the remainder in the early hours of 24 July) did much to restore morale. The orderliness and discipline encountered in the British ships were in stark contrast to the recent experiences of many of the evacuees. As the island's coast slipped by, bathed first by a spectacular setting sun and then lit by fiercely burning forest fires, those in *Olna* enjoyed a special diversion:

> We landed on *Olna*, a Fleet Auxiliary oil-tanker. Wonderful welcome, meals, first aid, messages home. . . . Incredible feeling of calm, security and total insulation from All That. Like a cruise ship, which in a sense it was. Plus one picturesquely improbable event. The ship carried a Russian troupe of dancers rescued from Kyrenia, who put on a floor show for us. We sat on planks across oil drums and watched wild Ukrainian dancing, while Cyprus and occasional flashings and burnings moved slowly past as a background. Quite surrealist.[21]

Andromeda's passengers were taken off on reaching Akrotiri and disembarkation of the remainder took place next morning. The organization was efficient and sympathetic:

> We were processed, registered, we filled up forms and were given cups of tea, bussed to an airfield *[Akrotiri]*, loaded into a plane, fed and flown to Fairford *[England]*. Then bus to Brize Norton, the main reception centre, and finally bus to Paddington *[London]*. Wherever we went there were people offering clothes, food, tea, information, help, It was marvellously done.[22]

Feelings of admiration and gratitude on the part of those rescued were matched by the sentiments of sailors of the Task Group:

> This day was summed up for me by Leading Seaman Wakeling *[coxswain of one of Andromeda's boats]* when I went . . . to tell him that he was to receive the Commander-in-Chief's Commendation. He said: "It was the most worth-while day of my life".[23]

For his part Gill reported:

All in all it was an exhausting but thoroughly worth-while and enjoyable day that appeared to speed by without a hitch, thanks to the magnificent professionalism of the Royal Navy.[24]

GILLFORCE had provided demonstration of how a few disciplined and well-led men can play a valuable part out of all proportion to their number, a circumstance common in UN peacekeeping forces in time of crisis. Without their assistance the highly successful British operation could not have been accomplished so smoothly, speedily or thoroughly. Nonetheless, UNFICYP's contribution received scant recognition: published UN documents omit all mention of it and no official expression of appreciation came from Britain. The latter's omission may have been due not only to preoccupation with its own problems but also to ignorance of the part played by GILLFORCE; that of the UN probably was attributable to two other circumstances. First was the generally negative attitude of the UN Secretariat in New York in publicizing the military activities of its peacekeeping forces, an attitude reflected in the inadequate provision at HQ UNFICYP for handling public information matters. The second, and perhaps more immediate, reason was that throughout 23 July attention at UN Headquarters was focused on serious developments at Nicosia airport (described in the following chapter) which were posing a major threat to the maintenance of the fragile general ceasefire. For New York the humanitarian operation being conducted under British auspices was not an immediate concern.

As Gill watched *Hermes* and *Rhyl* sailing west into the setting sun, he was already giving thought to what now needed to be done. Kyrenia was reported quiet and the Austrian UNCIVPOL detachment was ordered to re-establish its post in the town. Gill himself returned to the Dome Hotel, where he found about 200 Greek Cypriots, including a few members of the National Guard, as well as some Greek and other nationals who for various reasons had not wished to be evacuated by the Royal Navy. With the arrival in the town of Turkish troops all were apprehensive, if not frightened. Gill was concerned for their safety and for that of pockets of Greek Cypriots elsewhere now cut off in areas overrun by the Turks. Reporting this concern to HQ UNFICYP, he was ordered to leave a small UN party in the Dome Hotel as reassurance for people there, to send the Parachute Squadron, RAC, troop, back to Nicosia and to withdraw with the remainder of his team to Tjiklos for the night, ready to resume humanitarian tasks in and around Kyrenia in the morning. Throughout the next three weeks GILLFORCE maintained a UN presence in the Dome Hotel and, in a remarkable saga of humanitarian endeavour in the highest tradition of UN peacekeepers, brought succour and comfort in the face of numerous difficulties to many civilians of various nationalities throughout the area who now found themselves under Turkish sway.

CHAPTER FORTY-EIGHT

CRISIS AT NICOSIA AIRPORT

In the Nicosia area, after a quiet night, fighting developed in the vicinity of the airport at 0930 hours and continued throughout the morning until 1230 hours, when the Chief of Staff of UNFICYP arranged a ceasefire. The airport was declared a United Nations-controlled area, and was occupied by UNFICYP troops after National Guard troops had agreed to withdraw.

UN Secretary General, *S/11353/ADD.4*, 23 July 1974, para. 4.

Behind this laconic report lay a bold initiative on the part of General Prem Chand. Although next day it nearly plunged UNFICYP into a fight with the Turkish forces, with the grave international repercussions that this would have entailed, it proved in the event to have been an outstanding demonstration of effective peacekeeping action by a UN Force.

In July 1974 the Republic of Cyprus's only international airport was that at Nicosia[1] and was thus of importance to both sides. It also had a special significance for the Turkish Cypriots who since December 1963 had been allowed no part in its control or administration, these being in the exclusive hands of Greek Cypriot officials, some of whom were not averse to humiliating Turkish Cypriots passing through custom and immigration procedures. For these reasons capture of the airport was the third of the Turks' three initial objectives, but the slow progress of their forces had resulted in failure to seize it before the 1600hrs ceasefire accepted by Ankara was due to take effect. Whether or not Prime Minister Ecevit was aware of this failure is unclear. Some suspect that he had been assured by his generals that all three initial objectives would have been achieved by the 1600hrs deadline and that the generals, unwilling to admit this failure, were intent on rectifying it as soon as possible in disregard of the agreed ceasefire. Whatever the truth, subsequent events point to confusion in Ankara during the next 48 hours as to the situation at the airport.

The airstrike on it 45 minutes after the 1600hrs ceasefire can only have been deliberate, but at the time HQ UNFICYP was inclined to the view that the Turkish purpose was no more than pre-emptive: to ensure that the airport could not be used for another attempt to land reinforcements from Greece. Similarly, ground fighting which continued after 1600hrs as Turkish troops pushed south towards the airport could be attributed, we thought, to difficulties in passing ceasefire orders to those on the ground. UNFICYP had no reason to doubt the Turkish government's commitment to its agreement for a ceasefire and (despite sporadic

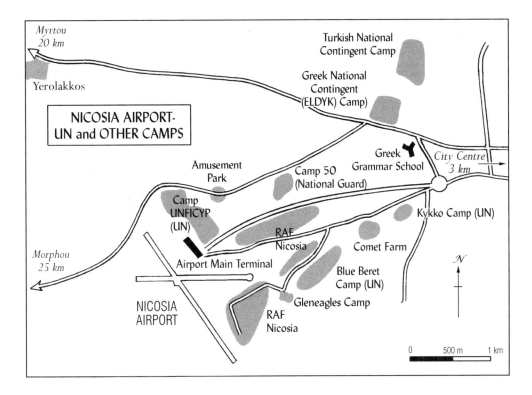

Myrtou
20 km

Yerolakkos

NICOSIA AIRPORT-
UN and OTHER CAMPS

Turkish National
Contingent Camp

Greek National
Contingent
(ELDYK) Camp)

Amusement
Park

Camp 50
(National Guard)

Greek
Grammar School

City Centre
3 km

Camp
UNFICYP
(UN)

RAF
Nicosia

Kykko Camp (UN)

Comet Farm

Morphou
25 km

Airport Main Terminal

Blue Beret
Camp (UN)

NICOSIA
AIRPORT

Gleneagles Camp

RAF
Nicosia

N

0   500 m   1 km

shooting in the area during the night of 22 July) no reason to suspect that the Turks were still intent on capture of the airport.

But early on 23 July, while GILLFORCE was making its way to Kyrenia, the situation took an ominous turn as Turkish troops, identified as part of the Turkish National Contingent, advanced towards the airport and some penetrated the perimeter wire fence into Camp UNFICYP which lay in their path. Major Barker (UK), Camp Commandant, described their reception:

> They were met by British soldiers . . . *[who]* did not threaten or point a weapon but said: "You can't come in here – this is a UN camp". The Turks could speak no English but the meaning was clear. In fact some could speak French or German. RSM Birch (UK) *[Camp Regimental Sergeant Major]* spoke the latter fluently and I managed to scratch up enough of the former to explain to one of their officers that everything in sight, bar the airport terminal building, was UN property. So they withdrew to the wood to the east of the camp.[2]

The approaching Turks, including at least one M47 tank and a M113 APC, had been seen by the National Guard in the airport and firing broke out, much of it passing over or through the UN camp. With a battle in prospect it became a matter of urgency for UNFICYP to halt the Turkish advance and the shooting to which it was giving rise; to this end the immediate despatch of a UN officer to each side was required. The gravity of the situation pointed the need for a senior officer to deal with the Turks and to coordinate the defence of UN camps in the immediate vicinity; this task was given to Colonel C.E. Beattie (Canada), the Force DCOS:

> Brigadier Henn asked me to go to the area to take command of local security arrangements and, if possible, to find the local Turkish commander and have the attack turned off. . . . I telephoned the CANCON Logistics Operations Centre in Blue Beret Camp and told the Duty Officer that I wanted a protection party organized – two Jeeps with troops and weapons. . . . The Jeeps arrived as ordered, one of them with a .30 calibre machine gun mounted on the hood. . . . I proceeded to Camp UNFICYP with this protection party. . . . I had told the Camp Commandant that we would come in under the wire . . . and using rifles we lifted the concertina wire over the Jeeps and quickly passed through. At the time there was shooting from the airport in the direction of the Morphou road, where the Turks were moving up, and from the National Guard in the JATC [*Joint Air Traffic Control*] building, which dominates the whole approach from the north. . . . We got into Camp UNFICYP without problem and I was met by the Camp Commandant, Major Barker.[3]

The officer sent to deal with the National Guard in the airport was Major J.R. Herbert (UK), the officer commanding UNFICYP's 7 Transport Squadron RCT based in Camp UNFICYP, who was already on good terms Major Papadopoulos, the airport's Greek commander.[4] He took with him his second-in-command, Captain B.W. Faulkener (UK):

> As Captain Faulkener and I drove towards the airport terminal, firing broke out on both sides. For the first time we were taken inside the terminal into a ground floor room facing the runway apron. . . . The situation was tense to say the least, and the scene in the room was made even more dramatic by the presence of a Russian-built T-34 tank which had been backed through the plate-glass window into the room. To add emphasis to its size the engine was running. The scene was one of pandemonium as 20 or so officers prepared for a battle which they fully intended to fight to the last man.[5]

Meanwhile Barker had briefed Beattie on the situation, shown him where the Turks had penetrated the perimeter wire of Camp UNFICYP and pointed out the small wood some 50m beyond into which they had withdrawn. He said that there had been some shooting on the Morphou road itself (along which several Greek civilian and military vehicles had been stopped) and he estimated that the Turks were in company strength in the area of the wood and a small amusement park and bar (known as the Arcadi Bar) just behind it, with the remainder of a battalion group closing up from a northerly direction. Beattie realized that he would have to go out through the wire in order to make personal contact with the local Turkish commander, ascertain his intentions and halt the advance that was drawing Greek fire. He decided to take with him his driver, Corporal Berikoff (Canada), carrying a man-pack radio and asked for a British representative to join them to give the party a multi-national complexion; Captain D.W. Miles (UK), Camp UNFICYP's Adjutant, at once volunteered to do so.[6] Brandishing a UN flag, the three crawled out under the wire and made a dash over open ground to the cover of the small wood, hurried on their way by Greek fire from the terminal and JATC buildings.

Turkish soldiers in the wood were surprised to see them, but not hostile, and amidst the noise and confusion Beattie tried to discover the whereabouts of the local Turkish commander. After some 25 minutes of fruitless search,during which the three twice had to go to ground as bullets came close, he saw a group of Turks at the amusement park which he thought might be the local command post. Making another dash over open ground, the three found it to be a collecting point where the Turks were holding about 35 prisoners taken from cars using the Morphou road, their occupants unaware that it had been cut by the advancing Turks:

> Some drivers who had tried to escape by driving on or firing at the troops had been killed and their bodies (approximately 14 in all) were strewn along the road for a distance of 400m. Shortly after our arrival . . . two cars, which included two women with children, were brought into the amusement park. I successfully negotiated their release by talking to a Turkish captain who understood some French. Then Captain Miles agreed to accompany them as escort along the Morphou road to the safety of Camp UNFICYP. By this time we had experienced communications difficulties *[the man-pack radio was not functioning]* and I requested that he also arrange suitable communications between our party and the airport in order that we could conduct negotiations with both sides. Captain Miles took the UN flag and successfully completed these tasks.[7]

Shooting had continued all the while and, when Beattie observed an estimated two companies of Turkish infantry and possibly a troop of tanks moving up to join those already in the wood, he realized that time was short if an attack on the airport was to be averted. Noticing a civilian telephone in a building in the amusement park, he persuaded the Turkish captain to kick in the door for him and found the telephone to be still working:

> I telephoned the Force Commander's office . . . and obtained the telephone number of the Turkish Embassy from his secretary. I also told the Force Commander where I was and what I was trying to do. Then I telephoned the Turkish Embassy and got hold of Mr Karaca, who was the Counsellor. I told him where I was and asked him to tell the Turkish captain to take me to his battalion commander; this he did. Thus I was able to get to the battalion commander.[8]

Noting that the battalion commander, Major Varol, had a radio-equipped Jeep (the Turkish infantry appeared to lack radios below the level of battalion HQ), Beattie asked to be taken at once to Varol's superior and was then whisked in this Jeep back to a villa near Orta Keuy some 6km away where he met Colonel Katircioglu, commander of the Turkish National Contingent – clear evidence that it was this officer who was directing the advance on the airport.[9] Beattie urged him to comply with the ceasefire accepted by Ankara and to halt the advance of his troops. Katircioglu was unforthcoming and Beattie returned to the area of the Morphou road without any such undertaking.

Beattie's telephone conversation with Prem Chand had suggested that the Turks either were unaware of the ceasefire agreement or were deliberately ignoring it, but there was still hope that his and Herbert's efforts might succeed. Miles had returned to the amusement park with Birch and the rest of Beattie's original party, bringing with them a replacement radio which allowed communication between Beattie and Herbert (messages being relayed through Barker in Camp UNFICYP). However, Beattie was experiencing difficulties with Varol:

> At about 1030hrs it was apparent to me that final preparations were being made to attack. He *[Varol]* kept going to his radio and didn't seem to be getting anything that he was prepared to tell me, and it didn't appear that he was prepared to turn off his preparations.[10]

When it became clear that the Turks were not to be stopped, Beattie and his party took cover to await the inevitable. At 1100hrs tank fire was opened:

> The firing just got heavier and they *[the infantry]* started to move . . . . I saw one of the first get hit and then there were more. The attack . . . advanced maybe 200m south of the road. At this point they started to take quite heavy casualties because of the firing from three directions – Camp 50, the JATC building, and the airport – and they were caught in the open field. . . . There was dry scrub and the ricochets started grass fires and these killed the wounded. Also the grass fires moved against the attackers and this didn't help them at all. At this point, as the attack faltered, I got word to *[Varol]* . . . that I would get the National Guard fire turned off if he would turn off the attack, and we went through a series of exchanges: "If they stopped shooting, we would pull back, etc." . . . We went through three unsuccessful ceasefire arrangements at about 20-minute intervals, and it was sometime after 1200 or 1215hrs that we actually got a ceasefire.[11]

Similar dangers and difficulties were encountered by Herbert in the airport terminal, where he was in contact with Barker by telephone:

> As the firing intensified and the wounded began to arrive at a medical aid post in the next room, tension mounted dramatically and the chances of negotiating a ceasefire receded in inverse proportions. Mutual hate and distrust were such that neither side was prepared to be the first to call a halt. Reasoned argument stood little chance in a room full of officers, by nature volatile and now agitated by anger and national fervour to the point of irrationality. Eventually the Camp Commandant *[Barker]* phoned to say that, as everything possible had been done to secure a ceasefire but without success, I should now try to get back to the camp. I decided, however, to make one final attempt and asked Mr Papioannou, the Airport Manager and a former RAF officer, to get Mr Papadopoulos back into the room.[12]

Pressing Papadopoulos to have the courage to order his men to stop firing, Herbert pointed to the futility of further fighting, which would only destroy the airport and cause more casualties to his own men and to the many civilians still in the building. He added, rashly, that, if the Greeks stopped firing, UNFICYP would ensure not only that the airport did not fall into Turkish hands but also that Turkish troops were withdrawn to north of the Morphou road. Quickly realizing that he had no authority to give any such undertakings, he then qualified what he had said. An angry Greek officer accused him of breaking his word and, when a soldier leapt forward, apparently to shoot him, Papadopoulos rushed between them and pushed the man aside. With tempers somewhat cooled, Papadopoulos decided to cooperate with Herbert and Beattie in exchanges that led to a tentative ceasefire at about noon.

It was clear by now that the Turkish action could not be attributed to an excess of zeal or ignorance of the ceasefire on the part of local Turkish commanders but was, rather, a deliberate attempt by the Turkish high command to make good the failure to capture the airport the previous day. It was no less clear that the Greeks were determined to prevent this. Throughout the morning they had been busy strengthening defences both at the airport and between it and Nicosia: UNFICYP observers reported buses and trucks rushing up infantry reinforcements, the movement of T-43 tanks and Marmon Harrington armoured cars, and the deployment of additional anti-tank and anti-aircraft guns. It was thus optimistic to expect that any local ceasefire achieved by Beattie and Herbert would prevail for long; the airport would remain a bone of contention. But any fight for it had serious implications: first was the danger to adjacent UN camps, especially Camp UNFICYP, which had already suffered in the crossfire[13] and which housed not only UNFICYP's logistic units and supplies but also the store of Czech weapons; the Greeks had been left in no doubt of UNFICYP's determination to resist by force any attempt to seize these weapons and there could be no question of allowing them to fall into Turkish hands. Second, the airport was now needed for the reception of UNFICYP reinforcements and civilian relief supplies: a battle was likely to inflict major damage and prevent its early use. Third, and for UNFICYP of overriding importance, any such fight would threaten maintenance of the already fragile island-wide ceasefire.

Earlier that morning (23 July) the National Guard commander, Brig. General Georgitsis, had visited HQ UNFICYP to discuss with Prem Chand the situation following the declaration of a ceasefire the previous day and had given assurances of the National Guard's cooperation to maintain this. As they spoke the situation at the airport seemed not to be giving Georgitsis undue concern, but the subsequent rapid deterioration alarmed the Greeks who feared not only loss of the airport but also the encirclement of Nicosia. These fears were voiced by Glafkos Clerides, then still President of the House of Representatives[14], in a telephone conversation with Prem Chand in which he suggested that, in order to avert a fight for the airport and consequential general breakdown of the ceasefire, the National Guard might withdraw from the airport and leave it in the hands of UNFICYP; he added that Georgitsis concurred in this suggestion.

Pondering the idea, Prem Chand recalled that in 1960 in the Congo the UN Force had taken over Leopoldville airport, a useful precedent, and he decided that the National Guard's willingness to cooperate rendered a take-over of Nicosia airport by UNFICYP a feasible proposition in spite of the Force's limited resources. The National Guard would be requested to vacate the airport forthwith and be replaced by UN troops, who would police it as a 'UN-protected area', to which entry would be denied to all others. It was a bold decision, for UNFICYP, already over-stretched and as yet lacking its promised reinforcements, would be able to muster only a small, almost token, force to take over the large airport. However, as is usual in UN peacekeeping operations, military weakness could be balanced in part by ensuring multi-national participation and consequential political strength. Nevertheless, the decision was a calculated gamble, for the likely Turkish reaction was an unknown factor.

Speed was essential. Prem Chand spoke at once by telephone to Mr George Sherry at UN Headquarters, New York, who in the absence of Waldheim (then consulting Kissinger in Washington) took it upon himself to give immediate approval for the intended action. Armed with this authority, HQ UNFICYP released a statement for promulgation by local radio and press, parallel messages being passed to both sides

> The United Nations Force in Cyprus is taking over the Nicosia International Airport temporarily after a new and serious breach of the ceasefire earlier this morning in the vicinity of the airport. The airport thus becomes a United Nations internationally protected area. This will at the same time facilitate the arrival of reinforcements for UNFICYP.[15]

No time was lost in mustering a multi-national UN group to take over from the National Guard. The British, Canadian and Finnish Contingents (those with men closest to the scene) were called upon and, since the airport lay within the operational boundary of the Canadians, Major J.D. Harries, Commander of the Canadian Logistic Base in Blue Beret Camp, was nominated to command the group; he at once organized an *ad hoc* company drawn from his own logistic personnel.

In the meantime Prem Chand had asked me to convene a meeting with the two opposing local commanders to inform them of UNFICYP's intention and notify them of the arrangements to be observed once the airport had come under UN protection. With the ceasefire achieved by Beattie soon after noon poised on a knife-edge, it was clear that the meeting needed to be held without delay. We decided that it should take place under the UN flag on neutral open ground about 200m east of Camp UNFICYP, and Beattie and Herbert were told to bring the respective local commanders to meet me there at once. Herbert acted quickly; leaving Faulkener in the terminal building as a communications link and taking Papadopoulos with him (as well as Papioannou as interpreter), he drove out from the airport proper to halt on the road skirting the southern edge of Camp UNFICYP. He has described the scene:

> To our rear over the crest of the rise was the airport terminal. On our right was the Joint Air Traffic Control Centre, which was being held as a strong point by the Greek airborne forces. On the left the ground was open and falling away into dead ground. Turkish infantry had been caught in heavy firing and a number of dead and wounded could be seen. The shelling had set fire to the grass and thick smoke and the smell of cordite enveloped us. It was apparent . . . that some members of the Turkish unit were still unaware of the ceasefire agreed by their commander and of the neutrality of the UN flag. . . . I walked back towards the corner of Camp UNFICYP which was being protected by Lieutenant Carter with B Troop, 7 Squadron RCT. I called for a UN flag; Lance Corporal Flay came out with one and together we walked back to the car with the flag prominently displayed. We noticed the Greek Special Forces moving from the JATC and Major Papadopoulos, realizing that this forward movement by his troops would jeopardise any possibility of maintaining the ceasefire, vigorously restrained his men. The Major and I stayed by the car while Lieutenant Carter walked further up the road to attempt to halt any further forward movement by the Greek soldiers.[16]

Concurrently I set out from Blue Beret Camp. Seeking to minimize tension by presenting a calm appearance, I drove without escort in my official black Mercedes flying its small UN flag, taking an additional driver, Lance Corporal Atkinson of 7 Squadron RCT, carrying a portable radio to allow me to speak to the JOC in Blue Beret Camp once we had left the radio-equipped car to go forward on foot to the meeting point (there had been no time to find a Turkish interpreter to accompany me, and the lack of one was to prove a handicap). Driving past the JATC building, where Greek soldiers eyed us suspiciously but did not halt us, we were met by Herbert. With much shouting and gesticulating at the Greeks in the JATC building, who were being frantically urged to halt all forward movement, we continued forward to the east corner of Camp UNFICYP to be greeted by the Camp's Quartermaster, Captain W.J. Bluck (UK), who emerged from the perimeter fence with a large UN flag. Dismounting and affecting to look as though nothing untoward was happening, we picked our way across rough ground to the proposed meeting point about 200m north of the road. Bluck led the way with his UN flag and was followed by me, Atkinson and the radio, Herbert with Papadopoulos and Papioannou, with Flay bringing up the rear. We were conscious of eyes at the airport, the JATC building and along the Morphou road watching our progress through drifting smoke, but no shots came from any direction. We reached a suitable position in this 'no man's land' just after 1230hrs and awaited the arrival of the local Turkish commander escorted by Beattie. It proved a long wait, as Beattie explained:

> We had trouble because the Turkish battalion commander didn't want to go forward to negotiate. I eventually convinced him to at least send a captain as a representative. I did so by climbing onto the roof of an abandoned bus and waving my UN flag. I then assured him that, as I had not been shot, then he would not be.[17]

Half an hour later Beattie appeared through the smoke with the French-speaking Turkish captain and the talking began, albeit hampered by the language problem.

There was no question of negotiations to secure agreement for UNFICYP's take-over of the airport: the unilateral decision to take this action had already been made by Prem Chand, endorsed by New York and announced publicly. It was, rather, a matter of agreeing conditions to be observed once the airport had become a UN-protected area. My plan was for UNFICYP to take over, not just the airport proper, but also the now abandoned premises of RAF Nicosia and its married quarters area, since these, together with the adjacent UN camps, formed a cohesive entity, most of which was bounded by an old wire perimeter fence (though broken in places). All these, I envisaged, would constitute the UN-protected area, to which all except UNFICYP would be denied access. I also intended that Greek Cypriot forces should be required to leave the airport within a stipulated time and that, following their replacement by UN troops, neither side should approach within a stipulated distance of the declared UN-protected area. With Papioannou interpreting, there was no problem in explaining this plan to the hoarse Papadopoulos. The latter was aware that Brig. General Georgitsis was willing to allow UNFICYP to take over the airport, but asked to return to the terminal building to consult about the conditions I proposed; his second-in-command was brought out to replace him. Discussion with the Turkish captain proved frustrating, not only due to language difficulties but also because it was clear that he had no authority to agree to anything. As time slipped by and we stood without shelter in the blazing midday sun in a temperature of over 40⁰ Centigrade, Bluck suggested that cool drinks might assist; a radio request to Camp UNFICYP produced the incongruous sight of two men in blue berets bearing a container of iced orange juice – welcome refreshment enjoyed by all, Greek and Turkish representatives included.

Meanwhile there had been little relaxation of tension, least of all in the airport terminal where Faulkener was experiencing difficulty in restraining the excitable Greek officers; at one point they even threatened his life. Matters became critical when he reported that the Greeks were claiming that they could see Turks advancing under cover of smoke and would not hold their fire any longer. I told him immediately to assure them that we were situated between the two sides and could see that there was no Turkish forward movement and no grounds for opening fire – the smoke was only burning grass; if they opened fire now, UNFICYP's efforts to arrange a peaceful settlement would be nullified. Faulkener replied that the Greeks accepted my assurance but that they remained much on edge. At this time the scratch company of Canadian logistic personnel under Harries had been halted at the JATC building by Greek troops who were refusing to allow it to go further. Harries judged that it would not be feasible to force a way through and was told to keep his men where they were, ready to move forward into the airport as soon as the outcome of my meeting was known.

I now learnt that the Turkish battalion commander, Major Varol, was ready to come forward to meet me, his earlier reluctance to do so having evidently been his need to obtain the necessary clearance from his superior. Beattie went back to bring him forward, returning with not only Varol but also Miles, Birch and a German-speaking Turkish corporal (like all others, they were required to divest themselves of their weapons before joining the discussion). By now it was about 1400hrs and we had been standing under the hot sun for one and a half hours. Rapid progress became possible. Through the medium of the German-speaking Birch and the German-speaking Turkish corporal, I told Varol of UNFICYP's decision, endorsed by New York, to take over the airport, and explained my plan to both sides:

- the whole of the airport complex, including RAF Nicosia, Camp UNFICYP and the RAF quarters area lying within the perimeter wire fence, was to be regarded as a UN-protected area.

- both sides must withdraw within one hour all troops to a point 500m beyond the perimeter wire and thereafter not approach within 500m of it.

- UNFICYP would patrol the perimeter by scout car and on foot at regular intervals.

- a UN officer would visit each side twice a day to see if either has any complaints or problems, and neither was to open fire before notifying these to the officer concerned.

- UNFICYP would establish check-points on the Morphou road to prevent Greeks in civilian cars from driving past Turkish posts along the road (this being the cause, so the Turks alleged, of the recent shooting).

The plan provoked little discussion and no objections and I reported to Prem Chand by radio that both local commanders had indicated acceptance and that in consequence all

Greek forces would vacate the airport by 1530hrs, when it would become a UN-protected area.

The meeting now dispersed, Beattie, Miles and Birch escorting the Turks back to the Morphou road, while the rest of us trudged back to our cars on the airport road. Urgent action was needed for time was short. With Harries and his company still held up (it took time for orders to reach the Greeks in the JATC building to allow them through), I told Herbert to continue to act as UNFICYP's LO in the airport and to hasten the departure of the National Guard within the stipulated one hour. He responded by organizing a UN escorting party for the departing Greeks and brought in some of his own men under Carter to take control of the terminal building. The Greeks were slow to withdraw but eventually left at about 1630hrs, the Greek officers shaking hands with Herbert and wishing him good luck. (Papadopoulos asked Herbert personally to escort him out of the area, which Herbert did.) The strength of the airport's Greek garrison, and the likely scale of the battle that had been averted, now became apparent. The departing National Guard force comprised two tanks, eight armoured cars, three APCs, five 100mm field guns, five vehicle-mounted quadruple MG and five towed Bofors AA guns, five Jeep-mounted 105mm recoilless anti-tank weapons, five truckloads of ammunition, and six busloads of troops. With them went some 60 civilian cars carrying members of the airport staff caught there for the past three days. All were escorted under Faulkener's command back into the city of Nicosia. As they left a Greek artillery battery withdrew from its position close to Blue Beret Camp and within the 500m zone.

Harries and his men were now able to enter the airport and were joined there by other UNFICYP troops, including a Finnish platoon from Kykko Camp and MPs of the Provost Company, who together with members of UNCIVPOL set up check-points on road approaches. A UN flag was hoisted over the terminal building, visible evidence that UNFICYP was now in occupation. The fact that the Force lacked the military strength to hold it in the face of determined attack was not of great consequence at this stage, for none thought that the Turks might try to eject UNFICYP. Nonetheless, prudence pointed the need for a defence plan consistent with the meagre resources available. Harries (in overall command) agreed with Herbert that the Canadians and Finns would be deployed in the area between the terminal and the Morphou road, their actions being coordinated with those of Barker's men in the adjoining Camp UNFICYP, while Herbert's British would be respon-sible for the airport's buildings and installations[18], for patrolling the rest of the airport, and for obstructing runways by placing airport vehicles and mobile equipment along them. Given the wide expanse of the airport, these were daunting tasks for the *ad hoc* force of no more than 150 lightly armed men. Ingenuity was the order of the day:

> Lieutenant Carter came up with the bright idea of using the fleet of fire tenders as patrol vehicles, and their searchlights and radio communication facilities enabled us to control effectively this very large area with a handful of men.[19]

A degree of calm now prevailed along the Morphou road, where Beattie, Miles and Birch were arranging to establish UN checkpoints to stop Greek cars from driving into the Turkish positions. To their dismay this calm was shattered at about 1700hrs when a mortar round landed just behind Turkish positions, towards which nine Turkish tanks could be seen advancing, causing the Turks to open fire in retaliation. Having established that the mortar had not been fired from the airport, Beattie and Birch drove in a Jeep along the road during a lull, shouting at the Turkish soldiers to stop firing. Their brave action had the desired effect, but no sooner was this situation dealt with than another required rapid action on their part. With all UN checkpoints not yet in place, a civilian car was seen approaching at speed from the direction of Nicosia:

> Knowing that others had been killed earlier in the day trying to race through the area, I pulled the Jeep directly in front of the car causing it to stop. In order to impress the Turks that the UN was controlling the road, I ordered the driver out of the car (having observed a loaded machine-gun on the front seat). When the driver delayed, RSM Birch quickly opened the door and helped *[sic]* him out. As he began to protest I told him to shut up and he might then escape with his life. By this time the Turkish soldiers were around us and wanted to kill the driver, who was obviously a National Guard reservist on his way home. We searched the car, finding some military equipment in the boot. After some hasty negotiations and assurances, I handed the machine-gun and military equipment to the Turks and directed the driver out of the area.[20]

The scene was repeated 15 minutes later, and again the two UN peacekeepers saved the Greek driver from almost certain death.

As darkness neared and with UN checkpoints and patrols now in place, attention turned to removing the wounded and dead of both sides, neither of which showed eagerness to do so:

> It was grisly work as many of the dead had been almost sliced in two by machine-gun fire. We loaded both the dead and wounded into our ambulance and sent it off to the General Hospital in Nicosia. We were congratulating ourselves on a job well done when our elation was deflated by a stinging rebuke from UNFICYP's Chief Medical Officer for misusing the ambulance to convey dead bodies.[21]

UN officers were surprised to discover the extent to which even rudimentary medical aid was lacking among the Turkish troops. At one point Miles and Birch were asked by the German-speaking corporal to try and find two of his friends:

> We found them quite quickly. Both were dead. The tragedy was that at least one of them could easily have been saved had he been given first aid. My overriding impression of the Turks during that day was that they were very brave and tough soldiers, but were totally lacking in administrative and medical back-up. I saw no evidence of even basic items such as field dressings.[22]

Although content that UNFICYP should remove their wounded and dead, the Turks refused to hand over prisoners held at the amusement park or to allow their names and addresses to be taken by UNFICYP. However, Beattie checked that they were being humanely treated and secured a Turkish officer's assurance that all would be released in due course through the auspices of the International Red Cross.

At the end of this eventful day a potentially grave threat to the maintenance of the general ceasefire had been averted, thanks to Prem Chand's bold initiative. No less credit was due to those members of UNFICYP who had displayed courage and initiative, at times under fire. Most of the latter were members of logistic units who would not normally have expected to be involved in such actions; it was a tribute to their professionalism that they responded with such discipline and competence. The day's events had provided a stark demonstration of the risks inherent in the peculiar third-party role of UN peacekeepers. The strangeness of it all struck one of those who returned that night to HQ UNFICYP close by:

> We ended up having supper in the mess in Blue Beret Camp. . . . I remember thinking how totally unreal the whole thing was, as at the time we had a number of refugees living in the mess, many of them female. When we walked into the mess in what must have been fairly dirty condition, we contrasted rather badly with the bright lights and pretty dresses.[23]

There was, however, a cloud on the horizon. HQ UNFICYP had protested the outbreak of shooting by Turkish troops along the Morphou road at about 1700hrs, stressing that this was a breach of the agreement with respect to the UN take-over of the airport accepted at local level a few hours earlier. The Turks replied that they did not recognize the validity of this agreement and said that their operations in the area would continue. Since UNFICYP's take-over was now a *fait accompli* and a Turkish attack against UN troops seemed unlikely, this reply was seen more as an expression of frustration than a threat. Indeed, we were reasonably confident that the situation around the airport had been stabilized with the bone of contention removed. We were not to know that this confidence would be short-lived and that within 24 hours we would be faced with a far more grave situation.

With benefit of hindsight greater weight should perhaps have been lent to reports from Oberwinkler, UNFICYP's LO to the Leadership, stating that there was constant talk amongst the Turks to the effect that they did not recognize any agreement alleged to have been reached with their local commander. Oberwinkler had added that Inhan himself had said that the Turks wanted the airport and were preparing to attack that evening. In the light of Inhan's emotional outbursts the previous day and his professed lack of direct communication with the Turkish Force Commander, we were disinclined to attach much credence to his words. Further assurance came in the early hours of 24 July when the US Embassy informed UNFICYP that the US Government had pressed the Turks to keep away from the airport. This information was received with what was to prove unfounded confidence in the degree to which Washington was able to influence Ankara.

CHAPTER FORTY-NINE

THE CRISIS DEEPENS

Brian Widlake: 'One of the things I find most striking in the book is something I don't think
  I have seen anywhere before – that at the time of the Turkish invasion of Cyprus you reck-
  oned that Britain was very close to war with Turkey.'
Sir Harold Wilson: 'I think within an hour of war.'
  BBC Radio: *The World This Weekend*, 14 October 1979.

The book in question (then recently published) was Harold Wilson's *Final Term – The Labour Government, 1974–1976*, in which his account of the crisis at Nicosia airport concluded with the comment that 'Apart from the lunacy at Suez, that was probably the nearest that Britain came to war with another nation since 1945'. Sir Harold (as by then he had become) was speaking five years after the event and his recollection may have been over-dramatic. Nonetheless, it certainly was the case that Turkey's refusal to accept the legitimacy of UNFICYP's action in taking over Nicosia airport and declaring it to be a UN-protected area generated acute international concern on account of the prospect of an imminent armed clash between the Turkish forces and the UN Force. Such a clash would have grave consequences not only for the UN and individual troop-contributor countries but also for NATO. That it was narrowly averted was due to two factors: first, the intense international pressures exerted on the Turks, and second, Kurt Waldheim's strong backing for UNFICYP's firm resolution in standing its ground.

The night of 23/24 July had been an uneasy one for UN troops in and around the airport. The National Guard attempted to remove a dump of ammunition brought in by the Greek airforce's operation two nights earlier (UNFICYP confiscated the ammunition) and in the early hours of 24 July there was some mortar and small-arms fire from the Turkish side, some striking the UN-occupied terminal building. This sporadic firing, which was interspersed with illuminating flares, continued until daylight, evidence of the nervousness of troops in the area.

The tactical importance of the airport, due to its position commanding the western approaches to Nicosia, remained unchanged. During the morning of 24 July Greek defence positions between the airport and the city suburbs were strengthened, providing clear evidence of Greek determination to prevent any Turkish attempt to outflank the capital from the west. This action implied, too, a lack of confidence in UNFICYP's ability, if not its resolve, to preserve the integrity of the UN-protected area in the face of Turkish pressure, whether military or political, which was reflected in National Guard protests that, in breach of what had been agreed the previous day, Turkish troops were still within 100m of Camp UNFICYP, preventing use of the main road between Nicosia and Morphou. The National Guard declared that, so long as this situation persisted, it did not consider itself bound by the agreement to keep its own men outside the 500m limit.[1]

Calm prevailed during the morning, but rumour persisted that the Turks remained intent on capture of the airport (Radio Ankara reported that it was already in Turkish hands) and this was confirmed by Inhan when Prem Chand and Weckman-Munoz called on him in mid-morning: this, he told them, was a prime Turkish objective. There was now real prospect of Turkish action to seize it, and events elsewhere, which demonstrated that Turkish forces were paying scant regard to observance of the general ceasefire, did nothing to lessen UNFICYP's disquiet. There could be no question of the UN Force not standing its ground. To do otherwise would not only breach the assurances given to both sides but also shatter the Force's credibility; rapid reinforcement of UNFICYP was needed. With speed vital, eyes were turned towards British forces in the SBAs, which alone were in a position to respond quickly. Prem Chand alerted New York to the urgency, requesting in particular that the promised British reinforcements now known to be arriving in the SBAs be sent forward to Nicosia at once.

Having experienced at close quarters the power of Turkish airstrikes, the prospect of these being unleashed on UN troops, who themselves lacked all air defence, was alarming. With Prem Chand's agreement and as Commander of the British Contingent, I represented to Olver, the British High Commissioner, UNFICYP's need not only for the promised ground reinforcements but also for air support in the event of a Turkish attempt to seize the airport. Stressing that this support could be provided quickly only by British Forces in the SBAs, I pointed out the effect on British public opinion if British troops, let alone those of other UN contingents, were subjected to Turkish airstrikes while the RAF at Akrotiri, a mere 60km away, was obliged to stand by without lifting a finger in their defence. Olver undertook to pass my representations to London at once.

Meanwhile, to dispel false reports that the airport was already in Turkish hands, Prem Chand convened a press conference at 1500hrs at HQ UNFICYP to demonstrate that it was under UNFICYP's exclusive control. TV and press correspondents were then conducted by Prem Chand personally to the airport to allow them see for themselves the true situation. And since Oberwinkler continued to report constant talk amongst the Turks of their intention to seize the airport, he was instructed to make the present situation plain to the Leadership, stressing that the airport was currently held in the name of the UN by British, Canadian, Finnish and Swedish troops (the last now added to the small garrison), who were under orders from the Secretary General to resist any attempt by either side to seize it from them. The Leadership confirmed that this message had been passed to Inhan, but doubted if it was within Inhan's power 'or even that of the Turkish Prime Minister' to avert the Turkish army's determination to take the airport, the reason being that the Greek media were claiming that the Turkish forces had failed to achieve their objectives in Cyprus, that such claims were an insult to Turkey and that its army was determined to uphold Turkey's honour. This reply gave no cause for optimism.

The situation had become so foreboding that, in accordance with UNFICYP's practice of positioning on the spot a senior officer to handle potentially difficult situations, Lieut. Colonel Manuel, the Canadian Commander of Nicosia District, was ordered to assume personal command at the airport. Beattie retained responsibility for coordinating the defence of UN camps in the area. The small airport garrison now included a platoon from Manuel's Observation company, two Canadian 106mm anti-tank RCLs, a scout car troop of the Parachute Squadron, RAC, and two sections of APC-mounted Swedes equipped with Carl Gustav anti-tank weapons; further reinforcement depended on the outcome of the representations made to New York and London.

Since the *coup* eight days earlier my responsibilities as Chief of Staff had held me at Force HQ in Nicosia, although as Commander of the British Contingent I was anxious to see for myself how the Coldstream Guards were faring in Limassol and Paphos Districts. Prem Chand agreed that I might now do so, visiting the Danes in Lefka District on my way back. Leaving by Sioux helicopter soon after lunch, I landed in turn at Polemidhia Camp, Limassol and St Patrick's Camp, Paphos, to discuss the local situation with Lieut. Colonel Willoughby in the former and his Company Commander, Major Macfarlane, in the latter. I found all in good heart and acting with energy and enterprise to cope with the many problems that had faced them over the preceding week. However, with resources stretched to the limit, Willoughby made a plea for reinforcement by that half of his battalion stationed in the Eastern SBA under British, not UN, command; neither of us knew then how soon his plea would be satisfied.

Flying on north-east to Xeros, extensive fires were visible below, destroying some of the island's most valuable forests. The acrid smell of smoke was pervasive and the intensity of the rising heat could be felt. On landing in Viking Camp I was greeted by a cheerful Lieut. Colonel Severinson and found his Danes in good heart, too, as they strove to maintain the ceasefire and watch over those Turkish Cypriots who had surrendered in Lefka town and those who remained defiant in the small coastal enclaves around Kokkina and Limnitis. The afternoon had provided a refreshing change from the pressures at Force HQ and encouraging confirmation of the high morale and devotion to their mission of our troops elsewhere. But on landing back in Blue Beret Camp at 1900hrs I learnt that the situation at the airport was giving continuing deep concern.

Although members of the world's media had seen for themselves that UNFICYP was in exclusive occupation of the airport and neither they nor Inhan had been left in any doubt of the Force's determination to resist any attempt by either side to enter it, it was becoming increasingly apparent that there was confusion in Ankara on both counts. Pronouncements emerging from the Turkish capital suggested that Prime Minister Ecevit had been kept in ignorance of the army's failure to capture the airport and was unaware that it was now a UN-protected area. Whether or not his generals had deliberately not so informed him, or even whether or not the generals themselves were not properly informed remain matters for speculation. What was of immediate concern to UNFICYP was that there had been no lessening of reports of Turkey's intention to take over the airport, possibly that very night, with or without UNFICYP's acquiescence.

Prem Chand had renewed appeals to New York for rapid reinforcement and for pressure to be exerted on Ankara to observe the agreed general ceasefire. As evening fell in Cyprus (then still early afternoon in New York) a troop of Turkish tanks advanced towards a UN check-point on the Morphou road. A stand-to was ordered in the UN camps and concern was increased by a puzzling message sent to Prem Chand by Inhan in which it was alleged that UNFICYP, having taken over the airport, had now vacated it. Further, Inhan stated that in the interests of their own security the Turkish forces had taken control of the airport and surrounding areas, that they would retain this control, repair the runways and open the airport to international traffic, and that they were ready to cooperate with and accept assistance from UNFICYP to these ends.[2] Even as this message was being passed we learnt that the Turks had told the British High Commission that they intended to seize the airport during the night, contradicting Inhan's message and adding to the confusion. Determined to demonstrate the true situation, UNFICYP arranged for five car-loads of media correspondents to be escorted by UN Military Police to the airport at about 2100hrs in order that they might see yet again that UNFICYP had not withdrawn and that there were no Turkish troops in the UN-protected area. If the Turks did, indeed, attempt to move into the airport during the night, at least it could be shown that the pretence that UNFICYP had withdrawn was false.

Alarm bells were now ringing in New York, Washington, London and Brussels with the realization that a fight between the Turks and the UN Force was looming perilously close. Waldheim was in Washington seeking Kissinger's support for action to restrain Turkey's continuing operations in Cyprus when he was told that the Turks were threatening to attack UNFICYP unless it had vacated the airport by morning:

> Time was short. It was already evening in Cyprus and the ultimatum would expire in a few hours. Fortunately there is no better worldwide communications system than that at the disposal of the American Secretary of State. . . . In a matter of minutes I was connected with the Turkish Prime Minister, Bulent Ecevit, in Ankara. He was not well informed; indeed, he was under the impression that Turkish troops had already occupied the airfield. Tersely, I gave him the facts. By an agreement worked out between UNFICYP, the Greek Cypriot National Guard and the local Turkish commander, the Guard had withdrawn from the airport and handed it over to the United Nations forces. Turkish military headquarters had now reversed that decision. Ecevit seemed genuinely surprised. He had not heard of any agreement with UNFICYP, he told me. I repeated that the National Guard had only relinquished the airport on my assurance that it would not fall into Turkish hands. If it was now attacked, his government would be responsible for the bloodshed. Ecevit stated that he would look into the matter at once and do his best to avoid violence.[3]

It was at this point that Waldheim made clear that UNFICYP was to reject any Turkish ultimatum to withdraw from the airport, but, if accounts other than his own are to be believed, Waldheim's meeting with Kissinger was less than helpful, the latter making clear that he was unwilling to threaten, much less to take, military action to halt the Turkish forces: they should be allowed to achieve what he (Kissinger) judged to be reasonable military objectives.

There was alarm in London as realization grew of the vulnerability of British troops at the airport. Foreign Secretary James Callaghan urged Waldheim formally to request the immediate despatch to UNFICYP of the reinforcements now in the SBAs and added his voice for pressure to be exerted in New York to dissuade the Turks from military action against UNFICYP, endorsing Waldheim's decision that any such action should be met by force. At British instigation, and now with Kissinger's approval, complementary pressure was exerted through NATO. Secretary General Luns warned the Turkish representative that any attempt to take the airport would involve a clash with the UN Force's British Contingent and a more specific warning was passed soon afterwards:

> Around midnight, Luns gave his assistant . . . the following message to deliver to Tulumen *[deputy Turkish representative]*: "The UN Peacekeeping Force has been instructed to resist any attempt by Turkish units to occupy Nicosia airport. We ask you to forward to your Government immediately our request that they order their forces not to go into action against the UN. We trust that they will listen to our appeal". This was an undisguised threat and seemed to Tulumen to violate all the rules of NATO procedure.[4]

Threat or not, this message added to the pressures fast building up on Ankara from all sides.

Events moved with gathering momentum. Waldheim confirmed to Callaghan that the British reinforcements should be sent to Nicosia without delay. Meanwhile Callaghan had spoken by telephone to Ecevit[5] and Foreign Minister Gunes, leaving them in no doubt of Britain's determination not to stand idly by in the event of Turkish action against British troops; the response of the two Turkish ministers was far from reassuring. Callaghan reported his fears to Kissinger before hurrying to urge Prime Minister Wilson to intervene personally by telephone with Ecevit:

> This I *[Wilson]* did and warned him strongly against the plan *[to take the airport]* but he refused to comply with what I asked; later he came back after, no doubt, consulting his military advisers. He had identified the exact location of the British forces, and undertook to avoid bombing the sector where they were. I said his proposal must be resisted. We had a responsibility, as the only UN member with forces close at hand, to defend UN troops. Furthermore, there were Canadians in the UN force. I was not entering into any collusion whereby British troops were safeguarded and the lives of Canadians endangered. He must realize that we must resist. If he proceeded with his design we should not hesitate to order our fighters to shoot down his aircraft. . . . He persisted in his decision.[6]

The prospect of British (and other) UN troops coming under Turkish air attack galvanized Whitehall. Orders were issued for immediate deployment to Akrotiri of 12 RAF Phantom aircraft of No. 38 Group based at Coningsby, Lincolnshire. Flying in pairs and refuelled in flight, the first pair reached the island at 0500hrs on 25 July; by 0645hrs eight aircraft were standing ready at Akrotiri, refuelled and armed, and the remaining four arrived soon afterwards. Since the aircraft were not placed under UN command, there had been no need to seek New York's agreement to this deployment and their status with respect to possible use in support of UN troops was not precisely defined. As Commander of the British Contingent, I was authorized, should I deem it necessary, to call for their support and told that any such call would be relayed immediately for a decision in Whitehall.[7] Although there seemed little doubt at the time that such a call would be approved, second thoughts might have prevailed, given the complexities, as Field Marshal Carver, then Chief of the Defence Staff, later explained:

> The political and military problems involved in a direct attack by RAF aircraft, operating under British national command, in support of the UN Force against the forces of a co-guarantor power, which was also a NATO and CENTO ally, the UN Force itself having been established primarily to protect the Turkish Cypriots, were intricate to say the least, not covered by the Security Council resolution, and certainly best not put to the test.[8]

No less swift action followed Waldheim's formal request for the British ground reinforcements to be sent to UNFICYP. CBFNE was instructed to coordinate arrangements direct with HQ UNFICYP and at about 2100hrs Major General Butler, GOC NEARELF, discussed these with me, confirming that the following were being sent from the SBAs:

- Regimental HQ 16th/5th Lancers together with its B and HQ Squadrons (armoured reconnaissance).

- C Squadron 4th/7th Dragoon Guards (air-portable armoured reconnaissance).

- Nos 2 (Support) and 3 Companies, 2nd Bn, Coldstream Guards (infantry).

B Squadron 16th/5th Lancers was equipped with Saladin armoured cars mounting 76mm guns with useful anti-tank and HE performance; C Squadron 4th/7th Dragoon Guards had only Ferret scout cars, but one troop was armed with Swingfire anti-tank guided missiles. Between them these two squadrons would give a significant boost to UNFICYP's hitherto weak anti-tank resources. Butler and I quickly agreed on routes and timings and I undertook to provide UNFICYP guides from the SBAs to Nicosia, where traffic control would be established by UN Military Police to ensure rapid and unimpeded movement through the city's suburbs to the airport. First to leave the SBAs were to be the Tactical Regimental HQ and B Squadron 16th/5th Lancers, who would reach Nicosia at 0100hrs; all the remainder were expected to have joined UNFICYP by 0900hrs. The 16th/5th Lancers' Commanding Officer, Lieut. Colonel R.Q.M. Morris, together with the Leader of his B Squadron, Major J.A. Wright, were to travel ahead and report to me as soon as possible. UNFICYP's CPLO, Lieut. Colonel Pennell (UK), and his staff lost no time in collecting together as many as possible of the requisite UN insignia (blue berets, badges, flags and vehicle stickers) for issue to the new arrivals as soon as they reached Nicosia. HQ National Guard was warned of the imminent troop movements, routes and timings, and requested to accord free passage through Greek checkpoints.

Morris and Wright reached Blue Beret Camp at 0015hrs and, having visited the airport an hour earlier to see the situation for myself, I lost no time in briefing them on their task. I told Morris that all the British reinforcements, together with those British troops already at the airport, were to come under his command, but that initially he himself was to be subordinate to Manuel as the overall commander of the airport defence. However, he was to take over this responsibility later in the morning, allowing Manuel to return to his post as Commander Nicosia District. With accurate information as to the strength of Turkish forces facing the airport scant ,I said that, if an attack took place, the most likely time would be after first light (we had noted that the Turks had shown little taste for night operations) and that it might involve an infantry battalion supported by tanks, artillery and FGA aircraft. I made clear that any Turkish move against the airport was to be resisted and that UNFICYP was authorized to open fire to this end, although the utmost care was to be exercised before resorting to this extreme; Morris was to ensure that fire was not opened unless the Turks fired first or refused to halt their advance. Information that a force of RAF Phantoms was on its way from the UK and would be available soon after first light to give support if necessary gave some comfort, as did the news that powerful international pressure was being exerted on the Turks not to attempt to dislodge UNFICYP from the airport. Finally, I told Morris that his regiment could use the currently vacant Gleneagles Camp (adjacent to both the airport and Blue Beret Camp) as its logistic base. Later Wright commented: 'Your briefing was one of the most sobering that I have ever been to. . . . I listed what the Turks were alleged to have . . . and what the UNFICYP airport task force had . . . . The equation did not seem to match.'[9]

No time was lost. Morris and Wright left immediately to seek out Manuel at the airport and agree with him a plan for deployment of the reinforcing troops. Their arrival was greeted with unconcealed relief, for the prospect of holding the airport in the face of a deliberate Turkish attack was a very different matter from the task hitherto envisaged: that of providing a token UN presence to deter casual trespass by either side.

By their nature airports extend over large areas of level open ground and to provide effective defence for the whole of this was out of the question. Manuel and Morris decided that, with the runways already obstructed and unusable, the main defence should be based on the terminal and other buildings which afforded not only observation over the airport and its northern approaches but also a degree of protection. To enhance their deterrent effect and serve as a trip-wire 16th/5th Lancer armoured cars were to be deployed forward to the airport perimeter at first light. Morris's Tactical HQ and B Squadron reached Nicosia soon after 0100hrs,when he issued orders accordingly. Wright then briefed his squadron:

> I next had an 'O' Group at my ACV and detailed specific tasks. I also laid down some rules of engagement. . . . As the troops left for their positions I got SHQ and others to start making bunkers. . . . Captain John Squire . . . set up on the roof with an ARC43 radio to act as FAC in case the RAF Phantoms were needed. We then waited as it became daylight for something to happen. I felt very vulnerable and extremely worried about my forward troops. For although we had put a brave face on it, I was not at all sure that our bluff would not be called.[10]

The arrival of the Lancers' Saladin armoured cars was greeted with a rousing cheer from Manuel's men.

Meanwhile the 16th/5th Lancers Second-in-Command, Major A.E.G. Gauntlett, was establishing the régiment's logistic base:

> Gleneagles Camp did nothing to restore our morale and confidence; it was pitch dark and derelict-looking and there was no one there to meet us. But shortly after our arrival a Land Rover appeared bearing a pile of blue berets, brassards and all the other paraphernalia, and in the dark we struggled to transform ourselves into United Nations troops. . . . At the height of the confusion the Commanding Officer appeared and called for instant orders. What he had to say was brief and to the point: "I have no time to waste. I have just seen the Brigadier and he expects the Turks will attack the airport at dawn – in a few hours time. They are at battalion strength and have a company of M47 tanks and artillery in support. We are to hold the airport with B Squadron and you are to take up defensive positions here. . . . Any questions?". After a stunned silence the Second-in-Command tentatively enquired as to which direction we might expect the enemy, and the Colonel replied in the grand traditional manner: "There is the enemy," he cried, flinging out his arm and pointing into the inky blackness, and then hastily departed.[11]

No. 2 Company of the Coldstream Guards reached Nicosia just as dawn was breaking. Major J.R. Heywood, its Commander, has described their breakneck journey from the Eastern SBA and instant conversion to UN troops:

> It was an unusually cold night for Cyprus in July but this was probably accentuated by the speed at which we drove . . . As we got nearer Nicosia we were left in no doubt that we were travelling through a country at war – vast areas of the countryside were burnt and charred, the smell of burning lingered in the air and the top half of telegraph poles hung tentatively and somehow grotesquely to the lines they were supposed to support, the bottoms of the poles having been burnt through. . . . As we approached the outskirts of Nicosia we were met by UN police who from then on manned all road junctions to ensure our smooth and still fast progress to the airport. . . . A few miles short of the airport we were waved into a lay-by, where in twenty minutes we converted ourselves into UN troops.[12]

UN berets and arm badges were quickly handed out and UN vehicle stickers issued all down the column, and Heywood's company then moved into the airport, spasmodic firing being heard as they did so. Heywood continues: 'I was taken to see the Colonel in charge of the Canadian detachment who was armed with two pistols and was sitting with his feet on his desk. Soon afterwards the Commanding Officer of 16/5L arrived and I learnt that my task was to defend the building against the very real threat of a Turkish attack.'[13] His guardsmen lost no time in putting the terminal building into a state of defence.

C Squadron 4th/7th Dragoon Guards, under Major P.J. Staveacre, which had only very recently arrived at Akrotiri from the UK, did not reach Nicosia until 1000hrs, when it came under Morris's command, its Swingfire troop being an especially welcome addition. (No.3 Company of the Coldstream Guards, under Major J.R. Crisp, had not been due to leave the Eastern SBA for Nicosia until 0800hrs, by which time, as described shortly, the situation at the airport had taken a significant turn for the better. Given the need for additional resources in Limassol and Paphos Districts, which my visit the day before had shown, the company was diverted instead to Polemidhia Camp, where later in the day it was joined by all remaining elements of 2nd Bn, Coldstream Guards hitherto stationed in the SBA under British command. Willoughby did not conceal his satisfaction to have now his complete battalion serving as part of UNFICYP.)

With the approach of dawn on 25 July, UN troops were stood to and both Morris and Wright surveyed the scene by helicopter, as the latter has written:

> Once airborne I was able to see for the first time the full panorama below. I was concerned at how close my forward Saladins were to the leading Turkish tanks – 8–10 yards! I also quickly established that there were only five tanks (a platoon?) in the vicinity – four M47s and one M48 – no M60s! We also confirmed that there was only a battalion of infantry dug in along the perimeter. . . . It was also fascinating to look down on the airport runway which was littered with debris, crashed aeroplanes and also quite badly cratered.
>
> We landed at the airport boundary road. I walked forward to talk to the Turkish battalion commander. I had to speak broken French to a Turkish NCO who translated for us both. We threatened each other politely for a short while without much effect. In the end I believe I convinced him by saying: "Look, we are not Greeks nor Finns nor Swedes. We are British soldiers lent by our government to help the UN in Cyprus. We are professional soldiers like you. We have been told to stop you taking the airport and that is exactly what we are going to do. Yesterday we were happy to defend Turkish Cypriot villagers in Pergamos [*the village adjoining the 16th/5th Lancers' camp in the SBA*], but today we are quite happy to die obeying our orders and fighting you. Just try it and see. Do not forget we have 12 RAF Phantom jets on call which are better than your Sabres and by themselves could destroy your battalion".
>
> He seemed very impressed and worried by this statement, and after some consultations on the radio he replied through the interpreter: "Yes, I quite understand. There will be no attack. We are friends of the USA too". It was then I realized that I had used the words "Etats Unis" instead of "Nations Unis"!
>
> After this was over I strolled over to Lieutenant Charles Orr-Ewing's troop. He was sitting on the top of his Saladin looking very relaxed as he looked down the 90mm barrel of a Turkish M47 a few yards away. . . . As the minutes passed the tension, which had been considerable, eased. We were all alive and hungry for breakfast, and quite frankly few of us had expected to be either.[14]

The proximity of the forward Turkish troops posed a dilemma as Squire, stationed on the roof of the terminal building to direct any strikes by the RAF Phantoms, explained:

> As dawn broke the tension became fairly high as troops reported enemy [*sic*] tanks and infantry at very close range. I could see Charles Orr-Ewing's Saladin and 50m in front of him two Turkish M47s. I remember thinking that it wouldn't make much difference which side opened fire first – one of the tanks would get the Saladin. I could not differentiate between the enemy front line and our own forward troops, and told the Squadron Leader [*Wright*] that, if a friendly airstrike was ordered, our men would probably receive as much fire as the enemy. He replied quite calmly that nothing could be done about this, and that the RAF would just have to do the best they could.[15]

During the morning HQ Squadron 16th/5th Lancers reached Gleneagles Camp from the Eastern SBA and the main elements of Morris's Regimental HQ joined his Tactical HQ in the airport's terminal:

> The building was in a state of complete shambles. Every office, shop and department had been looted and ransacked and the contents of drawers and cupboards mixed with personal belongings from passengers' luggage was strewn around the building. There was broken glass and debris everywhere – the aftermath of a few days previously when a large force of Greek National Guard held the airport . . . . The building had neither water nor electricity and the fridges and deep-freezers had long since given up the struggle to preserve their contents. The smell of rotting food that came up from the kitchens defies description. There was a lot to be done to clear this place up and make it habitable, but the first priority was to plan and prepare the defences.[16]

Meanwhile international pressures exerted on the Turks had taken effect. Ecevit, it seemed, had become alarmed by the contradictory information reaching him and was startled by clear declarations that any attempt to seize Nicosia airport would be met by force, not only by UNFICYP but also by Britain. Whatever the original Turkish objectives may have been, this was not a risk that could be ignored. In what must have been a painful climb-down, he telephoned Wilson in London and Waldheim in New York to assure both that Turkish forces would not attack UNFICYP and that the latter would be allowed to retain the airport. Culmination came in a meeting of the Security Council held in private at 2340hrs (by then 0540hrs on 25 July in Cyprus) when Waldheim announced that he had received a letter from Turun Gunes, Turkish Foreign Minister, the operative part of which read as follows:

> I am happy to be able to reaffirm the assurances conveyed earlier in the day to your Excellency by my Prime Minister. I would like to reiterate that, without prejudice to the contentions of the Turkish Government as to the legality of the United Nations presence at the Lefkosa (Nicosia) airport in Cyprus, the Government of Turkey undertakes not to attempt to assume possession of the Lefkosa (Nicosia) airport by force, the threat of force or other means of coercion. I hope, Mr Secretary General, that this letter will help to relieve the understandable tension under which we all lived today.[17]

The meeting had lasted a mere ten minutes. Writing of its outcome, Brian Urquhart observed that the Turkish Ambassador had proudly informed the Council that Turkey had settled the matter peacefully. Urquhart added tersely:

> It seemed cheap at the price to let him take the credit. For a lightly armed peacekeeping force it had been a dangerous moment.[18]

Waldheim's announcement was greeted with a sigh of relief in London, Brussels and Washington and when news of the Turkish climb-down reached UNFICYP the relief was no less. Although the unequivocal terms of Gunes's letter were accepted as a guarantee against any deliberate Turkish attack, UNFICYP could not risk dropping its guard against a casual or inadvertent incursion into the UN-protected area by either side. Nonetheless a reduction in the size of the airport garrison was necessary in view of UNFICYP's commitments elsewhere. Command was duly passed from Manuel to Morris, and the Canadians, Finns and Swedes were authorized to withdraw all their men from the airport except for one platoon each (which maintained the multi-national character of the garrison). Further, the 4th/7th Dragoon Guards squadron (less its Swingfire troop, which was retained at the airport) was redeployed to support the Finns on the eastern flank of the Turkish army's lodgement area.

With tension reduced, Morris set about demonstrating UNFICYP's determination not to be overawed by either the Turkish or the Greek forces. As a show of strength armoured car troops frequently moved from point to point around the UN-protected area and patrols probed out to north and west to show the UN flag and ascertain the situation in these areas. The experiences of B Squadron's 5th Troop led by Staff Sergeant De St Croix patrolling towards Yeralakkos (3km north-west of the airport) were typical:

> The village proved to be clear of Turkish tanks, so we stopped and had a chat with the local Greek soldiers. They complained that the Turks to the east had erected a road-block, stopping all traffic from using the road to the next village. We decided to have a talk to the Turks responsible and find out why they had put up the road-block. Apparently the Turks had been fired on from a passing car the previous night and didn't want it to happen again. During the following hour I tried to persuade the Turkish commander to at least remove the block during daylight hours to enable the civilian population to get to the next village. The Turks were quite adamant and refused to move it, so I returned to the airport to report what had happened.
>
> I was later sent back to the area . . . to try to sort something out. Shortly after returning we discovered a small Greek stronghold, consisting of eleven men and two young boys, directly behind the Turks. Although surrounded, they refused to move as they were sitting on the Turkish supply route. The Turks told us that the Greeks were well dug in and that if they didn't move by a certain time they would call in an airstrike and kill them all. The following two and a half hours were spent in trying to persuade the Greeks to move. This meant driving back and forwards between a Turkish colonel of the tank regiment and a Greek major in Yeralakkos. Eventually the Greeks decided to move out. The Turks then removed the road-block and everybody was happy.[19]

At the airport Heywood's guardsmen were no less active:

> We visited and patrolled the Turkish front line at frequent intervals, and at NCO level an exchange of cigarettes got some form of dialogue going. The front line troops were paratroopers, well disciplined though curiously they allowed their weapons to become very rusty. The soldiers were clearly very fearful of their officers, who thought nothing of delivering the odd kick or swipe with a stick to them as they passed on their rounds.[20]

Activities of this kind were evidence of the speed with which these well-trained professional soldiers adapted to their new role as UN peacekeepers. Ten days later Heywood and his company were released to rejoin their battalion at Polemidhia, leaving Morris's Lancers responsible for the UN-protected area.

Later, when time allowed, we pondered the reason for the convoluted and contradictory statements with respect to the airport that had emerged from the Turkish side during the preceding 48 hours. A credible explanation was that, discomfited by their failure to seize the airport before the time of the agreed ceasefire, the Turks had been determined to rectify this as soon as possible afterwards, but had unexpectedly been thwarted by Prem Chand's forestalling action. They had then decided, it seemed, to force out the UN troops, a task which they anticipated would be all too easy, and move in themselves, subsequently claiming that they had done so only because UNFICYP had already withdrawn. This plan may have misfired because that cover story had been put out too soon, allowing Prem Chand not only to demonstrate to all and sundry that UNFICYP had not withdrawn but also time to implement measures to frustrate the Turkish purpose.

Since UN Forces hitherto had rarely acted in such decisive fashion, the Turks may have expected UNFICYP to give way meekly in the face of an advance by their troops. But if Prem Chand had misjudged the Turkish mood following declaration of the airport as a UN-protected area, the Turks had misjudged no less his resolve and that of those he commanded. Representatives of both sides having been assured that UNFICYP would maintain exclusive control of the area, the Force was not going to default on that undertaking. It was an outstanding example of how a robust UN Force Commander, who is confident both in his troops and in the strength of his international support, can seize the peacekeeping initiative. Denial of the airport to the Turks was never the motive; the sole purpose was was to prevent a resumption of fighting that was likely to spread throughout the island. Nonetheless, UNFICYP's action was bitterly criticized by, and to this day has rankled with, the Turks, who argued that UN troops should have been protecting isolated Turkish Cypriot communities in the south rather than defending an airport which, they asserted, was no part of a UN force's business. What they could not, or would not, see was that the action had been taken solely in the interests of preserving the fragile ceasefire, a breakdown of which would have exposed those self-same Turkish Cypriot communities to much increased danger.

Prem Chand's action had entailed graver risks than could have been foreseen at the time (none anticipated that the Turkish forces might ignore a ceasefire accepted by their Prime Minister), but it can be seen in retrospect to have been highly successful in achieving its primary purpose. The success was not UNFICYP's alone. The rapidity with which international pressures on Ankara were mobilized in New York, Brussels, London and Washington, together with the speed with which Britain responded to calls for military support, all served to wrong-foot the Turks. Not least was the courage of Kurt Waldheim in taking responsibility upon himself without waiting for options to be debated at length in the Security Council.

For UN peacekeepers there was an important lesson. Having elected a course of action which is thought right for prevention of conflict, this must be carried through resolutely and quickly before opposition or delaying tactics are mobilized. No less clear is the lesson that, if his bluff is not to be called, a UN Force Commander must have the military resources to render his action militarily credible. At Nicosia airport it had been a close-run thing, but UNFICYP's clear determination to maintain the integrity of the declared UN-protected area, to which the timely arrival of the British Army reinforcements and the presence at Akrotiri of the RAF Phantoms gave credibility, was sufficient to persuade the Turks to hold back. There was also an important side-effect, the value of which became increasingly apparent during ensuing weeks. UNFICYP had given firm demonstration that it would not allow itself to be pushed around easily by the greatly superior Turkish forces. This not only induced grudging respect among the Turks (who had been inclined hitherto to brush aside the presence of UNFICYP as having no relevance to their operations), but also increased Greek Cypriot confidence in the UN Force. And within the Force morale was boosted by the effective international support it had enjoyed.

Something of a war of nerves was waged for some time afterwards. In places Turkish troops advanced close up to the perimeter of the UN-protected area, but never had the temerity to attempt to violate it. For reasons explained later, it proved impossible to agree on conditions acceptable to both sides for the airport to be brought back into use, and an action taken as a temporary peacekeeping expedient has left the airport ever since as a white elephant, unused and in the sole occupation of UNFICYP. However, at the time there was disquiet and criticism in some troop-contributor capitals of Prem Chand's unilateral decision, albeit backed by New York, to take over the airport and to deny it to both sides. Anxiety was much increased when the prospect of a fight between UNFICYP and the Turkish army loomed especially close, and doubts (which unsurprisingly the Turks shared) were expressed as to whether this was a proper role for the UN Force. These doubts were foremost in Waldheim's mind when subsequently consideration was being given as to whether or not the UN Force should attempt to halt the Turkish army's easterly expansion.

CHAPTER FIFTY

UNFICYP AND THE TURKISH FORCES

UNFICYP's mandate and its strength were not sufficient to resist the Turkish army. It had been intended only to control relations between the two Cypriot communities. To ask it to do anything more, I would need a much clearer directive from the Security Council. That directive was not forthcoming, so I took it upon myself, as cautiously as possible, to extend the very narrow mandate of UNFICYP – to act as a buffer between the Greek and Turkish communities – in order to mitigate as far as possible the hardships of a conflict it was unable to prevent.

Kurt Waldheim: *In the Eye of the Storm*, p. 85.

With a ceasefire now nominally in force, UNFICYP was kept at full stretch throughout 23 and 24 July, not only by events at the airport and helping in the rescue of foreign nationals along the north coast, but also in action to consolidate the fragile ceasefire and in dealing with a myriad of other problems. As the Force, its resources limited, grappled as best it could with many new demands, news from Athens and its consequences in Nicosia gave a glimmer of hope that the situation might take a turn for the better. The Greek colonels' control of events crumbled rapidly following Brig. General Ioannides's realization on 21 July that he could no longer browbeat his military colleagues, and the junta collapsed two days later, its demise brought about by the ignominious failure of its Cyprus policy: Turkey had regained a military foothold on the island while Greece had been obliged to look on in abject impotence. The nadir of seven years military rule had been reached; the call for restoration of democratic government in Greece was clear.

On the afternoon of 23 July President Gizikis summoned leading Greek politicians to a meeting at which the chiefs of the armed forces also were present. They agreed that the former President, Constantine Karamanlis, then in exile in Paris, should be pressed to return at once to head a constitutional government. He agreed to do so and Athens Radio announced the same evening that Greece was to return to civilian rule without further ado. This news was greeted with wild jubilation in the capital as realization spread that the junta's attempt to rid itself of Makarios had served only to bring about its own demise and the restoration of democracy in the mother country. An immediate consequence was the reversal of the junta's earlier refusal to meet Greece's co-guarantor powers, and a meeting of all three was quickly arranged to take place next day in Geneva (not Vienna, as previously proposed). Another consequence was a turn-about in international attitudes: distaste for the military dictatorship in Athens had hitherto generated all but unanimous sympathy for Turkey's intervention in Cyprus, but the return to power of the widely respected Karamanlis (which, to its credit, the Turkish government welcomed), coupled with reports by the world's media of the ruthless nature of the Turkish operation in Cyprus, still continuing despite the agreed ceasefire, caused sympathy to swing away from Turkey and towards Greece.

In Nicosia the collapse of the junta was quickly followed by the disappearance into oblivion of Nicos Sampson, who had never been more than an absurd puppet figure at the beck and call of the mainland Greek officers:

> At 1450hrs on 23 July the Force Commander received a telephone call from Mr Clerides, who stated that he had taken office as Acting President of Cyprus and informed UNFICYP that he wished to adhere strictly to the terms of the ceasefire. He stated that he was trying to get in touch with Vice President Denktash to enlist his cooperation in stopping violations of the ceasefire.[1]

As President of the House of Representatives Clerides was the person upon whom the office of Acting President legally devolved in the event of the death or incapacity of the President. He had declined to accept the office at the time of the *coup*, but that he was willing to do so now augured well for a return to constitutional government, at least in so far as the Greek community was concerned.[2] Given the long-standing friendship between Clerides and Denktash, it also held out prospect of a return to calmer relations between the two communities. Prem Chand and Weckman-Munoz lost no time in bringing the two face to face, all four meeting that same evening at Denktash's office in the Turkish quarter. The mood was constructive, giving rise to guarded optimism for maintenance of an effective ceasefire between the two Cypriot communities while a settlement was being sought of the situation that now confronted them. However, no mainland Turk was present and the unknown attitude of the Turkish army cast its shadow.

At 2100hrs on 23 July (then 0300hrs next day in Cyprus) yet another meeting of the Security Council, the fifth in eight days, was convened at the request of the Greek representative, Mr Panayotacos, who complained angrily of Turkish violations of the ceasefire and added:

> Unless immediate measures are taken to cause the Turkish armed forces to return to the positions they held on 22 July at 1600hrs (local time) and to stop their efforts to enlarge the territory occupied by them, the whole situation would inevitably deteriorate in such an explosive way that it could leads to a general conflagration.[3]

Waldheim confirmed that there had been numerous violations of the ceasefire, mostly around the edges of the main Turkish enclave, at the airport and along the Green Line in Nicosia, but also elsewhere. He added that UNFICYP was trying to re-establish OPs and to patrol the lines of confrontation wherever possible, was investigating complaints to the best of its ability and was rendering assistance to the victims of the fighting, both Cypriot and foreign nationals.

The stability of the ceasefire was cause for anxiety and Waldheim said that he had expressed concern on this account to several governments and had addressed the following message to Ecevit, Karamanlis and Clerides personally:

I fully realize that the first few days of a ceasefire after a bitter contest are always difficult. However, I am deeply concerned at information reaching me from my representatives in Cyprus that serious violations of the ceasefire are still taking place. I therefore ask you most urgently to give instructions to your military forces that no further violations of the ceasefire should take place and that, where territory has been taken over after the time of the ceasefire, that is 1600hrs, Cyprus time, on 22 July, troops should return to the positions which they occupied when the ceasefire came into effect.[4]

Waldheim had singled neither side out by name, but it was clear to all that his appeal was directed at the Turks as the prime culprits. Informing the Council of the instructions issued to Prem Chand following its meeting the previous day and of the reinforcement of UNFICYP now in train, he hoped that:

As reinforcements arrive and as the observance of the ceasefire allows for more extensive observation and patrol activity by UNFICYP, the Force will be able to carry out its great responsibilities with increasing effectiveness.[5]

Especially welcome to UNFICYP was his announcement that, following his personal approach to Ecevit, the Turks had agreed to appoint a senior officer to serve as a liaison link between the Commanders of the UN and Turkish forces.

Waldheim's introductory statement was followed by the unanimous adoption of a brief Resolution which, couched in language stronger than hitherto, *demanded* that:

All parties to the present fighting comply immediately with the provisions of paragraph 2 of Security Council Resolution 353(1974) calling for an immediate cessation of all firing in the area and requesting all States to exercise the utmost restraint and to refrain from any action which might further aggravate the situation.[6]

The swing of sympathy away from Turkey was apparent in the debate that followed. Criticism by the representatives of Greece and Cyprus was only to be expected, as was the Turks' reply in kind, but almost all other speakers pointed accusing fingers, albeit wrapped in diplomatic nicety, at the Turks as the prime transgressors of the Council's resolutions. Typical was the cold observation of Mr Ivor Richard for Britain:

It does no good for a government to say that it accepts a resolution unless its acceptance is effective, unless the fighting actually stops. But if a government says that it accepts Resolution 353(1974) which we adopted last Saturday, or if it says it will accept the Resolution that we have just adopted tonight and its forces do not stop firing, there is only one of two conclusions available to us: either that government is not in control of its own armed forces or, alternatively, its acceptance is not an honest one.[7]

and the general mood was reflected in the speech of the Austrian representative, Mr Jankowitsch, which concluded the debate:

> Every line of the Secretary General's report speaks of the suffering of innocent people, of blood-shed and the loss of human life. And throughout the report another spectre looms, much larger and much more dangerous for the future of the island: the spectre of communal strife which has been unleashed by the events of the past week.
>
> There can certainly be no peace, no stability and no justice in this most sensitive area of the eastern Mediterranean unless communal strife, the most powerful root-cause of the present crisis, can be eliminated; unless the Greek and Turkish communities of Cyprus and, to a larger context, the peoples of Greece and Turkey can live and co-exist in harmony. . . .
>
> We now feel that the time has come when all the parties – when all forces opposing each other – should heed the unanimous appeal of the world community acting through the Security Council. . . . The next steps are talks which should begin between the parties with the least possible delay.[8]

The Council rose just before midnight on 23 July, little knowing that, as already described, it would have to meet again within 24 hours following frantic international pressures to avert Turkish action against UNFICYP at Nicosia airport.

At this juncture Prem Chand's primary concern was to implement the Secretary General's instructions in the new situation that confronted UNFICYP. A Force Commander's Directive was issued setting out the new tasks, revised operational boundaries and various other operational and logistic details. The wedge of territory stretching from the north coast to Nicosia now controlled by the Turkish army had split in two UNFICYP's Kyrenia District, hitherto the responsibility of the Finns. Since movement by UN troops within or across this area was likely to prove difficult, two new UN operational Districts were created – one on each flank, to be known respectively as Kyrenia District (East) and Kyrenia District (West). The former remained the responsibility of the Finns, while the latter became that of the 16th/5th Lancers which was reinforcing the British Contingent. With a need to reconstitute a stronger Force Reserve, the complete Parachute Squadron, RAC, (most of which hitherto had been deployed in Limassol Zone) was concentrated back in Nicosia, its location until the reductions imposed on UNFICYP two months earlier.[9]

UNFICYP was confronted by two distinct but closely related situations. First were the difficulties caused by the Turkish army's determination despite the ceasefire to expand the area under its control; this was of direct concern to the Finns in Kyrenia District (East), the Canadians in parts of Nicosia District, and the 16th/5th Lancers in Kyrenia District (West). Second was the need to prevent a recurrence of intercommunal fighting else-where, especially attacks by Greek Cypriots on isolated Turkish villages; this involved the Swedes in Famagusta District, the Austrians in Larnaca District, the Coldstream Guards in Limassol and Paphos Districts, and the Danes in Lefka District (none of whom had so far been brought into direct contact with mainland Turkish ground forces), as well as the Canadians along the Nicosia Green Line and villages further south.

Waldheim had stressed the need for UNFICYP to establish an efficient control of the ceasefire. There were frequent violations around the edges of the main Turkish enclave and these were protested at once by UNFICYP, making clear that halting forward movement was as important as halting the shooting, since it was the former that more often than not gave rise to the latter. Turkish troops were the prime offenders as they sought to gain maximum territorial advantage while Foreign Ministers were meeting in Geneva. The constant Turkish advances provoked bitter complaint by the National Guard, who, although generally co-operative with UNFICYP and restrained in their reaction, often saw no alternative but to meet the blatant Turkish forward movement with fire. It was little surprise that in such cases UNFICYP's appeals to both sides were liable to fall on deaf ears.

On the morning of 25 July the SRSG, Weckman-Munoz, addressed a personal message to Inhan protesting against a fresh Turkish advance just north of Nicosia airport and concluding with these words:

> I would ask you, in conformity with the statement made by the Turkish representative at closed session of the Security Council meeting last night, to impress on Turkish army the urgent need of putting an end to continuous troop movements far beyond the date and hour when the cease-fire accepted by both governments became operational.[10]

Some hours later Inhan replied that Turkish forces would observe the agreed ceasefire so long as the National Guard and the Greek national contingent (ELDYK) did so too, but stressed that the ceasefire must not be limited to areas in the north: it should apply throughout Cyprus and UNFICYP should safeguard Turkish Cypriots everywhere. Weckman-Munoz confirmed that it was UNFICYP's understanding, too, that the ceasefire should apply island-wide, but pointed out that UN troops must be accorded freedom of movement in order to afford protection not only to Turkish Cypriots in Greek-controlled areas in the south but also to Greek Cypriots in Turkish-controlled areas in the north.

Their exchanges had been spread over a period of some seven hours, demonstrating the handicap under which UNFICYP had been labouring – the lack of a direct, reliable and quick means of communication with the Turkish Force Commander, General Ersin. Although Waldheim had informed the Security Council on 23 July of Ecevit's agreement to appoint a senior officer to liaise with UNFICYP, it was not until the evening of 26 July that Ersin invited Prem Chand to a meeting in the village of Boghaz, close to the Turkish HQ just south of the Kyrenia Pass, to discuss the matter. Prem Chand accepted with alacrity and took with him UNFICYP's DCOS, Colonel Beattie (Canada); those present with Ersin were Inhan and Colonels Katircioglu (commander of the Turkish national contingent) and Cakar (Ersin's DCOS). It was the first opportunity for a direct exchange of views on the roles of and relations between the two forces.

Prem Chand explained UNFICYP's mandate, adding that in spite of its small size the Force was well placed in the new situation to assist in maintenance of the ceasefire and conditions conducive to a settlement. Ersin replied that the purpose of his troops was similar: they had come to Cyprus to ensure a just peace. He accepted the need for a means of direct communication between himself and Prem Chand but would not agree to an exchange of LOs between their respective HQ (as the latter proposed). Instead he said that his LO, who was to be Cakar, would be located at the Turkish Embassy in Nicosia, where he could be contacted by UNFICYP's LO at the adjacent Vice President's Office. For UNFICYP this was a second-best arrangement, but at least the hitherto time-consuming procedure of relaying messages via Inhan and Ankara would be superseded.[11] Next, Prem Chand stressed the need to consolidate the ceasefire, suggesting that this would best be done by creating a buffer zone between Ersin's troops and the National Guard, policed by UNFICYP; this, he said, would entail both sides notifying the UN Force of the precise locations of their forward troops. When Ersin confessed that his units had become so intermingled that this information was not readily available, Prem Chand offered to send UN patrols to check forward positions with a view to delineating the buffer zone. Ersin would say only that he needed to examine the situation and await instructions from Ankara.

The Turkish Force Commander then took up the point made by Inhan the previous day – the need to take account of the situation throughout the island, not just that in the areas now under his control. He said that the Turkish government required all Turkish Cypriot villages now in Greek hands to be restored to Turkish control, emphasizing that the safety of Turkish Cypriots everywhere was a prime concern; the return of these villages would be an important step towards a peaceful settlement. Prem Chand replied that, if forward movement and shooting were halted, UN troops would be able not only to police areas of confrontation between the Turkish army and the National Guard but also to tackle the problem of the Turkish villages. When Ersin insisted that all the latter must be restored to their former status, Prem Chand said that UNFICYP would use its best endeavours to this end, but, he asked, did Ersin accept that the same principle should apply to Greek villages now in the hands of the Turkish forces? Ersin made no reply. The meeting concluded with Prem Chand proposing that both sides should agree to halt all further advances and all shooting as from 0800hrs next morning, 27 July; this, too, drew no response from Ersin. It was clear that without Ankara's authority he was not free to accept any of the UNFICYP Commander's proposals for consolidation of the ceasefire. This was not an encouraging outcome, but at least the two Force Commanders had met face to face, their exchanges had been conducted in friendly fashion and the establishment of a military channel of communication had been agreed. These were welcome gains.

Ever since the initial landings on 20 July there had been uncertainty as to the status of UNFICYP vis-à-vis the Turkish forces. The Secretary General had been able only to advise Prem Chand 'to play it by ear', but this was easier said than done, for the Turks demanded that UN troops withdraw from all areas under Turkish control on the grounds that there was no role for them in these areas. UNFICYP was not prepared to accept this demand for two reasons: first, because the relentless and continuing expansion of the Turkish-occupied area was making a travesty of the ceasefire, and second, on account of the Force's clear responsibility towards Cypriots of both communities. Waldheim had instructed Prem Chand to try to reach agreement with Ersin on this vital matter, but this having proving impossible, Waldheim was obliged to pursue it himself.

In a report to the Security Council on 25 July he had already drawn attention to the problem and had set out his own view as to how UNFICYP should conduct itself:

It has been my understanding that UNFICYP should, indeed must, use its best efforts to ensure, as far as its capabilities permit, that the ceasefire called for by the Council is maintained. Obviously a United Nations peacekeeping Force, in a deeply serious situation such as the one prevailing in Cyprus, cannot be expected to stand by and not make the maximum effort to ensure that a Resolution of the Security Council was put into effect. For this reason my Special Representative, the Force Commander and all the personnel of UNFICYP have, as reported by me to the Security Council, been engaged in numerous efforts to restore the ceasefire, to ensure that it was observed and to prevent any incidents from escalating into a full recurrence of fighting.[12]

It was clear that what was now needed was a fresh Security Council mandate. With this in mind, Waldheim sought the support of three of the Security Council permanent members, Britain, France and the United States, with whose representatives he met in private on 26 July. He sought in vain:

Although the Turkish advance was continuing, the delicate relationship of the Western powers with Turkey made them unwilling to put pressure on Turkey to halt its army. Waldheim, to his credit, felt strongly about this and . . . asked what could be done to deal with the expanding Turkish bridgehead. The three ambassadors were extremely reserved in their response. Waldheim was indignant. The Turks, he said, were happy in the knowledge that no one would lift a finger to save a small country caught in the turmoil of history. Without a clearer mandate from the Security Council UNFICYP was in an impossible situation, and one of the results would inevitably be a steady erosion of the efficacy of UN peacekeeping operations. A firmer lead from the Security Council was essential.[13]

At Waldheim's request, the Security Council met again next day, 27 July, just as a meeting of the guarantor powers was getting under way in Geneva. Referring to violations of the ceasefire and proposals for UNFICYP to be interposed between the two sides, he reminded the Council that UNFICYP's mandate had never envisaged that the Force might be deployed between the armed forces of another member state and those of Cyprus. Continuing, he said:

I have instructed my representative in Geneva, Mr Guyer, to discuss with the three Foreign Ministers in the negotiations the best way in which UNFICYP can actively assist in limiting further hostilities and ceasefire violations. Obviously any plan involving the interposition of UNFICYP would require the complete cooperation of both sides. . . . What is needed now is an agreement on how to stabilise the ceasefire throughout the island so that negotiations may make progress.[14]

In the debate that followed the many ceasefire violations were widely condemned, but there was no discussion of a fresh mandate and by common consent the question of the inter-position of UNFICYP was left for decision in Geneva.[15]

For UNFICYP the differences of view as to the legitimacy of its continuing presence and activity in areas under Turkish army control remained, the Turks becoming increasingly vociferous in objecting to all its activities, including those of a humanitarian nature, within these areas. Ersin demanded not only that UN patrols and relief convoys should not enter them without prior Turkish permission, but also that UN troops based within them (such as the Finns at Tjiklos) should be confined to the immediate vicinity of their camps. Culmination came on the morning of 29 July in a message from Ersin to Prem Chand requiring all UN troops, UN civilian police and all other UN civilians to be withdrawn from the Turkish-occupied area by that same evening. Ersin added that, if thereafter UN personnel entered the area without permission, the Turkish army would not accept responsibility for their safety. Prem Chand's reply to this veiled threat was swift and unequivocal:

> I am surprised to receive such a message in view of the cordial and understanding meeting we had on 26 July . . . . I have referred your message to the Secretary General of the United Nations in New York, who alone is authorized to issue instructions to UNFICYP on behalf of the Security Council. May I suggest that a similar approach be made by you to Ankara in view of the grave implications involved. In the meantime . . . I look to you personally and to your forces to afford full protection to all UN personnel in your areas.[16]

Waldheim's reaction was no less robust. He instructed Prem Chand that, regardless of the outcome of any further discussions with Ersin, UNFICYP was not to withdraw without further instructions from him following his own negotiations with Ankara. We accordingly issued orders that UN troops stationed within Turkish-controlled areas were to remain in existing locations, while adding that to minimize friction and avoid exacerbating relations with the Turkish forces movement should be restricted to what was judged to be really necessary.

Freedom of movement on the ground and in the air was a basic requirement to enable UNFICYP to operate effectively and its right to this was enshrined in the 1964 Status of Forces Agreement. Problems were few in areas under Greek control, the National Guard realizing that in the face of the far stronger Turkish forces it was to its advantage to cooperate with the UN Force. For safety reasons UN helicopter sorties over Greek territory were notified to the National Guard in advance, but otherwise UNFICYP's operations in these areas were conducted as before, except that to avoid misunderstandings prior notice was given at local level of convoys carrying relief supplies to isolated Turkish villages. Since Turkey had not been a party to the Status of Forces Agreement, it was unrealistic to suppose that UNFICYP could insist on a right to freedom of movement in areas controlled by the Turkish army, with which it was thus necessary to reach agreement on a *modus operandi*. This provided for UN personnel requiring to enter the Turkish area to do so via the Ledra Palace checkpoint in Nicosia and obtain a pass at the adjacent Vice President's Office. (Apart from occasional attempts at obstruction, this procedure worked to UNFICYP's satisfaction during the weeks that followed.)

From time to time difficulties, sometimes genuine and sometimes fabricated, were encountered with both sides due to arguments over identification of UN personnel, both alleging that the other was using UN flags, uniforms and insignia to disguise its own men; this was given as justification for halting UN patrols. The fact that some units in both the Greek and Turkish forces sported as part of their regulation uniform blue berets similar to those worn by UN troops exacerbated matters, as did the fact the UNFICYP's vehicles had hitherto been painted in the olive drab colour usual in most armies. To avoid future confusion, a crash programme was instituted in UNFICYP to paint its military vehicles white, (as has since become the practice in other UN peacekeeping forces).

It was in these circumstances that UNFICYP concentrated on the twin tasks of stabilizing the fragile ceasefire throughout the island while acting to alleviate the plight of those who were suffering in consequence of the fighting. The visible presence of disciplined UN soldiers, if few in number, and their activities to these ends exerted a steadying influence and helped to restore a degree of confidence while the outcome of negotiations in Geneva was awaited. The UN Force's mood at this juncture was well reflected by the US representative, Mr Bennett, who told the Security Council on 27 July:

> UNFICYP is on the job in Cyprus. It has been carrying out a thoroughly professional operation in an atmosphere of great uncertainty and great danger, and I have every confidence that the United Nations Force will continue to play a major role in peacemaking in Cyprus.[17]

CHAPTER FIFTY-ONE

BUYING TIME

Mr Callaghan can fairly defend the agreement as a commonsense buying of time.

A.M. Rendel, *The Times*, London, 31 July 1974.

The Foreign Ministers of Britain, Greece and Turkey, respectively, James Callaghan, George Mavros and Turan Gunes, gathered in Geneva on the evening of 24 July in response to the Security Council's call for the guarantor powers 'to enter into negotiations without delay for the restoration of peace in the area and constitutional government in Cyprus'.[1] The presence of Roberto Guyer of the UN Secretariat and William Buffum of the US State Department provided links to Waldheim and Kissinger, but neither Cypriot community was represented. The talks, conducted at times bilaterally and at others in plenary session, opened just as the crisis at Nicosia airport was at its most acute and continued for six days in a climate of tension created by reports of frequent ceasefire violations in Cyprus and relentless reinforcement and expansion of the Turkish held area.

Delegations had had little time to prepare and it was not surprising that in the circumstances exchanges were liable to be acrimonious and progress difficult. By common consent Callaghan assumed the role of chairman and honest broker, but this proved to be a frustrating and thankless task:

> *[George Mavros]* was . . . very conscious of the dignity of Greece, sometimes irascible when under strain (he occasionally threatened to walk out), but anxious to reach agreement with Turkey. Turan Gunes . . . was capable of repeating the same interminable argument time after time until the words lost their meaning. . . . He was an expert at obstruction. . . . *[I]* soon was convinced that he used stalling tactics merely to gain time and prevent progress. . . . It seemed to us that Gunes had little or no authority. Behind him stood the Turkish Cabinet, and behind the Cabinet stood the Turkish Generals. . . . The talks developed into a gruelling cliff-hanger with the Turks as well as the Greeks at times inclined to say that they were prepared to face war rather than "retreat" or "humiliation".[2]

Callaghan's purpose was twofold: first, to secure an effective ceasefire, and second, to lay the foundations for a settlement that would obviate justification for the retention of Turkish troops on the island. Mavros's first priority was similar: to halt the Turkish advances and troop build-up, but his second was more specific: he pressed for a return to the arrangements established by the 1960 treaties in accordance with the obligations incurred by all three guarantor powers. Gunes saw the latter demand as altogether unrealistic (it was clear that the Turks feared that acceptance of that *status quo* would deprive them of the spectacular strategic gain won by their military action), but for Turkey there was a more immediate military consideration – the vulnerability of its forces confined within a constricted area, most of which lay within range of the National Guard's artillery. For Ankara the overriding need was to ensure the security of these troops; constitutional matters could be relegated for settlement later when that imperative had been satisfied. It was this need that explained the unrelenting Turkish forward movement, and it was this movement and the inevitable ceasefire violations to which it gave rise that soured the atmosphere in Geneva and on occasion brought the talks to the verge of collapse.

Such a point was reached on the second day when Mavros declared that Greece would find continued participation difficult unless immediate and decisive action was taken to halt the Turkish advances. Underlying his declaration was the genuine fear that, unless a halt was called, the new and still insecure government of Karamanlis in Athens might not survive, allowing a return of military rule; war between Greece and Turkey might then follow. Gunes gave no ground, arguing that the Turkish army could not remain inactive while Turkish Cypriot communities remained at risk. Although his stand evidently gave rise to disquiet within his own team[3], he was adamant:

> We are not on the island with troops to occupy any area permanently or to impose our law on the Cypriot people. But we will not withdraw them so long as there are Turkish Cypriots in isolated villages where the water pipes have been turned off by Greek officers or the National Guard, food is not getting through, the villagers are starving, and irregular forces, including EOKA gunmen, are raping and shooting. Therefore we cannot accept the simple formula of Mr Callaghan and Mr Mavros that the first target of this conference should be a ceasefire with an immediate UN operation to freeze everything on the ground. That would leave isolated Turkish villages open to potential further attack.[4]

Gunes proposed that should Mavros or Callaghan decide for whatever reason to leave Geneva, then they should all meet again in a week's time to sign an agreement worked out in the meantime by officials, embodying a formula for a political settlement that would secure lasting peace in Cyprus. With the talks on the brink of collapse, Callaghan adjourned the session to permit further bilateral negotiations, meanwhile urging Kissinger to press both Ankara and Athens to moderate their demands.

Negotiations continued in this fashion for the next three days and nights, but with little progress, the Turks proving especially intransigent in the knowledge of the strength of their position. Nonetheless, both sides appreciated the risk in terms of international opinion of appearing responsible for a breakdown; this, coupled with Kissinger's and Callaghan's strong encouragement, ensured that the talks did not collapse. Demands and counter-demands did not lessen tensions and the possibility that Karamanlis might not survive in Athens and even of war between Greece and Turkey cast malign shadows. Callaghan's team played a positive part working tirelessly to hammer out proposals that might be acceptable to both sides and success was achieved in the early hours of 30 July when the text of a tri-partite Declaration was at last agreed. It was signed with due ceremony by all three ministers at 2200hrs (Geneva time) the same day amid protestations of mutual appreciation and good-will that rang somewhat hollow to those who had been privy to the gruelling drafting process.

In this document, referred to as 'The Geneva Declaration',[5] the three ministers declared that:

> They recognized the importance of setting in train, as a matter of urgency, measures to adjust and to regularise within a reasonable period of time the situation in the Republic of Cyprus on a lasting basis, having regard to the international agreements signed at Nicosia on 16 August 1960 and to Resolution 353(1974) of the Security Council.

Further, they stressed the need to stabilize the situation and called on all forces, including irregulars, to desist from all offensive or hostile activities and agreed that areas controlled by the opposing forces at the time of signature of the Declaration should not be extended (thus implicitly accepting the Turks' refusal to return to the positions held at the time of the cease-fire on 22 July). More specifically the three agreed that the following measures should be implemented immediately:

> - a security zone, the extent of which was to be determined by representatives of Greece, Turkey and Britain in consultation with UNFICYP, should be established at the limit of the areas occupied by Turkish forces at 2200hrs (Geneva time) on 30 July. This zone, once agreed and established, would not be entered by any forces other than UNFICYP, which would be responsible for ensuring observance. Until then existing areas between the Turkish and Greek forces should not be entered by any troops.

> - Greek forces should withdraw immediately from all Turkish Cypriot enclaves and areas, which should continue to be afforded protection by UNFICYP and allowed to retain their own previous security arrangements.

> - the security and policing of mixed villages should be the responsibility of UNFICYP.

> - military personnel and civilians taken prisoner in the recent fighting should be exchanged or released under the auspices of the International Red Cross as soon as possible.

Although not explicity so stated, it seemed that these measures were to apply only to Turkish and mixed villages within Greek controlled areas; the plight of Greek Cypriots who now found themselves within the area controlled by the Turkish army was not addressed. The need to implement Resolution 353 as soon as possible was reaffirmed and, looking further ahead, the ministers declared that:

> Within the framework of a just and lasting solution acceptable to all the parties concerned and as peace, security and mutual confidence are established in the island, measures should be elaborated which will lead to the timely and phased reduction of the number of armed forces and the amounts of armaments, munitions and other war material in the Republic of Cyprus.

This fine but ambiguous wording reflected a further Turkish gain, for it left open for Ankara's interpretation the circumstances and timing for any Turkish force reductions, much less total withdrawal from the island.

The three ministers agreed to meet again in Geneva on 8 August, nine days later, with a view to considering constitutional aspects of the problem and reaching a settlement that would secure peace in the region and restore constitutional order in Cyprus. This time representatives of the two Cypriot communities would be invited to participate in the constitutional discussions, in which connection the ministers noted 'the existence in practice in the Republic of Cyprus of two autonomous administrations, that of the Greek Cypriot community and that of the Turkish Cypriot community'. These words, which avoided reference to the Greek Cypriot administration as 'the Government', were further demonstration of the degree to which Turkey's hard line had prevailed. However, differences of view as to the legitimacy of Turkey's military intervention were indicated by a separate statement (issued in conjunction with the Declaration) in which all three foreign ministers affirmed that:

> The adherence of their Governments to the Declaration . . . in no way prejudiced their respective views on the interpretation or application of the 1960 Treaty of Guarantee or their rights and obligations under that Treaty.

Perceptions as to what had been achieved varied. Mavros was relieved by what he saw as the most important consequence: removal of the threat of war between Greece and Turkey and the risk of the return of military rule in Athens. Gunes boasted of victory for Turkish arms in Cyprus and Turkish diplomacy in Geneva (although Ankara gave some credit to Kissinger, who on several occasions had advised Ecevit by telephone); there was now no question, Gunes asserted, of a return to the old order in Cyprus. For his part Callaghan told the British Parliament:

> Greece and Turkey have, I believe, been brought back from the brink of war, and what we have done in Geneva will help to keep the peace and give everyone a chance of moving on to the second and more important phase of making peace – a peace which will last and which will create the essential confidence among the communities which has been lacking. . . . We must do our utmost to secure compliance with Resolution 353(1974) of the Security Council in all its aspects, including the military provisions, as well as resolution of the constitutional problems of Cyprus, in such a manner as will command the confidence of all its peoples.[6]

Callaghan was entitled to satisfaction on two counts: collapse of the talks had been averted and realism had compelled recognition of the *de facto* existence of two separate administrations on the island.

The texts of the Declaration and the associated statement were transmitted at once to the UN Secretary General, requesting him to take appropriate action. When the Security Council met next day, 31 July, Waldheim expressed the hope that the agreement reached in Geneva would be a first step towards the full implementation of Resolution 353 and drew attention to the new tasks now asked of UNFICYP. In this connection he stressed the need for clarification of the UN Force's role in areas now under the control of the Turkish army, adding:

> UNFICYP has been playing, and should continue to play, a most useful humanitarian role in all parts of the island of Cyprus in assisting the civilian population – Turkish and Greek Cypriot alike – who have been afflicted by the recent hostilities. This matter is now under discussion by UNFICYP with the Turkish military command in Cyprus.[7]

Waldheim said that he had asked Prem Chand for an assessment of the practical implications of the Declaration in so far as UNFICYP was concerned.

A draft Resolution formally requesting the Secretary General to take appropriate action in the light of the Geneva Declaration had been tabled at this meeting of the Council, but after more than six hours of debate, some of which was ill-tempered, the Soviet representative demanded that a vote be postponed, ostensibly to allow him to seek instructions from Moscow. Others saw no need for any delay; the consequence was a Soviet veto.[8] Controversy was prolonged when Waldheim intervened to read out a message (just received from HQ UNFICYP) addressed to him by General Ersin, the Turkish commander in Cyprus:

> Turkish Peace Force Commander is of the opinion that the United Nations Forces in the area have successfully completed their functions and should now move outside the Turkish-controlled area to the locations where their mandate is most needed. Such a move is felt to be consistent with the Geneva ceasefire agreement signed on 30 July. Therefore I kindly request your consideration of giving necessary instructions to the elements of UNFICYP and UNCIVPOL to leave the Turkish-controlled area within the earliest possible time.
>
> I must reiterate on this occasion my sincere appreciation and gratefulness for the efficiency and spirit of cooperation shown by your Forces in my area of responsibility during the accomplishment of their duties. I hope our relations with the United Nations Forces along the security areas, when established, would be as best as ever. I would be most happy if I could help United Nations-supported humanitarian activities in Turkish-controlled area in the future.[9]

Waldheim said that he intended to issue appropriate instructions to Prem Chand, since UNFICYP could only operate effectively with the full support of all parties concerned, but reaction on the part of the Greek Cypriot and Greek representatives was predictable and immediate. The former declared:

> This move by the Turkish commander violates all the agreements with regard to the presence of the United Nations Force in Cyprus and renders the work of the Force very difficult because it must occupy the positions it held before in order to protect the population on both sides.[10]

Detecting something more sinister in Ersin's message, the latter asked:

> What is really the intention of the reply of the commander of the Turkish forces in Cyprus? Is it that UNFICYP will operate in the territory which is not occupied by the Turkish forces and that it will not operate in the territory occupied by the Turkish forces? . . . Is there any intention that this territory should no longer be Cyprus territory?[11]

A sterile debate ensued with differing interpretations placed on the intentions at the heart of the Geneva Declaration. There was a consensus, nonetheless, that it should be left to the Secretary General to sort matters out, as the Turkish representative, Olcay, observed:

> The problem . . . is the question of the mandate of UNFICYP, which obviously is insufficient as it stands to cover all the situations *[cited in the debate]*. The Secretary General has had ample opportunity to indicate to the Council that, if he is to operate on behalf of peace, he needs something more than he has at present. That is the crux of the matter. The sooner this problem is solved the better we shall all be.[12]

Containing his frustration, Waldheim made no public reference to his failure five days earlier to obtain the support of Britain, France and the United States for a fresh mandate for UNFICYP but, as he later remarked, little could be done without their leadership in the Security Council. His freedom of action thus constrained, he had little choice but to pursue the problem in cautious and conciliatory fashion. He informed Ecevit that he accepted that UNFICYP's role in the area under Turkish control should be a strictly humanitarian one, and Ecevit responded by stating that instructions had been issued to Ersin that all UN posts, checkpoints and patrols were to be permitted to continue as hitherto on the understanding that their activities were for humanitarian purposes only.[13]

CHAPTER FIFTY-TWO

CONSOLIDATING THE CEASEFIRE AND OTHER TASKS (23 JULY –9 AUGUST)

Throughout the island United Nations Forces are re-deploying and re-establishing contact with the local population, re-occupying evacuated observation posts and base camps, and investigating charges and accusations from both sides.

My Special Representative, the Force Commander and all the personnel of UNFICYP have been engaged in numerous efforts to restore the ceasefire, to ensure that it was observed and to prevent any incidents from escalating into a full recurrence of fighting.

UN Secretary General, *S/11353/ADD.6*,
24 July, and ADD.7, 25 July 1974.

While the Foreign Ministers were buying time in Geneva, UNFICYP lost no time in implementing the Secretary General's instructions received late on 22 July. Despite the agreement for an island-wide ceasefire that day, the ensuing three weeks saw frequent exchanges of small arms, mortar, artillery and tank fire in many areas, most caused by the relentless advances of the Turkish army to the east and west . Throughout this period UNFICYP's frequent and detailed Situation Reports kept the Secretary General and members of the Security Council, to whom they were promptly circulated,[1] fully informed. Although not reproduced here, these demonstrated the intense pressures under which the UN Force was operating and the heavy demands placed on all its contingents.

The requirement was four-fold: first, to halt fighting in the north between the invading Turkish forces and the Greek Cypriot National Guard; second, to prevent retaliatory attacks by the National Guard against isolated Turkish Cypriot communities elsewhere; third, to do the utmost to ensure that prisoners and refugees on each side were being humanely treated; and fourth, to alleviate the hardships being experienced by the many others caught up in the conflict. UN District Commanders were instructed in particular to investigate the situation in Turkish and mixed villages in areas under National Guard control, and to endeavour to gain access for the same purpose to those Greek villages now behind Turkish army lines. Although reinforcements for all contingents, which eventually almost doubled the operational strength of UNFICYP,[2] were now arriving, the number and diversity of problems, facing the Force at this juncture strained its resources to the limit.[3]

Allegations of atrocities on both sides required prompt investigation in order to damp down passions; power and water supplies needed to be restored; calls came for relief to be taken to isolated communities short of food; negotiations were necessary to arrange for exchanges of wounded personnel; UNFICYP assistance was sought to deal with unexploded bombs; diplomatic missions asked for information or help in respect of missing foreign nationals; help was needed to deal with fires burning in sensitive locations, such as along the Green Line in Nicosia; there were requests for assistance in the repatriation of the dead from one side to the other; numerous untended animals in great distress on farms, from which owners had fled, needed to be watered and fed; reported but unmarked minefields required checking; assistance was requested to ensure delivery of supplies to bakeries; calls came for looting of abandoned premises to be prevented; help was sought for transport to hospital of the sick or injured now isolated in consequence of the fighting; escorts were requested for the carriage of money between banks and reports of dangerous chemicals left unguarded had to be investigated. All such problems, together with others too numerous to record here, were laid at UNFICYP's door. Since it was impossible for the Force to respond to every cry for help, the arrival in Nicosia on 23 July of a team from the International Committee of the Red Cross (ICRC) was most welcome. These diverse problems could not be allowed, however, to distract UNFICYP from the overriding priority, the need to halt any continuing fighting and to consolidate the ceasefire. The build-up of Turkish forces was continuing with daily deliveries by air of men and equipment into the main enclave, while tanks, artillery and additional troops were coming ashore on the north coast, and all the while the lodgement area was being expanded east and west. It was clear that Turkey was set on gaining maximum advantage both in the build-up of its forces and in seizure of territory pending the resumption of negotiations in Geneva on 9 August. This activity, opposed as best it could by the National Guard, gave rise to most of the continuing fighting, and was the main, but not sole, focus of UNFICYP's attention.

With the crisis at Nicosia airport resolved, it became possible to re-deploy part of its UN garrison in order to implement Waldheim's instruction that, wherever possible, UN troops should be interposed between the combatants with a view to establishing an efficient control of the ceasefire. Following their arrival during the night of 24/25 July to reinforce the airport defence, 16th/5th Lancers, the British armoured reconnaissance unit commanded by Lieut. Colonel R.Q.M. Morris, had been allotted operational responsibility for the newly created Kyrenia District (West), which included the airport and all the area between it and the north coast west of the main Turkish enclave. With reliable information as to the situation in this area scant,[4] there was an urgent need to discover the forward positions of the Turkish and Greek Cypriot forces. Finnish OPs in the Pendhadaktylos mountains were reporting artillery and mortar fire in the mountains and on the plain below, and the National Guard was protesting that Turkish troops with artillery and tanks were engaging their troops at Ayios Ermalaos (situated on one of the few roads leading west from the enclave) and advancing on other villages to its north and south.

16th/5th Lancers were accordingly ordered to patrol the road leading north-west from Nicosia through Yerolakkos to Myrtou and thence to the island's north coast at Ayios Yeorios (20km west of Kyrenia) with a two-fold mission: first, to ascertain the situation all along the enclave's west flank, and second, to stabilize this by inhibiting further Turkish advances. It was an ideal armoured reconnaissance mission, which Morris gave it to his B

Squadron led by Major J.A. Wright. Setting off from the airport early on 26 July, his troops (some of which suffered near misses from Turkish artillery fire) reported that the National Guard still held most of the dominant features east of the Squadron's axis, but that fighting was in progress in the area of Ayios Ermalaos with the National Guard falling back in the face of the Turks' superiority.

Told that some Greek wounded were thought to have been left behind in Ayios Ermalaos, the Lancer's Adjutant, Captain M.F.E. Radford, set out to rescue them, as Staff Sergeant De St Croix (leader of B Squadron's 5th Troop) later described:

> It was decided to put a couple of stretchers on the back deck of my Saladin armoured car and we would go in to bring out the wounded. Two Ferret scout cars, commanded by Captain Radford and L/Cpl Attwood, and my Saladin then proceeded . . . along the small road leading to Ayios Ermalaos. We passed the Greek front line about two miles from the village and drove very slowly not knowing what to expect. I was told to halt on the outskirts of the village while the Adjutant went in to investigate.[5]

Radford found the village deserted except for a few old people including one wounded, and the rest of his party entered. Splitting into pairs, they then carried out a house-to-house search on foot:

> I had finished my area and was returning to the square when we came under heavy small arms fire from the north-east. After picking ourselves up off the ground we made our way back to the vehicles and mounted very quickly. . . . At this stage I reported "Contact!" on the radio and decided it was time to pull out. I then realized that Captain Radford and his driver were missing. The firing had stopped, so I started calling for the Adjutant . . . . I received no answer, so along with L/Cpl Attwood we started out along the very narrow side streets . . . . On reaching the outskirts of the village I saw a house about 50m apart from the rest, and about 300m to the north was a M48 tank with its gun aimed directly at the house.[6]

De St Croix saw, too, that Radford had been pinned down behind the house and realized that the Turkish tank crew probably had mistaken them for Greeks. Covered by Attwood, he walked into the open flourishing a UN flag:

> Immediately the turret swung round my way and I braced myself for the shots. I walked to within 25m of the house and shouted to Captain Radford to get the hell out. This he did . . . . I gave a final wave with my UN flag and with heart in mouth retraced my steps to the village . . . . We all mounted up and very slowly drove out of the village with the old folk on my Saladin's back deck. In my opinion it was clearly a case of mistaken identity on the part of the Turks, but all the same we were very glad to get out safely.[7]

B Squadron gained valuable information throughout this day (26 July), but incidents such as this and the general uncertainties slowed progress to the point that it was not until the following afternoon that it reached the north coast at Ayios Yeoryios.

For the next 18 days Wright's troops maintained close watch along the whole length of the Turks' western flank. Reconnaissance patrols, which sometimes came under Turkish fire, were deployed forward to make contact with and monitor the movements of both the National Guard and the Turkish army with a view to stabilizing the situation.[8] To attempt to halt the Turkish advances lay neither within UNFICYP's legitimate role nor within its military capability, but the presence of these UN troops served in practice to inhibit them and to provide accurate information as to their extent. It also afforded opportunities, which the Lancers seized, to respond to appeals for help of various kinds from civilians of all communities in their area. The experiences of Lieut. Pickering were typical when his 4th Troop was sent to report on the situation in the Greek mountain village of Agridhaki, which had been subjected to Turkish artillery and mortar fire:

> It [Agridhaki] was being held by a 30-year-old Greek mainland officer with some 10 decent soldiers around him and possibly 30–40 others who weren't too happy with life. Their only defence against the Turks seemed to be an ancient .303 water-cooled Vickers MG and a .50 on an AA tripod. The Greek mainland officer was pretty unhappy with life, as he openly admitted to me that he had come over from the mainland in order to "help out" with the *coup*; this having gone completely haywire he found himself in the front line with now nothing to live for – his chances of returning to the mainland, he considered, were pretty remote; the Greek government didn't recognize him, the Nicosia government would have possibly shot him, except that they needed his skills against the Turks, and the SBA was too far away. . . . A few days later I witnessed the occupation of the village by the Turks. A creeping mortar barrage was used with the infantry fanned out in the standard V formation. Presumably the Greek officer died for a village he neither knew nor cared about.[9]

Expansion eastwards by the Turkish forces was no less relentless and complementary action on this flank was the task of the Finns under Lieut. Colonel Pullinen, now responsible for Kyrenia District (East). Since the Finns lacked an armoured reconnaissance capability, Major P.J. Staveacre's C Squadron, 4th/7th Dragoon Guards (less its Swingfire anti-tank missile troop, which was retained as part of the airport defence) was re-deployed in their support on 25 July. The Turks' easterly movement had four prongs: first, along the coast from Kyrenia to the villages of Kazaphani, Bellapais (where an estimated 1000 Greek Cypriot refugees had gathered), Ayios Epiktitos and Klepini; second, immediately south of the mountains along the road through Kato Dhikomo and on to Koutsovendis; third, on the plain in the area of Mandres; and fourth, north-east of Nicosia towards Mia Milea. All were supported by artillery and tanks (and by naval gunfire in the case of the first), with the National Guard imposing delay as best it could.[10] The Finns, with Dragoon Guards support, acted with initiative and courage in efforts to consolidate the ceasefire by inhibiting these Turkish advances, while providing valuable reports to HQ UNFICYP and rendering assistance to civilians in need.

A number of Greek Cypriot and Greek civilians, together with some wounded National Guard soldiers, were being held under UN protection by GILLFORCE at the Dome Hotel, Kyrenia, and about 5000 Greek Cypriots from surrounding areas had congregated in the village of Bellapais where there were some 100 wounded and an acute lack of medical supplies; to provide protection for the latter, Pullinen established a post nicknamed OP Bella in part of its ancient abbey. Although Turkish troops had bypassed the village earlier, on 28

July some 200 entered to search it and a captain demanded that the Finns withdraw, alleging that there were Greeks wearing UN uniform hiding in the village and that on this account the Finns might be shot by mistake. Lieutenant Markku Koli was sent from Tjiklos to handle the situation, only to have the same Turk hold a weapon to his head and demand that he and the men of OP Bella withdraw within five minutes on pain of being shot. Pullinen reacted with characteristic vigour: telling Koli to act as he judged best, he immediately made for Bellapais:

> Half a mile from the village there was a *[Turkish]* check-point with orders to stop all vehicles, but nothing said about men on foot. I walked alone to the village. Outside it I met the men of the OP who had withdrawn. They asked to return with me but I refused. I went into the village and met the captain who was very angry that I had been allowed through. There inside a building was a Turkish battalion CO who "couldn't help". All the inhabitants and the refugees were collected by the restaurant in the middle of the village which was surrounded by Turkish soldiers.[11]

At Pullinen's insistence OP Bella was re-established and a second Finnish post was established to its north. The Finns subsequently maintained watch over both Greek inhabitants and refugees until all were later deported by the Turks, most south to Nicosia but some males north to Turkey.

During late July heavy fighting took place between Turkish armoured forces and the National Guard on the east flank of the enclave, both along the coast and south of the mountains (Buffavento Castle itself was occupied by the Turks on 28 July). Although by early August Turkish expansion on this flank generally had not been as extensive as that in the west, HQ UNFICYP's constant protests that the Turks' continuing operations on both flanks were provoking frequent outbreaks of fighting were met by bland assertions that protection of Turkish Cypriot villages necessitated these advances. In this situation UNFICYP was able to do little more than to interpose its troops where possible in order to monitor and report. (Pullinen rejected Turkish demands for the withdrawal of those of his OPs, such as Martin's Mound, which lay in the path of Turkish advances.)

UNFICYP's contingents elsewhere, as yet not involved with mainland Turkish ground forces, acted with no less energy to prevent or to halt outbreaks of intercommunal fighting and to alleviate the hardships now being suffered by many in both communities. Of particular concern was the National Guard's action in surrounding and demanding the surrender of isolated Turkish villages; in these cases UN contingents endeavoured either by negotiation or by deployment of troops to ensure that bloodshed did not ensue. In Famagusta District Swedish patrols sent out by Lieut. Colonel Kristensson reported that the National Guard was in control of most of this large District, but that Turkish troops had not yet reached Kythrea (and its important water source) or the clutch of Turkish villages around Chatos. However, many Turkish Cypriots (apart from some of the old or infirm) had fled from small scattered villages to the security offered within the walls of Old Famagusta or in larger Turkish villages such as Galatia and Galinoporni on the Panhandle. Inhan's angry allegations of massacres by the National Guard of Turks at Chatos required urgent investigation. A Swedish patrol found that most of Chatos itself, together with the small villages to its west, had been abandoned, inhabitants having fled to Knodhara (5km east) where the village's normal population of about 630 had been swollen by refugees to about 4,000, including 15 severely wounded whom the Swedes evacuated to the Turkish hospital in Nicosia. The local Turkish leader assured the Swedes that there had been no massacres but that there were acute shortages of most necessities, including water, the supply from the Kythrea source having been turned off by the Greeks. Kristensson reacted quickly by providing what relief he could from within his Contingent's resources, the water supply was restored and his medical teams tended the sick and wounded, where necessary conveying them to hospital through National Guard lines. Some Turkish Cypriots remained in villages on the slopes of the Pendhadaktylos mountains and in the mixed village of Yenagra (10km south-east of Chatos), but the National Guard held other villages in the area, most of which were reported undamaged. Movement between TCF-held localities was difficult and short-ages of various natures including water continued, but a UN officer visiting Knodhara reported that morale among the Turkish Cypriots was remarkably high with no complaints of ill-treatment by the National Guard.

The plight of Turkish Cypriots congregated within the walls of the Old City of Famagusta (by 6 August these were estimated to number over 10,000, twice the normal population) also demanded attention. The Swedes' OP in Othello's Tower was re-established and a Liaison Officer was stationed in it to liaise with the local Turkish leader and a second was deployed to Colonel Kostas, the local National Guard commander; these liaison arrangements enabled Kristensson more than once to avert a recurrence of local fighting. A particular problem was caused by Greeks looting Turkish houses close to, but outside, the walls of the Old City, an activity visible to TCF stationed on the walls. To stop it Kristensson established temporary OPs in adjacent Turkish hamlets and these were augmented by UN patrols.[12] As at Knodhara, help was given to the sick and wounded (eight of the most serious were conveyed to the Nicosia Turkish hospital) and action was taken to meet urgent relief needs. Elsewhere patrols found Turkish refugees gathered at Galatia and Galinoporni also in need of food and water, which UNFICYP endeavoured to supply.

Although Kristensson reported on 27 July that the National Guard was holding about 90 TCF as prisoners in villages at the base of the Panhandle and that four National Guardsmen and one TCF had been killed in an outbreak of fighting at Ovgoros, the situation throughout the District more generally was calm. However, next day HQ National Guard protested that the TCF had attacked and captured the Greek village of Ayios Nikolaos and, more worry-ingly, that Turks inside Old Famagusta had opened a passage through the walls and were looting dockside warehouses. Next evening (29 July) Kristensson said that the situation had deteriorated. Turkish Cypriots using a bulldozer were building an earthwork across to the quayside, thus isolating the warehouses from National Guard positions, and Colonel Kostas was threatening action to stop this. There was little to be done that night but next morning I flew to Famagusta to see the situation for myself. Accompanied by Kristensson, I discussed the problem with the local Turkish leaders, who denied any looting of the warehouses and claimed that the new earthwork was necessary for defensive purposes.[13] Kristensson was reasonably optimistic that he would be able to exert sufficient pressure on Kostas to avert any action that might lead to fighting, although the National Guard was nonetheless far from satisfied.

For Lieut. Colonel Rieger's Austrians in Larnaca District the points of main concern lay in the town of Larnaca and in the area of Kophinou further west; some 740 Turkish Cypriots were being held in the former under the eyes of the Austrians, with a further 100 similarly held at Kophinou. However, National Guard attacks were reported to be continuing on some villages, such as Alaminos from which the Turkish inhabitants had fled[14], and there was some looting of Turkish property in the Scala area of Larnaca. Otherwise by early August the District was relatively calm.

In Limassol District, where by 5 August some 5300 Turkish Cypriots had fled isolated villages to seek sanctuary in the British SBA at Episkopi, the intercommunal situation generally was calm. In the town Lieut. Colonel Willoughby's Coldstream Guards had gained access to the stadium in which about 1,500 Turkish Cypriots were being held. The latter were regularly visited both by his guardsmen and by the Australian UN Civilian Police; food and water were found to be in adequate supply; tents were provided to give shelter; a Turkish and a Greek doctor were in attendance and sanitary facilities were reported satis-factory.[15] UNFICYP was thus able firmly to refute allegations made by the Turkish government and the Nicosia Leadership of maltreatment of those held in the stadium. Looting and wanton destruction on a considerable scale occurred in the Turkish quarter of Limassol town and in the villages of Evdhimou and Alekhtora, but otherwise Willoughby's patrols found the District generally to be quiet. However, he had been involved in a tiresome problem which, through no fault of his own, strained relations with Major General Butler, the Army Commander in the neighbouring British SBA.

When the National Guard had attacked the Turkish quarter of Limassol on 20 July, a mainland Turkish army colonel (the undercover commander of the local TCF), together with three other mainland officers, had sought asylum in Polemidhia Camp, the Coldstreams' main base just north of Limassol. Granting this in accordance with Waldheim's guidance, Willoughby kept the presence of the officers in his camp secret, but, learning soon afterwards that Greek civilian labour employed in the camp had discovered their presence and fearing that this might give rise to an attempt by the National Guard in the adjacent camp to seize them, he gave instructions for any such attempt to be met with full force. Nevertheless, the continuing presence of the Turks in his camp was an embarrassment and Willoughby considered how he might rid himself of them:

> I had occasion to visit General Butler and Colonel Woodford [a Staff Officer] and asked the General if he would provide refuge for the Turks if I was able to get them to the SBA. He agreed to do this. I considered the use of an ambulance but fortunately decided against it – the National Guard did stop one of our ambulances and carefully checked the occupants.[16]

His problem was solved by the arrival at Polemidhia on 24 July of a UN Whirlwind heli-copter; the four Turks were immediately put aboard this and flown into the SBA. Their arrival there proved most unwelcome and, when next day he learnt of it, Air Marshal Aiken, CBFNE, ordered them to be removed forthwith. Willoughby caught the blast:

An irate General Butler rang me up and asked what the devil I thought I was doing sending Turks into the SBA, and ordered me to remove them immediately. I reminded him of his agreement previously made to to accept them, which he admitted, but nevertheless I was to remove them. I presented this problem to *[UNFICYP's]* Chief of Staff, who much to my relief told me to do nothing, with the remark, "They're Butler's babies now".[17]

There had already been a disposition during the previous few days on the part of some at HQ BFNE to expect Willoughby and his battalion to comply with their directions. I made clear that as part of UNFICYP's British Contingent they were not subordinate in any way to HQ BFNE and that no orders emanating from that HQ were to be complied with without prior reference to me.

With HQ BFNE now saddled with the problem, I was requested to investigate the possibility of exchanging the Turks for mainland Greek officers currently held under UN protection at the Dome Hotel, Kyrenia. Without disclosing knowledge of the number or whereabouts of the Turkish officers, I asked the Counsellor at the Turkish Embassy, hypothetically, whether such an exchange might be arranged. The response was angry: if UNFICYP was holding Turkish officers they must be released at once; an exchange was irrelevant. I told him that no Turkish officers were being held by the UN Force and declined to give any further information. Before I could pursue the matter further I learnt that, on London's authority, the four Turks had been flown away from Cyprus under British arrangements for repatriation to Turkey.

Paphos District generally was calm. An allegation that a massacre of Turks had taken place at Polis was investigated by Major Macfarlane's company of the Coldstream Guards and found to have no substance. In those few areas, such as at the remote Turkish villages of Ayios Ioannis and Vrecha in the Troodos foothills, where from time to time there were isolated outbreaks of fighting, his guardsmen succeeded in bringing them to a halt. By 6 August all but six Turkish villages had surrendered to the National Guard, the males being held prisoner in the National Guard camp at Yeroskipos, where they were regularly visited by UNFICYP and ICRC representatives.

In Lefka District the Danish Contingent under Lieut.Colonel Severinson was succeeding in restoring a semblance of calm, and a number of its OPs previously withdrawn were re-established. A particularly watchful eye was being kept on those Turkish Cypriots in Lefka town who had surrendered to the National Guard, and those still holding out in the two small coastal enclaves at Kokkina and Limnitis.

Maintenance of the ceasefire along the Green Line in Nicosia continued to pose problems for the 1st Commando Group of the Canadian Airborne Regiment under Lieut. Colonel Manuel. On 23 July Turkish mortar fire fell in the vicinity of the British High Commission[18] and the Canadian Camp Kronborg on the west bank of the dry Pedhieos river, where the National Guard appeared to be attempting to move forward. Two Canadians were wounded in the crossfire and, to allow their evacuation, UN troops opened fire with heavy and light machine guns. Further fighting broke out next day not only along parts of the Green Line, but also close to the British High Commission and the nearby French Embassy; elsewhere the Greek and Soviet Embassies came under mortar fire, fortunately without casualties. The

Canadians succeeded in securing local ceasefires but not before the TCF had secured some advantages. The latters' attempts to limit the Canadians' access across the Green Line to premises previously occupied by them created new problems, which required tiresome negotiations with a Leadership now growing in confidence. Turkish allegations continued that the Ledra Palace Hotel was being used by snipers and, to refute these, representatives of the Turkish Embassy were conducted through it to prove that the building was now occupied solely by Canadians.

In late July the balance of the Canadian Airborne Regiment, augmented by other elements including airborne artillery, engineers, a troop of Lord Strathcona's Horse (armoured reconnaissance), and M113 APCs and Lynx reconnaissance vehicles, began to arrive to reinforce its 1st Commando Group, and the regimental commander, Colonel Lessard, took over command of Nicosia District from Lieut. Colonel Manuel on 2 August. Thus reinforced, the Canadians were able to operate with a new robustness:

> The Regiment was moving in with all the necessary "tools" to carry out its UN role and to ensure security of its own personnel including prevention of abuses against peacekeeping soldiers on the part of the belligerents. The Canadian Contingent was to have some "teeth". There were to be no more cases of Canadian soldiers being disarmed or being ignored. This point was made very clear when on more than one occasion road barricades put up by the Turkish army, TCF and Greek National Guard units were forcibly removed by our soldiers. In very specific areas we insisted on our freedom of movement and both sides learned to respect us for this stand . . . There was a great sense of pride among our Canadian soldiers; they felt more confident and were showing it.[19]

With sporadic exchanges of fire, especially in the area of the Ledra Palace Hotel, still taking place, Prem Chand appealed on 2 August to the commanders on both sides to do all they could to prevent any recurrence of fighting within the capital and offered UNFICYP's assistance to this end; the appeal was largely in vain. On the night of 6 August a Canadian soldier, Private Perron, on patrol in Nicosia was shot in the back near a TCF road-block and died as he was being evacuated. This incident may have been deliberate retaliation for the robustness now being displayed by the Canadians.[20]

Although the Turkish army's expansion in the north was continuing, the situation else-where on the island was stabilising and there was growing emphasis on humanitarian and relief operations. While movement in the Turkish-occupied areas was difficult, further south UNFICYP visited or established OPs at almost all Turkish Cypriot and mixed villages to ensure the safety of the inhabitants, especially where the TCF had surrendered their arms to the National Guard and requested UNFICYP protection. This improvement allowed UNFICYP to revert from Orange to the lower state of Blue Alert on 2 August and for some of the Force's families evacuated to Dhekelia 12 days earlier to return to Nicosia.

The future of the airport, taken over by UNFICYP as a temporary measure, now required consideration. There was a clear need to bring it back into use at an early date and to ensure in the meantime that technical installations and those aircraft still present were not allowed to deteriorate; further, there were calls for the reactivation of the Nicosia Joint Air Traffic

Control which was an integral element of the international Cyprus Flight Information Region. At a meeting convened at HQ UNFICYP on 4 August attended by representatives of the government (which since 1964 had exercised sole control of the airport) it was accepted that the airport should remain a UN-protected area for the time being, but that limited access should be allowed to technical personnel for specific purposes. These arrangements were notified to all concerned, including the Turkish side, in a Note issued the same day. It was met by immediate Turkish protest on the grounds that neither HQ UNFICYP nor the British Foreign Secretary had consulted the Leadership. Since Turkish troops were now in position to dominate the airport, it was not feasible to proceed as had been proposed; to attempt to do so in the face of Turkish opposition ran the risk of a breakdown in the ceasefire. In consequence it was necessary to continue to deny access to all except UNFICYP and certain RAF personnel.

Meanwhile UNFICYP was closely involved in action by the three guarantor powers to establish a security zone at the limit of the areas occupied by Turkish forces at 2200hrs (Geneva time) on 30 July, as required by the Geneva Declaration. This zone was to be delineated by a tripartite committee composed of representatives of Greece, Turkey and the United Kingdom, in consultation with UNFICYP. Those appointed to the committee (which was supported by a cartographic team provided by HQ British Forces, Episkopi) were Colonel Hunter (Defence Adviser to the British High Commission), who by common consent acted as Chairman, Major Tsolakis (the Greek army officer who was the National Guard's LO to HQ UNFICYP), and Colonel Cakar (the Turkish Force Commander's LO to UNFICYP); Colonel Beattie (Canada), UNFICYP's DCOS, was nominated as its representative. The committee's first meeting was held at HQ UNFICYP, which provided various facilities throughout, on 2 August, but its deliberations were not completed until 9 August.

Moving sometimes by helicopter and sometimes in vehicles or on foot and occasionally having to take cover from shooting close by, notably while surveying the Green Line in Nicosia, when UNFICYP troops helped to extricate its members unharmed, the committee tried to agree on the forward positions of each side. Problems were many and arguments frequent; for the most part they centred on the location of Turkish troops, about which Cakar often appeared poorly briefed, confirming General Ersin's admission to Prem Chand at their meeting on 26 July that he was uncertain of the exact positions of his forward units. In some places agreement was made difficult by the novel Turkish attitude that ground over which Turkish troops had observation had to be regarded as ground occupied by them, while at others problems were created when, no sooner had agreement been reached, than the Turkish troops moved forward. A UN officer present during one of the arguments commented later: 'Both sides were determined to dispute every acre, hectare, house and stubble field! Even the British full Colonel [Hunter] was losing patience since the Greek and Turk find it difficult to read a map.'[21] Indeed, the committee's work was often hampered by Turkish objections of one kind or another, giving rise to a growing suspicion that the Turks were playing for time before engaging in another round of fighting. On the Greek side there were few problems, for the National Guard recognized only too well its weakness vis-à-vis the Turkish army. Beattie's advice, based on accurate and impartial observation by UN troops and his own familiarity with the area, was sometimes crucial in resolving disagreements. After lengthy debate (with Cakar raising objections right up to the last moment) a report, in which differences of opinion were stated, was signed by all three members at HQ UNFICYP on 9 August in the presence of the press. It confirmed that the Turkish enclave had been expanded by some 10km both east and west and that in places the Green Line in Nicosia had been advanced by the Turks. Acting as courier for the three, Colonel Hunter delivered the report the same evening to Geneva, where the Foreign Ministers of the guarantor powers had re-convened for the second round of talks. It was quickly overtaken by events and nothing more was heard of it.

With the three Guarantor Powers re-convening in Geneva there was nervousness in New York lest UNFICYP take any action that might prejudice their deliberations. This was clear when the situation in Famagusta took a turn for the worse. Kristensson had been optimistic on 30 July that he could contain the situation, but the Turks were now sallying forth at night under cover of the new earthwork to loot warehouses on the quayside. The National Guard was not willing to tolerate this activity and Clerides, as acting President, warned Prem Chand on 5 August that, unless UNFICYP stopped the looting, the National Guard would act to do so. This was a clear intercommunal situation covered by the terms of UNFICYP's mandate (unlike that at Nicosia airport a fortnight earlier which had involved mainland Turkish forces).

Prem Chand decided that, unless the TCF agreed to demolish the earthwork and restore the *status quo*, UN posts should be interposed between the walls of the Old City and the warehouses to prevent further looting. His decision was notified that evening to both sides, making clear that UNFICYP did not intend to take control of the port itself. Clerides and the National Guard gave agreement, but the Leadership in the person of Dr Unel[22] questioned the proposed action and suggested that, instead, tripartite control should be established over the port; Prem Chand disagreed, considering this to be a matter for those about to meet in Geneva. The Leadership then asked for more time to consider the matter, no doubt in order to consult Ankara. However, guarded approval for UNFICYP's intended action came from New York with the hope expressed that there would be no shooting since this might upset deliberations in Geneva.

It was decided that I should go to Famagusta to take charge. I ordered a troop of 16th/5th Lancers (armoured cars), a platoon of Canadians and one of Finns (both carried in Canadian M113 APCs) to move under cover of darkness to Carl Gustav Camp to reinforce the Swedish Contingent and told Kristensson to organize a multi-national force including these troops ready to be interposed next morning (6 August); this he did, appointing as its Commander Lieut. Colonel Bertil Olsson, his second-in-command. I reached Carl Gustav Camp by helicopter as dawn was breaking and with Kristensson went at once to the Old City's Sea Gate, where at 0500hrs I met the local Turkish Cypriot leader, Mr Bessim, just outside the Walls. In the meantime Olsson's force was held unseen in the Swedish camp.

I pressed Bessim for TCF in the vicinity to be withdrawn and for the *status quo* to be restored by 0700hrs, and told him of UNFICYP's intention to establish UN posts between the Old City and the quayside warehouses to pre-empt any action by the National Guard. He said he would give me his reply by that time, but a marked increase in TCF activity and improvement of the disputed earthwork immediately followed. To demonstrate that we meant business, I ordered Olsson's Force to move forward and show itself just north of the Old City. (The sight of the Lancers' armoured cars and the Canadians' M113 APCs must have surprised the Turks, who hitherto had not been aware that the UN Force now included such armoured fighting vehicles.) When we met again at 0700hrs Bessim undertook only to consult the TCF commander (presumably a mainland Turkish officer), but gave his assurance that UNFICYP's proposed action would not be met by force. I thereupon told Prem Chand that I would now interpose the UN troops, only to be informed that in a telephone call from New York Brian Urquhart had emphasized the need to avoid any action that might complicate matters in Geneva. In view of this Prem Chand thought it prudent to discuss the matter with Unel further and for action to be deferred for the time being.

As time passed I held a third equally abortive meeting with Bessim and other Turks outside the Sea Gate while Prem Chand tried to speak to Unel. Meanwhile Olsson's Force was obliged to remain in frustrated inaction in full view of the Old City, where I visited it to explain the delay and warned the 16th/5th Lancer troop leader, Lieutenant C. Kenney-Herbert, that on no account during any subsequent action was fire to be opened with his armoured cars' 76mm main armament without my personal authority. After a long hot morning of stalemate, Prem Chand persuaded the Leadership in Nicosia, whose communications with the Turkish Cypriots inside the Old City had broken down, to send its Political Liaison Officer, Meri Hassan, to Famagusta to try to defuse the situation. Escorted by Major Bamford (Canada), one of HQ UNFICYP's operations officers, Hassan arrived in Carl Gustav Camp by UN Sioux helicopter in the early afternoon. In order to avoid the risk of taking him through National Guard lines I ordered him to be flown in to the Old City by the same helicopter.

The National Guard had become increasingly impatient at UNFICYP's apparent failure to interpose troops and, to explain the delay, I went together with Kristensson to meet its local commander, Colonel Kostas, at the badly bomb-damaged Aspelia Hotel on the seafront. Kostas, clearly under great emotional strain, declared that he had betrayed his honour as a Greek officer when on 22 July he had ordered artillery fire on the Old City to be halted two hours before the general ceasefire was due to take effect, and said that, since UNFICYP was evidently not prepared to act to halt the Turkish Cypriots' looting of the warehouses, he now must do so, not least to atone for his failure two weeks earlier. I replied that, contrary to what he thought of as a betrayal of his professional honour, he had actually acted in the highest tradition of military chivalry by halting the bombardment of helpless civilians when he knew that a ceasefire was in the offing. I gave my word that UNFICYP intended to take firm action to stop the looting by interposing UN posts and urged him on no account to take any step that might endanger the ceasefire or complicate the task of those in Geneva. Although not really mollified, he agreed.

On returning to Carl Gustav Camp from the Old City Hassan was singularly unforthcoming and, after further delay while Prem Chand spoke to Unel, he and Bamford flew back to Nicosia. In spite of my protestations Prem Chand still required the operation to be delayed to allow him to go with Hassan to meet Unel. This he did and at 1800hrs I received the order to abandon the operation. This decision was received with dismay. We had failed to remove an almost certain cause for renewed intercommunal violence (we were not to know that this would be overtaken by events a few days later) and in the process the UN Force generally and the Swedish contingent in particular had lost, at least temporarily, the confidence and respect of both sides. The situation was one that was properly covered by the terms of UNFICYP's mandate and the forces available made the intended operation credible. The failure could be attributed to a lack of resolution to act firmly and impartially, but above all quickly, before interested parties could muster counter-arguments and exert counter-pressures, as Ankara evidently had succeeded in doing. It was a low point in the high reputation hitherto enjoyed by UNFICYP.[23]

Despite acceptance by both sides of a ceasefire to take effect at 1600hrs on 22 July, and notwithstanding the subsequent declaration of the three Foreign Ministers at Geneva that in order to stabilize the situation the areas controlled by the opposing forces at 2200hrs (Geneva time) on 30 July should not be extended, throughout the 18 days before the Ministers re-convened the ceasefire was often little more than nominal. Outbreaks of fighting were numerous, the majority occurring in the north where artillery, mortar and tank fire was frequent as the Turkish army relentlessly expanded its lodgement area. There were also outbreaks of shooting locally elsewhere, notably on Nicosia's Green Line, in parts of Famagusta, Larnaca, Limassol and Paphos, and at a number of outlying (mostly Turkish) villages. Sometimes these could be attributed to the National Guard or Greek Cypriot irregulars angered by reports of the Turkish army's continuing actions in the north, and sometimes to defiant Turkish Cypriots attempting to alleviate their hardships, as demonstrated at Famagusta's Old City. Tempers in both communities were further inflamed by numerous reports of looting and wanton destruction of property, mostly in Turkish quarters of towns and villages but also in Greek areas now under Turkish control, and by some allegations of rape in both communities. All such matters demanded action or investigation by UNFICYP's contingents or its Civilian Police; they reacted throughout these exceptionally demanding days with admirable energy and practical commonsense, while simultaneously addressing the multitude of diverse humanitarian and relief demands described in the following chapter.

With Foreign Ministers due to meet again in Geneva on 9 August there was guarded hope that agreement might be reached then for a settlement that would bring some stability and an end to ongoing fighting and violence on the island. An ominous cloud loomed, however: the build-up of mainland Turkish forces by air and sea was continuing unabated. Suspicion grew that Turkey had yet to achieve its full military purpose.

CHAPTER FIFTY-THREE

HUMANITARIAN AND RELIEF OPERATIONS

The responsibilities devolving on the United Nations and the ICRC in Cyprus led to very close cooperation between the two institutions from the outset.

ICRC Memorandum, RO 570b/3, 8 August 1974.

The Secretary General's reminder that, in accordance with established UN peacekeeping practice, UNFICYP should render all possible humanitarian assistance to those caught up in the fighting had not been necessary. We had foreseen that this was likely to become a major commitment as soon as a ceasefire was achieved and had already appreciated the need to strengthen the Force HQ organization to cope. A new staff branch, named the Economics/Humanitarian Branch, was established with, as its nucleus, the existing small Economics Section of the Operations Branch, and New York was asked to provide an officer of Lieut. Colonel rank to head it. Ireland agreed to do so but there was a delay of three weeks before this officer reached Nicosia.[1] The task was shouldered in the meantime by the Force Economics Officer, Major M.W. Smith (Canada) under the supervision of the Senior Political Adviser, John Miles. When a ceasefire was accepted on 22 July, incomplete though this was, UN contingents throughout the island responded at once by doing their utmost within limited resources to ameliorate hardships being suffered in all communities. Humanitarian and relief operations quickly became a major commitment for the UN Force, second only to the need to consolidate the ceasefire. Fortunately UNFICYP was not left to bear this ever-growing and heavy burden alone.

On 20 July, within hours of the outbreak of fighting caused by Turkey's military intervention, the International Committee of the Red Cross (ICRC) had called upon the parties to respect the four Geneva Conventions of 1949 and, in conformity with these, to permit it to act on behalf of prisoners of war and the civil population. Both sides responded on 22 July by informing the ICRC of their desire to abide by the Conventions and by asking for its help in providing relief to victims of the fighting. The ICRC's reaction was swift. A DC-9 aircraft provided by the Swiss Confederation left Geneva for Akrotiri the same day. It carried a team of 14 delegates led by M. Pierre Gaillard[2], including three doctors, relief experts and a member of the Central Tracing Agency, together with three and a half tons of blood plasma and medical and other emergency supplies:

As soon as we landed, Pierre Gaillard and the doctors conferred with the chief surgeon of the *[RAF Akrotiri]* base hospital in order to gain an idea of immediate priorities. Then we went to

Limassol, the southernmost town of the island. When we arrived in the city it was already under curfew and we saw a few official cars on the road, their headlights extinguished because of the blackout. In the office of the *[Greek]* Cyprus Red Cross, converted into a hospital lit only with oil lamps, we saw immediately that medicaments, especially blood plasma, were tragically short. We decided to draw on the three tons of medical supplies brought from Geneva, and to forward the remainder at dawn to Nicosia, where needs were even greater.[3]

The team reached Nicosia early next morning and based itself in the Hilton Hotel,[4] its arrival warmly welcomed by UNFICYP's Chief Medical Officer, Colonel O'Carroll Fitzpatrick, and Major Smith. Cooperation between the ICRC and UNFICYP thereafter was close and harmonious.

This is not the place for a comprehensive account of the extensive ICRC operations in Cyprus (and in Turkey) in the weeks and months ahead[5], but the arrival of the team with its expertise and resources were a major boost for UNFICYP. For its part the UN Force played a critical role in ensuring the success of the ICRC operations; it knew the island well, had efficient radio communications, was able to discover where the problems lay and could provide essential physical resources, limited though these were, such as road transport. The Cyprus Red Cross and its Red Crescent counterpart at once joined the relief operations and practical support was given by the British High Commission and the US Embassy. Initially coordination was exercised by HQ UNFICYP, but on 30 July by mutual consent the ICRC assumed primary responsibility for providing relief and taking care of refugees, prisoners, missing persons, allegations of atrocities and similar problems that are traditionally within its terms of reference, while UNFICYP continued to play an active role that included carrying out investigations and local negotiations and generally assisting fully in relief operations.

Within a week of its arrival the ICRC team estimated that some 10,000 to 15,000 civilians were lacking almost everything and in urgent need of immediate help in the form of food and tentage, while a further 3,000 were reported short of food. By this time the ICRC had brought in some 42 tons of medical supplies, blankets, tents, milk powder and other needs,[6] and with the assistance of the Cyprus Red Cross and Red Crescent these were being distributed as soon as possible to those in need on both sides. UNFICYP obtained clearances for relief convoys and helped by providing guides and escorts and, where needed, the transport itself, especially where civilian drivers were unwilling to cross ceasefire lines. This assistance was crucial because, as the ICRC pointed out:

> The Greek and Turkish zones are scattered over the island like a leopard's spots, making it difficult to move from place to place and hampering the communications which the ICRC is trying to set up between its delegates and the inhabitants affected by the hostilities.[7]

The Secretary General reported to the Security Council on 30 July[8] that most of the Turkish Cypriot areas in Lefka, Limassol, Larnaca and Famagusta Districts were under the effective control of the Cyprus government and the National Guard. The Turkish Cypriots in some of the larger centres, such as Limassol and Paphos, had surrendered to the government and were being held in custody of some kind. Many of the smaller villages had been abandoned, their inhabitants having moved to larger Turkish Cypriot centres, such as the Old City of Famagusta and Knodhara. At some other locations, such as Larnaca, Turkish Cypriots were under United Nations protection. Those Greek Cypriot areas now occupied by Turkish forces mostly lay in Kyrenia District. Here approximately 500 Greeks were being held under UN protection in Kyrenia's Dome Hotel and about 2000 were detained by the Turks in Bellapais; Karmi, Kazaphani, Trimithi, Thermia and Mia Milea were other Greek villages now occupied by the Turks. Waldheim added that by 29 July ten UNFICYP convoys had delivered food, water, baby food, medical supplies and blankets to Kyrenia, Bellapais and other Greek villages in the north, as well as to Turkish Cypriots in the Old City of Famagusta and Knodhara and to those besieged in the small coastal enclaves at Kokkina and Limnitis in the north-west.

However, increasing difficulty was being experienced due to the Turkish army's obstruction of some relief convoys destined for Greeks in the north and its demand that all such relief should be channelled through it. This gave rise to growing National Guard irritation and protests that relief being provided to the Turkish Cypriots in the south displayed a lack of impartiality. Declaring that its cooperation in facilitating this relief was not being reciprocated by the Turks with respect to aid needed no less by Greeks in the Turkish-held north, the National Guard insisted on 30 July that relief convoys throughout the island be halted. Its complaint was not without justification and HQ UNFICYP warned the Leadership that the Turkish attitude was likely to restrict provision of aid to Turkish Cypriots in need in the south. This had the desired effect and the convoys were resumed next day.

By early August the areas of major concern were those Greek Cypriot villages in Kyrenia Districts (East) and (West) in which some Greeks, generally women and children and the old and infirm, remained, and those few Turkish Cypriot villages elsewhere that had not surrendered. About 5300 Turkish Cypriots had fled from the latter to the British SBAs, but some 1300 males were held prisoner in Limassol, to which those detained in Lefka District had been transferred, and another 500 were held under guard in Larnaca. All those thus held were regularly visited by UNFICYP troops, UN civilian police and ICRC representatives, whose reports confirmed that all were being humanely treated. Also by early August the majority of the male population of Greek villages in the north now in Turkish hands had been taken prisoner and were being held in the Boghaz, Geunyeli or Orta Keuy areas. Some women and children had been ordered to leave their villages and make their own way across ceasefire lines to National Guard-held territory, while others were transported without their possessions to Nicosia where they were set free and told to cross the Green Line into the Greek quarter.

As the relief operation gained momentum, a number of other problems demanded UNFICYP's attention. The situation in the Greek village of Bellapais, where some 5,000 Greeks had been gathered, was a point of friction between UNFICYP and the Turkish army, which asserted on 30 July that it would now take care of both Greeks and Turks in the area it controlled, and attempted to restrict the presence of the Finns in the village. UNFICYP insisted on its right to retain its posts there for humanitarian purposes and the next few days were marked by exchanges that culminated in Turkish demands that the Finnish presence, including its camp at Tjiklos, should be withdrawn from the north altogether. General Prem Chand was quick to remind the Turkish Force Commander in a personal message that:

> Prime Minister Ecevit specifically informed the Secretary General that all United Nations posts, check-points and patrols in the Turkish area will continue as before. These assurances were given on the understanding on both sides that activities by UNFICYP in the Turkish-controlled area would be basically for humanitarian purposes. . . . I have received reports today that these assurances are not being observed and that UN posts and patrols in the Turkish-controlled area around Kyrenia have had their movement restricted to such an extent that it is not possible for them to carry out the humanitarian activities which are in the interests of all concerned. Indeed, you had kindly offered *[in a personal message passed on 1 August]* to assist all UN-supported humanitarian activities in the Turkish controlled area. . . . I would be grateful if you would give such instructions as you consider necessary to the forces under your command to permit the UN activities to continue as before in fulfilment of the assurances conveyed to the Secretary General by your Prime Minister.[9]

This message made clear that the UN Force would accept orders only from the Secretary General. Nonetheless Turkish pressures continued with a view to restricting UNFICYP's presence and activities in the north.

There were many reports of looting and wanton damage, much of which was taking place in the south where, perhaps in reaction to the continuing Turkish operation in the north, Turkish Cypriot-owned property was the object of Greek Cypriot wrath. This was to be seen not only in the Turkish quarters of the main towns but also in some Turkish villages. Sometimes this activity could be attributed to National Guard indiscipline and sometimes to action by uncontrolled irregulars. For example, the Coldstream Guards reported that 'a platoon of irregulars, possibly EOKA, are burning, plundering and destroying the village of Evdhimou'.[10] Although this lawlessness was not strictly a matter for UNFICYP but for the Government, it was of concern because of the risk that it might afford Turkey grounds for action by its army or air force against Greeks in the south. For this reason UNFICYP pressed the National Guard to halt these excesses and with the support of UN contingents succeeded in most cases in doing so.

Looting was not confined to the south: Greek Cypriot, and in some cases foreign-owned, property in areas now occupied by the Turkish army was also suffering, primarily, it seemed, at the hands of Turkish Cypriots bent on revenge against their erstwhile Greek neighbours. On 23 July Captain Gerken RN had observed that in Kyrenia (not then in Turkish hands): 'Shutters were up everywhere, though where shop windows were not covered the glass was in good shape and unbroken with goods all on display', but a week later, the town having by then been taken by the Turkish army, Major Gill reported from the Dome Hotel that looting in the town 'was continuing'. Elsewhere in the Turkish-occupied north reports of looting also were common. For example, a Finnish officer on reconnaissance on 29 July noted that in Kato Dhikomo and various other areas 'Turkish soldiers were plundering villages. Domestic animals were straying and Turkish soldiers were collecting them, probably to be slaughtered',[11] and a Parachute Regt, RAC, patrol reported on 3 August seeing organized looting in the Greek village of Ayios Epiktitos. Given the Turkish army's attitude that there was no role, whether humanitarian or other, for UNFICYP in areas now under its control, there was little that the UN Force could do except to report such activities to New York, where subsequent unwelcome publicity was damaging to the reputation of Turkey's so-called 'Peace Force'.

On 26 July the Turkish Force Commander had accepted UNFICYP's proposal for the exchange of wounded or injured persons and asked for its assistance to this end. Requests for evacuation (usually by helicopter) of such people, mostly Turkish Cypriots in areas under National Guard siege, followed and were met wherever possible. But some proved hardly justified, as in the case of a man in the village of Kambyli (3km east of Myrtou). Pressing the urgency of his case, the Turkish Cypriot chief medical officer declared that the man had only an hour and a half to live – a check by a Parachute Sqn, RAC, patrol found that he only had a dental abcess, that there was a dentist in the village and that urgent evacuation was un-necessary. Other requests met by UNFICYP included the evacuation by helicopter from Kato Yialia, a small Turkish village 10km south of the Kokkina Turkish enclave, of an injured Turkish national contingent officer, an operation to which the National Guard readily gave consent. In addition to these humanitarian actions by UNFICYP, the ICRC organized the evacuation by air from Akrotiri of some casualties to Greece and also the repatriation of a few wounded Greek Cypriot prisoners from Turkey to Cyprus.

A major and growing task was posed by the problem of persons reported missing in all communities. UNFICYP, especially its Civilian Police, investigated cases wherever it could and sometimes found individuals, whose whereabouts were giving relatives anxiety, and succeeded in re-uniting them. However, the main task fell to the ICRC, which on 8 August reported:

> From the beginning of events in Cyprus the Central Tracing Agency has been inundated with enquiries from families worried about the fate of their loved ones. At the rate of more than a thousand a day the ICRC receives enquiries from countries all over the world. . . . The National Red Cross Societies too, particularly the Hellenic Red Cross in Athens, send us many enquiries. By telex and telegram the enquiries pour in, sometimes containing 2000 names. . . . The ICRC has been able to send out more than a thousand replies reassuring families in various countries. Another phase of these operations applies to persons held in detention as a result of these events. Lists of civilian and military prisoners from the Turkish Cypriot community have already been supplied by the authorities concerned. These detainees, numbering about 3000, have been visited by ICRC delegates.[12]

Other matters that necessitated action by UNFICYP included the problem of extinguishing fires burning in buildings on or close to the Nicosia Green Line. Sometimes one side or the other (and sometimes both) was disinclined to tackle these fires, but the Canadians were usually able to obtain clearance for fire brigades to attend the fires, and escorted them to these sensitive sites. There were similar problems over the restoration of electricity and water supplies in Nicosia, for these essential services took little account of the vagaries of the Green Line. In these cases the Canadians, as intermediaries, negotiated conditions under which repairs might be carried out (for example, technicians concerned should be unarmed and not wear uniform). In the case of a repair to the water supply UNFICYP procured and delivered to the Turkish side the necessary pipes and other equipment, having secured the prior agreement of both Government and Leadership. Water problems were not confined to Nicosia: the National Guard was reported to have cut the supply to the village of Stavrokono where the Turkish Cypriots continued to hold out; action by the Coldstream Guards ensured its restoration. Yet another matter in which UNFICYP's help was sought was the problem of unexploded artillery shells and mortar bombs, not only in the Nicosia area but also elsewhere, notably Famagusta. Since the UN Force did not itself possess the appropriate technical personnel, the assistance was enlisted of British Forces Near East, which readily responded as local situations allowed.

Of increasing concern were allegations by each side that the other was wearing UN insignia, for this was being used as justification for halting, attempting to search UN convoys and patrols and demanding to see UN identity cards. Contingents were instructed to refuse to show such cards but to refrain from any attempt to force their way through, while citing the Force's right to freedom of movement and reporting incidents where this was being denied.

Many of these matters were satisfactorily settled in discussions between HQ UNFICYP and HQ National Guard, but relations between the UN Force and the Turkish army were less close due to the liaison channel established on 26 July, whereby communication between the two was to be conducted via a Turkish colonel located at the Turkish Embassy in Nicosia. We believed that some matters could better be settled at a face-to-face meeting between General Ersin's Chief of Staff and myself as UNFICYP's Chief of Staff. Prem Chand sought Ersin's agreement on several occasions for such a meeting, but each time the latter declined it, saying that all matters of mutual interest could be satisfactorily dealt with by his officer at the Embassy.

With the return of the Foreign Ministers to Geneva on 8 August, the Secretary General issued an Interim Report which included details of agreements reached between Turkey, the Cyprus government and the ICRC for the release and/or exchange of prisoners. More generally Waldheim explained that:

> The current operations of UNFICYP are based on a framework of static posts . . . supplemented by frequent mobile patrols to all parts of Districts lying outside the Turkish-controlled area. The main purposes of this activity are to generate a feeling of confidence and to obtain information concerning the local situation, not least in order to ascertain those areas where humanitarian and relief measures are required. . . . Within the Turkish-controlled area UNFICYP activities are centred on humanitarian and relief measures in Kyrenia and certain surrounding villages, especially Bellapais. These activities include the delivery of food to a considerable number of small isolated groups.
>
> In all areas outside the Turkish-controlled area UNFICYP is making special efforts to prevent looting and harassment of civilians, especially in the major towns, although UNFICYP resources do not permit complete surveillance over all the areas concerned.
>
> [The Economics/Humanitarian Branch at HQ UNFICYP] has been most active in organizing and coordinating a wide range of humanitarian and relief measures for both communities. The Branch operates in close cooperation with the ICRC representatives in Cyprus. At the

present time all food relief convoys to all parts of the island are organized by this Branch, which also engages in many other humanitarian tasks, such as arranging the evacuation to hospitals of urgent medical cases, either by United Nations helicopter or by road ambulance.[13]

By this time humanitarian and relief operations carried out jointly by the ICRC and UNFICYP with the full cooperation of the Cyprus Red Cross, the Red Crescent and others had become well established. None were to know that within a week the heavy calls already made on them were about to be greatly increased following resumption of hostilities by the Turkish forces.

CHAPTER FIFTY-FOUR

FAILURE IN GENEVA

The second round of talks therefore began on 9 August in an atmosphere of charge and counter-charge. The Turks were flushed with success and their Government enjoyed a new-found popularity at home, while the Greek Government was too weak to be able to compromise.

James Callaghan: *Time and Chance*, p. 349.

The Foreign Ministers of the guarantor powers, George Mavros for Greece, Turun Gunes for Turkey and James Callaghan for the United Kingdom, re-convened in Geneva on 8 August. Others present included the UN Secretary General, Kurt Waldheim, and Under Secretary, Roberto Guyer, together with his Special Representative in Cyprus, Louis Weckman-Munoz, Arthur Hartman (US State Department) representing Henry Kissinger, and Mr Menin, the Soviet Union's observer. They were joined two days later by the leaders of the two Cypriot communities, Glafkos Clerides and Rauf Denktash. As before, Callaghan acted as chairman and, as before, it proved a frustrating business, typified at one point by a squabble over seating arrangements. As declared eight days earlier,[1] the purpose was to secure the restoration of peace in the area and the re-establishment of constitutional government in Cyprus. Attention was focused initially on the failure to implement two measures specifically agreed eight days earlier: the establishment of a security zone supervised by UNFICYP and the withdrawal of Greek forces from Turkish villages and enclaves. Gunes was especially insistent on early compliance with the latter. But from the outset he made plain that for the Turks a return to the constitutional arrangements guaranteed by the 1960 treaties was unrealistic; a physical separation of the two communities was required by the creation of a substantial autonomous Turkish zone in the north, or, possibly, a smaller such zone together with several Turkish cantons elsewhere, amounting in all to some 34% of the area of Cyprus. The continuing reinforcement of Turkish forces on the island left none in doubt that he spoke from a position of strength.

In his Interim Report[2] summarizing the action already taken pursuant to Security Council Resolution 355(1974), which by implication required the Secretary General to implement those provisions of the Geneva Declaration relevant to UNFICYP, Waldheim stated that the Force had endeavoured to carry out the role required of it by that Declaration, in particular to secure an effective ceasefire; that, although fighting generally had diminished and had ceased altogether in some areas, some intermittent fighting was continuing as Turkish forces expanded their area east and west, that Greek Cypriot forces had not yet evacuated all those Turkish villages or quarters occupied by them and that UNFICYP meanwhile was visiting not only these villages but also Greek villages now under Turkish control and assisting in the provision of relief where required. He added that the ICRC, in cooperation with UNFICYP, was endeavouring to arrange for the exchange or release of detained military personnel and civilians on both sides. He further stated that the military strength of UNFICYP was expected to have reached 4292 personnel by 14 August, which, he said, Prem Chand considered adequate, although recommending an increase in the civilian police element from 153 to 200. Finally Waldheim stressed that, in order effectively to carry out the role required of it, the Force needed a greater degree of cooperation; this applied particularly to consolidation of the ceasefire, the establishment of UNFICYP-supervised security zones and the withdrawal of Greek forces from occupied Turkish villages.

Detailed accounts[3] have been published of what proved to be ill-tempered and, ultimately, futile negotiations in Geneva. As the talking proceeded (more often bilaterally rather than in plenary session) it became ever more obvious that the Turks, bolstered by their initial military success, but concerned, nonetheless, that this was not affording adequate security for their troops now on the island, were playing for time and were determined to achieve, if necessary by force, seizure of a substantial part of the island and separation of the two communities in a federal arrangement. Every day brought fresh reports, not only of unrelenting action to expand the Turks' lodgement area, but also of the landing of more troops, heavy weapons and stores, by air into the main enclave and by sea on the north coast, so that by 13 August the Turkish force was estimated to number about 30,000 men with 200 tanks.[4] As each day passed in sterile negotiation, there was growing realization of the Turks' determination, when ready, to impose their will by military action, this despite protestations to the contrary:

> I must place on record that during these talks Gunes reassured me on two occasions that Turkey had no intention of her troops advancing nor of them remaining on the island.[5]

Against this background, and in the light of UNFICYP's recent action at Nicosia airport, pressure was exerted from Athens for UNFICYP to adopt a more forceful role vis-à-vis the Turkish forces. Mavros suggested to Callaghan that the UN Force, further reinforced by Britain, should be deployed to forestall any advance by the Turkish army eastwards towards Famagusta. Putting this to Waldheim, Callaghan said that Britain would be willing to supply troops equipped with anti-tank guns and heavy artillery:

> If we did so [Callaghan enquired], would the Secretary General seek authority for United Nations Forces to stand astride any Turkish line of advance, thus placing the onus on the Turks to decide whether to advance in the knowledge that British troops, acting under the authority of the United Nations, would not be pushed aside? Waldheim said that UNFICYP's original mandate did not extend to resisting the forces of a member state, but in the prevailing circumstances he did not believe that the Security Council would be an impediment to this. . . . He was very ready to cooperate, and I was heartened by his staunchness.[6]

Callaghan briefed the British press to this effect in the knowledge that his suggestion would quickly become public knowledge, as indeed it did, with consequential Turkish animosity.

In the early days after the ceasefire accepted for 22 July, when Turkish forces on the island were weaker, Prem Chand had himself contemplated action by UNFICYP to attempt to contain Turkish expansion eastwards, but had been discouraged from doing so by New York because the Force's recent action at Nicosia airport had caused disquiet to some troop-contributor governments. These were unhappy that their troops might become embroiled with mainland Turkish forces, a situation not covered by the agreement under which their contingent had been supplied to UNFICYP. But by 9 August, when the Turkish force had been substantially reinforced, we at UNFICYP HQ considered it unrealistic to suppose that, even if reinforced as envisaged by Callaghan (which would not have been feasible in the time – appropriate units were not available in the SBAs), the UN Force would be able to prevent an advance by a 30,000-strong Turkish army equipped with 200 tanks and supported by the Turkish airforce; at best it could only provide, as it was already doing, a deterrent screen which the Turks could all too easily brush aside. Waldheim, too, had been less receptive to the suggestion than Callaghan had supposed. Describing the British Foreign Secretary's suggestion as 'extraordinary', he said that he would have to consult with his colleagues in New York and look into the legal problems involved. These proved to be substantial and he informed Callaghan accordingly.

Kissinger, with whom Callaghan was in close touch, made plain his view that the position of the Turkish community required considerable improvement and protection and that there would be no American support for military action to oppose Turkey's intervention operation either by a naval blockade of the island's north coast to prevent further Turkish reinforcements or by action on land as envisaged by the Greeks and Callaghan. Nor was there any military support for such action in London, as Field Marshal Carver, Chief of the Defence Staff, has stated:

> The short and long term arguments against becoming directly involved were still strong, particularly against . . . military confrontation with the Turks, both on the widest politico-military grounds and on the narrow military one that they could bring much stronger forces to bear, especially in the air, to which the overcrowded [British Sovereign] bases would be vulnerable. The possibility of our establishing a naval and air blockade of the north coast . . . was considered and rejected for these reasons.[7]

Callaghan was thus obliged to abandon the suggestion.

Meanwhile Clerides had been looking elsewhere for military support. En route to Geneva he had met the Greek Minister of Defence, Mr Averof, in Athens in the hope of enlisting Greece's help, but:

> Despite my pressure that Greek reinforcements should be sent to Cyprus without delay, Mr Averof took the position that no reinforcements could be sent by sea or air because without air cover they would not reach Cyprus, and that the island was out of range of Greek fighter aircraft. He further stressed that no air protection could be provided from Crete for the Greek forces in Cyprus or for the National Guard because Greek fighter planes taking off from Crete would

only be able to stay over Cyprus for five minutes before returning to their bases, and that they could not land in Cyprus because of the proximity of the Turkish air bases from which attacks could be launched and reach Cyprus within minute, while the Greek planes were refuelling on the ground.[8]

Earlier, Clerides had raised with the Russian Ambassador in Nicosia, Sergei Astavin, the possibility of Soviet military assistance in the event of a further Turkish advance, only to be told that the Soviet Union would take such action only in collaboration with the Americans.[9] When on 13 August the Geneva negotiations came close to collapse and the Turkish forces were poised to advance, with no prospect of either the United States or Britain taking military action to prevent this, Clerides in desperation appealed again to the Russians for military support:

> The Soviet observer *[Menin]* wished to be informed if my request had been cleared with the US Government. It was obvious to me that there was no change in the Soviet attitude . . . and that unilateral Soviet military involvement was out of the question, *despite my offer to give the Soviet Union a base in Cyprus in return for Soviet military help.* [author's emphasis][10]

It was no secret that Clerides had been seeking Soviet military support, but, had it become generally known that he was offering the Russians a base on the island, this must have caused deep international alarm, especially within NATO.

The Turkish army's continuing advances east and west made a mockery of the tripartite committee's report delivered to the three ministers in Geneva on 9 August for the establishment of a security zone policed by UNFICYP. The Turks insisted that their advances were justified by the need to ensure the security of Turkish villages, but the numerous outbreaks of small-arms, mortar, artillery and tank fire, which were provoked as the National Guard attempted to contain them, threatened maintenance of the ceasefire more generally. At some points UNFICYP succeeded by peaceful, and sometimes courageous, action in inhibiting the Turkish expansion but in most cases UN troops – the Finns in the east and the British 16th/5th Lancers in the west – were able to do little more than to observe and report. National Guard tactics included the laying of mines, the locations of which were rarely properly recorded, causing much concern to the Turks, who feared being hemmed in by this means, and requiring great caution on the part of UN troops.[11] In these circumstances the proposed security zone could not be established and the matter was soon overtaken by events.

Elsewhere on the island UNFICYP was contending with numerous new problems both military and humanitarian, the visible presence of blue berets contributing to a restoration of some confidence among members of all communities. The arrival of the balance of the Canadian Airborne Regiment under Colonel C.H.G. Lessard allowed responsibility for the security of the UN-controlled area around the airport, which lay within the original boundary of UNFICYP's Nicosia District, to be handed back to the Canadians on 11 August, so freeing the 16th/5th Lancers to devote full attention to developments in Kyrenia District (West). A Turkish attack on the airport was thought unlikely in the light of Prime Minister Ecevit's assurances conveyed to Waldheim and the Security Council by Gunes's letter of 25 July[12] and UNFICYP was informed that reliance was no longer to be placed on British air support in such a contingency.

In Famagusta, where the National Guard continued to occupy its post in the isolated Pilot Tower adjacent to the walls of the Old City, a minor problem rapidly escalated when the Turks demanded that the Greeks withdraw from the tower and prevented supplies from reaching it. The National Guard responded with an ultimatum on 9 August: unless supplies were allowed through by noon, it would prevent relief supplies reaching Turkish Cypriots in need elsewhere. It was no empty threat; a convoy carrying Red Cross relief was halted soon after midday, but the Turks remained adamant that the National Guard post must be withdrawn. With the Greeks no less insistent that it must remain and be re-supplied, all relief convoys for isolated Turkish communities were blocked. At midnight the Swedes reported that the National Guard had taken up new positions at the harbour and around the Old City, that the Turks had stated that supplies to the Pilot Tower would be prevented by all means and that the Greeks had replied that they would retaliate with full force if fired at. A Swedish proposal that UNFICYP should deliver the necessary supplies was agreed in principle by those in Nicosia, but bickering then ensued at the local level as to how delivery should be effected. At one point the Swedes suggested that they might deliver supplies across the harbour by boat under the UN flag. Concerned by the failure to settle this relatively minor but potentially explosive matter and, conscious of its possible effect on proceedings in Geneva, Prem Chand appealed personally to Ersin, the Turkish Force Commander:

> There are military problems which UNFICYP cannot overcome immediately in supplying National Guard post direct from Othello Tower UN post *[as the Turks were proposing]* and it is therefore necessary to deliver these essential supplies by access to the Pilot Tower through the harbour area itself. . . . We should quickly solve this relatively small problem in the interests of all those of both communities both inside the area under your control and outside it, who otherwise are in danger of having essential food and other relief supplies denied to them.[13]

Ersin replied that re-supply should be carried out neither by UNFICYP nor by the National Guard, but by the Red Cross. The Greeks accepted this proposal and next day (11 August), so did the ICRC, who made a delivery that afternoon. Relief convoys to outlying Turkish villages were immediately resumed. But for UNFICYP's presence and mediation could this minor but potentially explosive matter have been settled thus?

The failure of Greek Cypriot forces to withdraw from occupied Turkish villages in the south, as required under the Geneva Declaration, was causing mounting Turkish anger in Geneva, but the Greek side was dragging its feet on this issue deliberately, not only because it considered the requirement unfair – no parallel action had been required of the Turks with respect of Turkish-occupied Greek villages in the north – but also because it saw the emphasis being laid on implementing this one aspect of the Declaration as unacceptably selective. Seeing the need to assuage Turkish tempers on this issue, which was threatening a collapse in Geneva, Callaghan prevailed upon Clerides to order Greek Cypriot forces to withdraw from the occupied Turkish villages without further delay; on Waldheim's instructions Prem Chand similarly pressed the National Guard in Nicosia. The urgency was clear and on the evening of 11 August the National Guard informed HQ UNFICYP that with-drawals would begin that same night. There were some initial difficulties caused by communication problems on the Greek side, but Lieut. Colonel Willoughby, Limassol Zone Commander, was able to report next morning that National Guard forces had withdrawn from six villages in Limassol and Paphos Districts and from the Turkish quarter of Paphos, while the Austrians confirmed that Greek forces had also vacated Larnaca's Turkish quarter. Waldheim immediately informed all concerned that 'in accordance with the role of UNFICYP pursuant to Security Council Resolution 355(1974), UNFICYP has assumed responsibility for the protection of those areas.'[14] Although by 12 August one of the major Turkish demands had thus been met, Gunes and the Turks were far from satisfied.

In spite of interventions by Kissinger and Waldheim and Callaghan's patient mediation, acute differences with respect to future constitutional arrangements for the island, especially the Turks' insistence on the creation of a Turkish Cypriot autonomous region in the north, prevented progress in Geneva. The Greeks argued that the meeting had no power to make fundamental changes to the constitution of the independent Republic of Cyprus as estab-lished in 1960. The Turks countered that, the Greeks having been in breach of it for the past ten years, the 1960 constitution could no longer be considered valid. After several threatened walkouts and near breakdowns, crisis point was reached on the evening of 13 August, when on firm instructions from Ankara, Gunes issued an ultimatum: unless Greece and the Greek Cypriots accepted Turkey's demand for the creation of a Turkish Cypriot zone covering the whole of northern Cyprus from Famagusta in the east to Morphou in the west , this to be established within the next three to four days, there was, he declared, no point in continuing the negotiations. The threat was clear: Turkey would now resort to force to achieve its demand. Both Mavros and Clerides declared that it was impossible for them to accept Gunes's demand without reference back to Athens and Nicosia and demanded an adjournment of 36 hours to permit this. Gunes refused point-blank.

The Turkish forces were now ready to resume operations to achieve the second phase of their intervention plan and had been ordered to do so at first light next morning (14 August). Gunes was therefore instructed by Prime Minister Ecevit to ensure that the Geneva negotiations were brought to a conclusion that night. In the event the talking continued into the early hours of 14 August, when Callaghan proposed an adjournment to the following day; all except Gunes and Denktash agreed. The conference had failed, as Callaghan later caustically reported:

> There was no formal end to the proceedings. Gunes rose from the table at which we sat, ungra-cious as ever, and departed, followed by his aides. The time was 2.25a.m. on the morning of 14 August. The rest of us shook hands and filed out wearily. I gave a press conference in which I did not spare the Turkish tactics. Even while I was speaking, the Turkish army was advancing once more, breaking the ceasefire. Gunes had played out time.[15]

As the reports reaching HQ UNFICYP from Geneva became ever more ominous, codeword VIKING was issued at 0400hrs on 13 August, placing the Force on Orange Alert, and UN District Commanders were summoned to a meeting at the Headquarters at 1700hrs that afternoon at which Prem Chand gave orders[16] for the policy to be adopted in the event of a final breakdown in Geneva and a resumption of hostilities by the Turkish forces. We anticipated that their purpose was likely to be to extend their existing area of control east to Famagusta and west to Lefka, thus embracing the whole of northern Cyprus, and that the National Guard would not only resist as best it could but also turn on Turkish Cypriot communities elsewhere. Experience during the first phase had shown that UNFICYP had neither the authority nor the military capability to oppose the Turkish army and that the lives of UN troops should not be risked to that end; halting the Turkish operation must be a task for the Security Council and others outside Cyprus. Prem Chand accordingly ordered that:

- All isolated detachments and posts, which in the opinion of District Commanders were exposed to danger from either the Turkish forces or those of the National Guard opposing them, were to be withdrawn to main UN camps at the discretion of the District Commander.

- Where detachments and posts were clearly not so exposed, they were to remain so long as in the judgement of District Commanders they could continue to serve a useful operational purpose.

- Re-deployment out of main camps was not to take place until a ceasefire had been agreed and orders to this effect were issued by the Force Commander.

Since the mandate continued to apply to intercommunal situations, he reminded District Commanders of UNFICYP's responsibility for the protection of Turkish Cypriots in those areas from which the National Guard had withdrawn on 11 and 12 August, adding that in other areas controlled by the National Guard every effort was to be made to prevent any recurrence of intercommunal fighting, especially action against Turkish Cypriot civilians or previously disarmed personnel. Saying that the situation was being assessed with great care and that he was maintaining close touch with New York and Geneva, Prem Chand warned against any premature disclosure of these instructions or any moves which might cause concern, if not panic, in the civilian population; action to implement his instructions was to be taken only on receipt of the codeword PICNIC from HQ UNFICYP.

Throughout 13 August reports flowed in to the JOC at UNFICYP HQ of Turkish movements in the north and of the National Guard constructing new defence positions, especially in the western outskirts of Nicosia. A powerful air of foreboding prevailed that a general resumption of hostilities was imminent. Those UN families who had returned to Nicosia from the safety of the Dhekelia SBA following the ceasefire on 22 July were evacuated to Dhekelia for a second time that evening.

CHAPTER FIFTY-FIVE

HOSTILITIES RESUMED –
THE SECOND TURKISH OFFENSIVE

> The only conclusion I could draw, having been shown the Turkish advance on a map, was
> that the battle for the north was lost before it began.
>
> Glafkos Clerides: *Cyprus: My Deposition*, Vol. 4, p. 85.

A message from Louis Weckman-Munoz in Geneva received at 0430hrs on 14 August warned General Prem Chand that the conference had broken down and that the British delegation expected that the Turkish forces would launch a new offensive within two hours. Numerous reports of Turkish troop movements to east and west as well as south down the Kyrenia road were already reaching UNFICYP Headquarters, and at 0450hrs salvos of artillery fire were resounding north of Nicosia. In the city itself the Canadians reported exceptional military activity on both sides, including the full manning of defensive positions and the readying of weapons and ammunition. These reports coupled with widespread Turkish air activity left no doubt that a second Turkish offensive was under way. At 0500hrs code-word PICNIC was flashed throughout UNFICYP authorizing the implementation of the orders issued by Prem Chand the previous evening.

Summary of the Turkish Operations[1]

The Turks' Sixth Corps (their 'peace force') under General Ersin, of which the 39th Infantry Division had initially provided the main element, had been reinforced by the 28th Infantry Division and supporting elements, and by 13 August was estimated to number some 40,000 men with about 200 M43, 47 or 48 tanks, APCs and 105mm and 155mm calibre artillery, for which the National Guard could be no match. As had already become apparent in Geneva, Ersin was just waiting for the order to execute the second phase of Ankara's plan – the expansion of the Turkish-controlled area east to Famagusta and the Panhandle by the 28th Division, and west to Morphou and Lefka by the 39th Division, thus taking control of all that part of Cyprus that lay north of the ineptly nicknamed Attila Line.[2] Each Division was to be supported by elements of the armoured, airborne or commando brigades and, as before, aircraft operating from bases in Turkey were to provide close air support; naval gunfire would engage coastal targets as required. When Gunes abruptly left the conference table at 0225hrs on 14 August with Ankara's game played out, Esrsin was ordered to launch the operation forthwith. As dawn broke in Cyprus, his forces began to move in overwhelming strength and with a confidence that had seemed lacking in the initial phase.

The Advance East and South

Widespread airstrikes were made on National Guard targets east and south of Nicosia and in the area of Angastina midway between it and Famagusta, and the Turkish 28th Division began to advance east on three axes, the group on each comprising tanks and infantry mounted in APCs. Movement seemed unduly cautious and, in the face of only light National Guard resistance, the groups were reported by 1030hrs to have advanced little more than a few kilometres from the recently enlarged Turkish enclave, with the National Guard retreating in disorganized fashion. As the Turkish advances continued in this ponderous manner, it became apparent that it was the Turks' deliberate tactic to allow Greek civilians the opportunity to flee before them, thus achieving the 'ethnic cleansing' of the area they intended to occupy. Widely publicized and generally well-substantiated reports of the harsh and often cruel treatment meted out to Greek Cypriots during the preceding days, not only by Turkish troops but also by some Turkish Cypriots, persuaded most of the prudence of fleeing.[3]

In the late afternoon of 14 August and after an advance of about 20km the Turkish troops halted on the general line Chatos – Marathovouno – Asha, with a reconnaissance element deployed 10km further forward near Prastio. This slow advance was resumed next morning, again encountering little resistance, and Famagusta was reached as dark was falling and four Turkish ships were visible in the offing. Varosha, the southern (Greek) part of the city, suffered three airstrikes during the morning of 15 August in retaliation for National Guard shelling of the Old City and harbour, parts of which were set ablaze. Most Greek Cypriot civilians had already fled Varosha and during the night of 15/16 August it was also abandoned by most of the National Guard; the few that remained were taken prisoner. Next morning, 16 August, Turkish forces entered unopposed and others continued north towards Boghaz and the Panhandle, from which National Guard troops had begun withdrawing on the evening of 14 August (Trikomo, 18km north of Famagusta, was reported to have come under naval gunfire earlier that day and Lefkoniko, 25km to its north-west, to have suffered an airstrike next morning). Early on 16 August the National Guard informed the Swedes that none of their troops now remained in Famagusta and the city was reported quiet, although fires continued to burn in the harbour area.

The Advance West

Airstrikes had been made on various targets west of Nicosia, including the radio station at Coral Bay (north of Paphos) and the Cyprus Mines jetty at Xeros. During the evening and night of 14 August part of the 28th Division's armoured support was re-deployed to the 39th Division, which had begun to advance west in similar deliberate fashion. Here the going was more difficult than on the plain of the the eastern Mesaoria and, although National Guard resistance again was weak, Turkish artillery and airstrikes were called into play. By the evening of 15 August Turkish troops had not advanced further than the general line Kalokhorio – Masari, a mere 15km, but next day they entered Morphou and by evening had reached Lefka, but stopped short of the small Turkish Cypriot coastal enclaves at Limnitis and Kokkina further west.

Fighting in the Nicosia Area

It was in this area, where the experiences of the Canadian and Finnish Contingents are described later, that some of the most intense fighting of the war was seen. In the city itself the TCF opened fire along the Green Line as soon as hostilities had been resumed at first light on 14 August; the National Guard responded strongly in kind. It seemed, however, that the TCF was not seeking major tactical gains but rather by these means to bolster the defence of the Turkish quarter. A British freelance photographer, who had spent the night of 13 August in the Saray Hotel in that quarter before accompanying the 28th Division next day during its advance east, reported Turkish Cypriots 'very frightened that the National Guard would come into the Turkish quarter'.[4] After three days of exchanges of fire, interspersed by several brief ceasefires negotiated by UNFICYP, the TCF had achieved only minor territorial gains along the length of the Green Line.

On the western outskirts of Nicosia a desperate battle developed, in this case between, on the one hand, two battalions of the Turkish 50th Infantry Regiment, one of which comprised the Turkish National Contingent, and on the other ELDYK, the Greek National Contingent, and elements of the National Guard. Both sides were supported by artillery and mortars and, in the case of the Turks, by tanks and close air support, which included the use of napalm. This battle took place close to UNFICYP Headquarters in Blue Beret Camp, the Force's logistics base in Camp UNFICYP and the Finns' base in Kykko Camp. Observers in all three were afforded a grandstand view of the fighting.

The Turkish objectives were to capture the village of Yerolakkos and ELDYK's camp (respectively 3km north-west and 3km north-east of the airport), both of which lay on the main road between Nicosia and Morphou, and to isolate the airport by cutting the road further south that linked it to the city; some suspected that the Turkish purpose may have been even wider.[5] Determined to halt the Turks and to prevent the possible encirclement of Nicosia from the west, the Greeks had established a key strongpoint in the Greek grammar school, a substantial three-storey building, situated in a dominating position 300m south-east of the ELDYK camp. Once Yerolakkos had been taken (not without difficulty) the Turks turned their attention to the ELDYK camp and the school. Their tactics entailed an attack up a shallow valley over the open ground of which the Greeks enjoyed excellent observation. For two days, on each occasion after preparatory airstrikes and intense artillery, mortar and tank fire, Turkish infantry attempted to advance up the valley towards the school, only to be halted by no less intense Greek small arms and artillery fire, the latter directed with telling effect by an OP officer sited on high ground near Kykko Camp. The action has been described by a Canadian officer:

It was interesting to watch, first of all the airstrike go into the grammar school . . . . An hour later the artillery would go in, then an hour later the tanks would open up. Then the PBI (poor bloody infantry) came on foot. The Turks tried and tried for a couple of days to secure the school. They finally did it on 16 August. That was when we first saw the Turkish flag on top. They lost about 200 soldiers and the Greek National Guard lost about 80 in that particular battle.[6]

Having at last captured the by now heavily damaged school, from which the courageous Greek troops had withdrawn, the Turks moved forward to a point just to its south, from which the airport road could be dominated; here they halted. Powerless to stop the fighting, those in the nearby UN camps had watched with fascination and admiration the courage of both Greeks and Turks, although unimpressed by the latters' rudimentary tactics.

Greek Cypriots' Responses

National Guard Headquarters had returned to Athalassa from its emergency location at Malounda on 23 July, but, as the news from Geneva became ever more ominous, and having experienced the ferocity of airstrikes on the Athalassa complex during the first round of the Turkish operation, a tactical headquarters was deployed on the evening of 13 August to another alternative location, this time near Pyrga, some 28km south of Nicosia. As before UNFICYP's LO, Commandant Flynn, went too:

> On this occasion Tsolakis *[the National Guard's LO to UNFICYP]* . . . and myself and my signal crew were situated in a small wood some 400yds from the HQ. . . . This HQ, which I think was in a monastery, seemed to have excellent communications with forward units throughout the island.[7]

It was to this headquarters that Clerides went on returning from Geneva to be briefed on the military situation. He had travelled via Athens where to his dismay he had been told by the Greek Prime Minister, Karamanlis, that no military support would be forthcoming from the motherland.[8] The morale of the National Guard, which, with the exception of its three elite Raiding Force Units, was not noted for its standard of training or discipline, was by now at a particularly low ebb in consequence of the events of the previous three weeks. At the Pyrga headquarters Clerides learned that, in the face of the overwhelming strength of the Turkish forces, all that the National Guard could muster were some 25 disorganized and demoralized infantry battalions, 11 out-dated Russian T-34 tanks and about 70 miscellaneous and mostly obsolescent artillery pieces; there were no aircraft and no warships. Small wonder that he considered the battle for the north already lost:

> All our forces could do was to fight a rearguard action, slowing down as much as possible the advance of the Turkish forces, giving us thus the necessary time to make diplomatic moves to bring a halt to the Turkish advance.[9]

That this was indeed the Greek Cypriot policy was confirmed in a message addressed to HQ UNFICYP by the Government spokesman:

National Guard has been ordered to retreat in an orderly manner from areas occupied by the Turkish army and open fire only in order to protect withdrawal or in self-defence. This applies to all areas north of the line occupied by the Turkish forces.[10]

Although the National Guard was neither willing nor able to offer resistance to the advancing Turks, there were no such inhibitions to prevent Greek Cypriots elsewhere (sometimes National Guard and sometimes ill-disciplined irregulars of EOKA-B type), angry and frustrated by their inability to prevent what was happening in the north and with passions exacerbated by reports of atrocities being committed by the Turks, from turning on Turkish Cypriot communities in the south. Such actions were liable to provoke the wrath of the Turkish air force, but in these areas the Greeks did not have to face the Turkish army. For example, before the Turkish army reached Famagusta, and in spite of temporary local cease-fires negotiated by the Swedes, the National Guard from time to time opened artillery and mortar fire on the Old City, now crowded with Turkish Cypriot refugees. The TCF retaliated with mortars and the Turkish air force came to their aid with airstrikes on Varosha on the afternoon of 14 August; these were repeated next morning, particular targets being the CYPOL station and the harbour area, the whole of which was reported to be burning. For good measure the Turkish airforce also attacked the National Guard camp at Karaolos, only 800m east of the Swedes' main base in Carl Gustav Camp. However, as night fell on 15 August the Swedes reported all quiet in Famagusta, although the harbour area was still ablaze, and that the Pilot Tower, the National Guard's occupation of which had been an earlier bone of contention, was now in Turkish hands. Karaolos Camp was taken by the Turks next morning and looting of Greek property was reported.

Early on 14 August the National Guard, fearing Turkish air or seaborne landings for the purpose of relieving Turkish Cypriots in Larnaca[11], demanded to move into Scala, the town's Turkish quarter. After discussions with Lieut. Colonel Rieger, the Austrian District Commander, it was agreed that his men would remain in Scala, but that the National Guard might temporarily take over Larnaca Castle and certain other Turkish buildings covering the sea front. Meanwhile the National Guard was reinforcing its troops both in Larnaca and on the Nicosia road further north and fighting had broken out at the village of Goshi (10km to the north), where efforts were being made to negotiate a local ceasefire; the National Guard was also demanding the surrender of Turkish Cypriots in the villages of Melousha and Tremetousha (both 17km north of Larnaca). Goshi was occupied by the National Guard at about 1430hrs and an hour later Turkish aircraft carried out a strike in its vicinity in which, as described later, three Austrians were killed. In the face of strong Austrian protests the National Guard rounded up Turkish males from the villages of Mari and Zyyi in the west of the District and transported them to Limassol. During the night of 14/15 August elements of the National Guard were observed withdrawing south from Famagusta[12] through Larnaca while others were moving east from the Limassol area.

The Austrians reported that by mid-morning a large number of men and vehicles, equivalent perhaps to two battalions, was gathered close to the coast in the area of the villages of Kiti and Mazotos about 10km south of Larnaca, but that Melousha was still in TCF hands. A considerable movement of National Guard vehicles during the night of 15/16 August suggested that an attempt was being made to redeploy the disorganized Greek Cypriot units, possibly with a view to holding the town of Larnaca and preventing an advance on Limassol by holding Kophinou, a key point where the roads from Nicosia and Larnaca met. On 16 August the Austrians reported Larnaca District to be generally quiet and that the National Guard was abandoning its headquarters and positions in the town itself, although CYPOL was continuing to man the police station.

From Limassol Lieut. Colonel Willoughby's Coldstream Guards reported in mid-morning on 14 August that the District was quiet and so it remained all day. In the town itself the National Guard was seen to be bringing prisoners to the stadium; these included the Turkish males whom the Austrians had reported being removed from Mari and Zyyi. Next morning the District was again reported quiet with National Guard and TCF positions unchanged. However, the Turkish airforce had made a reconnaissance over the area and the Greeks were reported to be laying mines in Limassol harbour. In late afternoon Ayios Ioannis, a remote Turkish village situated in the southern Troodos mountains, on the Paphos side of the inter-District boundary, came under Greek Cypriot attack in which four Turks were killed and some houses were looted and set on fire. A Coldstream Guards patrol was unable to establish who these Greek Cypriots were or where they had come from: there were suggestions that they were members of the National Guard from Limassol but may have been EOKA-B-type irregulars.[13] They warned that they would return later that night and that UN troops would not be allowed to enter. Willoughby ignored the warnings and a five-man Coldstream post was established in the village that evening.

If Limassol District was generally quiet, the same could not be said for Paphos District, where events gave Major Macfarlane's company of the Coldstream Guards concern from early on 14 August, when a Turkish aircraft strafed and bombed the radio station at Coral Bay 8km north of Paphos. This was quickly followed by reports that the National Guard intended to enter the Turkish village of Mandria 12km south-east of Paphos (which commanded the main road to Limassol and had seen bitter fighting only four weeks earlier) and 'within the hour' to attack Stavrokono, whose tough TCF defenders had held out against Greek demands for its surrender during the first round of Turkey's operation. Unable to persuade the Greeks not to attack, Macfarlane withdrew his post at Stavrokono when firing broke out soon afterwards.[14] The mixed village of Polis on Khrysokhou Bay in the north, also the scene of earlier fighting, remained quiet, but not Paphos itself, where six Turkish Cypriots were killed when the National Guard entered the Turkish quarter. During the after-noon a further Turkish airstrike took place, this time on a radio installation 4km north of the town. On the afternoon of 16 August Macfarlane reported that Paphos District generally was quiet.

On the morning of 14 August the Danes reported that in Lefka District heavy small-arms and mortar fire had broken out around the coastal enclaves at Limnitis and Kokkina. Summarizing the situation that evening, Lieut. Colonel Severinson, the Danes' Commander, said that an airstrike had been made during the morning on a Cyprus Mines Corporation installation only 50m from his Headquarters in Viking Camp and another that afternoon on the Greek village of Loutros (just south of the Limnitis enclave), that there had been shooting all day in the Limnitis area, but that the Danes had achieved a local ceasefire at 1740hrs. This was broken next morning when the Turkish air force returned to strike with bombs, rockets and napalm three national Guard posts around Limnitis (and close to the Danes' Limnitis camp). That afternoon the National Guard took 23 Turkish Cypriots prisoner from Angolemi and another 40 from Elea, both about 8km east of Lefka town (the Danes were able to obtain their names). As evening approached six Turkish aircraft attacked Morphou (from which National Guard troops and civilians had fled southwest), Kato Zodhia (4km south of Morphou) came under artillery fire, Loutros suffered a further airstrike and heavy fighting had been resumed around Limnitis. This continued next morning (16 August) as the besieged TCF stubbornly held their ground and the National Guard showed little inclination to advance. A Danish patrol entering Morphou in mid-morning reported that the town was clear of Greek and Turkish forces. By early afternoon the latter had reached Ghaziveran (8km beyond Morphou) and two Turkish frigates were observed in Morphou Bay. During the afternoon the National Guard abandoned Lefka and partially withdrew from around Limnitis as a force of some 20 Turkish tanks and two companies of motorized infantry neared Xeros and entered Lefka soon after 1715hrs, just before their 1800hrs ceasefire.

Henry Kissinger had been urging Prime Minister Ecevit to call a halt as soon as Turkey's military aims had been achieved, and on 15 August Ecevit authorized him to inform the Greek government that Turkish military operations would cease at noon (1800hrs in Cyprus) the following day, Turkish forces having expected that by then the whole of northern Cyprus from Famagusta in the east to Morphou Bay in the west would be under their control. This information was conveyed to all concerned in Cyprus and, although local shooting continued at some points, a general ceasefire came into being at that hour, with the Attila Line established at the positions on which Turkish forces had halted.[15] The National Guard played no part in determining the limits of this Line, having fallen back powerless and in no state to offer resistance. Indeed, had the Turkish advance not been halted, National Guard units, which had no final line of defence planned (much less prepared), might have been driven back into the sea. After three days of overwhelming Turkish military power the Greeks had no choice but to accept Turkey's unilaterally declared ceasefire and the humiliation of a *de facto* dividing line decided by Turkey. There had never been any realistic prospect of the National Guard holding back the Turkish forces, even if the Greek motherland had given military support.

Clerides and his government had left Nicosia for Limassol on the afternoon of 16 August, when the capital appeared to be in danger of being encircled by the Turks, but returned next day when the Turkish operation was halted. Formidable problems now faced them, especially the plight of some 180,000 refugees who had fled their homes in the face of the advancing Turkish army.

CHAPTER FIFTY-SIX

INTERNATIONAL REACTIONS

> The Security Council . . . *Demands* that all parties to the present fighting cease all firing and
> military action forthwith.
>
> *Resolution 357(1974),* 14 August 1974.

The breakdown at Geneva in the early hours of 14 August and the immediate resumption of
hostilities in Cyprus by the Turkish forces caused alarm in New York, where an urgent
meeting of the Security Council was convened at 0200hrs (New York time) the same
morning. By then it was already 0800hrs in Cyprus and the first of UNFICYP's frequent
situation reports had reached the Secretary General and been circulated to members of the
Council. Without further ado they adopted unanimously Resolution 357(1974), which
'deeply deplored' the resumption of the fighting, contrary to the provisions of Resolution
353(1974) (adopted on 20 July), and called for the resumption without delay of negotiations
for the restoration of peace in the area and constitutional government in Cyprus. Mr Richard
(UK), reminded members of the course of events in Geneva and appealed to the Turkish
government to comply with the provisions of Resolution 353 which it had itself accepted
only three weeks earlier. Mr Carayannis for Greece, quoting Turkish orders alleged to have
fallen into Greek hands, asserted that, even as the the Geneva Declaration was being signed
on 30 July, the Turkish army had already been planning to carry out a second phase of their
operation with a view to seizing the whole of the island's north. Why, he asked, was Turkey
demanding 34 per cent of its territory when Turkish Cypriots formed only 18 per cent of the
population? Because the Turkish army was there, he said, adding:

> The Government of Greece takes the attitude that no sovereign, independent State could accept
> such proposals at gun point from an outside country. . . . The situation is extremely serious.
> For Cyprus itself it is dramatic. For the United Nations it calls for a re-appraisal of its
> fundamental purposes.[1]

Continuing, he quoted a report carried by *The Washington Post* of 11 August:

> In Ankara a high Government official said that Turkey is determined to press for acceptance of
> its plan for a Cyprus solution even at the cost of renewed fighting on the island. "There will not
> be a third round of Geneva talks," said the official. "We will get peace either in Geneva talking
> or in Cyprus fighting".[2]

Mr Scali (US) reaffirmed Washington's conviction that only through negotiation could a settlement emerge that would restore constitutional government in Cyprus and peace and stability in the Eastern Mediterranean, but the Greek side drew no comfort from his declaration that:

> Turkey also has legitimate interests that must be fully recognized. My Government made clear yesterday in a public statement its view that the position of the Turkish community on Cyprus requires considerable improvement and protection, as well as a greater degree of autonomy.[3]

Mr Rossides (Cyprus) and Mr Olcay (Turkey) engaged in ritual argument and counter-argument, while the Council's President, Mr Malik (USSR), speaking as his country's representative, used this opportunity, and that offered by the two succeeding meetings, to argue that NATO interests lay at the heart of the crisis in Cyprus. The meeting rose at 0600hrs (New York time) and fighting on the island continued, the Council's latest Resolution ignored.

It met again at 1430hrs (New York time) the next day, 15 August, when Kurt Waldheim summarized events on the island since the previous meeting. Saying that reports he had received afforded no grounds for optimism, he added:

> UNFICYP has continued to do its utmost where possible to assist the population, to arrange local ceasefires and to de-escalate the fighting, to prevent the recurrence of intercommunal strife and to protect the civilian population who are in danger from such strife. . . . The successful discharge of the UNFICYP mandate depends upon the full co-operation of all the parties concerned. This especially applies to the implementation of the ceasefire called for by the Council. It is obvious that under its present mandate and at its present strength UNFICYP could not interpose itself between two armies engaged in full-scale hostilities.[4]

He expressed deep sympathy to those governments whose contingents on the island had suffered casualties (it was now known that these included three members of the Austrian Contingent killed the previous day in what had appeared to be a deliberate Turkish air attack) and said:

> I also wish to pay a tribute to my Special Representative in Cyprus, to the Force Commander and to all the personnel of UNFICYP – military, police and civilians – for their steadfast and courageous conduct during the current fighting.[5]

Waldheim despaired that the very credibility of the United Nations was at stake and stressed the need for all members to respect decisions of the Security Council, pointing out that, although they had called three times for a ceasefire, heavy fighting was continuing. The situation represented a threat to international peace and security and called into question the very essence of the Charter and the *raison d'être* of the Organization. The Council's response was the unanimous adoption of yet another Resolution, 358(1974), which again *'deeply deplored'* non-compliance with that adopted the previous day and *'insisted'* on full implementation with immediate effect of both it and the earlier Resolutions.

The meeting was then suspended for consultations on the terms of yet a further Resolution, which was tabled when the Council resumed at 2325hrs (New York time) and was adopted unanimously (China did not participate). Noting from Waldheim's reports that UNFICYP's casualties were increasing as a result of the continuing fighting, this further Resolution[6] was strongly worded: the Council *'deeply deplored'* (once again) that members of UNFICYP had been killed and wounded; *'demanded'* that all parties fully respect UNFICYP's international status and refrain from any action which might endanger their lives; *'urged'* the parties concerned to demonstrate in unequivocal manner their willingness to do so; *'demanded further'* that all parties cooperate with UNFICYP in carrying out its tasks, including humanitarian functions, in all areas of Cyprus and in regard to all sections of the island's populations; and, finally, *'emphasized'* the fundamental principle that the status and safety of the members of UNFICYP (or any other UN peacekeeping Force) must be respected in all circumstances.

Debate followed adoption of this further Resolution, during which old arguments and accusations were rehearsed and sympathy was expressed for the casualties suffered by UNFICYP. For Cyprus, Mr Rossides argued that the Force's mandate as enshrined in Resolution 186(1964) permitted

the use of the Force in situations arising not only from internal but also from international events, and the threat or use of force in international relations comes within that mandate. . . . Therefore the mandate of the United Nations Force in Cyprus includes its duties of deployment and interposition in the threatening situation between the forces of Turkey and the forces of Cyprus at the present juncture.[7]

This was a novel interpretation of the mandate which few shared, but Rossides was on firmer ground when he declared that Turkey was using the overwhelming weaponry in its possession as a member of the NATO alliance in an aggressive attack against a small non-aligned country, contrary to the purpose of NATO. Continuing, he said that the situation demonstrated that, by proceeding in accordance with Chapter VI of the Charter (providing for the pacific settlement of disputes) rather than invoking the provisions of Chapter VII (allowing the use of force), the Security Council was unable to function effectively. All were responsible that the Charter limitation was rendering the Organization lame. Mr Richard (UK) condemned the continuing fighting in Cyprus, stressing that they were not discussing an academic situation but one in which innocent people were being killed. The cost in human life and suffering was heavy, but whatever the rights or wrongs of the past might be, and he did not deny that there had been many wrongs, such action could not be justified. However, there was, he said, a need for impartiality in judgements on the situation and quoted the words of Mr Callaghan, British Foreign Secretary, following the breakdown in Geneva:

We must keep this in perspective, because the Turks have got a case. Despite what has been done by Turkey today, there is no doubt that the Turkish Cypriots have suffered as a result of the failure to observe the Constitution of Cyprus.[8]

These words echoed those uttered the previous day by Mr Scali (US), whose contribution on this occasion was anodyne. The Council's President, Mr Malik, speaking as before on behalf of the USSR, repeated at length Soviet criticism of NATO and called for the withdrawal of all military forces from Cyprus. Innocent people, he said, were were being killed and increased suffering was being inflicted on the Cypriot people who had fallen victim to the secret plans and designs of 'certain NATO circles', which in order to strengthen their military and strategic positions in the eastern Mediterranean were intent on sacrificing the independence, sovereignty and territorial integrity of the Republic of Cyprus. This was too much for Mr Richard, whose response was caustic:

> Originally we were told that NATO circles were on the side of the Greeks because they had engineered the expulsion of Makarios. Now we are told that NATO circles are on the side of the Turks. Is it one NATO circle we are complaining about or is it, perhaps, two? Or, indeed, are there more? Everywhere there seems to be the hand of NATO in something, if one is to take at face value what the representative of the Soviet Union insists on telling us so often.[9]

It was perhaps time, Richard said, that in relation to Cyprus the Soviet Union stopped turning its gaze on NATO and started looking at the realities of the situation. Indeed, instead of trying to hinder a settlement, it might be better if the Soviet Union devoted its great energies to trying to achieve one.

For Turkey Mr Olcay rehearsed the long-held Turkish view that the two communities in Cyprus should be treated as equals, neither a Greek majority nor a Turkish minority. Declaring that Turkey had always believed, and continued to believe, that international disputes can and must be solved through negotiation, he added:

> Everyone must be aware of the restraint and patience exercised by Turkey for the past 11 years. It was only when the independence of the island and the very life of the Turkish Cypriot community, already rendered hardly tolerable for a decade, were directly threatened that Turkey, upon the failure of consultations among the guarantor Powers, had to intervene.[10]

If a constitutional arrangement was accepted under which, in an independent State of Cyprus, the Turkish community would maintain its own autonomous administration in one part of the island and the Greek community its own in another, Turkey, he said, was willing to begin negotiations as soon as possible to determine the details.

The meeting was concluded on this note at 0130hrs (New York time) next morning, 16 August, by then 0730hrs in Cyprus, where fighting was continuing regardless of the three Resolutions so recently adopted by the Council. Those in UNFICYP, caught up in a conflict that was neither of their making nor within their power to halt, viewed with wry amusement (and a measure of cynicism) a cartoon published in *The Sun* (London) with, as its caption: '. . . And tell 'em if they don't stop, we'll send 'em another sharp note from the Security Council'.[11]

The abrupt breakdown in Geneva in the early hours of 14 August, following the refusal of Mr Gunes to allow any time for further negotiations and the immediate resumption of

'. . . And tell 'em, if they don't stop, we'll send 'em another sharp note from the Security Council.' (*The Sun*, London, 16 August 1974).

offensive operations by Turkish forces, caused anger and frustration in Athens, where the recently appointed Prime Minister, Mr Karamanlis, was compelled to recognize the military limitations of Greece's position:

> He *[Karamanlis]* did not have enough firepower to confront Turkey on Greece's [northern] border, and he could not mount any defence of Cyprus unless Britain provided air cover – and without American support this was impossible.[12]

This was a consequence of the Athens junta's dereliction over the previous seven years. In military impotence, Greek anger was vented on both the United States and NATO. The former because (it was held) Washington had lent tacit, if not active, support to the junta in its action to depose Makarios, but had then failed to prevent Turkey's consequential intervention, and, further, far from supporting international military action to halt a second Turkish offensive, the Americans had actually encouraged this by public statements that an expansion of the area under Turkish control was justified both politically and militarily.

As for NATO, Greek anger was generated by what was perceived to be a failure on the Alliance's part to prevent Turkey, a fellow member, from military action that lay far outside the purposes of the Alliance. Greek anger was not lessened by the knowledge that Turkish forces were employing aircraft and weapons supplied by the United States exclusively for operations conducted under NATO's auspices. Powerless to do more, Athens announced on 14 August that Greece was withdrawing immediately from NATO's military command, although not from its political wing. Its armed forces would no longer be at NATO's disposal, officers serving at various NATO headquarters were recalled and agreement for the use of naval and other facilities hitherto provided in Greece was cancelled. As a direct consequence of events in unaligned Cyprus, the long-held fear that a breakdown in Graeco-Turkish relations would seriously weaken NATO's southern flank had been realized. The Cold War was continuing and only the Soviet Union could view the situation with any satisfaction.[13]

The immediate concern for Britain, following the collapse of the Geneva negotiations, was the likely consequences for the SBAs. Orders were given at once for those families who had returned to dormitory towns to be withdrawn for a second time into the British bases and the evacuation of some back to the UK began. The withdrawal of some of the military reinforcements received in July was already in train, but that of Headquarters 19 Brigade and 40 Royal Marine Commando, together with supporting elements, was halted; by mid-August the British garrison strength was 5640 all ranks.[14] A new arrival was the 10th Gurkha Rifles (an integral part of the British Army) which joined 3rd Bn, Royal Fusiliers in the defence of the Eastern SBA. The legendary fighting reputation of the Gurkhas caused disquiet in Turkish circles until it was explained that their arrival was, in fact, part of the Army's normal troop rotation programme.

Two major concerns faced the authorities in the SBAs: first, the security of the Bases and second, the large numbers of Cypriot refugees, both Greek and Turkish, who sought refuge within them. Armed personnel, other than British and UN troops, were denied entry to the SBAs at checkpoints manned by soldiers. The security of the Western SBA, which was not affected by the operations of the Turkish army, was not a major problem, but the situation of the Eastern SBA became delicate as the Turks' eastward advance progressed. The first difficulty was caused by National Guard troops withdrawing from the Famagusta area attempting to do so through the SBA:

> Permission was given provided groups of not more than company strength loaded their weapons onto one vehicle in a convoy and the whole party was escorted by British troops through the Base. No heavy weapons or tanks were permitted to move through. Throughout one long night [of 15 August] this withdrawal took place and the Turkish forces arrived to find Famagusta an empty city.[15]

A second arose on 15 August when Turkish tanks approached Ayios Nikolaos, which lay within the northern boundary of the SBA and around which British flags had been hoisted. Having apparently failed to see these, a tank fired three rounds (all of which missed) at a Ferret scout car of 16th/5th Lancers and a vehicle carrying a BBC television team parked nearby beat a hasty retreat:

> An hour or so later a Turkish tank rumbled up the main road from Famagusta and stopped just short of the barrier where a disconsolate looking crew got out. An interpreter was sent forward and the crew commander said he had a few problems: he had run out of fuel, run out of main armament ammunition, his machine gun was jammed and his radio would not work. He was given some jerricans of fuel and told to go away.[16]

At the request of Air Marshal Aiken (CBFNE) I passed (via our liaison officer) a personal message from him to General Ersin, protesting the shooting incident and stressing the need to respect British sovereign territory. Ersin's reply came at once: 'Turkish troops were ordered not to enter British Sovereign Bases. I will investigate and stop immediately.'[17]

The rapidly growing number of refugees, especially those fleeing ahead of the Turkish army's eastward advance, was becoming a major problem, particularly in the Eastern SBA on which a flood of people descended in a continuous flow of cars, buses, tractors, bicycles and on foot. The emergency arrangements made in conjunction with the Cyprus government to care for these is described later.

In Nicosia fighting was continuing in the immediate vicinity of the British High Commission's main building, which became untenable:

> The front porch received a direct hit and HE *[Mr Olver]* withdrew the staff under fire to the Residence, which we had prepared as a fall-back position. This too was unhealthy and HE ordered a withdrawal to the Reserve High Commission alongside the Ops Room in Dhekelia on 16th August.[18]

Olver had decided on withdrawal on learning that the Cyprus government had already left Nicosia for Limassol that day. It had proved impossible to start Olver's official limousine and he was obliged to travel, escorted by 16th/5th Lancers' 7th Troop, in one of the regiment's Saracen APCs, which was as well as it was struck by machine-gun fire as they left. (The High Commissioner and a skeleton staff returned to Nicosia on 18 August.).

Throughout the three days of this second Turkish offensive those in the SBAs were at full stretch not only in coping with the influx of refugees but also in maintaining the Bases' security and meeting logistic commitments. These tasks were rendered all the more difficult by the disappearance of most locally employed civilians, but, nonetheless, logistic support for UNFICYP, even though by now the Force had been doubled in size, never wavered. Rations and petroleum needs (the latter greatly increased by the arrival of a considerable number of armoured vehicles) were met and transported in UN vehicles under UN escort. UNFICYP's casualties evacuated to the British base hospitals were willingly received and efficiently cared for until, where necessary, repatriated to home countries. Fortunately the only military casualty suffered by the British forces themselves was a Royal Marine reported wounded by Greek Cypriot small arms fire. For UNFICYP it was a different story.

CHAPTER FIFTY-SEVEN

UNFICYP AND THE SECOND TURKISH OFFENSIVE (14-16 AUGUST 1974)

> The resumption of heavy fighting on 14 August had placed UNFICYP units in an extremely difficult and dangerous position, resulting in severe casualties.
>
> *The Blue Helmets,* United Nations, 1990.

Those in UNFICYP who had witnessed at close quarters the operations of the Turkish forces (especially those of the airforce which enjoyed total air supremacy) during the first offensive had few illusions as to what was to be expected now that these forces had been substantially reinforced. Kissinger had made plain that the United States would not support international military action to halt a second Turkish offensive and there was no question of UNFICYP attempting to do so alone. Prem Chand's instructions, issued on the evening of 13 August and given effect by the issue of the codeword PICNIC at 0500hrs on 14 August, recognized that UNFICYP had neither the means nor the authority for any such action and that the lives of UN troops should not be put at risk to this end. He had authorized District Commanders at their discretion to withdraw any isolated detachments or posts that were exposed to danger by fighting between the Turkish forces and the National Guard, while retaining those not so exposed so long as they could continue to serve a useful operational purpose. Commanders were required to continue to act in the spirit of the mandate in so far as inter-communal situations were concerned and to the extent that their resources allowed.

By 14 August most of the planned reinforcements for UNFICYP had arrived, nearly doubling its military strength to a total of about 4100 men. Particularly welcome were the increased armoured and anti-tank capabilities represented by the British 16th/5th Lancer and 4th/7th Dragoon Guards squadrons and by the M113 APCs and Lynx tracked vehicles of the Canadian Airborne Regiment and Lord Strathcona's Horse.[1] However, there had been problems in finding accommodation, and in some cases other necessities such as vehicles, for some of the recent arrivals and not all had been deployed operationally by the time that the Turkish offensive was resumed.

Kyrenia District (East), covering the eastern flank of the Turkish lodgement area from the north coast southwards to the Turkish villages of Bey Keuy and Epikho 12km north-east of Nicosia, had been the operational responsibility since 24 July of the Finnish Contingent commanded by Lieut. Colonel Pullinen and supported by BRITCON's C Squadron, 4th/7th Dragoon Guards led by Major Staveacre (less its Swingfire guided weapons troop which remained part of the airport defence). The 220-man-strong Finnish Contingent had been reinforced by a further 400, consisting of two infantry companies from Finland. Since not all could be housed in Kykko Camp, the Finnish Contingent's base, accommodation for 2nd Company was found at the abandoned US monitoring station at Mia Milea, an industrial area 5km north-east of the capital, where, a Finn remarked, 'getting water was a problem and there was no electricity but all the more flies'. Pullinen's headquarters, his 3rd Company and logistic elements were located in Kykko Camp, which was also the base for Staveacre's squadron; the Finns' 1st Company continued to hold Tjiklos Camp at the head of the Kyrenia Pass.

From these bases posts were deployed at various points along this eastern flank both to observe and to provide a measure of reassurance to Turkish Cypriots in those villages not yet reached by the Turkish forces; in addition, the Finns continued to man OPs at Trakhonas and Omorphita on the northern outskirts of Nicosia and at Martin's Mound (which, lying inside Turkish-controlled territory, provided valuable information). Mobile patrols operated in the Pendhadaktylos mountains and in the area of Trapeza, a Turkish village north of the mountains. Thus on the morning of 14 August many of the Finns and their supporting 4th/7th Dragoon Guards found themselves in the direct path of the advancing Turkish 28th Division.

Heavy artillery, mortar and small arms fire broke out around Mia Milea early that morning, airstrikes followed and approaching Turkish tanks opened fire. As fighting spread, Pullinen recalled patrols from the mountains and Trapeza area, but his OPs in the vicinity of Turkish villages further south remained in position throughout the day, Turkish troops passing through without harming them. (These OPs were withdrawn to Mia Milea next day, since by then they were no longer serving any useful purpose.) The Trakhonas and Omorphita OPs also remained in position but, as described later, following discussions between UNFICYP and the Turkish command, the Finns at Bellapais and Martin's Mound were withdrawn to Tjiklos Camp. Turkish tanks had fired at clearly marked UN buildings in Omorphita and Mia Milea, wounding one Finn at the former and six at the latter. At nightfall on 14 August the only posts still occupied by Finns were at Trakhonas and Omorphita, all others, together with 4th/7th Dragoon Guard troops, had been withdrawn to Kykko or Tjiklos Camps or to Mia Milea, which was still held.

In Kyrenia District (West), the responsibility of BRITCON's 16th/5th Lancers under Lieut. Colonel Morris, armoured car troops of his B Squadron led by Major Wright, whose headquarters was in Myrtou, had for the previous three weeks been patrolling, observing and reporting on the changing situation all along the western flank, where Turkish troops constantly edged forward on the coast road, in the mountains and on the plain, giving rise to frequent breaches of the ceasefire as the out-gunned National Guard attempted to halt them. Sometimes Lancer patrols were able by their very presence to inhibit the Turkish advances, which on occasions resulted in them being straddled by Turkish artillery fire. Turkish operations were invariably halted at night and, in accordance with normal practice, armoured car troops then withdrew to a harbour area for maintenance and rest. Staff Sergeant De St Croix has described 5th Troop's task :

We spent three days at the Karavas crossroads *[on the coast road]*, our job being to report on Greek and Turkish movements to the west and east and on the Turkish fleet as it landed supplies and equipment in Kyrenia. The first day went without incident and we pulled back to a night RV at last light. On the afternoon of the second day the Turks moved up into houses about 150m from our position. . . . That night we pulled back again, leaving the Turks in their new positions. On the third day we arrived back to find that the Greeks . . . had also moved up and were digging in on the crossroads which meant that both sides were now only about 150m apart.[2]

De St Croix persuaded the Greeks to pull back about 500m, only to see them return two hours later, and as darkness fell on 13 August the two sides were once more only 150m apart. Noting the build up on the Turkish side and realizing that action was imminent, De St Croix prudently withdrew his troop that night to Vasilia, 6km further back. At 0500hrs next morning fighting erupted at Karavas. The second Turkish offensive had opened.

The first of the Lancers to suffer was B Squadron's 6th Troop consisting of three Ferret scout cars, led by 2nd Lieut. C.H.A. Goodwin. On the evening of 13 August the troop had withdrawn up a narrow steep track to the small Maronite village of Ayia Marina and established an OP at the village restaurant. There were no Greek forces in the village but it afforded good observation. Soon after 0400hrs on 14 August the sound of jet aircraft attacking in the direction of Nicosia alerted the troop and almost immediately three Super Sabres attacked Ayia Marina, presumably mistaking Goodwin's troop for National Guard:

> 6th Troop took the full force of the rocket attack and within seconds three of the six-man Troop had been wounded . . . Cpl Wilmore in the back, Tpr Wallbank in the leg and Tpr Kirkham in the abdomen. L/Cpl Wood hastily bandaged Kirkham's wounds and helped him into the scout car. He then drove the vehicle away but at the same time managed to operate the radio to keep his Troop and Squadron Leader informed. All three vehicles were able to extricate themselves, though not without difficulty, and they set off for Gleneagles Camp. On the way they were met by the Medical Officer, Capt Matheson, at the village of Yerolakkos which was then itself under heavy fire. The wounded were transferred into the ambulance and all returned to RHQ without further incident.[3]

Reports from other 16th/5th Lancer troops indicated that fighting had become widespread and that Turkish forces were on the move over a broad front. These, and the intense air activity, artillery, mortar and small arms fire that now could be both seen and heard near the airport and the Lancers' base in Gleneagles Camp, left Morris in no doubt that a full-scale Turkish offensive was under way. The airstrike on his 6th Troop illustrated the dangers to which B Squadron was exposed and, with codeword PICNIC received, he withdrew the squadron to Gleneagles. All were back in the camp by 0930hrs:

> For the next 72 hours as the battle raged around us we were in the incredible position of being on the touch-line and witnessing the heaviest fighting that took place in Cyprus. At times we became the "Aunt Sally" ourselves as we were entirely surrounded by Turkish and Greek positions and inevitably the odd stray round or bomb came close enough to remind us that the

UN flag was not bullet-proof. . . . The most impressive sight and sound of all came from the
Turkish Super Sabres. Using napalm, rockets and machine guns they attacked a variety of
targets close by causing buildings and gorse bushes to burn fiercely.[4]

Throughout these 72 hours the regiment was committed to maintaining the security of
Gleneagles, assisting in the defence of the airport area and in providing miscellaneous escorts
required for supply convoys and for ambulances evacuating casualties to the British Military
Hospital at Dhekelia.

Operational responsibility for Nicosia District, which included monitoring the Green
Line and defence of the UN protected area at the airport, lay with the Canadian Contingent.
The arrival in late July of the remainder of its Airborne Regiment and its supporting elements
had increased its strength to a total of 950 all ranks and given it significant new capability.
On 2 August its Commander, Colonel G. Lessard, took over as District Commander from
Lieut. Colonel D.S. Manuel.[5] The Contingent's main operational base was in Wolseley
Barracks, situated close behind the Ledra Palace Hotel and a mere 200m west of the Green
Line, its logistic elements were co-located with UNFICYP Headquarters in Blue Beret Camp
and a small detachment held Camp Kronborg on the west bank of the dry Pedhieos River.
Additional accommodation to house the new arrivals was found in a vacant United States
leisure compound situated in the Engomi area of south-west Nicosia, which became known
as Maple Leaf Camp.

Throughout 13 August the Canadians had reported constant Turkish military movement
north of Nicosia and, when darkness fell, that over 60 vehicles, including 38 tanks, were
concentrated at Geunyeli 3km north-west of the city. With a resumption of hostilities clearly
imminent, Lessard made plans for the withdrawal of non-essential personnel from the area
of Wolseley Barracks and the Ledra Palace. An overflight by an unidentified aircraft and the
dousing of lights in Geunyeli added to a feeling that events were fast moving to a climax; a
paratrooper remarked: 'the atmosphere of anticipation was not unlike that which is experienced prior to a parachute descent'.

Nicosia awoke early on 14 August to the sounds of mortar, machine-gun and small-arms
fire as fighting erupted all along the Green Line and to these were added the roar of Turkish
Super Sabre jets passing close overhead to bomb and strafe National Guard targets east and
west of the city. This and the next two days were a period of intense activity for the Canadians,
who were at full stretch in many directions, especially in efforts to secure local ceasefires.
Other tasks included rescuing UN civilians from two hotels (on one of which, the Cornaro, a
Canadian OP was sited and which was suffering from mortar and artillery fire with fighting in
close proximity), assisting diplomatic missions whose members and premises were under fire
from one side or the other, investigating complaints of military infringements of premises such
as the Hilton Hotel, declared by the ICRC as neutral and under its protection[6], restoring a
vital telephone link to the Leadership and receiving Greek Cypriot refugees handed over by
the Turks at the Ledra Palace checkpoint.[7] The Canadians' own OPs sometimes came under
mortar and small-arms fire (deliberately, some believed) and most had to be withdrawn.
(Three OPs on the city's north-west, including Cornaro, were subjected to this fire as early as
0515hrs and all three had been withdrawn by 0815hrs.)

Soon afterwards Lessard ordered the withdrawal of his easternmost OP around which intense fighting was taking place; a M113 APC, which had been stationed at the OP for the very purpose, came under small-arms fire as the men withdrew and was then disabled by an anti-tank mine laid in an unmarked minefield, compelling those inside to make their escape on foot.[8] By this time all Canadian posts except those at the airport and two in the city had also been withdrawn. (That at the Turkish village of Louroujina 20km south of Nicosia continued to be held.) At about 0900hrs heavy mortar, machine-gun and small-arms fire broke out in the area of Wolseley Barracks and the Ledra Palace Hotel and, when a Canadian soldier was wounded by a mortar bomb, all non-essential personnel were withdrawn to Blue Beret Camp. Lessard maintained contact locally with both sides and succeeded twice during the day in securing ceasefires within the city, the first of which lasted for only 25 minutes while the second was only partially observed and marked by sporadic firing for the rest of the day. However, in spite of sounds of occasional shooting, Nicosia was relatively quiet that night.

Throughout 14 August HQ UNFICYP's attention had been focused increasingly on the battle being fought on its doorstep as the Turks tried to take the Greek grammar school. Fighting died down during darkness, but next morning it flared again and by 1300hrs had spread further east, bringing Camp Kronborg under heavy mortar fire in which four Canadians were wounded. Most in the camp were evacuated by APCs, but, since Prem Chand regarded it important to retain a UN a presence at this point, one section of Canadians and an APC remained. Fighting was also resumed in the city where Lessard arranged another ceasefire to take effect at 1400hrs (which 'lasted for all of three minutes'). The Turks protested that National Guard mortars were firing on their positions in the north-east of Nicosia from behind the Hilton Hotel and threatened that airstrikes would be made on the city unless this was halted; HQ UNFICYP's pressure ensured that this firing ceased. Otherwise Nicosia generally was quieter than during the previous day, allowing the Canadians an opportunity to improve their defences in the Ledra Palace Hotel area and to re-man their OP on the Cornaro Hotel, which afforded excellent observation to north and west. In late evening Prem Chand passed a personal message to both sides calling for agreement for a ceasefire in the city and suburbs as from 1930hrs:

> This ceasefire should continue tomorrow in order to prevent further damage and casualties to innocent civilians of all communities. It should be both a ceasefire and cessation of forward movement by military forces on both sides in city area.[9]

The National Guard agreed, but the Turks replied that their commander had no authority to do so; they undertook only not to open fire unless the Greeks did. Thus nightfall on this second day once more saw relative calm prevailing in Nicosia.

Dawn on 16 August brought a resumption of airstrikes in the area of the grammar school, where the Turks resumed their attack in the face of determined Greek resistance, and fighting erupted again close to the Canadians' Cornaro OP, caused, it seemed, by a Turkish attempt to take the Central Prison 200m to its south. The prison was strongly defended by the National Guard and its capture not only would have compelled a Greek withdrawal back across the Pedhieos River but would also have threatened the security of the Canadian-held Camp Kronborg- Wolseley Barracks-Ledra Palace area. In the event the prison remained in National Guard hands, but those still manning OP Cornaro had to be withdrawn in APCs under fire, suffering a near miss by two 500lb bombs when Turkish aircraft attacked the prison. The Canadians now took determined action to maintain the security of the area mentioned:

> [Lessard] ordered Airborne HQ & Signal Squadron, 1 Commando and the engineer section attached to RHQ to prepare to defend the area and not to accept any "trespassing" on UN-controlled areas. The units were ready to execute the orders, support weapons were in position and barbed wire obstacles erected.[10]

Local commanders on both sides were warned that, while unarmed men entering the area would be given asylum, armed men would be prevented by force from doing so. Firm action of this kind, which earned the respect of both sides, was typical of the Canadian Airborne Regiment. The situation elsewhere in the city remained generally unchanged throughout this third day and, although sporadic firing continued, neither side attempted to advance across the Green Line. After Turkey's unilaterally declared ceasefire came into formal being at 1800hrs, some occasional shooting could still be heard in Nicosia throughout the night. Canadian casualties during the three days had been five wounded, of whom three were evacuated to the British Military Hospital at Dhekelia.

The battle for the Greek grammar school during the three days 14–16 August gave cause for deep concern to UNFICYP on account of the proximity of UN camps. The National Guard not only occupied defensive positions close to these camps but also deployed artillery or mortars in their immediate vicinity. Inevitably Turkish retaliatory fire and airstrikes were attracted with scant regard paid to the neutrality of UN camps, all of which suffered in some degree. Artillery or mortar rounds fell in Gleneagles Camp, Camp UNFICYP and in Blue Beret Camp, where the Military Police quarters and the UN Radio room, both in vulnerable positions on the camp's northern edge, had to be evacuated. The rocky nature of the ground, together with shortages of manpower and defence stores, prevented construction of effective shelters in these camps, in which, fortunately, there were no fatal casualties, although eleven men, all members of BRITCON[11], were wounded; two were evacuated to the British Military Hospital, Dhekelia and the remainder were treated in the Austrian Medical Centre in Blue Beret Camp.

Greatly concerned that casualties were being caused not only in these camps but also, as described later, to the Finns in Kykko Camp, Prem Chand protested strongly to the Turkish and National Guard Commanders that mortar and artillery fire was hitting UN camps. He urged them to respect UN premises, to refrain from firing on UN positions and to prevent troops entering UN property. Ersin replied that his forces were taking particular care not to fire at UN camps but wanted an assurance that no National Guard mortar positions were in the vicinity of the UN area. The National Guard replied that, as the Turks had broken the ceasefire since early that morning, 14 August, it would stop firing only on condition that the Turks did likewise. This impasse was no new experience for UNFICYP.

The plight of Lieut. Colonel Pullinen's Finns in Kykko Camp was serious. This camp was situated 900m south of the grammar school, with a small apartment block only 50m to its north, and between it and Blue Beret Camp lay a large chicken farm, known as Comet Farm. All three were situated on a tactically important ridge of high ground which afforded excellent observation and fire positions from which Turkish troops attacking up the valley towards the grammar school could be engaged.[12] For this reason the apartments and Comet Farm were both occupied by the National Guard; furthermore, a Greek artillery battery was deployed close behind the Finns' camp. All were targets for Turkish artillery, mortars and airstrikes, in which Kykko Camp inevitably suffered:

> The very first attack on the camp on the morning of 14 August was performed by Turkish Super Sabre aircraft. This attack could be considered a mistake as there was a similar Greek military camp in the vicinity, but the shelling of a certain Turkish mortar platoon had a definite aim: to scare the Finns away from the camp and at the same time the tactically very important hill. With the Battalion HQ, HQ Company, Logistics Company, the new Third Company, and the HQ and staff of 4th/7th Royal Dragoons inside its area, Kykko Camp was definitely overcrowded with about 330 all ranks.[13]

During the three days some 25 artillery or mortar rounds fell within the camp area which suffered also from aircraft cannon fire, fragments of exploding shells and spent anti-aircraft and small-arms rounds. The only protection in the camp was in shallow trenches hastily dug alongside buildings and protected with the few available sandbags. The growing number of casualties and damage in the camp (the medical centre and workshops were destroyed) caused great concern. On 14 August, in addition to the six wounded at Omorphita and Mia Milea, the Finns suffered twelve casualties in Kykko Camp, including the Medical Officer, and two members of the 4th/7th Dragoon Guards Squadron, one of whom was its second-in-command, were also wounded; Pullinen commented that only 'unbelievable luck' prevented more serious casualties. Ten of the wounded were evacuated the same day to the British Military Hospital, Dhekelia.

Repeatedly throughout 14–16 August Pullinen tried to secure local ceasefires by appealing both to Colonel Katircioglu, commander of the Turkish National Contingent (with whom he was on good terms) and officers of National Guard units operating in the vicinity. These appeals fell on deaf ears, not least because it was plain that the Greeks were using the cover of the UN camp from which to engage the Turks and, unsurprisingly, the latter refused to halt their counter-fire. Ultimately the National Guard were persuaded to withdraw from the Comet Farm, which was then incorporated in the UN Protected Area, but Pullinen's immediate concern was the Greeks' refusal to vacate the apartment block on Kykko Camp's doorstep, a particular target for the Turkish fire; this, he decided, must not be allowed to continue. Early on 15 August a party of Finns supported by a troop of the Dragoon Guards was ordered to evict the National Guard, if necessary by force:

> 0905. National Guard fired few angry shots at Finns but evacuated buildings without further resistance, and UN flag hoisted. Result: no further mortar fire fell in vicinity of Kykko and small arms fire became negligible.[14]

Pullinen took similar strong action to remove other National Guard elements that took up positions too close to his camp or, on occasions, even within its perimeter.

The battle for the grammar school continued with unabated intensity throughout this second day. Kykko Camp also suffered severely and, in order to minimize casualties, it was decided to evacuate those who were not fulfilling any operational purpose. It was too dangerous to attempt to do so while the fighting continued, but when this died down with the approach of darkness on 15 August 115 men of the Finns' recently arrived 3rd Company, some of whom had been shaken by their baptism of fire, were evacuated using the M113 APCs of the Canadian Contingent. Since Blue Beret Camp was already overcrowded, they were allotted transit accommodation in the abandoned RAF Nicosia

> The fact that about one third of the shells that landed inside the camp hit the area after the evacuation operation gives an adequate proof that the operation was a necessity.[15]

Waldheim received a message from the Turkish Prime Minister

> expressing the profound regrets of his government *[for casualties caused to members of UNFICYP]* and its assurances that the Turkish forces will exercise the utmost attention and care for the security of UN troops in Cyprus.[16]

but these assurances proved empty, for, when fighting flared again next morning (16 August) and came ever closer, some rounds, which could only have come from the Turkish side, fell either in or very near Kykko Camp, setting parts on fire. Since yet another urgent protest to Ersin had no evident effect, further evacuation of the camp became essential. With twelve Finns left as a guard, all the remainder were evacuated during the early afternoon to the abandoned RAF Nicosia premises. As before, the the Canadians' M113 APCs were used for the operation, during which an attack was made by Turkish aircraft using napalm and a Finnish officer was wounded. Kykko Camp was re-occupied by the Finns when the cease-fire declared by Turkey for 1800hrs on 16 August had taken effect.

The first day of the resumed Turkish offensive brought tragedy to the Austrians in Larnaca District at Goshi, a Turkish village situated close to the main Nicosia – Larnaca road and therefore of special importance in Greek eyes. After the first round of fighting in July Lieut. Colonel Rieger, the Austrian Commander, had negotiated an agreement whereby the TCF would withdraw to the western part of the village, allowing Greek traffic unhindered use of the road, with the Austrians establishing an OP near the road to ensure freedom of movement. When Turkey resumed the offensive on 14 August the Austrians observed a National Guard force in 30 lorries leaving Larnaca at about 1000hrs, evidently intent on attacking and securing Goshi. Rieger lost no time in despatching a patrol under Lieut. Itzay to reinforce his OP at the village and to attempt by negotiation to avert any fighting and bloodshed. Itzay succeeded in doing so for some two hours, during which time the Turks evacuated their families to the nearby Turkish village of Louroujina), but, when negotiations broke down at 1300hrs and a National Guard attack became imminent, he was ordered to withdraw his men to a position south of the village. Soon afterwards mortar fire was opened on Goshi which was then captured by the National Guard, the TCF retreating into hills south of Louroujina.

At about 1520hrs four Turkish F86 Sabres attacked with cannon and napalm not only Goshi but also the Austrian patrol then situated on the road some 1500m south of the village. Lieut. Itzay and two of his patrol, Sergeant Decombe and Lance Cpl. Isak, were burnt to death as they tried to escape; only the driver survived. It was difficult not to conclude that the attack had been deliberate, as Prem Chand made clear in a strong protest to Ersin:

> Soldiers were travelling in white-painted UN vehicle marked as such and carrying UN flag. Turkish aircraft made one pass before attacking, therefore there cannot have been mistaken identity. At second pass aircraft attacked with cannon fire and at third pass made napalm attack. Three Austrians died from burns. These facts confirmed by fourth surviving Austrian soldier. Request you take strong action against those responsible for this inhumane and irresponsible act against the United Nations.[17]

Ersin replied the same evening:

> There was not any planned air attack on any target in the vicinity of Goshi. Investigations are still being carried out to find out how the Goshi incident took place. Please convey my condolences to the Commander of AUSCON.[18]

The outcome of Ersin's investigations was never communicated to UNFICYP, but Turkey resented the Force's report to New York, which had left little doubt that the attack could only have been deliberate rather than a genuine mistake. The incident and the horrific manner in which the three Austrian peacekeepers had met their death profoundly affected everyone in the UN Force. A Memorial Service was held before the three bodies were returned to Austria; later a memorial was erected at the site.

Apart from a small area around Athienou and Arsos in the north of Larnaca District from which Greek Cypriots fled and which ultimately was incorporated in the Turkish-occupied area north of the Attila Line, the District did not experience Turkish ground action. Undaunted by the tragedy at Goshi, Rieger's Austrians, reinforced by a 60-strong infantry company, succeeded during the three days of the resumed Turkish operation in negotiating local, if temporary, ceasefires and in averting major intercommunal incidents either in Larnaca town, where they retained a presence in the Turkish quarter, or elsewhere in the District.

In Famagusta District it was a different story, for here the Turkish operation resulted eventually in the occupation of the whole District. By 14 August the Swedish Contingent, responsible for the District under Lieut. Colonel Kristensson's command, had been doubled in size by the arrival of a 200-strong infantry company. With its main base in Carl Gustav Camp, 2km north of the Old City of Famagusta, it retained its post in the Chatos area and manned a further eight posts in Turkish or mixed villages elsewhere; also retained were the Goldfish detachment just west of the Old City and the Othello Tower OP on the walls. But as the advancing Turkish army reached Turkish villages and Greeks Cypriots, apart from a few of the elderly or infirm, fled south from others, there was no longer any need to retain many posts. The Goldfish post, over which shooting was taking place, and temporary OPs in the harbour area were withdrawn to Carl Gustav Camp on 14 August as shelling, mortar fire and airstrikes developed; posts recently established further north were similarly withdrawn during the next two days. The Turks pressed for the removal of the long-established post at Chatos and, since it too no longer served a useful purpose, HQ UNFICYP authorized its withdrawal on 15 August; the situation around Carl Gustav Camp was too dangerous to effect this then, but next day its men reached the camp safely. On 15 August three National Guard T34 tanks and troops in APCs had drawn up just outside the camp and opened fire on approaching Turkish armour, exposing the Swedes to great danger. In yet another appeal Prem Chand urged both sides to keep away from the camp in order to avoid a situation similar to that suffered by the Finns in Kykko Camp. Turkish forces eventually encircled Carl Gustav Camp and elements of the National Guard who had failed to escape south. Next day, 16 August, the Turks occupied the latters' camp at Karaolos and at this juncture the Swedes found themselves virtually confined to Carl Gustav Camp by Turkish forces.[19]

Lieut. Colonel Willoughby's 2nd Bn, Coldstream Guards in Limassol District were not brought into contact with the Turkish army and continued to devote attention to intercommunal problems. As this second Turkish offensive was launched on 14 August six Turkish F84s bombed the radio station at Cape Aspro 4km west of the Western SBA, but otherwise the District was reported quiet throughout the day. Willoughby's guardsmen monitored the wellbeing of Turkish Cypriot males held prisoner by the National Guard in Limassol stadium, and also watched over the town's Turkish quarter, in which the women, children and the elderly remained. There was concern when Turkish aircraft overflew Limassol early next morning, but otherwise the District was reported quiet for the next two days, during which some 2000 Greek Cypriot refugees arrived in the town and were accommodated in a Greek school. On 16 August the Leadership in Nicosia protested that Turkish Cypriot prisoners had been transported to a 'concentration camp' in Limassol from Larnaca and Lefka Districts, that young and elderly males had been taken from the town's Turkish quarter to dig defensive positions and that the port had been mined. UNFICYP confirmed that Turkish Cypriot prisoners had arrived at the town's stadium from Larnaca and Lefka Districts but that no Turkish Cypriots had been forced to dig defences; the Leadership were not told that the National Guard was, indeed, laying mines at the harbour entrance.

In neighbouring Paphos District, also part of Willoughby's command as Zone Commander, his Coldstream Guards company under Major Macfarlane had a busier time. The airstrike early on 14 August on the Coral Bay radio station (8km north of Paphos) and the renewed Turkish offensive in the island's north angered the National Guard, which thereupon decided to re-occupy the Turkish quarter of Paphos and the Turkish village of Mandria, 12km to its south-east (both scenes of fighting during July) and threatened to attack the village of Stavrokono, a TCF stronghold in the Troodos foothills that had not surrendered earlier. Macfarlane did his utmost to persuade the locally strong National Guard not to enter the Turkish quarter, but lacked the resources to prevent it; in the fighting that ensued six Turkish Cypriots were killed and nine were wounded. At Stavrokono, where Lance Sergeant Denton, commanding the UN post, attempted to negotiate an agreement for a peaceful settlement, an exchange of fire took place, but, thinking better of it, the National Guard then declared that it did not intend to capture the village and withdrew, leaving only a platoon; sporadic firing continued that evening and next morning. During the afternoon of 14 August, to the further anger of the National Guard, two Turkish aircraft attacked a radio installation at Trimithousa, a Greek village a mere 4km north of Paphos. As darkness fell Macfarlane reported that UN posts were now deployed at Mandria, another at Kouklia (a mixed village in the south-east of the District, where Turkish Cypriots were reported short of food), and one in Paphos itself; the OP at Stavrokono was withdrawn at last light but returned next morning.

That same evening Willoughby had ordered a five-man Coldstream Guards post to be established in Ayios Ioannis, a remote Turkish village in the Troodos mountains, in which one of his patrols had reported four Turks killed with some houses looted and set on fire following an attack by either National Guard or EOKA-B elements, it was uncertain which. When next morning, 15 August, it was found that its TCF defenders had fled to Vrecha[20], another remote Turkish village in the mountains, Macfarlane deployed further Coldstream Guards posts to that village and to two other isolated Turkish villages, Lapithiou and Pelathousa; all were reported quiet. The mixed village of Polis near the north-west coast, where a Coldstream Guards detachment had supervised the intercommunal situation ever since the National Guard's occupation on 22 July, remained calm throughout these three days. Visiting his posts in isolated Turkish villages a few days later, Willoughby found:

> Guardsmen in really remote and quite beautiful places being treated by the local people as saviours, given grapes, eggs and all the 'goodies' that people, who themselves are short of food, could provide.[21]

He said that he had never seen his men so happy in spite of often having to endure somewhat squalid conditions. Describing especially warm and generous welcomes by Turkish Cypriots in Ayios Ioannis and Vrecha, he added:

> The offers of 'goodies', the cheering crowds of children, the men who stood up and waved as we drove through, really makes worthwhile all the endless hours of bothers and frustrations that we have had over the last four months.[22]

During early August the Danish Contingent in Lefka District under Lieut. Colonel Severinson had been reinforced by an infantry company from Denmark, increasing its strength to 425 all ranks. As soon as Turkish forces resumed the offensive early on 14 August, the National Guard opened fire on the two small Turkish coastal enclaves at Limnitis and Kokkina with mortars and heavy machine guns. Turkish airstrikes on a Cyprus Mines installation adjacent to the Danes' main base in Viking Camp at Xeros and on National Guard positions around Limnitis quickly followed. With codeword PICNIC received and his OPs now in danger from the fighting, Severinson ordered those around the two enclaves to withdraw into local company camps, although that at Limnitis was endangered by Greek mortar and small-arms fire aimed at the adjacent Turkish police station; at midday two Turkish aircraft using rockets and cannon attacked the Greek village of Loutros, which overlooked Limnitis. The Danes negotiated a local ceasefire that evening, but fighting at Limnitis and Kokkina was resumed next day; their resolute TCF defenders gave no ground, encouraged no doubt by further airstrikes with rockets, cannon and napalm on the besieging National Guard; airstrikes were also made on a National Guard local headquarters near Kambos, a Greek village 14km south of the coast, and the appearance in Morphou Bay of two Turkish frigates must have bolstered TCF confidence. On 15 August, as the westward advance of the Turkish ground forces drew closer and artillery fire and airstrikes were reported near Morphou and on the main Nicosia-Xeros road, Danish OPs at Ghaziveran and Elea, both situated in the path of the Turkish army, were withdrawn. By then all other Danish OPs, except that at Lefka, had also been withdrawn, although the Limnitis and Kokkina camps were still held.

Severinson was now concerned for the safety of those in Viking Camp, which lay in the path of any Turkish further westward advance. That evening he moved with his headquarters and supporting elements from Viking Camp to his company base established in the nearby Turkish town of Lefka after its surrender on 22 July. Shortly afterwards, a Turkish column comprising 16 tanks, 20 trucks and 25 jeeps reached Xeros and, in order to avert fighting, it was escorted by the Danes into Lefka. The National Guard had been withdrawing steadily south from the Morphou area and from Lefka and had also partially withdrawn from around Kokkina and Limnitis (although firing was reported at the latter during the evening and again next morning). Severinson and his headquarters returned to Viking Camp following the ceasefire declared by Turkey at 1800hrs on 16 August. The Turkish army was now in control of much of his District, but he resisted its demands that his men be confined to their camps. Tragedy struck UNFICYP once again that evening when the vehicle carrying five Danes on their way to relieve a newly established OP at Ambelikou, a Turkish village 3km south-west of Viking Camp, hit a land mine. The vehicle was destroyed, two of its crew, Sergeant Christensen and Private Andersen, were killed and the three others were seriously injured. Sadly, they were not the only Danish casualties that day – two others had been wounded during the battle being fought around UNFICYP Headquarters.

Throughout these three days there had been constant Turkish pressure for all UN personnel now in areas under Turkish army control to be withdrawn on the grounds that there was no longer a role for them consistent with UNFICYP's Security Council mandate. Earlier Waldheim had informed Prime Minister Ecevit that he accepted that the Force's role in such areas should be strictly a humanitarian one and Ecevit had responded by stating that instructions had been issued to Ersin that all UN posts, checkpoints and patrols were to be permitted to continue as hitherto on that understanding. Only in two places did this agreement now cause difficulty – at Bellapais and at the Dome Hotel, Kyrenia, at neither of which UN posts had been deployed before Turkish forces had landed on the island on 20 July. The removal of Greek Cypriots from Bellapais (males as prisoners to unknown destinations, women, children and the elderly to Nicosia) no longer justified the retention of the Finnish posts at the village, and agreement was reached with the Turks for their men to be withdrawn to Tjiklos Camp.

The situation at Kyrenia was different. On 23 July, after completion of the Royal Navy's evacuation from the north coast of foreign nationals wishing to leave, Major Gill (UK) had acted in accordance with HQ UNFICYP's instructions to take under his wing some 630 others – a mixed group of Greek Cypriots, Greek nationals and other nationals then gathered in the Dome Hotel. A UN flag was hoisted and the hotel was declared as UN-protected. The Turks would not recognize it as such, but nevertheless Gill and his team, assisted later by the ICRC, continued unmolested to care for all those who had sought refuge there, and during the next three weeks he established good working relations with the local Turkish authorities. He organized the daily administration within the hotel, including the provision of meals, and generally promoted a feeling of some security for those now in its overcrowded premises, some of whom were from time to time released back to Nicosia.

But the activities of Gill and his team, to which a troop of scout cars from the Parachute Squadron, RAC was added, were not limited to Kyrenia – outlying Greek villages and some expatriates, who had remained, were visited and humanitarian assistance delivered to them wherever possible. But these activities caused increasing irritation to Turkish commanders and, as the day neared for the launch of the second Turkish offensive, their demands became ever more insistent for a complete UN withdrawal. Matters came to a head on 14 August, soon after the Turkish operation began, when Gill was given a final ultimatum at 0800hrs requiring him and his team and all other UN personnel to evacuate the Kyrenia area forthwith. Protesting that he had received no authority to do so from either the UN Secretary General or UNFICYP Headquarters, he prevaricated for some nine hours. The Turks threatened force and the situation became so tense that Prem Chand decided that withdrawal must take place. A despondent Gill, who was deeply concerned for those left behind, was instructed accordingly:

> My headquarters had told me that I must conduct a dignified withdrawal but that I could not resort to or allow any form of violence or shooting. The lives of 450 civilians [by then the number of those at the Dome Hotel] also was at stake and we certainly could not resist to the point of exchanging fire. . . . We were eventually persuaded to move out. They were very polite and assured us that there was nothing personal in it, but they had their orders and in fact we were given a Guard of Honour with fixed bayonets by the Turkish army.[23]

The achievements of the team under Gill's outstanding leadership had been remarkable and added much to UNFICYP's fine humanitarian record.

Turkey's decision to declare a ceasefire to take effect at 1800hrs on 16 August was greeted with relief throughout UNFICYP. Since 20 July, during a conflict which it had neither the authority nor the means to halt, its casualties had been severe – a total of 9 men killed and 65 wounded.[24] A small UN Force, caught up in an all-out war between two armies, had paid a high price.

CHAPTER FIFTY-EIGHT

THE ISLAND DIVIDED
(AUGUST-OCTOBER 1974)

Cyprus was divided in two. There were atrocities on both sides, many missing persons and prisoners, and a large Greek Cypriot refugee problem. UNFICYP did its best to limit the disaster, to help the helpless, to protect the civilian population, and to evacuate foreign nationals. It eventually established a buffer zone across the island and maintained complete peace between the opposing armies. In all this Prem Chand was outstanding.

Brian Urquhart: *A Life in Peace and War*, p. 257.

The Security Council met at 1530hrs (New York time) on 16 August – by then three and a half hours after Turkey's declared ceasefire in Cyprus – to consider a revised draft resolution tabled by France which, with three abstentions, was adopted forthwith as Resolution 360(1974). This recorded the Council's 'formal disapproval of the unilateral military actions undertaken against the Republic of Cyprus' and urged the parties not only to comply with the earlier resolutions but also to resume without delay the negotiations called for in Resolution 353(1974), the outcome of which, the Council declared, 'should not be impeded or prejudged by the acquisition of advantages resulting from military operations'.

Introducing the draft resolution, Mr Lecompt (France) was scathing of Turkey:

> The events that led to the resumption of military operations in Cyprus, which resulted in the Turkish army cutting the island in two and once again plunging Cyprus into the horrors of war, are in everyone's mind, and we all mentioned them and condemned them, one after another, at the night meeting which followed the breakdown of the Geneva negotiations. It seems to me that those events are part of an inadmissible practice, a practice which one would have hoped had become outmoded thanks to the development of international cooperation: I am referring to what I shall describe as the ultimatum approach.[1]

Those who followed declared in similar, if less outspoken, terms their own country's support for the Resolution, but Mr Olcay for Turkey, not at that time a member of the Security Council and thus denied a vote, was incensed:

> I deplore the fact that this Resolution was ever tabled. I deplore the fact that it was accepted. I deplore the frame of mind of those who, in their Parisian ivory towers, even thought of such a biased approach in this issue at such a time.[2]

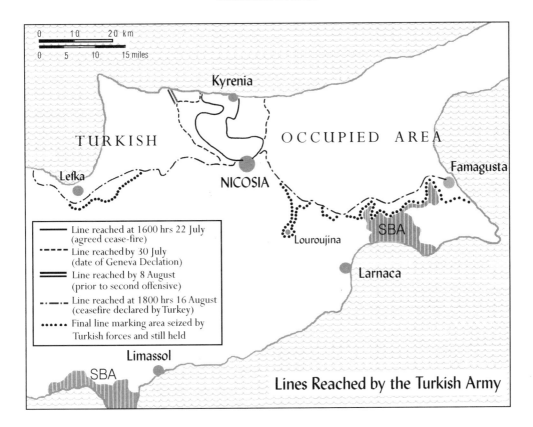

Lines Reached by the Turkish Army

This was strong stuff, but did not end there. Continuing in terms highly critical of France, Olcay concluded:

> I want to point out once more that Turkey does not enter into negotiations under conditions dictated on the basis of sentences extracted from statements dreamed up in Paris, even if it was in the Elysée Palace.[3]

The Council rose after five and a half hours of debate that had held little promise for any early agreement on what should be done. It was not a propitious beginning to the search for a permanent settlement of the Cyprus problem, which was still continuing three decades later.

Daunting problems faced not only UNFICYP but also the Greek Cypriot government, those in the SBAs and international relief agencies. An entirely new stage had been reached in the Cyprus saga; a fresh Security Council mandate for UNFICYP, although clearly required, was was not in prospect. The problem for UNFICYP was that, notwithstanding that the Security Council had demanded (by Resolution 358(1974)) only 24 hours earlier that 'all parties cooperate with UNFICYP in carrying out its tasks . . . *in all areas of Cyprus* [author's emphasis], Turkey took the view that its military intervention was a peacekeeping operation. There was thus no requirement, Turkey argued, for a UN peacekeeping Force in the area of northern Cyprus now under its control. (Turkey conceded nonetheless that there was a role for UNFICYP in policing a buffer zone and ceasefire lines.)

Pending a solution to this impasse, Waldheim informed Prem Chand that the Force's functions, as enshrined in its original mandate[4], remained in force in those areas under Cyprus government control where confrontation was continuing as between the National Guard and CYPOL on the one hand and Turkish Cypriots on the other. This function, he said, could be construed as authorizing an extension of effort by UNFICYP to protect the security of Turkish Cypriot villages and quarters of mixed villages. Adding that, for obvious reasons, UNFICYP could not for the time being perform the same functions on behalf of those Greek Cypriots still in areas under Turkish control, he directed that, where possible, UNFICYP should endeavour on a humanitarian basis to contribute, by negotiation, to the security of Greek Cypriot villages in the north. Waldheim appreciated, he said, that, wherever restrictions were imposed on UNFICYP's freedom of movement, his instructions could not be carried out, but it was important that the Force should make every effort to do so. More generally, and pending agreement as to what its long-term role should be, UNFICYP was to continue to assist pragmatically in maintaining the ceasefire and to take all possible measures to minimize intercommunal tension or a recurrence of intercommunal fighting. These were broad instructions to which Prem Chand and those under his command responded with initiative and energy.

There was much to be done, not least at UNFICYP Headquarters. On 17 and 18 August I visited UN Districts throughout the island, the Green Line in Nicosia, those defending the airport and UN camps and logistics units in its vicinity, and UNFICYP's small signals detachment in the Troodos mountains, which had continued valiantly to relay vital radio traffic, to see for myself the situation and discover local problems. Meetings were held to decide on future deployments, the possibility of repairing and opening the airport and of re-establishing civilian air traffic control; liaison was necessary with Commanders in the SBAs to examine common problems, as were meetings with international aid agencies, members of diplomatic missions and numerous other visitors, including politicians and journalists, seeking information or help. Not least, personal contact had to be maintained or re-established with National Guard headquarters, senior government officials and, less easily, the Leadership, whose mood was distinctly more confident in the light of the changed situation. It was a period of intense activity during which UNFICYP's operations, logistics, humanitarian and civilian police staffs all met the many new challenges with remarkable efficiency.

Contingents' operational responsibilities remained unchanged in the immediate aftermath of Turkey's ceasefire and District Commanders were notified of the principles by which UNFICYP's actions were now to be guided. It was clear that, if UNFICYP was going to be able to operate as required by the Security Council, the cooperation of those on both sides was necessary. To this end District Commanders were instructed to cultivate close liaison with military and civil authorities at all levels and, where possible, friendly personal relations with leaders concerned. The most pressing operational need was to stabilize the military situation, but here Waldheim had imposed a crucial *caveat*: until a settlement was reached, UNFICYP was not to take any action, such as the formal establishment of a cease-fire line, which might prejudice or prejudge the position of any of the parties. UNFICYP's role, he said, was to be essentially one of *ad hoc* assistance as the situation required, and in this process to be prepared to lend its good offices in any way that the parties might find useful.

Although the Turkish army's advance had been halted at 1800hrs on 16 August, the positions then reached did not mark the 'Attila Line' that ultimately divided north from south. There had not been any agreement with either the National Guard or UNFICYP as to the precise positions on which the Turkish army would halt, and during the succeeding days and weeks the Turks moved further forward in many areas. In Famagusta District they advanced in force close to the Eastern SBA boundary and eventually right up to the boundary itself, claiming that this was part of the area under their control, and in Nicosia District they thrust south from Pyroi to secure control of the Turkish village of Louroujina, resulting in the severing of the main Nicosia-Larnaca road and an awkward protrusion in the boundary between north and south; in Nicosia itself, however, the Canadians succeeded by negotiation in preventing Turkish expansion in the area of the golf course and just west of the Pedhieos River in the city's northern suburbs. In Lefka District the Turkish army pushed west from Xeros to link up with the Limnitis enclave and advanced south and east of Lefka to secure more territory.

In places these moves gave rise to fighting as the National Guard offered resistance, its morale and discipline improved following reinforcement by regular mainland Greek officers and the appointment of Major General Karayiannis as its new commander. In the light of Waldheim's important *caveat* UNFICYP could do little other than to urge both sides to stop the shooting and by mediation to seek agreement on the new positions to be held by each. Since movement in Turkish-controlled areas was severely restricted, UN patrols were obliged to probe cautiously forward through National Guard lines to make contact with local Turkish commanders, discover their precise locations and intentions, and, where feasible, to establish a UN OP to monitor the situation and provide some confidence to the nervous National Guard. When construction of semi-permanent defensive works and the laying of mines followed, it became evident that a degree of military stability had been achieved. Thus was the UN buffer zone, stretching for 120km right across the island from Famagusta in the east to Morphou Bay in the west, gradually established.[5]

Adjustments in UN Contingents' operational responsibilities were now required. The Finns still retained their bases at Tjiklos on the Kyrenia Pass and at Mia Milea north-east of Nicosia, but the rest of the Contingent now lacked an operational role. Lieut. Colonel Pullinen was accordingly instructed on 20 August to assume responsibility for the area west of Nicosia airport out to Peristerona, a front of 17km. With extensive reconnaissances being made by patrols of 4th/7th Dragoon Guards to discover the general situation, Pullinen deployed his 3rd Company under Major Jukka Hyle to monitor the new area. Hyle made contact with the Turkish troops to his the north and in due course established six OPs between the forward lines of the two sides.[6] This redeployment was formalized on 10 September, when the Canadians were instructed to take over all those parts of Nicosia and Kyrenia Districts lying east of the general line from Orta Keuy southwards, this to be known as 'Nicosia Zone (East)', and the Finns to assume responsibility for all parts of these two Districts lying west of that general line, this to be known as 'Nicosia Zone (West)', each being supported by a troop of the Parachute Sqn. RAC, now re-constituted as the Force Reserve. Elements of the British, Canadian and Finnish Contingents continued to safeguard the UN Protected Area around the airport and adjoining camps, with coordination remaining the responsibility of Colonel Beattie (Canada), UNFICYP's DCOS.

The Swedes remained responsible for Famagusta District, virtually all of which was now under Turkish army control. Although isolated in Carl Gustav Camp north of Famagusta, and in spite of Turkish army-imposed restrictions on their freedom of movement, they were increasingly successful in carrying out humanitarian tasks in various parts of the District. For the Austrians, who continued in Larnaca District, the main problem was in dealing with outbreaks of shooting as the Turkish army pressed forward to Louroujina and towards the Eastern SBA boundary north of Larnaca itself. The Danes in Lefka District, who like other contingents, experienced no difficulty in securing the cooperation of the National Guard, initially found themselves virtually confined to their camps by the Turkish army's denial of freedom of movement and became increasingly frustrated. Nevertheless, problems with the Turkish army were gradually overcome and by October the Danes had succeeded in establishing ten new OPs between the opposing forces.

The Coldstream Guards in Limassol Zone were concerned primarily to protect those Turkish Cypriots who still remained in small and sometimes remote villages where they were vulnerable to attack by roving bands of Greek Cypriot irregulars bent on revenge. Lieut. Colonel Willoughby deployed sections of guardsmen to protect such villages and asked for authority for them to use force to this end, if necessary. I told him that an attack on any village in which his men were present was to be treated as an attack on UNFICYP and that in such circumstances fire could be opened. The arrival in mid-September of the Queen's Royal Irish Hussars to join BRITCON allowed that regiment to assume responsibility for Paphos District and 2nd Bn Coldstream Guards then became responsible solely for Limassol District. At the same time the 16th/5th Lancers and C Squadron, 4th/7th Dragoon Guards, who had reinforced UNFICYP in July during the crisis at Nicosia airport, reverted to UK national command. Before they left Nicosia a farewell parade was mounted on 12 September at the airport at which Prem Chand, who to universal delight had been promoted to the rank of Lieutenant General five days earlier, thanked them warmly for their valuable contribution and announced that, in view of their excellent performance during the previous eight weeks, New York had agreed to make an exception in their case by waiving the six months' qualifying period for entitlement to the UN Medal 'In the Service of Peace'; this would now be awarded to them all.

Breaches of the ceasefire, mostly along the Green Line in Nicosia and areas immediately north and west of the Eastern SBA, continued, but by mid-September some stability had been established. An early trouble spot in Nicosia had been the area of the golf course just west of the Pedhieos River, which included the premises of the British High Commission and the French Embassy and was the scene of looting and similar lawless activity. On 17 August Colonel Lessard, Commander of the Canadian Airborne Regiment, went to the area to avert an imminent fight between a group of Turks and another of Greeks, facing each other at opposite ends of a street, by persuading both to withdraw. While so engaged a vehicle approached and its Turkish Cypriot civilian driver was was forced from it by the Greeks, who were about to shoot him. Lessard instantly placed himself between the civilian and the Greeks and, summoning a Canadian APC, sheltered him with his own body until he was safely inside the APC; Lessard's brave action undoubtedly saved the Turkish Cypriot's life. During the next few days the situation in this area was brought under control by the

Canadians, but on 10 September they suffered another fatality when Private Berger, engaged at the time on a humanitarian mission, was shot dead by the National Guard in an incident that probably was due to a case of mistaken identity.

Developments within the Greek Cypriot community were not one of UNFICYP's immediate concerns, although some anxiety was caused as anti-American feeling increasingly manifested itself among Greeks looking for a scapegoat for the calamity they now suffered. No matter that it had been the foolhardy rashness of the Athens junta that had brought this on their heads, there were many ready to believe that, had they so wished, the Americans could have prevented Turkey's invasion. These feelings were fanned by left-wing elements who on 19 August staged a demonstration outside the US Embassy in Nicosia, which turned violent with the burning of cars and flags and the stoning of the Embassy building. Under cover of the violence several ex-EOKA thugs armed with automatic weapons climbed to the second floor of an unfinished apartment building facing the Embassy building from another direction and from this fire was directed at the Ambassador's office. The Ambassador, Mr Rodger Davies, and a Cypriot secretary, Antoinette Varnava, both of whom had taken shelter in a corridor where they were protected from the demonstrators but not the EOKA gunmen, were killed.

The Embassy's warning to CYPOL that an anti-American demonstration was planned and its request for protection had been ignored. With the Ambassador dead and members of the staff in danger, an urgent appeal was made to UNFICYP to come to the rescue of those in the building. The Canadians were already on the alert and Colonel Lessard was instructed to be prepared to send M113 APCs to extricate those in the building, which was in danger of being set on fire. In the event this did not prove necessary, but there was some disquiet lest such action by UNFICYP might have exceeded the terms of its mandate and infringed the sovereignty of the host government. My view was that any such action would have been justified on humanitarian grounds, but, in order to remove doubts on this score, formal agreement was obtained later from the Government's Interior Minister, Mr Veniamin, for UNFICYP to assist in any future contingency where the safety of diplomatic missions was at stake.[7]

During September a rumour, which in the event proved false, gained ground of a possible Turkish 'Third Round', perhaps entailing a thrust by land from the Athienou area to the sea at Larnaca, coupled with sea or airborne operations to rescue Turkish Cypriots in the Limassol, Paphos and Polis areas. UN District Commanders were warned accordingly and told that UNFICYP's policy in that contingency would be the same as had been notified by the Force Commander on 13 August prior to the 'Second Round'; in the meantime, so as not to cause undue alarm in civilian circles, the Force was to remain at 'Increased Vigilance', to which it had reverted from 'Blue Alert' on 28 August. By mid-September UNFICYP, now some 4300 strong, was maintaining a UN presence at 36 locations in the area under Turkish control and at a further 93 locations in areas under Cyprus government control; these latter included 19 Turkish or mixed villages. (Most other Turkish and mixed villages in the south were visited by UN military or civilian police patrols daily.)[8] The Force was also increasingly undertaking a wide variety of other activities, ranging from escorting firemen to extinguish fires in buildings along the Green Line to feeding and watering abandoned farm animals, assisting in restoring water supplies and the electric power on which the pumps depended and numerous other humanitarian tasks; the calls for help were endless. All such activities contributed to a gradual return of confidence in Cypriots of all communities. Especially important were the comprehensive reports on conditions in villages both north and south which UNFICYP was able to provide, for the emphasis was changing from the military to the humanitarian and these factual reports formed the basis for much of the rapidly expanding relief programme.

The search for a political settlement of the situation currently exercising minds not only in New York but also in Washington, London, Ankara, Athens and Nicosia, was not one of UNFICYP's immediate concerns; its attentions were increasingly focused on calls for practical support for the aid agencies. The magnitude of the likely problems, especially that of the refugees, had become apparent even while the fighting was in progress, and, appreciating the need for UN co-ordination of the substantial international relief effort that was now required, Waldheim designated the UN High Commissioner for Refugees (UNHCR), Prince Sadruddin Aga Khan, to be the 'UN Co-ordinator of Humanitarian Relief Assistance for Cyprus'; two of his staff, John Kelly, who subsequently headed the UNHCR operations in Cyprus, and Nicholes Morris arrived in Nicosia from Geneva on 20 August.

Meanwhile Lieut. Colonel Gerry O'Sullivan (Ireland), recently arrived to take charge of HQ UNFICYP's new Economics/Humanitarian Branch, but engaged instead in drafting situation reports for New York while the fighting continued, lost no time. On the morning of 17 August, with the situation around Blue Beret and Kykko Camps still dangerous, he set out with Major Smith (Canada), hitherto Force Economics Officer and now his assistant, and Colonel O'Carroll-Fitzpatrick (UK), Force Chief Medical Officer, to ascertain what needed to be done and how UNFICYP could help:

> As we drove into Nicosia it was an eerie experience with the streets deserted, shops and houses closed up and just nobody on the streets. At the Hilton . . . we found that the ICRC had moved to the Cleopatra Hotel which was to be their operational HQ. We drove there and made contact with the Mission Chief, Laurent Martin and his Director of Operations, Francois Hohl. We discussed the situation and our mutual problems briefly but in those few hours we established a mutual understanding which stood the test of the difficult times to come. There was always a genuine cooperation between our two organizations, which was perhaps unique considering the basic military nature of UNFICYP and the strictly humanitarian function of the ICRC. At this first meeting a bond was established which was strengthened as our cooperation developed . . . there was never any question of rivalry but the common bond between two organizations of the need to relieve human suffering.[9]

This was an auspicious beginning to what quickly became a major international relief undertaking.

Prince Sadruddin himself arrived in Nicosia on 22 August and, with UNFICYP's assistance in the provision of helicopter and road transport (and escorts where necessary), he immediately undertook a tour to both north and south, including the SBAs, to see the problems at first hand. Speaking to the Press on his departure five days later, he said:

It is very difficult here. I think that . . . emphasis on the humanitarian role is extremely important . . . . As co-ordinator I have been able to see during my visit the plight of displaced persons – north, south, east and west of this island. It is difficult to really pinpoint individual suffering but what I can say, having met so many people, is that it goes across ethnic group, race and religion.

Many individual cases had, nonetheless, been brought to his notice, few more distressing than that of a young Greek Cypriot boy in the village of Voni (now under Turkish army control) who had been left untended with a bullet lodged in his head; Prince Sadruddin's quiet representations immediately led to the boy, and his sick sister, being treated in hospital. The Prince's sympathetic but firmly realistic approach to those he met was impressive, as I saw for myself when I escorted him to call, unannounced, on a group of Maronite refugees in the Troodos mountains and to visit isolated Turkish Cypriot villages further west.

Before leaving Cyprus Prince Sadruddin chaired the first UNHCR co-ordination meeting, held at the Ledra Palace Hotel on 27 August. The attendance was wide; it included diplomats from Canada, France, Federal Republic of Germany, Israel, Italy, Turkey, United Kingdom, United States, USSR, and representatives from the Cyprus Red Cross, ICRC, UN Development Programme (UNDP) and, of course, UNFICYP in the person of O'Sullivan; others who attended later meetings included representatives of the the UN Children's Fund, World Council of Churches, World Food Programme and World Health Organization. Closing the meeting, the first of many held under UNHCR auspices and chaired by John Kelly during succeeding weeks and months, Prince Sadruddin announced that he had given US $300,000 to the Cyprus Red Cross and a similar sum to the Turkish Red Crescent as an advance to meet immediate needs until an impending appeal was launched by the Secretary General, who, together with Brian Urquhart, had himself arrived in Nicosia two days earlier:

> [Travelling via Athens] . . . I arrived in Cyprus in the late afternoon of 25 August. I visited UNFICYP units in the Nicosia area and had lengthy discussions with my Special Representative, the Force Commander, and the High Commissioner for Refugees. On 26 August I had talks with Acting President Clerides and with Vice President Denktash. Before leaving Cyprus [on 26 August for Ankara] I presided over a joint meeting on humanitarian questions, at which Mr Clerides, Mr Denktash and the High Commissioner were present.[10]

The Secretary General's talks had covered a wide range of other matters, including UNFICYP's freedom of movement and future role, but none was left in doubt that the pressing humanitarian problems were receiving urgent attention at all levels and in many different quarters.

The extent of the refugee problem was summarized in Prince Sadruddin's report made on his return to Geneva from Nicosia:

> A large number of Greek Cypriot displaced persons, estimated at 163,800, have fled their homes in the northern part of the island and are now in the south. There are also an estimated 34,000 Turkish Cypriots in the south. Of these numbers, some 50,000 Greek Cypriots and some 7,800 Turkish Cypriots are in the British Sovereign Base Areas. In the south there is,

therefore, a total of some 197,800 persons in need. In the north there are an estimated 20,000 Greek Cypriots who did not or could not leave and a further 7,800 Turkish Cypriots who are homeless, making a total of 27,800 in need in the north and and a total of 225,600 in the whole island. These figures were given locally to the High Commissioner by the Red Cross and the Red Crescent. It should be noted that not all 225,600 are displaced, as most of the Greek Cypriots in the north are still in their own homes, but deprived of their livelihood. The great majority of these are, or shortly will be, in need of assistance.

Related to the present situation are also other problems, such as the care of large numbers of livestock left behind on Greek Cypriot farms in the north and the maintenance of the irrigation of the citrus plantations.[11]

Indeed, although the refugee situation was acute and pressing, the severe economic consequences, both short- and long-term, of Turkey's seizure of the north, were of no less concern. The catalogue was long:

> The territory controlled by Turkish forces at present is more than 40 per cent of the total area of the island. In this area the inhabitants were 80 per cent Greek and 20 per cent Turkish. The area comprises almost all the Mesaoria plain, east and west, the Kyrenia district and the Karpas peninsula. It is the almost exclusive cereal, carob and olive producing area and the main citrus, vegetable, meat, milk and egg producing area of Cyprus. It represents two-thirds of the tourist activities, 55 to 60 per cent of the industrial activity, 65 per cent of the cultivated land, 60 per cent of the underground water resources, 60 per cent of the mining and quarrying activities (almost 100 per cent of the latter), the main port of Cyprus at Famagusta, through which 85 per cent of the minerals were handled. In other words, the economic significance of this area is much more important than its size. It is estimated that about 70 per cent of total gross production from all sources emanates from this area, not to mention the immense wealth of physical assets, resources and structures situated there in the form of hotels and hotel apartments, houses, factories, orchards, arable and irrigated fertile land, mineral and quarrying resources, water resources and tourist land of great value.[12]

Cyprus had suffered a devastating blow.

Caring for the huge number of refugees who had fled south to seek refuge either in or close to the British SBAs was a task that initially fell entirely on the SBA authorities. A vast refugee camp, primarily for Greek Cypriots, was established in the Athna forest (actually a sparse area of trees and scrub) adjoining the northern edge of the Eastern SBA and basic needs, including medical care, were provided from SBA resources. All concerned, both military and civilian, rallied round under the leadership of Brigadier Robertson, SBA Commander, to ease the lot of the thousands of refugees of all ages who flooded into the camp. A particular concern for Robertson was to maintain security of both the SBA and the camp and, in view of the close proximity of the Turkish army,[13] to ensure that no incidents were created by any hot-headed Greeks. The refugee situation in the Western SBA was not so acute, but a camp, mainly for Turkish Cypriots who had fled from villages north of the SBA, was established in what was known as Happy Valley.

As the relief operation, efficiently coordinated by the UNHCR, gathered momentum, aid in the form of supplies and financial contributions flowed in from many governments and non-governmental organizations around the world, and the Cyprus government itself increasingly played a major part. The ICRC was engaged in its traditional role, begun as early as 23 July, in visiting prisoners and, where possible, arranging their repatriation, tracing individuals and families and passing on messages on their behalf, and distributing medical supplies, food and other aid to those in need in both the north and the south.

The relief operation grew rapidly and extended to all parts of the island.[14] UNFICYP's role was primarily supportive, especially in the provision of military transport (and of drivers where civilian drivers were reluctant to drive vehicles into Turkish-controlled areas), escorts and guides. For example, the Secretary General reported on 10 September:

> The UN Force continues to support the humanitarian relief programme in co-operation with the UNHCR, the ICRC, the UN Development Programme and local agencies. During the period *[26 August – 8 September]* a total of 67 truck-loads of relief supplies were delivered to villages, 63 to Turkish Cypriots and four to Greek Cypriots. From 2 August to 7 September UNFICYP delivered a total of 184 truck-loads, or the equivalent of 900 tons of food. Transportation is also provided for the movement to distribution areas of supplies from international sources received by UNHCR from Akrotiri.[15]

Most of this transport was provided by 7 Sqn, Royal Corps of Transport (the Force transport unit) but contingents' own vehicles also were used. Few problems were encountered, although there were difficulties when the National Guard protested that weapons were being transported to isolated Turkish Cypriot villages under the cover of relief supplies; we replied that UNFICYP did not have the manpower to unload every lorry to check whether or not weapons might have been concealed among the supplies. Some unusual tasks also came UNFICYP's way. One such was a request for the Force to obtain a large quantity of Greek-owned potatoes held in a store now in Turkish hands in east Nicosia, these being required for refugees in the Athna forest camp. In 'Operation Murphy' O'Sullivan successfully arranged for the release of these and their transport to the refugees. Less successful was a request by the SBA authorities for UNFICYP to recover a supply of rice, similarly owned and held in east Nicosia, required, it was said, for the Gurkhas now part of the SBA garrison; before an UNFICYP party arrived to collect the rice the store had been emptied. Otherwise UNFICYP's contingents were fully occupied in supervising the ceasefire and stabilizing the situation along the buffer zone, in numerous reconnaissances and escorts, in attending to farm animals in great distress, helping, in so far as technical resources allowed, in restoration of electricity and water supplies and in sundry other tasks. The wide-ranging activities of UNFICYP's men in blue berets drew much favourable comment, not least from agencies engaged in the relief effort.

From the moment that Turkish troops first put foot on the island on 20 July there had been reports of atrocities committed by both sides, not always in the heat of battle. The reports were numerous and there was little doubt that most were true. Some acts were alleged to have been committed by Turkish Cypriots in retaliation for long-held grievances against their Greek Cypriot compatriots, some by Turkish troops against National Guard soldiers taken prisoner and Greek Cypriots who had not fled their village, others by Greek Cypriot

National Guardsmen or irregulars against isolated and vulnerable Turkish Cypriot communities. By the time a nominal ceasefire had been declared on 16 August the number of atrocities reported to UNFICYP was considerable; they included incidents not only of murder but also of rape, sometimes multiple, and were committed against both groups and individual victims. In furtherance of its mission to minimize intercommunal tensions UNFICYP saw it as a duty to investigate these reports wherever possible. The task was undertaken by its UN Civilian Police, who were only able to carry out a partial investigation of many reports, their efforts being frustrated by the attitude of the Turkish authorities who generally were not willing to allow investigations by UNFICYP in areas under their control. The Government in its turn refused to let UNFICYP investigate those cases reported to have been committed in its area.[16]

A related problem, primarily the concern of the ICRC, was that of prisoners and the many missing persons, which included Greek Cypriots known to have surrendered or been captured and transported to Turkey, in some cases never to be heard of again. However, following talks between Clerides and Denktash, an exchange of prisoners, including the sick and wounded, teachers, students and all those under 18 years of age, began on 22 September and continued next day; it then was halted because a group of Greek prisoners due to return from Turkey did not appear and because the Turks refused to allow some released Greek Cypriots to return to their homes in the area now occupied by Turkish forces. The emotive question of the 'missing persons', which caused so much distress to their near and dear, was but one of the many that were to remain unresolved in the years ahead.

Numerous international missions of good offices, initiatives, inquiries, patient negotiations and new proposals failed to settle the deep constitutional, territorial and other differences that bedevilled the peoples of Cyprus throughout these many long years. Over all remained the brooding shadow of Turkey and the presence on the island of its powerful armed forces. Few in UNFICYP foresaw in October 1974 that 30 years later its thin blue line would still be marking a buffer zone dividing north from south.

*　　*　　*　　*

After two eventful years as UNFICYP's Chief of Staff and Commander of its British Contingent my tour of duty ended in October 1974. To leave the beautiful island and its friendly and hospitable people of all communities in such an unhappy state was cause for deep sorrow. Farewell visits were paid to all UN contingents to thank them for their invariably warm welcomes, comradeship and loyal support; it had been an inspiring experience to serve alongside the men of all these nations. Visits were paid, too, to those in the SBAs who had given vital logistic support to UNFICYP, especially in times of stress; to Government ministers and officials with whom contacts had been close in spite of occasional differences; and to those in the Leadership with whom sometimes difficult but nonetheless friendly negotiations had been conducted. Others of whom I took leave and thanked were members of diplomatic missions, in particular the British High Commission and the US Embassy, but also others, such as the Turkish, French, Italian and Russian Embassies, and good personal friends in both the Greek and Turkish communities.

It was a sadness to part from comrades, both military and civilian, in UNFICYP's Headquarters and supporting units with whom I had worked so closely. John Miles, the Australian Senior Political Adviser, had been a tower of strength; when he departed for another UN post in the Middle East in August 1974 the loss of his wise and ready counsel was keenly felt in the Headquarters. Colonel Beattie (Canada) succeeded me as Chief of Staff in the rank of Brigadier General; as DCOS he had displayed courage and negotiating skill in de-fusing several potentially explosive situations. Lieut. Colonel Pennell (UK), as Chief of Personnel and Logistics, had ensured that throughout the recent difficult days no contingent lacked essential supplies – indeed, to this end he and his staff had displayed admirable initiative, working quietly in ways to which it has not been possible to do justice in this book. Lieut. Colonel Skaarup, the Danish Chief Operations Officer, ran the Force's Joint Operations Centre, where pressures often were intense, with competence, supported by its UN Civilian Police members and helped especially by Major Baxter (UK), the Force Signals Officer, who was indefatigable in dealing on the radio with those whose command of English was not always perfect. It was sad also to say farewell to the UN civilian staff, male and female, the responsibility of Victor Mills (US), the Chief Administrative Officer ; they continued to work devotedly under conditions which normally only soldiers would be expected to endure. There were many others, especially my Personal Assistant, Staff Sergeant Peter Snow, who worked tirelessly for long hours under harsh, spartan and sometimes dangerous conditions in Blue Beret Camp to ensure that I was able to play my part. All would agree that at times it had been a business of rather more than a little heat.

Above all it was with the deepest regret that I said good-bye to General Prem Chand. He had been, and remained until his death in 2003, a valued and close friend; I greatly admired him as an outstanding UN Force Commander under whom it had been a privilege to serve. His personal example and high standards set the tone for the conduct of the whole Force. He did me the honour of parading a multi-national Guard of Honour as I left the Headquarters by helicopter for Akrotiri and handed me a letter not to be opened until I was aboard a RAF aircraft bound for England. As I opened and read it (Annex 7), memories were revived of stirring times but two points were foremost in my mind: first, I counted myself extraordinarily fortunate that a military career, which had begun on the outbreak of the Second World War and then progressed through a series of lesser conflicts, had ended with service in a UN Force whose sole purpose was peace. No matter that latterly we may not have been entirely successful, the progression gave hope for the future of mankind. Second, I left the island convinced that, however UNFICYP's recent performance might be judged by others, the sufferings of members of all communities in Cyprus would have been far more severe had the multi-national Force of men in blue berets not been there – indeed, it was not unrealistic to suppose that, but for their presence and actions, the Turkish forces might have felt it necessary to occupy the whole island in order to ensure the security of Turkish Cypriots isolated in the south. Seen in this light, the price paid by the Force in dead and injured had not been in vain.

POSTSCRIPT

The consequence of Turkey's military action in the summer of 1974 was the *de facto* partition of Cyprus that still persists thirty years later. Numerous initiatives on the part of the United Nations and others with a view to uniting the Turkish Cypriots in the north with the Greek Cypriots in the south in a federal republic, in which each would continue to enjoy a measure of self-government, have been frustrated by deep and complex differences. It seemed that more often than not the failures could be attributed to the intransigence of the Turkish Cypriots under Rauf Denktash; few doubted that he was acting other than at the bidding of Ankara, where determination not to surrender the strategic advantage won by its armed forces in 1974 was a potent factor.

However, two fresh developments held promise in early 2004 that a settlement might be attained. First was the European Union's agreement for the Republic of Cyprus to be admitted to membership on 1 May 2004, hopefully as a united island, but, if this had not been achieved by then, with the Turkish-occupied north excluded. Second, elections that had brought new governments to power in Athens and Ankara gave prospect of more cordial relations between the two, not least on account of Turkey's own aspiration to join the European Union. So long as the Cyprus problem remained unresolved, it was an obstacle in both contexts.

Exasperated by the failure after weeks of intensive diplomacy to secure a settlement acceptable to all the parties, the UN Secretary General, Kofi Annan, put forward what he declared to be his final plan to this end, which, if agreed, would have allowed both parts of the island to join the European Union together on 1 May 2004 as a federal republic. The parties remained deeply divided on key issues of the plan, but both agreed that it should be put to each community for decision in a referendum on 24 April 2004. The result was endorsement of the plan (which Kofi Annan had revised in the interim) by 64.9 per cent of Turkish Cypriot voters in the north, and its decisive rejection by 75.8 per cent of Greek Cypriot voters in the south. This outcome was a remarkable reversal of the positions displayed hitherto by the two communities. The Greek Cypriots' rejection, which occasioned international dismay, was centred primarily on a perception that the plan provided immediate satisfaction of Turkish Cypriot interests, whereas it held out only promise of satisfaction of their own at some future uncertain date. Proposals that Turkey should continue to station military forces on the island and that the Treaty of Guarantee should remain in force indefinitely were further provisions not acceptable to the Greek

Cypriots, who nonetheless declared their readiness to engage in renewed negotiations to reach agreement with their compatriots in the north. (It was of interest that Britain had stated that it would cede nearly half of the areas of the SBAs to Cypriot sovereignty if there was a settlement under the terms of Kofi Annan's plan.)

Thus the summer of 2004 found the UN Force of Cyprus, now in its forty-first year of duty on the island, still deployed to keep the peace along the line dividing north from south. With its strength reduced to 1230 all ranks, it was commanded by Major General Almandos of Uruguay; alone among its component Contingents, that of the United Kingdom had served throughout these years. (A Security Council resolution proposing the replacement of UNFICYP by a new UN mission of 2500 troops, 510 international police officers and a substantial civilian staff had been vetoed by Russia on 21 April 2004, but Kofi Annan stated, following rejection of his plan, that he expected the UN peacekeeping presence in Cyprus to continue in some form.)

The strategic importance of Cyprus, especially to Turkey, remains a constant factor, and, so long as the problem remains unresolved, the island will continue to be a cause for potential international instability. What does the future hold? Re-unification of north and south in a federal republic? Annexation of the north to Turkey? Or indefinite continuation of the present divide? And for how much longer must the patient peacekeepers of the United Nations remain?

FRH, September 2004.

ANNEX 1

RESOLUTION 186 (1964)

Adopted by the United Nations Security Council on 4 March 1964

The Security Council,

Noting that the present situation with regard to Cyprus is likely to threaten international peace and security and may further deteriorate unless additional measures are promptly taken to maintain peace and to seek out a durable solution,

Considering the positions taken by the parties in relation to the Treaties signed at Nicosia on 16 August 1960,

Having in mind the relevant provisions of the Charter of the United Nations and its Article 2, paragraph 4, which reads : "All Members shall refrain in their international relations from the threat or use of force against the territorial integrity or political independence of any State, or in any other manner inconsistent with the purposes of the United Nations",

1. *Calls upon* all Member States, in conformity with their obligations under the Charter of the United Nations, to refrain from any action or threat of action to worsen the situation in the sovereign Republic of Cyprus, or to endanger international peace;

2. *Asks* the Government of Cyprus, which has the responsibility for the maintenance and restoration of law and order, to take all additional measures necessary to stop violence and bloodshed in Cyprus;

3. *Calls upon* the communities in Cyprus and their leaders to act with the utmost restraint;

4. *Recommends* the creation, with the consent of the Government of Cyprus, of a United Nations Peace-Keeping Force in Cyprus. The composition and size of the Force shall be established by the Secretary-General, in consultation with the Governments of Cyprus, Greece, Turkey and the United Kingdom. The commander of the Force shall be appointed by the Secretary-General and report to him. The Secretary-General, who shall keep the Governments providing the Force fully informed, shall report periodically to the Security Council on its operation;

5. *Recommends* that the function of the Force should be in the interest of preserving international peace and security, to use its best efforts to prevent a recurrence of fighting and, as necessary to contribute to the maintenance and restoration of law and order and a return to normal conditions.

6. *Recommends* that the stationing of the Force shall be for a period of three months, all

costs pertaining to it to be met, in a manner to be agreed upon by them, by the Governments providing the contingents and by the Government of Cyprus. The Secretary-General may also accept voluntary contributions for that purpose.

7. *Recommends further* that the Secretary-General designate, in agreement with the Government of Cyprus and the Governments of Greece, Turkey and the United Kingdom, a mediator who shall use his best endeavours with the representatives of the communities and also with the aforesaid four Governments, for the purpose of promoting a peaceful solution and an agreed settlement of the problem confronting Cyprus, in accordance with the Charter of the United Nations, having in mind the well-being of the people of Cyprus as a whole and the preservation of international peace and security. The mediator shall report periodically to the Secretary-General on his efforts;

8. *Requests* the Secretary-General to provide, from funds of the United Nations, as appropriate, for the remuneration and expenses of the mediator and his staff.

Adopted unanimously at the 1102nd meeting.

UN CHAIN OF COMMAND AND CONTROL AND ORGANISATION OF UNFICYP HEADQUARTERS (JUNE 1972)

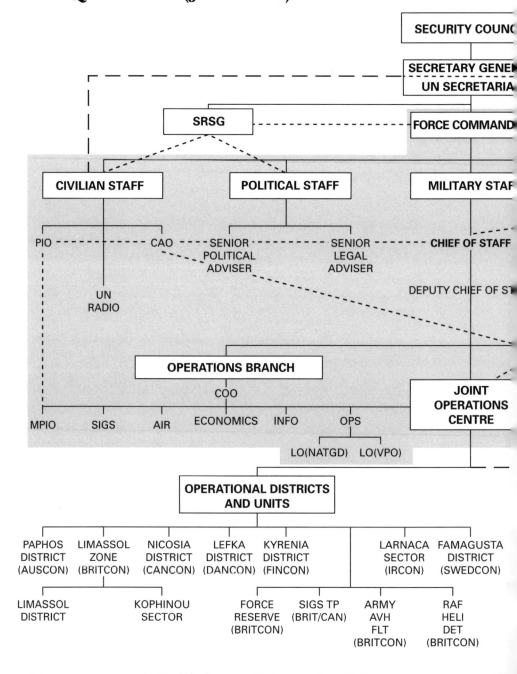

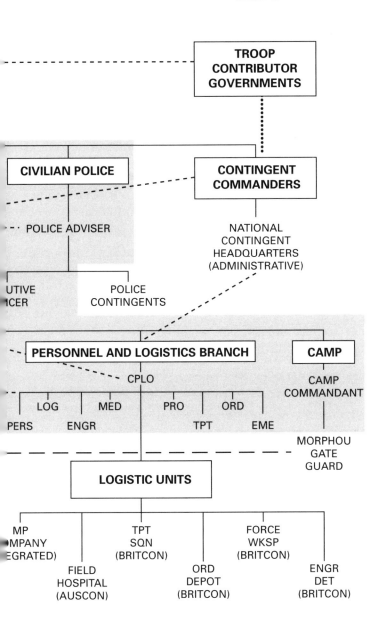

	Principal line of command and control
	Alternative line of control
	Liaison and coordination links
	National administration
	Elements comprising force headquarters

TROOP CONTRIBUTOR GOVERNMENTS

CIVILIAN POLICE

CONTINGENT COMMANDERS

POLICE ADVISER

NATIONAL CONTINGENT HEADQUARTERS (ADMINISTRATIVE)

UTIVE
ICER

POLICE CONTINGENTS

PERSONNEL AND LOGISTICS BRANCH

CAMP

CPLO

CAMP COMMANDANT

| LOG | MED | PRO | ORD |
PERS | ENGR | TPT | EME

MORPHOU GATE GUARD

LOGISTIC UNITS

MP
MPANY
EGRATED)

TPT SQN (BRITCON)

FORCE WKSP (BRITCON)

FIELD HOSPITAL (AUSCON)

ORD DEPOT (BRITCON)

ENGR DET (BRITCON)

GREEK CYPRIOT NATIONAL GUARD AND POLICE –1974

Composition of National Guard

Headquarters National Guard
Five Higher Military Command (HMC) Headquarters
Nine Tactical Group (TG) Headquarters
One Armoured Reconnaissance Battalion
One Medium Tank Batallion
One Armoured Personnel Carrier (APC) Battalion
Six Field Artillery Battalions
Two Anti-tank Artillery Battalions
Three Anti-aircraft Artillery Battalions
Fifteen Infantry Battalions
Nine Militia Infantry Battalions

Three Raiding Force Units (RFU)
One Service Battalion
Four Recruit Training Centres

Approximate Total Strength

Active	10,500*
1st Line Reserves	1,500
2nd Line Reserves	28,000
Total	**40,000**

* Includes permanent cadre of 1000, of which 650 were officers of the Greek army.

Outline Command Organization

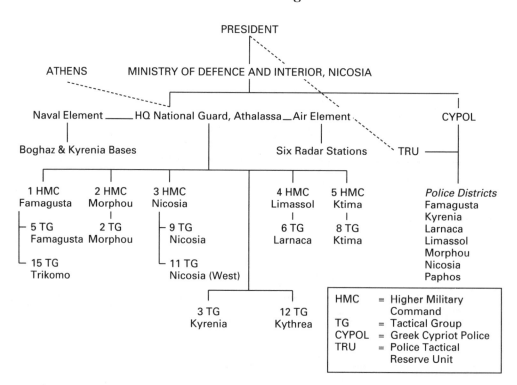

HMC	=	Higher Military Command
TG	=	Tactical Group
CYPOL	=	Greek Cypriot Police
TRU	=	Police Tactical Reserve Unit

TURKISH CYPRIOT FIGHTERS –1974

Approximate Strength

Active:	4,500*
1st Line Reserves	3,200
2nd Line Reserves	12,300
Total	**20,000**

*Including permanent cadre of 2,300 and 150 mainland Turks.

Outline Organization

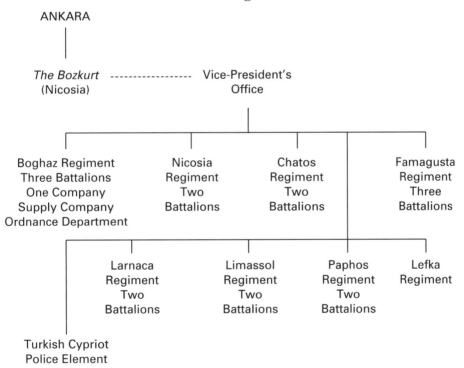

ANNEX 5

BRITISH FORCES IN OR NEAR CYPRUS IN JULY AND AUGUST 1974

Memorandum submitted by the Ministry of Defence*

1.   The Select Committee has asked for details of the disposition of British forces in or near Cyprus during July and August 1974.

2.   The garrison of the Sovereign Base Areas in early July 1974 comprised one infantry battalion (1 Bn Royal Scots), two infantry companies (of 2 Bn Coldstream Guards) and one armoured reconnaissance squadron (of 16/5 Lancers). An artillery battery was visiting Cyprus on exercise at the time. With supporting troops these forces totalled 2,995 men. The role of the garrison is the protection of the Sovereign Base Areas.

3.   Following the coup the garrison was reinforced by a brigade headquarters, one infantry battalion (3 Bn Royal Regiment of Fusiliers), one armoured reconnaissance regiment (Regimental HQ and one squadron 16/5 Lancers; one squadron 4/7 Dragoon Guards; and one squadron Royal Horse Guards/Dragoons), two Royal Marines Commando (40 Commando and 41 Commando) and support units. These reinforcements totalled 3,319 men. Some units were redeployed to UNFICYP, however, and this reduced the strength of the reinforced garrison to 5,553.

4.   41 Commando was withdrawn at the end of July 1974. 40 Commando began to withdraw on 8 August but, before the move was completed, returned with an artillery element between 11 and 15 August. 10 Gurkha Rifles deployed to Cyprus from 11 to 13 August. In mid-August the garrison strength was 5,640. The reinforcements were withdrawn progressively from September 1974.

5.   The following RAF forces with the task of protecting the Sovereign Base Areas and their approaches against air attack were based in Cyprus at the time of the coup: one squadron of Lightning interceptor aircraft, one squadron of Bloodhound surface-to-air missiles, and two squadrons of low level air defence guns. A Phantom detachment was deployed from the United Kingdom to RAF Akrotiri on 25 July.

6.   The resident air forces in Cyprus also included bomber aircraft (Vulcans), tactical support aircraft (Hercules and Argosy) and helicopters (Whirlwinds), to which were added

*Published as Appendix 6 to the Report from the House of Commons Select Committee on Cyprus, Session 1975–76.

additional transport aircraft for the evacuation of civilian residents and Service dependents, and Puma helicopters to support the army reinforcements. Nimrod maritime patrol aircraft and photo reconnaissance Canberras were available in Malta.

7.   The naval forces stationed permanently in the Mediterranean (excluding the Gibraltar Guard-ship) at the time of the coup comprised the guided missile destroyer HMS DEVONSHIRE and the frigates HMS RHYL and ANDROMEDA.

8.   HMS HERMES was not based in Cyprus. She left New York on 6 July and was programmed to call at Malta to disembark 41 Royal Marine Commando on 17–18 July before returning to the United Kingdom. On 16 July she was diverted to the Cyprus area and took part in the evacuation of refugees from the North of the Island on 23 July, following the Turkish invasion on 20 July. She remained in the area until the end of the month. HMS ANDROMEDA was in Malta, having arrived from Elba on 15 July. She sailed for Cyprus on 16 July. HMS DEVONSHIRE and HMS RHYL left Gibraltar on 15 July intending to visit Liverno but were also diverted to Cyprus on 16th July. These warships were supported by the Royal Fleet Auxiliary tankers OLNA and GOLD ROVER from 21 July.

9.   Three conventional submarines had been undertaking trials in the Mediterranean at the time of the coup. One, HMS ONSLAUGHT, was diverted from the Malta area to the area of Cyprus on 19 July. The other two returned to the UK as planned.

10.   The frigate HMS BRIGHTON was relieved by HMS GURKHA as Gibraltar Guard-ship on 22 July and was then deployed to the Eastern Mediterranean to join HERMES off Cyprus. GURKHA remained at Gibraltar until the end of the month. There were other HM ships in the Gibraltar area which could have been used if the need had arisen.

11.   HERMES, DEVONSHIRE, RHYL, BRIGHTON and ANDROMEDA were withdrawn from the Cyprus area at varying times between the end of July and early September 1974.

ORGANISATION AND CHAIN OF COMMAND OF TURKISH 'PEACE FORCE' JULY–AUGUST 1974

General Staff Headquarters, Ankara
(Chief of General Staff: General Sancar)
(Commander Land Forces: General Esref Akinci)

HQ 2nd Army, Konya
(General Suat Aktulga)

HQ 6 Corps (Turkish 'Peace Force'), initially at Adana, later at Aghirda, Cyprus
(Lieut. General Nurettin Ersin)

*39 Infantry Division (16,000)
(Maj. General Bedrettin Demirel)

14 Infantry Regt (three battalions)

49 Infantry Regt (three battalions)

50 Infantry Regt (three battalions)

*Airborne Brigade (2,600)
(Brig. General Sabri Everen)

Three battalions

*Commando Brigade (1,500)
(Brig. General Sabri Demirbag)

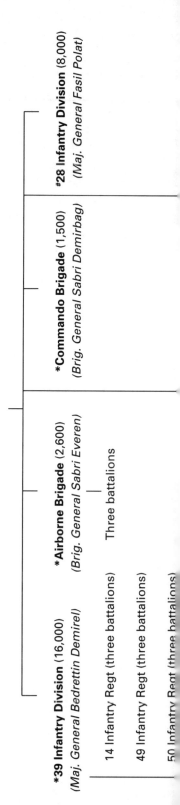

#28 Infantry Division (8,000)
(Maj. General Fasil Polat)

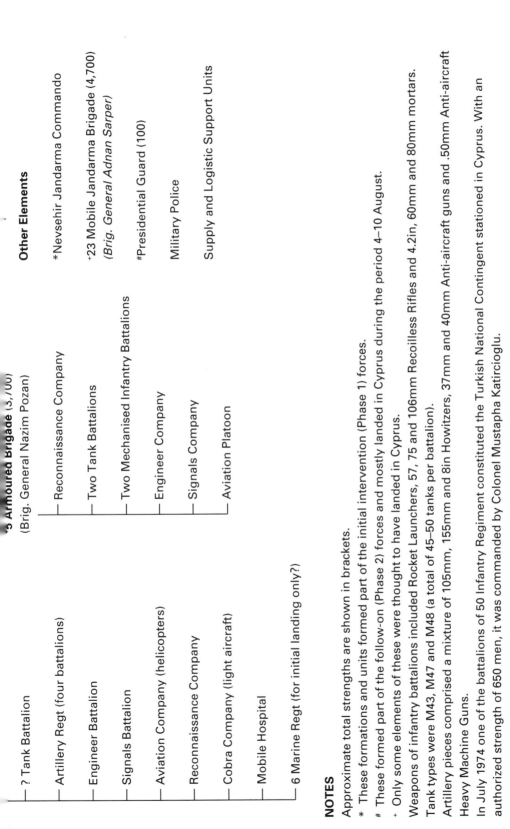

?3 Armoured Brigade (3,700)

(Brig. General Nazim Pozan)

— ? Tank Battalion
— Artillery Regt (four battalions)
— Engineer Battalion
— Signals Battalion
— Aviation Company (helicopters)
— Reconnaissance Company
— Cobra Company (light aircraft)
— Mobile Hospital
— 6 Marine Regt (for initial landing only?)

— Reconnaissance Company
— Two Tank Battalions
— Two Mechanised Infantry Battalions
— Engineer Company
— Signals Company
— Aviation Platoon

Other Elements

*Nevsehir Jandarma Commando

+23 Mobile Jandarma Brigade (4,700)
(*Brig. General Adnan Sarper*)

#Presidential Guard (100)

Military Police

Supply and Logistic Support Units

NOTES

Approximate total strengths are shown in brackets.

* These formations and units formed part of the initial intervention (Phase 1) forces.

\# These formed part of the follow-on (Phase 2) forces and mostly landed in Cyprus during the period 4–10 August.

+ Only some elements of these were thought to have landed in Cyprus.

Weapons of infantry battalions included Rocket Launchers, 57, 75 and 106mm Recoilless Rifles and 4.2in, 60mm and 80mm mortars. Tank types were M43, M47 and M48 (a total of 45–50 tanks per battalion).

Artillery pieces comprised a mixture of 105mm, 155mm and 8in Howitzers, 37mm and 40mm Anti-aircraft guns and .50mm Anti-aircraft Heavy Machine Guns.

In July 1974 one of the battalions of 50 Infantry Regiment constituted the Turkish National Contingent stationed in Cyprus. With an authorized strength of 650 men, it was commanded by Colonel Mustapha Katircioglu.

UNITED NATIONS   **NATIONS UNIES**

FORCE IN CYPRUS

Lieutenant General D. Prem Chand

<u>PERSONAL</u>   3 October 1974

Dear Frank,

    The time has come to say farewell and I am writing, on behalf of all of us serving with UNFICYP, to express to you our sincere gratitude for the splendid contribution you have made towards furthering the aims of the United Nations in Cyprus.   Your tenure as Chief of Staff of UNFICYP has been marked by important and indeed historical developments having international repercussions, and the stability, sense of balance, together with the steady course you were able to maintain at all times have been of the greatest assistance in many ways.   Cyprus, its good people and all of us owe you much.

    The recent emergency has over-shadowed somewhat the numerous problems we were up against during the summers of 1972/1973, when there was considerable violence in many parts of the Island, confronting us with many difficult and delicate situations.   I also remember well the move of four of our contingents to UNEF at such short notice, together with the reorganization and redeployment this necessitated.   In addition, we were required to take on a sizeable reduction in our strength, with further changes and moves, together with a reconsideration and recasting of our operating procedures and drills.   All this and more you took steadily, capably and well in your stride.

Brigadier F.R. Henn, C.B.E.
Chief of Staff
and
Commander of the British Contingent
United Nations Force in Cyprus

The recent operations constitute a chapter on their own, when we were faced with a totally new and unexpected situation, not visualized in our mandate. All this meant tackling a fast-changing set of operational situations day after day, without the normal organization, equipment, communications and set-up to take on a role of this nature. The pressures, stresses and strains at the time were heavy, and I know only too well the personal and devoted efforts you made to meet these situations, especially through your contacts at the High Commission, the Bases and at the Ministry of Defence in the United Kingdom. We were indeed fortunate to have you with us at such a time.

Personally, I shall look back upon our association here with the happiest of memories, and with special thanks for the loyalty, thoughtfulness and consideration you so kindly extended to me. Indeed, the fact that there has been so complete an identity in our views, thoughts and reactions all along is, if I may say so, an encouraging indication of the close association we have had in India with the United Kingdom, an association which I am glad to say still continues and grows in many fields. I have had the singular privilege and pleasure of getting to know and serve with some of the finest units of the British Army, their officers, NCOs and men, in Cyprus and may I add my personal appreciation and gratitude for the splendid way in which the British Contingent has played for the team under your captaincy.

With my warmest personal regards to Monica and yourself, and all the best,

Yours sincerely,

Prem Chand.

NOTES

Chapter 1 (pp 3–7)

1. William C. Heine: 'Interest in Peace is Mainly Military', *The London Free Press*, Ontario, 12 July 1973.
2. Cyprus was annexed to Britain in 1914 in retaliation for Turkey's entry into the First World War on Germany's side. It is one of the paradoxes surrounding the Cyprus story that, when in 1915 Britain offered to cede the island to Greece, the offer was refused and thereupon withdrawn. From 1914 to 1960 Cyprus held British colonial status.
3. On the other hand Cyprus lies more than 950km from mainland Greece. The nearest Greek airfield and seaport are located on the island of Rhodes, about 400km from Cyprus.
4. Quoted by Haluk Bayulken: 'The Cyprus Question', *Dis Politika*, February 1975, p. 85.
5. See Criton G. Tornaritis: 'Cyprus and Constitutional and Other Legal Problems', *Daily Bulletin*, Nicosia, 23 March 1984.
6. Professor Suat Bilge: 'The Cyprus Conflict and Turkey', *Turkey's Foreign Policy in Transition, 1950–1974*, ed. Kemal H. Karpat, E.J. Brill, Leiden, 1975, p. 184.
7. As reported by Costas Yennaris: *From The East – Conflict and Partition in Cyprus*, p. 61, Elliott & Thompson, London, 2003.
8. The remaining 4% comprised other small ethnic groups, including Armenians, Latins, Maronites and a number of British, American and other expatriates.
9. A contributory cause was discontent centred on a long-standing grievance that, notwithstanding annexation by Britain 17 years earlier, payment of the old Ottoman Debt Charge was still being exacted from the Cypriots.
10. Born Michael Christodoulos Mouskos on 23 August 1913 in Paphos District and apprenticed at the nearby Monastery of Kykko, he was ordained Priest in 1946, following which he spent two years in theological study at the University of Boston, USA. Recalled to Cyprus in 1948 to become Bishop of Kitium, he was elected Archbishop in October 1950 on the death of Makarios II; aged 37, he was the youngest ever to hold this office. During his enthronement he is said to have taken 'a holy oath' that during his lifetime he would bring about, as the Church's mission, the union of Cyprus with Greece.
11. Makarios fled the island on 16 July 1974 (see Chapters 28 and 30) but returned to resume the reins of office on 7 November the same year. He suffered a heart attack in April 1977 and, following a second attack, died in Nicosia on 3 August 1977, ten days short of his 64th birthday. He lies buried at a site chosen by himself high on a mountain-side, close to his birthplace and Kykko Monastery. Unusually in Cyprus in August, it rained on the day of his funeral. The

Greeks declared the downpour to be the tears of heaven, the Turks that rain attends the burial of a sinner to wash away his sins.

12. The Greek Cypriots are predominantly Christian Orthodox, the Turkish Cypriots are Moslems, the Armenians are also Christians but of another denomination, and the Maronites and Latins are Catholics. To these one could add also a few thousand British who came to the island after 1878 and who profess Protestantism. Yet, in spite of this religious amalgam, there is not even a single example of religious conflict in Cyprus. Throughout the troubled history of the country religion did not play a decisive role. ('Religious Tolerance and Freedom of Worship in Cyprus', *Daily Bulletin*, Nicosia, 30 March 1984).

Chapter 2 (pp 8–18)

1. See Nancy Crawshaw: *The Cyprus Revolt – An Account of the Struggle for Union with Greece.*
2. The Greek request followed an inept declaration in the British Parliament in July 1954 by Mr H.L. Hopkinson, Colonial Office Minister, who in response to a question about the future of Cyprus said that there were some colonial territories which, owing to their special situation, could *never* expect full independence.
3. The best remembered medieval folk epic concerns the exploits of a hero called Dighenis Akritas. During a battle in Asia Minor he is said to have fallen backward, caught his balance in Cyprus and left his handprint on a mountain before returning to the fray. A five-fingered peak north of Kyrenia is pointed out as confirmation of this superhuman feat. (Eugene K. Keefe *et al*: *Area Handbook for Cyprus, p. 141)*
4. Anti-Turkish feeling among Greek Cypriots was exacerbated by a belief that in a deliberate policy of 'divide and rule' successive British administrations had favoured the Turkish community.
5. What moved Athens and Ankara in 1958 seems to have been a sense of the increasing dangers of the Cold War confrontation in the Eastern Mediterranean. That in turn arose from crises in Lebanon, Jordan and Iraq, and a general sense that Soviet power was strengthening in the area. In effect, Athens and Ankara agreed on a *modus vivendi* over Cyprus during what seemed at the time a phase of general danger, and the local [*Cypriot*] communities had to go along. (Coral Bell: *The Diplomacy of Detente: The Kissinger Era*, p. 141).
6. The Lancaster House settlement was ratified by Greece on 28 February, by Turkey on 4 March and by Britain on 19 March. The State of Emergency was lifted on 4 December 1959.
7. There was criticism in the Turkish Parliament that Turkey had failed to secure a military base in Cyprus as Britain had done. Foreign Minister Zorlu replied that, had it done so, a similar base could not have been denied to Greece, which would have worked to Turkey's disadvantage.
8. This sum was duly paid in 1961–65, but no payments have been made since.
9. The first (and last) neutral President was the German jurist, Professor Ernst Forsthoff. He resigned in 1963, declaring that it had become plain that Makarios did not intend to abide by the Court's decisions on matters concerning the constitutional rights of the Turkish minority.
10. General Sir Kenneth Darling, personal, 11 April 1979.
11. *Ibid.*
12. The Turkish argument took scant account of the Treaty of Lausanne, 1923, by which as part of a wider settlement in the Eastern Mediterranean Turkey renounced for ever all claim to Cyprus. However, the Turks have maintained since that the terms of the Treaty implied that any future change in the status of Cyprus was a matter to be determined solely by Britain and Turkey. An interesting footnote was added by Victor Cavendish-Bentinck, 9th Duke of Portland, speaking in the British House of Lords 60 years later:

In July 1923 I was Secretary to the British Delegation to the Lausanne Conference. We were about to sign the Treaty . . . when Ismet Pasha, and later Inonu, put forward a demand for a clause to be included that, if we ever gave up Cyprus or left Cyprus, we would hand it back to Turkey. . . . Sir Horace Rumbold, who was the chief delegate, almost had an apoplectic fit with rage at the prospect of having to remain in Lausanne, and sent back a message that we would never give up Cyprus, which was vital to our interests, and he hoped the matter would not be pressed. He refused to put anything in writing. (*Official Report (Hansard)*, House of Lords, 16 November 1983, coln. 1310).

13. Bi-communal provisions were carried to such an extreme that in order to enjoy rights as citizens members of other ethnic minorities were required to elect to belong formally either to the Greek or to the Turkish community. All elected to be treated as Greeks.

14. It has been alleged that the British High Commissioner, Sir Arthur Clark, prompted Makarios to propose the thirteen Amendments.

15. It must be said in favour of these proposals that they streamlined the administration and removed features that laid stress on whether a Cypriot citizen was Greek or Turkish. But from the Turkish Cypriot point of view they removed almost all the props to their claim to be the "co-founders" of the Republic and demoted them to the status of a minority. (Keith Kyle: *Cyprus – Minority Rights Group Report No. 30*, p. 10).

16. Some believe that the thirteen Amendments were proposed as a deliberate *casus belli* to provoke intercommunal conflict as the first stage in implementing the 'Akritas Plan'. This plan was said to have been formulated earlier in 1963 with the connivance of Makarios, one of its principal authors being his Minister of the Interior, Polycarpos Georghadis (an ex-EOKA henchman who met a violent death in March 1970 – see Chapter 3). The plan had as its aim the dissolution of the Republic by stages, followed by full union with Greece; early steps included the neutralization of the Turkish community and abrogation of the Treaties of Alliance and Guarantee. (A purported copy of the plan was circulated to the UN Security Council as *S/12722*, 30 May 1978).

17. *Keesing's Contemporary Archives*, June 13–20 1964, p. 20115.

18. *Ibid.*

19. Makarios had announced abrogation of the Treaties of Alliance and Guarantee on 1 January 1964 but under pressure from Sandys was obliged to make a hasty retraction next day. (He explained lamely that his government had not abrogated them, but had decided to secure their termination by 'appropriate means'.)

20. The NATO peacekeeping Force was to have been responsible to a committee drawn from troop-contributor countries and sitting in London, which in Makarios's eyes was an added objection.

21. The text of Resolution 186(1964) is at Annex 1. In evidence to the House of Commons Foreign Affairs Committee in London on 18 November 1986, Denktash (who had been in New York during the Security Council's 1964 debate) stated that the Turkish side had expressed concern that references in the Resolution to 'the Government of Cyprus' might be taken to mean the Makarios administration composed only of Greek Cypriots. Oral assurances had been given, he said, that, although interpretation of the Resolution was a matter for the Security Council, references to 'the Government of Cyprus' could only mean the legitimate government as provided for in the 1960 Constitution – that is to say, a proper partnership of the two communities. Denktash added that the terms of the Resolution were accepted by the Turkish side on the basis of those assurances.

22. Makarios argued that with the formal establishment of UNFICYP on 27 March his consent the previous December for deployment of the Joint Truce Force automatically lapsed, and that there was no longer any legitimate right for the Turkish national contingent to remain outside its authorized camp.

23. As required by the terms of Resolution 186(1964), the composition of UNFICYP was decided in consultation with the governments of Cyprus, Britain, Greece and Turkey.

24. *S/5679*, 2 May 1964, para. 17.

Chapter 3 (pp 19–29)

1. Telegram to UN Secretary General (*S/5790*, 1 July 1964).

2. By late 1964 Turkish Cypriots had abandoned 136 of the 226 Turkish or mixed villages inhabited by them in 1960; during 1964–74 they returned to only a handful of these.

3. The Turks held that the National Guard was an illegal force since it was not provided for in the Constitution, but Dr Kuchuk's veto of the Bill to establish it was ignored.

4. In September 1964 the UN Secretary General reported with some under-statement: Although no cases of starvation have been noted in the Turkish Cypriot areas, serious inconveniences have been caused to the people subjected to these restrictions and in some cases conditions have reached the hardship stage. (*S/5950*, 10 September 1964, para. 20).

5. Memories of this black period convinced many Turkish Cypriots in 1974 that their future security and well-being could be assured only in an all-Turkish zone in northern Cyprus.

6. Polyvios G. Polyviou: *Cyprus – The Tragedy and the Challenge*, p. 53.

7. From inception to March 1966 the mandate was renewed for three months at a time, except in June 1965 when it was renewed for six months. From June 1966 it has been renewed for periods of six months, except for December 1967 and March 1968 when there was a reversion to three months.

8. Apart from several occasions in April and May 1964 when UN troops opened fire in self-defence, UNFICYP did not need to resort to the use of firearms until the crisis of July–August 1974.

9. Inonu's admission was made during an interview on 12 June 1964 (reported by C. Foley and W.I. Scobie: *The Struggle for Cyprus*, pp. 163–164). Johnson's letter was deeply resented by the Turks as an unwarranted interference in their affairs. The strained relations that resulted between the US and Turkey were a factor that influenced US policy during the 1974 crisis.

10. The Acheson Plan provided for the union of Cyprus with Greece, subject to compensations for the Turks. These included the transfer to Turkey of the small but strategically significant Greek island of Kastellorizon, close to Turkey's south coast; establishment of a sovereign Turkish military base area on the Karpasian peninsula (Cyprus's 'Panhandle'); the creation elsewhere of two Turkish Cypriot cantons under that community's administration; and the payment of compensation to Turkish Cypriots wishing to emigrate in consequence of the plan. The plan was accepted in principle by Athens and Ankara, but rejected by Makarios on the grounds that it entailed a form of partition.

11. Published as *S/6253*, 26 March 1965, this Report continues to repay study as an analysis of the Cyprus problem. Dr Galo Plaza, who was President of Ecuador 1948–52, died in 1987 aged 80.

12. In contrast to their action at Tillyria three years earlier, UN troops, although unable to prevent the National Guard attacks, stood their ground in and around the two villages in spite of coming under fire with some posts overrun. In consequence UNFICYP was much better placed to influence the situation and, after ten hours' fighting, to secure a ceasefire.

13. In January 1968 the Greek government announced that 6,400 men had been withdrawn but, although formed units had been withdrawn, some individuals in excess of the authorized 950-strong battalion remained. These continued to be a bone of contention, but it is doubtful if Turkey removed all its unauthorized personnel either.

14. In parallel elections Dr Fazil Kuchuk was returned unopposed as Vice President by the Turkish community.

15. Letter, 6 July 1974, to President of Greece.
16. On similar grounds AKEL opposed retention of the British SBAs, but since many of its members were employed in these Base Areas its opposition was equivocal and less than wholehearted.

Chapter 4 (pp 29–33)

1. There were other causes of friction between Greece and Turkey, in particular disputed oil rights in the Aegean.
2. The fact that Makarios long winked at American U-2 flights from the British Sovereign Base of Akrotiri in Cyprus and at the operation of CIA radio monitors along the northern coast near Kyrenia . . . rarely figured into evaluations of the Archbishop – perhaps for national security reasons. (Laurence Stern: 'Bitter Lessons: How We Failed in Cyprus', *Foreign Affairs*, Summer 1975, p. 58).
3. It has long been a Greek criticism of the North Atlantic Treaty that, while ensuring collective Alliance support in the event of aggression from outside the Alliance, it was no protection against attack by an ally – that is, by Turkey.
4. Both locals and tourists seem unaware of the high profile presence in the strategically vital island of Soviet diplomatic delegations. The Russians alone have more than 20 accredited diplomats, and on the Lady's Mile beach, near Limassol, Eastern bloc diplomatic cars are regularly spotted, their occupants meticulously recording British air movements to and from RAF Akrotiri. (*The Daily Telegraph*, London, 29 October 1985).
5. John Reddaway: *Memorandum for House of Commons Foreign Affairs Committee (2/80–81/FM)*, 10 November 1980.
6. *Ibid.*
7. Field Marshal Lord Harding of Petherton: *Memorandum for House of Commons Foreign Affairs Committee (64/80–81/FM)*, 16 January 1981. A Defence Review conducted in 1974 in Whitehall had concluded that Britain should withdraw altogether from Cyprus. When its conclusions were put to Dr Kissinger (then US Secretary of State):
   His one positive objection was to the proposed withdrawal from Cyprus. To this he was strongly opposed, not so much on the grounds of the loss of the facilities there, but because it would give the Russians the impression that the West was weakening its position and interest in the Eastern Mediterranean. (Michael Carver: *Out of Step*, pp. 454–5).
8. There was no Cypriot objection to the use of Akrotiri in December 1979 to facilitate deployment to Rhodesia of the Commonwealth Monitoring Force, but when in March 1981 Britain announced support for the planned US Rapid Reaction Force, the Cyprus government was quick to rule out use of the airfield by that force. There were no such objections when the facilities of both SBAs provided support for Coalition Forces operating under UN authority in the Gulf War nor for the later action in Afghanistan and Iraq.
9. Richard Crossman: *The Crossman Diaries – Selections from the Diaries of a Cabinet Minister*, Vol. 2.
10. *Daily Bulletin*, Nicosia, 7 April 1984.
11. *The Guardian*, London, 29 May 1984.

Chapter 5 (pp 37–42)

1. Kurt Waldheim: *Report on the Work of the Organization, 1978*, p. 11.
2. Javier Perez de Cuellar: *Report on the Work of the Organization, 1982*, p. 5.

3. *Ibid.*, pp. 8–9.
4. Lieut. General Ensio Siilasvuo (Finland), speaking at the Royal United Services Institute for Defence Studies, London, 20 July 1981.
5. *The Times*, London, 16 July 1981.
6. Part of a ditty popular in the messes of UNFICYP's British Contingent ran as follows:

> The island is a football pitch, the match is international;
> And we are all the linesmen, unbiased, fair and rational.
> Our aim is to ensure a draw, so play is rather slow;
> If any man should kick the ball, that breaks the status quo.
> If violence should erupt on field, we may not stop the game;
> Just duck our heads and wave our flags, and take the culprit's name.
> But what if we all quit the field, though life here is sublime?
> They'll quickly end the game themselves, but play in injury time!

7. The desirability for a degree of balance in geographical representation is an added factor but is not readily achievable since the field for selection is limited to those countries with the resources and willingness to participate.
8. Javier Perez de Cuellar: *op. cit.*, p. 9.

Chapter 6 (pp 43–47)

1. The costs of the Mediator and his staff were borne by UN funds.
2. These funding arrangements proved unsatisfactory (*see Chapter* 8) and were not adopted for later UN peacekeeping operations.
3. The Status of Forces Agreement, embodied in a formal exchange of letters between the Secretary General and the Cyprus Government, was published as *S/5634*, 31 March 1964, and subsequently was incorporated into Cyprus law as Law 29 of 1964, promulgated on 25 June 1964.
4. Contingents were accepted for service in UNFICYP on the basis of exchanges of letters between the Secretary General and troop-contributor governments by which the latter accepted the provisions of *Force Regulations*.
5. UNFICYP did not recognize a 'Turkish Cypriot Provisional Administration' and invariably declined to accept communications made in its name.
6. *S/6228*, 11 March 1965, para. 16.
7. In New York the Secretary General delegated day-to-day handling of the Cyprus operation to his two Assistant Secretaries General for Special Political Affairs, who in the period 1972–74 were Roberto Guyer and Brian Urquhart. Confidential communications between New York and HQ UNFICYP at this time were accordingly sent in the names of 'Guyer/Urquhart' and 'Osorio Tafall/Prem Chand' respectively, although on occasions Waldheim sent communications in his own name.
8. Additionally there was the usual flow of routine and less sensitive memoranda and cables, covering both operational and administrative matters, between the UN Secretariat in New York and staff branches in HQ UNFICYP.

Chapter 7 (pp 48–57)

1. The Force Commander served under contract to the UN and was paid and administered as a member of the UN staff. All other military personnel were nominated, administered and paid by their national government.
2. A British Commanding Officer wrote of General Prem Chand's first visit to his battalion:

> It was a great success and he charmed everyone, shaking hands and talking to every guardsman he could find. I have never seen an English general do better. (Lieut. Colonel The Hon. H.E.C. Willoughby, 2nd Bn, Coldstream Guards, *personal*, 26 May 1974.)

3. Prem Chand, whom the Indian Government promoted to the rank of Lieut. General in September 1974 in recognition of his role during the crisis of the preceding weeks, relinquished command of UNFICYP in December 1976, having held this for seven years. In 1977 he was appointed UN Representative for Rhodesia and Commander (Designate) of the UN force proposed under the Anglo-US plan (never implemented) to bring Rhodesia to independence as Zimbabwe. He was then appointed Commander (Designate) of the military force planned as part of the UN Transitional Assistance Group (UNTAG) for a similar task in Namibia. After long delays he assumed command of this Force when eventually this was established in March 1989 and held this until the successful completion of its mission in March 1990. As was the custom in the Indian Army under the British *raj*, Prem Chand had been attached to a British battalion for his first year of commissioned service; he then served in the Baluch Regt before transferring to the 1st Goorka Rifles. In recognition of his command of the many British troops who over the years had served under him in UNFICYP and UNTAG, he was received in audience by Queen Elizabeth II at Buckingham Palace, London in May 1990. He died in India in November 2003.

4. Born in Spain in 1903, Osorio-Tafall had held ministerial office in the Spanish Government before the advent of General Franco, when he left to adopt Mexican citizenship. A man of wide experience in the academic world, he first entered UN service in 1948, and held in succession senior posts in Chile, Indonesia, the United Arab Republic and the Congo, where he headed the UN operation from 1964–67. On retirement from UN service in 1974 at the age of 70, he was appointed Director General of the Centro De Estudios Economicos Y Sociales Del Tercer Mundo AC, Mexico, where he died in 1990. His ashes were interred in the family crypt in the country of his birth, Spain.

5. The author took over as Chief of Staff from Brig. General E.M.D. Leslie of Canada in July 1972 and was in turn succeeded in 1974 by a Canadian, Brig. General C.E. Beattie. (In 1991, for the first time, the appointment of Chief of Staff was filled by a Danish officer, the Force Commander being a Canadian and the Deputy Chief of Staff a British officer.)

6. This relay station was manned by a small British/Canadian detachment, whose voices were familiar throughout UNFICYP as they patiently relayed messages day and night under their call-sign 'Zero One'.

7. In the 1974 crisis the volume and length of signals between CANCON and Ottawa compelled a downgrading of their priority at HQ UNFICYP. In consequence the Canadians then established their own direct radio link.

8. Some contingents brought with them heavier weapons such as mortars and anti-tank launchers. Most ammunitions for such weapons were held on UNFICYP's behalf in secure conditions in the British SBAs.

9. The British and Canadian Contingents, the Commanders of which held respectively the posts of Chief and Deputy Chief of Staff, were exceptions.

10. '[Cyprus] is an island of mountains – the long narrow and elegant Kyrenia range that overshadows the inland capital of Nicosia runs just below the northern coastline; in the centre and west is the Troodos massif, including one of those heights which the Greeks named Olympus. Between these two is a plain 12 to 15 miles wide, which is very fertile provided the rains arrive – which they sometimes do not.' (Keith Kyle: *Cyprus*, p.4)

11. The Austrian Duke Leopold V had visited Cyprus on his way to the Third Crusade. In the Holy Land he was wounded in the assault on the Castle of Acre, when his white mantle was stained with blood. The White and Red national colours of Austria are said to derive from this incident.

12. Some Canadian OPs were located on the top of tall buildings, and the observation these afforded was demonstrated to visitors by 'the mirror trick' – at a given signal all OPs in sight flashed a mirror at the visitor's position.

13. In 1972 the Swedes possessed the only armoured vehicles in UNFICYP apart from the scout cars of the Force Reserve. These were Skania APCs (SKPF m/42) mounting twin 7.62mm machine guns and able to carry 13 men and a crew of two. They were large, cumbersome vehicles, but in spite of their obsolescence (they were first produced in 1945) they provided useful protection and mobility in the crisis of the summer of 1974.

14. Theobald Wolfe Tone was a maverick Irish protestant, who at the end of the 18th Century had founded the Society of United Irishmen in Belfast.

15. Responsibility for the Louroujina area was transferred to BRITCON in August 1972 and then to CANCON in January 1973.

16. This arrangement conformed to British practice for the command and control of air forces.

17. The Army Aviation Flight was moved from Camp UNFICYP to its own base within the RAF Nicosia Retained Site in the course of 1973, facilitating operational and administrative control of helicopter operations.

18. Apart from the transport squadron, which was rotated as a squadron each six months, these other units were maintained on a 'trickle posting' basis.

19. Miles left UNFICYP in August 1974 to serve as Political Adviser to the Coordinator of UN Forces and Missions in the Middle East. Subsequently he held senior posts with UNWRA in New York and in the field. He died in Australia in 1992. As Legal Adviser, Prieto, a Spanish national, was concerned primarily with constitutional and legal aspects of the intercommunal negotiations. Possessed of a sceptical sense of humour and a realistic understanding of the problems, he could be relied upon for shrewd advice. Jean Back, the PIO, left UNFICYP in December 1972 and was not replaced, his role being carried out by Miles, assisted by the Force's MPIO. The lack of a PIO was much felt when crisis flared in July 1974 and the world's media descended on Cyprus.

CHAPTER 8 (pp 58–61)

1. For many years deadlock in the UN Military Staff Committee, established under Article 47 of the Charter with these purposes in mind, obliged the Secretariat (assisted by a small group of junior military officers) to assume these responsibilities. Matters were improved in 1993 when a Department of Peacekeeping Operations was established at UN Headquarters, New York.

2. Rikhye et al.: The Thin Blue Line, p. 116.

3. In 1972 UNFICYP still had some 20 old UN-owned vehicles transferred to it from Gaza on the demise of the first UNEF in 1967; these were being rapidly wasted-out or disposed of on the local market.

4. For example, the British Army baked several varieties of bread to suit different contingent appetites. It claimed, too, to be able to procure and deliver any special items of diet demanded by contingents at lower cost and more quickly than the national authorities of contingents concerned could do.

5. UNFICYP employed a considerable number of locally hired civilians at Force HQ, in its logistic units and in contingents. These were administered and paid on its behalf by the British Army, thus avoiding invidious differences as between those working for UNFICYP and those serving the British forces.

6. In 1972 about 500 men (one sixth of UNFICYP) were still living under canvas at a cost in tentage of £2,000 per month. The last tented base camp was that of the Danes at Limnitis, which was

replaced by hutted accommodation, erected by self-help, in 1974 – 10 years after the arrival of UNFICYP on the island.

7. *S/6534*, 31 March 1964, para. 19.

8. In the period 1972–74, when the island's economy was booming and UNFICYP's financial position was steadily worsening, the Cyprus Government was obliged to recognize that this attitude was not easily defensible. Pressure exerted by HQ UNFICYP persuaded the Government to be more forthcoming in early 1974.

9. Items required by contingents from national sources were usually imported by air, the Canadians using its weekly flight from Canada (via Lahr, Germany) and the Danes and Swedes sharing a fortnightly special flight from Scandinavia. (After the establishment of UNEF 2 on the Suez Canal in 1973 these flights were extended from Nicosia to Cairo to serve national contingents in that Force.) The Austrian, Finnish and Irish Contingents were usually re-supplied with such items in the course of routine six-monthly troop rotations. The British Contingent was able to draw freely on stocks held in the SBAs.

10. *Report of the Secretariat Review Team on the United Nations Peacekeeping Force in Cyprus, S/21982*, 7 December 1990, para.36. (Agreement has since been reached to permit UNFICYP's funding on a more general basis.)

11. This arrangement had been concluded in the context of the HQ for Nicosia Zone being provided in the early days by the Canadians; it proved an astute move since CANCON's logistic needs hardly warranted a weekly service, the spare capacity of which was used to carry those who wished to visit Cyprus for purposes not strictly connected with UNFICYP.

12. The Federal Republic of Germany became a member of the UN in September 1973. The Swiss Government, in addition to financial contributions, provided an executive jet aircraft much used by senior UN officials travelling on UN business throughout the Mediterranean region.

13. The attitude of these three countries reflected reservations at that time as to the propriety of the UN undertaking peacekeeping operations.

Chapter 9 (pp 62–65)

1. Rikhye *et al.* : *The Thin Blue Line*, p. 267.
2. James A. Stegenga: *The United Nations Force in Cyprus*, pp. 84–85.
3. Ibid, p. 85.
4. Feelings of this nature were not confined to members of UNFICYP. When visiting the Force in 1973 the Chief of the Canadian Defence Staff, General A. Dextrase, remarked that British support for UNFICYP was due to the UK's concern for the security of its SBAs. It was necessary to remind him that UNFICYP served a far wider interest that was as much Canada's as Britain's – the prevention of conflict between two NATO allies, Greece and Turkey.
5. *S/5653*, 11 April 1964, para. 13.
6. Very senior officers of the Ministry of Defence, Directors of Arms and Services represented in BRITCON, Colonels of Regiments, and specialist and technical advisers all had legitimate reasons for visiting, and these were welcomed.
7. The Parachute Regiment's unpopularity increased after the 'Bloody Sunday' tragedy of 20 January 1972, when in the space of twenty minutes a company of the 1st Battalion shot dead thirteen Catholics and wounded fourteen more after a civil rights march in Londonderry. (Henry Stanhope: *The Soldiers – An Anatomy of the British Army*, p.201.)

Chapter 10 (pp 66–71)

1.   Lieut. General G. Denizis took over command from Lieut. General Charalambopoulos in August 1973; both were on the Greek army's reserve list, which preserved the fiction that their orders were not dictated by Athens. From July 1972 to June 1974 the post of Chief of Staff was held by Brig. General P. Papadakis (promoted to Major General in December 1973) who was said to be related by marriage to Brig. General D. Ioannides, nominally Chief of Military Police in Athens, but from November 1973 the shadowy and sinister directing force behind the junta.

2.   The bi-communal Cyprus army, envisaged under the 1960 Constitution, was never established except in token form. Nonetheless, Colonel Athos Myrianthopoulos was appointed its commander; during 1972–74 his role was unclear but appeared to include acting as senior Aide de Camp and Military Adviser to Archbishop Makarios as Head of State.

3.   In addition the National Guard possessed some early generation surface-to-air guided weapons of Soviet origin, acquired from Egypt in 1964–65 but by 1974 of doubtful serviceability (no such weapons were used against the Turkish airforce in 1974). That the National Guard also possessed surface-to-surface anti-tank guided weapons was discovered fortuitously by UNFICYP in early 1974 (see Chapter 16).

4.   This economic consideration was one of the obstacles encountered by UNFICYP when seeking to secure a reduction in the size of the TCF with a view to reducing intercommunal military confrontation.

5.   Under the 1960 Constitution the offices of Vice President and Minister of Defence were reserved to Turkish Cypriots, who continued to hold onto these empty titles as demonstration of fictitious adherence to that Constitution. The post of Minister of Defence was held by Mr Osman Orek, who was based in the VPO.

6.   UNFICYP had reason to believe that two field guns had been smuggled into the island in 1971–72; it is probable that these were held by the Turkish national contingent, contrary to the provisions of the Treaty of Alliance, rather than by the TCF.

7.   This spring, Kephalovryso, reputedly the best water source on an island where water is a highly valued commodity, yields 2–5 million gallons a day and never fails even in time of severe drought. Some believe the water originates in the mountains of Anatolia, reaching Cyprus by subterranean aquafer. Throughout the island's history it has been of strategic military significance.

8.   Under the 1960 Treaty of Establishment the Cyprus Government undertook to keep Tymbou airfield and its related facilities in being. The UK had the right to use it as a reserve landing ground for Nicosia airport and agreed to contribute to the costs of its maintenance. In August 1974 it was captured by Turkish forces and subsequently was developed as the main airport (named Ercan Airport by the Turks) serving the Turkish occupied area of northern Cyprus.

9.   During the period 1972–74 CYPOL was commanded by Mr S. Antoniou; he was removed during the 1974 coup d'état but reinstated soon afterwards. During the same period the TCPE was commanded by Mr M. Refik. Both maintained good working relations with each other and with UNFICYP, due in no small measure to the personal link provided by the latter's Police Adviser, Dr Hans Wagner (Austria).

10. When a candidate attempted to stand against Mr Rauf Denktash in the election for Vice President in February 1973, he was abruptly removed in circumstances that were unsavoury. It was widely believed that the Bozkurt had ordered this action.

Chapter 11 (pp 72–78)

1. *S/5920*, 29 August 1964, para. 4.
2. The proximity of the two camps was a consequence of the treaty's intention that the two contingents, together with the planned but never established Cyprus army, should constitute a tripartite force under a tripartite headquarters.
3. The Turks asked for UNFICYP protection for their troops during this intended rotation, but the request was refused on the ground that at the time UNFICYP had no mandate to provide this.
4. *S/6102*, 12 December 1964, para. 8.
5. For example, in May 1974 the Secretary General reported:
   > A partial rotation of the Turkish National Contingent took place on 26 February 1974, after the Governments of Cyprus and Turkey had requested UNFICYP's good offices in the rotation. UNFICYP assisted in the negotiations and provided the customary transport, escorts and observers. With the cooperation of both parties, the rotation was completed without incident. (*S/11294*, 22 May 1974, para. 25).
6. The Turkish Government did not reimburse the UN for the considerable costs incurred by UNFICYP in providing transport and other services twice a year.
7. Production of a list was a considerable task. The Turks' description of many items, which included spare parts for vehicles and weapons, uniform, medical stores and special varieties of food, often was unclear. The list had to be scrutinized by UNFICYP specialists, who, after identifying each item, drew up a revised one using British military nomenclature.
8. At the February 1974 rotation the Greeks proposed that electronic detectors be passed over the sealed bags. The Turks held this to be 'inspection' and refused to allow it.
9. A particular point of dispute centred on the quantities of small-arms ammunition imported, the Greeks demanding that for every round brought in one empty case should be exported (their fear being that 'empties' were being reloaded on the island by the Turks, thus building up stocks). UNFICYP held this to be unreasonable, and a formula was agreed on the proportion of 'empties' to be exported against imports. This required tedious counting of large quantities of 'empties' by UNFICYP (these having been expended legitimately by the Turks during training).

Chapter 12 (pp 79–85)

1. *S/5950*, 1 September 1964, paras. 8 and 10.
2. 'Agreements', 'Arrangements' and 'Understandings' were well understood gradations in the scale, ranging from the formal written to the informal oral. Irrespective of point on the scale, it was UNFICYP policy to ensure that both parties observed provisions to which they had assented.
3. In the case of the TCF this usually was a Turkish Cypriot 'front man' since the mainland Turks who commanded at most levels declined direct contact with UNFICYP.
4. Major J.R. Macfarlane, Coldstream Guards, Commander Paphos District May – August 1974, speaking to the British Army Staff College, Camberley, 21 July 1975.
5. Although as a matter of courtesy usually referred to as 'Ambassador', the senior Turkish diplomat in Nicosia (at this time Mr Asaf Inhan) was in fact a *Chargé d'Affaires*. This was because Turkey objected to accrediting an ambassador to a government which it regarded as unconstitutional and, further, was unwilling to oblige its ambassador to present his Letters of Credence to Archbishop Makarios as its Head.

6. Pilots of the UNFICYP Army Aviation Flight (BRITCON) were trained military observers who as a matter of routine watched out for useful information, such as the number of armoured vehicles to be seen in camps near their flight path.

7. In 1973 a series of small-scale exercises was initiated to practice the rapid assembly of a reserve group drawn from two or more contingents. Other inter-contingent exercises included training with the helicopters and armoured reconnaissance troops of BRITCON.

8. There were added complications when the British or Canadian Contingents included a parachute unit, the men of which needed to maintain parachuting skills while serving with UNFICYP. Appropriate training was arranged in the SBAs using C130 aircraft of the RAF's 70 Squadron based at Akrotiri. On one occasion this gave rise to a Soviet complaint that UNFICYP and British forces in the SBAs were colluding clandestinely for some unstated purpose.

9. UNIFIL's Spokesman, press briefing, June 1978.

Chapter 13 (pp 86–92)

1. A contingent provided by New Zealand was withdrawn in 1967. The inclusion of civilian police contingents in UNFICYP had been due to the Secretary General's foresight in seeing the need for them, even though not specifically authorized by the Security Council.

2. *S/7611*, 8 December 1966, para. 84.

3. *S/10842*, 1 December 1972, paras. 35–36. Both sides accepted UNFICYP's verdict in this incident. Subsequently the Government had paid compensation to the dead Turkish Cypriot's family.

4. *S/11294*, 22 May 1974, para. 43.

5. The Government claimed that by mid-1974 the sum owed for electricity by Turkish villages had reached a total of £3.5 million.

6. The drought was broken the following winter, and the spring of 1974 brought a galaxy of colour throughout the island as shrubs and plants, some of which had lain dormant for many years, burst into flower.

7. Wherever resources allowed, UNFICYP contingents readily and without charge delivered water to needy villages.

8. UNFICYP's pressure was not entirely without effect, for in 1973 the Government instituted a limited programme for the repair of Turkish-owned houses in a handful of villages. During the same year this pressure was reinforced by the Cyprus Resettlement Project – an international study group sponsored by Haverford College, USA – which spurred the Government to resume resettlement plans for displaced Turkish Cypriots. Surveys and estimates for repairs were made during the early part of 1974, but by May the Government had still not taken any further positive action. The events that took place two months later put paid to the project.

9. *S/10940*, 31 May 1973, para. 64.

10. *S/11137*, 1 December 1973, para. 66.

11. Both projects were halted by the events of the summer of 1974 but were resumed later.

Chapter 14 (pp 93–105)

1. The Green Line Agreement had been reached in December 1963, when British troops under Major General Young had been deployed to Nicosia and before UNFICYP was established. Although it cannot have been in anyone's mind that the Line was anything more than a temporary expedient to separate the combatants, 40 years later it still existed, altered a little here

and there, but for the most part unchanged from that delineated by General Young's green pencil.

2.   At one point a Turkish sentry, finding himself in high summer standing in the hot glare of the sun, crossed the narrow street which at that point constituted the Green Line to stand in the shade. Seeing this as a breach of the Agreement, the Greeks immediately threatened reaction. The situation was defused by a compromise reached through UNFICYP's mediation, which allowed the sentry to cross into the shade, provided that he did not take his rifle with him. It became a routine duty of Canadian patrols to check that this understanding was observed.

3.   The Greek Cypriot Church was exempt from taxation and much of its wealth derived from commercial activities, especially in the tourist industry.

4.   A tunnel under the Roccas Bastion had been revealed, much to Turkish embarrassment, when part of the wall gave way. To discourage further tunnelling at this point the Canadians occasionally drove a truck across the Bastion. It was rumoured that on one such occasion a section of tunnel collapsed, killing a Turkish Fighter inside it. In later years some Canadian sentries claimed that the post was haunted at night – presumably by the spirit of this Turk. A Canadian chaplain was said to have cured the problem by a rite of exorcism. (Heavy rain in December 2001 destroyed part of the Bastion. Through UN mediation the Turkish Cypriot authorities agreed to undertake repairs in conjunction with the Cyprus Department of Antiquities.)

5.   A dramatic example was to be seen at St Hilarion Castle, perched on a peak 600m above Greek-controlled Kyrenia. On high days and holidays a huge Turkish flag was strung on cables running from the Castle across a valley to another peak, clearly visible to all in and around the town 3km away.

6.   A TCF commando-trained detachment was stationed in Mandria, such was its importance to the Turks.

7.   When asked at a subsequent meeting of District Commanders to describe what had happened. the reply of Lieut. Colonel Alphonse Kloss, the Austrian Commander, was succinct: 'Both sides were so frightened that they dirtied their trousers'.

8.   Tourists were allowed to visit St Hilarion Castle, but were refused access to its highest part.

9.   In 1973 the Leadership protested to UNFICYP against a decision by the Government to include within the municipal boundary of Kyrenia town an area regarded as belonging to Temblos village. The Greeks argued that this was necessary in the interests of better administration, but there was a strong suspicion that the action was being taken with commercial tourist interests in view.

10. The Austrians (who replaced the Irish in Larnaca in November 1973) succeeded in lowering tension along the Artemis Road by persuading both sides to accept simultaneous UN inspection of military posts on each side of the road to confirm that there were no changes in the *status quo*. This procedure was instituted in May 1974.

11. Containing the tomb of Umm Haram ('Respected Mother'), an aunt of the Prophet Mohammed, it was considered to be the holiest Islamic shrine after Mecca and Medina. According to Muslim tradition she had died in Cyprus while accompanying an Arab invasion of the island and was buried at this spot in about 647 AD.

12. Limassol, Famagusta and Larnaca were 'dormitory towns' for British personnel stationed in the SBAs. A large number of British service families lived in these towns.

13. The Leadership had not formally been a party to the Status of Forces Agreement but had accepted its provisions in so far as the Turkish community was concerned.

14. The resultant agreement was reported to the Security Council by the Secretary General in December 1964:

The whole of the island is now open to UNFICYP with the exception of certain stipulated areas, namely:

(a) Twenty-three areas, mostly around the coast, which may be visited by the Force Commander only after consultation with General Grivas, and which cover 45 square miles or 1.25 per cent of the total area of the country;

(b) Sixty-three areas, scattered throughout the island, which may be inspected by UNFICYP Zone and District Commanders, not below the rank of lieutenant colonel, if prior notice is given to the local National Guard Commander. These areas cover 15 square miles or 0.4 per cent of the total area of the country.

These restrictions do not apply to twelve bathing beaches situated inside the areas referred to under (a) above. (*S/6102*, 12 December 1964, para. 127)

Chapter 15 (pp 106–110)

1. During the 1980s the Turks built a fast modern and more direct road between Nicosia and the southern end of the Kyrenia Pass, bypassing villages on the old road.

2. This narrow road ran through one of the National Guard's sensitive areas to which access by UNFICYP was restricted by the agreement of December 1964 and was closed to all civilian traffic. As Chief of Staff I was entitled to use the road and regularly did so, encountering no difficulties and invariably receiving appropriate courtesies as I drove past the Raiding Force Unit camp near Bellapais.

3. Published as Annex 1 to *S/6102*, 12 December 1964.

4. *S/6102*, 12 December 1964, paras. 15 and 17.

5. Lieut. Colonel J. Pullinen: *End of Tour Report*, 22 October 1975 (unpublished).

Chapter 16 (pp 111–119)

1. *S/11294*, 22 May 1974, para. 77.

2. *S/5828*, 23 July 1964, Section E.

3. Since dock labour forces at Famagusta and Limassol were mostly Turkish Cypriot, it is likely that the Leadership was kept informed of the movement of Greek military material through these ports.

4. Brig. General E.M.D. Leslie, *personal*.

5. Some at least of these armaments were taken into use by Greek Cypriots during the events of July-August 1974.

6. In 1992 Glafkos Clerides revealed that:

    I accepted to go to Czechoslovakia, where I negotiated a deal for the purchase of a large quantity of arms and armoured cars . . . . The arms were delivered . . . . The order for armoured cars was cancelled by the Government of Czechoslovakia at the request of the Soviet Union, after protests from Turkey. (Glafkos Clerides: *Cyprus: My Deposition*, Nicosia, 1992, Vol. 4, Footnote pp. 124–125)

7. Such was the anger of the Athens junta that the Colonels issued an ultimatum to Makarios demanding surrender of the arms to the National Guard, removal from his Cabinet of opponents to the Athens régime and replacement by others sympathetic to it, and acknowledgement of the authority of Athens as 'the National Centre' and arbiter of Hellenic policy concerning Cyprus. Pressure by Washington on Athens not to precipitate armed conflict and on Makarios not to afford the junta any pretext for this led the junta to soften its demands and Makarios to accept the custodial arrangements described in this chapter. After a decent face-saving interval, two ministers were removed from the Cyprus cabinet, one of whom was the Foreign Minister, Mr

Spyros Kyprianou (who became President on the death of the Archbishop in 1977), his place being taken by Mr I.Cl. Christofides, but Makarios refused to dismiss his Director of Public Information, Mr Miltiades Christodoulou, a founder member of AKEL and regarded by the junta as a crypto-communist.

8. *S/10564, Add.2*, 21 April 1972, para. 3.

9   When suspicious movement was seen one night close to the perimeter wire of Camp UNFICYP, the patrolling sentries challenged and, receiving no reply, opened fire. The camp was stood-to but no trace of intruders was found. It may have been a false alarm, but provided a salutary demonstration of UNFICYP's determination not to allow the weapons to be seized from within its camp.

10. The weapons were smeared in grease in a state of 'heavy preservation'. From time to time all were unpacked, cleaned and re-greased under the supervision of Phylactis and UNFICYP's Force EME; this took several days and allowed UNFICYP to note the serial number on each weapon. In May 2002 UNFICYP 'decommissioned' 4500 of these weapons with the agreement of the Government.

11. I demanded to inspect the weapons so that, hopefully, I might establish dates of manufacture and possibly trace the channel by which they had reached the TCF. Eventually, with much reluctance, one M72 was produced, but all manufacturer's markings had been carefully obliterated.

12. It was difficult to accept that these vehicles could have passed undetected through customs inspection without a degree of connivance on the part of Greek Cypriot officialdom. Inquiries by the British High Commission in Nicosia led to action in the British courts against the exporter for failing to comply with British regulations covering exports of military equipment.

13. We considered more drastic immobilization measures, such as withdrawing half-shafts, but knew that no such measures by themselves could guarantee permanent immobilization. As in the case of the Turkish weapons stored in the Saray Police Station, the moral onus imposed by the double lock and key system was the best safeguard.

14. 'Snapper' was a truck-mounted wire-guided ground-to-ground anti-tank missile system, using missiles weighing 22kg with a range of 500–2300m and a velocity of 50m per second.

15. *S/10940*, 31 May 1973, para. 40.

16. *S/11137*, 1 December 1973, para. 46.

Chapter 17 (pp 120–124)

1. *S/10940*, 12 May 1973, para. 99.

2. 'During the nine years that the Austrian Field Hospital has served with UNFICYP it played a most important part by providing medical care for personnel of all contingents and of UNFICYP Headquarters. It also provided emergency medical facilities to Cypriots of all communities in accordance with the highest traditions of the medical profession.' (*S/11137*, 1 December 1973, para.6)
    While serving with UNFICYP the Austrian Field Hospital had treated over 6,000 in-patients, 35,500 out-patients and 26,500 dental patients, and had carried out some 3,100 surgical operations:

3. *S/10940*, 31 May 1973, para. 93.

4. The risks inherent in this action were judged at the time to be acceptable in order to promote deconfrontation and create conditions in which further troop reductions and financial savings within UNFICYP would be possible. But when Turkish forces intervened in July 1974 and bullets began to fly, there was criticism that some UN posts and the men in them had been left far too vulnerable. With hindsight this was a valid criticism, not only because the lives of UN

soldiers are too valuable to be thus exposed, but also because it became necessary to withdraw some posts, thus limiting the Force's operational effectiveness at a critical juncture.

5. Since the small Irish Contingent was not replaced in UNFICYP, the Austrian, Danish, Finnish and Swedish Contingents were each allowed a ceiling of 215 men, but the net effect was an even larger overall reduction of 820 men (26%).

6. Kurt Waldheim: *Introduction to the Report of the UN Secretary General on the Work of the Organization, 1974*, p. 10.

Chapter 18 (pp 125–132)

1. Major J.R. Macfarlane, Coldstream Guards, speaking to the British Army Staff College, Camberley, 21 July 1975.

2. Operations Officer, 2nd Bn, Royal Canadian Regt., writing in *2 RCR Cyprus Tour, Oct 73 – Apr 74*.

3. See, for example, Rikhye *et al.*: *The Thin Blue Line*, p. 266 *et seq.*

4. Operational elements of the Force functioned round-the-clock every day.

5. The *Status of Forces Agreement* stipulated that;

    Members of the Force shall normally wear their national uniform with such identifying United Nations insignia as the Commander may prescribe. The conditions on which the wearing of civilian dress is authorized shall be notified by the Commander to the Government . . .

    and *Force Regulations* stated that:

    Civilian dress may be worn at such times and in accordance with such conditions as may be authorized by the Commander.

    The matter was thus within the discretion of the Force Commander.

6. There were exceptions, such as a Swedish OP which became a tourist attraction on account of its location on the Othello Tower. Built in the 15th Century as part of the massive fortifications of old Famagusta and bearing to this day over its entrance the effigy of the Winged Lion of Venice, the tower is so named in the belief that Famagusta was Shakespeare's 'seaport of Cyprus' in his play *Othello, The Moor of Venice*.

7. Some of these sporting facilities were available only in the SBAs but were open to members of UNFICYP through the generosity of the British forces.

8. The Force observed customary religious festivals and international holidays, especially UN Day on 24 October. Contingents also observed their own national holidays.

9. Exceptionally General Prem Chand invited others to take a Medal Parade on his behalf. The honour was extended to Dr Osorio-Tafall and to myself before our respective departures.

10. The Cyprus government established a duty-free shop for UNFICYP in Nicosia but the range of goods was small and in some cases prices were little different from those in shops outside.

11. Members of BRITCON and CANCON donated blood to British hospitals in the SBAs, and UNFICYP as a whole donated blood to Cypriot hospitals (in 1973 280 litres were so donated to the latter; far more could have been supplied but this would have defeated efforts to persuade Cypriots themselves to donate more blood to their own hospitals).

Chapter 19 (pp 135–139)

1. 'In 1973 by calling an Alert we kept the Soviets out of the Middle East'– Richard Nixon, interviewed on BBC TV's Panorama, 28 April 1980.

2. General George Keegan, former head of US Air Force Intelligence, asserted in an interview on BBC TV's *Newsnight*, 11 July 1985, that during the early stages of the Yom Kippur War a

telephone conversation had been intercepted between Israeli Ministers and Service Chiefs, in which the latter had asked that nuclear weapons be deployed from their factory at Dimona in the Negev Desert. He also stated that a Soviet freighter carrying nuclear weapons had sailed from Odessa through the Bosphorus (tracked by the Turks) to arrive on 15 October 1973 at Alexandria, where it was immediately surrounded by underwater defences while the weapons were unloaded; meanwhile Soviet officers from two SCUD Missile units had arrived in Egypt by air. These weapons (he said) remained in Egypt for some time, always under exclusive Soviet control, but were eventually returned to Russia.

3.   The situation there [*Cyprus*] was becoming unstable and emotional, so we were taking a consider-
      able risk. Kurt Waldheim: *In the Eye of the Storm*, pp. 64–65.
4.   Within UNFICYP, for example, contingency planning was confined to an emergency with-
      drawal of the Force from Cyprus should cancellation of its mandate or any other development
      so require.
5.   All other contingents were similarly affected. The Irish 25th Infantry Group had taken over from
      the 24th only three days earlier; the advance party of 5th Royal Inniskilling Dragoon Guards,
      who were to relieve 1st Bn, Parachute Regt, had arrived on the island the previous day; the Danes
      were due to rotate their battalion in three weeks time; and in CANCON 2nd Bn, Royal Canadian
      Regt had taken over in Nicosia less than three weeks earlier. Thus it was already a period of
      turbulence and change within UNFICYP.
6.   That so many volunteered nonetheless was a tribute both to their enthusiasm for and belief in
      the value of UN service and to the leadership of their commanders.

Chapter 20 (pp 140–145)

1.   Commonly known in the British army as an 'O' Group.
2.   New York's request for estimates of stores to be moved could not be satisfied immediately, but
      in any case was overtaken as soon as it was known that the airlift was to be provided by the RAF
      from Akrotiri, with whom HQ UNFICYP then dealt direct on the matter.
3.   'The process of working out agreement [*on arrangements for logistic support in UNEF 2*]
      dragged on for three weeks while troops in the field subsisted on improvisation, good luck and
      considerable hardship.' Brian Urquhart: *A Life in Peace and War*, p. 242. In the event it was six
      weeks before even a rudimentary logistic supply organization was established in UNEF 2.
4.   At the time the strength of each's battalion in UNFICYP was about 275 men.
5.   These rations, and various other stores, were to be drawn in bulk by UNFICYP from depots in
      the Eastern SBA and transported to Akrotiri, where they were to be issued to contingents as they
      arrived to emplane.
6.   Lieut. General E. Siilasvuo, speaking to the Seminar for Nordic UN Personnel, Gurrehus,
      Denmark, February 1977.
7.   The Cyprus government normally would not permit air traffic to and from the Republic to use
      Akrotiri rather than Nicosia Airport, not only because this was contrary to the Treaty of
      Establishment but also because of the consequential loss of revenue. In any case the British were
      reluctant to allow use of Akrotiri except in an emergency since it was a busy military airfield. In
      the crisis of the summer of 1974, when Nicosia Airport became unusable, Akrotiri served for a
      prolonged period as the island's main airport for both civil and military traffic. Makarios himself
      was obliged to use it to escape from Cyprus and for his subsequent return.
8.   Subsequently this arrangement was made permanent. There were no difficulties.
9.   Siilasvuo had been Chief of Staff of the UN Truce Supervisory Organization (UNTSO) in the
      Middle East since 1970. His HQ was in Jerusalem, but he had gone to Cairo on 24 October in

order to redeploy UNTSO officers withdrawn from their posts along the Suez Canal on the outbreak of the Yom Kippur War.

Chapter 21 (pp 146–151)

1. British military term for parties of men of a given number, depending on aircraft capacity.
2. In the event the Swedes preceded the Austrians, whose arrival at Akrotiri had been delayed.
3. The shortages were a legacy of recent industrial disputes in the UK. The British government lost no time in directing that any vehicles leased to UNFICYP for use in Cyprus but taken to Egypt in Operation DOVE were to be treated as outright sales to the UN and charged for accordingly.
4. Major D.M. Bond, *op.cit.*
5. Captain J.D. Fielden, *personal*, 9 April 1979.
6. The CAO's staff at HQ UNFICYP was kept busy for the next six months trying to account for items ranging from refrigerators to cooking-stoves alleged to have been taken to Cairo.
7. Captain J.D. Fielden, *op. cit.*
8. Colonel C.E. Beattie, *personal*, 20 October 1977.
9. The reason was that the Swedes had decided to send their UN stand-by battalion to UNEF 2. On its arrival in Egypt the men sent from Cyprus were to be returned to the island for rotation as scheduled.
10. For the distinction between high- and low-cost contingents see Chapter 8. Since the costs of UNEF 2 were to be treated as a charge on the UN as a whole, it did not face the financial problems that beset UNFICYP.

Chapter 22 (pp 152–154)

1. Lieut. General E. Siilasvuo, *op. cit.*
2. UNFICYP's small Irish Contingent arrived on 31 October and Siilasvuo immediately deployed it on the Israelis' side of the Canal's northern sector – an astute move prompted by a lesson of 1956–1967, when the Israelis had refused to allow UNEF troops to be stationed on their side of the Armistice Demarcation Line.
3. It emerged later that in fact their Third Army was not in such dire straits as the Egyptians would have had others believe.
4. The first Sinai Disengagement Agreement, reached with General Siilasvuo's help, was signed on 18 January 1974. This provided for the withdrawal of Israeli troops from the Canal's west bank and consequential relief of the Egyptian Third Army.
5. Lieut General E. Siilasvuo, *op. cit.* The UN Depot at Pisa, Italy, was established at the time of the first UNEF. In October 1973 it held only some obsolete vehicles recovered when that Force was hurriedly withdrawn, some limited equipment for UN Observer teams, items of UN clothing such as blue berets, and UN flags and insignia. In his *A Life in Peace and War* (p. 242), Brian Urquhart makes much of the difficulty experienced in securing Canadian agreement to establish a joint Canadian – Polish logistic organization to support UNEF 2, and states that discussions to this end occupied three weeks.
6. Kurt Waldheim: *Report of the Secretary General on the Work of the Organization, 1979*, p.10.
7. Rikhye *et al.*: *The Thin Blue Line*, p. 323.

Chapter 23 (pp 155–159)

1. *S/11056*, 28 October 1973, para. 4.
2. The journey by helicopter was some 130km each way, entailing a climb of more than 1800m over the Troodos mountains; the journey by road, whether through the mountains or by the coast road, was a tedious one of several hours each way.
3.   'I will arise and go now, and go to Innisfree,
        And a small cabin build there, . . .
        And I shall have some peace there, . . .
                W.B. Yeats: *The Lake Isle of Innisfree*'
4. Trees and shrubs were donated to all contingents for planting in their camps by the Cyprus Forestry Department's forward-looking Director Mr Seraphim.
5. There were ample precedents for the redeployment of UN contingents from one part of Cyprus to another. In earlier years the Irish had been moved from Famagusta to Paphos and Lefka and later to Larnaca; the Danes from Nicosia to Lefka; the Swedes from Paphos to Famagusta and the Canadians from Kyrenia to Nicosia.
6. The British treated service in UNFICYP as temporary operational duty; camps were maintained to a reasonable standard of accommodation, but time and money were not spent on the refinements that some other contingents thought appropriate.
7. *Regulations for the United Nations Force in Cyprus* (*ST/SGB/UNFICYP/1*, 25 April 1964, para. 11.)

Chapter 24 (pp 163–170)

1. Rauf Denktash, letter to Glafkos Clerides, 9 August 1971, para. 2. (reproduced by Clerides: *Cyprus: My Deposition*, Vol. 3, p. 108).
2. The constitutional adviser appointed by Greece was Judge Dekleris and that by Turkey was Professor Aldikacti.
3. Subsequent meetings took place alternately in the offices of Mr Clerides and Mr Denktash.
4. Polyvios G. Polyviou: *Cyprus – In Search of a Constitution*, p. 184.
5. *S/10842*, 1 December 1972, para. 71.
6. Glafkos Clerides, *op.cit.*, p. 204.
7. *Ibid.*, p. 206.
8. Archbishop Makarios was re-elected President unopposed. Dr Kuchuk having decided not to stand again, Mr Denktash was proclaimed the elected Vice-President, the only other candidate, Mr Ayhan Berberoglu, having withdrawn under pressure from the Turkish *Bozkurt* and in circumstances that gave rise to disquiet in diplomatic circles in Nicosia. (Dr Kuchuk died in London in January 1984 aged 77 years).
9. Glafkos Clerides, *op. cit.*, p. 267.
10. *S/10940*, 31 May 1973, para. 81.
11. *S/11137*, 1 December 1973, para. 77.
12. *S/11294*, 22 May 1974, para. 61.
13. Statement to the French *Le Point*, 19 February 1973.
14. It was reported that during his visit to Moscow in July 1971 Makarios was given a pledge of Soviet support for the independence of Cyprus.
15. Polyvios G. Polyviou, *op. cit.*, p.255.

Chapter 25 (pp 171–176)

1. Quoted by Dr P.N. Vanezis: *Makarios – Life and Leadership*, p. 130.
2. Glafkos Clerides did not entirely subscribe to this view – see his *Cyprus: My Deposition*, Vol.3, p. 114.
3. Dr P.N. Vanezis, *op. cit.*, p. 129
4. *ibid.*, p. 131.
5. Dr Vassos Lyssarides was Makarios's personal physician and confidant. He played an active part in various political and covert activities and had contacts in the Arab world. He was leader of EDEK, a radical left-of-centre party, and editor of *Ta Nea* (*News*), a left-wing daily newspaper.
6. UNFICYP's lack of a conventional intelligence capability was a handicap, but the deficiency was remedied to some extent by reports in the local press and by contacts with well-informed members of some diplomatic missions in Nicosia.
7. In a public statement made on 30 March 1973 Makarios explained that the government had decided to strengthen the security forces and that to this end an 'auxiliary police force' was being established, the main task of which would be to 'follow and combat unlawful activities and terrorism wherever coming from, in cooperation with the regular police force'. He added that the ultimate strength of the new police unit, which would be integrated within the existing force, would 'depend on developments and prevailing conditions'. (*S/10940*, 31 May 1973, paras. 28–29).
8. It is likely that the 1-ton Humber armoured trucks, hurriedly moved from Limassol to the CYPOL barracks at Athalassa early in 1973, were destined for the TRU's use.
9. UNFICYP could not ignore the terms of Security Council Resolution 186(1964) (Annex 1) which recognized that the government of Cyprus 'has the responsibility for the maintenance and restoration of law and order'.
10. Dr P.N. Vanezis, *op. cit.*, pp. 131–133.
11. An incident at Ayios Seryios (near Famagusta) on 7 October 1973, when a bomb was exploded on the route taken by a car carrying Makarios, has been cited as evidence that EOKA-B was intent on his life. If seriously so intended, the attempt was ineptly executed; more likely it was intended as a threatening gesture.
12. There is reason to believe that a confidant, who attended Grivas in a professional medical capacity, assured the Archbishop that the General's death was due to natural causes.
13. Dr P.N. Vanezis: *Cyprus – The Unfinished Agony*, p. 50
14. Laurence Stern: 'Bitter Lessons: How We Failed in Cyprus, *Foreign Affairs*, Summer 1975, p. 35.

Chapter 26 (pp 177–182)

1. *S/10842*, 1 December 1972, para. 79.
2. The dead man was reported to be Abad al-Chair, a member of 'Black September', killed in reprisal for the murder of Israelis at the 1972 Olympic Games in Munich.
3. The lull in external terrorist activity lasted until 1985 when in one incident three Israelis were shot at Larnaca marina and in another an Iraqi airline manager was murdered by a bomb in Nicosia.
4. UNFICYP's actions rankled the Turks more than was evident at the time. An article published in the Turkish Cypriot *Bozkurt* nearly a year later complained that 'General Prem Chand raised an outcry when a Turk set about building a house beside Piknik 2 but he did nothing about the extension of the Ledra Palace . . . .' (*Special News Bulletin*, Nicosia, 14 August 1974, p. 3)
5. *S/11294*, 22 May 1974, paras. 75, 76, 79.

Chapter 27 (pp 183–191)

1. *Le Monde*, Paris, 18 September 1974.

2. *Ibid*.

3. See, for example, Coral Bell's *The Diplomacy of Detente: The Kissinger Era* (Chapter 8) and Laurence Stern's article 'Bitter Lessons: How We Failed in Cyprus', *Foreign Affairs*, Summer 1975. A report published in 1974 by the American Hellenic Institute stated:

    > ... there is abundant evidence suggesting that the US knew of the impending coup well in advance. ... Trying to establish what happened at this period is complicated by the fact that the US was apparently in the habit of communicating with the junta via the CIA station chief, while the regular Embassy channels in Athens were rarely used. ('Crisis on Cyprus' – *Report prepared for the Subcommittee to Investigate Problems Connected with Refugees and Escapees of the Committee on the Judiciary of the United States Senate*, p.14)

4. *Le Monde*, Paris, 18 September 1974.

5. An example was the case of the commander of the National Guard camp at Skylloura who was reported to have 'disappeared' after participating in a theft of weapons from his camp's armoury.

6. That same evening, 18 June, I attended a farewell reception hosted by the Commander of the National Guard for his departing Chief of Staff, Maj. General Papadakis, who was leaving ostensibly to assume command of a Division on the Graeco-Turkish frontier, but actually (it was later alleged) to join the *coup* planners in Athens. Most of the National Guard's Greek officers were present and the atmosphere was tense. The Cypriot Foreign Minister, Mr I. Christophides, recently so humiliated by the 'Snapper' episode, declined to attend.

7. One of the dead was a Briton, Mr M. Howell, killed when the Land Rover he was travelling in was fired upon in the dark just west of Limassol in circumstances never fully explained. His British companions, a man and two women, were wounded.

8. *Le Monde*, Paris, 18 September 1974.

9. A senior minister told me that the letter was drafted by Makarios personally and its terms had been approved by ministers, although not all had supported the decision to make the contents public.

10. Some Turkish Cypriots claimed later that on 13 July – two days before the *coup* – members of ELDYK wearing National Guard uniform had taken over guard duties on some official buildings in Nicosia. If true, this would not have been apparent to UN patrols, but could not have escaped public notice and would have been reported in the local press. There were also reports later that during early July some Greek officers sent their families home to Greece.

11. The Commander (Colonel Georgitsis) and Operations Officer (Major Soulis) of the National Guard 3rd Higher Military Command located in Nicosia were exceptionally busy during early July. At a meeting with them on 12 July FINCON's Commander, Lieut. Colonel Pullinen, found both tired and irritable. It emerged later that Georgitsis had assumed command of the National Guard in the rank of Brig. General that very day on the departure of General Denizis for Athens, and that it was he who was the *coup's* mastermind in Cyprus. Unknown to UNFICYP at the time was the recall to Nicosia from leave in Greece of Colonel C. Kombokis, Commander of the National Guard's elite Raiding Force Units. Landing at Nicosia airport in a small aircraft and accompanied by several others, all in civilian dress, he took an unobtrusive back route out of the airport, but not before he was spotted by the government's Chief of Protocol, Mr George Pelaghias, who challenged him with the words: 'I thought you were on holiday?'. Kombokis replied lamely that his wife missed the sun of Cyprus. Pelaghias warned the Archbishop that trouble was brewing.

12. P. Stavrou, Under-Secretary to President Makarios, quoted in *Sunday Eleftherotypia*, Athens, 8 July 1979.

13. Colonel M.E. Jessup, *personal*, 6 February 1978.

14. *Ibid.*

15. See *Report from the Select Committee on Cyprus, Session 1975–76*, p. 56. This has been confirmed by Field Marshal Carver, then Chief of Defence Staff ('Peacekeeping in Cyprus', *Cyprus in Transition 1960–1985*, p. 33).

16. James Callaghan: *Time and Change*, p. 335.

17. Henry Kissinger: *Years of Renewal*, p. 204.

18. Such was the Turks' misreading of the situation that Prime Minister Ecevit adhered to a planned visit on 15 July to Afyon in western Turkey, Foreign Minister Gunes left Ankara on a visit to China, the Turkish Ambassador to Athens embarked for a cruise in the Aegean and the Chief of the General Staff left for Istanbul.

19. Interview published in *To Vema*, Athens, 24 July 1977.

20. Mr Arthur Hartman, Assistant Secretary for European Affairs.

21. *Le Monde*, Paris, 18 September 1974.

22. Some believe that General Denizis (who did not return to Cyprus) was placed under house arrest in Athens because he was not in sympathy with the impending action, but his recall may have been a stratagem to suggest that the hand of Athens was not behind the National Guard's action.

23. *Sunday Eleftherotypia*, Athens, 8 July 1979.

24. Laurence Stern, *op. cit.*, pp. 55–56.

Chapter 28 (pp 192–196)

1. Interview published in *Aghon*, Nicosia, 26 July 1977. Commenting later to the author on the timing of the *coup*, CYPOL's commander, Mr Antoniou, observed that by 0800hrs Nicosia could be expected to be relatively quiet with most people already at work, the Archbishop in his office and his guards reduced in number and relaxed after being on duty all night.

2. The relatively few Greek Cypriot officers (who in any case were permitted only to fill junior and non-sensitive posts) had either been sent on leave or confined at National Guard HQ shortly beforehand.

3. To the chagrin of his opponents Dr Lyssarides himself found safe refuge in the Syrian Embassy in Nicosia.

4. The plotters must have been tempted to deal with Makarios as he passed the gate of the ELDYK camp on his way back from the Troodos, but to have done so would have given the lie to the pretence that Athens had no hand in the *coup*. (Makarios used the Presidential Palace for official business as President but resided in the Archbishopric, situated within the walls of old Nicosia, travelling between the two under strong escort.)

5. Two members of BRITCON's Parachute Sqn RAC, who were observing events at the airport, reported seeing at least 10 members of the TRU shot dead; they were obliged to withdraw when bursts of MG were directed at them.

6. Lieut. Colonel S. Kristensson, *personal*, 3 January 1978.

7. J. Bowyer Bell: *Violence at a Distance: Greece and the Cyprus Crisis*, p. 791.

8. UNFICYP officers who saw Sampson at National Guard HQ on this and subsequent days reported that the he was in awe of the Greek officers, who treated him more like an office boy than President of Cyprus. In 1976 Sampson was tried in Nicosia for his part in the *coup* and sentenced to 20 years imprisonment. His Defence Counsel told the Court:

> Sampson had not physically taken part in the anti-Makarios *coup* and was not connected with the

organizers. He happened to be passing the National Guard Headquarters and was appointed "President" by Brigadier Ioannides, then head of the Greek military police, when five prominent Cypriots had either refused to accept the post or could not be found. (*The Daily Telegraph*, London, 1 September 1976).

After serving three years in prison Sampson was allowed to leave Cyprus for health reasons on condition that he returned on completion of medical treatment; he did not do so but lived instead in self-imposed exile in Paris. However, in June 1990, then aged 54, he unexpectedly returned and was taken into custody to serve the remainder of his sentence. Following an appeal, he was released in 1991, immediately re-arrested, and then released again in April 1992 by decree of President Vassiliou.

Chapter 29 (pp 197–208)

1. An official 'UN Flag Code' stipulated when, where, by whom and in what fashion UN flags could be displayed. The code did not cater for the type of emergency in which UNFICYP now found itself, and throughout the following weeks its provisions were ignored.

2. One of UNFICYP's few military telephone lines ran between the Canadians in Wolsely Barracks and the Leadership at the VPO.

3. Commandant J. Flynn, *personal*, 16 December 1977.

4. The bus carrying the children had been halted by a burst of fire from a T-34 tank. Two RAF wives in charge of the children subsequently received The Queen's Commendation for Brave Conduct.

5. The Canadian Logistics Company in Blue Beret Camp, which contributed to the security of Force HQ, was also placed on short alert.

6. During the morning Manuel himself made a helicopter reconnaissance over Nicosia but air surveillance was discontinued soon after midday, a Bofors AA gun having been observed trained on a UN helicopter.

7. Broadcasting over 'Radio Bayrack' (the Turkish station in Nicosia regarded by the Government as illegal), Denktash assured his community that the *coup* was an internal matter for the Greek Cypriots. This did not accord with Ankara's view, and Denktash had his knuckles rapped accordingly.

8. The weapon was recovered that afternoon after Manuel visited the scene and protested to the local Greek commander.

9. Lieut. Colonel The Hon. H.E.C. Willoughby, speaking to the Army Staff College, Camberley, 21 July 1975.

10. *Ibid.*

11. The text of the message, which HQ UNFICYP relayed to New York without delay, read as follows:

    Following message for Cyprus Representative in United Nations, Mr Zenon Rossides. Quote. Request by President of Cyprus Republic, Archbishop Makarios, to call forthwith the Security Council of the United Nations to condemn the military government of Greece for the scandal (*sic*) armed intervention against the lawful government of the Republic of Cyprus which took place this morning. Stop. And to ask United Nations to take immediate measures to stop intervention. Unquote. Bishop of Paphos.

12. A week earlier Kristensson had warned Stockholm that he thought a *coup* was a possibility. Later he told me that he had found it remarkable that Prem Chand, at the meeting of District Commanders on the afternoon of 15 July, had said that the *coup* had come as a complete surprise. It is fair to say that it was the timing rather than the event itself which had taken us by surprise, but

this point illustrates the sensitivities that beset UN Forces. Had Prem Chand suggested earlier, even in confidence, to his subordinate commanders that a *coup* was a possibility, this risked being reported to home governments and finding its way into UN circles in New York. Protests from the Cyprus government would have followed and Prem Chand would have been taken to task for speculating so openly on a political matter that lay outside UNFICYP's mandate. These sensitivities had been demonstrated three months earlier, when Lieut. Colonel C. Clausen (Austria), UNFICYP's Chief Operations Officer, had submitted to me a draft operational instruction to meet the contingency of a *coup* in Cyprus. After consultations with my colleagues in the HQ's 'top corridor' I told him:

> In view of the very delicate situation which this covers we have decided . . . that it would not be desirable to issue now guidance of this nature. Although not entirely satisfactory, we consider that on balance it will be better to issue any guidance at the time, accepting the risks that this might entail.

13. At Severinson's request a helicopter was sent to Xeros to bring him to Force HQ so that he might report in person on this incident. By the time he reached Blue Beret Camp the information he brought concerning Archbishop Makarios had been overtaken by that received from Macfarlane in Paphos.

14. UN Secretary General: *Statement to the Security Council, SC/3546*, 16 July 1974.

15. For example, a T-34 tank was observed with its main armament at full elevation firing to no apparent purpose in a direction that must have caused rounds to fall on the Turkish side un-observed by its crew. Similarly a mortar base-plate position was located from which rounds were being fired towards the Turkish quarter.

16. Assessing the situation that faced him on assuming the post of Acting President on 23 July 1974, Glafkos Clerides has written:

> General Yiorgitsis *[sic]* was a small-built man with a narrow head and narrower mind. He was sent to Cyprus a few days before the *coup* for the purpose of executing it. My impression was that he had no time to study and digest the plans which existed for the defence of Cyprus, had no knowl-edge of the topography of the island and no idea of what reserves were available in men and material. He must have been assured that there would be no Turkish military reaction to the coup and therefore did not bother to take even the most rudimentary measures for the defence of the island. I made a mental note that he should be replaced as soon as this was feasible. *Cyprus: My Deposition*, Vol. 4, p. 31.

17. Flynn remained at National Guard HQ throughout the night, noting much troop movement with occasional shooting and tracer in the night sky. Relieved at intervals by Captain Granlund (Sweden) (with radio nickname 'LOCUST') this radio link was maintained until the evening of 19 July, when the National Guard requested its withdrawal, telephone communications having been restored.

18. Pandelakis himself was taken into custody, but when five days later the Turks landed in Cyprus he was released and given command of a National Guard unit.

19. N. Harvey and family: *A Holiday to Remember*, circulated privately, 2 August 1974. Of this fire they wrote:

> We thought at the time that this was an accident, but were later told that some of Makarios's supporters had started it to cut off a Greek army post on the mountains from EOKA-B supporters of the *coup* in the villages at the bottom of the mountains.

19. Next day we learnt that there were some 20 seriously wounded ELDYK men in the Nicosia General Hospital. There was an ugly report that members of EOKA-B had gone through some wards knocking away blood plasma bottles from wounded Makarios supporters.

Chapter 30 (pp 209–217)

1. P. Stavrou, interview, *Sunday Eleftherotypia*, Athens, 8 July 1979.
2. *To Vema*, Athens, 23 July 1977. Visiting the Presidential Palace in 1980 (by then rebuilt) I was shown by Mr P. Stavrou the Archbishop's escape route.
3. The frightened children were eventually brought out of the Palace unharmed, as were the adults. But some of the latter, in particular Vakis (who had been kidnapped and released two months earlier), suffered rough treatment.
4. *To Vema*, Athens, 23 July 1977.
5. *Ibid.* Stavrou (*op. cit.*) has told how, while held at the Palace, he heard these conversations on radios seized by the National Guard, and how the latter thought they were a trick, the Archbishop's voice having been recorded in anticipation of a *coup*.
6. Apparently traffic on the CYPOL radio net had been monitored in the SBAs, leading a senior officer at HQ BFNE to suspect that, anticipating the *coup*, a wily Makarios had remained at Troodos while sending his car back to Nicosia with a decoy. On learning that a *coup* had taken place (so this story went), the Archbishop had gone straight to Kykko Monastery and from there to Paphos. My later investigations confirmed that there are no grounds to support any such suspicion.
7. *To Vema*, Athens, 23 July 1977.
8. In his haste to leave the Palace the Archbishop had been unable to don either and had left behind his pendant Cross. To maintain a dignified appearance he later borrowed the latter from the Bishop of Paphos.
9. Major J.R. Macfarlane, speaking to Army Staff College, Camberley, 21 July 1975.
10. *Ibid.*
11. The Treaty of Establishment provided for free movement through the SBAs of the armed forces of the Republic. HQ BFNE did not attempt to prevent the passage of this motley group because (it was said) insufficient British troops were on hand to do so.
12. Some casualties from this and later fighting in Limassol went to the RAF Hospital at Akrotiri but were refused admission 'because they had not been processed through the civil hospital in Limassol'. Lieut. Colonel Willoughby acted quickly to sort out this procedural nonsense, pointing out to the SBA authorities that any who presented themselves to the Limassol hospital 'risked having their head amputated'.
13. Lieut. Colonel H.E.C. Willoughby, *Report to Regimental HQ Coldstream Guards*, London, 18 July 1974.
14. This broadcast, in which he appealed 'to all freedom loving nations', was heard as far afield as Cairo, Malta, Tel Aviv and Rhodes.
15. *To Vema*, Athens, 23 July 1977.
16. *Ibid.*
17. When Lieut. Colonel Willoughby remarked to a senior Greek Cypriot official that it was ironic, given past history, that it was to the British that Makarios had turned in his hour of need, the official replied that this should occasion no surprise: Cypriots knew well on whom they could rely in a crisis. (Events in the next few weeks may have led him to revise that view.)
18. With scant regard for UNFICYP's interests or the safety of RAF helicopters serving the UN Force and without informing General Prem Chand, Air Marshal Aiken instructed the pilot to fly a course to Paphos which would suggest that it had come from Nicosia and not from Akrotiri.
19. At his trial in 1976 Nicos Sampson made the absurd claim that he had spared the life of Makarios as he fled from Paphos:

    A young officer at Paphos, speaking to me over the field telephone, said: "Mr President, I can see

Makarios running to a British helicopter. I have him within range of my rifle. Shall I shoot him? shall I shoot him?". I replied: "No, don't shoot him. Let him live. Let him go!". (*The Daily Telegraph*, London, 1 September 1976).

20.   Major J.R. Macfarlane, *op. cit.*

21.   *To Vema*, Athens, 23 July 1977.

Chapter 31 (pp 218–227)

1.   The British High Commission, US Embassy and Turkish Cypriot Leadership all rejected similar approaches, although Dimitriou was received in a personal capacity when he knocked on the door of the British High Commission.

2.   The assignments of diplomatic representatives abroad come within the purview of "foreign affairs" and as such require my prior approval as the Vice President of the Republic of Cyprus under Articles 49(D) and 50 of our Constitution. (*S/11352*, 20 July 1974, circulating copy of letter from Rauf Denktash.)

3.   An exasperated Lieut. Colonel Willoughby told the District Officer, Limassol that the irrational and truculent behaviour of the 'cowboys' was a potential intercommunal threat and that, so long as they were allowed to drive around in uncontrolled fashion, he would not press the Turks to take down their barricades.

4.   Lieut. Colonel Willoughby, *personal*, 17 July 1974.

5.   *Ibid.* Returning to Paphos two days later, Willoughby reported:

I had an interesting morning talking to the Turkish Cypriot leader, Mr Fellahoglu . . . . He was in cracking form and obviously delighted that the Greeks were killing each other.

6.   Major J.R. Macfarlane, *report to Regimental HQ Coldstream Guards.*

7.   The Danes visited the 25 men in National Guard custody daily and confirmed that they were being well treated. All were released and re-absorbed into the National Guard when Turkish forces landed in Cyprus three days later.

8.   On 19 July the Austrians inspected all positions along the Artemis Road. Those of the National Guard were found to be unchanged but five new TCF posts were found; the Austrians required these to be dismantled.

9.   Mr Paralikis, the District Officer, who previously had been such a great man, looked more like a dog with his tail between his legs. (Lieut. Colonel Kristensson, *personal*, 3 January 1978.)

10.   A Canadian officer's letter to his family, 18 July 1974, printed in *The Maroon Beret*, January 1975.

11.   *Ibid.*

12.   Both were found unharmed under guard in their own homes.

13.   UNFICYP established that there were 21 Turkish Cypriot convicts in the prison. Their names were given to the Leadership with the information that visits by relatives would be permitted.

14.   UNFICYP has not seen this ammunition since, and it must be assumed that most (if not all) was expended in the fighting of the following weeks.

15.   UNFICYP officers were denied entry to the Greek General Hospital in Nicosia, and no information was forthcoming as to the number of casualties being treated. At the Turkish Hospital it was learnt that eight casualties had been admitted, all but two of whom had already been discharged. *Estia*, Athens, carried an unconfirmed report on 17 July 1974 that 300 people had died in the violence of the two preceding days. In 1980, Mr Antoniou, Chief of CYPOL, told the author that about 20 members of the Police TRU had been killed during the *coup*. Contrary to assertions in later years, there were no reports of any Turkish Cypriot having been killed during the period 15–19 July 1974.

16. Hearing the sound of shooting from the direction of the Presidential Palace on the morning of 15 July, Belaiev and the Military Attaché had gone to investigate; a bullet through the windscreen had made them turn back.
17. Major I.McK. Robertson, *personal*, 15 January 1978.
18. PIO Nicosia, *Press Release No. 8*, 18 July 1974.
19. *Ibid.* An Encyclical, signed by the three prelates unfrocked in 1973 at the instigation of Makarios, was published on 19 July 1974 declaring that an election for a new Archbishop would be held soon.

Chapter 32 (pp 228–237)

1. *House of Commons Official Report (Hansard)*, 15 July 1974.
2. *Ibid.*
3. *The Times*, London, 16 July 1974.
4. M.A. Birand: *30 Hot Days*, p. 3. (Turkish officialdom is notoriously secretive and authoritative information concerning political and military actions on the Turkish side during the Cyprus crisis of 1974 is not readily obtainable. Mehmet Ali Birand is a well-informed Turkish journalist of repute and those well qualified to judge consider his *30 Hot Days* to be a reliable and balanced account of events as seen from the Turkish viewpoint).
5. The Sahin Line was believed to be that which Turkish Forces were required to secure in the first phase of their intervention operation.
6. Laurence Stern, *Foreign Affairs*, Summer 1975, p. 57.
7. *The Times*, London, 16 July 1974.
8. *SC/3546*, 16 July 1974.
9. In fact this routine troop rotation was scheduled for 17 July but in the event it took place on 19 July, closely observed by UNFICYP.
10. During the second half of July alone the NATO Council met in special session to consider the Cyprus situation on some 30 occasions, once three times in a single day.
11. For the wording of Article IV see Chapter 2.
12. Foreign Minister Gunes did not return to Ankara from his visit to Peking until 19 July.
13. *The Times*, London, 18 July 1974.
14. Makarios and Ecevit did not meet in London. It was another of the Cyprus paradoxes that at the UN in New York at this juncture Turkey was supporting the Archbishop, hitherto an arch enemy.
15. *To Vema*, Athens, 24 July 1974. One of those who called upon the Archbishop in his hotel was Lord Caradon, who as Sir Hugh Foot had been the last British Governor of Cyprus. Caradon had been invited to record a radio tribute on the reported death of Makarios but had been obliged to revise this when he learnt that the latter had survived. On being thanked by Makarios for the generous terms of this (revised) tribute, Caradon replied: 'You should know, Your Beatitude, that I said much nicer things about you when I thought you were dead'.
16. Questioned in 1976 by the House of Commons Select Committee on Cyprus, Callaghan declined to be drawn on what had passed between British ministers and the Turks.
17. M.A. Birand, *op. cit.*, pp. 7 8.
18. Bulent Ecevit, letter to *The Sunday Times*, London, 6 June 1976.
19. James Callaghan: *Time and Chance*, p. 340.
20. Giving evidence in 1975 to the House of Commons Select Committee on Cyprus, Roy Hattersley (Minister of State) said:
    What we possessed on the island were troops sufficient to defend the perimeters of the sovereign

bases and provide some logistic support for the United Nations forces; but we did not possess on the island at any time troop levels which would have enabled us meaningfully to intervene either in the invasion or before or during the Sampson coup. (*Report From The Select Committee on Cyprus, Session 1975–76*, London, 1976)

21. During his Middle East shuttle Kissinger had a brief meeting in May in Nicosia with Soviet Foreign Minister Gromyko. His somewhat patronizing account of the presence of Makarios at their meeting throws unconscious but revealing light on Kissinger's own estimate of the signifi-cance of 'the obscure island' and its problems in the realm of international affairs. (See Henry Kissinger: *Years of Upheaval*, pp 1063–4).

22. Henry Kissinger, *op. cit.*, p. 1190. Interviewed on BBC television on 21 November 1979, he confessed that 'the handling of the Cyprus crisis could have been more effectively done'.

23. M.A. Birand, *op. cit.*, p. 11.

24. *Ibid.*

25. James Callaghan, *op. cit.*, p. 341.

26. Details of British forces deployed in or near Cyprus during July and August 1974 are given at Annex 5. Throughout the 1974 crisis the British Forces Broadcasting Service (BFBS) Cyprus provided a valuable means of passing information and advice, not only to British servicemen and their families but also to English speaking people throughout the island.

27. From 21 July this Royal Navy group was supported by the Royal Fleet Auxiliary (RFA) tankers *Olna* and *Gold Rover*; a third Auxiliary, *Regent*, was sailed from UK to provide additional backing.

Chapter 33 (pp 241–247)

1. Turkey was estimated to have the capability to land in Cyprus one tank and two artillery battalions in one sea lift and 2,000 men by parachute in a single air lift, with a further 6,000 men airlanded within 12 hours. Recent NATO exercises suggested that seaborne landings would be conducted with reasonable efficiency.

2. *The Daily Telegraph*, London, 22 July 1974, quoted a British tourist on holiday with his family in Famagusta:

   > On Friday just before the Turkish invasion an assistant at the High Commission came out to see us at the hotel. He said everything was perfectly okay and that we should not worry. He did not tell us to get ready to go. There were two old ladies who asked if it was all right to go to Kyrenia, and he said that it was – just before the Turks landed. The British authorities in the island left it too late. Most of Famagusta was still full of holidaymakers when the Turks landed. But the Army and the RAF were excellent.

3. Given Greek attitudes and UNFICYP's very limited resources, the suggestion that it should take over control of the National Guard was unrealistic. Nonetheless, Hattersley said that the Government would follow it up with all speed; nothing more was heard of it.

4. *House of Commons Official Report (Hansard)*, 19 July 1974.

5. HQ BFNE also requested a signals detachment to provide secure radio communication between it and the High Commission in Nicosia. This link was to prove invaluable.

6. HQ BFNE was in principle a unified tri-Service Command, but because naval units were not a normal element of the Command it was composed in practice only of Army and RAF personnel, the Royal Navy being represented by a single officer of Commander rank. *Hermes* and *Rhyl* were due to be joined by *Andromeda* and *Devonshire* next day (20 July), by RFAs *Olna* on 21 July and *Olwen* and *Regent* later.

7. Routine maritime reconnaissance patrols were made by RAF Nimrod aircraft based on Malta and by Vulcan aircraft based at Akrotiri.
8. The wide beaches in Famagusta Bay, their proximity to the port of Famagusta and its sizable Turkish community, the good going across the Mesaoria Plain (allowing rapid link-up with the Turkish villages that dotted it, the Turkish-controlled area around Chatos and the Turkish quarter of Nicosia, only 45km to the west) all made a landing at this point an attractive military option. In contrast, a landing on the north coast, where the only port was the small and limited Kyrenia, entailed a fight to break out from the narrow coastal strip and across the mountain barrier of the Pendhadaktylos with difficult going for tanks before a link-up could be effected with the main enclave and the Turkish quarter of the capital 20km to the south. However, in each case airborne forces might be employed to seize vital areas ahead of the seaborne troops.
9. Whether by accident or design, contacts between HQ UNFICYP and the US Embassy were less close than usual during this period (possibly due to the absence in the UK of the US Military Attaché, Colonel Jessup) and the UN Force was not made privy to the Embassy's assessment of the situation.
10. *Security Council 1780th Meeting*, 19 July 1974.
11. *S/11346/REV.1*, 19 July 1974.
12. Major H. Oberwinkler, *personal*, 10 March 1981.
13. The first two nights of this week had been spent on a camp-bed in my office at UNFICYP HQ, which became my home in the weeks that followed.

Chapter 34 (pp 248–253)

1. A smaller group of seven ships was still in the vicinity of Cape Andreas, its purpose unclear.
2. Red Alert, the highest state, was not declared because it required certain measures that were inappropriate and might at that stage have proved more of a hindrance than help to contingents.
3. Other US communications installations were located at Mia Milea (3km north-east of Nicosia) and Yerolakkos (7km to its west). All three were to find themselves caught up in the fighting and had to be abandoned.
4. Ersin handed over command of the 'Peace Force' to Demirel in August 1974 following completion of the first phase of the Turkish operation.
5. Elements of 6th Marine Regt may also have taken part under the command of 39th Division. The planned landing east of Kyrenia did not take place on 20 July, but may have been made on the afternoon of 22 July, when a troop transport and escorting destroyer were observed inshore off Karakoumi.
6. Brian Urquhart: *A Life in Peace and War*, p. 256.
7. HQ 3TC was destroyed by this airstrike and command of National Guard units in the Kyrenia area was then assumed by HQ 3HMC in Nicosia.

Chapter 35 (pp 254–260)

1. The Greeks claimed to have shot down five Turkish aircraft during the first day. UNFICYP saw none brought down but received reports that one had come down in the sea and that others were found damaged on landing back in Turkey.
2. The Cypriot Turks were seized with frenzied excitement when they saw the paratroopers jumping. Only a few of the islanders had known with certainty that military intervention was scheduled. . . . People ran into the fields to welcome them with food and drink. A fleet of cars . . . was hastily mobi-

lized to transport the soldiers to the battle front. Even a bread truck on its early rounds was pressed into service. (Vamik D. Volkan: *Cyprus – War and Adaptation*, pp. 111–112).

3. V.M. Mills, *personal*, 10 March 1981.

4. Major H.J. Oberwinkler, *personal,* 10 March 1981.

5. The Turks estimated (erroneously) that three National Guard infantry battalions opposed their seaborne landing.

6. National Guard HQ main building suffered only minor damage, but during the afternoon the Mental Hospital 2000m to its south was hit, causing heavy casualties and Greek anger.

7. This alternative HQ was situated in underground bunkers believed to have been constructed in the days before 1967, when Grivas commanded the National Guard.

8. Calling on the National Guard's Chief of Staff on 19 July, the US Military Attaché, Colonel Jessup, had remarked that units were still deployed to support the aftermath of the *coup*, whereas the threat now was from the Turkish army – was the National Guard ready to meet this? Yiannikodemos had replied that, if the Turks came, they would be defeated – Greece would not forsake Cyprus. Wishful thinking, indeed.

9. The Finns reported seeing three Greek aircraft, identified by blue crosses on their wings, attacking the TCF HQ in Boghaz, but this was not corroborated by any other source. If such an attack took place, it was the only demonstration of military support by the motherland during this first day.

10. N. Harvey and Family: *A Holiday to Remember* (circulated privately), 2 August 1974.

11. During this attack the National Guard lost three tanks and three armoured cars. Some National Guard batteries were firing from positions close to the married quarters of RAF Nicosia in which British families were living. They and those in adjacent UN camps listened expectantly for Turkish counter-battery fire, but this never came, for at that stage the Turks lacked the necessary capability.

12. M.A. Birand: *30 Hot Days*, p. 29. This and the following extracts exaggerate the strength of the Greek opposition, valiant though this was.

13. *Ibid.*, pp. 31–32.

14. On the morning of 20 July all five of Cyprus Airways' only aircraft were at Nicosia airport. During the fighting one was destroyed and three others were damaged. Arguments with respect to insurance liabilities (which touched on the role of UNFICYP and its legal standing on the island) were settled out of court in London ten years later. Also at the airport on 20 July was a Norwegian C130 aircraft which operated the routine SCACYP support service for UNFICYP's Nordic contingents; it escaped harm and was flown out later despite damaged runways. A Canadian C130 en route from Lahr (West Germany) to Nicosia was diverted in flight. Aircraft of other commercial airlines had all left Cyprus before the first Turkish airstrikes.

15. Major J.R. Herbert: 'The United Nations Takeover of Nicosia International Airport, July 1974', *The Royal Corps of Transport Review*, May 1975, pp. 7–8.

Chapter 36 (pp 261–273)

1. Major Oberwinkler was tireless during the ensuing 48 hours in conveying messages to and from HQ UNFICYP. From 22 July he was relieved from time to time by Major Ottesen (Denmark) or Captain Linholm (Sweden).

2. Commandant Flynn had returned to HQ UNFICYP when telephone communications had been restored the previous evening. (The island's telephone system continued to function in the weeks that followed, allowing individuals on each side of the fighting to speak to one another.)

3. Major Evangalos Tsolakis was an able officer who throughout the crisis days of July and August

1974 was indefatigable in so far as his liaison duties were concerned. Reliable and courteous, even when tired and under pressure, he earned the respect of officers at UNFICYP HQ.

4.   The first physical contact between Denktash and the newly arrived Turkish troops took place at about 1000hrs on 20 July:

> A Turkish colonel and two junior officers, all still in their paratroopers' regalia, very tough-looking with dusty faces, turned up to make the first contact with Mr Denktash. They all kissed one another and when they came to me they tried to kiss me too- they must have mistaken my blue UN beret for a Turkish para beret – but that would have been going too far! (Major H.J. Oberwinkler, *personal*, 10 March 1981).

5.   Beattie, with Flynn beside him, was in danger as air attacks on Athalassa were repeated. From time to time he consulted me by telephone. On one occasion, as they lay prone on the floor, conversation was difficult due the noise of aircraft coming in low to release bombs and fire cannons, AA fire from every available ground weapon and excited shouts all around. A particularly loud explosion caused Beattie to exclaim 'What was that?' Flynn's Irish voice was heard to reply, 'It wasn't the Leprechauns!' – 'the what?' – 'the Leprechauns – the Little People!'.

6.   3HMC was the operational HQ that controlled National Guard units in Nicosia. The location of the main TCF HQ at this time was in the Turkish school, Haydar Street, inside the walled city.

7.   *Nicosia District JOC Log, 20 July 1974*. The 'civilian' was Colonel Athos Myrianthopoulos, well know to HQ UNFICYP as the Greek Cypriot nominally in command of the Cyprus army (envisaged in the 1960 Constitution but never properly established). An upright and respected figure, he had acted in the intervening years as ADC and Military Adviser to Makarios. During the crisis days of July and August 1974 he appeared to use his influence to persuade the National Guard's mainland officers to accord the interests of Cyprus as much weight as those of Greece.

8.   Commandant Flynn was hard put to it to maintain radio contact with HQ UNFICYP as, uninvited, he followed at break-neck speed. At Malounda he was refused entry to the subterranean HQ and was obliged to operate at a distance outside it.

9.   Colonel J.J. Hunter, *personal*, 1 December 1977. Hunter had returned to Nicosia from London late on 15 July. His wife and two young daughters were sheltering in the sub-basement of his house during 20 July.

10.   Peter Pringle and Colin Smith: 'Our Hotel Becomes a Stronghold', *The Sunday Times*, London, 21 July 1974.

11.   *Ibid.*

12.   Lieut. Colonel A.C. Simonds, *personal*, 27 February 1980.

13.   Major A.C. Napier, *personal*, 2 August 1974.

14.   They included Mr Osorio-Tafall, erstwhile SRSG, and his wife, who had returned to Cyprus and their apartment in Kyrenia only the day before.

15.   Colonel J. Pullinen: *End of Tour Report*, 22 October 1975.

16.   Major J.R. Herbert: 'The United Nations Take-Over of Nicosia International Airport, July 1974', *The Royal Corps of Transport Review*, May 1975.

17.   *Ibid.*

18.   *Ibid.*

19.   In the event these weapons remained in secure UNFICYP custody until May 2002, when they were 'de-commissioned' with the consent of the Cyprus government (see chapter 16, note 10).

Chapter 37 (pp 274–281)

1.   The old city of Famagusta is enclosed in well-preserved walls built by the Venetians. On the landward side a dry moat, in places 100m wide, runs outside the walls; on the seaward side

lies the harbour. Averaging 15m in height and 8m in width, the walls still constitute formidable defence works. Air raid sirens were sounded in Famagusta and the nearby SBA at 0615hrs.

2. Given the still tenuous foothold of the Turkish forces on Cyprus on the evening of 20 July, not to have adopted this strategy was a major Greek error. However, limited transport resources and Turkish air supremacy may have led the National Guard to conclude that such a strategy was impracticable.

3. Reporting from Chatos that TCF morale was high with victory believed to be assured, Hansson said that he had even been invited to a party that night to welcome the invading Turks.

4. One of the vessels caught in Famagusta harbour was the Danish *Mette Steen*, then about to discharge its cargo. Her Master, Captain Rolf Jensen, described events:

    There was panic in the port and all work stopped completely. We heard ambulances and the sound of machine guns. The fighting continued furiously all day on Saturday *[20 July]*. Word went round that several ships in the harbour had been hit. At 1400hrs a sudden jolt shook the ship and glass scattered in all directions. We realized we had been hit by a shell. I went immediately with my six-man crew to inspect the damage and make repairs. . . . Throughout Saturday night and all day Sunday fighting continued and fires were breaking out in many places. (*Lloyds List*, London, 24 July 1974.)

    (*Mette Steen* left the port on the night of 21 July with a hole in her hull and anchored off Beirut next day.)

5. Anders Wendelberg (Ed.): *With the Swedish Contingent in Cyprus*, p. 37.

6. At this time these were the only armoured vehicles held by UNFICYP, apart from the Ferret scout cars of the UK's Force Reserve squadron. Their value was amply demonstrated during the events of July and August 1974.

7. Several Swedes in the camp suffered minor wounds. The worst casualty was Private Nilsson who received a bullet in the head when, finding the heat in his shelter stifling, unwisely looked outside. He was evacuated to the British Military Hospital, Dhekelia, and thence flown back to Sweden. Miraculously he survived, albeit with the loss of one eye.

8. The police station suffered severe damage and the nearby Turkish hospital was destroyed by fire.

9. On learning that sanitary problems within the old city were acute due to the Greeks having turned off its water supply, Kristensson acted firmly:

    I threatened him *[Colonel Kostas, National Guard Commander]* more or less with Court Martial if he did not change his criminal way of warfare and turn on the water again. (Lieut. Colonel Kristensson, *personal*, 3 January 1978).

10. To preserve security the Austrians used a different radio frequency to their LO on each side and spoke in a broad Austrian dialect that was likely to be incomprehensible to others.

11. Some rounds fell in Duke Leopold V Camp, but no casualties were suffered.

12. The National Guard requested UNFICYP to maintain surveillance of the coast to give warning of any impending landing by mainland Turkish forces. Rieger rightly declined to do so.

13. In 2002 the remains of 14 Turkish Cypriots killed in the 1974 hostilities were found in a multiple grave in the village of Alaminos.

Chapter 38 (pp 282–291)

1. The remainder of the battalion comprised elements of Battalion HQ and Nos. 2 (Support) and 3 Companies, all of which were stationed at Dhekelia. All rejoined their battalion and became part of UNFICYP on 25 July 1974.

2. At this juncture two Ferret scout car troops were located in Camp UNFICYP, Nicosia, as a small Force Reserve.

3. Lieut. Colonel H.E.C. Willoughby, *Report to Regimental HQ, Coldstream Guards*, 30 July 1974.

4. HQ 4 HMC was normally located next to the main police station in Limassol but was moved early on 20 July to the National Guard camp at Ayia Phyla (immediately east of the UN's Polemidhia Camp). Colonel Rossis was seen during the day directing operations in the town from a Command Post established in a bar on the Limassol bypass road.

5. Lieut. Colonel H.E.C. Willoughby, *op. cit.*

6. At Air Marshal Aiken's request I informed HQ National Guard in Nicosia that, unless this agreement was forthcoming, Aiken would deploy British troops to ensure safe passage of the evacuation convoys. HQ National Guard replied that the necessary instructions had been passed to its commander in Limassol on the understanding that UNFICYP would not permit the TCF to exploit the temporary ceasefire to its own advantage.

7. Lieut. Colonel H.E.C. Willoughby, *personal*, 21 July 1974.

8. During the afternoon the Australian CIVPOL also were withdrawn to Polemidhia Camp from their station in the town.

9. The firm discipline usual in the TCF may have been lacking because the four mainland Turkish army officers hitherto in command had already decided that discretion was the better part of valour and had absconded to Polemidhia Camp, where they sought and were given asylum by the Coldstream Guards.

10. Lieut. Colonel H.E.C. Willoughby, *op. cit.*

11. *Ibid.*

12. *Ibid.*

13. Speaking to the Army Staff College, Camberley on 21 July 1975, Macfarlane described how his guardsmen viewed the combatants:

    We had a silent admiration for the Turkish Cypriot fighters. They were always smart, well turned-out and we had watched their training periods, which were conducted with admirable professionalism; their mobilization arrangements also were good. In contrast the National Guard were a shambles – terribly scruffy and slovenly, and with no evidence of much discipline or training.

14. Major J.R. Macfarlane, *Report to HQ Coldstream Guards*. (So concerned was Macfarlane at the seemingly unbalanced state of Gravenes that he asked HQ UNFICYP to take up the matter with HQ National Guard in Nicosia.)

15. A military telephone line between St Patrick's Camp and Villa OP remained in operation and was used by Fellahoglu after the OP was withdrawn.

16. Press reports suggested that this was a ship of the Hellenic navy, but more likely it was the Greek Cypriot gunboat *Levantis*.

17. As darkness was falling an aircraft carrier was visible off the coast near Mandria. This was the British HMS *Hermes*, but, with its identity unknown, the sighting did nothing to allay Greek fears of a Turkish landing in this area.

18. Major J.R. Macfarlane, *op. cit.*

19. 2 HMC also controlled National Guard units in the west of Kyrenia and Nicosia Districts. When later there was a threat of it being overrun by Turkish forces, this HQ moved south, first to Kato Koutraphas and then to Platania Forest Station.

20. So named on account of its proximity to the Greek village of Mosphileri.

Chapter 39 (pp 292–297)

1. Field Marshal Carver, Chief of Defence Staff at this time, wrote later of the problem of families living outside the British bases:

   > After this experience, coming on top of that ten years before, I was determined that we should not again find our freedom of action in Cyprus so totally restricted by the vulnerability of large numbers of women and children living outside the bases. (Michael Carver: *Out of Step*, p. 466.)

2. A list of British forces in or near Cyprus in July and August 1974, including those reinforcements sent from the UK, is given at Annex 5.

3. *The Thistle*, Journal of The Royal Scots (The Royal Regiment), November 1974, p. 5.

4. Later CBFNE established a communications link with Ankara using a Vulcan aircraft and NATO and US channels.

5. *The Thistle*, November 1974, pp. 5–6. The piper was Piper Malcolm Halliday, who wrote: 'They say the families were glad to see me; well, I was more than glad to see them arrive safely and I enjoyed playing for them all'.

6. Major P.E.W. Gibbs: *Report to Regimental HQ Coldstream Guards for Period 13–25 July 1974*.

7. Captain C.R.P.C. Branson RN, *personal*, 22 September 1978. ('FOCAS' was Flag Officer Carriers and Amphibious Ships – Rear Admiral Cassidi; 'CTF 321' was Commander Task Force 321; and 'CTG 321.1' was his subordinate, Commander Task Group 321.1.)

8. *Ibid.*

9. *The Western Mail*, Cardiff, 1 August 1974.

10. This (expurgated) entry is from a detailed record of events in the Kyrenia area during the period 15 July – 28 September 1974 maintained in diary form by its expatriate author. Unconsciously it reveals a remarkable story of how an elderly British couple, with total unselfishness and much courage, did their utmost to care for their frightened and bewildered Cypriot village neighbours. The author has since died, and, in the interests of those expatriates who stayed behind under Turkish rule in this part of Cyprus, permission for publication of major extracts has been withheld.

Chapter 40 (pp298–303)

1. Sisco is reported to have said of the junta: 'This is the goddamnest government I have ever had to dealt with.' (Lawrence Stern: 'Bitter Lessons: How We Failed in Cyprus', *Foreign Affairs*, Summer 1975, p. 65). The US Ambassador, Tasca, took a similar view: 'You cannot imagine how uninformed and incompetent Ioannides and his civilian ministers were.' (*Newsweek*, 2 September 1974).

2. Although reported to have been strongly worded, Nixon's message was not in this respect comparable to the stern letter addressed by President Johnson to Prime Minister Inonu in 1964.

3. The *Sunday Mirror*, London, 21 July 1974, reported that such was Callaghan's haste to reach the Foreign Office that he hitched a ride with a passing baker's van rather than await his official car.

4. On adoption the draft resolution became Resolution 353(1974).

5. This and succeeding quotations are from the provisional record of the Security Council's meeting (*S/PV. 1781*, 20 July 1974).

6. Safronchuk also took the opportunity to read out a *TASS* statement denying an *Agence France Presse* report that Soviet forces had been placed on a war footing in response to an alleged NATO alert.

Chapter 41 (pp 304–310)

1. M.A. Birand: *30 Hot Days*, p. 32.
2. A Turkish officer later confided to a Finnish officer that the 39th Division had been expected to capture Kyrenia and effect a link-up with airborne units in the enclave within the first 24 hours.
3. Pullinen ordered shelters to be dug in Kykko Camp following the first airstrikes on 20 July but:

    > With the infantry equipment it turned out to be impossible to dig through the rock shelf covering the hills in the camp area, and the poor shelters were built beside the buildings and in the ditches and were covered only partly with a very small number of sandbags. The only somewhat sturdy building in the camp, the ammunition store, was emptied to shelter the 30 wives and children who were evacuated from the city early in the morning. The temperature inside the store was about 50°C but the families stayed in the shelter until the evening. (Lieut. Colonel J. Pullinen: *End of Tour Report*, 22 October 1975.)

    Pullinen added that when visiting Kykko Camp while the Greek battery was firing, General Prem Chand had remarked : 'What a noise! Better make sure that the trousers stay up!'.
4. The situation in the Ledra Palace Hotel steadily deteriorated:

    > The civilians began to be gripped with panic and the sergeant of the *[Canadian]* reconnaissance platoon who was in the hotel tried to calm them and made them go down into the basement. He also endeavoured to stop the National Guard from shooting; they were as nervous as the civilians. ... By the middle of the morning the situation in the hotel became more acute. Water and food were rationed, damage to the building increased and the civilians wanted to leave. Some journalists had already left the premises. The National Guard platoon, 40 in number, refused to leave the hotel, the soldiers becoming more and more threatening. ('L'Intervention Turque à Chypre', *Le Beret Marron, Le Journal du Regiment Aeroporte du Canada*, January 1975, pp. 4–6.)

5. When HQ UNFICYP protested this attack to Inhan, he replied that a mistake had been made – the target had been neighbouring Omorphita.
6. A Canadian was wounded at this time while trying to extinguish a fire in Wolseley Barracks; he was the Contingent's ninth casualty.
7. A Canadian officer positioned near the hotel reported that a FAC was indeed nearby, but that the controller stated that he had no authority to abort the mission.
8. Some of these RAF personnel manned the airport's Air Traffic Control Centre jointly with Greek Cypriots.
9. Apparently the British High Commission in Nicosia was not consulted, warned or informed either.
10. To ensure reliable communications between UNFICYP HQ and the British High Commission Captain J.G. Longfield, second-in-command of the now grounded Army Aviation Flight, was deployed with radio to the latter during the afternoon.

Chapter 42 (pp 311–321)

1. Rieger made plain to Mehmet that UN protection would be extended only to those who complied with UN instructions. Mehmet had difficulty in persuading some members of the TCF of the worth of this protection, but in the event there was no instance in which it failed. Rieger reported that those TCF who surrendered direct to the National Guard were being treated correctly.
2. Due to a misunderstanding an Austrian patrol began to disarm a National Guard platoon close to the Turkish quarter but halted the action as soon as the error was realized, the Greek platoon then being advised to withdraw.

3. By the morning of 22 July the Austrians were holding about 600 surrendered TCF in the school. Later the total rose to 846, some 200 more than the National Guard had believed to be in Larnaca.

4. Rieger also arranged for the early release of elderly men and school-age youths among the TCF, and later for that of others, such as butchers, bakers, electricians and even bank clerks, required for restoration of services in the Turkish quarter.

5. *The Thistle*, Journal of The Royal Scots (The Royal Regiment), November 1974, p. 6. ('Sergeant Deakin' was in fact Sergeant D.G. Deighan.)

6. Major J.R. Macfarlane, *Report to Regimental HQ Coldstream Guards.*

7. *Ibid.*

8. *Ibid.*

9. With some 100 civilians of various nationalities already sheltering in St Patrick's Camp and supplies running short, Willoughby requested a helicopter to deliver more from Polemidhia. Since Turkish air action at Nicosia airport compelled continuing grounding of all UN helicopters, his request could not be met. (All these civilians were safely evacuated by road to the Western SBA later in the day.)

10. The identity of this shipping was unknown to Macfarlane, who surmised that it might be related to rumours of impending Greek landings on the west coast (in fact it was related to the events described in Chapter 44).

11. Major J.R. Macfarlane, speaking to the Army Staff College, Camberley, 21 July 1975. In view of the peril in which these airstrikes placed the Turkish hostages, HQ UNFICYP pressed the Leadership in Nicosia to have them stopped. Given the inadequacy of communications on the Turkish side it is doubtful if the message reached the commander of the Turkish forces.

12. *Ibid.*

13. Turkish Cypriot casualties at Mandria were believed to have been heavy; they included some 60 wounded.

14. About midday there was a rumour (unfounded) of an imminent landing by Turkish forces on the Akamas peninsula near Polis; this may have encouraged its TCF to stand firm.

15. With evacuation by UN helicopter impossible, he was taken by ambulance to the British Military Hospital, Dhekelia, which reported that his condition was satisfactory.

16. They included a party from Kent University, USA, on an archaeological mission, some British and Brazilian civilians, and some of the Danes' own families on a temporary visit to Cyprus.

17. Kristensson remarked later to the author that both officers deserved medals for gallantry but that in the Swedish armed forces such awards were not made.

18. Kristensson also asked for information on the state of the Finnish contingent, Helsinki having asked Stockholm to obtain this through him (the Finns' own communications with Finland had broken down). HQ UNFICYP told him that the Finns had no major problems, that they had supplies for seven days and that a full report was being sent to Helsinki via the UN Radio.

Chapter 43 (pp 322–327)

1. Major P.E.W. Gibbs, *Report to Regimental HQ Coldstream Guards (13–25 July 1974).* The ten-year-old boy who died was Michael Farley, the only fatality suffered by British Service families during the 1974 crisis.

2. *Ibid.*

3. Since the government of Nicos Sampson was not recognized by the UN or the UK, there was no question of seeking its consent for this operation by British troops on the territory of the Republic of Cyprus.

4. For reasons not explained these orders permitted British troops to fire back only if their own

vehicles were fired at; they were not authorized to do so if vehicles they were escorting were so attacked.

5.   He *[Cheeseman]* performed a minor miracle and was superb – an unsung hero. (Major J.A. Wright, *personal*, 26 November 1977.)

6.   One of those sheltering in the married quarters of RAF Nicosia has described conditions:
> With darkness Kim *[Mrs Lloyd]* and I opened the shutters to see the Kyrenia hills ablaze from end to end. Bits of metal and things hit the bungalow all night and made sleep impossible. With the dawn came more parachute drops towards the Kyrenia hills, and between the bombing Kim and I stood on the verandah watching the Turkish planes screaming overhead and attacking the gun positions. (Mrs S. Pennell, *personal*, 25 January 1978.)

7.   Colonel J.J.G. Hunter, *personal*, 1 December 1977.

8.   Signor V. Manfredi, *personal*, 24 February 1978.

9.   Levant Correspondent, *The Economist*, London.

10.   Captain J.E. Squire, *personal*, 26 November 1977.

11.   Major J.A. Wright, *personal*, 26 November 1977.

12.   Captain J.E. Squire, *op. cit.*

13.   Major E.B. Hutchings, *personal*, 29 March 1978. (He returned to HQ UNFICYP next day, bringing with him those UN vehicles used to transport families to the SBA.)

14.   It was announced on 26 July that families of British servicemen with less than three months to serve in Cyprus would be flown to the UK, starting on 28 July, and that the families of those with less than six months to serve would be placed on stand-by for evacuation if the situation did not improve.

15   Passengers were also required to sign a certificate giving consent for the British government to reclaim later the cost of the flight to the UK; in the event the British government made no such claims.

16.   Brigadier W.P.W. Robertson, *personal*, 9 November 1977.

17.   *Security Council 1782nd Meeting*, 22 July 1974.

Chapter 44 (pp 328–333)

1.   Unknown at the time, even to the Chiefs of the armed forces, was that President Gizikis had agreed at the insistence of the still powerful Brig. General Ioannides that Greece should declare war on Turkey.

2.   The Turks began to evacuate some villages in Thrace, and some people were reported leaving Aegean seaboard towns such as Bodrum.

3.   See Chapter 39 regarding exclusion zones declared by Turkey.

4.   The US 6th Fleet told Sisco that the existence of the 'convoy' could be neither confirmed nor denied. Asked by Ankara on the afternoon of 21 July about the identity of shipping off Paphos, HQ BFNE replied that it was unable to investigate owing to Turkish air activity in the area.

5.   On one occasion, Kissinger later told American newsmen off the record, Ecevit awoke him in the early hours of the morning to complain that a Greek armada was steaming towards Turkey. "Those perfidious Greeks – you know what they are doing? They are flying Turkish flags to try to fool our aircraft". Nancy Kissinger grumbled sleepily to her husband, "Why don't you tell him to shut up and sink the goddamned thing?" (Laurence Stern, Foreign Affairs, Summer 1975, pp. 65–66.)

6.   M.A. Birand: *30 Hot Days*, p. 40.

7.   More than 24 hours later the Turkish representative was telling the Security Council:
> Ankara has told me that a force of eight Greek vessels is now at Paphos attempting to land troops. (*Security Council 1782nd Meeting*, 22 July 1974).

8.   Captain R.W.F. Gerken RN, *personal*, 18 August 1978.

9. In addition to those picked up by the Israelis, *Andromeda* and *Berk*, a number of others were picked up towards the African coast by Italian and Libyan ships. Of *Kocatepe's* full complement of about 230, some 54 were lost.

10. Captain R.W.F. Gerken RN, *op. cit.*

11. *Ibid.*

12. Use of this air corridor without warning or consent gave rise to British concern both on grounds of flight safety and because Turkey might see it as British complicity in the Greek operation. (First reports from RAF Akrotiri suggested that the incoming aircraft consisted of a force of helicopters, prompting speculation that the Turks might be mounting a heli-borne operation from this new direction).

13. To make room for it in the hangar a Cyprus Airways BAC 1-11 aircraft was towed out, but it was thought that a Turkish reconnaissance aircraft had observed the operation. In view of the risk created for Camp UNFICYP, the National Guard was prevailed upon to remove the Noratlas, which was then positioned to obstruct the main runway. It became a target for Turkish air action and what remained of it was set on fire by the National Guard that evening.

Chapter 45 (pp 334–344)

1. M.A. Birand: *30 Hot Days*, p. 44.

2. Henry Kissinger: *Years of Upheaval*, p. 1192.

3. Inhan told Oberwinkler that he thought that airstrikes on Nicosia that day were unlikely. Asked about the Turkish army's build-up, Inhan told him that some artillery had now been landed.

4. *HQ UNFICYP Operations Log*, 22 July 1974.

5. Commandant J.J. Flynn, *personal*, 6 October 1978. (Captain Granlund was Assistant Force Economics Officer and WO McCowat was Chief Clerk of the Operations Branch, HQ UNFICYP).

6. A half-troop (two Ferret scout cars) of the Parachute Squadron RAC was under his command at this time; the other half-troop joined it later in the day.

7. Rosen was assisted by Sergeant J. Anderson, a BRITCON Military Policeman who was invaluable in providing liaison with the SBA British staff.

8. This decision gave rise later to unjustified criticism of the Swedes in some West German and US newspapers.

9. They included six British, one Tunisian, four French and six Greek Cypriots with British passports.

10. On arrival in the SBA the Scandinavians were processed for onward movement in the same way as other foreign nationals and were then flown in Swedish military aircraft to Cairo, where they were looked after by the Swedish contingent in UNEF 2 until flown to Stockholm. The Swedes expressed generous praise for British arrangements in the SBA, and Brigadier Robertson and his staff were grateful to Kristensson and his UN soldiers for undertaking the tasks described.

11. The quandary of Colonel Kostas at this time, when he knew that a general ceasefire was due to take effect within two hours, was revealed in a conversation with the author two weeks later (see Chapter 52).

12. Prem Chand appreciated the importance of investigating allegations of atrocities as quickly as possible in order to prevent unfounded rumours that might inflame intercommunal tempers.

13. *War Diary, 1st Rifle Coy, Austrian 5th UN Battalion*, 22 July 1974.

14. The Austrians removed the unexploded round next morning and then persuaded the National Guard platoon to move away.

15. The TCF spoke well of the Greek officer, Captain Valentinos, in command at the stadium and Willoughby reported that Turks admitted to the Greek hospital were being well treated.

16. Major J.R. Macfarlane, *Report to Regimental HQ, Coldstream Guards.* (This demonstrates the responsibilities that not infrequently devolve on young and junior members of UN peacekeeping forces.)

17. A Greek soldier, cut off from his unit, tried to seek shelter in the Danish camp but was prevented by the Turks from doing so; the Danes found his corpse later.

18. In consequence the Canadians (who were inclined to inordinately lengthy signals) established their own radio link to Ottawa, the necessary equipment being flown in to Akrotiri on 22 July. The British High Commission, aware of the pressure on UNFICYP's communications, offered to transmit urgent traffic over UK channels but this did not prove necessary. Later the carriage of some of UNFICYP's diplomatic pouches between Nicosia and New York was effected in British aircraft.

Chapter 46 (pp 347–354)

1. The Secretary General refers to 'the ceasefire agreement', but there was no formal written agreement embodying specific conditions, merely agreement on the the part of the Greek and Turkish governments to halt fighting between their forces in Cyprus at the time stated.

2. *UN Security Council 1782nd Meeting,* paras. 25–26.

3. *Ibid.,* paras. 10–11.

4. *Ibid.,* paras. 113–114.

5. HQ UNFICYP had recommended to New York that all contingents should be provided with some APCs and armoured scout cars, the value of which had been demonstrated during preceding days, but it was given no indication as to whether or not troop-contributor governments had been informed accordingly.

6. Major M.M. Barker, *personal,* 18 November 1977. The Czech arms store was sited approximately in the centre of Camp UNFICYP. The young REME soldier was duly 'admonished' and then presented with a copy of the unusual charge-sheet as a memento.

7. The intense pace of traffic on this radio net had already led to the recording of conversations for transcription into the HQ Operations Log during quieter interludes, and Inhan was not to know that his outbursts were already being recorded (copies of the relevant tapes are extant and provide ample evidence of his emotional state).

8. Greece complained to the Secretary General of 15 major Turkish violations of the ceasefire during its first three hours. (*S/11361,* 23 July 1974).

9. It is probable that these were some of the many Cypriots who held British passports.

10. This was an example of how the parties may use a UN force to gain intelligence. UN peacekeepers need to treat such requests with care in order not to prejudice their third-party status. In this case there was clear need to quash unfounded reports that might otherwise have threatened the fragile ceasefire.

11. HQ UNFICYP succeeded in negotiating agreement for free access by UN personnel to those parts of RAF Nicosia hitherto used by UNFICYP's helicopters. (Inspection revealed relatively minor damage to installations; the bulk aviation fuel dump was intact but unusable due to a lack of electric power.)

Chapter 47 (pp 355–365)

1. Captain C.R.P.C. Branson RN, *personal*, 22 September 1978. During the morning HQ National Guard protested that HMS *Hermes* was positioned behind Turkish ships off Kyrenia, preventing Greek defensive fire; HQ UNFICYP replied that there were no British warships west of Cape Andreas. 40 Commando RM had arrived in the Western SBA by air direct from the UK on 21 July.

2. The island's civil telephone system continued to function throughout this period.

3. The author must remain anonymous for reasons explained in Note 10 to Chapter 39.

4. Major P.N. Gill, *transcript of tape-recorded report*, August 1974.

5. Captain C.R.P.C. Branson RN, *op. cit.*

6. Captain R.W.F. Gerken RN, *personal*, 18 August 1978.

7. *Ibid.*

8. Captain C.R.P.C. Branson RN, *op. cit.*

9. *Ibid.* Although Turkish troops had reached Kyrenia the previous evening, the situation in the town early on 23 July was unclear. For this reason, and because there had been no fighting along the coast east of Kyrenia, Gill thought it prudent to concentrate initially on Six Mile Beach as the main evacuation point.

10. *The Western Morning News*, Plymouth, 7 August 1974.

11. The presence of these Soviet nationals was an embarrassment for the Royal Navy, which was unwilling to embark them in HM warships.

12. Captain R.W.F. Gerken RN, *op. cit.*

13. Of the Turkish tanks I saw and heard nothing. It was about halfway through the evacuation that my UN (British) Major mentioned that the Turks were parked a couple of streets away from the Dome, and that he and others were having some problems with them over the castle. My reaction was to ask him to tell nobody else and to do his very best to hold the ceasefire, and I was so relieved that this is exactly what happened. (Captain R.W.F. Gerken RN, *ibid.*)

14. The Ukrainian dance troupe was embarked in the Royal Fleet Auxiliary *Olna*. Gerken had to explain that, due to helicopter limitations, each person was limited to one suitcase and that the troupe's properties and costumes, packed in large hampers, would have to be left behind.

15. Captain R.W.F. Gerken RN, *op. cit.* Branson had intended to transfer the Press party from *Hermes* to *Andromeda* for early passage to Akrotiri, 'but these very individualistic characters took so long to assemble their bits and pieces that I transferred them later to *Rhyl* instead.' (Captain C.R.P.C. Branson RN, *op. cit.*)

16. Captain C.R.P.C. Branson RN, *op. cit.*

17. N. Harvey and Family: *A Holiday to Remember* (circulated privately), 2 August 1974.

18. Major P.N. Gill, *personal*, 27 January 1978.

19. During the morning the British High Commission stated that Greek nationals holding Greek passports *could* be evacuated by the Royal Navy, but there was some confusion on this point, with the result that some Greek nationals were obliged to remain behind in the Dome Hotel.

20. Captain C.R.P.C. Branson RN, *op. cit.* The 1530 people came from 23 different countries.

21. N. Harvey and Family, *op. cit.*

22. N. Harvey and Family, *op. cit.*

23. Captain R.W.F. Gerken RN, *op. cit.* Letters of appreciation from people in Britain and abroad flowed in to the Royal Navy and national newspapers. The following was typical:

    It is of course impossible to thank them adequately, and I can only say that it was the most wonderful sight of our lives when we saw the British warships off Kyrenia on Tuesday morning and realized that help was at last on hand. From the moment of sighting the ships we took for granted the superb efficiency and co-ordination with which the whole operation was carried out –

but what overwhelmed us completely was the fantastic kindness, courtesy and cheerfulness of every single person involved, with everything taken care of from the first welcoming cup of tea in the hangar of HMS *Hermes* to the final hospitality at Brize Norton. We were all made to feel such honoured guests that what started off as a nightmare ended as an enriching experience which we shall never forget. (Letter published in *The Daily Telegraph*, London, 30 July 1974.)

24.   Major P.N. Gill, *op. cit.*

Chapter 48 (pp 366–377)

1.   The disused airfield at Tymbou (named Ercan by the Turks) had yet to be developed, and those at Larnaca and Paphos (on the Greek side) and at Lefkoniko (on the Turkish side) had not been built.

2.   Major M.M. Barker, *personal*, 18 November 1977. The troops concerned were from the Turkish national contingent, to whom men of UNFICYP were a familiar sight.

3.   Colonel C.E. Beattie, *personal*, 20 October 1977.

4.   Earlier that morning Herbert had given Papadopoulos some penicillin tablets to alleviate his severe throat infection.

5.   Major J.R. Herbert: 'The United Nations Take-Over of Nicosia Airport', *The Royal Corps of Transport Review*, May 1975.

6.   Fearing that the appearance of Beattie and his party, armed and in combat gear, might be misunderstood by the Turks, Barker suggested that Beattie should leave behind the remainder of his group in Camp UNFICYP and go forward on foot without arms. The three accordingly went out through the wire equipped only with a UN flag tied to a broom-stick, a man-pack radio and a pair of binoculars.

7.   Colonel C.E. Beattie, *op. cit.*

8.   *Ibid.*

9.   At this time the Turkish national contingent was found by 1 Bn, 50 Infantry Regt at augmented strength. Colonel Katircioglu was an engineer officer.

10.   Colonel C.E. Beattie, *op. cit.*

11.   *Ibid.* Barker has described the process:

> Both sides demanded that the other stopped first. Greeks insisted that the Turks withdrew. Turks refused, and we pointed out that it was unreasonable to expect them to do so under fire. The Turks kept threatening to shoot their prisoners if the Greeks did not stop firing. After about two hours both agreed to cease fire at a given time, we synchronized watches and waited for the moment. There was a slight lull, followed by fierce firing and accusations from each that the other side had not stopped. (Major M.M. Barker, *op. cit.*)

12.   Major J.R. Herbert, *op. cit.*

13.   A British signalman manning a sand-bagged OP on top of the camp's water tower was hit in the leg. Disregarding the danger, others climbed the tower, rendered first aid and lowered him to the ground, where he was quickly evacuated to the Austrian Medical Centre in Blue Beret Camp. In spite of this casualty there was no lack of volunteers to man this vantage point, which throughout succeeding days proved a valuable source of information for HQ UNFICYP.

14.   Following the flight of Makarios on 16 July, Clerides as President of the House of Representatives should properly have assumed as a temporary measure the office of President of the Republic, as provided for in the Constitution. On the morning of 23 July it was not known that he would actually do so later that day.

15.   *S/11353/ADD.4*, 23 July 1974, para. 4. That the action was intended only as a temporary peace-keeping expedient is clear.

16. Major J.R. Herbert, *op. cit.*
17. Colonel C.E. Beattie, *op. cit.*
18. One of Herbert's concerns was to safeguard the contents of the duty-free and other shops and stores in the terminal, most of which had been broken into before the arrival of UN troops.
19. Major J.R. Herbert, *op. cit.*
20 Colonel C.E. Beattie, *op. cit.*
21. Major B.L. Brett, *personal*, 24 November 1977.
22. Captain D.W. Miles, *personal*, 6 May 1978.
23. *Ibid.*

Chapter 49 (pp 378–390)

1. HQ National Guard asked UNFICYP if, subject to an assessment of its state, the airport might be used to bring in urgently needed medical supplies. HQ UNFICYP replied that there was no objection to the landing of such supplies under UN supervision but, since the Force did not have the technical expertise necessary for an assessment of the damage, HQ BFNE was being asked to make this. (The latter agreed to do so during 25 July, but the situation then necessitated postponement to the following day).
2. On being asked to transmit this message, Oberwinkler (UNFICYP's LO at the VPO) suggested to Inhan that he (Oberwinkler) should escort a Turkish representative to the airport to allow the latter to see for himself that what was alleged in the message was not true. Inhan rejected the suggestion, insisting that Turkish forces were already holding the airport.
3. Kurt Waldheim: *In the Eye of the Storm*, p. 84.
4. See M.A. Birand, *30 Hot Days*, p.56.
5.   We had an acrimonious conversation, at the end of which Ecevit undertook to look into the matter personally, saying that Ankara did not always know what was taking place on the island. (James Callaghan: *Time and Chance*, p. 347).
6. Harold Wilson: *Final Term*, pp. 63–64.
7. Use of SKYNET (a British military secure voice communications system) would (I was told) allow this to be done within minutes – perhaps even while the aircraft were already airborne en route to Nicosia.
8. Michael Carver: *Out of Step*, p. 464.
9. Major J.A. Wright, *personal*, 26 November 1977.
10. *Ibid.* HQ BFNE stated that a Forward Air Controller (FAC) was not immediately available. Fortunately Squire had received the necessary training some years earlier and took on the task until relieved later in the day by an RAF officer from Akrotiri. The latter was replaced on 28 July by an Army FAC team from 19 Brigade in the UK.
11. Major A.E.G. Gauntlett, writing in *The Scarlet and Green* (Regimental Journal of 16th/5th Lancers), Vol. IX, No. 4, 1974/75, p. 9. (His reference to 'the grand traditional manner' was to Captain Nolan's contemptuous reply which sealed the fate of the Light Brigade in its gallant charge at the Battle of Balaclava, 1854. Gauntlett added that with the coming of dawn came realization that in the dark the Colonel had erred by 180° in his direction.)
12. Major J.R. Heywood, *personal*, 7 October 1977.
13. *Ibid.*
14. Major J.A. Wright, *op. cit.*
15. Captain J.A. Squire, *personal*, 26 November 1977.
16. Major A.E.G. Gauntlett, *op. cit.*
17. *S/PV.1784*, 24 July 1974.

18. Brian Urquhart: *A Life in Peace and War*, p. 256.
19. Staff Sergeant De St Croix, *personal*, 26 November 1977.
20. Major J.R. Heywood, *op. cit.*

Chapter 50 (pp 391–399)

1. *S/11353/ADD.4*, 23 July 1974, para. 14.
2. The Turkish government announced that it recognized Clerides as Leader of the Greek Cypriot community but not as President of Cyprus.
3. Security Council *1783rd Meeting*, 23 July 1974, para.7.
4. *Ibid*, para. 8.
5. *Ibid*, para. 13.
6. Security Council *Resolution 354(1974)*. (*Resolution 353* was that adopted on 20 July 1974).
7. Security Council *1783rd Meeting*, 23 July 1974, para. 77.
8. *Ibid*, paras 100, 101, 104.
9. Since Gleneagles Camp, previously the Force Reserve base, was now occupied by 16th/5th Lancers, the Parachute Squadron, RAC took over part of the now abandoned RAF Nicosia accommodation.
10. HQ UNFICYP *Operations Log*, 25 July 1974.
11. Cakar appeared at the Turkish Embassy next morning. Thereafter this channel of communication, if not ideal, served adequately.
12. *S/11353/ADD.7*, 25 July 1974, para. 11.
13. Brian Urquhart: *A Life in Peace and War*, p. 257. Urquhart added that the meeting had pinpointed a central weakness of the UN – the frequent lack of leadership or consensus in the Security Council at critical times.
14. *S/PV. 1785*, 27 July 1974.
15. In fact UNFICYP was already acting on the Secretary General's instructions received on 22 July to make every effort to interpose itself in crucial areas on ceasefire lines.
16. HQ UNFICYP *Operations Log*, 29 July 1974. (Ersin's reply came in a message passed through HQ UNFICYP to the Secretary General, which the latter read out to the Security Council at its meeting on 31 July – see Chapter 51.)
17. *S/PV. 1785*, 27 July 1974.

Chapter 51 (pp 400–405)

1. *Security Council Resolution 353* adopted on 20 July.
2. James Callaghan: *Time and Chance*, pp. 348–349.
3. The Turkish delegation, too, was disturbed by the ceasefire violations and the continued advance of our forces. In private they were saying to each other: 'These advances are having an adverse effect on world opinion and are reducing our negotiating powers at the conference table. It is time they stopped, (M.A. Birand: *30 Hot Days*, p. 64.)
4. Report by Patrick Keatly, *The Guardian*, London, 27 July 1974.
5. *Annex to S/11398*, 30 July 1974.
6. As quoted by Ivor Richard (UK), Security Council, *1788th Meeting*, 31 July 1974, para. 41.
7. Security Council *1788th Meeting*, 31 July 1974, para. 9.
8. The draft resolution was adopted next day, 1 August, as Resolution 355(1974). (The Geneva Declaration itself 'was never formally adopted by the Security Council, in large part because the government of Cyprus was dissatisfied with it, regarding it as insufficiently condemnatory of Turkey.' Rosalyn Higgins: *United Nations Peacekeeping*, Vol. 4, Europe 1946–1949, p. 381).

9. Security Council *1788th Meeting*, 31 July 1974, para. 219. (General Ersin's message to the Secretary General was the consequence of General Prem Chand's firm reply to Ersin's ultimatum received on 29 July – see Chapter 50).

10. *Ibid.*, para. 242.

11. *Ibid.*, para. 248.

12. *Ibid.*, para. 267

13. Waldheim did not issue specific instructions reflecting this position to Prem Chand but his exchanges with Ecevit had been copied to HQ UNFICYP in the expectation that the UN Force's future activities within the Turkish controlled area would be governed accordingly.

Chapter 52 (pp 406–418)

1. See *S/11353/ADDs 1–33*, 21 July – 20 August 1974).

2. See Chapter 46. The arrival of so many reinforcements posed major logistic problems both for individual contingents and for UNFICYP as a whole. HQ UNFICYP's logistics staff was obliged to improvise solutions.

3. During the afternoon of 25 July the Turkish government formally requested UNFICYP to provide immediate relief for and 'to control the situation of' *[sic]* Turkish Cypriots in Knodhara, Famagusta, Galatia, Galinoporni and Ovgoros (all in Famagusta District), Kokkina, Limnitis and Ambelikou (all in Lefka District), and Polis, Mandria and Paphos/Ktima (all in Paphos District), in all of which the inhabitants were said to be surrounded by the National Guard and suffering shortages of food and water.

4. Unconfirmed reports suggested that Turkish troops had advanced as far west as Ayios Vasilios (some 16km NW of Nicosia), Syklloura and even Myrtou, and that these villages had been abandoned by their Greek inhabitants. Such reports, which seemed to have emanated from demoralised retreating National Guard soldiers, were soon found to be false.

5. Staff Sergeant De St Croix, *personal,* 1977.

6. *Ibid.*

7. *Ibid.*

8. The HQ of B Squadron was established on a hill above Ayia Marina, a small Maronite village 15km north-west of the airport. Its inhabitants were quick to point out that they were neither Greeks nor Turks but neutral, and displayed touching faith in in the protection that they believed was offered by the UN's blue flag. That this was misplaced was demonstrated later when Turkish aircraft attacked B Squadron's 6th Troop, then manning an OP in the village.

9. Lieut. R.A. Pickering, *personal*, 1977.

10. During the fighting the Finns noted that five Turkish tanks had been destroyed by 'Snappers', the wire-guided anti-tank missiles which in 1973 the National Guard had insisted were no longer serviceable.

11. Lieut. Colonel J. Pullinen, *personal*, 22 October 1975.

12. The Finns assisted in these patrols since Swedish reinforcements were not due to arrive until 4 August.

13. I took this opportunity to tour the Old City to see the plight of the refugees. Conducted by the local Leadership, I visited a number of buildings in which they were sheltering and was impressed by the air of order, discipline and calm. Mosques, schools and public buildings had been put to use, an official wearing a red armband was in charge of each and the organization appeared admirable. Considerable damage caused by National Guard shelling and mortaring was evident, casualties had been caused and the supply situation was giving cause for anxiety.

14. Alaminos had been attacked on 23 July. Most of its Turkish inhabitants fled, but seven men were reported missing, believed captured by the National Guard and allegedly shot. An Austrian post

was established in the village on 31 July, following which there was a gradual return of some inhabitants.

15. The stadium was visited on 28 July by ICRC delegates, who inspected conditions and distributed blankets.

16. Lieut. Colonel H.E.C.Willoughby, *personal*, 12 October 1977.

17. *Ibid.*

18. Nobody was shooting at us but we were in the direct line of fire for both sides. The building was hit frequently. Colonel J.J.G. Hunter; *Defence Adviser's Diary*.

19. *The Maroon Beret*, Newsletter of The Canadian Airborne Regiment, January 1975, p. 7. (Lynx were tracked reconnaissance vehicles operated by Lord Strathcona's Horse).

20. On 7 August a sergeant manning a Canadian OP in Nicosia was warned by a member of the TCF that, if his men continued to report Turkish activities, what had happened the previous night to Private Perron would happen to them. (*HQ UNFICYP Situation Report*, 8 August 1974).

21. Captain Lord Morpeth, *personal*, 1977.

22. Dr Unel, formally Vice President of the House of Representatives (a post reserved under the Constitution for a Turkish Cypriot), was chief medical officer of the Turkish hospital in Nicosia and one of Denktash's close associates.

23. Three days later the Secretary General blandly reported: 'The Turkish Cypriot leadership have stated that the stores in Famagusta harbour have been secured by them for safekeeping.' (*S/11353/ADD. 18*, para. 5, 9 August 1974).

Chapter 53 (pp 419–425)

1. Ireland provided Lieut. Colonel G. O'Sullivan, a high-grade officer destined to achieve the rank of Lieut. General as Chief of the Irish Defence Forces. He reached Nicosia on the evening of 13 August:

> On the morning of 14th August the second phase *[of the Turkish operation]* broke out, and when I arrived at the Ops Centre you said to me: "I'm afraid there will not be much humanitarian activity for a few days. Would you cooperate with John Miles in coordinating incoming operational messages and preparing cables to keep New York informed". So I was occupied for three days until the ceasefire on Friday 16th August. (Lieut. Colonel G. O'Sullivan, *personal*, 24 October 1977.)

Thereafter he took control of the Force's humanitarian and relief operations with outstanding success.

2. Pierre Gaillard was relieved by M. Laurent Marti in early August.

3. Article by Hubert de Senerclens, ICRC Press Officer, *ICRC Memorandum RO 570b/2*, 30 July 1974.

4. On 14 August, when the second phase of Turkey's operation began *(chapter 55)*, the ICRC declared the Hilton Hotel to be a neutral zone, to which entry by military personnel (other than UNFICYP) was not allowed. It also declared two other neutral zones in Nicosia. All were marked by prominently displayed symbols of the Red Cross.

5. The ICRC issued detailed periodic Memoranda *(RO 570b/1, 26 July 1974, et seq.)* reporting on its activities (including those of a small team sent to Turkey where its purpose was to visit Greek Cypriot prisoners transferred there from Cyprus). A summary is contained in its publication *ICRC Action In Cyprus, July-October 1974*. ICRC operations in Cyprus continued well into 1975.

6. These 42 tons included gifts in kind from Red Cross and Red Crescent Societies in many countries in Europe and the Near East as well as from international bodies such as UNICEF and UNWRA. In succeeding weeks further generous support came from many other countries and organizations.

7. *ICRC Memorandum RO 570b/3*, 8 August 1974.

8. *S/11353/ADD.15*, 5 August 1974.

9. *UNFICYP Operations Log*, 2 August 1974. UNFICYP reconnaissance patrols, especially those of the Parachute Sqn. RAC (the Force Reserve), were displaying initiative (and incurring Turkish displeasure) by locating and giving succour and comfort to those (mostly British) expatriates who had declined evacuation by the Royal Navy and remained isolated in the Turkish-controlled north.

10. *Ibid.*, 4 August 1974,

11. *Ibid.*, 29 July 1974. This officer, Lieut. Paaso, added that he had released eight horses and two oxen in need of water and fodder.

12. *ICRC Memorandum RO 570b/3*, 8 August 1974.

13. *S/11433*, 10 August 1974, paras. 16–19.

Chapter 54 (pp 426–432)

1. The Geneva Declaration *(Annex to S/11398*, 30 July 1974).

2. *S/11433*, 10 August 1974.

3. See, for example, Callaghan's *Time and Chance*, pp. 349–355 (this is especially scathing of Turkish attitudes as displayed by Gunes). First-hand Greek Cypriot accounts are given in Clerides's *Cyprus: My Deposition* and in Polyviou's *Cyprus: In Search of a Constitution*. A Turkish account is contained in Birand's *30 Hot Days*.

4. Turkish reinforcements included 28th Infantry Division (see Annex 6).

5. Callaghan, *op. cit.*, p.350.

6. *Ibid.*, p.351

7. Carver: *Out Of Step*, p.465.

8. Clerides: *Cyprus: My Deposition*, Vol. 4, p. 45.

9. The internal aspect of the problem appeared of no interest at all to the Soviet Government. . . . The Russian concern appeared to be on matters affecting the balance of power of the super-states in the area. (*Ibid*, p. 48)

10. *Ibid*, p.69.

11 Mines were the cause of a tragic incident on 8 August when a group of American and British journalists, ignoring a warning by a 16th/5th Lancers patrol, drove into a minefield on the coast road west of Kyrenia with the result that one was killed and five were injured. Fearing that it lay in a minefield, the Turks left the corpse of the dead man where he had fallen; several hours later it was recovered by Lieut. Colonel Morris (16th/5th Lancers Commanding Officer), Major Wright (B Squadron Leader) and Captain Matheson (Regimental Medical Officer). Two of the injured were evacuated by the Turkish forces and the remaining two by the 16th/5th Lancers. On 16 August two members of the Danish Contingent were killed and two were seriously injured when in darkness their vehicle drove over a mine near Ambelikou (5km west of Lefka). These were the only casualties suffered by UNFICYP due to mines.

12. *S/PV.1784*, 24 July 1974. See Chapter 49.

13. HQ UNFICYP *Operations Log*, 10 August 1974.

14. *S/11353/ADD.20*, 12 August 1974, para. 3.

15. Callaghan, *op. cit.*, p. 355.

16. These orders were confirmed in writing (*HQ UNFICYP Ops 2802*, 13 August 1974).

Chapter 55 (pp 433–439)

1. HQ UNFICYP cabled at frequent intervals, sometimes every 15 minutes, detailed Situation Reports to New York on the progress of the fighting. Most were at once circulated as Security Council documents (see *S/11353/ADD.21*, 14 August – *ADD.29*, 16 August 1974) and are not reproduced here.

2. See Chapter 32 for a reference to 'the Sahin and Attila lines'. In selecting the name 'Attila' the Turks evidently were unaware of its connotation in European minds.

3. There were many well authenticated cases of atrocities committed by both sides.

4. Michael Blackman, *Interview*, 15 June 1978.

5. We were convinced that one of the Turkish objectives . . . was to take out the northern edge of Nicosia from the airport, down the airport road to the Pedhieos river bridge. That they failed to achieve this was a relief to us as the area includes the [British] High Commission, the Residence and many other High Commission quarters. (Colonel J.J.G. Hunter: *Defence Adviser's Diary*).

6. Captain Ian Nicol: 'Cyprus and the Canadian Airborne Regiment', *Sentinel*, 1974/8, p. 20.

7. Commandant J.J. Flynn, *personal,* 6 September 1978. Flynn added that Tsolakis and his team returned to Athalassa on 18 August, as he himself also did, but that a Tactical Headquarters remained at Pyrga until early September.

8. Detailed reasons for not providing military support to the Greek Cypriots were recorded in the minutes of meetings held on 13 and 14 August between Prime Minister Karamanlis and the Chiefs of the Greek Armed Forces, extracts from which have been quoted by Glafkos Clerides: *Cyprus: My Deposition*, Vol. 4. pp. 81–83.

9. *Ibid*, p. 85. On assuming the post of Acting President on 23 July, Clerides had anticipated that: with the forces and ammunition avalable we would hold the Nicosia front, falling slowly back to the Troodos mountains after defending Nicosia to the last street. I estimated that street fighting in Nicosia could be waged for a few days and that civilian casualties would not be heavy as most of the population of the town had already taken refuge in mountain villages. *ibid*, p. 32.

10. HQ UNFICYP, *Operations Log*, 15 August 1974.

11. Unofficial pleas were made to the Austrians by local civilians, who feared Turkish air attacks or landings from the sea, for Larnaca to be declared 'an undefended zone', *Ibid*.

12. HQ BFNE informed HQ UNFICYP early on 15 August that 400 members of the National Guard withdrawing from Famagusta had moved through the Dhekelia SBA to Larnaca, having allowed themselves to be disarmed as they moved through the SBA. *Ibid*.

13. After the *coup* a month earlier some pro-Makarios supporters, still armed, had taken to the mountains and may have been acting in this fashion to discredit the National Guard. Such activities gave much concern to UNFICYP.

14. Although some sporadic shooting continued and intentions remained unclear, the National Guard informed Macfarlane that it did not intend to attack Stavrokono and it withdrew all but one platoon from its vicinity. The UN post was re-established at first light next morning in spite of continuing sporadic fire.

15. Some fighting developed later as the Turkish forces made local advances in modification of the Attila Line.

Chapter 56 (pp 440–446)

1. *Security Council 1792nd Meeting,* 14 August 1974, para. 51.

2. *Ibid.,*para. 54.

3. *Ibid.*, para. 70.

4. *Security Council 1793rd Meeting*, 15 August 1974, para. 11.
5. *Ibid.*, para. 16.
6. Resolution 359(1974).
7. *Security Council 1793rd Meeting*, 15 August 1974, paras. 52 and 53.
8. *Ibid.*, para. 82.
9. *Ibid*, para. 111.
10. *Ibid.*, para. 128.
11. In poking fun, this cartoon by Rigby (p. 444) illustrated the disenchantment with which UN peacekeeping operations were viewed by some in the public at large.
12. Brendan O'Malley and Ian Craig: *The Cyprus Conspiracy*, p.218.
13. In October 1974 the influential American Greek lobby succeeded in persuading Congress, contrary to Kissinger's strong advice, that military aid to Turkey should be halted. The embargo was implemented in February 1975 (with the result that Turkey closed nearly all US military installations on its territory) but was eventually lifted in April 1978. Greece resumed full participation in NATO military activities in January 1980.
14. See Annex 5 – British Forces in or near Cyprus in July and August 1974.
15. Brigadier W.P.W. Robertson, Commander Eastern SBA, *personal*, 9 November 1977.
16. *Ibid.*
17. *HQ UNFICYP Operations Log*, 15 August 1974.
18. Colonel J.J.G. Hunter: *Defence Adviser's Diary.*

Chapter 57 (pp 447–459)

1. Reinforcements included an airborne battery of eight 81mm mortars, eight 106mm RCLs, and an airborne engineer squadron, together with first line and seven day reserves of ammunition. The armoured vehicles were shipped to Cyprus from Germany and the men flown in from Canada.
2. Staff Sergeant De St Croix, *Personal*, 1977.
3. *The Scarlet and Green Journal*, 1974/75 (Regimental journal of 16/5th Lancers). The three wounded were evacuated to the British Military Hospital, Dhekelia the same day. (The Maronite owner of the restaurant where the UN OP was located had pleaded to be given a UN flag to display over it but had been assured that this was unnecessary – the presence of the clearly identified UN patrol would suffice to ensure it was not attacked. He was reported to have been killed in the airstrike.)
4. *Ibid.*
5. On 14 August Lieut. Colonel Manuel assumed command of the defence of the airport.
6. At the Hilton Hotel in Nicosia, where reporters and many refugees were gathered, a rocket from an aircraft landed in front of the entrance at about 1100 hours. At 1145 hours an aircraft attacked the area adjacent to the hotel where there were a National Guard camp and a technical school. Rockets from the plane set the area on fire. National Guard soldiers who attempted to enter the Hilton Hotel, which the ICRC had declared a neutral area, were successfully prevented from doing so. *S/11353/ADD.25*, 14 August 1974, para. 7.

   At 1830 the Turkish command informed UNFICYP that it had agreed to the request that the Hilton and Cleopatra Hotels be regarded as Red Cross neutral areas. *Ibid*, para. 19.
7. On this and succeeding days further groups of Greek Cypriots expelled by the Turks from the north were received at the Ledra Palace checkpoint by the Canadians and handed over to the Greek Cypriot authorities.

8. An armoured group was sent to recover the M113 next day, only to have one of the escorting Lynx also disabled on another mine. After careful checks for further mines both vehicles were successfully recovered.
9. HQ UNFICYP *Operations Log*, 15 August 1974.
10. *The Maroon Beret*, January 1975.
11. Those wounded included Flight Lieut. Anderton, UNFICYP's Air Liaison Officer, and two RAF officers of the Force's Whirlwind helicopter detachment.
12. The UN Protected Area surrounding the airport, which already included Blue Beret Camp, Camp UNFICYP and Gleneagles Camp, was subsequently extended along the length of the ridge to include Kykko Camp and the Comet Farm.
13. Lieut Colonel Pullinen, *End of Tour Report*, 22 October 1975.
14. *War Diary, 23 July–22 September 1974*, C Sqn, 4th/7th Dragoon Guards.
15. Lieut. Colonel Pullinen, *op. cit.*
16. *HQ UNFICYP Operations Log*, 15 August 1974.
17. *Ibid*, 14 August 19 74.
18. *Ibid*. A personal message from the Turkish Ambassador, Asaf Inhan, also expressed deep regret for casualties to UN personnel caused during the day as a result of Turkey's military operations and his assurance that these had not been deliberate. (A fragment of napalm casing recovered at Goshi showed clearly that it had been manufactured in the US.)
19. During the morning of 16 August the Swedes reported that Turks had raped a Greek Cypriot woman just north of their camp and that this had been verified by their MO. When the Turks demanded that she and her elderly father be handed over to them, HQ UNFICYP instructed the Swedes not to do so; the two were later evacuated to Dhekelia. (This was one of a long list of atrocities alleged to have been perpetrated by both sides during this and later periods.)
20. Vrecha had come under attack, in which six were reported killed and six wounded, within hours of the ceasefire agreed for 1600hrs on 22 July. On that occasion the National Guard suggested that the attack was the work of EOKA-type irregulars not under its control (see Chapter 46).
21. Lieut. Colonel Willoughby, *personal*, 22 August 1974.
22. *Ibid*.
23. Major P. Gill, *Report on UNFICYP Operations in Kyrenia and Dome Hotel July-August 1974*, tape-recorded August 1974.
24. *S/11568*, 6 December 1974, para. 36.

Chapter 58 (pp 460–471)

1. *Security Council 1794th Meeting*, para. 26.
2. *Ibid*, para. 93.
3. *Ibid*. para. 101.
4. *Resolution 186(1964)*, para. 5 (text at Annex 1).
5. The buffer zone, as established in September 1974, remained virtually unchanged and policed by UNFICYP for the next 30 years.
6. The Finnish success in establishing these posts allowed some 10,000 people to return to their homes and factories, some of which were even located inside the buffer zone.
7. Ambassador Davies was a charming man, with delightful children, who had been in post only six months. In 1976 the Americans persuaded Makarios to allow an American investigator to work with CYPOL to carry out a thorough investigation into this incident, as a result of which four Greek Cypriots were convicted and imprisoned for various terms. (An official American

source furnished me with what he described as 'the most comprehensive account of the Davies case in existence outside the classified files of the US Government'.)

8. *S/11468/ADD.1*, 10 September 1974.

9. Lieut. Colonel G. O'Sullivan, *personal*, 24 October 1977. (Murray remarked that in view of the uncertain situation, perhaps they should have taken a Padre with them.)

10. *S/11473*, para. 2, 28 August 1974. While in Nicosia Waldheim addressed a gathering of representatives from all of UNFICYP's contingents, explaining the present situation with respect to the Force's role and the political questions that now faced all concerned.

11. Annex to *S/11488*, 4 September 1974, paras. 4–5.

12. Letter from representative of Cyprus to Secretary General, *S/11467*, 23 August 1974, para. 3(b).

13. There was an incursion into SBA territory by six Turkish tanks on 21 August. This was found to be due to a map reading error and the tanks withdrew.

14. Details may be found in the following published documents: *ICRC Action in Cyprus, July – October 1974; Minutes of Weekly Coordinating Meetings held by UNHCR, 27 August – 17 December 1974*; UN Secretary General's reports, *S/11468* (27 August 1974), ADD.1 (10 September 1974) and ADD.2 (18 September 1974).

15. *S/11468/ADD.1*, 10 September 1974, para. 6.

16. *Ibid*, paras. 12–17.

BIBLIOGRAPHY

Published material relating not only to Cyprus and its problems but also to United Nations peace-keeping generally is extensive. Listed here is a selection directly relevant to the subject of this book.

Documents and Records

Proceedings and Reports of the United Nations Security Council are too numerous to be listed in detail. Many are quoted in this book and are identified by the prefix 'S/' in the references.

Some quotations are also made from the Official Reports (Hansard) of debates in the Houses of the British Parliament and references to these are given in Notes. Two Parliamentary Reports are especially relevant:

House of Commons, Report from the Select Committee on CYPRUS, Session 1975-76.
House of Commons Foreign Affairs Committee, Third Report, Session 1986-87, CYPRUS.

Books

Adams, T.W. *AKEL: The Communist Party of Cyprus*, Hoover Institution Press, USA, 1971

Bell, Coral *The Diplomacy of Detente – The Kissinger Era*, Martin Robertson, London, 1977

Bell, J Bowyer *Violence at a Distance; Greece and the Cyprus Crisis*, Orbis, USA, 1974

Birand, M.A. *30 Hot Days*, Rustem & Brother, Nicosia, 1985

Callaghan, James *Time and Chance*, Collins, London, 1987

Carver, Michael *Out of Step*, Hutchinson, London, 1989

Clerides, Glafkos *Cyprus: My Deposition*, Vols. 3 & 4, Alithia Publishing, Nicosia, 1990 and 1992

Crawshaw, Nancy *The Cyprus Revolt – An Account of the Struggle for Union with Greece*, George Allen & Unwin, London, 1978

Durrell, Lawrence *Bitter Lemons*, Faber and Faber, London, 1957

Ertekun, N.M. *The Cyprus Dispute and the Birth of the Turkish Republic of Northern Cyprus*, Rustem & Brother, Nicosia, 1981

Faulds, A. (Ed.) *Excerpta Cypria for Today*, Rustem & Brother, Nicosia, 1988.

Foley, C. & Scobie, W.I. *The Struggle for Cyprus*, Hoover Institution Press, USA, 1975

Foot, Sir Hugh *A Start in Freedom*, Hodder & Stoughton, London, 1964

Harbottle, Michael *The Impartial Soldier*, Oxford University Press, Oxford, 1970

Higgins, Rosalyn *United Nations Peacekeeping. Documents and Commentary. Vol. 4. Europe 1946–1979*, Oxford University Press, Oxford, 1981 (for the Royal Institute of International Affairs)

Hitchens, Christopher *Cyprus*, Quartet Books, London, 1984

Hunt, Sir David *On the Spot – An Ambassador Remembers*, Peter Davies, London, 1975

James, Alan *Peacekeeping in International Politics*, Macmillan, London, 1990

Jokihaara, M *Kyprokseu Kniisi 1974*, published privately, Maalishuu, Finland, 1975

Karpat, Kemal H. (Ed.) *Turkey's Foreign Policy in Transition, 1950-1974*, E.J. Brill, Leiden, 1975

Keefe, Eugene (*et al.*) *Area Handbook for Cyprus*, The American University, USA, 1971

Kellner, P & Hitchens, C. *Callaghan – The Road to Number 10*, Cassell, London, 1976

Kinross, Lord *The Ottoman Centuries – The Rise and Fall of the Turkish Empire*, Jonathan Cape, London, 1977

Kissinger, Henry *Years of Upheaval*, Weidenfeld & Nicolson and Michael Joseph, London, 1982

Kissinger, Henry *Years of Renewal*, Weidenfeld & Nicolson, London, 1999

Kitson, Frank *Bunch of Five*, Faber & Faber, London, 1977

Koumoulides, J.T.A. (Ed.) *Cyprus in Transition 1960-1985*, Trigraph, London, 1986

Markides, Kyriacos C. *The Rise and Fall of the Cyprus Republic*, Yale University Press, USA, 1977

Mirbagheri, Farid *Cyprus and International Peacemaking*, C. Hurst, London, 1998

Mouskos, Charles C. *Peace Soldiers: The Sociology of a United Nations Military Force*, University of Chicago Press, USA, 1976

Nedjatigil, Zaim M. *The Cyprus Conflict – A Lawyer's View*, Rustem & Brother, Nicosia, 1981

O'Malley B. & Craig I. *The Cyprus Conspiracy – America, Espionage and the Turkish Invasion*, I.B. Tauris, London, 1999

Papandreou, A. *Democracy at Gunpoint*, André Deutsch, London, 1971

Parsons, Anthony *From Cold War to Hot Peace – UN Interventions 1947-1994*, Michael Joseph, London, 1995

Plaza, Dr. Galo *Report by the UN Mediator in Cyprus*, United Nations, New York, S/6253, 26 March 1965

Polyvios, G. Polyviou *Cyprus: The Tragedy and the Challenge*, Nicosia, 1975

Polyvios, G. Polyviou *Cyprus: In Search of a Constitution*, Nicosia, 1976

Reddaway, John *Burdened with Cyprus – The British Connection*, Weidenfeld & Nicolson, London, 1986

Richmond, Oliver P. *Mediating in Cyprus – The Cypriot Communities and the United Nations*, Frank Cass, London, 1998

Rikhye, Indar Jit *et al.* *The Thin Blue Line*, Yale University Press, USA, 1974

Rikhye, Indar Jit *The Theory and Practice of Peacekeeping*, C. Hurst, London, 1984

Scott Gibbons, H. *Peace Without Honour*, ADA Publishing House, Ankara, 1968

Siilasvuo, Ensio *In the Service of Peace in the Middle East, 1967–1979*, C. Hurst, London, 1992.

Stegenga, James A. *The United Nations Force in Cyprus*, Ohio State University Press, USA, 1968

Theodoracopulos, Taki *The Greek Upheaval – Kings, Demagogues and Bayonets 1967- 1976*, Stacey International, London, 1976

Thubron, Colin *Journey into Cyprus*, Heinemann, London, 1975

United Nations *The Blue Helmets – A Review of United Nations Peacekeeping*, United Nations, New York, 1990

Urquhart, Brian *A Life in Peace and War*, Weidenfeld & Nicolson, London, 1987

Vanezis, Dr. P.N. *Cyprus – The Unfinished Agony*, Abelard-Schuman, London, 1977

 Makarios: Life and Leadership, Abelard-Schuman, London, 1979

Verrier, Anthony *International Peacekeeping – United Nations Forces in a Troubled World*, Penguin Books, London, 1981

Volkan, Vamik D. *Cyprus – War and Adaptation. A Psychoanalytic History of Two Ethnic Groups in Conflict*, University Press of Virginia, USA, 1979

Von Horn, Carl *Soldiering for Peace*, Cassell, London, 1966

Wainhouse, D.W. *International Peacekeeping at the Crossroads – National Support – Experience and Prospects*, John Hopkins University Press, USA, 1973,

Waldheim, Dr. Kurt *In the Eye of the Storm – The Memoirs of Kurt Waldheim*, Weidenfeld & Nicolson, London, 1985

Welin, G & Ekelund, C FN på Cypeiu, Protus Förlag HB, Stockholm, 1999 (Published in English as The UN in Cyprus – Swedish Peace-Keeping Operations, 1964–1993, C. Hurst, London, 2004.)

Wilson, Harold *Final Term – The Labour Government 1974-1976*, Weidenfeld & Nicolson and Michael Joseph, London, 1979

Wilson, Sir James *Unusual Undertakings – A Military Memoir*, Leo Cooper, London, 2002

Woodhouse, C.M. *The Rise and Fall of the Greek Colonels*, Granada, London, 1985

Articles.

Numerous articles, in addition to those quoted in this book, have been published in a variety of journals. The following is a selection

Clogg, R. *Greece and the Cyprus Crisis*, The World Today (Royal Institute of International Affairs)

Coufoudakis, V. *United Nations Peacekeeping and Peacemaking and the Cyprus Question*, Western Political Quarterly, 1976

Crawshaw, Nancy *Cyprus: A Failure in Western Diplomacy*, The World Today, February 1984 (Royal Institute of International Affairs)

Dent, O. *The Miracle of Cyprus. Four Weeks in Summer*, Army Quarterly, 1975

Dobell, W.M. *Where Greeks and Turks Meet Confrontation Politics Emerge*, International Perspectives, 1974

The Economist *Cyprus, The Makarios Years*, July 1974

Fischer, A.J. *Cyprus, The Island Republic: Background to the Crisis*, Contemporary Review, 1974

Gill, P.N. *Island of Tragedy: Cyprus – Summer 1974*, Army Air Corps Journal, 1975

Henn, F.R. *Guidelines for Peacekeeping – Another View*, British Army Review, April 1981

Henn, F.R. *The Nicosia Airport Incident of 1974: A Peacekeeping Gamble*, International Peacekeeping, Spring 1994

Henn, F.R. *UN Peacekeeping: The Mirror Should Be Polished*, Contemporary Review, June 1994

International Institute for Strategic Studies *The Cyprus Crisis*, Strategic Survey, 1975

Jackson, R.J. *Political Intransigence Means Tragedy for the Troubled Island*, International Perspectives, 1974

Kourvetaris, G.A. *Survey Essay on the Cyprus Question*, Journal of Political and Military Sociology, Spring 1976

Legault, A. *Strategic Triangle Formed by Athens, Ankara and Nicosia*, International Perspectives, 1974

Leslie, E.M.D. *Cyprus: After Ten Years of UNFICYP the Basic Problems Remain*, International Perspectives, 1974

Linley, T.A. *Cyprus Demarcation Task, 1974*, Royal Engineers Journal, September 1976

McIntyre, Sir G. *Cyprus as a United Nations Problem*, Australian Outlook, April 1976

MacLeish, Kenneth *Cyprus Under Four Flags: A Struggle for Unity*, National Geographic Magazine,
    March 1973

Mazza, U. *Operation Attila*, Armies and Weapons, November/December 1974

Park, W. *Cyprus: The Time Bomb in the Mediterranean*, World Press, 1974/75

Pennell, M.R. *Kibris Taksim*, Royal Green Jackets Chronicle, 1974

Rodnick, D. *NATO and the Cyprus Crisis: Pressure Groups vs Power Politics*, Round Table,
    April 1977

Tuck, F.M.K. *Sappers in Cyprus, 1974-76*, Royal Engineers Journal, March 1977

INDEX